CHESS-PLAYERS'

HANDBOOK

Howard Staunton

© COPYRIGHT 1980 AND PUBLISHED BY
COLES PUBLISHING COMPANY LIMITED
TORONTO — CANADA
PRINTED IN CANADA

CONTENTS

CHAPTER   PAGE

PREFACE TO THE PRESENT EDITION . . . ix

PREFACE TO THE FIRST EDITION x

BIOGRAPHICAL NOTE xiii

BOOK I

INTRODUCTION

I. DESCRIPTION OF THE CHESS BOARD AND MEN—AR-
RANGEMENT OF THE MEN—THE KING—THE QUEEN
—THE ROOKS OR CASTLES—THE BISHOPS—THE
KNIGHTS—AND THE PAWNS—THEIR MOVEMENTS,
POWERS, METHOD OF CAPTURING AN ADVERSE MAN,
ETC. 1

II. CHESS NOTATION 15

III. TECHNICAL TERMS 22

IV. ON THE RELATIVE VALUE OF THE CHESS FORCES . 34

V. THE LAWS OF THE GAME 35

VI. GENERAL RULES AND OBSERVATIONS . . . 39

VII. MAXIMS AND ADVICE FOR AN INEXPERIENCED PLAYER 45

BOOK II

I. THE KING'S KNIGHT'S OPENING 61

II. THE PHILIDOR DEFENCE—ANALYSIS . . . 64

GAMES 70

CHAPTER		PAGE
III.	THE PETROFF DEFENCE—ANALYSIS	91
	GAMES	98
IV.	GRECO COUNTER GAMBIT—ANALYSIS	107
	GAMES	111
V.		113
VI.	GIUOCO PIANO—ANALYSIS	115
	GAMES	128
VII.	EVANS' GAMBIT—ANALYSIS	147
	GAMES	152
VIII.	EVANS' GAMBIT DECLINED—ANALYSIS	161
	GAMES	164
IX.	THE TWO KNIGHTS' DEFENCE—ANALYSIS	166
	GAMES	168
X.	RUY LOPEZ—ANALYSIS	173
	GAMES	185
XI.	THE DOUBLE RUY LOPEZ, AND FOUR KNIGHTS' GAME —ANALYSIS	199
	GAMES	200
XII.	SCOTCH GAMBIT—ANALYSIS	204
	GAMES	213
XIII.	PONZIANI'S OR STAUNTON'S OPENING—ANALYSIS	224
	GAMES	225

BOOK III

I.	KING'S BISHOP'S OPENING—ANALYSIS	231
	GAMES	241
II.	THE CENTRE GAMBIT—ANALYSIS	254
	GAMES	257

CHAPTER		PAGE
III.	Danish Gambit—Analysis	258
	Games	260
IV.	Queen's Bishop's Pawn Opening—Analysis	261
	Games	262

BOOK IV.

		PAGE
I.	The King's Knight's Gambit—Analysis	265
	Games	268
II.	Cunningham Gambit—Analysis	274
	Games	276
III.	The Salvio Gambit—Analysis	278
	Games	285
IV.	The Cochrane Gambit—Analysis	280
	Games	285
V.	The Muzio Gambit—Analysis	289
	Games	298
VI.	The Allgaier Gambit—Analysis	304
	Games	306
VII.	The Kieseritsky Gambit—Analysis	308
	Games	314
VIII.	The King's Rook's Pawn's Gambit—Analysis	321
IX.	The Bishop's Gambit—Analysis	322
	Games	341
X.	The King's Gambit Declined—Analysis	353
	Games	357

BOOK V

CHAPTER   PAGE
   I. THE QUEEN'S GAMBIT—ANALYSIS   362
                              GAMES   363
  II. THE QUEEN'S GAMBIT DECLINED—ANALYSIS   .   . 366
                                    GAMES   .   . 370
 III. THE SICILIAN DEFENCE—ANALYSIS   .   .   . 378
                              GAMES   .   .   . 383
  IV. THE FRENCH DEFENCE—ANALYSIS   .   .   . 390
                              GAMES   .   .   . 393
   V. THE CENTRE COUNTER—ANALYSIS   .   .   . 399
                              GAMES   .   .   . 402
  VI. THE VIENNA GAME—ANALYSIS   .   .   . 404
                              GAMES   .   .   . 407
 VII. MISCELLANEOUS OPENINGS—ANALYSIS   .   . 413
                                  GAMES   .   . 417

SYNOPSIS OF BOOK VI.   424

BOOK VI

              THE END GAME   .   .   . 425

APPENDIX
By R. F. GREEN

INDEX TO THE OPENINGS   521

INDEX TO PLAYERS   543

PREFACE TO THE PRESENT EDITION.

WHEN another edition of Staunton's "Handbook" was called for, it was thought desirable to simplify the system of notation which he employed in order to make the variations more readily accessible to chess players. Consequently, in the present edition the fractional system, in columns, is adopted; and where the opening moves of two or more variations are the same, these moves are not repeated, thus showing at a glance where a particular variation branches off. The great economy of space thus effected made it possible to incorporate in the present edition all the chief variations and many of the games from the "Chess Praxis," thus embodying in one volume the chief of Staunton's analytical researches. When this had been done it was found that some openings which figure prominently in modern tournaments, had been inadequately treated by Staunton, and in these cases the original analyses have been strengthened by the addition of many recent accredited lines of play. This was particularly necessary in the case of the Ruy Lopez, to which nearly forty new variations have been added.

In order to disturb Staunton's work as little as possible, some few openings, now rarely heard of, and even more rarely played, have been retained. On the other hand a few, entirely unnoticed by him, have been added.

A feature of the present edition is the large collection of games, about 250 in all, including some by nearly all the greatest players from Philidor to Capablanca.

The usual signs are used, including 0—0 and 0—0—0 for Castles on the King's and Queen's sides respectively.

A few chapters have been rewritten and enlarged or condensed, in accordance with the requirements demanded by the absorption of the "Praxis" by the "Handbook."

E. H. B.

PREFACE TO THE FIRST EDITION.

WIDE as is the field of theory which comprehends the manifold varieties of openings and endings in the game of Chess, its every part has been explored in modern times with so much skill and perseverance, that little now remains for a follower in this walk beyond the adaptation and arrangement of materials which have been garnered by his predecessors. The pretensions of this treatise can therefore take no lofty ground. Adopting the common basis founded by the earlier writers, Lopez, Salvio, Greco, Cozio, Lolli, &c., and superadding the important discoveries brought to light in the works of Bilguer and Jaenisch, I have aimed only at producing an instructive compendium available by the large majority of English players to whom those works are inaccessible. In my labours of collation and compression, I have not, however, indolently acquiesced in the opinions of those distinguished authorities, but have subjected every variation they have given to the test of repeated investigation, and hence it will be found that I have occasionally deviated from the course prescribed by them, and ventured on a route which they have overlooked. For these digressions, put forth without the advantage of revision by other players, I may reasonably solicit the indulgence that should be shown to any one who devotes himself to a task so difficult as that of devising new combinations in openings which have already undergone the ordeal of laborious examination by the most penetrating and industrious intellects.

In a work of this description, intended as well for the

general as the scientific reader, it was thought desirable
to adhere to the notation in common use among the
players of this country, but in a more elaborate and
expansive treatise, it would certainly be desirable, perhaps
indispensable, to adopt such a modification of the system
as would admit of tabular demonstrations. Who that has
ever attempted the wearisome exertion of threading his
way through the ramifications of a leading opening from
an English book, can ever forget the bewilderment and
confusion which its endless references to "Variations 1, 2,
3," and "A, B, C," and "Games 5, 6, and 7," have
occasioned him? And yet such references for the most
part are needful, and indeed inseparable, from our method
of recording the moves in columns, rather than on tables.
Mindful of these obstacles to the progress of the student,
I have been at some pains to lessen his difficulties in the
present work. In the first place, by discarding all unnecessary variations, and abridging, where curtailment
was practicable, the remainder ; and secondly, by distinguishing the accredited methods of attack and defence
from the subordinate or doubtful ones, by a difference of
type. Thus the reader who has not leisure to pursue an
opening through its several deviations, and is content to
follow the moves which have been pronounced the best,'
has only to play over the column of larger type, and may
reserve for a future opportunity the study of the many
beautiful and suggestive variations which are given in the
smaller letter.

By these means much of the irksomeness complained of
in the practice of playing from book may be avoided, and
I have hopes that the mere learner will be enabled in a
short time to master an opening of "The Handbook,"
variations and all, and derive not only profit but even
pleasure from the task.

I must not omit the present opportunity to acknowledge
the profound obligations this volume is under to its great
namesake "The Handbuch" of Bilguer and V. der Laza,
a production—whether considered in reference to its research, its suggestiveness, or the methodical completeness
of its arrangement,—which stands unrivalled and alone.

Nor can I forego the gratification of tendering my warmest thanks to Messrs. Angas and Finley, of Durham, for their invaluable assistance in the shape of translations and corrections, and to my esteemed friend the Rev. H. Bolton, and to those gentlemen who have kindly seconded his efforts, for the series of exquisite problems which so appropriately concludes the work.

H. S.

London, June, 1847.

BIOGRAPHICAL NOTE.

HOWARD STAUNTON, the author of this "Handbook" and one of the greatest chess players that any country has produced, was born in 1810, probably in London. Little is known of his early life, and that little is not creditable to his parents. His education was neglected, and he was allowed to do pretty much what he liked. This freedom enabled him to early take an interest in the stage, which, after an interregnum of 20 years devoted to chess, he resumed in his emendations of the text of Shakspere. That he acted as an amateur in his young days is evident, for later in life he used to tell how he played Lorenzo to the Shylock of Edmund Kean. But how, where or when this happened is not known. He went to Oxford, but it is doubtful if he received any education there, or was even a member of the University, and he certainly did not take a degree. On coming of age in 1831 Staunton received "a few thousand" pounds from his father, and, as might be expected from one who was so little accustomed to restraint, he very quickly spent this sum. He became a regular habitué of Simpson's Divan in the Strand, Kilpack's in Covent Garden, Ries' Divan and Goode's Chess Rooms in Ludgate Hill—famous London chess resorts during the early Victorian period. Here, for any one who showed ability at the game it was possible to meet the strongest English players of the day, and occasionally a continental master. Staunton's great natural penetration, which he was ultimately to turn to other account than just playing chess, gained for him the reputation of one

of the strongest players in London. From 1840 to 1842
he met all classes of English players, but especially
Cochrane, with whom he played a great number of
games—winning most of them. Staunton might now be
said to have arrived at master rank, but he had yet to
prove his ability outside London. For a young ambitious
player with merely a "local habitation and a name" he
did the correct thing—he accepted the most formidable
challenge open to him.

Excepting the aged Deschappelles, St. Amant was
generally regarded as the finest player in France, if not in
Europe. From the middle ages France had enjoyed a
reputation for skill at chess second to none. In the
absence of international tournaments it was impossible to
determine the nationality of the greatest players, but
certainly none were so celebrated as the French masters.
Hence, when Staunton accepted St. Amant's challenge in
1843, the odds were wholly in favour of the latter, whose
strength was well known.

Staunton had not crossed swords in a match with any
of the continental players of repute, and he showed no
little temerity in meeting the greatest of them. The
match was to go to the first winner of 11 games, for
£100 a side, to be played in Paris. Staunton's style was
somewhat unusual in those days, for he showed a decided
preference for the close game, thus anticipating chess
fashion by a complete generation.

The match was played at the Chess Circle during
November and December, 1843. Staunton started
brilliantly by winning three out of the first four games,
the other one being drawn. Later St. Amant did better,
particularly towards the close of the match, when Staunton
won only two of the last nine games. But the French-
man could not overtake his rival's strong lead, and at the
end of a memorable struggle the score stood—

Staunton .	.	.	11
St. Amant	.	.	6
Drawn .	.	.	4
			—
			21

The result was an undoubted surprise, particularly to the Parisians, who regarded their champion as vastly the superior player of the two. Staunton's friends, however, such as Cochrane, knew better, but even they can hardly have hoped for such a handsome victory as is indicated by the score of 11 to 6. Altogether it was a great and lasting triumph for English chess, such as it never got before, and has hardly needed since.

Staunton was now the foremost player of his day. At 33 years of age he achieved a position for himself which, a generation later, would have justified the title of chess champion of the world. Indeed, he was generally regarded as such, though the title was not formally recognised. Steinitz formally assumed it 23 years later on no better ground. For the first time in its history Staunton had raised British chess to the level of the continental game. By the defeat of St. Amant and, four years later, the publication of his "Handbook," Staunton did more for chess in this country than any other man before or since. The game acquired a popularity it never before had, and it has not since lost. Chess clubs multiplied rapidly, tournaments were held, and — surest sign of all — the literature of the game made great strides. Chess columns were started in some papers which, at the present day, number amongst them some of the greatest dailies and weeklies in the country. For ten years after his defeat of St. Amant Staunton's industry in the cause of chess was indefatigable. In 1846 he played matches with both Horwitz and Harrwitz in Germany, which he won. He subsequently played the latter two more matches, conceding odds of Pawn and Pawn and move respectively, winning one and losing the other. He published his "Handbook," in 1847, the "Chess Players' Companion" and the "Chess Players' Text Book" in 1849, and "The Chess Tournament of 1851" in 1852. In 1849 Staunton invented the graceful chessmen now almost universally used and called after him. His interest in chess was retained to the last, for even after he had turned his attention to other literary work he published his "Chess Praxis" in 1860, and left his "Theory and Practice of

Chess " in MS.- at his death, which was published by
R. B. Wormwald in 1876.

Meanwhile Staunton had started a monthly magazine
wholly devoted to the game—the *Chess Players' Chronicle*,
which he owned and edited from 1841 to 1854. The
Illustrated London News had started the first chess column
in this country in 1842, and two years later Staunton
assumed the editorship of it, which he retained till his
death. Chess journalism demands something more than
exceptional skill over the board, and some great players
have edited quite insipid columns. Staunton was not of
these. As he was one of the earliest chess journalists in
this country he was also one of the best. Indeed, a very
pleasant hour can always be spent by turning up
Staunton's old column in the *Illustrated London News*.
His annotations were sound, his notes informative, and
his answers to correspondents were characterised by
perfect candour, as the following few examples, taken at
random, will show :—

"F.G.C. Your solution (?) is all wrong." A week
later. " F.G.C. should learn the simple rules of the game ;
the very first move of his intended solution is a flagrant
violation of them." To a critic. " A lover of chess, con-
fessedly knowing little or nothing of the game, would it
not be well for the amateur to devote the time he can
spare for chess to his own improvement, rather than to
animadversions on games the beauties of which he does
not seem to understand ? *Get Lewis's ' Chess for
Beginners.'* " To a would-be problem composer. " 225.
The position sent in is childish, mate can be forced in two
moves instead of six." To another. " R.S.L. Your
problem of three moves can be solved in one ! " " Had
Philo-Philidor bestowed one-fiftieth part of the attention
on the Problem No. 97 that we have, he would have
spared us the necessity of telling him he has discovered a
' mare's nest.' " To a correspondent who belittled the
chess capacity of ladies. " Homo. There is neither justice
nor gallantry in the supposition. We have the pleasure
of knowing several ladies who play chess admirably,
and there are two in England who, we believe, could

give the odds of a Knight to three-fourths of our male correspondents."

These answers betray an impatience—not indeed without cause—which Staunton did not display over the board, where indeed patience and restraint were two of the qualities that made him the formidable player he was. They also throw an interesting light on the awakening of the English people to chess during the middle of the last century. No chess journalist of to-day has to deal with the comments and queries that Staunton had to answer week by week, which show that most of his correspondents were beginners.

During the year 1850, Staunton's time was largely devoted to promoting the great Chess Tournament of 1851 —the first international tournament ever held. As this event marked an epoch in the history of chess, and Staunton was its originator and prime mover, a few details of it may not be out of place here.

To the present generation who are so familiar with international chess tournaments, the difficulties that faced Staunton may not be obvious. It must be remembered that, apart from the difficulty of bringing the chess masters of the world together for the first time, there were minor obstacles that had to be overcome. For instance, the rules of chess were not uniform, and a fault that proved a great embarrassment during the tournament and for many years afterwards, was the absence of a time limit. This latter cost Staunton quite a number of games, especially against Williams.

Another trouble was the opposition of an influential club, the members of which desired a national, rather than an international, tourney. But these obstacles were finally surmounted, and invitations were extended to the leading players in Europe. In the absence of championships, the tournament had to be open to all comers, and this, in conjunction with the "knock out" principle on which it was conducted, led to some absurd results. Thus Anderssen and Kieseritsky, two of the greatest players of all time, were drawn together in the first round, with the result that Kieseritsky disappeared early, while two second-rate amateurs, who nowadays would not be allowed to appear in such company at all, survived to figure in the prize list! Staunton did not do himself justice. Hard work, bad health, and worry over the tournament spoiled his chances of success, even if his temperament now were such as to placidly abide a player taking two or even three hours over *one move*. The first prize, £183, justly fell to Anderssen, whom Staunton had personally gone out of his way to bring over, but the rest of the prizes were not, owing to the conditions of play, so equitably bestowed by fate.

The tournament itself was Staunton's own reward. Although it failed to rectify anomalies in the rules of play which Staunton had hoped to effect, it organised chess for the first time, and made the modern tournament possible. It gave an impetus to the game that developed into a permanent expansion. Much indeed had yet to be done. But the first step, and that against the huge mass of inertia that all new enterprises must move, was taken. And the inception, accomplishment and chief credit is due to Howard Staunton.

For over a year he was busy preparing the "Chess Tournament" for publication. This work, which is a permanent record of the tournament, may be reckoned a chess classic, not only on account of the unique event it represents, but also for the fine collection of games.

Though Staunton retained his interest in the game to the end, during the last twenty years of his life he divided his enormous energies between chess and literature—particularly the study of Shakspere. To the curiosity of youth he had added the scholarship and research of middle age. No details were too small for him to note. His articles in the press displayed an extraordinary knowledge of the stage of Shakspere's day. Almost immediately after the publication of "The Chess Tournament" he set to work on an edition of Shakspere. This was published between 1857 and 1860 in monthly parts, with illustrations by Sir John Gilbert. It at once became recognised as a standard—possibly the best edition of Shakspere till then published. Unlike some modern commentators, Staunton did not strain after subtle psychological explanations of Shakspere's meaning. He brought his unrivalled knowledge of the people of Shakspere's Day—their customs, lives, and modes of speech—to assist him, with the result that his notes are sensible and sound. This is not a kind of work that will individually live. Every generation brings its own Shakspere commentators, and the best of subsequent generations will be he who, to a judicious selection of the best from all his predecessors, adds perhaps a trifle that is new. In this way the researches of Staunton will filter through from edition to edition, till they become diffused and lost as the work of an individual. Thus the utility of his studies will survive long after his own name has ceased to appear on an edition of Shakspere.

While Staunton was engaged on his edition of Shakspere, an event took place in the chess world which directed attention to him in his old capacity of chess champion. This was the meteoric rise of Paul Morphy, who is generally regarded as the greatest chess player that the world has ever seen. When, in 1857, rumours reached Europe of the chess exploits of an American youth of barely twenty years, little notice was taken of them. America had yet to show she contained *any* players of master rank, and the fact that Morphy had vanquished everybody he had met on the other side of the Atlantic proved nothing. Nowadays, extraordinary skill can readily be tested. Its possessor can beat the champion of his own country and thus qualify for international honours, where he may demonstrate his title to go even further, and challenge the chess champion of the world. But in the fifties of last century it was different. Players had to rely on individual engagements to prove their prowess, and for this purpose Morphy came to Europe in 1858. He met successively Lowenthal, Harrwitz and Anderssen, easily defeating them all—winning, in fact, three games for every one he lost. Great hopes were placed on Anderssen in particular, for since the 1851 tournament he was regarded as the strongest player in Europe, with the possible exception of Staunton. Since Anderssen's defeat, then, Staunton was the last hope of Europe. But he steadily

declined to meet Morphy. Heavy literary work, bad
health, and want of practice were indeed a serious
handicap for such an encounter, even if he were willing
to meet the American master. But Staunton refused to
be drawn, and Morphy left Europe never to return.

It will ever remain a matter for regret that Staunton
did not see his way to meet Morphy in a match. Morphy
was modest to a fault. Unlike some modern masters, he
imposed no exacting conditions, such as heavy stakes or
the playing of a match in two hemispheres. He was
satisfied that "the play's the thing" that counts, and
was prepared to accommodate Staunton in any way he
could. That they never played was Staunton's fault.
As an offset against the disadvantages that Staunton
would have laboured under, the immaturity of Morphy
may be mentioned. It is hardly possible that he had
reached his best at twenty-one, while his *knowledge* of
the game—apart from sheer skill—was probably inferior
to Staunton's. Neither therefore was at his best.
Staunton's refusal to play Paul Morphy has injured
his reputation as a sportsman without increasing it as a
player. It is a pity he did not follow the chivalrous
example of Anderssen, who, like Staunton, had more or
less retired from hard play, and emerge to meet the new
conqueror, for the sake of the game he had done so much
to advance. But time has granted to Morphy that which
Staunton could not withhold. Few players now doubt that
Staunton would have met with a reverse in a match with
the American, and one cannot help thinking that it was
this lurking conviction in Staunton's mind that prevented
the contest from ever taking place. It is a thousand pities
that the spirit in which he met Harrwitz fourteen years
earlier, when he said of himself—

> "He either fears his fate too much,
>   Or his deserts are small,
> Who dares not put it to the touch
>   To win or lose by all,"

was lacking when it came to Morphy.

Truth to tell, Staunton's character exhibits a trait not
uncommon amongst artists of every sphere. He had a

very high opinion of his own powers, while frequently belittling those of others. He almost invariably referred to his contest with St. Amant as "The great Match between England and France," whereas it had no official international significance whatever. In one of the games of his match with Harrwitz, which Staunton lost, he referred to his own play as being "so deplorably bad, that it would be waste of time to comment on it in detail"— denying poor Harrwitz all credit! He frequently referred to Cochrane as "the *second* player in England." He unnecessarily accentuated his unsportsmanlike attitude towards Morphy by some of the notes to his games. Again, the notes attached to Anderssen's celebrated game with Dufresne—justly regarded as a gem of chess genius —were quite unworthy of Staunton.

The same year that Staunton completed his edition of Shakspere, 1860, he published his "Chess Praxis." This work carried the analysis of the "Handbook" still further, and added to Staunton's reputation as a master of theory. Probably no English writer on the game has left so many original lines of play, and Staunton did not shrink from departing from accepted theories where he thought they were wrong. The visit of Morphy more than ever impressed chess players with the importance of the "book"; for Morphy's knowledge of the openings was immense, and many of his games were scored by relentlessly pressing home an advantage gained in the opening. From the "Praxis," Staunton turned again to Shakspere. In 1864 he published a lithograph quarto of the first edition of "Much Ado About Nothing," and in 1866 he brought out his facsimile edition of the 1823 folio. He also published his "Memorials of Shakspere." Meantime he maintained his position as a chess journalist, his column in the *Illustrated London News* being the leading chess column in England. From 1865 to 1869 he edited and owned the *Chess World*. The former year also saw his "Great Schools of England"—a painstaking historical account of the famous public schools.

For two years prior to his death, Staunton was contributing a valuable series of papers to the *Athenæum* on

" Unsuspected Corruptions of Shakspere's text," to be embodied in a new edition of the poet's works, which, however, was never accomplished. These papers, perhaps more than anything else he had written, displayed Staunton's extraordinary powers of research. During these years, too, he was engaged on that new work on the game he had made a life study, which, as mentioned above, was finished and published two years after his death by R. B. Wormwald. This completed Staunton's contributions to the literature of the game. Half a dozen text books, several magazines wholly devoted to chess—which, however, did not live—and thirty years' continuous chess journalism—a splendid achievement! No other English writer has at all approached this record. Staunton found the game in England but little practised, with a meagre literature, and English players with no hope of holding their own with the continental masters. He left it enriched by his own researches, enormously increased as a pastime, and with exponents equal to the best in Europe. He was himself the first player to vindicate the capacity of his country to hold its own.

Death overtook this indefatigable worker literally in harness. He was actually engaged writing a letter to the *Athenæum* when his heart failed, and he was found dead, sitting at his writing-table, 22nd June, 1874, aged sixty-four.

Although Staunton was "the keenest Shaksperean critic of his day," it is probable that it will be by his connection with chess that he will be longest remembered. His knowledge of early English drama was truly remarkable. He was saturated, as it were, in the life of Elizabethan England, and this, combined with his natural acuteness, gave him great pre-eminence as a critic. But others have arisen to dispute his position in this field, while it is doubtful if England has ever produced his equal as a chess player, and certainly not as a theorist. Staunton's style of play belonged more to the modern school than to the gambit days of yore. He was essentially a sound player, fond of the " close " game. Of the ten games in which he had the move in his match with St. Amant, he only played 1. P—K 4 in two of them. In all the others he played either 1. P—Q 4 or 1. P—Q B 4. Walker characterised his play as showing " brilliancy of imagination, thirst for invention, judgment of position, eminent view of the board, and untiring patience." He was well acquainted with the modern principles of pawn play, and he was very rarely led into showy but unsound combinations. For this reason Staunton has left few, if any, games of outstanding brilliance. His are not the games a student would play over so much for amusement as for profit. He showed great resource in defence, restraint in complicated positions, and a rare knowledge of the end game.

In private life, Staunton was an agreeable man. His conversation was brilliant, and he had a great facility for apt quotation, particularly from Shakspere. He was an excellent story-teller, with that greatest of all boons in a raconteur, that he never repeated himself.

Staunton married early in the fifties Mrs. Nethersole, but left no family. Mrs. Staunton died in 1882.

The impetus that chess received from Staunton's achievements over the board, no less than from his instruction, has caused it to become as indissolubly blended in the hearts of his countrymen, as chess itself is with the name of Howard Staunton.

E. H. B.

The
Chess=Player's Handbook.

BOOK I.

INTRODUCTION.

CHAPTER I.

DESCRIPTION OF THE CHESS BOARD AND MEN—
ARRANGEMENT OF THE MEN—THE KING—THE
QUEEN—THE ROOKS OR CASTLES—THE BISHOPS—
THE KNIGHTS—AND THE PAWNS—THEIR MOVE-
MENTS, POWERS, METHOD OF CAPTURING AN
ADVERSE MAN, ETC.

THE game of Chess, the most fascinating and intellectual
pastime which the " wisdom of antiquity " has bequeathed
to us, is played by two persons, each having at command
a little army of sixteen men, upon a board divided into
sixty-four squares, eight on each of the four sides. The
squares are usually coloured white and black, or red and
white, alternately; and custom has made it an indispensable regulation in this country, that the board shall
be so placed that each player has a white square at his
right-hand corner. (a)

(a) This arrangement is merely conventional. In the earlier ages
of chess, the board was simply divided into sixty-four squares, without any difference of colour ; and there is good reason for believing
that the chess-men were then alike in form and size, and distinguish-
able only by an inscription or sign on each.

The following diagram represents the board with all the men arranged in proper order for the commencement of a game :—

No. 1.

BLACK.

WHITE.

Each player, it will be observed, has eight superior Pieces or officers, and eight minor ones which are called Pawns ; and for the purpose of distinction, the Pieces and Pawns of one party are of a different colour to those of the other.

The eight superior Pieces, on each side, are—

A King .   .   .   .   ♔ ♚

A Queen   .   .   .   .   ♕ ♛

Two Rooks, or Castles . . . . . ♖ ♜
   (as they are indiscriminately called)

Two Bishops . . . . ♗ ♝

Two Knights . . . . ♘ ♞

And each of these Pieces has his Pawn or ♙ ♟
   Foot-soldier . . . . . .

making in all an array of sixteen men on each side.

On beginning a game, these Pieces and Pawns are disposed in the manner shown on the foregoing diagram. The King and Queen occupy the centre squares of the first or "royal" line, as it is called, and each has for its supporters a Bishop, a Knight, and a Rook, while before the whole stand the Pawns or Foot-soldiers in a row. (To prevent a common error among young players, of misplacing the King and Queen on commencing a game, it is well to bear in mind that at the outset each Queen should stand on a square of her own colour.) The Pieces on the King's side of the board are called the King's, as King's Bishop, King's Knight, King's Rook; and the Pawns directly in front of them, the King's Pawn, King's Bishop's Pawn, King's Knight's Pawn, and King's Rook's Pawn. The Pieces on the Queen's side are, in like manner, called the Queen's Bishop, Queen's Knight, and Queen's Rook; and the Pawns before them, Queen's Pawn, Queen's Bishop's Pawn, Queen's Knight's Pawn, and Queen's Rook's Pawn.

MOVEMENT OF THE PIECES AND PAWNS.

A knowledge of the moves peculiar to these several men is so difficult to describe in writing, and so comparatively easy to acquire over the chess-board, from any competent person, that the learner is strongly recommended to avail himself of the latter means when practicable: for the use, however, of those who have no chess-playing acquaintance at command, the subjoined description will, it is hoped, suffice.

THE KING.

The King can move one square only at a time (except in "Castling," which will be explained hereafter), but he can make this move in any direction, forwards, backwards, laterally, or diagonally (*a*). He can take any one of the adversary's men which stands on an adjoining square to that he occupies, provided such man is left unprotected, and he has the peculiar privilege of being himself exempt from capture. He is not permitted, however, to move into check, that is, on to any square which is guarded by a Piece or Pawn of the enemy, nor can he, under any circumstance, be played to an adjacent square to that on which the rival King is stationed. Like most of the other Pieces, his power is greatest in the middle of the board, where, without obstruction, he has the choice of eight different squares. At the sides, he may play to any one of five, but when in the angles of the board, three squares only are at his command.

THE QUEEN.

The Queen is by much the most powerful of the forces. She has the advantage of moving as a Rook, in straight lines, forwards, backwards, and sideways, to the extent of the board in all directions, and as a Bishop, diagonally,

---

(*a*) The original movement of the King, or "Rey," as he was first called in Europe, appears to have been very limited, since he was restricted from moving at all, except by the necessity of extricating himself from an adverse check. About the beginning of the thirteenth century, he had the power of playing one square directly, but was not permitted to move or capture angularly; this limitation, however, lasted but a short period, and then the Rey had the privilege of moving and taking in any direction, as at present, but his range of action never extended beyond one square.

with the same range. To comprehend her scope of action, place her alone in the centre of the board; it will then be seen that she has the command of no less than twenty-seven squares, besides the one she stands on. (See diagram No. 4.)

 THE ROOK.

The Rook, or Castle, is next in power to the Queen. He moves in a straight line, forwards, backwards, or sideways, having a uniform range, on a clear board, of fourteen squares, exclusive of the one he occupies. (See *Castling*, page 22.)

 THE BISHOP.

The Bishop moves diagonally forwards or backwards, to the extent of the board. It follows, therefore, that he travels throughout the game only on squares of the same colour as the one on which he stands when the game begins, and that each player has a Bishop running on white squares, and one on black squares. When placed on a centre square of a clear board, he will be found to have a range of thirteen squares.

 THE KNIGHT.

The action of the Knight is peculiar, and not easy to describe. He is the only one of the Pieces which has the privilege of leaping over another man. The movements of the others are all dependent on their freedom from obstruction by their own and the enemy's men. For example, when the forces are duly ranged in order of battle before the commencement of the game, the Knight is the only one of the eight capital Pieces which can be played before the Pawns are moved—King, Queen, Bishop, and Rook are all hemmed in by the rank of Pawns, which they cannot overleap; but the Knight, having the liberty of springing over the heads of other men, can be brought into the field at once. In this case, as his move is one square *in a straight line*, and *one in an oblique direction*, if the King's Knight were to begin the game, he must be played either to King's Rook's third square, or to King's Bishop's third square; and if the Queen's Knight commenced, he must be moved to Queen's Rook's third square, or to Queen's Bishop's third square.

The following diagram will serve, perhaps, to make his action better understood. (See also pages 11 and 42, for a description of the powers and peculiarities of this Piece.)

No. 2.

BLACK.

WHITE.

In this position we have the Knight surrounded by Pawns in a way which would render any other Piece immovable. A King, Queen, Rook, or Bishop, so encompassed by their own forces, could never stir until one of the men were moved to make an outlet; and, if thus shut in by *adverse* Pawns, could escape only by being enabled to capture one or other of them. But the Knight clears such impediments at a bound, and can here be played to any one of the eight white squares around. It is worth remarking, that if he is stationed on a *white* square in the centre of the board, he has then eight *black* squares at his choice; because, from the peculiarity of his move, it is impossible for him to spring from one white square to another white one, or from a black square to a black square. On placing him on any square at the side of the board, it will be seen that his scope of action is much diminished, and when standing on either of the four corners, or Rook's squares, as they are called, he has then only two squares to which he can leap.

The Pawn.

The Pawn moves only one square at a time, and that *straight forward*, except in the act of capturing, when it takes one step diagonally to the right or left file on to the square occupied by the man taken, and continues on that file until it captures another man. A power has been conceded to it, however, in latter times, of going *two steps when first played* in the game, *provided no hostile Pawn commands the first square over which he moves*, but, in that case, the adverse Pawn has the option of taking him in his passage, *as if he had moved one step only* (see the diagram, No. 9). A Pawn is the only one of the forces *which goes out of his direction to capture*, and which has not the advantage of moving backwards; but it has one remarkable privilege, by which on occasions it becomes invaluable, *whenever it reaches the extreme square of the file on which it travels, it is invested with the title and assumes the power of any superior Piece, except the King, which the player chooses*. From this circumstance it frequently

happens that one party, by skilful management of his
Pawns, contrives to have two, and sometimes even three,
Queens on the board at once, a combination of force
which of course is irresistible.

ON CAPTURING AN ADVERSE MAN.

The "Pieces," by which title the eight superior officers
are technically designated, in contradistinction to the
"Pawns," all take in the same direction in which they
move. This act consists in removing the adverse Piece
or Pawn from the board, and placing the captor on the
square the former occupied. To make this clear, we will
begin with the King, and show his mode of capturing an
adverse man.

No. 3.

BLACK.

WHITE.

Supposing the above to be the position of the men towards the conclusion of a game, and it being either party's turn to play, he could take the adverse Pawn from the board, and place his King on the square it occupied; and by doing so, the King would not depart from the order of his march, which, as we have before said, permits him to move *one step* in every direction. In each of these instances we have placed the Pawn in *front* of the King, but he would be equally entitled to take it were it standing on any other of the eight squares immediately surrounding him, *always provided it was not sustained or guarded by some other Piece or Pawn.*

The next diagram will exhibit the power of the Queen in capturing an enemy.

No. 4.

BLACK. 2

7   WHITE. 6

Thus placed in the middle of the board, the range of the Queen is immense. She has here the option of taking any one of eight men if they were placed at the extremities of the board, on the squares respectively numbered 1, 2, 3, 4, 5, 6, 7, and 8, should her line of march be unobstructed; and if these men were nearer, on any of the intermediate squares, indicated by the dotted lines, she would be equally enabled to take any one of them at her choice. Like all the other Pieces and Pawns she

No. 5.

BLACK.

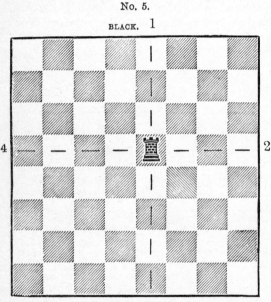

WHITE.

effects the capture by removing the man from the board, and stationing herself on the vacated square.

The Rook has the same power in taking as the Queen, forwards, backwards, and sideways, but he cannot, like her, take any man diagonally.

For example, place the Rook in the centre of the board, and an opposing man on each of the squares numbered, and the Rook has the power of taking any one of the four; and he has the same power if the Pieces are on any of the intervening squares as indicated.

The BISHOP takes, as he moves, diagonally, either forwards or backwards, his range extending, on unobstructed squares, to the extent of the diagonal line on which he travels.

No. 6.

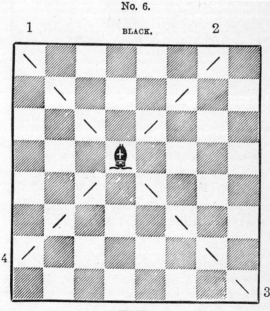

WHITE.

The KNIGHT, as we have seen before, moves or leaps one square forward and one obliquely, his action being a combination of the shortest move of the Rook and the shortest move of the Bishop. In other words, he moves to the next square but one—of a different colour. His power and method of taking an opponent's man will be seen from the diagram subjoined.

No. 7.

BLACK.

WHITE.

In this situation, in the centre of the board, he would have the power of taking any one of the men stationed on the squares numbered, by removing the man and placing himself on the vacant square. (a)

(a) There is no evidence, we believe, to show that the Knight has undergone any variation in action or power, since the first introduction of chess into Europe. His move appears to be supplementary to the range of the other forces, and to comprehend just those squares of the board over which none of them, similarly placed, would have command.

The PAWN, as we have previously observed, is the only man which captures in a direction different from his line of march. He is permitted to move only one square forward at a time, except on his first move, and is not allowed to take any Piece or Pawn which may impede his path. If, however, he meets with any of the adverse force on a point diagonal, one step either to the right or left of the square he occupies, he is at liberty to capture that man and take his place on the next file; for example:—

No. 8.

BLACK.

WHITE.

Suppose, at the opening of the game, White begins by playing P — K 4 (see the article on Notation, p. 15), Black may reply in the same manner with P — K 4, and neither Pawn can do more than remain an obstruction to the onward march of the other. But if Black instead played P—Q 4 as in Diagram 8, then White, if he likes, may take the adverse Pawn from the board and place his own in its stead. To exemplify another peculiarity of the Pawn, suppose White in this situation preferred playing the Pawn on to K 5, instead of taking Black's Pawn, the following would be the aspect of the board:—

No. 9.

BLACK.

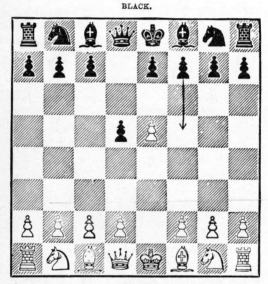

WHITE.

If, now, Black chose to play P—K B 4 as shown by the arrow, White has the option of taking that Pawn (in passing, as it is called), just as if Black, instead of playing it two steps, had moved it to K B 3 only. White, in fact, might arrest it in its leap over the King's Bishop's third square, take it off the board, and station his King's Pawn on the said Bishop's third square, as in an ordinary case of capture. But if he omit to exercise this power at once, he is not allowed to do so after another move has been made (a).

This privilege of the Pawn to take, in passing, another Pawn which attempts to advance two steps when first moved, is so very imperfectly understood by beginners, and is the cause of so much misunderstanding, that every one should comprehend it thoroughly before he begins to play a game in earnest.

CHAPTER II.

CHESS NOTATION.

IT will be obvious that without an easy method of re-cording games, chess players would not only be precluded from studying the games and analysis of their con-temporaries, but would also be shut out from the great republic of chess literature that centuries of skill and industry have accumulated. Notation is, in short, the language of the game, and it has taken many years to evolve the present simple form of recording games. Various systems have from time to time been tried. But here—this not purporting to be a history of notation—we shall but briefly mention two, which will suffice for all practical purposes for the student.

The ENGLISH NOTATION, adaptations of which are used in various foreign countries, is based on naming each

(a) The reason for this power of taking *en passant* will be readily understood when it is remembered that formerly Pawns were only allowed to move one square at a time. To accelerate the opening of a game Pawns were given the privilege of either moving one or two squares on the first move, at the will of the player. This privilege, however, does not override the much older *right* of an opposing Pawn to capture as if the Pawn had only been played one square; hence the *en passant* rule.

file from the piece that stands on it at the beginning of the game, and numbering the eight squares of the file from one to eight from each side of the board, as in the following diagram:—

No. 10.

FILES.

BLACK.

QR1 / QR8	QKt1 / QKt8	QB1 / QB8	Q1 / Q8	K1 / K8	KB1 / KB8	KKt1 / KKt8	KR1 / KR8
QR2 / QR7	QKt2 / QKt7	QB2 / QB7	Q2 / Q7	K2 / K7	KB2 / KB7	KKt2 / KKt7	KR2 / KR7
QR3 / QR6	QKt3 / QKt6	QB3 / QB6	Q3 / Q6	K3 / K6	KB3 / KB6	KKt3 / KKt6	KR3 / KR6
QR4 / QR5	QKt4 / QKt5	QB4 / QB5	Q4 / Q5	K4 / K5	KB4 / KB5	KKt4 / KKt5	KR4 / KR5
QR5 / QR4	QKt5 / QKt4	QB5 / QB4	Q5 / Q4	K5 / K4	KB5 / KB4	KKt5 / KKt4	KR5 / KR4
QR6 / QR3	QKt6 / QKt3	QB6 / QB3	Q6 / Q3	K6 / K3	KB6 / KB3	KKt6 / KKt3	KR6 / KR3
QR7 / QR2	QKt7 / QKt2	QB7 / QB2	Q7 / Q2	K7 / K2	KB7 / KB2	KKt7 / KKt2	KR7 / KR2
QR8 / QR1	QKt8 / QKt1	QB8 / QB1	Q8 / Q1	K8 / K1	KB8 / KB1	KKt8 / KKt1	KR8 / KR1

RANKS. RANKS.

WHITE.

FILES.

It will be seen that the files have the same name for each player, but the numbers are different. Thus White's King's Bishop's Square, or K B 1 as it is concisely written, is Black's King's Bishop's Eighth, or K B 8. White's K 3 is Black's K 6, etc. It may be thought that this double numbering would lead to confusion, but it rarely does; and very little practice will enable the student to visualise any square on the board.

The Pawns are named after the Piece in front of which each stands. That in front of the King is the King's Pawn, K P; that in front of the Queen's Rook is the Queen's Rook's Pawn, or Q R P, etc.

Having now a separate name for each square on the board, moves are recorded by naming the Piece to be moved and the square to which it is played. The first three moves of the Ruy Lopez opening would be written as follows :—

WHITE.	BLACK.
1. King's Pawn to King's Fourth Square.	1. King's Pawn to King's Fourth Square.
2. King's Knight to King's Bishop's Third Square.	2. Queen's Knight to Queen's Bishop's Third Square.
3. King's Bishop to Queen's Knight's Fifth Square.	3. King's Knight to King's Bishop's Third Square.

This is the notation fully written, and as it is to be found in the old books. It was seen that all this is unnecessary, so it was contracted thus :—

WHITE.	BLACK.
1. K P to K 4th	1. K P to K 4th
2. K Kt to K B 3rd	2. Q Kt to Q B 3rd
3. K B to Q Kt 5th	3. K Kt to K B 3rd.

As in the vast majority of cases only one Piece or Pawn can be played to the same square, it is therefore unnecessary to state the particular Piece or Pawn, *i.e.*, King's Bishop or Queen's Bishop. By substituting a dash—for the word "to" the English notation, as generally written, becomes :—

WHITE.	BLACK.
1. P—K 4	1. P—K 4
2. Kt—K B 3	2. Kt—Q B 3
3. B—Kt 5	3. Kt—B 3

Occasionally the dash is omitted and the move simply written, P K 4 ; but the dash, by distinguishing the Piece from the square, is an assistance to the student.

It will be observed that with regard to the first move,

since only one Pawn can be played to K 4, it is unnecessary to say King's Pawn, so the K is omitted.
With regard to the second move, each Knight could be
played to its Bishop's Third, hence K or Q, according as
it is the King's or Queen's Knight is moved, must be
added. Sometimes this move would be written K Kt—B 3
instead of Kt—K B 3, but the latter is perhaps more
consistent.

In the above example White's third move is written
simply B—Kt 5 : had his Queen's Pawn been previously
played to Q 4, so that either of his Bishops could move to
Kt 5 (the *King's* Bishop to *Queen's* Knight 5 or the
Queen's Bishop to *King's* Knight 5), it would have been
necessary to show which Bishop he intended to move.
The move actually taken would be then recorded B—Q Kt 5
or K B—Kt 5—preferably the former. It will be noticed
that at his third move, Black, having already played one
Kt to B 3, only one can now be played there, so it is
merely stated Kt—B 3.

If a piece is to be taken the multiplication sign × is
used, as B × Kt, P × P, etc. When check is written,
ch. is written after the move, thus, B—Kt 5 ch., R × P ch.,
etc. If double check is given (*i.e.*, check by two or more
pieces), db. is inserted before the ch., as Kt—B 4 db. ch.
Sometimes the sign + denotes check, but as this sign is
used in the analysis of the present work to show when
either side has a superiority, its double use was not
thought advisable. Discovered check is shown—d. ch.

When this notation was first introduced one would
come across such legends as the following, in the middle
of a game, to denote a simple move.

King's Bishop's Pawn takes King's Knight's Pawn.

With initials only this reads :—

K B P × K Kt P.

It is, however, only in extremely rare cases, that all this
is essential. The rare case is—when *both* of Black's
Knight's Pawns can be taken, and both can be taken
withal, by *either of two Pawns of White*. Ordinarily, P × P
would be sufficient, but if more than one Pawn can take,

and more than one Pawn can be taken, the exact Pawns concerned must then be indicated. The rule therefore for modern English notation, is to give what is essential to describe the move, and *no more*. It sometimes happens that two Pieces can take the same Piece or Pawn, or move to the same square. The square on which the Piece stands that is to be moved is then placed in brackets, thus :—

Kt (K 4) × B.

This means that either of White's Knights could take a Black Bishop, and he does so with the one on K 4.

The GERMAN NOTATION is founded on numbering and lettering the board as in the following diagram :

No. 11.

BLACK.

WHITE.

The moves are shown by giving the squares on which the Piece stands, and the one to which it is to be moved. In the case of the Pawns the squares merely are given, but with Pieces the initial letter of the Piece (in capitals) is also given, though this is not essential. The first few moves in the Giuoco Piano Opening read thus in the German notation :—

1. *e* 2—*e* 4   *e* 7—*e* 5
2. S *g* 1—*f* 3   S *b* 8—*c* 6
3. L *f* 1—*c* 4   L *f* 8—*c* 5
4. *d* 2—*d* 3   *d* 7—*d* 6

At first this form of naming the squares is puzzling. With a little practice, however, they become as easy to locate as in the English system, possibly easier, since neither ranks nor files are duplicated. It is more consistently concise too, for since no two Pieces can stand on the same square at the same time, naming the square which a Piece leaves as well as that to which it goes, precludes all possibility of misunderstanding. In this system × means takes ; + check ; † takes with a check ; ‡ mate.

Both the English and the German systems of notation are commonly used in fractional form, the moves of the White Pieces being recorded above the line, and Black below, as follows :—

1. $\frac{P-K 4}{P-K 4}$ 2. $\frac{Kt-K B 3}{Kt-Q B 3}$ 3. $\frac{B-B 4}{B-B 4}$ 4. $\frac{P-Q 3}{P-Q 3}$, etc.

1. $\frac{e\, 2-e\, 4}{e\, 7-e\, 5}$ 2. $\frac{S\, g\, 1-f\, 3}{S\, b\, 8-c\, 6}$ 3. $\frac{L\, f\, 1-c\, 4}{L\, f\, 8-c\, 5}$ 4. $\frac{d\, 2-d\, 3}{d\, 7-d\, 6}$, etc.

It will be observed that in the present work this form is adopted for the analysis, while the ordinary method of writing the moves opposite each other is used in the illustrative games.

It now but remains to mention an exceedingly simple method of recording positions, problems, etc. Starting at white's Q R 8 read the rank across from left to right, then the next rank, and so on down the board. White's

Pieces and Pawns are denoted by capitals, Black's by small letters, and the vacant squares by numbers. At the end of a rank it is convenient to draw a stroke / to save confusion by running into the next rank. Below we give a celebrated position in a game between Morphy and Paulsen, in Diagram, and also in the Forsyth notation— so called after Mr. David Forsyth, its inventor.

No. 11A.

BLACK.

WHITE.

$$4r1k/p1pb1ppp/Qbp1r3/8/$$
$$1P6/2PQ1B2/R2P1PPP/2B2RK1$$

The simplicity of this method of recording positions is self-evident, and it has proved extremely useful for taking down adjourned games.

CHAPTER III

TECHNICAL TERMS.

CASTLES or Castling (a).—Although, as a general rule, the move of the King is restricted to one square at a time, he has the privilege, under certain conditions, once in the game, of moving in conjunction with either of the Rooks two squares. This peculiar movement is called *Castling*, and is performed in the following manner:—If a player wishes to castle on his King's side of the board, he simultaneously moves the King to King's Knight's square and his King's Rook to King's Bishop's square. If he castles on the Queen's side, he simultaneously plays his King to Queen's Bishop's square, and Queen's Rook to Queen's square.

A player may not Castle:—1. If his King is in check. 2. If either the King or the Castling Rook has moved. 3. If the King has to move over or on to a square commanded by the enemy. 4. If there is any Piece, either of his own or the adversary's, between the King and the Rook.

In exemplification of the importance of castling, to escape from an attack, and to retort one on the adversary, see, presently, the diagram, No. 12.

The following diagram illustrates the operating of Castling:—

(a) The practice of castling is a European innovation of comparatively modern origin. In the oriental nations, the birthplace of chess, castling was unknown, and the earliest authors upon the game in Europe, Damiano (1512), and Lopez (1561), make no allusion to it, but mention only the "leap of the King," a peculiar privilege derived from the Eastern game, which permitted the King, on his being first played, provided he had not been checked, to move and even make a capture like a Knight.

No. 12.

BLACK.

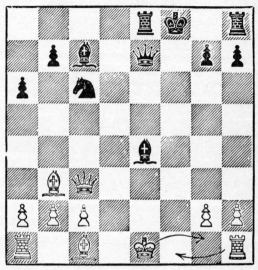

WHITE.

In this situation the White King is threatened with what is called "a discovered check," that is, his opponent, by removing the Bishop would *discover* check from the Queen. Not being at the moment in check, however, and having moved neither King nor Rook, and there being no Piece between them, White may castle as indicated, incidentally giving check.

Check.—The King is said to be in *check* when he is attacked by any Piece or Pawn.

Though it is usual to do so, the attacking party is not obliged to announce "check."

Checkmate (or merely "mate") occurs when the attacked King cannot legally move, *i.e.* when he cannot move out of check.

DOUBLED PAWN.

When two Pawns of the same colour are on the same file the front one is called a *doubled Pawn*.

DRAWN GAME.

When neither party can give checkmate, the game is drawn. This may arise from several causes, as :—1st. *Perpetual check.* 2nd. Where there is not sufficient force to effect a mate, as a King and a Knight only, or a King and two Knights, etc. 3rd. Where one party has force sufficient, but is ignorant of the proper mode of applying it, and thus fails to checkmate his helpless adversary within the fifty moves prescribed. 4th. Where both parties persist in repeating the same move from fear of each other. 5th. Where both parties are left with the same force at the end, as a Queen against a Queen, a Rook against a Rook, and the like, when, except in particular cases, the game should be resigned as a drawn battle. And 6th. When one of the Kings is *stalemated*.

EN PRISE.

When a Piece or Pawn is in a situation to be taken by the enemy, it is said to be *en prise.* To put a Piece *en prise*, is to play it so that it may be captured.

THE EXCHANGE.

When a player gains a Rook for a Bishop or a Knight, it is termed *winning the exchange.*

FALSE MOVE.

Any illegal move, such as castling when the King has been moved or is in check, moving a Rook diagonally, or a Bishop like a Knight, is called a false or an "impossible" move.

FOOL'S MATE.

This is the simplest of all checkmates, being accomplished in two moves in the following manner :—

WHITE.	BLACK.
1. P—K Kt 4	1. P—K 4
2. P—K B 4	2. Q—R 5, mate.

It cannot possibly be given by the first player.

FORCED MOVE.

When a player has only one legal move at command, it is said to be a *forced move*.

GAMBIT.

This word is derived from an Italian phrase in wrestling, and signifies a movement by which the adversary is tripped up. In chess, this is attempted by the first player putting a Pawn *en prise* of the enemy early in the game, by which he is enabled more rapidly and effectually to develop his superior Pieces. There are several gambits, but the most important, and one which includes many others, is the King's gambit, commenced as follows :—

WHITE.	BLACK.
1. P—K 4	1. P—K 4
2. P—K B 4	2. P×P.

The Pawn offered by the first player here at his second move is called the Gambit Pawn, and when taken by the adversary the opening becomes a gambit.

The varieties of the gambits are often designated by the names of the players who invented or first brought them into vogue—as the *Muzio* gambit, the *Salvio* gambit, the *Allgaier* gambit, the *Lopez* gambit ; while others obtain their names from the opening moves of the first player, as the King's Bishop's gambit, which begins thus :—

WHITE.	BLACK.
1. P—K 4	1. P—K 4
2. P—K B 4	2. P×P
3. B—B 4	

and is so called because the King's Bishop is played out at the third move instead of the King's Knight.

There is also the Queen's gambit, of which the opening moves are :—

WHITE.	BLACK.
1. P—Q 4	1. P—Q 4
2 P—Q B 4	2. P×P.

The gambits are the most brilliant and animated of all the openings, full of hair-breadth escapes and perilous vicissitudes, but affording an infinitude of beautiful and daring combinations.

GIUOCO PIANO.

A solid and instructive modification of the King's Knight's game. The opening moves are :—

WHITE.	BLACK.
1. P—K 4	1. P—K 4
2. K Kt—B 3	2. Q Kt—B 3.
3. B—B 4	3. B—B 4.

TO INTERPOSE.

When the King is checked, or any valuable Piece in danger from the attack of an enemy, you are said to *interpose* a man when you play it between the attacked and attacking Piece.

ISOLATED PAWN.

A Pawn which stands alone, without the support and protection of other Pawns, is termed an *isolated* Pawn.

J'ADOUBE.

A French expression, signifying " I arrange," or " I replace," which is used by a player when he touches a man merely to adjust its position on the board, without intending to play it.

MINOR PIECES.

The Bishop and Knight, in contradistinction to the Queen and Rook, are called *minor Pieces*.

THE OPPOSITION.

An important manœuvre in playing the King, by which one player is enabled to occupy certain key squares, and thus compel the adverse King to abandon a favourable position.

PARTY.

From the French *partie*. Frequently used by modern writers instead of the word "game."

PASSED PAWN.

A Pawn is said to be a *passed* one when the adversary has no Pawn to obstruct its march on the same file, or on either of the next files to the right or left.

PION COIFFÉ OR MARKED PAWN.

This is a description of odds but rarely given, and only when there is a vast disparity between the skill of the players. It consists in one party placing a *cap* or ring on one of his Pawns, and undertaking to checkmate his opponent with that particular Pawn. He is not allowed to *Queen* the Pawn, and if he loses it, or happens to checkmate his opponent with any other man, he forfeits the game. The Pawn usually *capped* is the King's Knight's, because it can be more readily and effectually surrounded by protecting Pieces.

TO QUEEN A PAWN, OR TO ADVANCE A PAWN TO QUEEN.

When a player has contrived to advance a Pawn to the eighth or last square of the file, it assumes the rank and power of a Queen, or any other Piece he chooses, and he is then said to have *Queened* his Pawn.

SCHOLAR'S MATE.

A checkmate occasionally given at the opening of a game by a practised player to one but little tutored in the science.   The following are the moves :—

WHITE.	BLACK
1. P—K 4	1. P—K 4
2. B—B 4	2. B—B 4
3. Q—R 5	3. P—Q 3
4. Q×P, mate.	

SMOTHERED MATE.

A checkmate which is sometimes given by the Knight, when the adverse King is hemmed in, or *smothered*, by his own forces.   (See diagram No. 16.)

STALEMATE.

When one party has his King so circumstanced that not being at the moment in check, he cannot play him without going into check, and at the same time has no other Piece or Pawn to move instead he is said to be *stalemated*, and the game is considered drawn.   (See diagram No. 17.)

TAKING A PAWN EN PASSANT, OR IN PASSING.

It has been shown before, in speaking of the action of the Pawn, that he is limited in his march to one square forward at a time, when not capturing, and one square forward diagonally, either to the right or left, when he takes an adversary, but that he has the privilege, on being first played in the game, to advance two squares, unless in so doing he passes a square which is attacked by a hostile Pawn; in which case the opponent may, at his option, permit him to make the two steps forward, and there remain, or may capture him in his passage in the same way as if he had moved but one step.   (See diagram No. 9.)

CHECKMATE.

No. 13.

BLACK.

WHITE.

White to move and mate in two moves.

Above is an example of mate. White plays Q × P ch. Black can now only save his King in two ways, either by taking White's Q with his P, or by interposing his B. If Black plays P × Q, White replies with B — Kt. 6 mate,— since Black cannot move his King out of check, nor interpose a Piece, nor take White's Bishop. If instead of taking the Q, Black had interposed his B by playing it to K 2, White would simply take the B with his Q, giving mate again. Black cannot take White's Q, for it is protected by a Bishop.

DISCOVERED CHECK AND CHECKMATE.

No. 14.

BLACK.

WHITE.

The above diagram illustrates both *discovered check*, and also *checkmate*. White has the move, and it will be seen that his own Rook prevents his Bishop from attacking the Black King. He therefore plays R—Kt 6 giving *discovered check*. Black cannot move his King out of check, he must therefore *interpose* his Queen on Kt 2, between his own King and the White Bishop. White now plays R × R *mate*—since Black cannot take the Rook nor interpose any Piece between it and his King.

PERPETUAL CHECK.

No. 15.

BLACK.

WHITE.

This position is a modification of the preceding one, to illustrate *perpetual check*. White has the move, and having less force than Black, is satisfied to get a drawn game. He therefore plays Q—B 6 check. Black cannot move his King out of check, so therefore he must interpose his Queen again on Kt 2. White now plays Q—K 8 check, and Black, still not being able to move his King out of check, must bring back his Queen to Kt 1, and White repeats the previous move, thus giving perpetual check and gaining a draw.

SMOTHERED MATE.

No. 16.

BLACK.

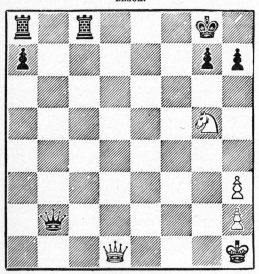

WHITE.

This is a familiar example of *smothered mate*, which you will find can be effected by no other Piece than the Knight. White's first move is, Queen to her 5th square, checking. Black is obliged to retreat his King to the Rook's square, because, were he to play him to his Bishop's square, the Queen would checkmate at once. Upon the King retiring, White gives check with his Knight at K B 7; this brings the King back again to Knight's square, and affords to White an opportunity of giving *double check*, which he does by moving the Knight to K R 6, checking with both Queen and Knight; as before, the King must go to Rook's square; and now follows a

beautiful move—White plays his Queen down to *K Kt* 8
(next square to the Black King), giving check; the King
cannot take on account of the Knight; he is compelled,
therefore, to capture with his Rook, and the Knight then
gives the *smothered mate* at K B 7.

STALEMATE.

No. 17.

BLACK.

WHITE.

White has the move. He cannot move his Queen from
in front of his King, for then the latter would be in
check. He has nothing better to do than to take Black's
Rook, but then the latter is stalemated, since his King is
not in check. He cannot move it without going into
check, and he has no other move.

CHAPTER IV.

ON THE RELATIVE VALUE OF THE CHESS FORCES.

AN attempt to establish a scale of powers whereby the relative values of the several men could be estimated with mathematical exactitude, although it has frequently engaged the attention of scientific minds, appears to be an expenditure of ingenuity and research upon an unattainable object. So ever varying, so much dependant on the mutations of *position* which every move occasions, and on the augmented power which it acquires when combined with other forces, is the proportionate worth of this with that particular man, that it would seem to be beyond the reach of computation to devise a formula by which it can be reckoned with precision. But still an approximation to correctness has been made, and the result arrived at gives the following as the ultimate respective values :—

$$
\begin{aligned}
\text{Pawn} &= 1 \cdot 00 \\
\text{Knight} &= 3 \cdot 05 \\
\text{Bishop} &= 3 \cdot 50 \\
\text{Rook} &= 5 \cdot 48 \\
\text{Queen} &= 9 \cdot 94
\end{aligned}
$$

The King, from the nature of the game, which does not admit of his being exchanged or captured, is invaluable, and he is not, therefore, included in the calculations.

The Pawn, it is seen, is the least valuable of all the men, the Knight being worth at least three Pawns.

The Bishops and Knights are practically considered of equal value, although there is a difference in the estimate here given.

A Rook is of the value of five Pawns and a fraction and may be exchanged for a minor Piece and two Pawns. Two Rooks may be exchanged for three minor Pieces.

The Queen is usually reckoned equal, in average

situations, to two Rooks and a Pawn, but towards the end of a game she is hardly so valuable as two Rooks.

These comparative values may be of service to the student in general cases of exchanging men, but he will find in practice the relative worth of his soldiers is modified by so many circumstances of time, opportunity, and position, that nothing but experience can ever teach him to determine accurately in every case "which to give up and which to keep."

Chapter V.

THE LAWS OF THE GAME.

The following Laws, with some trifling variations, have been in general use for the last hundred years. They have been embodied in the British Chess Code, and are now universally adopted by all the chess clubs of Great Britain.

I.

The chess-board must be so placed that each player has a white square at his right-hand corner of the board. If the board has been improperly placed, either player may require the game to be annulled, provided the game has not been finished, and that *four* moves on each side have not been played, but not afterwards.

II.

If a Piece or Pawn be misplaced at the beginning of the game, either player may require the game to be annulled, if it is not finished, and before the second player has played his fourth move, but not afterwards.

III.

Should a player, at the commencement of the game, omit to place all his men on the board, either player may require the game to be annulled, if it is not finished, and before the second player has played his fourth move, but not afterwards.

IV.

If a player, undertaking to give the odds of a Piece or Pawn, neglect to remove it from the board, his adversary, after four moves have been played on each side, has the choice of proceeding with or recommencing the game.

V.

When no odds are given, the players must take the first move of each game alternately, drawing lots to determine who shall begin the first game. Unless otherwise arranged the first player in each game shall take White.

VI.

The player who gives the odds has the right of moving first in each game, unless otherwise agreed. Where a Pawn, Knight, Bishop or Rook is conceded, unless otherwise agreed it shall be the King's Bishop's Pawn, the Queen's Knight, the Queen's Bishop, or the Queen's Rook.

VII.

A Piece or Pawn touched must be played, unless immediately before touching it the player announces his intention of adjusting it; *but if a Piece or Pawn be displaced by accident, it may be restored to its place without penalty.*

VIII.

While a player holds the Piece or Pawn he has touched, he may play it to any other than the square he took it from; but, having quitted it, he cannot recall the move.

IX.

Should a player touch one of his adversary's Pieces or Pawn's other than for adjusting it, his adversary may compel him to take it; but if it cannot be legally taken, he may oblige him to move the King; if his King, however, cannot be legally moved, his opponent may indicate a man which he must move.

X.

If a player takes one of his adversary's men with one of his own that cannot legally take it, his antagonist may require him to replace the man, and then (a) take it with a legal move if he can ; (b) if he cannot, then to move his King; (c) if he cannot move his King, his opponent can indicate a Piece to be moved.

XI.

Should a player take one of his own men with another, his adversary has the option of obliging him to move either.

XII.

If a player makes an illegal move, his opponent may require him to (a) move that man legally; (b) or if he cannot, move his King; (c) or if he cannot move his King, his opponent can indicate a Piece to be moved.

XIII.

Should a player move out of his turn, his adversary may require him to replace the man and then when his turn to play comes, (a) move it; or (b) if he cannot, move his King; or (c) if he cannot move his King, his opponent can indicate a man to be moved.

XIV.

When a Pawn is first moved in a game, it may be played one or two squares ; but in the latter case the opponent has the privilege of taking it *en passant* with any Pawn which could have taken it had it been played one square only. A Pawn cannot be taken *en passant* by a Piece. See page 14.

XV.

A player cannot castle in the following cases :—
1. If the King or Rook have been moved.
2. If the King be in check.
3. If there be any Piece between the King and Rook.
4. If the King passes over any square attacked by one of the adversary's Pieces or Pawns.   See page 22.

XVI.

If a player touch a Piece or Pawn that cannot be moved without leaving the King in check, he must replace the Piece or Pawn and move his King; but if the King cannot be moved, he may be required to move a man selected by his opponent.

XVII.

Every Pawn which has reached the eighth or last square on the chess-board, must be immediately exchanged for a Queen or any other Piece (of the same colour) the player may think fit, even though all the Pieces remain on the board.   It follows, therefore, that he may have two or more Queens, three or more Rooks, Bishops, or Knights.

XVIII.

A player may claim a game as drawn if he can prove that the last fifty moves on each side have been made without a Pawn being moved or a Piece taken.

XIX.

If a player agree to checkmate with a particular Piece or Pawn, or on a particular square, or engage to force his adversary to stalemate or checkmate him, he is not restricted to any number of moves.

XX.

A stalemate is a drawn game.

XXI.

If a player make an illegal move, the adversary must take notice of such irregularity before he touches a Piece or Pawn, or he will not be allowed to inflict any penalty.

CHAPTER VI.

GENERAL RULES AND OBSERVATIONS.

CONCERNING THE KING.

IT is generally advisable to castle the King pretty early in the game, and to do so on the King's side, because he is less subject to an attack, and better able to repel one on that side than the other—nevertheless, it frequently happens, that a player by castling on the Queen's side, is enabled to make a formidable assault on the adverse King, by throwing forward his King's flank Pawns. When the Queens are exchanged off early in the game, it is often well to move the King to K B 2, and in that way bring the Rooks into play, instead of castling, because there is then less danger to the King, and he may become a valuable auxiliary during the remainder of the fight. In castling, move the King before you touch the Rook.

Be fearful, when castled on the King's side, of permitting an adverse Knight to gain safe possession of your K B 4 square, and remember that it is seldom prudent in an inexperienced player to advance the Pawns on the side on which his King has castled.

Be cautious of playing your Queen in front of your King. Never subject yourself to a discovered check. It is better when check is given to your King to interpose a man that attacks the checking Piece than with one that does not. Beware of giving useless checks to your adversary's King, but when, by checking, you can oblige him to move, and thus deprive him of the right to castle, it is generally good play to do so. It is sometimes useful to give a series of checks, and even sacrifice a Piece, to force the King into the middle of the board, where he may be subjected to the attacks of your other men.

Do not in all cases take an enemy's Pawn which stands before your King—it may serve sometimes as a protection to him; and bear in mind that towards the termination of a game, especially when the superior Pieces have been taken off the board, the King should be made to compensate for his previous inactivity, by being busily engaged. The fate of the game is then dependant for the most part on the skill displayed in the management of the King.

CONCERNING THE QUEEN.

The Queen is so powerful and important a Piece at chess that she should rarely be employed to defend or attack any point if you can do it as well with a subordinate.

It is not good to play the Queen out into the game at the beginning, because she can be attacked by inferior Pieces, and is compelled to retire with the loss of many moves.

Be careful, too, when about to capture a distant Pawn or Piece, that you do not remove your Queen too far from the immediate point of action. A clever player will often permit you to win a Pawn with the Queen, that he may prevent her returning in time to rescue your King from his attack. The power of the Queen is wonderfully greater when she is aided and protected by other Pieces than when she goes forth unsupported; it is generally injudicious, therefore, to make an attack with her unless in combination with some other of your forces.

CONCERNING THE ROOK.

The Rook is a most important officer, yet few players even among the best avail themselves sufficiently of his power. He has seldom much scope for action in the early part of the engagement, but when the field is thinned no time should be lost in bringing him into action. You should then endeavour to *double* your Rooks, that is, to place them one before the other on the same file: in this situation, mutually sustaining one another, their power on a clear board is equal to the Queen's—sometimes superior.

It is usually good play to get command of an open file, that is to say, a file which is occupied by no other man, by stationing a Rook at one end of it. When you have thus gained possession of the file, should your opponent try to dispossess you of it, by playing one of his Rooks on to the same file, it is frequently better to defend with your other Rook than to take his or remove your own. You will often embarrass your adversary, too, if you can manage to post a Rook on his second rank, say at your K 7 or Q 7. In this position he generally makes an attack on the Pawns unmoved, and compels the enemy to lose time in defending them, while you can bring more forces into action.

One of the strongest reasons for playing out your Pieces early in the battle, is, that while at home they are not only themselves inactive, but they utterly retard the movements of your Rooks. In an unskilfully developed game it is a common occurrence to see the victory won before the defeated player's Rooks have been moved.

CONCERNING THE BISHOP.

When the game is opened by each party with P—K 4, the King's Bishop is somewhat superior to the Queen's because it can be sooner brought into play, and may be made to bear immediately on the adversary's weak point, the K B P. It is desirable therefore generally to exchange your Q B or Q Kt for the adversary's K B. The K B should rarely or never be played to the Q 3 before the Queen's Pawn is moved. His best position, as we have remarked above, is Q B 4, where he attacks the opponent's K B P. If your antagonist then challenges an exchange of Bishops by moving B—K 3, it is not always prudent to accept it, because although you may double the Pawns on his King's file, you at the same time afford him an open range for his King's Rook, when he has castled. The best play in such a case is, therefore, to retreat your B to Kt 3.

Be careful, as a general rule, in an open game, not to move P—Q 3 *before* you bring out the K B, as by so doing he can only be played to K 2, and there his position is defensive rather than attacking.

If strong in Pawns towards the conclusion of the game, endeavour to get rid of the enemy's Bishops, because they can impede the march of your Pawns more readily than either the Rooks or Knights.

When the other men are exchanged off, and you remain with a Bishop and two or three Pawns, it is often proper to keep your Pawns on squares of a different colour to those on which your Bishop travel, as he can then prevent the opposing King from approaching them. If, however, you have the worst of the game, it is generally better then to keep them on the same colour as the Bishop, that he may defend them.

Supposing you have Pawns only at the end of a game, and the adversary has a Bishop, it is generally advisable to move the Pawns to squares of a different colour to the Bishop.

Do not indiscriminately exchange your Bishops for Knights, or *vice versâ*. Two Bishops at the finish of a game are stronger than two Knights, and one Knight generally more useful than a single Bishop.

CONCERNING THE KNIGHT.

The Knight is at once the most striking and most beautiful of all the Pieces. The singularity of its moves, by which it is enabled to overleap the other men and wind its way into the adverse ranks, and if attacked leap back again within the boundary of its own, has rendered it the favourite Piece of leading players in every country.

The assault of the Knight is more subtle and dangerous than that of any other Piece, because he attacks without putting himself *en prise*, and his attack can never be resisted by the interposition of another man.

At the commencement of a game, the best place for the King's Knight is at K B 3; it there attacks your adversary's King's Pawn, if it has been played to K 4, and offers no impediment to the playing out your King's Bishop, and prevents the adversary from placing his Queen on K R 5, where she would often be a source of restraint and danger to your King. Many persons prefer playing the Kt to K 2 at the second move, from the mistaken notion that the K B P should be moved before the Knight is played to B 3; this is an error, and generally leads to a bad game.

When you have brought out your Q Kt to B 3, it is frequently advisable, at a proper opportunity, to get him round *viâ* K 2 to K Kt 3, where he exercises a very important influence, by threatening Kt—B 5.

Other things being equal, a Knight with three or four Pawns, at the end of a game, has an advantage over a Bishop with an equal number of Pawns, because he can leap from white to black, and thus attack the Pawns on either coloured squares, whereas the Bishop can attack them only when they move on squares of the colour of his diagonals. In similar circumstances, however, he is not so useful in defending as a Bishop or a Rook, since if forced to remove he ceases to defend, while the Rook or Bishop may retreat and still protect.

CONCERNING THE PAWNS.

Struck by the scope and power of the higher Pieces, young players commonly overlook the Pawns, or deem them scarcely worthy of regard, and are amazed to learn that the combinations of these simple elements are among the most refined and arduous studies of the game. Yet such is the fact, and without a thorough comprehension of their quiet but remarkable predominance in almost every circumstance of the game, it is impossible for any one to attain a high degree of excellence.

It is generally advantageous for your Pawns to occupy

the middle of the board, because when there they greatly
retard the movements of the opposing forces. The K P
and Q P at K 4 and Q 4 respectively, are well posted,
but it is not easy to maintain them in that position, and
if you are driven to advance one of them, the power of
both is much diminished. It is well, therefore, not to be
too eager to establish two Pawns abreast in the centre
until you are fully able to sustain them there.

When you have two Pawns abreast, as at K 4 and Q 4,
should the adversary attack one of them with a Pawn, it
is occasionally better to advance the Pawn that is attacked
than to take the Pawn.

The Pawns, however, should seldom be far advanced,
unless they can be properly sustained by the Pieces.
Pawns at their fourth squares are therefore generally
more powerful than at their sixth.

The K B P, having no support but that of the King, is
usually the point to which the first attack is directed, and
more than ordinary care should be taken to preserve it.
It is rarely good play to move it to B 3 early in the game.

As a general rule it is not advisable to move the
Knight's Pawns early in the game. P—K Kt 3 will often
allow your adversary to play his Q B—R 6, a dangerous
move when you have castled on King's side.

After castling, it is generally proper not to move the
Knight's Pawn that is before your King, until you are
obliged.

In a diagonal line of Pawns you should endeavour to
preserve the Pawn at the head of them. Pawns, when
united, have great strength ; but when separated, their
power is much lessened.

A passed Pawn is greatly strengthened when supported
by another Pawn.

A doubled Pawn is not in all cases a disadvantage,
especially if it is united with other Pawns. The worst
kind of doubled Pawn is one on a Rook's file; while the
most advantageous is the K B P doubled on the King's
file, because it strengthens your middle Pawns and opens
a file for your K R.

The Pawn being less important than a Piece, it is

usually better to defend with it than with a Piece. For the same reason it is likewise better to protect a Pawn with a Pawn than with a Piece. No Piece can interpose between the attack of a Pawn, it can therefore frequently check the King with great advantage.

Be cautious generally of advancing the Pawns far on either side, till you see on which your opponent castles; and remember, when approaching the end of a game, where you have Pawns, or even a Pawn, against a minor Piece, that *you may win*, but that your opponent, except in very rare cases, cannot, and that two Pawns in any situation can protect themselves against the adverse King.

Chapter VII.

MAXIMS AND ADVICE FOR AN IN-EXPERIENCED PLAYER.

There is nothing that will improve you so much as playing with good players; never refuse, therefore, when any one offers you odds, to accept it; you cannot expect a good player to feel much interest in playing with you upon even terms, and as you are sure to derive both amusement and instruction from him, it is but fair that he should name the conditions. It will soon happen that you yourself will be able to give odds to many amateurs whom you meet; when this is the case, avoid, if possible, playing them even, or you are likely to acquire an indolent, neglectful habit of play, which it will be very difficult to throw off. Be always careful, before beginning a game, that the men on both sides are properly arranged.

Never permit your hand to hover over the board, or indeed to approach it, until you have completely made up your mind what Piece to move; a contrary habit begets a feeling of indecision that is fatal to success. Play invariably according to the laws of the game, neither taking back a move yourself, nor allowing your opponent to recall one. Do not exhibit impatience when your adversary is long in making his move. His slowness is a tacit compliment to your skill, and enables you to play with proportionate quickness, because while he is meditating on his next step you can take advantage of the time to consider what shall be your rejoinder; besides, it is absolutely necessary for every one desirous of excelling at chess to play slowly. Mr. Lewis aptly remarks, " It is no doubt desirable to play well and quickly, but I scarcely ever knew a very good player who was not also a slow one; and indeed, how can it well be otherwise ? A fine player examines occasionally from five to twenty or more moves on each side; can this be done in a moment ? It is easy enough to play quick against inferior play; but against equal and very good play one cannot play quick without losing."

Learn to play indifferently either with the white or black men. Do not play too many games at a sitting— and never suffer the loss of a game to occasion you much disquietude. Think of how many thousand games a Philidor must have lost before he attained his highest excellence; besides, the loss of one well-fought game with a fine player will do more towards your improvement than the gain of ten light skirmishes with weaker players than yourself. Endeavour to play all your Pieces equally well. Many young players have a predilection for a particular Piece, as the Knight or the Queen, and lose both time and position in trying to prevent exchanges of their favourite. In opening your game, endeavour to bring the Pieces into action speedily, but avoid all premature attacks. Take care not to play a Piece to a square where it impedes the action of another, and beware of venturing an unsupported Piece in the adversary's game.

If subjected to a violent attack, you may often disconcert your opponent by compelling the exchange of two or three Pieces. When, however, you are about to exchange, you must calculate not only their ordinary value, but their peculiar worth in the situation in question; for example, a Rook is generally more valuable than a Knight or a Bishop; but it may happen, that by exchanging a Rook for one of the latter you may greatly improve your game.

It is generally good play to exchange the Pieces off when you are superior in power, so that when you have the odds of a Piece given to you by a strong player, you should endeavour to exchange as often as you can consistently with safety.

When an exchange of two or more Pieces appears inevitable, look closely to see whether it is better for you to take first or to compel your opponent to do so. When one of the enemy is completely in your power, do not be too eager to make the capture—there may perhaps be a move of importance which you can make before you take him. Beware also of snatching hastily a proffered man, it may be only given as a bait to catch a more important advantage from you.

If at the end of a game you remain with Pawns against a Knight and find it difficult to evade his repeated checks, recollect that by placing your King on the same diagonal as the Knight, but with one intervening square between them, that you cannot again be checked under three moves.

When you have lost a game which has cost you great attention, it is a good practice to play it over afterwards in private, and endeavour to discover where the error occurred through which your opponent gained his first advantage. This custom will improve both your memory and your play.

Appearances notwithstanding, chess is an exciting game. This is perhaps the most surprising feature that the beginner, who had thought it so dull, will notice. It will cause many of his blunders. First-class players lose " won " games every day by reason of it. So that it is extremely important for the student to acquire as much self-command as he possibly can from the very commencement of his chess career. So important is this that Steinitz, for twenty-eight years chess champion of the world, laid it down as a rule for himself, that whenever he saw a good move he did not take it—until he had looked all over the board for a better. Even Steinitz felt the necessity for checking himself from making hasty moves. Good moves are not at all obvious; in fact, the reverse is a pretty general rule. Hence they will not be easily seen, and least of all by those in a hurry. Beginners, therefore, take time, *even when you see a mate on the move*. Mates are elusive, and a would-be mating move is often the turning point in the novice's game. Caution should be borne in mind throughout the entire game, but particularly at the climax when coolness may be worth a piece to the player who possesses it.

Join a club. Practically no progress will be made by playing with friends at home, and often a very bad style is acquired by too frequently meeting the same opponent.

Avoid " skittles "—games played in a hurry. Players have rightly tabooed calling this chess. Some players pore over the board all the time, whether it is their turn to play or not. Others never look at the position till it is their turn to move. A judicious compromise of these extremes is probably best. While waiting for your opponent during a long game it is often advantageous to completely divert your mind for a few minutes by strolling round the room or otherwise, and then come back to the board with a fresh aspect of the position. It is then often seen to contain possibilities that you did not see before.

Always play against the board; that is, give your opponent credit for playing the best move every time, and try and meet it accordingly. Even when you know your opponent to be a weak player do not take liberties with him which his calibre might justify, but—just play, not him, but the board. His little fusilades will be futile enough, and against correct play he will soon succumb. This is not easy to do; especially where there is great disparity between the players. The stronger is often inclined to take risks in order to win quickly, trusting to the inability of his opponent to take advantage of them. This is unwise, for it induces the habit of loose play, and the day will come when you will take the risks—and the other fellow the game. When your opponent moves, before you put your own ideas into effect, try and see the object of his move. This will be most difficult to do against very strong and very weak players. The very strong will be too deep—the very weak purposeless. For the object of the former you may, and for the latter you certainly will, look in vain. When you see his idea, fortify yourself against it before proceeding with your attack, unless you are absolutely sure you can mate him before he can you, when you may disregard his move— except of course it is a check. Do not be discouraged by players who, when defeated, exclaim, " If I had been just a move sooner I would have had you." They are found in every club.

In playing weak players do not study their tactics, except as things to be avoided. If your opponent reconnoitres the board exhaustively with a solitary knight, he is giving you every opportunity to gain time—and possibly the knight also.

To play chess well demands patience and restraint. The man who easily loses heart or head will never make a strong player. It is beautiful to watch a resourceful player who, after early reverses, drags the remnants of a shattered attack together, welds a number of disunited pieces and pawns by combination into a position that ultimately allows him to enter the end game on equal terms with his opponent. Such a player will go far, and his reverses will become beautifully less.

Strength at chess may be variously acquired. Natural insight and continuous hard practice produce the greatest players. A few of these may rightly be regarded as geniuses, but it would be a mistake to say that every man who achieved master rank was. A natural gift for the game is easily detected. It will manifest itself among beginners by original, unexpected moves, even though they may be unsound. But the surest sign that a player has natural chess capacity is to note that, after being shown once or twice *why* a bad move in the openings is bad, how carefully he eschews that move in future. The mere wood shifter will make the same blunder a thousand times ; not indeed because he does not *know* that it is

wrong—for he has often been told so—but simply because
he cannot see *why* it is so.   Thus, after playing—

1. P—K 4	P—K 4
2. B—B 4	B—B 4
3. Q—R 5	

the gifted beginner will only require to be shown a couple
of times why 3. Q—R 5 is useless, but your stubborn fellow
will persist in his futile attempts to take your King
unawares.

If in the opening you find that your opponent has
moved seven men in seven moves, and you have only
moved two, be sure you! will soon find out an alarming
difference in your positions.   You have been doing much
wood shifting with very little progress.

Great progress may be made by a judicious study of
the books—particularly in conjunction with club practice.
Dr. Lasker, the chess champion of the world, is probably
the best end game player living.   It is the one portion of
the game that can be played with almost mathematical
certainty.   Every player then can improve this portion of
his game within his sphere—and about half the great
chess struggles are decided on the end game.   Go carefully through the treatise on the end game and try and
grasp the underlying *principles*, and apply them.   The
significance of subtle moves will in time become apparent,
and the ability to win an ordinary ending with, say, a
pawn up, will lead to the accomplishment of greater
things.

While to try and memorise the openings is worse than
useless, it is nevertheless essential to know the book in
order to get out of it successfully.   That is to say, it is
necessary to know the first 8 or 10 moves in a few of the
chief lines of play so that you may " get out of the opening," as it is termed, without compromising your game.
In the absence of book knowledge work on principle.
See that nothing is attacked that needs defending, and
then develop your Pieces.

An excellent way for gaining all round insight into
position and at the same time learning the openings is the

habit of playing over master games. It is hardly possible to overrate the value of this pleasant though little-practised pastime. It is far better, and often more enjoyable, than playing with beginners, and, done systematically, improves one's play immensely. The handiest way is perhaps to play with a pocket board, but of course any board will do. Two methods may be followed. First, put yourself on the side of the winning party and study the development of *his* game, giving less attention to the other side, for practice has shown that it is not advisable to try and keep in touch with both sides at the same time. Cover the score of the side you are playing, say White, and after every move of Black try and discover what White's reply will be before looking at the score. At first you will not divine many of his moves, but later on, you will be gratified to see how often you would have played the same move in such and such a position as, say, Tarrasch. The deep moves alone will elude you, and even these will occasionally be discovered.

The second plan is to take one player to yourself as before, but do not look whether he has won or lost the game. Cover the score. Then, during the progress of the play try and see how he is faring—you not knowing the result. Practice will enable you in time to recognize a gradual advantage (or the reverse) which he may have accumulated. It is the ability to recognize such changes in position that makes the good player.

Games of the old masters are unsurpassed for brilliancy of combination and middle game play generally. In playing over games, especially those of modern experts, the student will incidentally acquire a sound knowledge of the openings. An interesting feature in playing recorded games is to note the characteristics of various exponents. As in literature so in chess, every master has his style. Some play the open, some play the close game. Some are content to attempt nothing, keeping the draw well in sight, and hoping for their opponent to make a slight mistake. The enterprising, however, will set out on a plan of attack, and court intricacies. They will even sacrifice material to produce a position after their fancy.

These variations are possible, because chess puts no limit
on a man's fancy, and individual—even national—traits,
find expression in the game as in music.   Thus the
modern school, led by the Germans, is sound, deep, and
theoretically correct.   The Italian school, on the other
hand, is more brilliant and showy, though not so accurate
and lasting.   The highest expression of chess skill is a
judicious combination of the two.

Another good plan for strengthening play, and more
exciting than it sounds, is correspondence chess.   This
is specially to be commended to players living in out-of-
the-way parts of the country, where it is not easy to
get a game over the board.   It generates the habit of
deliberate play, particularly with those who rightly *think
out* some of the minor variations, rather than playing
them all over the board, before despatching a move.

If the student will bear some of these hints in mind he
will be surprised to find that the study of chess, commonly
regarded as both dull and slow, can be made both interesting and rapid.   His progress need meet with no checks,
for chess itself is inexhaustible.   The only limit it knows
are those of the human mind.   So that at chess a man
may demonstrate his superiority against all the world
more conclusively, perhaps, than at any other game.

Comparing small things with great ones, never forget
that in chess, as in modern warfare, one of the most
important stratagems is the art of gaining *time* upon the
enemy.   In this respect, as indeed in many others, the
broad principles which are laid down by the highest
military authorities as the basis of operations in a
campaign are applicable to the management of your forces
on the chess field.   From the *Traité de Grand Tactique*
of General Jomini, we gather that the art of war, as
exemplified by Buonaparte, consisted in the proper
application of three combinations—first, the art of disposing the lines of operation in the most advantageous
manner; secondly, in a skilful concentration of the forces
with the greatest possible rapidity upon the most important point of the enemy's line of operations; and
thirdly, that of combining the simultaneous employment

of this accumulated force upon the position against which it is directed. No player of great skill can fail to see that we have here the key to the basis of offensive movements in the battle of chess. Nor, to carry on the parallel, are the principles which direct defensive operations on the grander field in any degree less capable of application. "It is an acknowledged principle," says another able writer on the subject, "that the base of a plan of attack should form the best possible line of defence; and this fundamental rule cannot be violated with impunity, since nothing is more embarrassing than a sudden transition from offensive to defensive operations, when false measures or an unfortunate turn of affairs may have overset the plans of an assault."

With every allowance for the amazing disparity in the importance of the individuals and the magnitude of the objects at stake, there is an analogy observable, too, in the abilities requisite for the command of armies and the perfectly first-rate manœuvring of the mimic warriors of the chess-board. The commander of an army must possess not less a profound acquaintance with the general principles which regulate the conduct of a long and tedious campaign, than with those that are called into requisition in actual conflict. He must be able equally to arrange the plan of preliminary operations—to act at once and with decision in cases of the most pressing emergency, and on the occurrence of the most unforeseen events—to judge of the importance of a position and of the strength of an intrenchment — to discover from the slightest indications the designs of the enemy, while his own are impenetrable—and at the same time to preside with unshaken self-possession over the tumult of the battle-field, and the raging fury of an assault. The qualifications of a really finished chess-player, however less in degree, are somewhat similar in kind. To a perfect mastery of the difficult art of selecting and occupying, with the utmost rapidity, a " good position," he must add a thorough knowledge of all the complicated varieties of stratagems and snares which he is called upon alternately to invent and to defeat. He must, in short, to some extent, display the same energies on the smaller scale which are so indispensable on the grander one.

Marshal Saxe, a great general (and an enthusiastic lover of chess, by the way), in his summary of the attributes required in a commander-in-chief, gives him genius, and courage, and health. The first of these qualities is unquestionably called for in the highest order of chess skill; and if by courage is implied, not so much mere physical bravery as entire self-possession, promptitude of decision, and undaunted perseverance; and by health is meant the preservation of a sound mind, to which a sound body is so important an adjunct, then indeed both courage and health will be found to exercise a powerful influence upon the success of the chess-player, as well as upon the fortunes of a Marlborough or a Wellington.

These comparisons might be extended to more minute particulars, but the general analogy observable may suffice to show you that great mental activity is called into requisition, and much attention and perseverance are necessary for the attainment of the highest excellence, even in the strategy of chess-playing.

Chapter VIII.

PRELIMINARY GAME.

PREPARATORY to the investigation of the several openings treated of in the following Chapters, it may not be uninstructive to give a short game which shall exhibit the application of some technical phrases in use at chess, and at the same time show a few of the most prominent errors into which an inexperienced player is likely to fall.

In this game, as in all the analyses which follow, the reader will be supposed to play the White Pieces and to have the first move, although, as it has been before remarked, it is advisable for you to accustom yourself to play with either Black or White.

WHITE.	BLACK.
1. P—K 4	P—K 4

When the men are first arranged in battle order, it is seen that the only Pieces which have the power of moving are the Knights, and that to liberate the others it is necessary to move a Pawn. Now, as the K P, on being moved, gives freedom both to the Q and to the K B, it is more frequently played at the beginning of the game than any other. You will remember, in speaking of the Pawns it was shown that on certain conditions they have the privilege of going either one or two moves when they are first played.

| 2. B—B 4 | B—B 4 |

Thus far the game illustrates the *King's Bishop's* opening. Each party plays his K B thus, because it attacks the most vulnerable point of the adverse position, viz. the K B P.

| 3. P—Q B 3 | Kt—Q B 3 |

In playing this Pawn your object is afterwards to play P—Q 4, and thus establish your Pawns in the centre ; but Black foresees the intention and seeks to prevent its execution by bringing another Piece to bear upon the square.

| 4. P—Q 4 | P×P |
| 5. P×P | B×P |

Here you have played without due consideration. Black's third move of Kt—Q B 3 was a bad one, and afforded you an opportunity of gaining a striking advantage, but omitting this, you have enabled him to gain a valuable Pawn for nothing. Observe, now, your reply to his third move was good enough (4. P—Q 4), but when he took your Pawn with his, instead of taking again, you ought to have played B×P ch.; the game would then most probably have gone on thus :—

5. B×P ch.	K×B
6. Q—R 5 ch.	K—B 1
7. Q×B ch.	

In this variation, you see Black has lost his K B P, and
what is worse, *has lost his privilege of castling,* by being
forced to move his King; and although for a moment he
had gained a Bishop for a Pawn, it was quite clear that
he must lose a Bishop in return by the check of the
adverse Queen. It is true that he need not have taken
the Bishop, but still his King must have moved, and
White could then have played B×Kt, having the better
position.

But now to proceed with the actual game :—

6. Kt—K B 3	Q—B 3

Bringing out the Knight is good play; you not only
threaten to win his Bishop, but you afford yourself an
opportunity of castling whenever it may be needful.
Black would have played better in retiring the Bishop to
Kt 3 than in supporting it with the Queen.

7. Kt×B	Q×Kt

Both parties played well in their last moves. You rightly
took off the Bishop, because supported by the Queen he
menaced your Q Kt P, and Black properly retook with
his Queen instead of with the Knight, because having a
Pawn ahead, it was his interest to exchange off the
Queens.

8. Kt—Q 2	Kt—B 3

You played correctly here in not exchanging Queens, and
also in protecting your Bishop and your King's Pawn,
both of which were attacked by the adverse Queen; but
all this might have been done without impeding the
movements of any of your Pieces, by simply playing
Q—K 2; as it is, the Knight entirely shuts your Queen's
Bishop from the field. Black properly brings another
Piece to the attack of your King's Pawn :—

9. P—B 3	Kt—K 4

In protecting the Pawn with your K B P you are guilty of
a very common error among young players; as you
improve, you will find that it is rarely good to play

P—K B 3. In the present instance, for example, you have deprived yourself of the power of castling, at least for some time, since Black's Queen now commands the very square to which your King, in castling on his own side, has to move. Black's last move is much more sensible. He again attacks your Bishop, and by the same move brings his Q's Knight into co-operation with the King's, on the weak point of your position :—

10. P—Q Kt 3	Q × R

This is a serious blunder indeed. In your anxiety to save the threatened Bishop, which you feared to withdraw to Kt 3, on account of Black playing Kt—Q 6 ch., you have actually left your Rook *en prise !* Black takes it, of course, and having gained such an important advantage, ought to win easily.

11. 0—0	Kt × B
12. Kt × Kt	0—0
13. Q—Q 2	P—B 4

Your last move is very subtle ; finding the mistake that Black had committed in not retreating his Queen directly after winning the Rook, you determine, if possible, to prevent her escape by gaining command of all the squares she can move to. Seeing the danger, Black throws forward this Pawn to enable him, if possible, to bring the Queen off, by playing Q—Q 5 ch.

14. B—Kt 2	Q × P

This move of the Bishop is well-timed : it does not, to be sure, prevent the Queen from escaping for a move or two, but it gives you an attack, and very great command of the field.

15. Q—Kt 5	Kt—K 1

Very well played on both sides. By playing Q—Kt 5 you threatened to win his Knight by at once taking it with your Bishop, which he could not retake without opening check on his King. Instead of so moving, you might have played Kt—R 5, in which case, by afterwards moving

R—R 1, it would have been impossible for his Queen to get away.

16. Q—K 3   P—K R 3

You prudently retreated your Queen to guard her Knight's Pawn, which it was important to save, on account of its protection to the Knight. Black played P—K R 3 to prevent your Queen returning to the same post of attack.

17. P—R 3   K—R 1

Here are two instances of what is called "lost time" at chess, neither move serving in the slightest degree to advance the game of the player. That you should have overlooked the opportunity of gaining the adverse Queen (by R—R 1) was to be expected. Similar advantages present themselves in every game between young players, and are unobserved.

18. P—B 4   P—Q Kt 3

Again you have failed to see a most important move ; you might have taken the R P with your Queen, giving check safely, because Black could not take your Queen, as his P is "pinned" by your B. All this time, too, your opponent omits to see the jeopardy his Queen is in, and that as far as practical assistance to his other pieces is concerned, she might as well be off the board.

19. P—K Kt 4   P—Q Kt 4

Your last move is far from good. By thus attacking your Knight, Black threatens to win a Piece, because upon playing away the Knight you must leave the Bishop unprotected.

20. P—Kt 5   P×Kt

Although your Knight was thus attacked, it might have been saved very easily. In the first place, by Q×P, threatening to take his Rook, on his removing which, or interposing the Q P, you could have taken the Pawn which attacked your Knight ; or, in the second place, by moving your Queen to B 2. In the latter case, if Black ventured to take the Knight, you would have won his

Queen by B×P ch. Black would have been obliged to parry the check, either by taking the Bishop or moving his King, and you would then have taken his Queen. This position is very instructive, and merits attentive examination.

21. B—B 3	P×Q Kt P
22. P—R 4	P—Kt 7

In such a position, the advance of your King's flank Pawns is a process too dilatory to be very effective.

23. P—B 5	P—Kt 8 (Q)

Now the fault of your tortoise-like movements with the Pawns becomes fatally evident. Black has been enabled to make a second Queen, and has an overwhelming force at command.

24. R×Q	Q×R ch.

You had no better move than to take the newly-elected Queen, for two Queens must have proved irresistible.

25. K—Kt 2	Kt—Q 3
26. P—Kt 6	P×P
27. P×P	B—Kt 2

Here you have given another remarkable instance of lost opportunity. At your last move you might have redeemed all former disasters by checkmating your opponent in two moves. Endeavour to find out how this was to be accomplished.

28. P—R 5	Kt×P
29. B—K 5	Kt—Kt 4 d. ch.

Up to Black's last move you had still the opportunity of winning the game before mentioned.

30. K—Kt 3	R—B 6 ch.
31. K—R 4	Q—B 4

At this point you were utterly at the mercy of your antagonist, but fortunately he wanted the skill to avail himself properly of his vast superiority in force and position, or he might have won the game in half a dozen different ways.

32. Q×R	Q×Q
33. B×P ch.	K×B

This was your last chance, and its success should serve to
convince you that in the most apparently hopeless situations of the game there is often a latent resource, if we
will only have the patience to search it out. By taking
the Bishop, Black has left your King, which is not in
check, no move without going into check, and as you
have neither Piece nor Pawn besides to play, you are
stalemated, and the game is DRAWN.

If thoroughly acquainted with the information contained
in the preceding Chapters, you may now proceed to the
consideration of the openings.

BOOK II.

Chapter I.

THE KING'S KNIGHT'S OPENING.

1. $\dfrac{\text{P—K 4}}{\text{P—K 4}}$ 2. $\dfrac{\text{Kt—K B 3}}{}$

White's second move gives the name to this opening, which is one of the most popular and instructive of all the various methods of commencing the game. The Kt, it will be observed, at once attacks the adverse Pawn, and the defence, recommended by the best authors and the leading players of Europe, is for Black to reply 2. $\dfrac{}{\text{Kt—Q B 3}}$. He has, however, many other ways of playing, and as the examination of these comparatively simple variations will serve to prepare you for the more complex and elaborate combinations of the best defences, it will be advisable to consider them previously. In the first place, then, Black may sustain his Pawn by playing—

(a) 2. $\dfrac{}{\text{P—K B 3}}$ (c) 2. $\dfrac{}{\text{Q—B 3}}$

(b) 2. $\dfrac{}{\text{B—Q 3}}$ (d) 2. $\dfrac{}{\text{P—Q 3}}$

or, in the second place, he may leave it unprotected, and play—

(e) 2. $\dfrac{}{\text{Kt—K B 3}}$ (g) 2. $\dfrac{}{\text{P—K B 4}}$

(f) 2. $\dfrac{}{\text{B—B 4}}$ (h) 2. $\dfrac{}{\text{P—Q 4}}$

He has thus eight feasible modes of play at his command, besides the move of Kt—Q B 3 in answer to White's second move of Kt—K B 3. Each of these will form the subject of a separate analysis.

	(1)	(2)	(3)
1.	P—K 4 / P—K 4	—	—
2.	Kt—K B 3 / P—K B 3	—	—
3.	Kt×P / P×Kt (?)	—	—
4.	Q—R 5 ch. / P—Kt 3	—	/ K—K 2
5.	Q×K P ch. / Q—K 2	—	Q×K P ch. / K—B 2
6.	Q×R / Kt—K B 3	Q×P ch.	B—B 4 ch. / P—Q 4 (!)
7.	P—Q 4 (!) / Q×P ch.	K—Q 1 / P—Q 4	B×P ch. / K—Kt 3
8.	B—K 3 / Q×B P	B—Kt 5 ch. / K—Q 1 (!)	P—K R 4 / B—Q 3
9.	Q×Kt / Q×Kt P	R—K 1 / B—Kt 5 ch.	P—R 5 ch. / K—R 3
10.	B—Q B 4 / B—Kt 5 ch.	P—B K 3 and wins	P—Q 4 d. ch. / P—K Kt 4
11.	Kt—Q 2 / Q×R ch.		P×P e.p. d. ch. / K×P
12.	K—K 2 and wins		W. mates in 2

	(4)	(5)	(6)
1.	—	P—K 4 / P—K 4	P—K 4 / P—K 4
2.	—	Kt—K B 3 / B—Q 3 ?	Kt—K B 3 / Q—B 3
3.	/ Q—K 2 !	B—B 4 / Kt—K B 3	B—B 4 / Q—Kt 3
4.	Kt—B 3 ! (a) / P—Q 4	P—Q 4 / Kt—B 3 (b)	0—0 / Q×K P

(a) If 4. Q—R 5 ch. / P—Kt 3 ; 5. Kt×P / Q×P ch. and Q×Kt next move.

(b) If 4. P×P / Kt×P ; 5. P×P / B—B 4 ; 6. Q—Q 5 / B×P ch. ; 7. K—K 2 / 0—0 ; 8. Q×Kt / B—Kt 3 ;
9. Kt—Kt 5 + ;

	(4)	(5)	(6)
5.	P–Q 3 / P×P	P×P / B×P (a)	B×P ch. / K–Q 1 (b)
6.	P×P / Q×P ch.	Kt–Kt 5 / 0–0	Kt×P / Kt–K B 3
7.	B–K 2 / B–K B 4	P–B 4 / B–Q 5	R–K 1 / Q–K B 4
8.	Kt–Q 4 / Kt–Q B 3	P–K 5 / Q–K 2	B–Kt 6 / Q–K 3
9.	Kt×B / Q×Kt	Q–K 2 / Kt–K 1	Kt–B 7 ch. wins Q
10.	0–0 / B–Q 3	B–Q 5 / B–Kt 3	
11.	B–Q 3+ /	Kt–Q B 3+ /	

	(7)	(8)	(9)
1.	P–K 4 / P–K 4	—	—
2.	Kt–K B 3 / B–B 4	—	—
3.	Kt×P / Q–K 2	—	—
4.	P–Q 4 / B–Kt 3	B–Q 3	P–Q 3
5.	B–Q B 4 / Kt–K B 3	P–K B 4 / P–K B 3	Kt×P / Q×P ch.
6.	B×P ch. / K–B 1	Kt–B 4 / Q×P ch.	B–K 3 / Kt×Kt
7.	B–Kt 3 / Kt×P	K–B 2 / Kt–Q B 3	P×B / P×P

(a) If 5. Kt×P / ; 6. Kt×Kt / B×Kt ; 7. P–B 4 / B–Q 3 ; 8. P–K 5 / Q–K 2 ; 9. Q–K 2 / winning a piece.

(b) If 5. K–K 2 / ; 6. R–K 1 / Q–B 5 ; 7. R×P ch / K×B (7. K–B 3 ; 8. P–Q 4 (!)); 8. P–Q 4 / Q–B 3 ; 9. Kt–Kt 5 ch. / K–Kt 3 ; 10. Q–Q 3 ch / K–R 4

11. P–Kt 4 ch. and mate next move.

	(7)	(8)	(9)
8.	$\underline{0-0}$ +	$\dfrac{B-Q\ 3}{Q \times Q\ P\ ch.}$	$\dfrac{Q-R\ 5\ ch.}{K-B\ 1}$
9.		$\dfrac{B-K\ 3}{Q-Q\ 4}$	$Q \times P\ (B\ 5)\ ch.$ +
10.		$\underline{B-Kt\ 6\ ch.}$ +	

			(10)		(10) (contd.)
1.	—	4.	$\overline{P-K\ B\ 3}$	7.	$\dfrac{K-Q\ 1}{Q \times Kt}$
2.	—	5.	$\dfrac{Q-R\ 5\ ch.}{P-Kt\ 3}$	8.	$\underline{Q \times B}$ +
3.	—	6.	$\dfrac{Kt \times P}{Q \times P\ ch.}$	9.	

CHAPTER II.

THE PHILIDOR DEFENCE—ANALYSIS.

	(1)	(2)	(3)
1.	$\dfrac{P-K\ 4}{P-K\ 4}$	—	—
2.	$\dfrac{Kt-K\ B\ 3}{P-Q\ 3}$	—	—
3.	$\dfrac{P-Q\ 4}{P-K\ B\ 4}$	$\dfrac{B-B\ 4}{P-Q\ B\ 3}$	$\dfrac{P-Q\ 4}{P-K\ B\ 4}$
4.	$\dfrac{P \times K\ P}{P \times K\ P}$	$\dfrac{P-Q\ 4\ (!)}{P-Q\ 4}$	$\dfrac{P \times K\ P}{P \times K\ P}$
5.	$\dfrac{Kt-Kt\ 5}{P-Q\ 4}$	$\dfrac{P \times Q\ P}{P-K\ 5}$	$\dfrac{Kt-Kt\ 5}{P-Q\ 4}$
6.	$\dfrac{P-K\ 6}{Kt-K\ R\ 3}$ (see diagram)	$\dfrac{Kt-K\ 5}{P \times P}$	$\dfrac{P-K\ 6}{Kt-K\ R\ 3}$ (see diagram)

	(1)	(2)	(3)
7.	$\dfrac{\text{P—K B 3}}{\text{Kt—B 3 } (a)}$	$\dfrac{\text{B—Kt 5 ch.}}{\text{B—Q 2}}$	$\dfrac{\text{Kt—Q B 3}}{\text{P—B 3 } (c)}$
8.	$\dfrac{\text{B—Kt 5}}{\text{Q—Q 3}}$	$\dfrac{\text{Kt} \times \text{B}}{\text{Kt} \times \text{Kt}} =$	$\dfrac{\text{Kt} \times \text{R P}}{\text{B} \times \text{P !}}$
9.	$\dfrac{\text{Kt—B 3}}{\text{B} \times \text{P}}$		$\dfrac{\text{Kt} \times \text{B}}{\text{K} \times \text{Kt}}$
10.	$\dfrac{\text{Kt} \times \text{B } (b)}{\text{Q} \times \text{Kt}}$		$\dfrac{\text{Kt} \times \text{K P}}{\text{Kt—Kt 5}}$

Nos. 1 and 3—6.   Position after Black's 6th move.

BLACK.

WHITE.

(a) If (see diagram) 7. $\dfrac{\text{P—K B 3}}{\text{P} \times \text{B P}}$; 8. $\dfrac{\text{Q} \times \text{P (B 6)}}{\text{R—Kt 1}}$; 9. $\dfrac{\text{Kt—B 3 !}}{\text{P—B 3}}$;
10. $\dfrac{\text{Q—B 7 ch.}}{\text{Kt} \times \text{Q}}$; 11. $\dfrac{\text{P} \times \text{Kt ch and wins}}{}$; or, 7. $\dfrac{\text{P—K B 3}}{\text{B—K 2}}$; 8 $\dfrac{\text{P} \times \text{P}}{\text{B} \times \text{Kt}}$;
9. $\dfrac{\text{Q—R 5 ch.}}{\text{P—Kt 3}}$; 10. $\dfrac{\text{Q} \times \text{B}}{\text{Q} \times \text{Q}}$; 11. $\dfrac{\text{B} \times \text{Q}}{\text{Kt moves}}$; 12. $\dfrac{\text{P} \times \text{Q P}}{}$ +

(b) If 10. $\dfrac{\text{Q Kt} \times \text{K P}}{\text{Q—K 4 !}}$; 11. $\dfrac{\text{P—K B 4}}{\text{Q—B 4}}$; 12. $\dfrac{\text{Kt—K Kt 3}}{\text{Q—Kt 3}}$;
13 $\dfrac{\text{Q—K 2}}{\text{K—Q 2}}$; 14. $\dfrac{\text{B} \times \text{Kt ch.}}{\text{P} \times \text{B}}$ +

(c) If 7. $\dfrac{}{\text{B—Kt 5}}$; 8. $\dfrac{\text{Q—R 5 ch.}}{\text{K—B 1}}$; 9. $\dfrac{\text{Kt—B 7}}{\text{Q—K 1}}$; 10. $\dfrac{\text{Q} \times \text{P}}{\text{Kt} \times \text{Kt}}$;
11. $\dfrac{\text{P} \times \text{Kt}}{\text{Q—B 3}}$; 12. $\dfrac{\text{B—Q B 4}}{}$ +

	(1)	(2)	(3)
11.	$\dfrac{Q \times P}{Q \times Q}$		$\underline{Kt-Kt\ 5\ +}$
12.	$\dfrac{Kt \times Q}{0-0-0}$		
13.	$\underline{P \times K\ P\ +}$		

	(4)	(5)
1.	—	—
2.	—	—
3.	—	—
4.	—	—
5.	—	—
6.	—	—
7.	—	$\dfrac{P-K\ B\ 3}{B-B\ 4}$
8.	$\dfrac{K\ Kt \times K\ P}{P \times Kt}$	$\dfrac{P \times P}{0-0}$
9.	$\dfrac{Q-R\ 5\ ch.}{P-K\ Kt\ 3}$	$\dfrac{P \times P\ (a)}{R-B\ 4}$
10.	$\dfrac{Q-K\ 5}{R-Kt\ 1}$	$\dfrac{Kt-Q\ B\ 3}{R-K\ 4\ ch.\ (b)}$
11.	$\dfrac{B \times Kt}{B \times B}$	$\dfrac{Q\ Kt-K\ 4}{R \times Q\ P}$
12.	$\dfrac{Q\ R-Q\ 1}{Q-K\ 2}$	$\dfrac{B-Q\ 2}{B \times P}$
13.	$\dfrac{Kt \times P}{B \times P}$	$\dfrac{B-Q\ B\ 4}{Kt-Q\ R\ 3}$

(a) If 9. $\dfrac{Q \times P}{Q-K\ 2}$; 10. $\dfrac{B-Q\ B\ 4}{Kt-Q\ B\ 3}$ +

(b) If 10. $\dfrac{}{R \times Kt}$; 11. $\dfrac{B \times R}{Q \times B}$; 12. $\underline{Q-K\ B\ 3}$

	(4)	(5)
14.	$\dfrac{\text{R}-\text{Q } 6 \ (a)}{\text{B}-\text{K B } 4}$	Q−B 3 +
15.	$\dfrac{\text{Kt}-\text{B } 6 \text{ ch.}}{\text{K}-\text{B } 1 \ !}$	
16.	$\dfrac{\text{R}-\text{Q } 8 \text{ ch.}}{\text{K}-\text{B } 2}$	
17.	$\dfrac{\text{B}-\text{B } 4 \text{ ch.}}{\text{B}-\text{K } 3 \ !}$	
18.	$\dfrac{\text{Kt} \times \text{R} \text{ and wins.}}{}$	
19.		

	(6)	(7)	(8)
1.	$\dfrac{\text{P}-\text{K } 4}{\text{P}-\text{K } 4}$	—	—
2.	$\dfrac{\text{Kt}-\text{K B } 3}{\text{P}-\text{Q } 3}$	—	—
3.	$\dfrac{\text{P}-\text{Q } 4}{\text{K}-\text{K B } 3}$	$\dfrac{\text{B}-\text{Kt } 5 \ (c)}{}$	$\dfrac{\text{P} \times \text{P}}{}$
4.	$\dfrac{\text{B}-\text{K Kt } 5}{\text{B}-\text{Kt } 5 \ (b)}$	$\dfrac{\text{P} \times \text{P}}{\text{B} \times \text{Kt}}$	$\dfrac{\text{Q} \times \text{P}}{\text{B}-\text{Q } 2 \ (e)}$
5.	$\dfrac{\text{P} \times \text{P}}{\text{B} \times \text{Kt}}$	$\dfrac{\text{Q} \times \text{B} \ (d)}{\text{P} \times \text{P}}$	$\dfrac{\text{B}-\text{K B } 4}{\text{Kt}-\text{Q B } 3}$
6.	$\dfrac{\text{Q} \times \text{B}}{\text{P} \times \text{P}}$	$\dfrac{\text{B}-\text{Q B } 4}{\text{Q}-\text{B } 3}$	$\dfrac{\text{Q}-\text{Q } 2}{\text{B}-\text{K } 2}$
7.	$\dfrac{\text{Q}-\text{Kt } 3}{\text{P}-\text{Q Kt } 3}$	$\dfrac{\text{Q}-\text{Kt } 3}{\text{P}-\text{Q Kt } 3}$	$\dfrac{\text{Kt}-\text{Q B } 3}{\text{Kt}-\text{B } 3}$

(a) If 14. $\dfrac{\text{Q}-\text{Q } 4}{\text{Q}-\text{K } 2}$; 15. $\dfrac{\text{B}-\text{K } 2 \ +}{}$

(b) If 4. $\dfrac{}{\text{P} \times \text{P}}$; 5. $\dfrac{\text{Q} \times \text{P}}{\text{B}-\text{K } 2}$; 6. $\dfrac{\text{Kt}-\text{B } 3}{\text{0}-\text{0}}$; 7. $\dfrac{\text{0}-\text{0}-\text{0} \ +}{}$

(c) If 3. $\dfrac{}{\text{P} \times \text{P}}$; 4. $\dfrac{\text{Q} \times \text{P}}{\text{Kt}-\text{Q B } 3}$; 5. $\dfrac{\text{B}-\text{Q Kt } 5}{\text{B}-\text{Q } 2}$; 6. $\dfrac{\text{Q}-\text{Q } 1}{\text{Kt}-\text{K } 4}$

$\left(\text{or } 6. \ \dfrac{}{\text{Kt}-\text{Kt } 5}; 7. \ \dfrac{\text{B}-\text{Q B } 4 \ !}{}\right)$; 7. $\dfrac{\text{Kt} \times \text{Kt} \ +}{}$

(d) Or 5. $\dfrac{\text{P} \times \text{B}}{\text{P} \times \text{P}}$; 6. $\dfrac{\text{Q} \times \text{Q} \text{ ch.}}{\text{K} \times \text{Q}}$; 7. $\dfrac{\text{P}-\text{K B } 4}{}$

(e) If 4. $\dfrac{}{\text{Kt}-\text{Q B } 3}$; 5. $\dfrac{\text{B}-\text{Q Kt } 5}{\text{B}-\text{Q } 2}$; 6. $\dfrac{\text{B} \times \text{Kt}}{\text{B} \times \text{B}}$ 7. $\dfrac{\text{B}-\text{Kt } 5}{}$

	(6)	(7)	(8)
8.	$\dfrac{\text{B-Q B 4}}{\text{Q-Q 2}}$	$\dfrac{\text{Kt-B 3}}{\text{P-B 3}}$	$\dfrac{\text{B-B 4}}{\text{0-0}}$
9.	$\dfrac{\text{B} \times \text{Kt}}{\text{P} \times \text{B}}$	$\dfrac{\text{0-0}}{\text{B-Q 3}}$	0-0 =
10.	$\dfrac{\text{Kt-B 3}}{\text{B-Kt 2}}$	$\dfrac{\text{P-K B 4}}{\text{P} \times \text{P}}$	
11.	$\dfrac{\text{R-Q 1}}{\text{Q-K 2}}$	$\dfrac{\text{Q B} \times \text{P}}{\text{B} \times \text{B !}}$	
12.	$\dfrac{\text{B-Kt 5 ch.}}{\text{P-B 3}}$	$\dfrac{\text{P-K 5}}{\text{B} \times \text{P ch.}}$	
13.	Kt-Q 5 +		

	(9)	(10)	(11)
1.	—	—	
2.	—	—	—
3.	—	—	—
4.	$\dfrac{\text{Kt} \times \text{P}}{\text{P-Q 4}}$	—	—
5.	$\dfrac{\text{P-K 5}}{\text{P-Q B 4 }(a)}$	—	—
6.	$\dfrac{\text{B-Kt 5 ch.}}{\text{B-Q 2 !}}$	—	—
7.	$\dfrac{\text{P-K 6}}{\text{P} \times \text{Kt}}$	$\overline{\text{Q-K 2}}$	$\overline{\text{P} \times \text{P}}$
8.	$\dfrac{\text{P} \times \text{B ch.}}{\text{Kt} \times \text{P}}$	$\dfrac{\text{B} \times \text{B ch.}}{\text{Kt} \times \text{B}}$	$\dfrac{\text{Kt} \times \text{P}}{\text{Q-K 2 !}}$
9.	$\dfrac{\text{Q} \times \text{P}}{\text{Kt-B 3}}$	$\dfrac{\text{0-0}}{\text{P} \times \text{Kt !}}$	$\dfrac{\text{B} \times \text{B ch.}}{\text{Kt} \times \text{B !}}$
10.	$\dfrac{\text{0-0}}{\text{B-K 2 !}}$	$\dfrac{\text{P} \times \text{Kt ch.}}{\text{Q} \times \text{P}}$	$\dfrac{\text{0-0}}{\text{Q} \times \text{Kt}}$
11.	$\dfrac{\text{Kt-B 3}}{\text{P-Q R 3}}$	$\dfrac{\text{R-K 1 ch.}}{\text{B-K 2}}$	$\dfrac{\text{K R-K 1}}{\text{Kt-K 4}}$
12.	$\dfrac{\text{B-R 4}}{\text{P-Q Kt 4}}$	Q×P +	Q-R 5 ch +
13.	B-Kt 3 +		

(a) If 5. $\dfrac{}{\text{B-Q B 4}}$; 6. $\dfrac{\text{Kt-Q B 3}}{\text{Kt-K 2}}$; 7. $\dfrac{\text{B-K 2}}{\text{0-0}}$; 8. $\dfrac{\text{0-0}}{} +$

	(12)	(13)
1.	—	$\dfrac{\text{P—K 4}}{\text{P—K 4}}$
2.	—	$\dfrac{\text{Kt—K B 3}}{\text{P—Q 3}}$
3.	—	$\dfrac{\text{B—B 4}}{\text{P—Q B 3 } (a)}$
4.	—	$\dfrac{\text{P—Q 4}}{\text{P—Q 4}}$
5.	—	$\dfrac{\text{P} \times \text{Q P}}{\text{P—K 5}}$
6.	—	$\dfrac{\text{Kt—K 5}}{\text{P} \times \text{P}}$
7.	$\overline{\text{B} \times \text{B}}$	$\dfrac{\text{Q—R 5 } (b)}{\text{P—K Kt 3 } (c)}$
8.	$\dfrac{\text{P} \times \text{P ch.}}{\text{K} \times \text{P}}$	$\dfrac{\text{Kt} \times \text{P}}{\text{B P} \times \text{Kt}}$
9.	$\dfrac{\text{Kt} \times \text{B}}{\text{Q—R 4 ch.}}$	$\dfrac{\text{Q—K 5 ch.}}{\text{Q—K 2 !}}$
10.	$\dfrac{\text{Q Kt—B 3}}{\text{P—Q 5}}$	$\dfrac{\text{Q} \times \text{R } (d)}{\text{P} \times \text{B}}$
11.	$\dfrac{\text{Q—R 5 ch.}}{\text{P—Kt 3}}$	$\dfrac{\text{Q} \times \text{Kt}}{\text{B—K 3}}$
12.	$\dfrac{\text{Q—Q 5}}{\text{K—K 1 !}}$	$\dfrac{\text{Q—R 8}}{\text{Kt—Q 2 or B 3}} =$
13.	$\dfrac{\text{Kt} \times \text{P}}{}$	

(a) If 3. $\dfrac{}{\text{B—K 3}}$; 4. $\dfrac{\text{B} \times \text{B}}{}$, followed by 5. $\dfrac{\text{P—Q B 3}}{}$; or, if

3. $\dfrac{}{\text{Kt—K B 3}}$; 4. $\dfrac{\text{Kt—Kt 5}}{}$

(b) If 7. $\dfrac{\text{B—Kt 5 ch.}}{\text{B—Q 2}}$; 8. $\dfrac{\text{Kt} \times \text{B}}{\text{Kt} \times \text{Kt}} =$

(c) If 7. $\dfrac{}{\text{B—K 3}}$; 8. $\dfrac{\text{B—Kt 5 ch.}}{\text{K—K 2 !}}$; 9. $\dfrac{\text{Q—R 4 ch.}}{} +$

(d) If 10. $\dfrac{\text{B—Kt 5 ch.}}{\text{B—Q 2}}$; 11. $\dfrac{\text{Q} \times \text{R}}{\text{B} \times \text{B}}$; 12. $\dfrac{\text{Q} \times \text{Kt}}{\text{B—B 3}}$; 13. $\dfrac{\text{Kt—Q B 3}}{}$

THE PHILIDOR DEFENCE—GAMES.

	(1)	(2)	(3)
	(By Philidor)	Attwood / Wilson (b)	M. de la Bourdonnais (d) / M. Boncourt
1.	P—K 4 / P—K 4	P—K 4 / P—K 4	P—K 4 / P—K 4
2.	Kt—K B 3 / P—Q 3	Kt—K B 3 / P—Q 3	Kt—K B 3 / P—Q 3
3.	P—Q 4 / P—K B 4	P—Q 4 / P—K B 4	B—B 4 / P—K B 4
4.	P×K P / P×K P	P×K P / P×K P	P—Q 3 / P—B 3
5.	Kt—Kt 5 / P—Q 4	Kt—Kt 5 / P—Q 4	Kt—B 3 / B—K 2
6.	P—K B 4 (a) / B—Q B 4	P—K 6 / Kt—K R 3	0—0 / Kt—B 3
7.	P—B 4 / P—B 3	Kt—Q B 3 / P—B 3	Q—K 2 / P—Q Kt 4
8.	Kt—Q B 3 / Kt—K 2	K Kt×K P / P×Kt	B—Kt 3 / P—Kt 5
9.	P—K R 4 / P—K R 3	Q—R 5 ch. / P—Kt 3	Kt—Q 1 / P×P
10.	Kt—R 3 / 0—0	Q—K 5 / R—Kt 1	P×P / B—R 3
11.	Kt—R 4 / B—Q Kt 5 ch.	B×Kt / B×B	B—Q B 4 / B×B
12.	B—Q 2 / B×B ch.	R—Q 1 / Q—K 2	Q×B / P—Q 4
13.	Q×B / P—Q 5	B—B 4 / B—Kt 2	P×P / P×P
14.	P—Q B 5 / P—Q Kt 4	Q×P / R—B 1 (c)	Q—K 2 / P—K 5
15.	P×P e.p. / R P×P	Q Kt—Kt 5 / P×Kt	Kt—Q 4 / Q—Q 2
16.	P—Q Kt 3 / B—K 3	B×P ch. / Kt—B 3	Kt—K 3 / Kt—B 3

(a) He should play P—K 6.
(b) Contemporaries of Philidor.
(c) Black should have played B×Kt ch.
(d) M. de la Bourdonnais playing blindfold.

	(1)	(2)	(3)
17.	B—K 2 / Kt—B 4	B×Kt ch. / P×B	Kt×Kt / Q×Kt
18.	Kt—Kt 1 / Kt—Kt 6	Q×B P ch. / B—Q 2	Kt—B 5 / B—B 1
19.	R—R 2 / P—K 6	Q×R ch. / Q—Q 1	B—K 3 / Q—Q 2
20.	Q—Kt 2 / P—Q 6	P×B ch. / K—K 2	Kt—Q 4 / B—Q 3
21.	B—B 3 / R×P	Q—K 4 ch. and wins.	P—K B 4 / 0—0
22.	0—0 / R (B 5)×Kt		P—K R 3 / P—K R 4
23.	P×R / R×P		Q R—Q 1 / B—B 4
24.	P—Q R 3 / R—B 5 ch.		P—B 5 / Q R—K 1
25.	K—Kt 1 / R—B 7		P—B 4 / P×P e.p.
26.	Q—Kt 4 / Kt—R 3		P×P / R—K 4
27.	Q—K B 4 / Kt—B 4		P—B 4 / B×Kt
28.	Q×Kt / B—R 7 ch. and mate next move		B×B / R×P
29.	—		R×R / Q×R
30.	—		B×Kt / Q×B
31.	—		P×P / Q—K 4

(3) (contd.)

32.	P—Q 6 / P—K 6
33.	P—Q 7 / R—Q 1
34.	Q—B 4 ch. / K—R 2
35.	R—Q 5 / Q—R 8 ch.
36.	K—R 2 / P—K Kt 3
37.	Q—Q B 5 / Q—K B 3
38.	Q×K P / R—K B 1
39.	R—K 5 / Q—Q 3
40.	P—K Kt 3 / R—K B 2

Drawn.

	(4)	(5)	(6)
	Captain Kennedy / Mr. Buckle	Staunton / Horwitz	E. Williams / Rev. Lock
1.	P—K 4 / P—K 4	P—K 4 / P—K 4	P—K 4 / P—K 4
2.	Kt—K B 3 / P—Q 3	Kt—K B 3 / P—Q 3	Kt—K B 3 / P—Q 3

	(4)	(5)	(6)
3.	P—Q 4 / P×P	P—Q 4 / P×P	P—Q 4 / P—K B 4
4.	Q×P / Kt—K B 3	Kt×P / Kt—K B 3	P×K P / P×K P
5.	B—K Kt 5 / B—K 2	Q Kt—B 3 / B—K 2	Kt—Kt 5 / P—Q 4
6.	Kt—B 3 / 0—0	B—K 2 / 0—0	P—K 6 / B—Q B 4 (d)
7.	0—0—0 / Kt—B 3	P—B 4 / P—B 4	Kt—Q B 3 (e) / Q—B 3
8.	Q—Q 2 / B—K 3	Kt—B 3 / Kt—B 3	Q×P / B×P ch.
9.	Kt—Q 4 / Kt×K Kt	0—0 / B—Kt 5 (a)	K—Q 1 / P—K 6
10.	Q×Kt / P—B 4	B—K 3 / P—Q R 3	Q Kt—K 4 / Q—K 2
11.	Q—Q 2 / Q—R 4	P—Q R 3 / B×Kt	B—Kt 5 ch. / P—Q B 3
12.	P—Q R 3 / P—Kt 4	B×B / R—B 1	Kt—Q 6 ch. / K—B 1
13.	B×Kt / B×B	Kt—K 2 / Q—B 2 (b)	Q—B 3 ch. / Kt—B 3
14.	Kt—Q 5 / Q×Q	Kt—Kt 3 / K B—K 1 (c)	Kt×B / Q—Q 1 ch.
15.	R×Q / Q B×Kt	P—B 3 / Q R—Q 1	B—Q 3 / Q×Kt ch.
16.	R×B / K R—Q 1	Q—B 2 / B—B 1	Kt×P (f) / R×Kt
17.	B×P / Q R—Kt 1	Q R—Q 1 / P—Q Kt 3	B×R / Q×P

(a) With the hope of planting his Kt at Q 5.

(b) Intending presently, if an opportunity occur, to play Q Kt—Q 5, and, after the exchanges, take Q B P with his Q.

(c) Had he played the Kt over to Q 5, before protecting the B, he would have lost at least a Pawn.

(d) The ordinary defence at this point is Kt—K R 3.

(e) Kt×K P is the correct move, and if the Kt be taken, Q—R 5 (ch.) recovering the Piece with the better game.

(f) This was not well advised. White's Knight is of more value than Black's Rook, which is locked up. He ought to have seized the opportunity of getting rid of the dangerous Pawn at K 3.

	(4)	(5)	(6)
18.	P—Q R 4 / P—Q R 3	P—Kt 4 / Kt—R 2	B—Q 3 / Q Kt—Q 2
19.	B×P / B×P ch.	P—B 4 / P×P	K—K 2 / Kt—K 4
20.	K—Q 2 / R—Kt 5	P×P / P—Q 4 (b)	Q—B 5 / Kt×P (e)
21.	B—Kt 5 / R×K P	Q—B 2 (c) / Kt—B 1 (d)	Q×Kt / Q—Kt 5 ch.
22.	P—Q B 3 / P—B 5 (a)	B P×P / B×P	K—B 1 / R—K 1
23.	R—Q Kt 1 / B—Q R 6	P—K 5 / Kt—Q 2	Q—K 2 / Q—K B 4
24.	P—K B 3 / R—R 5	P—Q 6 / Q—Kt 1	P—K Kt 4 / Kt×P
25.	P—R 3 / R—Kt 1	B—B 6 / P—Kt 3 (f)	K—Kt 2 / R—K 5

(a) The only move to save the B.

(b) The exchange of Pawns, with the subsequent advance of this Pawn, appears, at first sight, a skilful conception, and one that must turn the scale in favour of the second player. Upon examination, however, it turns out to have been made without any consideration of the move White had in store, which renders the whole combination worse than nugatory.

(c) This rejoinder was certainly not foreseen by Black when he played on the Q P.

(d) He would have got an equally bad position by taking the K P with P.

(e) Very pretty. If White take the Queen he loses a piece.

(f) As the sacrifice of the Q Kt at this crisis had many advocates when the game was over, it may be well to examine briefly the consequences of that move. Suppose, then, instead of "P—K Kt 3," that Black had played

25. Kt×Q P

White then has several ways of playing.

IN THE FIRST PLACE.

26	B×Kt	R×B
27.	K—R sq	Q R—K 2 (1)
28.	P×Kt	R×B
29.	P—Q 7 winning easily.	

IN THE SECOND PLACE.

26.	R×Kt	B×R
27.	P×B	Q×P
28.	B×Kt	R×B
29.	B×P, and White ought to win.	

(1) If he support the Q R, White may at once take off the Kt

	(4)	(5)	(6)
26.	R—K 1 / K—B 1	K—K 4 / R—K 3	R—Q 1 / Kt×P
27.	R—K 4 / R×R	Q—R 4 / Kt—R 2	P—Kt 3 (b) / R—Kt 5 ch.
28.	P×R / K—K 2	B×Kt / R×B	K—R 1 / Q—K 5 ch.
29.	R—Q 4 / R—Q B 1	Kt—Kt 5 / P—K R 4	K×Kt / Q—R 2 mate
30.	R×B P (a) / R×R	Kt×R / P×Kt	
31.	B×R / P—R 4	P—B 5 / P—R 4	
32.	P—R 5 / P—R 5	P×K P / R—K Kt 2	
33.	P—R 6 / B—B 4	P—K 7 / Resigns.	
	Drawn.		

	(7) Jaenisch / Schumoff	(8) Morphy / Harrwitz	(9) Morphy / Harrwitz
1.	P—K 4 / P—K 4	P—K 4 / P—K 4	P—K 4 / P—K 4
2.	Kt—K B 3 / P—Q 3	Kt—K B 3 / P—Q 3	Kt—K B 3 / P—Q 3
3.	P—Q 4 / P×P	P—Q 4 / P×P	P—Q 4 / P×P
4.	Q×P / Kt—Q B 3	Q×P / Kt—Q B 3	Q×P / Kt—Q B 3

IN THE THIRD PLACE.

26.	P×Kt	R×B
27.	Q×R	B—B 4
28.	R—Q 4	Kt—K B 3
29.	K R—Q sq	R×P
30.	Kt—B 5	B×R
31.	R×B, retaining a Piece more than Black.	

(a) He should have played B×P.

(b) Too late. White should have liberated his pieces on the Queen's side sooner, and he might then have saved the game.

	(7)	(8)	(9)
5.	B—Q Kt 5 / B—Q 2	B—Q Kt 5 / B—Q 2	B—Q Kt 5 / B—Q 2
6.	Q—Q 1 / Kt—B 3	B×Kt / B×B	B×Kt / B×B
7.	Kt—B 3 / Kt—K 4	B—Kt 5 / P—K B 3	B—Kt 5 / Kt—B 3
8.	B—K 2 / B—B 3	B—K R 4 / Kt—R 3	Kt—B 3 / B—K 2
9.	B—K Kt 5 / B—K 2	Kt—B 3 / Q—Q 2	0—0—0 / 0—0
10.	B×Kt / B×B	0—0 / B—K 2	K R—K 1 / P—K R 3
11.	Kt—Q 4 / 0—0	Q R—Q 1 / 0—0	B—R 4 / Kt—K 1
12.	0—0 / Kt—Kt 3	Q—B 4 ch. / R—B 2	B×B / Q×B
13.	P—B 4 / Q—K 2	Kt—Q 4 / Kt—Kt 5	P—K 5 / B×Kt
14.	Kt×B / P×Kt	P—K R 3 / Kt—K 4	P×B / Q—Kt 4 ch.
15.	B—Q 3 / Q R—Kt 1	Q—K 2 / P—K Kt 4 (d)	K—Kt 1 / P×P
16.	R—Kt 1 / B—Q 5 ch.	B—Kt 3 / R—Kt 2	R×P / Q—Kt 7
17.	K—R 1 / Q—B 3	Kt—B 5 / R—Kt 3	Kt—Q 5 / Q×R P
18.	P—K 5 (a) / P×P	P—B 4 / P×P	K R—K 1 / Q—Q 3
19.	Kt—K 4 / Q—K 2	R×P / K—R 1	R—Kt 1 / K—R 2
20.	P—B 5 / Kt—B 5	R—R 4 / B—B 1	Q—K 3 / P—K B 4
21.	P—B 6 (b) / Q—Q 2 (c)	B×Kt / B P×B	Kt—B 4 / Q—Q Kt 3

(a) By the sacrifice of this Pawn he is enabled to bring his Kt into effective co-operation with the other forces immediately.

(b) All this is good chess.

(c) Taking Pawn with Pawn would have been highly dangerous.

(d) Very imprudent in such a position and against such an opponent. It must be admitted, however, that Black has no good move at this crisis.

	(7)	(8)	(9)
22.	$\dfrac{\text{R} \times \text{Kt} \ (a)}{\text{P} \times \text{R}}$	$\dfrac{\text{R} - \text{B} \ 1}{\text{Q} - \text{K} \ 3}$	$\dfrac{\text{Q} - \text{K} \ 2}{\text{R} - \text{B} \ 2}$
23.	$\dfrac{\text{Q} - \text{R} \ 5}{\text{Q} - \text{Q} \ 4}$	$\dfrac{\text{Kt} - \text{Kt} \ 5}{\text{Q} - \text{Kt} \ 1}$	$\dfrac{\text{Q} - \text{B} \ 4}{\text{Q} - \text{B} \ 3}$
24.	$\dfrac{\text{Q} - \text{Kt} \ 4}{\text{P} - \text{Kt} \ 3}$	$\dfrac{\text{R} - \text{B} \ 2}{\text{P} - \text{Q} \ \text{R} \ 3}$	$\dfrac{\text{Kt} - \text{K} \ \text{R} \ 5 \ (f)}{\text{Q} - \text{K} \ 2}$
25.	$\dfrac{\text{Q} \times \text{P} \ (\text{B} \ 5)}{\text{Q} - \text{K} \ \text{R} \ 4}$	$\dfrac{\text{Kt} \times \text{B} \ \text{P} \ (b)}{\text{R} - \text{B} \ 1}$	$\dfrac{\text{Q} \ \text{R} - \text{K} \ 1}{\text{Q} - \text{Q} \ 2}$
26.	$\dfrac{\text{P} - \text{K} \ \text{Kt} \ 4}{\text{Q} - \text{R} \ 5}$	$\dfrac{\text{Q} \ \text{Kt} - \text{Q} \ 5}{\text{B} \times \text{Kt}}$	$\dfrac{\text{P} - \text{R} \ 3}{\text{Kt} - \text{Q} \ 3}$
27.	$\dfrac{\text{P} - \text{Q} \ \text{Kt} \ 3}{\text{K} \ \text{R} - \text{K} \ 1}$	$\dfrac{\text{P} \times \text{B}}{\text{Q} \ \text{R} - \text{B} \ 2 \ (c)}$	$\dfrac{\text{Q} - \text{Q} \ 4}{\text{R} - \text{K} \ \text{Kt} \ 1}$
28.	$\dfrac{\text{R} - \text{K} \ \text{B} \ 1}{\text{B} - \text{K} \ 4}$	$\dfrac{\text{P} - \text{B} \ 4}{\text{B} - \text{K} \ 2}$	$\dfrac{\text{R} - \text{Kt} \ 2}{\text{P} - \text{Q} \ \text{Kt} \ 3}$
29.	$\dfrac{\text{Q} - \text{Q} \ 2}{\text{P} - \text{K} \ \text{R} \ 4}$	$\dfrac{\text{R} - \text{R} \ 5}{\text{Q} - \text{K} \ 1}$	$\dfrac{\text{R} - \text{Kt} \ 1}{\text{Kt} - \text{K} \ 1}$
30.	$\dfrac{\text{Kt} - \text{Kt} \ 5}{\text{B} \times \text{R} \ \text{P}}$	$\dfrac{\text{P} - \text{B} \ 5 \ (d)}{\text{R} \times \text{P}}$	$\dfrac{\text{Q} - \text{B} \ 3}{\text{P} - \text{B} \ 5 \ (g)}$
31.	$\dfrac{\text{Kt} - \text{B} \ 3}{\text{B} - \text{B} \ 5 \ \text{d. ch.}}$	$\dfrac{\text{R} \times \text{P ch.}}{\text{K} \times \text{R}}$	$\dfrac{\text{R} - \text{R} \ 1 \ (h)}{\text{P} - \text{Kt} \ 3}$
32.	$\dfrac{\text{Kt} \times \text{Q}}{\text{B} \times \text{Q}}$	$\dfrac{\text{Q} - \text{R} \ 5 \ \text{ch.}}{\text{K} - \text{Kt} \ 1}$	$\dfrac{\text{R} \ (\text{R} \ 1) - \text{Kt} \ 1}{\text{Q} - \text{Q} \ 4}$
33.	$\dfrac{\text{Kt} \times \text{P}}{\text{P} \times \text{P}}$	$\dfrac{\text{Kt} \times \text{B ch.}}{\text{K} - \text{Kt} \ 2 \ (e)}$	$\dfrac{\text{Q} - \text{K} \ 1}{\text{Q} \times \text{Kt}}$

(a) This is better, I believe, than the more obvious course of taking the K Kt P.

(b) Perfectly sound, as the sequel shows.

(c) Taking the Pawn would have been injudicious, for example :

27.	—	Q × P
28.	R × K R P ch.	K × R (best)
29.	Q — R 5 ch.	B — R 3
30.	Kt × B	R × Kt
31.	Q — K B 5 ch	Anything
32.	Q × Q R, &c.	—

(d) The first step in a combination of admirable daring and ingenuity.

(e) Had he taken the Knight it would have cost him his Queen.

(f) This looks promising, but does not turn out well. He had better, perhaps, have played R — K Kt 6.

(g) Well played. White must now beware, for his Knight is in sore peril.

(h) This will not save the Knight. The best move apparently was R — K Kt 4.

	(7)	(8)	(9)
34.	$\dfrac{\text{Kt}-\text{K 7 ch.}}{\text{R}\times\text{Kt}}$	$\dfrac{\text{Kt}-\text{B 5 ch.}}{\text{K}-\text{Kt 1}}$	$\dfrac{\text{R}-\text{Kt 5 }(a)}{\text{Q}\times\text{P}}$
35.	$\dfrac{\text{P}\times\text{R}}{\text{R}-\text{K 1}}$	Kt$\times$Q P and wins.	$\dfrac{\text{Q}-\text{K 5}}{\text{R}-\text{B 3}}$
36.	$\dfrac{\text{R}-\text{K Kt 1}}{\text{R}\times\text{P}}$	**(7)** *(contd.)*	$\dfrac{\text{Q}-\text{K 7 ch.}}{\text{R}-\text{Kt 2}}$
37.	$\dfrac{\text{R}\times\text{P ch.}}{\text{K}-\text{B 1}}$	43. $\dfrac{\text{B}\times\text{R}}{\text{K}-\text{B 3}}$	$\dfrac{\text{Q}\times\text{Kt}}{\text{P}\times\text{R}}$
38.	$\dfrac{\text{R}-\text{K R 4}}{\text{P}-\text{R 4}}$	44. $\dfrac{\text{B}-\text{K 4}}{\text{P}-\text{B 4}}$	$\dfrac{\text{Q}-\text{K 1}}{\text{Q}-\text{B 3}}$
39.	$\dfrac{\text{P}-\text{R 4}}{\text{R}-\text{K 3}}$	45. $\dfrac{\text{K}-\text{B 3}}{\text{K}-\text{K 4}}$	$\dfrac{\text{P}-\text{K B 3}}{\text{R}-\text{K 3}}$
40.	$\dfrac{\text{K}-\text{Kt 2}}{\text{R}-\text{B 3}}$	46. $\dfrac{\text{B}-\text{Q 3}}{\text{P}-\text{B 4}}$	$\dfrac{\text{Q}-\text{B 2}}{\text{R (Kt 2)}-\text{K 2}}$
41.	$\dfrac{\text{R}-\text{R 5}}{\text{K}-\text{K 2}}$	47. $\dfrac{\text{B}-\text{R 6}}{\text{K}-\text{Q 5}}$	Resigns.
42.	$\dfrac{\text{R}-\text{K B 5}}{\text{R}\times\text{R}}$	48. $\dfrac{\text{B}-\text{Q 3}}{\text{P}-\text{B 5}}$ Drawn.	

	(10)	(11)	(12)
	$\dfrac{\text{Boden}}{\text{Morphy}}$	$\dfrac{\text{Barnes}}{\text{Morphy}}$	$\dfrac{\text{Szen}}{\text{Hampe}}$
1.	$\dfrac{\text{P}-\text{K 4}}{\text{P}-\text{K 4}}$	$\dfrac{\text{P}-\text{K 4}}{\text{P}-\text{K 4}}$	$\dfrac{\text{P}-\text{K 4}}{\text{P}-\text{K 4}}$
2.	$\dfrac{\text{K}-\text{K B 3}}{\text{P}-\text{Q 3}}$	$\dfrac{\text{Kt}-\text{K B 3}}{\text{P}-\text{Q 3}}$	$\dfrac{\text{Kt}-\text{K B 3}}{\text{P}-\text{Q 3}}$
3.	$\dfrac{\text{P}-\text{Q 4}}{\text{P}\times\text{P}}$	$\dfrac{\text{P}-\text{Q 4}}{\text{P}-\text{K B 4}}$	$\dfrac{\text{P}-\text{Q 4}}{\text{P}\times\text{P}}$
4.	$\dfrac{\text{Q}\times\text{P}}{\text{B}-\text{Q 2}}$	$\dfrac{\text{P}\times\text{K P}}{\text{P}\times\text{K P}}$	$\dfrac{\text{B}-\text{B 4}}{\text{Kt}-\text{Q B 3}}$
5.	$\dfrac{\text{B}-\text{K 3}}{\text{Kt}-\text{Q B 3}}$	$\dfrac{\text{Kt}-\text{Kt 5}}{\text{P}-\text{Q 4}}$	$\dfrac{\text{Kt}\times\text{P}}{\text{Kt}\times\text{Kt}}$
6.	$\dfrac{\text{Q}-\text{Q 2}}{\text{Kt}-\text{B 3}}$	$\dfrac{\text{P}-\text{K 6}}{\text{B}-\text{B 4 }(b)}$	$\dfrac{\text{Q}\times\text{Kt}}{\text{B}-\text{K 3}}$

(*a*) Merely desperate.

(*b*) The usual move here is 6. $\dfrac{\text{Kt}-\text{K R 3}}{\quad}$, and the safest and strongest move for White is 7. $\dfrac{\text{Kt}-\text{Q B 3}}{\quad}$.

	(10)	(11)	(12)
7.	B—Q 3 / B—K 2	Kt—B 7 (a) / Q—B 3	Kt—B 3 / B×B
8.	Kt—B 3 / 0—0	B—K 3 (b) / P—Q 5	Q×B / Q—Q 2
9.	0—0 / P—K R 3	B—K Kt 5 / Q—B 4	B—K 3 / Kt—B 3
10.	P—K R 3 / Kt—R 2	Kt×R / Q×B	0—0—0 / Q—B 3 (e)
11.	P—K Kt 4 / P—K R 4	B—B 4 / Kt—Q B 3	Q×Q / P×Q
12.	Kt—R 2 / R P×P	Kt—B 7 / Q×P	B—Q 4 / Kt—Kt 5
13.	P×P / Kt—K 4	R—B 1 / Kt—B 3	P—B 3 / Kt—K 4
14.	P—B 3 / P—K Kt 4	P—K B 3 / Kt—Q Kt 5	B×Kt / P×B
15.	K—Kt 2 / P—Q B 4	Kt—R 3 / B×P (c)	R—Q 3 / B—Q 3
16.	R—R 1 / K—Kt 2	B×B / Kt—Q 6 ch.	Kt—Q 1 (f) / 0—0
17.	Kt—B 1 / R—R 1	Q×Kt (d) / P×Q	Kt—K 3 / P—P 3
18.	Kt—Kt 3 / P—B 3	0—0—0 / B×Kt	Kt—B 5 / B—B 4
19.	Kt—Q 5 / Kt—B 1	B—Kt 3 / P—Q 7 ch.	R—Q 7 / R—B 2
20.	Kt—R 5 ch. / K—B 2	K—Kt 1 / B—B 4	R×R / K×R
21.	Q R—Q 1 / Kt (B 1)—Kt 3	Kt—K 5 / K—B 1	R—Q 1 / P—Kt 3

(a) Better to have played 7. $\dfrac{\text{Kt} \times \text{K P}}{}$, regaining the Piece by Q—R 5 ch.

(b) The worst defence he could adopt. Q—Q 2, followed by Q—B 4, was the proper move.

(c) Highly ingenious.

(d) The only move to escape instant defeat.

(e) Whence this eager desire to exchange Pieces, even at a disadvantage, which Mr. Hampe exhibits ? One would have supposed that Mr. Szen's acknowledged skill in Pawn end-games would have prompted his antagonist to retain his officers as long as possible.

(f) Kt—R 4, with the object of afterwards playing his Q R—B 3, would also have been good play.

	(10)	(11)	(12)
		Kt—Q 3	Kt—Kt 3
22.	**B—K 2** / Kt—R 5 ch.	R—K 1	B—K 6 ch.
		Kt×B	K—Kt 1
23.	K—B 2 / B—B 3	Q×R	K—K 3
		Resigns.	R—Q 3
24.	Kt×B / Q×Kt		B—Q 5
			Kt—K 2
25.	Q×P / P—Kt 3		P—Q B 4
			R—R 3 (b)
26.	Q×Q ch. (a) / K×Q		P—Q R 4
			Kt×B ch.
27.	Kt—Kt 3 / K—B 2		K P×Kt
		(10) (contd.)	P—B 3
28.	R—Q 6 / K—K 2	38. R—Q 6 ch. / K—B 2	K—Q 3
		39. B—R 5 ch. / K—K 2	K—B 2
29.	R—Q 2 / K—B 2		K—B 3
		40. B×P ch. / K—B 1	P×P
30.	P—K B 4 / P×P		P×P
		41. R—B 1 ch. and wins.	R—R 4
31.	B×P / Kt (R 5)—Kt 3		K—B 4
			P—Q Kt 4 ch. (c)
32.	B—R 6 / R—R 2		K—Kt 4
			R×P ch.
33.	K—K 3 / Q R—R 1		R×R
			P×R
34.	Kt—B 5 / Kt—K 2		K×P
		(12) (contd.)	P—B 4
35.	Kt×Kt / K×Kt	38. P×P / K—B 3	K—Kt 4
			K—Q 3
36.	P—Kt 5 / K—K 3	39. P—Q R 4 / K—B 4	P—Q B 4
			P—K 5 (d)
37.	K R—Q 1 / P×P	40. P—R 5 and wins	P×P

(a) Better, I believe to have taken Kt with K R; the attack then, apparently, would have been irresistible.

(b) P—Q B 3 looks a better move.

(c) The termination is played by Mr. Szen with the ingenuity which he always displays in endings of this description.

(d) He now obtains two passed Pawns, as he foresaw, when he forced an exchange of Rooks; and it is impossible for the Black King to stop *both*.

	(13) Szen / Hampe	(14) Lowenthal / Allies	(15) De Riviere / Laroche
1.	P–K 4 / P–K 4	P–K 4 / P–K 4	P–K 4 / P–K 4
2.	Kt–K B 3 / P–Q 3	Kt–Kt B 3 / P–Q 3	Kt–K B 3 / P–Q 3
3.	P–Q 4 / P×P	P–Q 4 / P×P	P–Q 4 / P×P
4.	Kt×P / P–Q 4	Q×P / Kt–Q B 3	Q×P / Kt–Q B 3
5.	P–K 5 (a) / B–Q B 4	B–Q Kt 5 / B–Q 2	B–Q Kt 5 / B–Q 2
6.	B–K 3 / Kt–K 2	B×Kt / B×B	B×Kt / B×B
7.	P–K 6 (b) / P×P	B–Kt 5 / Kt–B 3 (d)	B–Kt 5 / P–B 3 (f)
8.	Kt×P / B–Kt 5 ch.	B×Kt / Q×B	B–R 4 / P–K R 4 (g)
9.	P–Q B 3 / B×Kt (c)	Q×Q / P×Q	P–B 4 / Q–Q 2
10.	P×B / 0–0	Q Kt–Q 2 / R–K Kt 1	Kt–B 3 / 0–0–0
11.	B–Q 3 / B–B 4	0–0 / B–R 3	0–0 (h) / K–Kt 1
12.	0–0 / Kt–Q B 3	K R–K 1 / K–Q 2 (e)	P–Q K 4 / P–Q Kt 3

(a) The first player may also retreat the Kt—K B 3 advantageously.

(b) Better to have brought out his Pieces.   Exchanging the centre Pawn for the adversary's K B P is not a profitable barter usually, and in this case White subjects himself to the necessity of doubli g a Pawn on his Queen's side into the bargain.

(c) He might even have gained a Pawn now without any danger, beyond that of bringing his opponent's Q Kt into the field.

(d) In a similar position, which occurred in the match won by Harrwitz of Lowenthal, the former here played P—K B 3.

(e) I am rather inclined to believe that the Allies would have done better in Castling.

(f) For the result of Kt—K B 3, see the preceding game.

(g) The usual move is Kt—K 2 or K R 3, but in either case the second player's game is grievously constrained.

h) By taking the R P he would have placed his Queen too far out of play.

	(13)	(14)	(15)
13.	P—Kt 5 / Kt—K 4	Kt—Kt 3 / P—B 4	P—R 4 (e) / P—K Kt 4 (f)
14.	B×B / Kt×B	Q R—Q 1 / Q R—K 1	B×P (g) / P×P
15.	B—K B 4 / Kt (K 4)—Kt 3	K Kt—Q 2 / B×Kt (b)	Q×R / B—K Kt 2
16.	Q—Q 2 / P—Q 5 (a)	R×B / P×P	Q×P / B×Kt
17.	B—Kt 5 / Q—Q 3	P—Q B 4 / P—Kt 3 (c)	Q R—Kt 1 / B×K P
18.	Q—Q 3 / Kt—K 4	R—K 3 / P—B 4	R—Kt 3 / Kt—B 3 (h)
19.	Q—Kt 3 ch. / K—R 1	R—R 3 / R—K 2	Q×P / R—Kt 1
20.	Kt—Q 2 / Q—K Kt 3	P—Kt 3 / K—B 1 (d)	Q—K 3 / R×P ch.

(a) Threatening to take the Bishop, and then play Kt—K 6, winning the exchange.

(b) It is pretty obvious that Black would have gained nothing by taking the Pawn, for suppose—

15.	—	P×P
16.	Kt×P	B×Kt
17.	R×B	R×R
18.	Kt—B 5 ch.	K moves.
19.	Kt×R, &c.	—

(c) If Black had now taken the K Kt P, they would have lost a Piece, e.g. :—

17.	—	R×P ch.
18.	K×R	P—K 6 d. ch.
19.	R—Q 5, &c.	—

(d) This serves to corroborate the opinion expressed in the note to Black's 12th move.

(e) Mr. de Riviere remarked that he should rather have played Q R—Q, threatening to advance P—Q Kt 5, P—R 4, &c.

(f) Mr. Laroche now commences a counter-attack on the King's flank, and pursues it with such spirit and decision, that in a few m ves Black is completely routed, horse and foot.

(g) He appears to have nothing better to do. Advancing the Pawns on the Queen's side would be quite futile.

(h) The terminating moves on the Black side are very clever from this moment.

	(13)	(14)	(15)
21.	B—B 4 / Kt—R 5	Kt—Q 4 / B—Q 2	K—R 1 (g) / R×P ch.
22.	B—Kt 3 / R—B 5 (a)	R—R 4 / R—Kt 5	K×R / Kt—Kt 5 ch.
23.	K R—K 1 / R—K 1 (b)	R×R / P×R	K—Kt 3 / Kt×Q
24.	K—R 1 / R×P	Kt—B 2 / P—K R 4	P×Kt / Q—Kt 2 ch.
25.	Kt—B 4 / Q R—K B 1	Kt—K 3 / B—K 3	Resigns
26.	Kt×Kt / Q—K 5 (c)	K—B 1 / K—Q 2	
27.	Kt—B 3 / Q—Kt 5	R—Q 4 / B—B 2	
28.	Kt×Kt / Q—K 7 (d)	Kt—Q 5 / R—K 3	
29.	B×R and wins	P—Kt 3 (e) / K—Q 1 (f)	
30.		Kt—B 4 / R—K 4	
31.		K—K 2 / B—Kt 1	
32.		K—K 3 / B—R 2	

(14) (contd.)

33.	R—Q 5 / K—K 2
34.	R×R ch. / P×R
35.	Kt—Q 5 ch. (h) / K—Q 3
36.	Kt—B 6 / B—Kt 3
37.	P—Kt 4 / P—R 4
38.	P—Q R 3 / P×P

(a) This is an ingenious manœuvre to avoid giving up the attack; but a very hazardous one.

(b) The position is full of difficulties for Black, and this move certainly does not lessen them. Perhaps his best plan was to play the Q Kt—Q 6; and if White then attacked his Queen with the Rook, to play the Kt—Q B 4.

(c) A truly gallant defence this of Mr. Hampe's, and worthy of a better result.

(d) Bad; but he has no good move left.

(e) White protects his Q B P that he may be enabled safely to take the K P with his Rook; and if his Rook were captured, give check with Kt—B 6.

(f) To prevent the capture of their K P. I believe, however, they might have played P—Q B 3 advantageously.

(g) It is indifferent whether he take or not. His game cannot be saved.

(h) Had he taken the K R P, it would have cost his Kt.

(14) *(contd.)*

39. $\dfrac{P \times P}{P - B\,4}$ *(a)*

40. $\dfrac{P - Kt\,5}{K - B\,2}$ *(b)*

41. $\dfrac{Kt - Q\,5\ ch.}{K - Kt\,2}$

42. $\dfrac{Kt - B\,6}{K - B\,2}$

43. $\dfrac{Kt \times P}{B - B\,2}$

44. $\dfrac{Kt - Q\,2}{K - Q\,3}$

45. $\dfrac{P - B\,4}{B - Kt\,3}$

46. $\dfrac{Kt - K\,4\ ch.}{K - K\,3}$

47. $\dfrac{Kt - B\,3}{P \times P\ ch.}$

48. $\dfrac{P \times P}{P - R\,5}$ *(c)*

49. $\dfrac{Kt - R\,4}{B - B\,7}$ *(d)*

50. $\dfrac{Kt \times Kt\ P}{B - Kt\,6}$

51. $\dfrac{P - B\,5\ ch.}{K - K\,4}$ *(e)*

52. $\dfrac{P - B\,6}{K \times P}$

53. $\dfrac{K - B\,4}{P - Kt\,6}$

54. $\dfrac{P \times P}{P \times P}$

55. $\dfrac{K \times P}{K - K\,2}$

56. $\dfrac{K - B\,4}{K - Q\,3}$

57. $\dfrac{K - K\,3}{K - B\,2}$

58. $\dfrac{Kt - Q\,5\ ch.}{K - Kt\,2}$

59. $\dfrac{K - Q\,3}{B - R\,5}$

60. $\dfrac{K - B\,3}{K - R\,2}$

Drawn.

	(16)	**(17)**	**(18)**
	B., M., W.	Morphy and Barres	Brien
	H., M., Z.	Staunton and Owen	Z—
1.	$\dfrac{P - K\,4}{P - K\,4}$	$\dfrac{P - K\,4}{P - K\,4}$	$\dfrac{P - K\,4}{P - K\,4}$
2.	$\dfrac{Kt - K\,B\,3}{P - Q\,3}$	$\dfrac{Kt - K\,B\,3}{P - Q\,3}$	$\dfrac{Kt - K\,B\,3}{P - Q\,3}$

(a) I should have preferred advancing this Pawn to P—Q B 3 only.

(b) Most important, or White, by playing his Kt—Q 5, would have won the Q Kt P.

(c) The game is played throughout attentively; but the latter portion manifests extreme care and forms a very interesting and instructive ending.

(d) The only move to save the day.

(e) Well conceived. If Black take, the reply is Kt—Q 7; and White apparently must win.

	(16)	(17)	(18)
3.	$\dfrac{\text{P}-\text{Q 4}}{\text{P}\times\text{P}}$	$\dfrac{\text{P}-\text{Q 4}}{\text{P}-\text{K B 4}}$	$\dfrac{\text{P}-\text{Q 4}}{\text{P}\times\text{P}}$
4.	$\dfrac{\text{Q}\times\text{P}}{\text{B}-\text{Q 2}}$	$\dfrac{\text{P}\times\text{K P}}{\text{P}\times\text{K P}}$	$\dfrac{\text{Q}\times\text{P}}{\text{B}-\text{Q 2}}$
5.	$\dfrac{\text{B}-\text{K B 4}}{\text{Kt}-\text{Q B 3}}$	$\dfrac{\text{Kt}-\text{Kt 5}}{\text{P}-\text{Q 4}}$	$\dfrac{\text{B}-\text{K B 4}}{\text{Kt}-\text{Q B 3}}$
6.	$\dfrac{\text{Q}-\text{Q 2}}{\text{B}-\text{K 2}}$	$\dfrac{\text{P}-\text{K 6}}{\text{Kt}-\text{K R 3}}$	$\dfrac{\text{Q}-\text{Q 2}}{\text{B}-\text{K 2}}$
7.	$\dfrac{\text{Kt}-\text{B 3}}{\text{Kt}-\text{B 3}}$	$\dfrac{\text{Kt}-\text{Q B 3}}{\text{P}-\text{B 3}}$	$\dfrac{\text{Kt}-\text{Q B 3}}{\text{Kt}-\text{B 3}}$
8.	$\dfrac{\text{B}-\text{K 2 }(a)}{\text{0}-\text{0}}$	$\dfrac{\text{K Kt}\times\text{K P}}{\text{P}\times\text{Kt}}$	$\dfrac{\text{B}-\text{K 2 }(e)}{\text{0}-\text{0}}$
9.	$\dfrac{\text{0}-\text{0}-\text{0}}{\text{Kt}-\text{K Kt 5}}$	$\dfrac{\text{Q}-\text{R 5 ch.}}{\text{P}-\text{Kt 3}}$	$\dfrac{\text{P}-\text{K R 3 }(f)}{\text{P}-\text{Q R 3}}$
10.	$\dfrac{\text{K R}-\text{B 1}}{\text{B}-\text{K 3}}$	$\dfrac{\text{Q}-\text{K 5}}{\text{R}-\text{Kt 1}}$	$\dfrac{\text{P}-\text{K Kt 4}}{\text{P}-\text{Q Kt 4}}$
11.	$\dfrac{\text{P}-\text{K R 3}}{\text{Kt}-\text{K 4}}$	$\dfrac{\text{B}\times\text{Kt}}{\text{B}\times\text{B}}$	$\dfrac{\text{P}-\text{Q R 3}}{\text{B}-\text{K 3}}$
12.	$\dfrac{\text{P}-\text{K Kt 4}}{\text{B}-\text{B 3}}$	$\dfrac{\text{R}-\text{Q 1}}{\text{Q}-\text{Kt 4 }(c)}$	$\dfrac{\text{P}-\text{Kt 4 }(g)}{\text{Kt}-\text{Q 2}}$
13.	$\dfrac{\text{Kt}-\text{Q 5}}{\text{B}\times\text{Kt}}$	$\dfrac{\text{Q}-\text{B 7}}{\text{B}\times\text{P}}$	$\dfrac{\text{R}-\text{Q 1}}{\text{B}-\text{B 3}}$
14.	$\dfrac{\text{P}\times\text{B}}{\text{Kt}\times\text{Kt}}$	$\dfrac{\text{Q}\times\text{Kt P}}{\text{P}-\text{K 6 }(d)}$	$\dfrac{\text{Kt}-\text{Q 5}}{\text{B}\times\text{Kt}}$
15.	$\dfrac{\text{B}\times\text{Kt}}{\text{Kt}-\text{K 4}}$	$\dfrac{\text{P}-\text{B 3}}{\text{Q}-\text{K 2}}$	$\dfrac{\text{P}\times\text{B}}{\text{Kt}-\text{K 4}}$
16.	$\dfrac{\text{B}-\text{K 4}}{\text{Kt}-\text{B 5 }(b)}$	$\dfrac{\text{Q}\times\text{R}}{\text{K}-\text{B 2}}$	$\dfrac{\text{Kt}-\text{Q 4}}{\text{Kt}-\text{Q Kt 3}}$

(a) I am not sure that this is so good as playing the B—Q 3.

(b) An obvious and a very serious error.

(c) This very obvious move is not sound, but it has the merit of retarding the attack for some time.

(d) Very well played.

(e) In the present form of the opening, this Bishop should occupy B 4.

(f) 0—0 is much better.

(g) This seems objectionable.

	(16)	(17)	(18)
17.	$\dfrac{\text{B} \times \text{P ch. } (a)}{\text{K—R 1}}$	$\dfrac{\text{Kt—K 4 } (b)}{\text{B—B 5}}$	$\dfrac{\text{B} \times \text{Kt}}{\text{B} \times \text{B}}$
18.	$\dfrac{\text{Q—Q 3}}{\text{B} \times \text{P ch.}}$	$\dfrac{\text{B—K 2}}{\text{K—Kt 2}}$	$\dfrac{\text{Kt—B 6}}{\text{Q—K 1}}$
19.	$\dfrac{\text{K—Kt 1}}{\text{P—Q Kt 4}}$	$\dfrac{\text{0—0}}{\text{Q—B 2}}$	$\dfrac{\text{P—K B 4 } (c)}{\text{Kt—B 5}}$
20.	$\dfrac{\text{Q—B 5}}{\text{P—Kt 3}}$	$\dfrac{\text{Kt—B 5}}{\text{B} \times \text{P ch.}}$	$\dfrac{\text{Q—B 1}}{\text{B—Kt 7}}$
21.	$\dfrac{\text{B} \times \text{Kt P}}{\text{P} \times \text{B}}$	$\dfrac{\text{K—R 1}}{\text{B—B 1}}$	$\dfrac{\text{Q—Kt 1}}{\text{Q—K 5}}$
22.	$\dfrac{\text{Q} \times \text{P}}{\text{Q—B 3}}$	$\dfrac{\text{R—Q 4}}{\text{B—Kt 6}}$	$\dfrac{\text{0—0}}{\text{Q} \times \text{B}}$
23.	$\dfrac{\text{Q—R 5 ch.}}{\text{K—Kt 1}}$	$\dfrac{\text{R—K 4}}{\text{K—R 1}}$	$\dfrac{\text{R—K 1}}{\text{Q—B 6}}$
24.	$\dfrac{\text{Q—Kt 5 ch.}}{\text{Q} \times \text{Q}}$	$\dfrac{\text{R—Q 1}}{\text{Q—K Kt 2}}$	$\dfrac{\text{R—Q 3}}{\text{Q} \times \text{B P}}$
25.	$\dfrac{\text{B} \times \text{Q}}{\text{R—B 6}}$	$\dfrac{\text{R—K R 4}}{\text{B} \times \text{R}}$	$\dfrac{\text{R—K B 1}}{\text{Q—Kt 4}}$
26.	$\dfrac{\text{R—Q 3}}{\text{Q R—K B 1}}$	$\dfrac{\text{Q} \times \text{Kt}}{\text{B—R 3}}$	$\dfrac{\text{R (Q 3)—K B 3}}{\text{Q R—K 1}}$

(a) They appear to have had nothing better to do under the circumstances.

(b) Over-confident in the superiority of their position, White now played without due consideration. By simply moving R—Q 4, the game, I believe, is their own without trouble, for suppose:

17. R—Q 4   P—K 7, or (A.)
18. B×P   B—K 6
19. R—K 4, and wins.

(A.)

17.   —   R—Q B sq., or (B.)
18. B—B 4   —

And again Black has no resource.

(B.)

17.   —   K—Kt 2
18. R—K 4

With an easy winning game.

Black has other modes of play, but all tend to the same result.

(c) Clearly an oversight; Kt×B is the correct move.

(16)	(17)	(18)
27. $\dfrac{R \times R \ (a)}{R \times R}$	$\dfrac{Q-R \ 2}{B \times B}$	$\dfrac{P-B \ 3}{Q \times Q \ P}$
28. $\dfrac{P-K \ R \ 4}{B-B \ 3}$	$\dfrac{R-Q \ 7}{Q-R \ 3}$	$\dfrac{R-B \ 5}{Q \times Kt}$
29. $\dfrac{\text{Resigns.}}{}$	$\dfrac{Kt-K \ 4}{B-B \ 5}$	$\dfrac{R-R \ 5}{Q-K \ 5}$
30.	$\dfrac{Kt-B6}{P-K \ 7}$	Resigns.
31.	Resigns.	

(19)	(20)	(21)
Amateur	Lowenthal	Max Lange
Amateur	Harrwitz	Dr. Hoffmann
1. $\dfrac{P-K \ 4}{P-K \ 4}$	$\dfrac{P-K \ 4}{P-K \ 4}$	$\dfrac{P-K \ 4}{P-K \ 4}$
2. $\dfrac{Kt-K \ B \ 3}{P-Q \ 3}$	$\dfrac{Kt-K \ B \ 3}{P-Q \ 3}$	$\dfrac{Kt-K \ B \ 3}{P-Q \ 3}$
3. $\dfrac{P-Q \ 4}{P-K \ B \ 4}$	$\dfrac{P-B \ 4}{B-K \ 2 \ (b)}$	$\dfrac{B-B \ 4}{B-K \ 2}$
4. $\dfrac{P \times K \ P}{P \times K \ P}$	$\dfrac{Kt-B \ 3}{Kt-K \ B \ 3}$	$\dfrac{0-0}{B-Kt \ 5}$
5. $\dfrac{Kt-Kt \ 5}{P-Q \ 4}$	$\dfrac{P-Q \ 3}{0-0}$	$\dfrac{P-Q \ 4}{Kt-Q \ B \ 3}$
6. $\dfrac{P-K \ 6}{Kt-K \ R \ 3}$	$\dfrac{P-K \ R \ 3}{Kt-B \ 3}$	$\dfrac{P-Q \ 5}{Kt-Q \ 5}$
(see diagram)		

(a) Had they played the R—Kt 3, the following neat mate was on the cards :—

27. R—Kt 3　　　　　　　R × B P
28. R × R　　　　　　　　R × R
29. R × B

A·d black mates in four moves

(b) This, or P—Q B 3, is perhaps the best move at the present moment. If Black plays the latter, and White should reply with P—Q 4, Black may obtain a tolerably free game, by playing P—Q 4 also.

	(19)	(20)	(21)
7.	$\dfrac{\text{P—K B 3}}{\text{B—B 4 }(a)}$	$\dfrac{\text{B—K Kt 5}}{\text{B—K 3 }(d)}$	$\dfrac{\text{B—K 3}}{\text{Kt} \times \text{Kt ch.}}$
8	$\dfrac{\text{P} \times \text{P}}{\text{0—0}}$	$\dfrac{\text{B} \times \text{Kt }(e)}{\text{B} \times \text{B}}$	$\dfrac{\text{P} \times \text{Kt}}{\text{B—Q 2 }(f)}$
9	$\dfrac{\text{P} \times \text{P}}{\text{B—B 7 ch. }(b)}$	$\dfrac{\text{B—Kt 3}}{\text{Kt—K 2}}$	$\dfrac{\text{P—B 4}}{\text{Kt—B 3}}$
10.	$\dfrac{\text{K—K 2}}{\text{B—Q 2}}$	$\dfrac{\text{Kt—K 2}}{\text{P—B 3}}$	$\dfrac{\text{P} \times \text{P}}{\text{P} \times \text{P}}$
11.	$\dfrac{\text{P} \times \text{B }(c)}{\text{Q—K 2 ch.}}$	$\dfrac{\text{B} \times \text{B}}{\text{P} \times \text{B}}$	$\dfrac{\text{Kt—B 3}}{\text{Kt—Kt 5}}$

BLACK.

WHITE.

(a) This defence may be adopted without danger, and appears to me to enable Black to overcome all the difficulties of his position; for this reason I prefer the method of continuing the attack beginning with 7 Kt—Q B 3, which in every case gives an advantage to the first player.

(b) This is good for Black; he may also play 9 R—K B 4 advantageously.

(c) This is somewhat rashly played.

(d) The defence adopted by Mr. Harrwitz gives him a constrained game for a long time, but under this disadvantage he fights very ably.

(e) This appears to give the enemy more freedom than is desirable, and yet I doubt if he could have done better.

(f) The best square to retreat the Bishop to.

	(19)	(20)	(21)
12.	$\dfrac{\text{K—Q 3}}{\text{Kt}\times\text{P}}$	$\dfrac{\text{P—B 3}}{\text{P—Q 4}}$	$\dfrac{\text{Q—Q 2}}{\text{0—0}}$
13.	$\dfrac{\text{Q—K 2}}{\text{Kt—B 4 ch.}}$	$\dfrac{\text{Q—Kt 3}}{\text{Q—Kt 3}}$	$\dfrac{\text{P—B 4}}{\text{P}\times\text{P}}$
14.	$\dfrac{\text{K—B 4}}{\text{P—Kt 4 ch.}}$	$\dfrac{\text{0—0}}{\text{Kt—Kt 3}}$	$\dfrac{\text{B}\times\text{P}}{\text{P—B 4 ch.}}$
15.	$\dfrac{\text{K}\times\text{P}}{\text{Q R—Kt 1 ch.}}$	$\dfrac{\text{Q}\times\text{Q}}{\text{P}\times\text{Q}}$	$\dfrac{\text{K—R 1}}{\text{P—Q B 3}}$
16.	$\dfrac{\text{K—B 4}}{\text{R—Kt 5 ch.}}$	$\dfrac{\text{P—K Kt 3}}{\text{P}\times\text{P}}$	$\dfrac{\text{Kt—R 4}}{\text{Kt—B 7 ch.}}$
17.	$\dfrac{\text{K}\times\text{R}}{\text{Kt—Q 6}}$ db. ch. and wins	$\dfrac{\text{P}\times\text{P}}{\text{R—R 5 }(a)}$	$\dfrac{\text{R}\times\text{Kt}}{\text{B}\times\text{R}}$
18.		$\dfrac{\text{Kt—Q 2}}{\text{B—Kt 4}}$	$\dfrac{\text{Q}\times\text{B}}{\text{P—Q Kt 4}}$
19.		$\dfrac{\text{P—Kt 3 }(b)}{\text{R—R 3}}$	$\dfrac{\text{R—K Kt 1}}{\text{P}\times\text{P}}$
20.		$\dfrac{\text{K R—Q 1}}{\text{P—Kt 4 }(c)}$	$\dfrac{\text{B—R 6}}{\text{P—Kt 3}}$
21.		$\dfrac{\text{P—K R 4}}{\text{B}\times\text{Kt}}$	$\dfrac{\text{Q—Q 4}}{\text{P—B 3}}$
22.		$\dfrac{\text{R}\times\text{B}}{\text{K R—R 1}}$	$\dfrac{\text{B}\times\text{R}}{\text{K}\times\text{B}}$
23.		$\dfrac{\text{Kt—B 1}}{\text{Kt—B 1 }(d)}$	$\dfrac{\text{P}\times\text{P}}{\text{B}\times\text{P }(e)}$
24.		$\dfrac{\text{R—Kt 1}}{\text{P—B 4}}$	$\dfrac{\text{Q—B 5 ch.}}{\text{Q—K 2}}$

(a) The attack obtained by this move compensates, in some degree, for the ugly doubled Pawns on Black's side.

(b) The position, it will be remarked, is very critical for White, and without great care he would certainly have suffered some loss at this point.

(c) R—Q 1 would only have been a loss of time, as White could have replied at once Kt—K B 3.

(d) This Knight is badly posted, and the difficulty of bringing him into play is a more serious drawback to Black's game than even his doubled Pawns.

(e) Black gives up a Piece for the chance of making a drawn game through the exposed position of White's King. If he had played 23. $\dfrac{}{\text{B—K 3}}$; then 24. $\dfrac{\text{P—B 4}}{\text{Q—K 2}}$; 25. $\dfrac{\text{Kt—B 5}}{\text{B—B 2}}$; 26. $\dfrac{\text{Kt—Q 7 ch.}}{\text{K—Kt 2}}$; 27. $\dfrac{\text{R—B 1}}{}$, with an irresistible attack.

	(19)	(20)	(21)
25.		R(Kt 1)—Kt 2 / K—B 2	Q×B / R—Q 1
26.		P—Q B 4 (a) / R—R 4	Kt—B 3 / R—Q 7
27.		P—Q Kt 4 / B P×P	Q×P (B 5) / Q—K 4
28.		R×P / R—Q B 1	Q—B 8 ch. / K—Kt 2
29.		Kt—Q 3 (b) / P×P	Q—R 3 / R×P
30.		R×P ch. / K—B 3	R—Q 1 / P—K R 4

(a) At this juncture, I think that White had a winning game.
Instead of the move made I believe he should have played Kt—Q 3;
in which case the following is the most probable continuation:—

   27. Kt—Q 3   Kt—Q 2
     (I see no better or more likely move.)
   28. Kt—Kt 4   P×Kt
  (Again this seems his most feasible mode of playing.)
   29. R×Kt (ch)   K—K 1
   30. R×P   P×P (or A)
   31. R—B 2   R—B 3
   32. R×P   R—Q 1
   33. K—B 1   R—Q 7
If he play R—Q 5, White can safely take the King's Pawn.
   34. R×R   P×R
   35. K—K 2

      And White wins easily.

         A.

   30.   R×P
   31. R×R   R×R
   32. P×P   R—Kt 7
   (If R—K 7, then follows P—K B 3, &c.)
   33. R×P
    (Winning without much trouble.)

(b) Instead of this move he ought, I believe, to have played the
Kt—Kt 3, in which case the game would, most likely, have been
carried on as follows:—

   29. Kt—Kt 3   R to his 5
   30. R×P   R×P
(If he take this Pawn with the other Rook, White must win, I think,
      without much trouble.)
   31. R×P ch.
And White has a Pawn more, and a better situation than his
adversary.

	(19)	(20)	(21)
31.		R—B 2 / R—R 6	Q—Kt 3 / Q—K 2
32.		Kt—Kt 2 (a) / R×P	R—K Kt 1 / P—Kt 4
33.		R×B P / R×Kt	R—K 1 / Q—Kt 5
34.		R×R / R×R	P—K 5 / Q—Kt 2 ch.
35.		R×Kt ch. / K—K 2	Kt—K 4 / R×Kt P
36.		R—Q R 8 (b) / R—Kt 5	P×P ch. / K—B 2
37.		P—B 3 / R—Kt 7 (c)	Q—B 3 / K—Kt 3
38.		R—R 5 / K—B 3	R—K B 1 / Q—Kt 1
39.		P—Kt 4 / P—R 3	W. mates in 4.
40.		R—R 7 / P—Kt 4	
41.		P—R 5 / R—Kt 7 ch. (d)	

(a) Even here, most good players in White's position would have won the game. He should, if I make no mistake in my calculation, have played his Kt—K 1 ; then to K Kt 2, and afterwards to K 3, threatening a deadly check at K Kt 4. Such is the helplessness of Black's position that these moves could hardly be prevented.

(b) R—B 3, allowing his King an opportunity of coming into the field, would surely have been better Chess.

(c) A good move, as it paralyzes the action of the White King for some time.

(d) Drawn ; for if K × R stalemate.

Chapter III.

THE PETROFF DEFENCE—ANALYSIS.

	(1)	(2)	(3)
1.	P—K 4 / P—K 4	—	—
2.	Kt—K B 3 / Kt—K B 3	—	—
3.	P—Q 4 / P×P	—	—
4.	P—K 5 / Kt—K 5 !	—	Q—K 2
5.	Kt×P / P—Q 3 !	B—Q 3 / Kt—B 4	Q—K 2 ! / Kt—Q 4
6.	P×P / B×P	Kt×P / P—Q 3	Kt×P / P—Q 3
7.	B—Q B 4 / B—Q B 4	P×P / B×P	P×P / Q×Q ch.
8.	B—K 3 / O—O	O—O / O—O (a)	B×Q / B×P
9.	O—O / Kt—Q 2 =		O—O / O—O
10.			P—Q B 4 / Kt—B 5
11.			B—B 3 / P—Q B 3
12.			Kt—B 3 / Kt—Q 2
13.			Kt—K 4 / B—B 2 =

(a) If instead 8. B×P ch. ; 9. K×B / Q×Kt ; 10. B—Kt 5 ch. , etc.

	(4)	(5)	(6)
1.	$\dfrac{\text{P--K 4}}{\text{P--K 4}}$	$\dfrac{\text{P--K 4}}{\text{P--K 4}}$	—
2.	$\dfrac{\text{Kt--K B 3}}{\text{Kt--K B 3}}$	$\dfrac{\text{Kt--K B 3}}{\text{Kt--K B 3}}$	—
3.	$\dfrac{\text{P--Q 4}}{\text{Kt}\times\text{P}}$	$\dfrac{\text{Kt}\times\text{P}}{\text{Kt}\times\text{P}}$	—
4.	$\dfrac{\text{B--Q 3}}{\text{P--Q 4}}$	$\dfrac{\text{Q--K 2}}{\text{Q--K 2}}$	—
5.	$\dfrac{\text{Kt}\times\text{P}}{\text{Kt--Q 3}}$	$\dfrac{\text{Q}\times\text{Kt}}{\text{P--Q 3}}$	—
6.	$\dfrac{\text{P--Q B 4}}{\text{P}\times\text{P}}$	$\dfrac{\text{P--Q 4}}{\text{P--K B 3}}$	—
7.	$\dfrac{\text{Kt}\times\text{P}}{\text{B--K 3}}$	$\dfrac{\text{P--K B 4}}{\text{Kt--Q 2 }(a)}$	—
8.	$\dfrac{\text{Kt--K 3}}{\text{B--K 2}}$	$\dfrac{\text{Kt--Q B 3}}{\text{Q P}\times\text{Kt}}$	$\dfrac{\text{B P}\times\text{Kt}}{\text{B P}\times\text{P}}$
9.	$\dfrac{\text{0--0 +}}{\text{0--0}}$	$\dfrac{\text{Kt--Q 5}}{\text{Q--Q 3}}$	$\dfrac{\text{P}\times\text{P}}{\text{Kt--Q o}}$
10.		$\dfrac{\text{Q P}\times\text{P}}{\text{P}\times\text{P}}$	$\dfrac{\text{Kt--K B 3}}{\text{B--Kt 5 ch.}}$
11.		$\dfrac{\text{P}\times\text{P}}{\text{Q--B 3}}$	$\dfrac{\text{P--B 3}}{\text{Kt}\times\text{Kt ch.}}$
12.		$\dfrac{\text{B--Q Kt 5}}{\text{Q--Q B 4}}$	$\dfrac{\text{P}\times\text{Kt !}}{\text{B}\times\text{P ch.}}$
13.		$\underline{\text{P--Q Kt 4 +}}$	$\dfrac{\text{K--Q 1 !}}{\text{B--Q 2}}$
14.			$\dfrac{\text{P--Q R 4}}{\text{0--0--0}}$
15.			$\dfrac{\text{P}\times\text{B}}{\text{Q}\times\text{B P}}$
16.			$\dfrac{\text{R--R 3}}{\text{B}\times\text{P ch.}}$
			$\dfrac{\text{R}\times\text{B}}{\text{P}\times\text{P d. ch.}}$
			$\dfrac{\text{B--Q 2}}{\text{P--K 6}}$
			$\overline{\text{B--R 3 ch.}}$

(a) If instead 7. $\dfrac{}{\text{Q P}\times\text{Kt}}$; 8. $\dfrac{\text{B P}\times\text{P}}{\text{P}\times\text{P}}$; 9. $\dfrac{\text{Q}\times\text{P}}{}$, &c.

	(4)	(5)	(6)
20.			$\dfrac{\text{K—Kt 1}}{\text{R—R 2}}$
21.			$\dfrac{\text{R} \times \text{B ch.}}{\text{R} \times \text{R}}$
22.			$\text{P} \times \text{R} +$

	(7)	(8)	(9)
1.	$\dfrac{\text{P—K 4}}{\text{P—K 4}}$	—	—
2.	$\dfrac{\text{Kt—K B 3}}{\text{Kt—K B 3}}$	—	—
3.	$\dfrac{\text{Kt} \times \text{P}}{\text{P—Q 3}}$	—	—
4.	$\dfrac{\text{Kt—K B 3}}{\text{Kt} \times \text{P}}$	—	$\dfrac{\text{Kt} \times \text{P}}{\text{K} \times \text{Kt}}$
5.	$\dfrac{\text{P—Q 4}}{\text{P—Q 4}}$	—	$\dfrac{\text{B—B 4 ch.}}{\text{B—K 3}}$
6.	$\dfrac{\text{B—Q 3}}{\text{B—K 2}}$	$\overline{\text{B—Q 3}}$	$\dfrac{\text{B} \times \text{B ch.}}{\text{K} \times \text{B}}$
7.	$\dfrac{\text{0—0}}{\text{Q Kt—B 3}}$	$\dfrac{\text{0—0}}{\text{0—0}}$	$\dfrac{\text{P—Q 4}}{\text{K—Q 2 (a)}}$
8.	$\dfrac{\text{P—B 4}}{\text{B—K 3}}$	$\dfrac{\text{P—B 4}}{\text{B—K 3}}$	$\underline{\text{P—K 5}}$
9.	$\dfrac{\text{P—Q R 3}}{\text{0—0}}$	$\dfrac{\text{Q—B 2}}{\text{P—K B 4}}$	
10.		$\underline{\text{Q—Kt 3} +}$	

(a) If 7. $\overline{\text{K—B 2}}$; 8. $\dfrac{\text{Kt—B 3}}{\text{B—K 2}}$; 9. $\dfrac{\text{Q—K 2}}{\text{R—B 1}}$; 10. $\dfrac{\text{B—K 3}}{\text{K—Kt 1}}$;
11. $\underline{\text{0—0—0}} +$

	(10)	(11)	(12)
1.	—	—	—
2.	—	—	—
3.	—	$\dfrac{\text{B}-\text{B}4}{\text{Kt}\times\text{P}}$	—
4.	—	$\dfrac{\text{Q}-\text{K}2}{\text{P}-\text{Q}4}$	—
5.	$\overline{\text{P}-\text{Q}4}$	$\dfrac{\text{Kt}\times\text{P}}{\text{B}-\text{Q B}4\,!}$	—

Nos. 11, 12, and 13.   Position after White's 6th move, P—Q 3.

BLACK.

WHITE.

	(10)	(11)	(12)
6.	$\dfrac{\text{B}-\text{Kt}3}{\text{Q}-\text{K}1}$	$\dfrac{\text{P}-\text{Q}3\ (\text{see diagram})}{\text{B}\times\text{P ch.}\ (a)}$	$\overline{\text{P}\times\text{B}}$
7.	$\dfrac{\text{P}-\text{Q}3}{\text{B}-\text{K}3}$	$\dfrac{\text{K}-\text{Q}1\,!}{\text{B}-\text{Kt}3}$	$\dfrac{\text{Q}\times\text{Kt}}{0-0}$

(a) If 6. $\overline{\text{Kt}\times\text{P}}$; 7. $\dfrac{\text{Kt}-\text{B}6\text{ d. ch.}}{\text{K}-\text{Q}2}$; 8. $\dfrac{\text{Kt}\times\text{Q}}{\text{R}-\text{K}1}$; 9. $\dfrac{\text{Q}\times\text{R ch.;}}{\text{K}\times\text{Q}}$

10. $\dfrac{\text{B}\times\text{P}}{\text{Kt}\times\text{R}}$; 11. $\dfrac{\text{Kt}\times\text{B P}}{\text{Kt}-\text{B}7}$; 12. $\text{P}-\text{K R}3+$

	(10)	(11)	(12)
8.	$\dfrac{\text{P} - \text{K} 5}{\text{P} - \text{Q} 5}$	$\dfrac{\text{Kt} \times \text{P}}{\text{B} - \text{Kt} 5\,(a)}$	$\dfrac{\text{Q} \times \text{P (B 5)}}{\text{Q} - \text{K} 2}$
9.	$\dfrac{\text{P} - \text{Q B} 4}{\text{P} \times \text{P } e.p.}$	$\dfrac{\text{Kt} \times \text{Q}}{\text{B} \times \text{Q ch.}}$	$\dfrac{\text{P} - \text{B} 4}{\text{Kt} - \text{B} 3}$
10.	$\dfrac{\text{Kt} \times \text{P}}{\text{K Kt} - \text{Q} 2}$	$\dfrac{\text{K} \times \text{B}}{\text{Kt} - \text{B} 7}$	$\dfrac{\text{Q} - \text{K} 4}{\text{R} - \text{K} 1}$
11.	$\dfrac{\text{Q} - \text{B} 3 \text{ ch.}}{\text{K} - \text{Kt} 1}$	$\dfrac{\text{R} - \text{B} 1}{\text{P} \times \text{B}}$	$\dfrac{\text{K} - \text{Q} 1 \text{ (see dia-}}{\text{Q} - \text{R} 5 \qquad \text{gram).}}$
12.	$\dfrac{\text{Q} \times \text{Kt P}}{\text{Kt} - \text{Kt} 3}$	$\dfrac{\text{Kt} - \text{K} 6}{\text{P} \times \text{P ch.}}$	$\dfrac{\text{P} - \text{K Kt} 3}{\text{Q} - \text{R} 4 \text{ ch.}}$
13.	$\dfrac{\text{Kt} - \text{Q} 5}{\text{Q} - \text{B} 3}$	$\dfrac{\text{P} \times \text{P}}{\text{K} - \text{K} 2}$	$\dfrac{\text{K} - \text{Q} 2}{\text{Kt} \times \text{Kt}}$

Nos. 12 and 13.   Position after Black's 10th move, R — K 1.

BLACK.

WHITE.

(a) If 8. $\overline{\text{K} \times \text{Kt}}$;   9. $\dfrac{\text{Q} \times \text{Kt}}{\text{B} - \text{K} 3}$;   10. $\dfrac{\text{R} - \text{B} 1 \text{ ch.}}{\text{K} - \text{K} 2}$;   11. $\dfrac{\text{B} - \text{Kt} 5 \text{ ch.}}{\text{K} - \text{Q} 2}$;

12. $\dfrac{\text{B} \times \text{P}}{\text{Q} \times \text{B}}$;   13. $\dfrac{\text{Q} \times \text{B ch.}}{\text{K} - \text{Q} 1}$;   14. $\dfrac{\text{B} \times \text{P} +}{}$

	(10)	(11)	(12)
14.	$\dfrac{\text{Kt} \times \text{B P}}{\text{B} \times \text{B}}$	$\dfrac{\text{Kt} \times \text{Kt P}}{\text{R} - \text{Kt 1}}$	$\dfrac{\text{P} \times \text{Kt}}{\text{R} \times \text{P}}$ and wins.
15.	$\dfrac{\text{Q} \times \text{Q}}{\text{Kt} \times \text{Q}}$	$\dfrac{\text{Kt} - \text{B 5 ch.}}{\text{K} - \text{K 3}}$	
16.	$\text{Kt} \times \text{R} +$	$\dfrac{\text{B} - \text{K 3}}{\text{B} \times \text{B}}$	
17.	—	$\dfrac{\text{Kt} \times \text{B}}{\text{Kt} - \text{Kt 5}}$	

Nos. 14 to 19.   Position after White's 4th move.

BLACK.

WHITE.

	(13)	(14)	(15)
1	---	$\dfrac{\text{P} - \text{K 4}}{\text{P} - \text{K 4}}$	—
2	---	$\dfrac{\text{Kt} - \text{K B 3}}{\text{Kt} - \text{K B 3}}$	—
3.	—	$\dfrac{\text{B} - \text{B 4}}{\text{Kt} \times \text{P}}$	---
4.	—	$\dfrac{\text{Kt} - \text{Q B 3}}{\text{Kt} \times \text{Kt}}$ (see diagram)	—

	(13)	(14)	(15)
5.	—	$\dfrac{Q\,P\times Kt\ !}{P-Q\,3}$	
6.	—	$\dfrac{Kt\times P\ (a)}{P\times Kt}$	$\overline{Q-K\,2}$
7.	—	$\dfrac{B\times P\ ch.}{K-K\,2}$	$\dfrac{B\times P\ ch.}{K-Q\,1}$
8.	—	$\underline{B-Kt\,5\ ch.\ and\ wins}$	$\dfrac{0-0}{Q\times Kt}$
9.	—		$\dfrac{R-K\,1}{B-Kt\,5\ !}$
10.	—		$\dfrac{R\times Q}{B\times Q}$
11.	—		$\dfrac{B-Kt\,5\ ch.}{K\ moves}$
12.	$\dfrac{Q\,Kt-Q\,2}{Q-R\,4\ ch.}$		$\underline{R\times B\ +}$
13.	$\dfrac{Q\,Kt-K\,B\,3\ !}{B-K\,Kt\,5\ +}$		

	(16)	(17)	(18)	(19)
1.	—	—	—	—
2.	—	—	—	—
3.	—	—	—	—
4.	—	—	—	$\overline{Kt-K\,B\,3}$
5.	$\dfrac{P-K\,B\,3}{0-0}$	—	$\dfrac{B-K\,2}{Kt\times P}$	$\dfrac{Kt\times P}{P-Q\,4}$
6.	$\dfrac{Kt-B\,3}{Kt-R\,4}$	$\overline{P-K\,Kt\,3}$	$\dfrac{0-0}{0-0}$	$\dfrac{B-Kt\,3}{B-Q\,3}$
7.	$\overline{Kt-K\,2}$	$\dfrac{R-K\,1}{P-Q\,3}$	$\underline{0-0}$	$\dfrac{P-Q\,4}{P-Q\,4}$

(a) If 6. $\dfrac{Kt-Kt\,5}{B-K\,3}$; 7. $\dfrac{B\times B}{P\times B}$; 8. $\dfrac{Q-B\,3}{}$, &c.

H

	(16)	(17)	(18)	(19)
8.	B—Q 3 / P—K Kt 3	Kt—Kt 5 / P×Kt		
9.	P—K B 4 +	R×P ch. / B—K 2		
10.		R—K 2 / P—K R 3		
11.		Q—Q 4 and wins.		

THE PETROFF DEFENCE—GAMES.

	(1) Buda Pesth Paris (Played by correspondence)	(2) M. Petroff Amateurs	(3) Van der Lasa Jaenisch
1.	P—K 4 / P—K 4	P—K 4 / P—K 4	P—K 4 / P—K 4
2.	Kt—K B 3 / Kt—K B 3	Kt—K B 3 / Kt—K B 3	Kt—K B 3 / Kt—K B 3
3.	Kt×P / P—Q 3	P—Q 4 / Kt×P	Kt×P / P—Q 3
4.	Kt—K B 3 / Kt×P	B—Q 3 / P—Q 4	Kt—K B 3 / Kt×P
5.	P—Q 4 / P—Q 4	Kt ×P / B—Q 3	P—Q 3 / Kt—K B 3
6.	B—Q 3 / B—Q 3	0—0 / 0—0	P—Q 4 / P—Q 4
7.	0—0 / 0—0	P—Q B 4 / P—K B 4	P—K R 3 / B—Q 3
8.	P—B 4 / B—K 3	P—B 4 / P—B 3	B—K 3 / 0—0
9.	Q—B 2 / P—K B 4 (a)	B—K 3 / B—K 3	B—K 2 / Q—K 2

(a) If this be the best move left for Black, their Monarch totters already.

	(1)	(2)	(3)
10.	$\dfrac{\text{Q—Kt 3 }(a)}{\text{P}\times\text{P}}$	$\dfrac{\text{P}\times\text{P}}{\text{P}\times\text{P}}$	$\dfrac{\text{P—B 3}}{\text{P—B 4}}$
11.	$\dfrac{\text{Q}\times\text{Kt P }(b)}{\text{P—B 3}}$	$\dfrac{\text{Kt—Q B 3}}{\text{Kt—Q B 3}}$	$\dfrac{\text{Q—B 2}}{\text{Kt—B 3}}$
12	$\dfrac{\text{B}\times\text{Kt}}{\text{P}\times\text{B}}$	$\dfrac{\text{R—B 1}}{\text{R—B 3 }(f)}$	$\dfrac{\text{Q Kt—Q 2}}{\text{B—K 3}}$
13	$\dfrac{\text{Kt—Kt 5}}{\text{B—K B 4}}$	$\dfrac{\text{B}\times\text{Kt}}{\text{B P}\times\text{B}}$	$\dfrac{\text{P}\times\text{P}}{\text{B (Q 3)}\times\text{P}}$
14.	$\dfrac{\text{Kt—Q B 3}}{\text{Q—Q 2 }(c)}$	$\dfrac{\text{Kt—Kt 5}}{\text{Kt—K 2}}$	$\dfrac{\text{B}\times\text{B}}{\text{Q}\times\text{B}}$
15.	$\dfrac{\text{Q}\times\text{Q}}{\text{Kt}\times\text{Q}}$	$\dfrac{\text{Kt}\times\text{B}}{\text{Q}\times\text{Kt}}$	$\dfrac{\text{Kt—Kt 3}}{\text{Q—Kt 3}}$
16.	$\dfrac{\text{K Kt}\times\text{K P}}{\text{B—B 2}}$	$\dfrac{\text{P—K Kt 4}}{\text{P—K Kt 3 }(g)}$	$\dfrac{\text{0—0}}{\text{Q R—B 1}}$
17.	$\dfrac{\text{R—K 1}}{\text{Q R—Kt 1}}$	$\dfrac{\text{P—B 5 }(h)}{\text{P}\times\text{P}}$	$\dfrac{\text{Q—Q 2}}{\text{K R—Q 1}}$
18.	$\dfrac{\text{R—K 2}}{\text{Kt—Kt 3 }(d)}$	$\dfrac{\text{B—Kt 5}}{\text{R (B 3)—B 1}}$	$\dfrac{\text{Q R—Q 1}}{\text{P—Q R 3}}$
19.	$\dfrac{\text{Kt—B 5}}{\text{B—Q 3}}$	$\dfrac{\text{B—R 6}}{\text{R (B 1)—B 1 }(i)}$	$\dfrac{\text{K R—K 1}}{\text{R—Q 2}}$
20.	$\dfrac{\text{Kt (B 5)—K 4}}{\text{B—B 2 }(e)}$	$\dfrac{\text{Q—Q 2 }(j)}{\text{Q—Q 1}}$	$\dfrac{\text{B—Q 3}}{\text{R (B 1)—Q 1}}$

(a) These moves result from a profound investigation of the opening. The sort of *coup de repos*, to await the advance of the enemy's K B P, was a master touch.

(b) This and many moves to come form connecting links in the admirable combination of the Hungarians, and were evidently foreseen when the Q was played to her B 2.

(c) Is there anything better to be done by Black at this juncture? B—Q B square would compel the Queen to take the Rook. But *cui bono?* Could she then be caught? We doubt it.

(d) With the view to plant the Kt at Q 4.

(e) The same moves, Kt—B 5 and B—B 2, were persisted in for weeks by both parties. Pesth having the first game virtually won, were content to draw this without further trouble. In the end, Paris, as they must lose equally whether they drew or lost the present party, decided on venturing another move.

(f) This unfortunate counter attack is admirably taken advantage of by M. Petroff.

(g) They do not appear to have had a better move.

(h) Well played.

(i) It would have been better to leave the Rook *en prise*, and advance the Pawn to K B 5.

(j) After this move, the game of Black was beyond redemption

	(1)	(2)	(3)
21.	Kt (K 4)—B 5 / B—Q 3	R×R / R×R	Kt (Kt 3)—Q 4 / R—K 1
22.	Kt (B 5)—K 4 / B—B 2	P×P / Kt×P	R—K 2 / R (Q 2)—K 2
23.	Kt (K 4)—B 5 / B—Q 3	Q—K Kt 2 ch. / K—R 1	R (Q 1)—K 1 / P—R 3
24.	Kt (B 5)—K 4 / B—B 2	R×Kt / Q—Kt 1	Q—B 4 / Kt—Q 1
25.	Kt (K 4)—B 5 / B—Q 3	R—B 6 / B—R 6	B—B 5 / Q—B 4
26.	Kt (B 5)—K 4 / B—B 2	Q—Kt 3 / Q×Q	K Kt—K 5 / B×B
27.	Kt (K 4)—B 5 / B—Q 6	P×Q / Resigns.	Kt×B / Kt—K 3
28.	R—K 3 / B—B 7		Kt×R ch. / R×Kt
29.	Kt—K 6 / R—B 2		Q—B 5 / P—Q 5
30.	Kt×B / R×Kt	(1)—(contd.)	R—Q B 2 / P—Q 6
31.	R—K 2 (a) / B—Q 6	38. P—Q R 3 / B—Kt 3	Q×P / Kt—B 5
32.	B—B 4 / B×R	39. P—K B 3 (b) / K—B 2	Q—Q 4 / Q×Q
33.	B×R / R—K 1	40. K—B 2 / K—K 3	P×Q / Kt (B 3)—Q 4
34.	B×Kt / P×B	41. K—K 3 / P—R 3	P—R 3 / P—K Kt 4
35.	R—K 1 / B—R 4	42. P—K Kt 4 / K—Q 4	Kt—B 3 / R×R ch.
36.	R×R ch. / B×R	43. Kt—B 3 ch. / K—Q 3	Kt×R / K—Kt 2
37.	Kt—K 4 / P—Q Kt 4	44. P—B 4 / B—K 1 (c)	R—B 5 / P—Kt 3

(a) All this denotes an admirable insight of the position. White see clearly that every exchange now strengthens the advantage they have acquired.

(b) Not only protecting the Kt, but affording a speedier route for the King to sustain his Pawns.

(c) B—Q 6 would permit the White to play their Q Kt P one square, with advantage.

	(1)	(1)—(contd.)			(3)
45.	$\dfrac{\text{P—B 5}}{\text{B—Q 2}}$	49.	$\dfrac{\text{P—K R 4}}{\text{B—Q 4}}$	38.	$\dfrac{\text{R—B 6}}{\text{Kt—K 3}}$
46.	$\dfrac{\text{Kt—K 4 ch.}}{\text{K—K 2}}$	50.	$\dfrac{\text{P—Kt 5}}{\text{P×P}}$	39.	$\dfrac{\text{R—Q 6}}{\text{Kt (Q 4)—B 5}}$
47.	$\dfrac{\text{K—B 4}}{\text{B—K 1}}$ (a)	51.	$\dfrac{\text{P×P}}{\text{B—Kt 1}}$	40.	$\dfrac{\text{Kt—B 2}}{\text{Kt—Q 6}}$
48.	$\dfrac{\text{K—K 5}}{\text{B—B 2}}$	52.	$\dfrac{\text{P—Kt 6}}{\text{Resigns.}}$ (b)	41.	$\dfrac{\text{R×P}}{\text{Resigns.}}$

	(4)	(5)	(6)
	Staunton	Staunton	Staunton
	Horrwitz	Horrwitz	Horrwitz
1.	$\dfrac{\text{P—K 4}}{\text{P—K 4}}$	$\dfrac{\text{P—K 4}}{\text{P—K 4}}$	$\dfrac{\text{P—K 4}}{\text{P—K 4}}$
2.	$\dfrac{\text{Kt—K B 3}}{\text{Kt—K B 3}}$	$\dfrac{\text{Kt—K B 3}}{\text{Kt—K B 3}}$	$\dfrac{\text{Kt—K B 3}}{\text{Kt—K B 3}}$
3	$\dfrac{\text{B—B 4}}{\text{Kt×P}}$	$\dfrac{\text{B—B 4}}{\text{Kt×P}}$	$\dfrac{\text{B—B 4}}{\text{Kt×P}}$
4.	$\dfrac{\text{Kt—B 3}}{\text{Kt×Kt}}$	$\dfrac{\text{Kt—Q B 3}}{\text{Kt×Kt}}$	$\dfrac{\text{Kt—B 3}}{\text{Kt—Q 3}}$
5	$\dfrac{\text{P×Kt}}{\text{P—K B 3}}$	$\dfrac{\text{Q P×Kt}}{\text{P—K B 3}}$	$\dfrac{\text{B—Kt 3}}{\text{P—K 5}}$
6.	$\dfrac{\text{0—0}}{\text{Kt—B 3}}$	$\dfrac{\text{0—0}}{\text{P—K Kt 3}}$ (c)	$\dfrac{\text{Q—K 2}}{\text{B—K 2}}$
7.	$\dfrac{\text{Kt—R 4}}{\text{Kt—K 2}}$	$\dfrac{\text{R—K 1}}{\text{P—Q 3}}$	$\dfrac{\text{Kt×P}}{\text{Kt×Kt}}$
8.	$\dfrac{\text{B—Q 3}}{\text{P—Q 4}}$	$\dfrac{\text{Kt—Kt 5}}{\text{P×Kt}}$ (d)	$\dfrac{\text{Q×Kt}}{\text{0—0}}$
9.	$\dfrac{\text{Q—R 5 ch.}}{\text{K—Q 2}}$	$\dfrac{\text{R×P ch.}}{\text{B—K 2}}$	$\dfrac{\text{P—Q 4}}{\text{B—B 3}}$ (e)

(a) The Black have no resource left.

(b) Longer resistance would be frivolous and vexatious, and the Frenchmen with good grace resign.

(c) To guard against the consequences of White's playing Kt—R 4.

(d) This looks trebly hazardous, but on examination I am induced to believe it perfectly sound.

(e) B—K 5 ch., followed by R—K 1, would have been imprudent.

(4)	(5)	(6)
10. $\dfrac{\text{P--K B 4}}{\text{P--K 5}}$	$\dfrac{\text{R--K 2}}{\text{P--K R 3}}$ (a)	$\dfrac{0\text{--}0}{\text{P--B 3}}$
11. $\dfrac{\text{B}\times\text{P}}{\text{P}\times\text{B}}$	$\dfrac{\text{Q--Q 4}}{\text{R--B 1}}$ (b)	$\dfrac{\text{P--B 4}}{\text{P--Q 3}}$
12. $\dfrac{\text{R--Q 1 ch.}}{\text{Kt--Q 4}}$	$\dfrac{\text{Q--Kt 7}}{\text{B--B 4}}$	$\dfrac{\text{B--B 4}}{\text{Kt--R 3}}$
13. $\dfrac{\text{Q}\times\text{Kt ch.}}{\text{B--Q 3}}$	$\dfrac{\text{Q}\times\text{R P}}{\text{Kt--Q 2}}$ (c)	$\dfrac{\text{K R--K 1}}{\text{Kt--B 2}}$
14. $\dfrac{\text{Kt--B 5}}{\text{K--K 1}}$	$\dfrac{\text{B}\times\text{P}}{\text{Kt--K 4}}$	$\dfrac{\text{Q R--B 1}}{\text{Kt--K 3}}$
15. $\dfrac{\text{Kt}\times\text{P ch.}}{\text{K--B 1}}$	$\dfrac{\text{B}\times\text{B}}{\text{Q}\times\text{B}}$	$\dfrac{\text{B--B2}}{\text{P--K Kt 3}}$
16. $\dfrac{\text{Kt--B 5}}{\text{B}\times\text{Kt}}$	$\dfrac{\text{P--B 4}}{0\text{--}0\text{--}0}$ (d)	$\dfrac{\text{B--Kt 3}}{\text{Kt--Kt 4}}$ (e)
17. $\dfrac{\text{Q}\times\text{B}}{\text{Q--K 2}}$	$\dfrac{\text{P}\times\text{Kt}}{\text{P}\times\text{P}}$	$\dfrac{\text{Q--B 4}}{\text{Kt}\times\text{Kt ch.}}$
18. $\dfrac{\text{B--K 3}}{\text{P--Kt 3}}$	$\dfrac{\text{Q--K 3}}{\text{K--Kt 1}}$	$\dfrac{\text{Q}\times\text{Kt}}{\text{B}\times\text{P}}$
19. $\dfrac{\text{P--Q Kt 4}}{\text{R--K 1}}$	$\dfrac{\text{Q}\times\text{K P}}{\text{Q}\times\text{Q}}$	$\dfrac{\text{Q R--Q 1}}{\text{P--Q B 4}}$
20. $\dfrac{\text{B--Q 4}}{\text{K--B 2}}$	$\dfrac{\text{R}\times\text{Q}}{\text{B}\times\text{P}}$	$\dfrac{\text{P--Kt 4}}{\text{Q--Kt 3}}$
21. $\dfrac{\text{Q--R 5 ch.}}{\text{K--B 1}}$	Q R--K 1 and won	$\dfrac{\text{P}\times\text{P}}{\text{Q}\times\text{P}}$
22. $\dfrac{\text{Q--R 6 ch.}}{\text{K--B 2}}$	after many more	$\dfrac{\text{R--K 7}}{\text{B--K 3}}$
23. $\dfrac{\text{R--K 1}}{\text{Q--K 3}}$	moves	$\dfrac{\text{Q}\times\text{P}}{\text{Q}\times\text{P}}$
24. $\dfrac{\text{Q--R 5 ch.}}{\text{K--B 1}}$		$\dfrac{\text{B--Kt 3}}{\text{Q--K 7}}$
25. $\dfrac{\text{P--B 5}}{\text{Q--K 2}}$		$\dfrac{\text{B}\times\text{P}}{\text{B}\times\text{P ch.}}$

(a) Apparently indispensable.

(b) If to K R 2, White's answer would probably have been Q—B 6, followed by B—Kt 8.

(c) Black's best move here appears to be Kt—B 3.

(d) He might also have played P—K Kt 4, with an irresistible attack.

(e) Very well played.

	(4)	**(6)**		**(6)**—*(contd.)*
26.	Q—R 6 ch. / K—B 2	K—R 1 / Q R—Q 1 (a)	34.	Q—B 2 / B×B
27.	R×P / B×P ch.	Q—Kt 4 / B—R 5	35.	P×B / R—Q 7
28.	K×B / Q—Q 3 ch.	Q×B / R×B	36.	Q—K 3 / Q—R 7
29.	R—B 4 / QR—Kt 1	R—K 1 / Q—R 3 (b)	37.	Q—Kt 3 / Q—R 2
30.	R—K 1 / R—Kt 4	Q—Kt 3 / R—Q 6	38.	Q—K 3 / Q—R 7
31	P—Kt 3 / R(R 1)—Kt 1	R×P / Q—Kt 4	39.	Q—Kt 3 / Q—R 2
32.	QR—K6 / R(Kt 4)—Kt 3	R—Kt 7 / Q—R 3	40.	Q—K 3 / Q—R 7 (c)
33.	Q×P ch. and wins.	R—Kt 6 / Q—R 4	41.	Q—B 3 / R—Q 1
			42.	R—K B 1 and won ultimately.

	(7) Morphy (blindfold) / Potier	**(8)** Cochrane / Brahmin Moheschunder Bonnerjee	**(9)** Schallopp / Mieses
1.	P—K 4 / P—K 4	P—K 4 / P—K 4	P—K 4 / P—K 4
2.	Kt—K B 3 / Kt—K B 3	Kt—K B 3 / Kt—K B 3	Kt—K B 3 / Kt—K B 3
3.	B—B 4 / Kt×P	Kt×P / P—Q 3	Kt×P / P—Q 3
4.	Kt—B 3 / Kt—K B 3	Kt×P / K×Kt	Kt—K B 3 / Kt×P
5.	Kt×P / P—Q 4	B—B 4 ch / K—K 1	P—Q 4 / P—Q 4

(a) Mr. Horrwitz was of opinion, afterwards, that he should have played B—R 5.

26.   B—R 5
27. R×B   P×R
28. B×R   R×B
29. R—K Kt 1   B—B 7
30. Q—K 7, and wins.

(b) A fine move.

(c) Hoping White would submit to a drawn battle.

	(7)	(8)	(9)
6.	B–Kt 3 / B–K 2	0–0 / P–B 4	B–Q 3 / B–K 2
7.	P–Q 4 / P–B 3	P–K R 3 / Q–B 2	0–0 / 0–0
8.	0–0 / Kt–Q 2	P–B 4 / Kt–B 3	P–B 4 / Kt–K B 3
9.	P–B 4 / Kt–Kt 3	Kt–B 3 / P–Q R 3	Kt–B 3 / B–K Kt 5
10.	Q–B 3 / P–K R 4	P–Q R 4 / Q–K 2	P×P / Kt×P
11.	P–B 5 / Q–B 2	Kt–Q 5 / Q–Q 1	B–K 4! / Kt×Kt
12.	B–K B 4 / B–Q 3	P–Q 4 / P×P	P×Kt / P–Q B 3
13.	Q R–K 1 / K–B 1	P–K 5 / Kt×Kt	P–K R 3 / B–R 4
14.	Q–Kt 3 / P–K R 5	B×Kt / P×P	Q–Kt 3 / Q–B 2
15.	Kt–Kt 6 ch. (a) / K–Kt 1	B×Kt ch. / P×B	R–Q Kt / P–Q Kt 3
16.	B×B / P×Q	Q–R 5 ch. / K–Q 2	Kt–K 5 / B–Q 3
17.	B×Q / P×Kt	P×P / K–B 2	P–K B 4 / K–R 1
18.	P×P (Kt 6) / P×P ch.	R–B 7 ch. / K–Kt 1	P–Kt 4 / B–Kt 3
19.	K–R 1 / B–Kt 5	P–K 6 (c) / B–Q 3 (d)	P–B 5 / P–B 3
20.	R–K 7 / Q Kt–Q 2	B–Kt 5 / Q–Kt 3	Kt×B ch. / P×Kt
21.	B–K 5 / K–B 1	P–Q R 5 / Q–B 4	P×P / Q–K 2
22.	R–B 7 ch. (b) / K–Kt 1	P–Q Kt 4 / Q–K 4	R–B 5 / Resigns.

(a) Finely played.
(b) The termination of this game is extremely elegant and finished.
(c) The attack is characteristic of Mr. Cochrane.

(d) If 19. B×P ; 20. Q–K 5 ch. / R–Q 3 ; 21. Q×B / R–R2

	(7)	(8)	(9)
23.	Kt×P / P×Kt	B—B 4 / Q×P (a)	
24.	B×P / Kt—Kt 3	Q—Q B 5 / Q×R	
25.	B—Q Kt 3 / Resigns.	B×B ch. / Q—B 2	
26.		Q—Kt 6 ch. / B—Kt 2	
27.		Q×Q ch. / K—R 2	
28.		B—B 5 mate.	

	(10) Tchigorin / Pillsbury	(11) Pillsbury / Schlechter
1.	P—K 4 / P—K 4	P—K 4 / P—K 4
2.	Kt—K B 3 / Kt—K B 3	Kt—K B 3 / Kt—K B 3
3.	P—Q 4 / P×P	P—Q 4 / Kt×P
4.	P—K 5 / Kt—K 5	B—Q 3 / P—Q 4
5.	Q×P / P—Q 4	Kt×P / Kt—Q B 3
6.	P×P e.p. / Kt×Q P	Kt×Kt / P×Kt
7.	Kt—B 3 / Kt—B 3	Q—K 2 / Q—K 2
8.	Q—K B 4 / B—B 4	O—O / P—Kt 3
9.	B—Kt 5 / B—K 2	B×Kt / Q×B
10.	Kt—Q 4 / B—Q 2	Q×Q / P×Q

(a) Taking the Queen would have been evidently fatal.

	(10)	(11)
11.	$\dfrac{\text{B} \times \text{Kt}}{\text{B} \times \text{B} \ (a)}$	$\dfrac{\text{R} - \text{K} \ 1}{\text{P} - \text{K B} \ 4}$
12.	$\dfrac{\text{Kt} \times \text{B}}{\text{P} \times \text{Kt}}$	$\dfrac{\text{P} - \text{K B} \ 3}{\text{B} - \text{K Kt} \ 2}$
13.	$\dfrac{0 - 0}{0 - 0}$	$\dfrac{\text{P} - \text{B} \ 3}{0 - 0}$
14.	$\dfrac{\text{B} - \text{Kt} \ 3}{\text{R} - \text{Kt} \ 1}$	$\dfrac{\text{B} - \text{B} \ 4}{\text{P} - \text{B} \ 4}$
15.	$\dfrac{\text{Q R} - \text{Kt} \ 1}{\text{Kt} - \text{B} \ 1}$	$\dfrac{\text{P} \times \text{P}}{\text{R} - \text{Kt} \ 1}$
16.	$\dfrac{\text{Q} - \text{B} \ 3}{\text{Q} - \text{Q} \ 2}$	$\dfrac{\text{R} - \text{K} \ 2}{\text{B} - \text{Q R} \ 3}$
17.	$\dfrac{\text{Q R} - \text{Q} \ 1}{\text{B} - \text{Q} \ 3}$	$\dfrac{\text{R} - \text{K B} \ 2}{\text{P} - \text{K} \ 6}$
18.	$\dfrac{\text{P} - \text{Q Kt} \ 3}{\text{Q} - \text{K} \ 3}$	$\dfrac{\text{B} \times \text{K P}}{\text{K R} - \text{K} \ 1}$
19.	$\dfrac{\text{Kt} - \text{K} \ 4 \ (b)}{\text{Kt} - \text{K} \ 2}$	$\dfrac{\text{B} - \text{Q} \ 2}{\text{R} \times \text{P}}$
20.	$\dfrac{\text{K R} - \text{K} \ 1 \ !}{\text{Q} - \text{Kt} \ 3}$	$\dfrac{\text{Kt} - \text{R} \ 3}{\text{B} - \text{K B} \ 1 \ !}$
21.	$\dfrac{\text{B} \times \text{P}}{\text{Q R} - \text{K} \ 1}$	$\dfrac{\text{B} - \text{K} \ 3}{\text{R} \times \text{B}}$
22.	$\dfrac{\text{Kt} \times \text{B}}{\text{P} \times \text{Kt}}$	$\dfrac{\text{R} \times \text{R}}{\text{B} \times \text{P}}$
23.	$\dfrac{\text{P} - \text{B} \ 4}{\text{P} - \text{Q B} \ 4 \ !}$	$\dfrac{\text{K} - \text{R} \ 1}{\text{B} \times \text{Kt}}$
24.	$\dfrac{\text{B} - \text{Kt} \ 6}{\text{Kt} - \text{B} \ 4}$ and wins.	$\dfrac{\text{R} - \text{Kt} \ 8 \ \text{ch.}}{\text{K} - \text{B} \ 2}$
25.		$\dfrac{\text{P} - \text{R} \ 4}{\text{B} - \text{B} \ 4}$
26.		$\dfrac{\text{P} - \text{Q B} \ 4}{\text{R} - \text{B} \ 6}$ and wins.

(a) If 11. $\dfrac{\quad}{\text{P} \times \text{B}}$

       12. Q — B 3   P — Q B 4

       13. Kt. — B 6

(b) If 19. $\dfrac{\text{Q} \times \text{Q B P}}{\quad}$; $\overline{\text{B} \times \text{P}}$ ch.

CHAPTER IV.

GRECO COUNTER GAMBIT—ANALYSIS.

	(1)	(2)	(3)
1.	$\dfrac{P-K4}{P-K4}$	—	—
2.	$\dfrac{Kt-KB3}{P-KB4}$	—	—
3.	$\dfrac{Kt \times P\,!}{Q-B3\,!}$	—	—

Nos. 1, 2, and 3.   Position after White's 6th move.

BLACK.

WHITE.

4.	$\dfrac{P-Q4}{P-Q3}$	—	—
5.	$\dfrac{Kt-B4}{P \times P}$	—	—
6.	$\dfrac{Kt-B3 \text{ (see diagram)}}{P-B3}$	—	—
7.	$\dfrac{Kt \times KP\,!}{Q-K3}$	—	—
8.	$\dfrac{Q-K2}{P-Q4}$	—	—

	(1)	(2)	(3)
9.	$\dfrac{\text{Kt (K 4) – Q 6 ch.}}{\text{K – Q 2}}$	$\dfrac{\text{Kt (B 4) – Q 6 ch.}}{\text{K – Q 1}}$	$\dfrac{\text{Kt (K 4) – Q 6 ch.}}{\text{K – Q 1}}$
10.	$\dfrac{\text{Kt – B 7}}{\text{P × Kt}}$	$\dfrac{\text{Kt – K Kt 5}}{\text{Q × Q ch.}}$	$\dfrac{\text{Kt × P ch.}}{\text{K – B 2}}$
11.	$\dfrac{\text{Q – Q ch.}}{\text{K × Q}}$	$\dfrac{\text{B × Q}}{\text{B × Kt}}$	$\dfrac{\text{Q × Q}}{\text{B × Q}}$
12.	$\dfrac{\text{B × P ch.}}{\text{K – K 2}}$	$\dfrac{\text{Kt – B 7 ch.}}{\text{K – K 2}}$	$\dfrac{\text{Kt (B 4) – R 5}}{\text{K – Kt 3 !}}$
13.	$\dfrac{\text{Kt × R}}{\text{B – K 3}}$	$\dfrac{\text{Kt × R}}{\text{B – K 3}}$	$\dfrac{\text{B – Q 2}}{\text{Kt – Q 2}}$
14.	$\dfrac{\text{B – Q 3}}{\text{Kt – B 3}}$	$\dfrac{\text{B – Q 3}}{\text{Kt – B 3}}$	$\dfrac{\text{P – Q Kt 4}}{}$ +
15.	$\dfrac{\text{B – K Kt 5}}{\text{B – Kt 1}}$	$\dfrac{\text{Kt – Kt 6}}{\text{P × Kt}}$	
16.	$\dfrac{\text{O – O}}{}$ +	$\dfrac{\text{B × P}}{}$ +	

	(4)	(5)	(6)
1.	—	—	—
2.	—	—	—
3.	$\dfrac{\text{Q – K 2}}{}$	—	—
4.	$\dfrac{\text{Q – K 5 ch.}}{\text{P – Kt 3}}$	—	—
5.	$\dfrac{\text{Kt × P}}{\text{Q × P ch.}}$	—	—
6.	$\dfrac{\text{B – K 2 !}}{\text{K Kt – B 3}}$	$\dfrac{\text{Kt – K 2}}{}$	$\dfrac{\text{Q – Kt 3}}{}$
7.	$\dfrac{\text{Q – R 3 !}}{\text{P × Kt}}$	$\dfrac{\text{P – Q 5}}{\text{Q – Kt 3}}$	$\dfrac{\text{P – B 3 !}}{\text{K Kt – B 3}}$ (a)

(a) If 7. $\dfrac{}{\text{P × P}}$; 8. $\dfrac{\text{Q × P}}{\text{K Kt – B 3}}$; 9. $\dfrac{\text{B – Q 3}}{\text{Q – Kt 5}}$; 10. $\dfrac{\text{Q – K 3 ch.}}{\text{B – Q 2}}$; 11. $\dfrac{\text{O – O}}{}$ +

	(4)	(5)	(6)
8.	Q×R / Q×Kt P	Q—Q 4 / B—B 4	P×P / Kt×P
9.	R—B 1 / K—B 2	Kt—Kt 5 winning a P.	Q—K 2 / B—B 4
10.	Q—R 4 +		Kt—Q 2 / Q Kt—B 3
11.			K Kt×Kt / Kt×Q P
12.			Q—Q 3 +

	(7)	(8)	(9)
1.	P—K 4 / P—K 4	—	—
2.	Kt—K B 3 / P—K B 4	—	—
3.	Kt×P / Q—B 3	B—B 4 / P×P	B—B 4 / P—Q 3
4.	P—Q 4 / P×P	Kt×P / Q—Kt 4 (c)	P—Q 4 ! / P×K P
5.	B—Q B 4 / P—B 3 (a)	Kt—B 7 ! / Q×Kt P	Kt×P / P×Kt
6.	B—B 7 ch. / K—K 2 (b)	R—K B 1 / P—Q 4	Q—R 5 ch. / K—Q 2
7.	P—K R 4 / P—K R 3	Kt×R / P×B (d)	Q—B 5 ch. / K—B 3
8.	Q—R 5 / K—Q 3	Q—R 5 ch. / P—Kt 3	Q×P (K 5) / P—Q R 3

(a) If 5. —/Kt—K 2 ; 6. Kt—Q B 3 / Q—B 4 ; 7. Kt—Kt5 / Kt—R 3 ; 8. Kt—K B 7 / — winning the R.

(b) If 6. —/K—Q 1 ; 7. B×Kt / R×B ; 8. B—Kt 5 / —

(c) If 4. B×Kt / R×B ; 5. Kt×P / Q—Kt 4 ; 6. Kt—Kt 4 / P—Q 4 +

(d) If 7. B×P / B—R 6 ; 8. Q—K 2 / Kt—K B 3 ; 9. B—B4! / Kt—B 3 ; 10. Kt×R / Kt—Q 5 +

	(7)	(8)	(9)
9.	$\dfrac{\text{B—Kt 5}}{\text{P} \times \text{B}}$	$\dfrac{\text{Q} \times \text{R P}}{\text{B—K 3}}$	$\dfrac{\text{P—Q 5 ch.}}{\text{K—Kt 3 } (a)}$
10.	$\dfrac{\text{Q} \times \text{R} +}{}$	$\dfrac{\text{Q} \times \text{P ch.}}{\text{Q} \times \text{Q}}$	$\dfrac{\text{B—K 3 ch.}}{\text{B—B 4}}$
11.		$\text{Kt} \times \text{Q} +$	$\dfrac{\text{B} \times \text{B oh.}}{\text{K} \times \text{B}}$
12.			$\dfrac{\text{P—Kt 4 ch.}}{\text{K} \times \text{P } (b)}$
13.			$\dfrac{\text{Kt—Q 2}}{\text{P—Q Kt 4 } (c)}$
14.			$\dfrac{\text{R—Kt 1 ch.}}{\text{K—R 4}}$
15.			$\dfrac{\text{Q—Q 4}}{\text{Q—Q 3}}$
16.			$\dfrac{\text{Kt—Kt 3 ch. and}}{\text{wins.}}$

	(10)	(11)
1.	—	—
2.	—	—
3.	$\dfrac{\text{P} \times \text{P !}}{\text{P—Q 3}}$	$\dfrac{\text{Q—B 3}}{}$
4.	$\dfrac{\text{P—Q 4}}{\text{P—K 5}}$	$\dfrac{\text{Q—K 2}}{\text{Kt—B 3}}$
5.	$\dfrac{\text{Kt—Kt 5}}{\text{B} \times \text{P}}$	$\dfrac{\text{P—Q 4}}{\text{P—Q 3}}$
6.	$\dfrac{\text{Q—K 2}}{\text{P—Q 4}}$	$\dfrac{\text{P} \times \text{P}}{\text{P} \times \text{P}}$
7.	$\dfrac{\text{Q—Kt 5 ch.}}{\text{Kt—Q B 3}}$	$\dfrac{\text{B—K B 4}}{\text{B—Q 3}}$
8.	$\dfrac{\text{Q} \times \text{Kt P}}{\text{Kt} \times \text{P}}$	$\dfrac{\text{P—K Kt 4}}{\text{Kt—K 2}}$

(a) If 9. $\dfrac{}{\text{K—B 4}}$ white mates in four.

(b) If 12. $\dfrac{}{\text{K} \times \text{B}}$ white mates in four.

(c) If 13. $\dfrac{}{\text{K—B 4}}$ white mates in three.

	(10)	**(11)**
9	$\dfrac{\text{B}-\text{Kt 5 ch.}}{\text{Kt}\times\text{B}}$	$\dfrac{\text{B}-\text{K Kt 5}}{\text{Q}-\text{B 2}}$
10.	$\dfrac{\text{Q}\times\text{Kt ch.}}{\text{Q}-\text{Q 2}}$	$\dfrac{\text{P}-\text{K R 3}}{\text{P}-\text{K R 4}}$
11.	$\dfrac{\text{Q}-\text{Kt 7}}{\text{R}-\text{B 1}}$	$\dfrac{\text{B}-\text{Kt 2}}{\text{P}\times\text{P}}$
12.	$\dfrac{\text{Q}\times\text{R P}}{\text{P}-\text{K R 3}}$	$\dfrac{\text{P}\times\text{P}}{\text{R}\times\text{R}}$
13.	$\dfrac{\text{Kt}-\text{K R 3}}{\text{B}\times\text{Kt}}$	$\dfrac{\text{B}\times\text{R}}{\text{P}-\text{K Kt 3}}$
14.	$\dfrac{\text{P}\times\text{B}}{\text{Q}\times\text{P} +}$	$\dfrac{\text{B}\times\text{K Kt}}{\text{Q}\times\text{B}}$
15.		$\dfrac{\text{P}\times\text{P}}{\text{B}\times\text{Kt P} +}$

GRECO COUNTER GAMBIT—GAMES.

	(1)	**(2)**
	Martinez	Duras
	Pollock	Newmann
1.	$\dfrac{\text{P}-\text{K 4}}{\text{P}-\text{K 4}}$	$\dfrac{\text{P}-\text{K 4}}{\text{P}-\text{K 4}}$
2.	$\dfrac{\text{Kt}-\text{K B 3}}{\text{P}-\text{K B 4}}$	$\dfrac{\text{Kt}-\text{K B 3}}{\text{P}-\text{K B 4}}$
3.	$\dfrac{\text{P}-\text{Q 4}}{\text{P}\times\text{K P}}$	$\dfrac{\text{Kt}\times\text{P}}{\text{Kt}-\text{Q B 3}}$
4.	$\dfrac{\text{Kt}\times\text{P}}{\text{Kt}-\text{K B 3}}$	$\dfrac{\text{Kt}\times\text{Kt}}{\text{Q P}\times\text{Kt}}$
5.	$\dfrac{\text{Kt}-\text{Kt 4}}{\text{P}-\text{Q 4}}$	$\dfrac{\text{P}-\text{Q 4}}{\text{Kt}-\text{B 3}}$
6.	$\dfrac{\text{Kt}\times\text{Kt}}{\text{Q}\times\text{Kt}}$	$\dfrac{\text{P}-\text{K 5}}{\text{Kt}-\text{K 5}}$
7.	$\dfrac{\text{Q}-\text{R 5 ch.}}{\text{Q}-\text{B 2}}$	$\dfrac{\text{B}-\text{K 3}}{\text{P}-\text{B 4}}$
8.	$\dfrac{\text{Q}\times\text{Q ch.}}{\text{K}\times\text{Q}}$	$\dfrac{\text{P}-\text{K Kt 3}}{\text{P}\times\text{P}}$
9.	$\dfrac{\text{B}-\text{K B 4}}{\text{P}-\text{B 3}}$	$\dfrac{\text{Q}\times\text{P}}{\text{B}-\text{Q 2}}$

	(1)	(2)
10.	$\dfrac{\text{Kt}-\text{Q 2}}{\text{B}-\text{K B 4}}$	$\dfrac{\text{B}-\text{Q B 4}}{\text{P}-\text{B 4}}$
11.	$\dfrac{\text{O}-\text{O}-\text{O}}{\text{Kt}-\text{Q 2}}$	$\dfrac{\text{Q}-\text{Q 5}}{\text{Q}-\text{R 4 ch.}}$
12.	$\dfrac{\text{B}-\text{K 2}}{\text{P}-\text{B 4}}$	$\dfrac{\text{B}-\text{Q 2}}{\text{Kt}\times\text{B}}$
13.	$\dfrac{\text{B}-\text{K 3}}{\text{R}-\text{B 1}}$	$\dfrac{\text{Q}-\text{B 7 ch.}}{\text{K}-\text{Q 1}}$
14.	$\dfrac{\text{Kt}-\text{B 1 !}}{\text{P}\times\text{P}}$	$\dfrac{\text{Kt}\times\text{Kt}}{\text{B}-\text{K 2}}$
15.	$\dfrac{\text{B}\times\text{P}}{\text{B}-\text{B 4}}$	$\dfrac{\text{O}-\text{O}-\text{O}}{\text{R}-\text{K B 1}}$
16.	$\dfrac{\text{Kt}-\text{K 3}}{\text{B}-\text{K 3}}$	$\dfrac{\text{Q}\times\text{Kt P}}{\text{Q}-\text{B 2}}$
17.	$\dfrac{\text{B}\times\text{B}}{\text{Kt}\times\text{B}}$	$\dfrac{\text{Kt}-\text{K 4 !}}{\text{P}\times\text{Kt}}$
18.	$\dfrac{\text{Kt}\times\text{P}}{\text{Kt}-\text{R 5}}$	$\dfrac{\text{P}-\text{K 6}}{\text{P}-\text{Kt 4}}$
19.	$\dfrac{\text{Kt}-\text{B 4}}{\text{B}\times\text{P ?}}$	$\dfrac{\text{B}\times\text{P}}{\text{B}-\text{Q 3}}$
20.	$\dfrac{\text{R}-\text{Q 7 ch.}}{\text{K}-\text{B 3}}$	$\dfrac{\text{R}\times\text{B}}{\text{Q}\times\text{R}}$
21.	$\dfrac{\text{Kt}-\text{R 5 ch.}}{\text{K}-\text{Kt 3}}$	$\dfrac{\text{R}-\text{Q 1}}{\text{Q}\times\text{R ch.}}$
22.	$\dfrac{\text{K R}-\text{Q 1}}{\text{R}-\text{B 3}}$	$\dfrac{\text{K}\times\text{Q}}{\text{B}\times\text{B}}$
23.	$\dfrac{\text{R}\times\text{P ch.}}{\text{K}-\text{R 3}}$	$\dfrac{\text{P}-\text{K 7 ch.}}{\text{Resigns.}}$
24.	$\dfrac{\text{P}-\text{Kt K 4 and wins.}}{}$	

Chapter V.

(1)	(2)	(3)	(4)
1. $\dfrac{\text{P—K 4}}{\text{P—K 4}}$	—	—	—
2. $\dfrac{\text{Kt—K B 3}}{\text{P—Q 4}}$	—	—	—
3. $\dfrac{\text{P} \times \text{P !}}{\text{Q} \times \text{P}}$	$\dfrac{}{\text{P—K 5}}$	$\dfrac{\text{Kt} \times \text{P}}{\text{Q—K 2 !}}$	$\dfrac{}{\text{P} \times \text{P}}$
4. $\dfrac{\text{Kt—B 3}}{\text{Q—K 3}}$	$\dfrac{\text{Q—K 2}}{\text{Q—K 2}}$	$\dfrac{\text{P—Q 4}}{\text{P—K B 3}}$	$\dfrac{\text{B—B 4}}{\text{Q—Kt 4 !}}$
5. $\dfrac{\text{B—Kt 5 ch.}}{\text{B—Q 2}}$	$\dfrac{\text{Kt—Q 4}}{\text{Kt—K B 3}}$	$\dfrac{\text{Kt—Kt 4}}{\text{B} \times \text{Kt}}$	$\dfrac{\text{P—Q 4}}{\text{Q} \times \text{Kt P}}$
6. $\dfrac{\text{0—0}}{\text{B} \times \text{B}}$	$\dfrac{\text{Q Kt—B 3}}{\text{Q—K 4}}$	$\dfrac{\text{Q} \times \text{B}}{\text{Q} \times \text{P ch.}}$	$\dfrac{\text{R—B 1}}{\text{B—K 3 ! } (a)}$
7. $\dfrac{\text{Kt} \times \text{B}}{\text{B—Q 3}}$	$\dfrac{\text{Kt—B 3}}{\text{Q—K 2}}$	$\dfrac{\text{Q} \times \text{Q ch.}}{\text{P} \times \text{Q}}$	$\dfrac{\text{P—Q 5}}{\text{B—R 6}}$
8. $\dfrac{\text{R—K 1}}{\text{P—K B 3}}$	$\dfrac{\text{Kt—K Kt 5}}{\text{B—B 4}}$		$\dfrac{\text{B—B 4}}{} =$
9. $\dfrac{\text{P—Q 4}}{\text{P—B 3}}$	$\dfrac{\text{Q—Kt 5 ch. }+}{}$		
10. $\dfrac{\text{P} \times \text{P}}{\text{P} \times \text{P}}$			
11. $\dfrac{\text{K Kt} \times \text{P }+}{}$			

ILLUSTRATIVE GAMES.

(1)	(2)
Cochrane	Jaenisch
$\overline{\text{Staunton}}$	$\overline{\text{Petroff}}$
1. $\dfrac{\text{P—K 4}}{\text{P—K 4}}$	$\dfrac{\text{P—K 4}}{\text{P—K 4}}$
2. $\dfrac{\text{Kt—K B 3}}{\text{P—Q 4}}$	$\dfrac{\text{Kt—K B 3}}{\text{P—Q 4}}$

(a) If 6. $\dfrac{}{\text{B—R 6}}$; 7. $\dfrac{\text{B} \times \text{P ch.}}{}$

	(1)	(2)
3.	$\dfrac{\text{Kt} \times \text{P}}{\text{Q} - \text{K} 2}$	$\dfrac{\text{Kt} \times \text{P}}{\text{Q} - \text{K} 2}$
4.	$\dfrac{\text{P} - \text{Q} 4}{\text{P} - \text{K B} 3}$	$\dfrac{\text{P} - \text{Q} 4}{\text{P} - \text{K B} 3}$
5.	$\dfrac{\text{Kt} - \text{Q B} 3}{\text{P} \times \text{Kt}}$	$\dfrac{\text{Kt} - \text{K B} 3}{\text{P} \times \text{P}}$
6.	$\dfrac{\text{Kt} \times \text{P}}{\text{Q} - \text{B} 2}$	$\dfrac{\text{Kt (B 3)} - \text{Q} 2}{\text{P} - \text{K B} 4}$
7.	$\dfrac{\text{B} - \text{Q B} 4}{\text{B} - \text{K} 3}$	$\dfrac{\text{B} - \text{K} 2}{\text{Kt} - \text{Q B} 3}$
8.	$\dfrac{\text{O} - \text{O}}{\text{P} - \text{B} 3}$	$\dfrac{\text{Kt} - \text{Kt} 3}{\text{Kt} - \text{B} 3}$
9.	$\dfrac{\text{P} - \text{B} 4}{\text{P} \times \text{Kt}}$	$\dfrac{\text{O} - \text{O}}{\text{Q} - \text{B} 2}$
10.	$\dfrac{\text{P} \times \text{K P}}{\text{Q} - \text{Q} 2}$	$\dfrac{\text{P} - \text{Q B} 4}{\text{B} - \text{Q} 2}$
11.	$\dfrac{\text{P} \times \text{P}}{\text{B} \times \text{P}}$	$\dfrac{\text{B} - \text{B} 4}{\text{O} - \text{O} - \text{O}}$
12.	$\dfrac{\text{P} - \text{K} 6}{\text{Q} - \text{B} 3}$	$\dfrac{\text{Kt} - \text{B} 3}{\text{P} - \text{K R} 3}$
13.	$\dfrac{\text{Q} - \text{R} 5 \text{ ch.}}{\text{P} - \text{Kt} 3}$	$\dfrac{\text{P} - \text{Q R} 3}{\text{P} - \text{K Kt} 4}$
14.	$\dfrac{\text{Q} \times \text{B}}{\text{Kt} - \text{K} 2}$	$\dfrac{\text{B} - \text{Q} 2}{\text{P} - \text{B} 5}$
15.	$\dfrac{\text{Q} - \text{K} 5}{\text{Q} \times \text{B}}$	$\dfrac{\text{P} - \text{Q} 5}{\text{Kt} - \text{K} 4}$
16.	$\dfrac{\text{Q} \times \text{R}}{\text{Kt} - \text{B} 4}$	$\dfrac{\text{Kt} - \text{Q} 4}{\text{B} - \text{Q B} 4}$
17.	$\dfrac{\text{B} - \text{R} 6}{\text{Q} - \text{Kt} 5}$	$\dfrac{\text{B} - \text{K} 1}{\text{K R} - \text{Kt} 1}$
18.	$\dfrac{\text{Q} \times \text{B ch.}}{\text{Q} \times \text{Q}}$	$\dfrac{\text{P} - \text{Q Kt} 4}{\text{B} - \text{K} 2}$
19.	$\dfrac{\text{B} \times \text{Q}}{\text{K} \times \text{B}}$	$\dfrac{\text{P} - \text{B} 3}{\text{P} - \text{K} 6}$
20.	$\dfrac{\text{P} - \text{K Kt} 4}{\text{Resigns.}}$	$\dfrac{\text{Q} - \text{Kt} 3}{\text{P} - \text{Kt} 5}$

(2) *(contd.)*

21. $\dfrac{P-B\,5}{P \times P}$

22. $\dfrac{Kt \times P}{Kt \times Kt \text{ ch.}}$

23. $\dfrac{B \times Kt}{Kt-Kt\,5}$

24. $\dfrac{Q-B\,4}{K-Kt\,1}$

25. $\dfrac{Q-K\,4}{Q\,R-K\,1}$

26. $\dfrac{P-Q\,6}{B-Q\,B\,3}$

27. $\dfrac{Q-Q\,4}{B \times B}$

28. $\dfrac{R \times B}{B-Kt\,4}$

29. $\dfrac{Kt-Kt\,5}{P-B\,3}$

30. $\dfrac{P-Q\,7}{R-K\,3}$

31. $\dfrac{B-Kt\,3}{P \times Kt\ (a)}$

32. $\dfrac{B \times P \text{ ch.}}{Kt-K\,4}$

33. $\dfrac{B \times Kt \text{ ch.}}{R \times B}$

34. $\dfrac{Q \times R \text{ ch}}{K-R\,1}$

35. $\dfrac{R \times Q}{P-K\,7}$

36. $\dfrac{Q-K\,8 \text{ ch.}}{R \times Q}$

37. $\dfrac{P \times R}{}$ and Queens ch. and wins.

CHAPTER VI.

GIUOCO PIANO—ANALYSIS.

(1)	(2)	(3)
1. $\dfrac{P-K\,4}{P-K\,4}$	—	—
2. $\dfrac{Kt-K\,B\,3}{Kt-Q\,B\,3}$	—	—
3. $\dfrac{B-B\,4}{B-B\,4}$	—	—

(a) If Black had played 31. $\overline{P \times B}$ he would have lost equally, thus—

31. $\dfrac{}{P \times B}$; 32. $\dfrac{Q \times Kt}{P \times P \text{ ch.}}$; 33. $\dfrac{K-R\,1}{Q \times Q\ P}$; 34. $\dfrac{Q-Kt\,3 \text{ ch.}}{}$ and wins.

	(1)	(2)	(3)
4.	$\dfrac{\text{P}-\text{B}\,3}{\text{Kt}-\text{B}\,3\,!}$	—	—
5.	$\dfrac{\text{P}-\text{Q}\,4\,(a)}{\text{P}\times\text{P}}$	—	—
6.	$\dfrac{\text{P}-\text{K}\,5}{\text{P}-\text{Q}\,4\,!}$	—	$\overline{\text{Kt}-\text{K}\,5}$
7.	$\dfrac{\text{B}-\text{Q}\,\text{Kt}\,5\,(b)}{\text{Kt}-\text{K}\,5}$	—	$\dfrac{\text{B}-\text{Q}\,5}{\text{Kt}\times\text{K}\,\text{B}\,\text{P}}$

Nos. 1 to 5. Position after White's 6th move.

BLACK.

WHITE.

| 8. | $\dfrac{\text{B}\times\text{Kt ch.}}{\text{P}\times\text{B}}$ | — | $\dfrac{\text{K}\times\text{Kt}}{\text{P}\times\text{P d.c.}}$ |

(a) If 5. $\dfrac{\text{Kt}-\text{Kt}\,5}{0-0}$; 6. $\dfrac{\text{P}-\text{B}\,4}{\text{P}-\text{Q}\,4\,!}$; 7. $\dfrac{\text{P}\times\text{Q}\,\text{P}\,!}{\text{Kt}\times\text{P}}$; 8. $\dfrac{\text{B}\times\text{Kt}}{\text{Q}\times\text{B}}$;

9. $\overline{\text{K R}-\text{Q}\,1\,!}\,+$
$\dfrac{}{\text{Q}-\text{B}\,3}$

(b) If 7. $\dfrac{\text{P}\times\text{Kt}}{\text{P}\times\text{B}}$; 8. $\dfrac{\text{P}\times\text{P}}{\text{R}-\text{Kt}\,1}+$

	(1)	(2)	(3)
9.	$\dfrac{P \times P}{B - Kt\,3}$ (a)	—	$\dfrac{K - Kt\,3}{P \times P}$
10.	$\dfrac{0 - 0}{B - Kt\,5}$	$\dfrac{Kt - Q\,B\,3}{P - K\,B\,4}$ (b)	$\dfrac{Q\,B \times P}{Kt - K\,2}$
11.	$\dfrac{B - K\,3}{0 - 0} =$	$\dfrac{P \times P\ e.p.}{Q \times P}$	$\dfrac{Q - B\,2}{P - Q\,3}$
12.		$\dfrac{Kt \times Kt}{P \times Kt}$	$\dfrac{B - K\,4}{Kt - Kt\,3}$
13.		$\dfrac{Kt - K\,5}{0 - 0\ +}$	$\dfrac{Q\,Kt - Q\,2}{P - Q\,B\,3}$
14.		—	$\dfrac{Q\,R - Q\,1\ +}{}$

	(4)	(5)	(6)
1.	—	—	—
2.	—	—	—
3.	—	—	—
4.	—	—	—
5.	—	—	—
6.	—	—	$\dfrac{P \times P}{B - Kt\,5\ ch.}$
7.	—	—	$\dfrac{B - Q\,2}{B \times B\ ch.}$ (c)
8.	—	—	$\dfrac{Kt\ (Kt\,1) \times B}{P - Q\,4}$

(a) If 9. $\dfrac{}{B - Kt\,5}$ ch.; 10. $\dfrac{B - Q\,2}{B \times B\ ch.}$; 11. $\dfrac{Q\,Kt \times B}{P - K\,B\,4}$; 12. $\dfrac{R - Q\,B\,1}{}$

(b) If 10. $\dfrac{0 - 0}{P - K\,B\,4}$

(c) If 7. $\dfrac{Kt - B\,3}{Kt \times K\,P}$; 8. $\dfrac{0 - 0}{B \times Kt}$; 9. $\dfrac{P \times B}{P - Q\,4}\ +$

	(4)	(5)	(6)
9.	$\dfrac{\text{K}-\text{K 1}}{\text{P}\times\text{P}}$	$\dfrac{\text{K}-\text{B 1}}{\text{P}\times\text{P}}$	$\dfrac{\text{P}\times\text{P}}{\text{Kt}\times\text{P}}$
10.	$\dfrac{\text{Q B}\times\text{P}}{\text{Kt}-\text{K 2}}$	$\dfrac{\text{Q B}\times\text{P}}{0-0}$	$\dfrac{\text{Q}-\text{Kt 3}}{\text{Q Kt}-\text{K 2}}$
11.	$\dfrac{\text{B}-\text{K 4}}{\text{P}-\text{Q 4}}$	$\dfrac{\text{Kt}-\text{Q 2}}{\text{P}-\text{Q 3}}$	$\dfrac{0-0}{0-0}$
12.	$\dfrac{\text{P}\times\text{P } e.p.}{\text{Q}\times\text{P}}$	$\dfrac{\text{Kt}-\text{K 4}}{\text{Kt}-\text{K 2}}$	$\dfrac{\text{K R}-\text{K 1}}{\text{Kt}-\text{K B 5}}$
13.	$\dfrac{\text{Q}\times\text{Q}}{\text{P}\times\text{Q}}$	$\dfrac{\text{Kt}\times\text{B}}{\text{P}\times\text{Kt}}$	$\dfrac{\text{R}-\text{K 4}}{\text{Q Kt}-\text{Kt 3}}$
14.	$\dfrac{\text{Kt}-\text{B 3}}{\text{B}-\text{B 4}}$	$\dfrac{\text{B}-\text{K 4 }(a)}{\text{B}-\text{B 4}}$	$\underline{\text{Q R}-\text{K 1}}$
15.	$\underline{\text{K}-\text{K 2 }+}$	$\dfrac{\text{Q}-\text{B 2}}{\text{B}\times\text{B}}$	
16.		$\dfrac{\text{Q}\times\text{B}}{\text{Q}-\text{Q 4}}$	
17.		$\underline{\text{Kt}-\text{Kt 5 }+}$	

	(7)	(8)	(9)
1.	—	$\dfrac{\text{P}-\text{K 4}}{\text{P}-\text{K 4}}$	—
2.	—	$\dfrac{\text{Kt}-\text{K B 3}}{\text{Kt}-\text{Q B 3}}$	—
3.	—	$\dfrac{\text{B}-\text{B 4}}{\text{B}-\text{B 4}}$	—
4.	—	$\dfrac{\text{P}-\text{B 3}}{\text{Kt}-\text{B 3}}$	—
5.	—	$\dfrac{0-0}{\text{Kt}\times\text{P}}$	—
6.	—	$\dfrac{\text{Q}-\text{K 2 }(b)}{\text{P}-\text{Q 4}}$	$\dfrac{\text{P}-\text{Q 4}}{\text{P}\times\text{P}}$

(a) Not 14. $\dfrac{\text{B}\times\text{P ch.}}{\text{K}\times\text{B}}$

(b) If 6. $\dfrac{\text{B}-\text{Q 5}}{\text{K Kt}-\text{B 3}}$; 7. $\dfrac{\text{B}\times\text{Kt}}{\text{Kt P}\times\text{B}}$; 8. $\underline{\text{Kt}\times\text{P}}$

	(7)	(8)	(9)
		$\dfrac{\text{B—Kt 5}}{0—0}$	
7.	$\dfrac{}{\text{Kt}\times\text{K P}}$		$\dfrac{\text{R—K 1}}{\text{P—Q 4}}$
8.	$\dfrac{\text{B}\times\text{B}}{\text{Kt}\times\text{B}}$	$\dfrac{\text{B}\times\text{Kt}}{\text{P}\times\text{B}}$	$\dfrac{\text{P}\times\text{P}}{\text{B—Q Kt 5}}$
9.	$\dfrac{\text{B}\times\text{P } e.p.}{\text{K}\times\text{B}}$	$\dfrac{\text{Kt}\times\text{P}}{\text{B—Kt 2}}$	$\dfrac{\text{B—Q 2}}{0—0}$
10.	$\dfrac{\text{Q—Kt 3 ch.}}{\text{P—Q 4}}$	$\dfrac{\text{P—Q 4}}{\text{B—Kt 3}}=$	$\dfrac{\text{B}\times\text{B}}{\text{Kt}\times\text{B}}$
11.	$\dfrac{}{\text{Q}\times\text{Kt ! } (a)}$		$\dfrac{\text{Q—Kt 3}}{\text{P}\times\text{B}}$
12.			$\dfrac{\text{Q}\times\text{Kt}}{\text{Kt—Q 3 }+}$

	(10)	(11)	(12)
1.	—	—	—
2.	—	—	—
3.	—	—	—
4.	—	—	—
5.	$\dfrac{}{0—0}$	$\dfrac{}{\text{P—Q 3 !}}$	$\dfrac{\text{P—Q 3}}{\text{P—Q 3}}$
6.	$\dfrac{\text{P—Q 4}}{\text{B—Kt 3 !}}$	$\dfrac{\text{P—Q 4}}{\text{P}\times\text{P}}$	$\dfrac{\text{P—Q 4}}{\text{P}\times\text{P}}$
7.	$\dfrac{\text{P}\times\text{P}}{\text{Kt}\times\text{K P}}$	$\dfrac{\text{P}\times\text{P}}{\text{B—Kt 3}}$	$\dfrac{\text{P}\times\text{P}}{\text{B—Kt 3}}$
8.	$\dfrac{\text{P—Q Kt 4}}{\text{K—R 1 !}}$	$\dfrac{\text{Kt—B 3 } (b)}{\text{B—K Kt 5}}$	$\dfrac{\text{Kt—B 3}}{\text{B—Kt 5}}$
9.	$\dfrac{\text{P—Q R 4}}{\text{P—Q R 3}}$	$\dfrac{\text{P—Q 5}}{\text{Kt—K 4}+}$	$\dfrac{\text{P—Q 5}}{\text{Kt—K 4}}=$
10.	$\dfrac{\text{B—Q 5}}{\text{P—K B 4}}$		
11.	$\dfrac{}{\text{R—R 2}+}$		

(a) If 11. $\dfrac{\text{Kt—K 5 ch.}}{\text{K—B 3}}$; 12. $\dfrac{\text{Q}\times\text{Kt}}{\text{P—B 4}}$; 13. $\dfrac{\text{Q—R 4}}{\text{Q—K 1}}+$

(b) Or 8. $\dfrac{\text{B—Q Kt 5}}{}$

	(13)	(14)	(15)
1.	—	P—K 4 / P—K 4	—
2.	—	Kt—K B 3 / Kt—Q B 3	—
3.	—	B—B 4 / B—B 4	—
4.	—	P—B 3 / P—Q 3	—
5.	P—Q 4	P—Q 4 / P×P	—

Nos. 14 to 20.   Position after White's 6th move.

BLACK.

WHITE.

6.	P×P / Kt×P	P×P / B—Kt 5 ch.	B—Kt 3
7.	Q—Kt 3 / B—K 3	B—Q 2 / B×B ch.	P—K R 3 (a) / Kt—B 3
8.	Q×P / Kt—K 2	Q Kt×B / Kt—B 3	B—K Kt 5 / P—K R 3

(a) Or 7. $\dfrac{\text{Kt—Q B 3}}{}$.

	(13)	(14)	(15)
9.	$\dfrac{B \times B +}{P \times B}$	$\dfrac{Q-Kt\ 3}{0-0}$	$\dfrac{B \times Kt\ (a)}{Q \times B}$
10.		$\dfrac{0-0}{Kt-Q\ R\ 4}$	$\dfrac{B-Kt\ 5}{0-0}$
11.		$\dfrac{Q-B\ 2}{Kt \times B}$	$\dfrac{B \times Kt}{P \times B}$
12.		$\dfrac{Q \times Kt}{Kt \times P}$	$\dfrac{0-0}{P-B\ 4}$
13.		$\dfrac{Kt \times Kt}{P-Q\ 4}$	$\dfrac{P-K\ 5}{Q-Kt\ 3}$
14.		$\dfrac{Q-K\ 2}{P \times Kt}$	
15.		$\overline{Q \times P}$	

	(16)	(17)	(18)
1.	—	—	—
2.	—	—	—
3.	—	—	—
4.	—	—	—
5.	—	—	—
6.	$\overline{B-Kt\ 5\ ch.}$		—
7.	$\dfrac{K-B\ 1}{B-Kt\ 5}$	$\overline{Q-Q\ 2}$	$\overline{B-Kt\ 5}$
8.	$\dfrac{Q-R\ 4}{B \times Kt}$	$\dfrac{Q-R\ 4}{B-R\ 4}$	$\dfrac{P-Q\ 5}{B \times Kt}$
9.	$\dfrac{P \times B}{Q-Q\ 2}$	$\dfrac{Kt-R\ 3\ (b)}{B-Kt\ 3}$	$\dfrac{Q-R\ 4}{B \times P}$

(a) Not 9. $\dfrac{B-R\ 4}{P-Kt\ 4}$; 10. $\dfrac{B \times P}{}$, &c.

(b) Not 9. $\dfrac{P-Q\ 5\ ?}{Kt-K\ 4\ !}$

	(16)	(17)	(18)
10.	$\dfrac{\text{B}-\text{Q Kt 5}}{\text{0-0-0}}$	$\dfrac{\text{B}-\text{Q Kt 5}}{\text{P}-\text{Q R 3}}$	$\dfrac{\text{P}\times\text{Kt}}{\text{P}-\text{Q Kt 4}}$
11.	$\dfrac{\text{K}-\text{Kt 2}+}{\quad}$	$\dfrac{\text{P}-\text{Q 5}}{\text{P}\times\text{B}}$	$\dfrac{\text{B}\times\text{Kt P}}{\text{B}\times\text{Kt}}$
12.		$\dfrac{\text{Q}\times\text{R}}{\text{Kt}-\text{R 4 }(a)}$	$\dfrac{\text{Q}\times\text{B}}{\text{B}-\text{B 4}}$
13.		$\text{P}-\text{Kt 4}+$	

	(19)	(20)	(21)
1.	—	—	$\dfrac{\text{P}-\text{K 4}}{\text{P}-\text{K 4}}$
2.	—	—	$\dfrac{\text{Kt}-\text{K B 3}}{\text{Kt}-\text{Q B 3}}$
3.	—	—	$\dfrac{\text{B}-\text{B 4}}{\text{B}-\text{B 4}}$
4.	—	—	$\dfrac{\text{P}-\text{B 3}}{\text{P}-\text{B 4}}$
5.	—	—	$\dfrac{\text{P}-\text{Q 4}}{\text{P}\times\text{K P}}$
6.	—	—	$\dfrac{\text{Kt}\times\text{P}}{\text{B}-\text{Kt 3}}$
7.	$\dfrac{\quad}{\text{B}-\text{R 4}}$	—	$\dfrac{\text{Q}-\text{R 5 ch.}}{\text{P}-\text{Kt 3}}$
8.	$\dfrac{\text{Q}-\text{R 4}}{\text{B}-\text{Q 2}}$	$\dfrac{\quad}{\text{P}-\text{Q R 3}}$	$\dfrac{\text{B}-\text{B 7 ch.}}{\text{K}-\text{B 1}}$
9.	$\dfrac{\text{P}-\text{Q 5}}{\text{Kt}-\text{Q 5 }(b)}$	$\dfrac{\text{P}-\text{Q 5}}{\text{P}-\text{Q Kt 4}}$	$\dfrac{\text{B}-\text{R 6 ch.}}{\text{Kt}\times\text{B}}$
10.	$\dfrac{\text{Q}\times\text{B}}{\text{Kt}-\text{B 7}}$	$\dfrac{\text{Q}-\text{R 3}}{\text{P}\times\text{B}}$	$\dfrac{\text{Q}\times\text{Kt ch.}}{\text{K}-\text{K 2}}$
11.	$\dfrac{\text{Q}-\text{B 3}}{\text{Kt}\times\text{R}}$	$\dfrac{\text{P}\times\text{Kt}}{\text{B}-\text{Kt 3}}$	$\dfrac{\text{B}\times\text{P}}{\text{Kt}\times\text{Kt}}$
12.	$\dfrac{\text{P}-\text{Kt 3}}{\text{Q}-\text{B 3}}$	$\dfrac{\text{Q}-\text{B 3}}{\quad}$	$\text{Q}-\text{Kt 5 ch. }+$
13.	$\dfrac{\text{B}-\text{Kt 2 or}}{\text{P}-\text{K 5}+}$		

(a) If 12. $\dfrac{\quad}{\text{Q Kt}-\text{K 2}}$; 13. $\dfrac{\text{B}-\text{K 3}}{\quad}$

(b) If 9. $\dfrac{\quad}{\text{Kt}-\text{K 4}}$; 10. $\dfrac{\text{Q}\times\text{B}}{\text{Kt}\times\text{B}}$; 11. $\dfrac{\text{Q}-\text{B 3}}{\text{B}-\text{Kt 4}}$; 12. $\dfrac{\text{Q}\times\text{Kt P}}{\quad}$

	(22)	(23)	(24)
1.	—	—	—
2.	—	—	—
3.	—	—	—
4.	—	Q—K 2	—
5.	P×Q P	P—Q 4 / B—Kt 3	P×P
6.	Kt—Kt 5 / P—Q 4	P×P / Kt×P	0—0 / Kt—K 4
7.	B×P / P×K P	Kt×Kt / Q×Kt	Kt×Kt / Q×Kt
8.	B×K Kt / R×B	0—0 / P—Q 3	P—B 4 / P×P d. ch.
9.	Q—R 5 ch. / P—Kt 3	K—R 1 / B—K 3	K—R 1 / P×P
10.	Q×R P / Q—Q 4		P×Q / P×R (Queen's)
11.	P—Q B 4 / Q×P (a)		Q—Q 5 +
12.	Kt—Q 2 / B—Q Kt 5		
13.	K Kt×P +		

	(25)	(26)	(27)
1.	—	P—K 4 / P—K 4	—
2.	—	Kt—K B 3 / Kt—Q B 3	—
3.	—	B—B 4 / B—B 4	—
4.	B—Kt 3	0—0 / P—Q 3	—

(a) If 11 B—Kt 5 ch. ; 12. B—Q 2

	(25)	(26)	(27)
5.	P—Q 4 / P—Q 3	P—B 3 / B—K Kt 5	—
6.	P×P / P×P	Q—Kt 3 / B×Kt	Q—Q 2
7.	Q×Q ch. / K×Q	B×P ch. / K—B 1	Q×P / R—Kt 1
8.	B×P +	P×B / Q—B 3	Q—R 6 / B×Kt
9.		B—R 5 / P—K Kt 3	P×B / R—Kt 3
10.		B—Kt 4 / B—Q Kt 3	Q—R 4 / Q—R 6
11.		Q—Q 1 +	B—K 2 ! +

	(28)	(29)	(30)
1.	—	—	—
2.	—	—	—
3.	—	—	—
4.	—	Kt—B 3	—
5.	Kt—K B 3	R—K 1 / 0—0	—
6.	P—Q 4 / P×P	P—B 3 / R—K 1	P—Q 1
7.	P×P / B—Kt 3	P—Q 4 / B—Kt 3	P—Q 4 = / B—Kt 3
8.	Kt—B 3	Kt—Kt 5 / R—K 2	

GIUOCO PIANO (MAX LANGE ATTACK)—ANALYSIS.

	(31)	(32)	(33)
1.	$\dfrac{\text{P}-\text{K 4}}{\text{P}-\text{K 4}}$	—	—
2.	$\dfrac{\text{Kt}-\text{K B 3}}{\text{Kt}-\text{Q B 3}}$	—	—
3.	$\dfrac{\text{B}-\text{B 4}}{\text{B}-\text{B 4}}$	—	—
4.	$\dfrac{\text{0}-\text{0}}{\text{Kt}-\text{B 3}}$	—	—
5.	$\dfrac{\text{P}-\text{Q 4 } (a)}{\text{P}\times\text{P ! } (b)}$	—	—

Nos. 31 to 37.   Position after White's 8th move.

BLACK.

WHITE.

(a) Max Lange's move.

(b) If 5. $\dfrac{}{\text{Q Kt}\times\text{P}}$; 6. $\dfrac{\text{Kt}\times\text{P}}{}$; or, if 5. $\dfrac{}{\text{B}\times\text{Q P}}$; 6. $\dfrac{\text{Kt}\times\text{B}}{\text{Kt}\times\text{Kt}}$

$\left(\text{if 6 } \dfrac{}{\text{P}\times\text{Kt}}; \text{ 7. } \dfrac{\text{P}-\text{K 5}}{}\right)$; 7. $\dfrac{\text{P}-\text{K B 4}}{\text{P}-\text{Q 3}}$; 8. $\dfrac{\text{P}\times\text{P}}{\text{P}\times\text{P}}$; 9. $\dfrac{\text{B}-\text{K Kt 5}+}{}$

	(31)	(32)	(33)
6.	$\dfrac{\text{P—K 5}}{\text{P—Q 4}}$	—	—
7.	$\dfrac{\text{P}\times\text{Kt} \ (a)}{\text{P}\times\text{B}}$	—	—
8.	$\dfrac{\text{R—K 1 ch.}}{\text{K—B 1}}$	—	—
9.	$\dfrac{\text{P}\times\text{P ch.}}{\text{K}\times\text{P}}$	—	—
10.	$\dfrac{\text{Kt—K 5}}{\text{R—K 1}}$	—	$\dfrac{}{\text{B—K 3}}$
11.	$\dfrac{\text{B— R 6 ch.}}{\text{K—Kt 1}}$	—	$\dfrac{\text{Q—R 5}}{\text{B—B 1}}$
12.	$\dfrac{\text{Kt}\times\text{Kt}}{\quad\ \text{or Kt}\times\text{P (B 4)}}$	$\dfrac{\text{Q—B 3}}{\text{Kt}\times\text{Kt}}$	$\dfrac{\text{Kt—Kt 4}}{\text{P—K R 3}}$
13.		$\dfrac{\text{R}\times\text{Kt}}{\text{R}\times\text{R}}$	$\dfrac{\text{B}\times\text{P ch.}}{\text{K—Kt 1}}$
14.		$\dfrac{\text{Q—Kt 3 ch}}{\text{Q—Kt 4 !}}$	$\dfrac{}{\text{R}\times\text{QB and wins}}$
15.		$\dfrac{\text{Q}\times\text{Q ch.}}{\text{R}\times\text{Q}}$	
16.		$\dfrac{\text{B}\times\text{R}}{\text{B—B 4}+}$	

	(34)	(35)	(36
1.	—	—	—
2.	—	—	—
3.	—	—	—
4.	—	—	—
5.	—	—	—
6.	—	—	—

(a) Or 7. $\dfrac{\text{B—Kt 5}}{}$

	(34)	(35)	(36)
7.		—	—
8.	B—K 3 (a)	—	—
9.	$\dfrac{\text{Kt—Kt 5}}{\text{Q—Q 4}}$	—	—
10.	$\dfrac{\text{Kt—Q B 3}}{\text{Q—B 4}}$	—	—
11.	$\dfrac{\text{P—K Kt 4}}{\text{Q—Kt 3}}$	—	—
12.	$\dfrac{\text{Kt×B}}{\text{P×Kt}}$	$\dfrac{\text{R×B ch.}}{\text{P×R}}$	$\dfrac{\text{Kt—K 4 !}}{\text{B—Kt 3}}$
13.	$\dfrac{\text{R×P ch.}}{\text{K—B 2}}$	$\dfrac{\text{Kt×P}}{\text{P×Kt}}$	$\dfrac{\text{P—B 4}}{\text{0—0—0}}$
14.	$\dfrac{\text{Kt—Q 5}}{\text{B—Q 3+}}$	$\dfrac{\text{Q—K 2}}{\text{Kt—K 4}}$	$\dfrac{\text{P—B 5}}{\text{B×P}}$
15.	—	$\dfrac{\text{Q×Kt}}{\text{Q×P ch.}}$	$\dfrac{\text{P×B}}{\text{Q×P}}$
16.	—	$\dfrac{\text{K moves}}{\text{B—Q 3+}}$	

	(37)	(38)
1.	—	$\dfrac{\text{P—K 4}}{\text{P—K 4}}$
2.	—	$\dfrac{\text{Kt—K B 3}}{\text{Kt—Q B 3}}$
3.	—	$\dfrac{\text{B—B 4}}{\text{B—B 4}}$
4.	—	$\dfrac{\text{P—Q 3}}{\text{P—Q 3}}$
5.	—	$\dfrac{\text{P—B 3}}{\text{Q—B 3 (b)}}$
6.	—	$\dfrac{\text{B—Kt 5}}{\text{Q—Kt 3}}$

(a) If 9. $\dfrac{\text{Kt—K Kt 5}}{\text{Q—Q 4}}$

(b) If 5. $\dfrac{}{\text{B—K Kt 5}}$; 6. $\dfrac{}{\text{Q—Kt 3+}}$

	(37)	(38)
7.	---	$\dfrac{0-0}{\text{B}-\text{K Kt 5}}$
8.	—	$\dfrac{\text{Q Kt}-\text{Q 2}}{\text{Kt}-\text{R 3}}$
9.	—	$\dfrac{\text{P}-\text{Kt 4}}{\text{B}-\text{Kt 3}}$
10.	—	$\dfrac{\text{P}-\text{Q R 4}}{\text{P}-\text{Q R 4 !}}$
11.	$\dfrac{}{\text{Q}\times\text{P (B 3)}}$	$\dfrac{\text{P}-\text{Kt 5}}{\text{Kt}-\text{Q 1}}$
12.	$\dfrac{\text{Kt}-\text{Q 5}}{\text{Q}-\text{Q1}}$	$\dfrac{\text{B}-\text{Q 5 +}}{}$
13.	$\dfrac{\text{R}\times\text{B ch.}}{\text{P}\times\text{R}}$	
14.	$\dfrac{\text{Kt}\times\text{K P}}{\text{Q}-\text{Q3 }(a)}$	
15.	$\dfrac{\text{B}-\text{K B 4}}{\text{Kt}-\text{K 4 }(b)}$	
16.	$\dfrac{\text{Q}-\text{K 2 and wins}}{}$	

GIUOCO PIANO—GAMES.

	(1)	(2)	(3)
	Horwitz	Staunton	Horwitz
	$\overline{\text{Staunton}}$	$\overline{\text{Horwitz}}$	$\overline{\text{Staunton}}$
1.	$\dfrac{\text{P}-\text{K 4}}{\text{P}-\text{K 4}}$	$\dfrac{\text{P}-\text{K 4}}{\text{P}-\text{K 4}}$	$\dfrac{\text{P}-\text{K 4}}{\text{P}-\text{K 4}}$
2.	$\dfrac{\text{Kt}-\text{K B 3}}{\text{Kt}-\text{Q B 3}}$	$\dfrac{\text{Kt}-\text{K B 3}}{\text{Kt}-\text{Q B 3}}$	$\dfrac{\text{Kt}-\text{K B 3}}{\text{Kt}-\text{Q B 3}}$
3.	$\dfrac{\text{B}-\text{B 4}}{\text{B}-\text{B 4}}$	$\dfrac{\text{B}-\text{B 4}}{\text{B}-\text{B 4}}$	$\dfrac{\text{B}-\text{B 4}}{\text{B}-\text{B 4}}$
4.	$\dfrac{\text{P}-\text{B 3}}{\text{Kt}-\text{B 3}}$	$\dfrac{\text{P}-\text{B 3}}{\text{P}-\text{Q 3}}$	$\dfrac{\text{P}-\text{B 3}}{\text{Kt}-\text{B 3}}$
5.	$\dfrac{\text{P}-\text{Q 4}}{\text{P}\times\text{P}}$	$\dfrac{\text{P}-\text{Q 4}}{\text{P}\times\text{P}}$	$\dfrac{\text{P}-\text{Q 3}}{\text{P}-\text{Q 3}}$

(a) If 14. $\dfrac{}{\text{Q}-\text{Q 2}}$; 15. $\dfrac{\text{Q}-\text{K B 3}}{}$

(b) If 15. $\dfrac{}{\text{Q}-\text{Q 2}}$; 16. $\dfrac{\text{Kt}\times\text{P ch.}}{\text{K moves}}$; 17. $\dfrac{\text{Kt}\times\text{B}}{}$

	(1)	(2)	(3)
6.	P—K 5 / P—Q 4	P×P / B—Kt 3	Kt—Kt 5 / 0—0
7.	B—Q Kt 5 / Kt—K 5	Kt—B 3 / B—Kt 5	P—B 4 / P—Q 4
8.	P×P / B—Kt 3	B—K 3 / Kt—B 3	P×Q P / Kt×P
9.	0—0 / 0—0	P—Q R 3 / 0—0	B×Kt / Q×B
10.	P—K R 3 / P—B 3	B—K 2 / R—K 1	Q—B 3 / R—Q 1 (c)
11.	Kt—B 3 / P×P	P—Q 5 / Kt—K 4	Q×Q / R×Q
12.	B×Kt / P×B	Kt×Kt / B (Kt 5)×B	K—K 2 (d) / B—Kt 5 ch.
13.	Kt×K P / B—R 3	Q×B / R×Kt	Kt—B 3 / Q R—Q 1
14.	Kt—K 2 (a) / P—B 4 (b)	B×B / R P×B	P—Q 4 (e) / P×Q P

(a) We should have taken off the Knight in preference. Black, then, as his best move, would probably have taken the Knight (for taking the Rook would be dangerous, on account of " Kt—Kt 5 "), and then the game might have proceeded thus:—

WHITE.	BLACK.
14. Kt×Kt	P×Kt
15. Q—Kt 3 ch.	Q—Q 4
16. Q×Q	P×Q
17. R—Q 1	

The position, however, would even then have been much in favour of the second player, from the commanding situation of his two Bishops.

(b) This is stronger play, we believe, than taking the Kt. After advancing the doubled Pawn, Black remarked that, had his position been less favourable, and the advantages springing from this move less obviously certain, he should have much preferred the more enterprising play of taking the P with his Kt,—a sacrifice, as he demonstrated in an after-game, which leads to many strikingly beautiful situations.

(c) From this point we look upon the game as virtually lost for White.

(d) Probably his best move. Had he played P—Q Kt 4, Black might have taken it with his Kt, and upon the B P retaking, have moved B—Q 5, winning the exchange.

(e) As good a move, perhaps, as he had on the board. By playing R—Q 1 he would evidently have lost a Piece.

	(1)	(2)	(3)
15.	$\dfrac{\text{B—K 3}}{\text{P}\times\text{P}}$	$\dfrac{\text{0—0}}{\text{Kt}\times\text{K P}}$	$\dfrac{\text{P—Q B 4}}{\text{R—K 1 ch.}}$
16.	$\dfrac{\text{B}\times\text{P }(a)}{\text{B}\times\text{Kt}}$	$\dfrac{\text{Kt}\times\text{Kt}}{\text{P—K B 4}}$	$\dfrac{\text{K—B 2 }(g)}{\text{R—Q 2}}$
17.	$\dfrac{\text{Q}\times\text{B}}{\text{B}\times\text{B}}$	$\dfrac{\text{P—B 3}}{\text{P}\times\text{Kt}}$	$\dfrac{\text{Q Kt—Q 2}}{\text{P—Q 6 d. ch.}}$
18.	$\dfrac{\text{Kt—B 6}}{\text{Q—B 3 }(b)}$	$\dfrac{\text{P}\times\text{P}}{\text{Q—K 2}}$	$\dfrac{\text{K—Kt 3}}{\text{B}\times\text{Kt}}$
19.	$\dfrac{\text{Kt}\times\text{B}}{\text{Q}\times\text{Kt}}$	$\dfrac{\text{Q R—K 1}}{\text{Q R—K 1}}$	$\dfrac{\text{Kt}\times\text{B}}{\text{R—K 7}}$
20.	$\dfrac{\text{Q R—Q 1}}{\text{Q—B 4}}$	$\dfrac{\text{R—B 4}}{\text{P—K R 3 }(c)}$	$\dfrac{\text{B—Q 2}}{\text{R—Q 3}}$
21.	$\dfrac{\text{R—B 1}}{\text{Q—Q Kt 3}}$	$\dfrac{\text{Q—B 3 }(d)}{\text{R}\times\text{Q P}}$	$\dfrac{\text{Q R—Q 1}}{\text{R —Kt 3 ch.}}$
22.	$\dfrac{\text{P—Q Kt 3}}{\text{Kt—Kt 6}}$	$\dfrac{\text{R—K B 1 }(e)}{\text{R—K 4}}$	$\dfrac{\text{K—R 3 }(h)}{\text{R—R 3 ch.}}$
23.	$\dfrac{\text{Q—Q 3}}{\text{Kt}\times\text{R and wins.}}$	$\dfrac{\text{R—B 7}}{\text{Q—K 3 }(f)}$	$\dfrac{\text{Kt—R 4}}{\text{B—K 2}}$
24.		$\dfrac{\text{R}\times\text{B P}}{\text{R}\times\text{P}}$	$\dfrac{\text{P—K Kt 3}}{\text{Kt—Q 5}}$

(a) This move loses a clear Piece. Play as he could, however, the game was irredeemable.

(b) A move White overlooked, unfortunately, when he took the P with Bishop.

(c) Black would have gained no advantage by taking the Q P at this juncture, or by playing P—K Kt 4, to attack the Rook. The move in the text was not made without due deliberation, and we believe it the best on the board.

(d) White designedly gives up the Queen's Pawn, to get a counter attack with his combined forces.

(e) Q—Kt 3 would have been worse than useless.

(f) Had he gone to Q 1, to protect his threatened Pawn White would have won a Pawn (e.g.)—

	WHITE.	BLACK.
23.		Q—Q 1
24.	R×P ch.	K×R
25.	Q—B 7 ch.	K—R1
26.	R—B 6	R—R 4
27.	Q×R (R 4)	Q×R
28.	Q×R ch., &c.	

(g) Well conceived. Tempting Black to open the discovered check, which would cost him " the exchange."

(h) Interposing the Kt and then pushing the B P on the Rook afterwards, would have been unwise on account of B—Q 3 ch., &c.

	(2)	(2) (contd.)	(3)

25. $\dfrac{\text{R×Q Kt P}}{\text{P—Q 4}}$ 37. $\dfrac{\text{Q—Q 5 ch.}}{\text{Q×Q}}$ 25. $\dfrac{\text{B—B 3}}{\text{Kt—K 3 (e)}}$

26. $\dfrac{\text{P—K R 3 (a)}}{\text{R—K 8}}$ 38. $\dfrac{\text{R×Q}}{\text{K—B 2}}$ 26. $\dfrac{\text{K—Kt 4}}{\text{B×Kt}}$

27. $\dfrac{\text{R×R ch.}}{\text{Q×R}}$ 39. $\dfrac{\text{R—Q Kt 5}}{\text{K—K 2}}$ 27. $\dfrac{\text{P×B}}{\text{R—K 5}}$

28. $\dfrac{\text{Q—B 1 (b)}}{\text{Q—K 6 ch.}}$ 40. $\dfrac{\text{P—K Kt 4}}{\text{K—Q 2}}$ 28. $\dfrac{\text{K R—B 1}}{\text{R—Kt 3 ch.}}$

29. $\dfrac{\text{Q—B 2}}{\text{Q—B 8 ch.}}$ 41. $\dfrac{\text{K—Kt 3}}{\text{K—B 3}}$ 29. $\dfrac{\text{K—B 5}}{\text{R—K 6}}$

30. $\dfrac{\text{K—R 2}}{\text{R—K B 1}}$ 42. $\dfrac{\text{R—K 5}}{\text{R—Q 3}}$ 30. $\dfrac{\text{P—R 5}}{\text{R—Kt 7}}$

31. $\dfrac{\text{Q—Q 4}}{\text{R—B 3 (c)}}$ 43. $\dfrac{\text{R—K 3}}{\text{K—B 4}}$ 31. $\dfrac{\text{P—Q R 4}}{\text{Kt—B 4 (f)}}$

32. $\dfrac{\text{Q×P ch.}}{\text{K—R 2}}$ 44. $\dfrac{\text{P—K R 4}}{\text{P—Kt 3}}$ 32. $\dfrac{\text{K R—K 1 (g)}}{\text{P—K Kt 3 ch.}}$

33. $\dfrac{\text{Q—K 5}}{\text{R—Kt 3 (d)}}$ 45. $\dfrac{\text{K—B 4}}{\text{K—Q 5}}$ Black mates in two.

34. $\dfrac{\text{R—K 7}}{\text{Q—Q7}}$ 46. $\dfrac{\text{R—K 4 ch.}}{\text{K—Q 4}}$

35. $\dfrac{\text{Q—K 4}}{\text{Q—Q 3 ch.}}$ 47. $\dfrac{\text{R—K 8}}{\text{R—K B 3 ch.}}$

36. $\dfrac{\text{R—K 5}}{\text{K—Kt 1}}$ 48. $\dfrac{\text{K—K 3}}{\text{K—B 5}}$

(a) A most important move. Black dare not now advance his Q P on account of Q—B 7 ch., which would enable White to double his Rooks on the adversary's K Kt P, and thus win easily.

(b) K—R 2 would have been very bad play, because Black would have checked with his Q at K 4 ; and if then the Queen were interposed, he would have taken the Q and played R—K 6 ch., and afterwards R—Q Kt 6.

(c) He could not save all the Pawns attacked.

(d) Threatening to take the Kt P with his Rook, and then check with the Queen at B 3.

(e) Threatening, if White took the Q P, to win a Piece.

(f) He might also have checked with Kt P, and after the exchange of Pawns when the K was driven to his B 6, have played Kt×P The move in the text, however, appears as effectual as any.

(g) If B—K 5, Black rejoined with Kt—Q 2, &c.

(2) *(contd.)*

49. R–K 4 ch. / K–Q 4	57. K–K 2 / R–R 6	65. R–K R 4 / K–B 4
50. R–K B 4 / R–B 3	58. R–K B 4 / R×K R P	66. P–Kt 6 / R–R 2
51. R–Q Kt 4 / R–K 3 ch.	59. R–B 6 ch. / K–Kt 4	67. K–B 5 / P–Kt 4
52. K–Q 3 / R–K B 3	60. R×Kt P / R–R 7 ch.	68. R–K Kt 4 / P–Kt 5 (b)
53. R–Kt 5 ch. (a) / K–B 3	61. K–B 3 / R×P	69. P–Kt 7 / R×P
54. R–K 5 / K–Q 3	62. R×R P / R–Kt 6 ch.	70. R×R / P–Kt 6
55. R–Kt 5 / K–B 3	63. K–B 4 / R×P	71. K–K 4 / K–Kt 5
56. R–Kt 4 / R–B 6 ch.	64. P–Kt 5 / R–R 8	72. K–Q 3 / Resigns.

	(4)	(5)	(6)
	Staunton	Ralli	Amsterdam
	St. Amant	Lowenthall (Played by correspondence)	London (Played by correspondence)
1.	P–K 4 / P–K 4	P–K 4 / P–K 4	P–K 4 / P–K 4
2.	B–B 4 / B–B 4	Kt–K B 3 / Kt–Q B 3	Kt–K B 3 / Kt–Q B 3
3.	Kt–K B 3 / Kt–Q B 3	P–Q 4 / P×P	P–Q 4 / P×P
4.	P–B 3 / Q–K 2	B–B 4 / B–B 4	B–B 4 / B–B 4

(a) K–K 3 would have been better.

(b) This was ill-judged. He should have played R–K Kt 2, or Q R 1.

	(4)	(5)	(6)
5.	P-Q 4 / P×P (a)	P-B 3 / Kt-B 3	P--B 3 / Kt-B 3
6.	0-0 / Kt-K 4	P-K 5 / P-Q 4	P-K 5 / P-Q 4
7.	Kt×Kt / Q×Kt	B-Q Kt 5 / Kt-K 5	B-Q Kt 5 / Kt-K 5
8.	P-B 4 / P×P d. ch.	B×Kt ch. / P×B	B×Kt ch. / P×B
9.	K-R 1 / Q-Q 5 (b)	P×P / B-Kt 3	P×P / B-Kt 3
10.	Q-Kt 3 / Kt-R 3	Kt-B 3 / 0-0 (e)	Kt-B 3 / P-K B 4
11.	Kt×P / 0-0	B-K 3 (f) / P-B 4	P-K R 4 (k) / 0-0
12.	P-K R 3 (c) / P-Q B 3	Q-B 1 (g) / B-Kt 3 (h)	B-B 4 / P-Q B 4
13.	P-B 5 / Q-B 3	Kt-K Kt 5 / P-B 5 (i)	K-B 1 / R-Kt 1
14.	P-K 5 (d) / Q-R 5	B×P / R×B (j)	Kt-Q R 4 / P×P

(a) The proper move is B—Kt 3. Taking the Pawn gives an immediate advantage to White.

(b) The ill consequences attendant on P×P have been shown in the preceding analysis.

(c) If White play P—B 5 at this point, his opponent may move Kt—K Kt 5, threatening to play afterwards Q—Kt 8 ch., and then mate with his Kt to B 7.

(d) From this move the attack is very lively and interesting.

(e) Many now play P—B 4, but Castling appears to be equally good.

(f) This game, though began as a Scotch Gambit, is so soon resolved into a Giuoco Piano that it may be fairly classed among the games that illustrate that opening.

(g) Better to have Castled or taken the Pawn in passing.

(h) This prevents White from Castling, and hampers him sadly.

(i) From this point to the end, Mr. L. plays very cleverly.

(j) Daring, but sound and well calculated.

(k) The first of a series of fantastic manœuvres on the part of White, who appear to have been utterly paralysed by their opponent's unexpected *coup* on the preceding move. Their best play, as we have seen, was to take the Pawn in passing; but Castling would also have been better than the move made.

	(4)	(5)	(6)
15.	$\dfrac{B \times Kt}{Q \times B}$	$\dfrac{Kt-K\,6}{Kt \times Kt\,(b)}$	$\dfrac{K\,Kt \times P}{Q-K\,1\,(f)}$
16.	$\dfrac{Kt-K\,4}{B-Q\,5}$	$\dfrac{Q \times R\,(c)}{Kt-K\,7}$	$\dfrac{P-Q\,Kt\,3}{P-Q\,B\,4}$
17.	$\dfrac{Kt-Q\,6}{Q-R\,4}$	$\dfrac{Kt \times Q}{Kt \times Q}$	$\dfrac{Kt-B\,2}{P-Q\,5}$
18.	$\dfrac{B \times P\ \text{ch.}}{R \times B}$	$\dfrac{Kt \times P}{B-Kt\,2}$	$\dfrac{R-B\,1}{B-R\,3\ \text{ch.}}$
19.	$\dfrac{P-K\,Kt\,4}{B \times K\,P\,(a)}$	$\dfrac{Kt-Kt\,4}{B \times P}$	$\dfrac{K-Kt\,1}{B-Kt\,4}$
20.	$\dfrac{Q\,R-K\,1}{Q \times P\ \text{ch.}}$	$\dfrac{P-K\,Kt\,3\,(d)}{Kt-R\,6}$	$\dfrac{Kt-R\,3\,(g)}{B \times Kt}$
21.	$\dfrac{Q \times Q}{B \times Kt}$	$\dfrac{P-B\,4}{B \times Kt\,P}$	$\dfrac{P \times B}{B-Q\,B\,2}$
22.	$\dfrac{R-K\,8\ \text{ch.}}{B-B\,1}$	$\dfrac{R-Kt\,1}{P-Q\,5\,(e)}$	$\dfrac{P-B\,3}{Kt-B\,6}$
23.	$\dfrac{K\,R-K\,1}{P-Q\,4}$	$\dfrac{R \times B}{B \times R}$	$\dfrac{Q-B\,2}{B \times K\,P}$

(a) There appears to be nothing better, bad as this is.

(b) A *coup d'état !*

(c) His best play apparently, under the circumstances. If he had taken the Queen, the following very striking variation would most probably have occurred :—

16. Kt × Q	R—K 5 ch.
17. K—Q 2	Kt—K 7
18. Q—Kt 1 !	

(If 18. Q—B 2, Black replies with B—R 4 ch., and wins easily. If 18. Q × B P, Black also answers with B—R 4 ch., winning the Queen in a move or two afterwards, and having an excellent position).

18.	R × P ch.
19. K—K 1	B—R 4 ch.
20. P—Q Kt 4	R × Q Kt P and wins.

If White at move 20 plays K—B 1, Black equally wins by playing Kt—B 8 d.ch.

(d) Well conceived.

(e) It would have been better for him to have played B—B 6 ch., and then P—Q 5.

(f) The object of Black's 10th move is now apparent. They here commence an attack on White's K P, which being isolated must fall in the end.

(g) It is difficult to see why Amsterdam thus allowed a Pawn to be doubled at the side of the board.

	(4)	(5)	(6)
24.	R—Q 8 / R—Q 2	Kt—R 6 / R—Q B 1	R—K 1 / B×B (*b*)
25.	K R—K 8 / R×R	Kt—B 5 / P—Kt 4	R×Q / R×R
26.	R×R / P—Q Kt 3	P—B 5 / P—Kt 5	K—B 2 (*c*) / R—K 7 ch.
27.	Q—K 3 / Q B—Kt 2	R—Kt 4 / Kt—Kt 4	Q×R / Kt×Q
28.	R×R / B×R	P—K 6 / Kt—K 5	K×Kt / R—K 1 ch.
29.	Q—K 6 ch. / K—R 1	R×P (*a*) / Kt×Kt	K—B 2 / P—Q 6
30.	Q—B 7 / Resigns.	R×P ch. / K—B 1	R—Q 1 / P—Q 7
31.		R—B 4 / Kt—K 5	K—B 1 / B—Kt 6
32.		P—Kt 4 / B—B 6	Kt—B 2 / R—K 8 ch.
33.		P—B 6 / R—Kt 1 and wins.	R×R / P×R (Queens) ch.
34.			Kt×Q / B×Kt
35.			K×B / K—B 2 and wins.

	(7)	(8)	(9)
	Jaenisch / Prince Ouroussoff	Schumoff / Prince Ouroussoff	Buckle / Schulder
1.	P—K 4 / P—K 4	P—K 4 / P—K 4	P—K 4 / P—K 4
2.	Kt—K B 3 / Kt—K B 3	Kt—K B 3 / Kt—Q B 3	Kt—K B 3 / Kt—Q B 3
3.	B—B 4 / B—B 4	B—B 4 / B—B 4	B—B 4 / B—B 4

(*a*) Mere desperation. The game is past hope.
(*b*) The sacrifice of the Queen leads to a speedy victory.
(*c*) This was imperative, since Black threatened to play B—Kt 6 with fatal effect.

	(7)	(8)	(9)
4.	$\dfrac{\text{P—B 3}}{\text{Kt—B 3}}$	$\dfrac{\text{P—B 3}}{\text{Kt—B 3}}$	$\dfrac{\text{Kt—B 3} (d)}{\text{Kt—B 3}}$
5.	$\dfrac{\text{P—Q 4}}{\text{P} \times \text{P}}$	$\dfrac{\text{P—Q 3}}{\text{P—Q 3}}$	$\dfrac{\text{P—Q 3}}{\text{P—Q 3}}$
6.	$\dfrac{\text{P—K 5} (a)}{\text{P—Q 4}}$	$\dfrac{\text{B—K Kt 5}}{\text{P—K R 3}}$	$\dfrac{\text{0—0}}{\text{P—K R 3}}$
7.	$\dfrac{\text{B—Q Kt 5}}{\text{Kt—K 5}}$	$\dfrac{\text{B—R 4}}{\text{P—K Kt 4}}$	$\dfrac{\text{Kt—K 2}}{\text{Kt—Q R 4} (e)}$
8.	$\dfrac{\text{B} \times \text{Kt ch.}}{\text{P} \times \text{B}}$	$\dfrac{\text{B—Kt 3}}{\text{P—Q R 3}}$	$\dfrac{\text{B—Kt 3}}{\text{P—Q Kt 4}}$
9.	$\dfrac{\text{P} \times \text{P}}{\text{B—Kt 3}}$	$\dfrac{\text{P—Q Kt 4}}{\text{B—R 2}}$	$\dfrac{\text{Kt—Kt 3}}{\text{B—Kt 3}}$
10.	$\dfrac{\text{Kt—B 3}}{\text{P—B 3}}$	$\dfrac{\text{P—Q R 4}}{\text{Kt—K 2}}$	$\dfrac{\text{K—R 1}}{\text{P—B 4}}$
11.	$\dfrac{\text{B—K 3}}{\text{0—0}}$	$\dfrac{\text{Q—Kt 3}}{\text{R—K R 2} (b)}$	$\dfrac{\text{B—Q 2}}{\text{Kt—B 3}}$
12.	$\dfrac{\text{P—K R 3}}{\text{P—K B 4}}$	$\dfrac{\text{Q Kt—Q 2}}{\text{Kt—Kt 3}}$	$\dfrac{\text{P—Q R 4}}{\text{P—Kt 5}}$
13.	$\dfrac{\text{0—0}}{\text{P—B 5}}$	$\dfrac{\text{P—Q 4}}{\text{P—Kt 5} (c)}$	$\dfrac{\text{B—Q B 4} (f)}{\text{Kt—K 2}}$

(a) Major Jaenisch remarks on this move : " At this time I am inclined to believe that in the Giuoco Piano opening, the first player acquires a better game by taking the Q Pawn with his Q B P, as was done by the old players, than in advancing the King's Pawn to attack the adverse Knight."

(b) There is a freshness and originality about the games of the Princes Ouroussoff, that render them as delightful as they are instructive to the chess student.

(c) A capital counter-move.

(d) The present variation in the Giuoco Piano opening has not received much attention at the hands of chess authors. It may be adopted I believe in perfect safety ; and now that the combinations springing from the usual move of 4 P—B 3 have been analyzed to exhaustion, 4 Kt—B 3 presents an agreeable variety.

(e) If played for the express purpose of taking the adverse K B, this move is unobjectionable, but, as Black does not exchange Pieces, it is somewhat puzzling to account for his placing the Knight in such a position.

(f) I do not see that Mr. Buckle derives any more advantage from the Bishop being posted here than from his standing at Q Kt 3 ; and if not, this must be considered " a lost time." If I mistake not, he might have played Kt—R 4 at once. For suppose :—

	(7)	(8)	(9)
14.	B—B 1 / B—Kt 2	Kt—R 4 / Kt×Kt	Kt—R 4 / B—Kt 5 (f)
15.	P—Q R 4 / P—Q R 4	B×Kt / P×P	P—K B 3 / B—K 3
16.	R—K 1 / P—B 4	P—K5 (b) / P×B P	B×B / P×B
17.	Kt×Kt / P×Kt	Kt—K 4 (c) / Kt×Kt (d)	P—K B 4 / P×P
18.	P×P / B×P	B×Q / B×P ch.	R×P / Q—Q 2
19.	Q×Q / Q R×Q	K—K 2 / P—Kt 6	Kt—R 5 (g) / Kt (K 2)—Kt 1
20.	Kt—Kt 5 / Q R—K 1 (a)	P—R 3 / K×B	Kt—Kt 6 / R—R 2
21.	B—Q 2 / R×P	B×B P / B—K B 4 (e)	P—R 5 / B—B 2
22.	P—R 4 / P—K 6	B—Q 5 / R—K 2	P—B 3 / P×P
23.	P×P / P×P	P—K 6 / P—B 3	B×P / P—K 4
24.	B—B 3 / P—K 7 d. ch.	B×Kt / R×P	R—B 5 (h) / R—Kt 1

---

13. Kt—R 4   Kt×K P (if)
14. B×P ch.   K×B

(If he plays K—B 1, or K 2, White may check with his Knight at Kt 6, &c.).

15. Q—R 5 ch.   K—Kt 1
16. P×B

And White has much the advantage.

(a) Black has now a winning advantage through the freedom of his Pieces, and the strength of his advanced Pawns in the centre of the field.

(b) All these moves are excellently conceived.

(c) White might also have taken the Pawn with his Queen.

(d) This, though perhaps unsound, is played with remarkable ingenuity.

(e) From this point Black plays in great style.

(f) Cui bono ?

(g) Threatening, the young player may be told, to take the Knight with his Rook for nothing ; since if Black captured his Rook in return, he would lose his Queen.

(h) The game now increases in animation move by move, until it attains a climax of remarkable interest and beauty.

	(7)	(8)	(9)
25.	K–R 2 / R–K 6	K R–Q 1 (a) / R×B ch.	Q–Kt 4 (b) / Q–K 3 (c)
26.	B×R P / R–B 7	K–B 1 / P–B 7	Kt×Kt ch. / Kt×Kt (d)
27.	R–K Kt 1 / B–Q 3 ch.	R×P ch. / K–K 2	R×P (e) / Q×R (f)
28.	K–R 1 / P–K R 3	R–Q 2 / B–K 3	Q–R 3 (g) / Kt×P
29.	Resigns.	Q×P / B–B 5 ch.	P×Kt / Q×P
30.		R–Q 3 / R–B 1	R–K 1 / Q×R
31.		Q×Q B / R×Q	B×Q and wins.
32.		Resigns.	

	(10) Schumoff / Jaenisch	(11) Buckle / Anderssen	(12) Max Lange / Ehrich
1.	P–K 4 / P–K 4	P–K4 / P–K 4	P–K 4 / P–K 4
2.	Kt–K B 3 / Kt–Q B 3	Kt–K B 3 / Kt–Q B 3	Kt–K B 3 / Kt–Q B 3
3.	B–B 4 / B–B 4	B–B 4 / B–B 4	B–B 4 / B–B 4
4.	P–B 3 / Kt–B 3	P–B 3 / Kt–B 3	0–0 / Kt–B 3

(a) Q×P seems a better move.

(b) This move can evidently be made with impunity.

(c) Running into the lion's mouth ! He should rather have played Q–B 2, I believe.

(d) If he had taken with the Kt P, White would have captured the K P with his Rook even still more advantageously.

(e) Very well conceived.

(f) This was a fatal error. He should have taken the Queen with his Knight, although, even in that case, Black would have had the better game.

(g) A masterly *coup de repos*, almost compelling White to immolate himself. After this the game is hopeless.

(10)	(11)	(12)
5. $\dfrac{0-0}{Kt \times P}$	$\dfrac{P-Q\,4}{P \times P}$	$\dfrac{P-Q\,4}{P \times P}$
6. $\dfrac{P-Q\,4}{P \times P\ (a)}$	$\dfrac{P \times P}{B-Kt\,5\ ch.}$	$\dfrac{P-K\,5}{P-Q\,4}$
7. $\dfrac{P \times P}{B-Kt\,3\ (b)}$	$\dfrac{B-Q\,2}{B \times B\ ch.}$	$\dfrac{P \times Kt}{P \times B}$
8. $\dfrac{B-Q\,5\ (c)}{Kt-B\,3}$	$\dfrac{Kt \times B}{P-Q\,4}$	$\dfrac{R-K\,1\ ch.}{K-B\,1}$
9. $\dfrac{R-K\,1\ ch.}{Kt-K\,2}$	$\dfrac{P \times P}{Kt \times P}$	$\dfrac{P \times P\ ch.}{K \times P}$
10. $\dfrac{Kt-B\,3}{B-R\,4\ (d)}$	$\dfrac{Q-Kt\,3}{Kt\,(B\,3)-K\,2}$	$\dfrac{Kt-K\,5}{B-K\,3}$
11. $\dfrac{P-Q\,Kt\,4}{B \times P}$	$\dfrac{0-0}{0-0}$	$\dfrac{Q-R\,5}{Q-K\,2}$
12. $\dfrac{B \times P\ ch.}{K-B\,1}$	$\dfrac{R-K\,1}{Kt-B\,5}$	$\dfrac{B-Kt\,5}{P-B\,3}$
13. $\dfrac{Q-Kt\,3}{B \times Kt}$	$\dfrac{R-K\,4}{Kt\,(K\,2)-Kt\,3}$	$\dfrac{Q-R\,6\ ch.}{K-Kt\,1}$
14. $\dfrac{Kt-Kt\,5}{B \times R\ (K\,1)}$	$\dfrac{Q\,R-K\,1\ (e)}{Q-B\,3}$	$\dfrac{B \times P}{Q-B\,1}$
15. $\dfrac{B-R\,5}{B \times P\ ch.}$	$\dfrac{Kt-K\,5}{Q-Kt\,4\ (f)}$	Q—Kt 5 ch. and wins.
16. $\dfrac{K \times B}{P-Q\,4}$	$\dfrac{B \times P\ ch.}{K-R\,1}$	
17. $\dfrac{B-R\,3}{Kt \times B}$	$\dfrac{Kt \times Kt\ ch.}{P-Kt}$	

(a) He should rather have played P—Q 4.

(b) Equally faulty with his last move. His best play would have been 7. B—K 2, by which he might have maintained the Pawn with a tolerably safe though somewhat confined game.

(c) R—K 1 would have been better; *ex. gr.*, 8. $\dfrac{R-K\,1}{P-Q\,4}$; 9. $\dfrac{B \times Q\,P}{Q \times B}$; 10. $\dfrac{Kt-B\,3}{}$, regaining the Pawn.

(d) White cleverly takes advantage of this error in his next few moves.

(e) These three moves with the Rooks give White a very fine position.

(f) Black risks too much on this counter-attack, Kt×Kt would have been better play.

	(10)	(11)	(12)
18.	$\dfrac{\text{R}-\text{K 1}}{\text{Q}-\text{Q 2}}$	$\dfrac{\text{Q}-\text{Kt 3 }(b)}{\text{Q}\times\text{Q}}$	
19.	$\dfrac{\text{R}\times\text{Kt}}{\text{Q}\times\text{R}}$	$\dfrac{\text{R P}\times\text{Q}}{\text{R}\times\text{B}}$	
20.	$\dfrac{\text{Q}\times\text{Q P }(a)}{\text{K}-\text{K 1}}$	$\dfrac{\text{R}\times\text{Kt}}{\text{K}-\text{Kt 1 }(c)}$	
21.	$\dfrac{\text{B}\times\text{Q}}{\text{K}\times\text{B}}$	$\dfrac{\text{R}-\text{K 8 ch.}}{\text{Resigns,}}$	
22.	$\dfrac{\text{Q}-\text{K 5 ch.}}{\text{K}-\text{B 1}}$		
23.	$\dfrac{\text{Q}\times\text{B P}}{\text{B}-\text{K 3}}$		
24.	$\dfrac{\text{Q}-\text{Q 6 ch.}}{\text{K}-\text{K 1}}$		
25.	$\dfrac{\text{Q}\times\text{B ch.}}{\text{K}-\text{Q 1}}$		
26.	$\dfrac{\text{Kt}-\text{B 7 ch.}}{\text{K}-\text{B 2}}$		
27.	$\dfrac{\text{Q}-\text{Q 6 ch.}}{\text{K}-\text{B 1}}$		
28.	$\dfrac{\text{Kt}\times\text{R}}{\text{Kt}-\text{B 3}}$		
29.	$\dfrac{\text{Q}-\text{B 8 ch.}}{\text{Resigns.}}$		

	(13)	(14)	(15)
	$\dfrac{\text{Max Lange}}{\text{Heineman}}$	$\dfrac{\text{Max Lange}}{\text{Heineman}}$	$\dfrac{\text{Taubenhaus}}{\text{Burn}}$
1.	$\dfrac{\text{P}-\text{K 4}}{\text{P}-\text{K 4}}$	$\dfrac{\text{P}-\text{K 4}}{\text{P}-\text{K 4}}$	$\dfrac{\text{P}-\text{K 4}}{\text{P}-\text{K 4}}$
2.	$\dfrac{\text{Kt}-\text{K B 3}}{\text{Kt}-\text{Q B 3}}$	$\dfrac{\text{Kt}-\text{K B 3}}{\text{Kt}-\text{Q B 3}}$	$\dfrac{\text{Kt}-\text{K B 3}}{\text{Kt}-\text{Q B 3}}$
3.	$\dfrac{\text{B}-\text{B 4}}{\text{B}-\text{B 4}}$	$\dfrac{\text{B}-\text{B 4}}{\text{B}-\text{B 4}}$	$\dfrac{\text{B}-\text{B 4}}{\text{B}-\text{B 4}}$

(a) Now the position becomes highly interesting, but if White had been satisfied with the obvious move of B×Q, he would soon have lost all his advantage.

(b) Well played.

(c) A palpable oversight, but the position is lost.

	(13)	(14)	(15)
4.	$\dfrac{0-0}{\text{Kt}-\text{B }3}$	$\dfrac{0-0}{\text{Kt}-\text{B3}}$	$\dfrac{\text{P}-\text{Q }3}{\text{P}-\text{Q }3}$
5.	$\dfrac{\text{P}-\text{Q }4}{\text{B}\times\text{P}}$	$\dfrac{\text{P}-\text{Q }4}{\text{Kt}\times\text{Q P}}$	$\dfrac{\text{P}-\text{B }3}{\text{Kt}-\text{B }3}$
6.	$\dfrac{\text{Kt}\times\text{B}}{\text{Kt}\times\text{Kt}}$	$\dfrac{\text{Kt}\times\text{P}}{\text{Kt}-\text{K }3}$	$\dfrac{\text{B}-\text{K }3}{\text{B}-\text{Kt }3}$
7.	$\dfrac{\text{P}-\text{B }4}{\text{Kt}-\text{K }3}$ (a)	$\dfrac{\text{B}\times\text{Kt}}{\text{B P}\times\text{B}}$ (c)	$\dfrac{\text{Q}-\text{K }2}{\text{Kt}-\text{K }2}$
8.	$\dfrac{\text{P}\times\text{P}}{\text{Kt}-\text{Kt }1}$ (b)	$\dfrac{\text{Kt}-\text{Q }3}{\text{Q}-\text{K }2}$ (d)	$\dfrac{\text{Q Kt}-\text{Q }2}{\text{Kt}-\text{Kt }3}$
9.	$\dfrac{\text{R}\times\text{P}}{\text{K}\times\text{R}}$	$\dfrac{\text{B}-\text{Kt }5}{\text{P}-\text{K }4}$ (e)	$\dfrac{\text{P}-\text{K R }3}{\text{P}-\text{B }3}$
10.	$\dfrac{\text{B}\times\text{Kt ch.}}{\text{K}\times\text{B}}$	$\dfrac{\text{Kt}-\text{B }3}{\text{P}-\text{B }3}$	$\dfrac{\text{B}-\text{Kt }3}{0-0}$
11.	$\dfrac{\text{Q}-\text{Q }5\text{ ch.}}{\text{K}-\text{K }2}$	$\dfrac{\text{B}\times\text{Kt}}{\text{P}\times\text{B}}$	$\dfrac{\text{P}-\text{Kt }4}{\text{P}-\text{Q }4}$
12.	$\dfrac{\text{B}-\text{Kt }5\text{ ch.}}{\text{Kt}-\text{B }3}$	$\dfrac{\text{Q}-\text{R }5\text{ ch.}}{\text{K}-\text{Q }1}$	$\dfrac{\text{P}\times\text{P}}{\text{Kt}\times\text{P}}$
13.	$\dfrac{\text{Kt}-\text{B }3}{\text{R}-\text{B }1}$	$\dfrac{\text{Kt}\times\text{B}}{\text{Q}\times\text{Kt}}$	$\dfrac{\text{B}\times\text{Kt}}{\text{P}\times\text{B}}$
14.	$\dfrac{\text{R}-\text{K B }1}{\text{P}-\text{Q }3}$	$\dfrac{\text{Q R}-\text{Q }1}{\text{K}-\text{B }2}$	$\dfrac{\text{Kt}-\text{B }1}{\text{P}-\text{Q }5}$

(a) If 7. $\dfrac{}{\text{P}-\text{Q }3}$; 8. $\dfrac{\text{P}\times\text{P}}{}$. If 7. $\dfrac{}{\text{Kt}-\text{B }3}$; 8. $\dfrac{\text{B}\times\text{P ch.}}{}$

(b) It would have been unwise to take the K P, on account of 8. $\dfrac{\text{Q}-\text{B }3}{\text{Kt}-\text{Kt }4}$; 9. $\dfrac{\text{B}\times\text{Kt}}{\text{Kt}\times\text{B}}$; 10. $\dfrac{\text{B}\times\text{P ch.}}{}$, &c.

(c) It is clear that 7. $\dfrac{}{\text{Q P}\times\text{B}}$ is bad.

(d) 8. $\dfrac{}{\text{Kt}\times\text{P}}$ loses a Piece. He might, however, play 8. $\dfrac{}{\text{B}-\text{Kt }3}$ or 8. $\dfrac{}{\text{B}-\text{K }2}$. In both cases White replies with $\dfrac{\text{P}-\text{K }5}{}$ and gets the better game. Lastly, if 8. $\dfrac{}{\text{P}-\text{Q }3}$; 9. $\dfrac{\text{Kt}\times\text{B}}{\text{P}\times\text{Kt}}$; 10. $\dfrac{\text{Q}-\text{K }2}{0-0}$, and White has the better game.

(e) To prevent P—K 5. If 9. $\dfrac{}{\text{P}-\text{Q }3}$; 10. $\dfrac{\text{Kt}\times\text{B}}{\text{P}\times\text{Kt}}$; 11. $\dfrac{\text{P}-\text{K }5}{}$ wins.

	(13)	(14)	(15)
15.	P×Kt ch. ‾P×P‾	K—R 1 ‾Q—K 2‾	B—Q 2 ‾P×P‾
16.	R×P ‾R×R‾	P—B 4 ‾P—Q 3‾	P×P ‾B—Q 2‾
17.	P—K 5 ‾B×K 3‾	B P×P ‾Q P×P‾	Kt—Kt 3 ‾B—Kt 4‾
18.	B×R ch. ‾K—B 2‾	R—B 2 ‾R—B 1‾	P—B 4 ‾B—B 3‾
19.	Q—B 3 ‾Q—Kt 1‾	Q R—K B 1 ‾B—K 3‾	0—0 ‾P—B 3‾
20.	Kt—K 4 ‾P×P‾	Q—R 4 ‾R—B 2‾	Kt—B 5 ‾Q—Q 2‾
21.	B—Q 8 d. ch. and wins.	R×P ‾Q R—K B 1‾	P—K R 4 ‾Q R—Q 1 (b)‾
22.		R×R ‾R×R‾	P—R 5 ‾Q×P‾
23.		R×R ‾Q×R‾	Q×Q ‾R×Q‾
24.		P—R 3 ‾Q—B 8 ch.‾	P×Kt ‾B×Kt‾
25.		K—R 2 ‾Q—B 5 ch.‾	B—Kt 4 ‾R—K 1‾
26.		Q×Q ‾P×Q‾	P×P ch. ‾K×P‾
27.		P—K 5 (a) ‾B—B 4‾	P—B 5 ‾B—B 2‾
28.		Kt—K 2 ‾B×P‾	Kt—Q 6 ‾R—K R 1‾
29.		Kt×P ‾K—Q 2‾	Kt—B 7 ‾R—Q 5‾
30.		P—Q Kt 4 ‾P—Q R 3‾	Kt×R ‾R×P ch.‾
31.		K—Kt 3 ‾P—Kt 4‾	K—R 2 ‾P—K 5 d. ch.‾
32.		K—B 3 ‾P—B 4‾	K—R 3 [wins (c) ‾P—K Kt 4‾ and

(a) The right move, overlooked apparently by Black when he forced the exchange of Queens.

(b) The beginning of a very subtle combination.

(c) A neat finish to a splendidly played game.

(14) *(contd.)*

33. $\dfrac{P \times P}{K-B\,3}$ 36. $\dfrac{P-B\,6\ ch.}{K \times K\,P}$ 39. $\dfrac{Kt \times P}{B \times P}$

34. $\dfrac{P-K\,6}{P-Kt\,5}$ 37. $\dfrac{Kt-Q\,5\ ch.}{K-Q\,3}$ 40. $\dfrac{Kt-Kt\,4}{B-R5}$

35. $\dfrac{P-K\,7}{K-Q\,2}$ 38. $\dfrac{Kt \times P}{B-Q\,R\,5}$ 41. $\dfrac{\quad}{P-Kt\,4\ \text{and wins}}$

	(16)	(17)	(18)
	Schiffers	Kolisch	Marshall
	Harmonist	Paulsen	Burn
1.	$\dfrac{P-K\,4}{P-K\,4}$	$\dfrac{P-K\,4}{P-K\,4}$	$\dfrac{P-K\,4}{P-K\,4}$
2.	$\dfrac{Kt-K\,B\,3}{Kt-Q\,B\,3}$	$\dfrac{Kt-K\,B\,3}{Kt-Q\,B\,3}$	$\dfrac{Kt-K\,B\,3}{Kt-Q\,B\,3}$
3.	$\dfrac{B-B\,4}{B-B\,4}$	$\dfrac{B-B\,4}{B-B\,4}$	$\dfrac{B-B\,4}{B-B\,4}$
4.	$\dfrac{P-B\,3}{Kt-B\,3}$	$\dfrac{0-0}{Kt-B\,3}$	$\dfrac{P-B\,3}{Kt-B\,3}$
5.	$\dfrac{P-Q\,4}{P \times P}$	$\dfrac{P-Q\,Kt\,4}{B \times P\ (b)}$	$\dfrac{P-Q\,4}{P \times P}$
6.	$\dfrac{P \times P}{B-Kt\,5\ ch.}$	$\dfrac{P-B\,3}{B-K\,2}$	$\dfrac{P \times P}{B-Kt\,5\ ch.}$
7.	$\dfrac{B-Q\,2}{B \times B\ ch}$	$\dfrac{P-Q\,4}{P \times P}$	$\dfrac{K-B\,1}{Kt \times K\,P}$
8.	$\dfrac{Q\,Kt \times B}{P-Q\,4\ (a)}$	$\dfrac{P \times P}{K\,Kt \times P}$	$\dfrac{P-Q\,5}{Kt-K\,2\ (c)}$
9.	$\dfrac{P \times P}{K\,Kt \times P}$	$\dfrac{P-Q\,5}{Kt-Q\,R\,4}$	$\dfrac{Q-Q\,4}{Kt-K\,B\,3}$
10.	$\dfrac{Q-Kt\,3}{Q\,Kt-K\,2}$	$\dfrac{B-Q\,3}{Kt-Q\,B\,4}$	$\dfrac{B-K\,Kt\,5}{Kt-Kt\,3}$

(a) If 8.   Kt × K P
      9. P−Q 5 !   Kt × Kt
    10. Q × Kt   Kt−K 2
    11. P−Q 6   P × P
    12. Q × P   0−0
(b) Turning the game into an Evans Gambit.
(c) If 8.   Kt−R 4
      9. B−Q 3 !

	(16)	(17)	(18)
11.	$\dfrac{0-0}{0-0}$	$\dfrac{B-R\ 3}{Kt \times B}$	$\dfrac{Q\ Kt-Q\ 2}{P-K\ R\ 3}$
12.	$\dfrac{K\ R-K\ 1}{P-Q\ B\ 3}$	$\dfrac{Q \times Kt}{0-0}$	$\dfrac{R-K\ 1\ ch.}{K-B\ 1}$
13.	$\dfrac{P-Q\ R\ 4}{Q-B\ 2}$	$\dfrac{P-Q\ 6}{P \times P}$	$\dfrac{B-Q\ 3}{B-K\ 2}$
14.	$\dfrac{Q\ R-B\ 1}{Kt-B\ 5}$	$\dfrac{Kt-Q\ B\ 3}{P-Q\ Kt\ 3}$	$\dfrac{K\ B \times Kt}{R\ P \times B}$
15.	$\dfrac{Kt-Kt\ 5}{Kt\ (K\ 2)-Kt\ 3}$	$\dfrac{Kt-Q\ 5}{Kt-Q\ Kt\ 2}$	$\dfrac{Kt-K\ 5\ !}{P \times B}$
16.	$\dfrac{R-K\ 8\ !\ (a)}{R \times R}$	$\dfrac{B-Kt\ 2}{Kt-Q\ B\ 4}$	$\dfrac{Kt \times Kt\ P\ ch.}{K-B\ 2}$
17.	$\dfrac{B \times P\ ch.}{K-R\ 1}$	$\dfrac{Q-K\ 3}{Kt-K\ 3}$	$\dfrac{R \times B\ ch.}{K \times Kt\ (d)}$
18.	$\dfrac{B \times R}{Kt-K\ 7\ ch.}$	$\dfrac{Kt-Q\ 4\ !\ (b)}{B-K\ B\ 3}$	$\dfrac{Q-Q\ 3\ ch.}{K-R\ 3}$
19.	$\dfrac{K-R\ 1}{Kt \times R}$	$\dfrac{Kt-Q\ B\ 6\ !!\ (c)}{P \times Kt}$	$\dfrac{P-K\ R\ 4\ (e)}{P-Kt\ 5\ (f)}$
20.	$\dfrac{Kt-B\ 7\ ch.}{K-Kt\ 1}$	$\dfrac{Kt \times B\ ch.}{P \times Kt}$	$\dfrac{P-R\ 5}{Kt \times R\ P}$
21.	$\dfrac{Kt-R\ 6\ d.\ ch.}{K-B\ 1}$	$\dfrac{Q-R\ 6}{P-Q\ 4}$	$\dfrac{Q-B\ 5}{\text{Resigns.}}$
22.	$\dfrac{Q-Kt\ 8\ ch.}{K-K\ 2}$	$\dfrac{B \times K\ B\ P}{Q-Q\ 3}$	
23.	$\dfrac{B \times Kt}{P \times B}$	$\dfrac{P-K\ B\ 4}{R-K\ 1}$	
24.	$\dfrac{Q \times P\ ch.}{K-Q\ 1}$	$\dfrac{R-K\ B\ 3}{\text{Resigns.}}$	

(a) Capital !
(b) The beginning of a magnificent combination.
(c) Super-excellence. If 19.   Q—K 1
         20. Kt × B ch., &c.
(d) If 17.   K—Kt 1
        18. Kt—K 4   Kt—R 4 (or K 1)
        19. Q × P ch., and mate next move.
(e) Threatening mate.
(f) If 19.   Q × R
        20. P × P ch.   K × P
        21. Kt—B 3 ch.   K—B 5
        22. P—Kt 3 ch.   K—Kt 5
        23. Q—Kt 6 ch.   K × Kt
        24. Q—B 5 mate.

(16)   (17)   (18)

25. $\dfrac{\text{Q}-\text{B 8 ch.}}{\text{K}-\text{Q 2}}$

26. $\dfrac{\text{Kt}-\text{K 4 ! } (a)}{\text{Q}-\text{Q 1}}$

27. $\dfrac{\text{Q}-\text{Q 6 ch.}}{\text{K}-\text{K 1}}$

28. $\dfrac{\text{Kt}-\text{B 6 ch.}}{\text{Resigns.}}$

(19)	(20)
$\dfrac{\text{Steinitz}}{\text{Bardeleben}}$	$\dfrac{\text{Lasker}}{\text{Steinitz}}$

1. $\dfrac{\text{P}-\text{K 4}}{\text{P}-\text{K 4}}$ $\dfrac{\text{P}-\text{K 4}}{\text{P}-\text{K 4}}$

2. $\dfrac{\text{Kt}-\text{K B 3}}{\text{Kt}-\text{Q B 3}}$ $\dfrac{\text{Kt}-\text{K B 3}}{\text{Kt}-\text{Q B 3}}$

3. $\dfrac{\text{B}-\text{B 4}}{\text{B}-\text{B 4}}$ $\dfrac{\text{B}-\text{B 4}}{\text{B}-\text{B 4}}$

4. $\dfrac{\text{P}-\text{B 3}}{\text{Kt}-\text{B 3}}$ $\dfrac{\text{P}-\text{Q 3}}{\text{P}-\text{Q 3}}$

5. $\dfrac{\text{P}-\text{Q 4}}{\text{P}\times\text{P}}$ $\dfrac{\text{Kt}-\text{B 3}}{\text{Kt}-\text{B 3}}$

6. $\dfrac{\text{P}\times\text{P}}{\text{B}-\text{Kt 5 ch.}}$ $\dfrac{\text{B}-\text{K 3}}{\text{B}-\text{Kt 3}}$

7. $\dfrac{\text{Kt}-\text{B 3}}{\text{P}-\text{Q 4}}$ $\dfrac{\text{Q}-\text{Q 2}}{\text{Kt}-\text{Q R 4}}$

8. $\dfrac{\text{P}\times\text{P}}{\text{K Kt}\times\text{P}}$ $\dfrac{\text{B}-\text{Kt 5 ch.}}{\text{P}-\text{B 3}}$

9. $\dfrac{\text{0}-\text{0}}{\text{B}-\text{K 3}}$ $\dfrac{\text{B}-\text{R 4}}{\text{B}\times\text{B}}$

10. $\dfrac{\text{B}-\text{K Kt 5 !}}{\text{B}-\text{K 2}}$ $\dfrac{\text{P}\times\text{B}}{\text{P}-\text{Q Kt 4}}$

11. $\dfrac{\text{B}\times\text{Kt}}{\text{Q B}\times\text{B}}$ $\dfrac{\text{B}-\text{Kt 3}}{\text{Q}-\text{Kt 3}}$

12. $\dfrac{\text{Kt}\times\text{B}}{\text{Q}\times\text{Kt}}$ $\dfrac{\text{0}-\text{0}}{\text{Kt}-\text{Kt 5}}$

(a) A truly splendid finale.

	(19)	(20)
13.	$\dfrac{B \times B}{Kt \times B}$	$\dfrac{Q\ R - K\ 1}{P - B\ 3\ !}$
14.	$\dfrac{R - K\ 1}{P - K\ B\ 3\ (a)}$	$\dfrac{P - K\ R\ 3}{Kt - R\ 3}$
15.	$\dfrac{Q - K\ 2}{Q - Q\ 2}$	$\dfrac{Kt - K\ 2}{Kt \times B}$
16.	$\dfrac{Q\ R - B\ 1}{P - B\ 3}$	$\dfrac{R\ P \times Kt}{0 - 0}$
17.	$\dfrac{P - Q\ 5\ !}{P \times P}$	$\dfrac{Kt - Kt\ 3}{P - Q\ R\ 4}$
18.	$\dfrac{Kt - Q\ 4}{K - B\ 2}$	$\dfrac{P - Q\ 4}{Kt - B\ 2}$
19.	$\dfrac{Kt - K\ 6}{K\ R - Q\ B\ 1}$	$\dfrac{Q - B\ 2}{R - R\ 2}$
20.	$\dfrac{Q - Kt\ 4}{P - K\ Kt\ 3}$	$\dfrac{R - Q\ 1}{P - R\ 5}$
21.	$\dfrac{Kt - Kt\ 5\ ch.}{K - K\ 1}$	$\dfrac{P - Kt\ 4}{Q - B\ 2}$
22.	$\dfrac{R \times Kt\ ch.\ !}{K - B\ 1\ (b)}$	$\dfrac{Kt - K\ 1}{P - Q\ B\ 4\ !}$
23.	$\dfrac{R - B\ 7\ ch.}{K - Kt\ 1}$	$\dfrac{Q - Q\ 2}{B - K\ 3\ !}$
24.	$\dfrac{R - Kt\ 7\ ch.\ !}{K - R\ 1}$	$\dfrac{P - Q\ 5}{B - Q\ 2}$
25.	$\dfrac{R \times P\ ch.}{\text{Resigns.}\ (c)}$	$\dfrac{R - R\ 1}{P \times P}$
26.		$\dfrac{Q \times P}{R - B\ 1}$
27		$\dfrac{Q - Q\ 2}{Q - B\ 5}$
28		$\dfrac{R - B\ 2}{Kt - Kt\ 4\ \text{and wins.}}$

(a) To prevent Kt — K 5.
(b) If 22. $Q \times R$
    23. R × R ch., and wins.
(c) Sternitz demonstrated mate in ten moves, beginning with
26. R — Kt 7 ch.

Chapter VII.

EVANS' GAMBIT—ANALYSIS.

	(1)	(2)	(3)
1.	$\dfrac{\text{P—K 4}}{\text{P—K 4}}$	—	—
2.	$\dfrac{\text{Kt—K B 3}}{\text{Kt—Q B 3}}$	—	—
3.	$\dfrac{\text{B—B 4}}{\text{B—B 4}}$	—	—

Nos. 2, 3, 4, and 5. Position after White's 8th move, Q—Kt 3

BLACK.

WHITE.

	(1)	(2)	(3)
4.	$\dfrac{\text{P—Q Kt 4}}{\text{B} \times \text{Kt P}}$	—	—
5.	$\dfrac{\text{P—B 3}}{\text{B—R 4}}$	—	—
6.	$\dfrac{\text{0—0}}{\text{P—Q 3}}$	—	—
7.	$\dfrac{\text{P—Q 4}}{\text{P} \times \text{P}}$	—	—
8.	$\dfrac{\text{P} \times \text{P}}{\text{B—Kt 3}}$	$\dfrac{\text{Q—Kt 3}}{\text{Q—K 2}}$	$\overline{\text{Q—B}}$

	(1)	(2)	(3)
9.	B—Kt 2 / Kt—B 3	P—K 5 / P×K P	P×P / B—Kt 3
10.	P—Q 5 / Kt—K 2	R—K 1 / B—Kt 3	P—K 5 / P×P
11.	B×Kt / P×B	B—R 3 / Q—B 3	P×P / Q—Kt 3
12.	Kt—Q 4 / B×Kt	Kt×K P / Kt×Kt	Kt—Kt 5 / Kt—Q 1
13.		B×P ch. / K—Q 1	
14.		Q—Q 5 ch. / B—Q 2	
15.		R×Kt+	

	(4)	(5)	(6)
1.	—	—	P—K 4 / P—K 4
2.	—	—	Kt—K B 3 / Kt—Q B 3
3	—	—	B—B 4 / B—B 4
4.	—	—	P—Q Kt 4 / B×Kt P
5.	—	—	P—B 3 / B—B 4
6.	—	—	P—Q 4 / P×P
7.	—	—	P×P / B—Kt 3
8.	Q—Q 2	B—K 3	0—0 / P—Q 3
9.	P—K 5 / P×K P	B×B / P×B	P—Q 5 / Kt—K 2
10.	Kt×K P / Kt×Kt	P×P / Q—Q 2	B—Kt 2 / Kt—B 3
11.	R—K 1 / P—KB 3	P—Q 5 / Kt—Q 1	B×Kt / P×B

	(4)	**(5)**	**(6)**
12.	$\dfrac{\text{B} \times \text{Kt}}{\text{P} \times \text{B P}}$	$\dfrac{\text{P} \times \text{P}}{\text{Kt} \times \text{P}}$	$\dfrac{\text{Kt} - \text{R 4}}{\text{Kt} - \text{Kt 3}}$
13.	$\dfrac{\text{B} \times \text{R P}+}{}$	$\dfrac{\text{Q} \times \text{Kt P}+}{}$	$\dfrac{\text{Kt} - \text{B 5}}{\text{B} \times \text{Kt}}$
14.			$\dfrac{\text{P} \times \text{B}}{\text{Kt} - \text{K 4}}$
15.			$\dfrac{\text{R} - \text{K 1}}{0-0}$
16.			$\dfrac{\text{B} - \text{Kt 3}}{}$

	(7)	**(8)**	**(9)**
1	—	—	—
2	—	—	—
3.	—	—	—
4	—	—	—
5.	—	—	—
6.	—	—	—
7.	$\dfrac{0-0}{\text{P} - \text{Q 3}}$	—	—
8.	$\dfrac{\times \text{P}}{\text{B} - \text{Kt 3}}$	—	—
9.	$\dfrac{\text{Kt} - \text{B 3}}{\text{B} - \text{Kt 5}}$	—	—
10.	$\dfrac{\text{Q} - \text{R 4}}{\text{B} \times \text{Kt}}$	$\dfrac{}{\text{K} - \text{B 1}}$	$\dfrac{}{\text{B} - \text{Q 2}}$
11.	$\dfrac{\text{P} - \text{Q 5}}{\text{B} - \text{Kt 5}!}$	$\dfrac{\text{P} - \text{Q 5}}{\text{Q Kt} - \text{K 2}}$	$\dfrac{\text{Q} - \text{Kt 3}}{\text{Kt} - \text{R 4}}$
12.	$\dfrac{\text{P} \times \text{Kt}}{\text{P} \times \text{P}}$	$\dfrac{\text{B} - \text{K 2}}{\text{B} \times \text{Kt}}$	$\dfrac{\text{B} \times \text{P ch.}}{\text{K} - \text{B 1}}$
13.	$\dfrac{\text{P} - \text{K 5}}{\text{P} \times \text{P}}$	$\dfrac{\text{B} \times \text{B}}{\text{Kt} - \text{Kt 3}}$	$\dfrac{\text{Q} - \text{Q 5}}{\text{Kt} - \text{K B 3}}$
14.	$\dfrac{\text{Q} \times \text{P ch.}}{\text{B} - \text{Q 2}}$	$\dfrac{\text{K} - \text{R 1}}{\text{Kt} - \text{K 4}}$	$\dfrac{\text{Q} - \text{Kt 5}}{\text{K} \times \text{B}}$

	(7)	(8)	(9)
15.	$\dfrac{\text{Q—Q 5}}{\text{B—K 3}}$	$\dfrac{\text{B—K 2}}{\text{Q—R 5}}$	$\dfrac{\text{P—K 5}}{\text{Kt—Kt 5}}$
16.	$\dfrac{\text{Q×K P}}{\text{B—Q 5}}$	$\dfrac{\text{P—B 4}}{\text{Kt—Kt 5}}$	$\dfrac{\text{Q—B 4 ch.}}{\text{K—Kt 1}}$
17.	$\dfrac{\text{B—Kt 5 ch.}}{\text{K—B 1}}$	$\dfrac{\text{B×Kt}}{\text{Q×B}}$	$\dfrac{\text{Kt—Kt 5}}{\text{Kt—R 3}}$
18.	$\dfrac{\text{B—R 3 ch.}}{\text{Kt— K2}}$	$\underline{\text{P—K 5}}$	$\dfrac{\text{P—K 6}}{\text{B—K 1}}$
19.			$\dfrac{\text{Kt—Q 5}}{\text{Kt—B 3}}$

	(10)	(10a)	(11)
1	—	—	—
2.	—	—	—
3.	—	—	—
4.	—	—	—
5.	—	—	$\overline{\text{B—R 4}}$
6.	$\dfrac{\text{0—0}}{\text{P—Q 3}}$	—	$\dfrac{\text{0—0}}{\text{Kt—B 3}}$
7.	$\dfrac{\text{P—Q 4}}{\text{P×P}}$	—	$\dfrac{\text{Kt—Kt 5}}{\text{0—0}}$
8.	$\dfrac{\text{P×P}}{\text{B—Kt 3}}$	—	$\dfrac{\text{P—B 4}}{\text{P—Q 4}}$
9.	$\dfrac{\text{B—R 3}}{\text{Kt—B 3}}$	$\dfrac{\text{P—Q 5}}{\text{Kt—R 4}}$	$\dfrac{\text{P×Q P}}{\text{Kt×P}}$
10.	$\dfrac{\text{P—K 5}}{\text{P×P}}$	$\dfrac{\text{B—Kt 2}}{\text{Kt—K 2}}$	$\dfrac{\text{P—Q 4}}{\text{P—K R 3}}$
11.	$\overline{\text{Q—Kt 3+}}$	$\dfrac{\text{B—Q 3}}{\text{0—0}}$	$\dfrac{\text{Q—Kt 3}}{\text{P×Kt}}$
12.	—	$\dfrac{\text{Kt—B 3}}{\text{P—Q B 4}}$	$\dfrac{\text{B×Kt}}{\text{K P×B P}}$
13	—	$\dfrac{\text{Kt—K 2}}{\text{P—B 3}}$	$\dfrac{\text{P—Kt 3}}{\text{K —K 2+}}$
14.	—	$\dfrac{\text{K—R 1}}{\text{Kt—Kt 3}}$	

	(12)	(13)	(14)
1.	—	$\dfrac{\text{P—K 4}}{\text{P—K4}}$	—
2.	—	$\dfrac{\text{Kt—K B 3}}{\text{Kt—Q B 3}}$	—
3.	—	$\dfrac{\text{B—B 4}}{\text{B—B 4}}$	—
4	—	$\dfrac{\text{P—QK t 4}}{\text{B}\times\text{Kt P}}$	—
5.	—	$\dfrac{\text{P—B 3}}{\text{B—R 4}}$	—
6.	—	$\dfrac{\text{0—0}}{\text{Kt—B 3}}$	—
7.	$\dfrac{\text{P—Q 4}}{\text{P}\times\text{P}}$	$\dfrac{\text{P—Q 4}}{\text{0—0}}$	—
8.	$\dfrac{\text{P—K 5}}{\text{Kt—K 5}}$	$\dfrac{\text{P}\times\text{P}}{\text{Kt}\times\text{K P}}$	—
9.	$\dfrac{\text{Q—Kt 3}}{\text{0—0}}$	$\dfrac{\text{Q—B 2}}{\text{P—Q 4}}$	—
10.	$\dfrac{\text{B—R 3}}{\text{P—Q 3}}$	$\dfrac{\text{R—Q 1}}{\text{B—K 3}}$	—
11.	$\dfrac{\text{P}\times\text{P (Q 5)}}{\text{B—Kt 3}}$	$\dfrac{\text{B—K 3}}{\text{P—B 4}}$	—
12.	$\dfrac{\text{Q—K 3}}{\text{B—K B 4}}$	$\dfrac{\text{B}\times\text{P}}{\text{B}\times\text{B}}$	—
13.	$\dfrac{\text{B—Q 5+}}{}$	$\dfrac{\text{P—Q B 4}}{\text{Kt—Q Kt 5}}$	—
14.		$\dfrac{\text{Q—Kt 3}}{\text{P—B 5}}$	$\dfrac{\text{Q—Kt 2}}{\text{P—B 5}}$
15.		$\dfrac{\text{B—Q B 1}}{\text{Kt—B 4}}$	$\dfrac{\text{B—Q B 1}}{\text{Kt}\times\text{B P}}$
16.		$\dfrac{\text{Q—R 3}}{\text{Kt—Q 6+}}$	$\dfrac{\text{K}\times\text{Kt}}{\text{B—Kt 3 ch.}}$
17.			$\dfrac{\text{K—K 1}}{\text{B}\times\text{Kt}}$
18.			$\dfrac{\text{R}\times\text{Q}}{\text{R}\times\text{R+}}$

	(15)	(16)	(17)	(18)
1.	—	—	—	—
2.	—	—	—	—
3.	—	—	—	—
4.	—	—	—	—
5.	—	—	—	—
6.	P—Q 4 / P×P	—	—	—
7.	O—O / P×P	—	—	—
8.	Q—Kt 3 / Q—B 3	—	Kt—B 3 / B—R 3	P—Q 3 / Q—Kt 3
9.	P—K 5 / Q—Kt 3	—	P—Q 3 / P—K 5	Q—B 3 / P—K 5
10.	Kt×P / K Kt—K2!	—	P—Q 4 / B—Kt 5	P×P / R—K 1
11.	B—R 3 / R—Q Kt 1!	R—Q 1 / P—Kt 4		B—Q 2 / B—K Kt 5
12.	Q R—Q 1	Kt×P / R—Q Kt 1		Q—B 4 / Q×Kt P
13.		B—Q 3 / Q—Kt 5		

EVANS' GAMBIT—GAMES.

	(1) Staunton / Cochrane	(2) Horwitz / Kieseritsky	(3) Anderssen / Kipping
1.	P—K 4 / P—K 4	P—K 4 / P—K 4	P—K 4 / P—K 4
2.	Kt—K B 3 / Kt—Q B 3	Kt—K B 3 / Kt—Q B 3	Kt—K B 3 / Kt—Q B 3
3.	B—B 4 / B—B 4	B—B 4 / B—B 4	B—B 4 / B—B 4

	(1)	(2)	(3)
4.	$\dfrac{\text{P}-\text{Q Kt 4}}{\text{B}\times\text{Kt P}}$	$\dfrac{\text{P}-\text{Q Kt 4}}{\text{B}\times\text{Kt P}}$	$\dfrac{\text{P}-\text{Q Kt 4}}{\text{B}\times\text{Kt P}}$
5.	$\dfrac{\text{P}-\text{B 3}}{\text{B}-\text{R 4}}$	$\dfrac{\text{P}-\text{B 3}}{\text{B}-\text{Q 3}\ (c)}$	$\dfrac{\text{P}-\text{B 3}}{\text{B}-\text{B 4}}$
6.	$\dfrac{\text{0}-\text{0}}{\text{B}-\text{Kt 3}}$	$\dfrac{\text{0}-\text{0}}{\text{Q}-\text{K 2}}$	$\dfrac{\text{P}-\text{Q 4}}{\text{P}\times\text{P}}$
7.	$\dfrac{\text{P}-\text{Q 4}}{\text{P}\times\text{P}}$	$\dfrac{\text{P}-\text{Q 4}}{\text{Kt}-\text{Q 1}}$	$\dfrac{\text{P}\times\text{P}}{\text{B}-\text{Kt 3}}$
8.	$\dfrac{\text{P}-\text{K 5}\ (a)}{\text{P}-\text{Q 4}}$	$\dfrac{\text{P}\times\text{P}}{\text{B}\times\text{P}}$	$\dfrac{\text{0}-\text{0}}{\text{P}-\text{Q 3}}$
9.	$\dfrac{\text{P}\times\text{P}\ e.p.}{\text{Q}\times\text{P}}$	$\dfrac{\text{Kt}\times\text{B}}{\text{Q}\times\text{Kt}}$	$\dfrac{\text{P}-\text{Q 5}}{\text{Q Kt}-\text{K 2}}$
10.	$\dfrac{\text{R}-\text{K 1 ch.}}{\text{B}-\text{K 3}}$	$\dfrac{\text{Q}-\text{Q 3}}{\text{K Kt}-\text{B 3}}$	$\dfrac{\text{P}-\text{K 5}\ (d)}{\text{P}\times\text{P}}$
11.	$\dfrac{\text{B}-\text{R 3}}{\text{Q}-\text{Q 2}}$	$\dfrac{\text{P}-\text{B 4}}{\text{Q}\times\text{K P}}$	$\dfrac{\text{Kt}\times\text{P}}{\text{Q}-\text{Q 3}}$
12.	$\dfrac{\text{Kt}-\text{Kt 5}}{\text{P}\times\text{P}}$	$\dfrac{\text{Q}\times\text{Q}}{\text{Kt}\times\text{Q}}$	$\dfrac{\text{Q}-\text{K 4}}{\text{B}-\text{Q 5}}$
13.	$\dfrac{\text{Kt}\times\text{B}\ (b)}{\text{Q}\times\text{Q}}$	$\dfrac{\text{R}-\text{K 1}}{\text{P}-\text{K B 4}}$	$\dfrac{\text{B}-\text{B 4}\ (e)}{\text{B}-\text{K B 4}\ (f)}$
14.	$\dfrac{\text{Kt}\times\text{Kt P d. ch.}}{\text{K}-\text{Q 2}}$	$\dfrac{\text{Kt}-\text{Q 2}}{\text{Kt}-\text{K 3}}$	$\dfrac{\text{B}-\text{Q Kt 5 ch.}}{\text{P}-\text{B 3}}$
15.	$\dfrac{\text{R}\times\text{Kt ch.}}{\text{K}-\text{B 1}}$	$\dfrac{\text{Kt}\times\text{Kt}}{\text{P}\times\text{Kt}}$	$\dfrac{\text{P}\times\text{P}}{\text{0}-\text{0}-\text{0}}$
16.	$\dfrac{\text{Kt}\times\text{P}}{\text{B}-\text{Q 5}}$	$\dfrac{\text{R}\times\text{P}}{\text{P}-\text{K Kt 3}}$	$\dfrac{\text{P}\times\text{P ch.}}{\text{K}\times\text{P}}$
17.	$\dfrac{\text{R}\times\text{B}}{\text{Kt}\times\text{R}}$	$\dfrac{\text{B}-\text{R 3}}{\text{K}-\text{B 2}}$	$\dfrac{\text{Kt}-\text{Q 2}}{\text{B}\times\text{Kt}}$
18.	$\dfrac{\text{B}\times\text{P}}{\text{Kt}-\text{R 3}}$	$\dfrac{\text{R}-\text{K B 1}}{\text{P}-\text{Q 3}}$	$\dfrac{\text{B}\times\text{B}}{\text{Q}\times\text{Kt}}$

(*a*) This variation, which was played, for the first time, in the present game, attracted the attention of the celebrated Indian player, Ghuiam Kassim, who took the pains to analyse it very carefully, and forwarded the result to the writer.

(*b*) This is an instructive situation.

(*c*) This is not at all a commendable defence to the Evans' Gambit

(*d*) The usual move is B—Kt 2.

(*e*) Very ingenious. If Black takes the Rook White wins easily by B—Kt 5 ch.

(*f*) B—Q 2 would have been much better.

	(1)	(2)	(3)
19.	$\dfrac{\text{K B}-\text{Kt 3}}{\text{Kt}\times\text{B}}$	$\dfrac{\text{P}-\text{Kt 4}}{\text{K R}-\text{Kt 1}}$	$\dfrac{\text{B}-\text{R 6 ch. } (b)}{\text{K}-\text{R 1}}$
20.	$\dfrac{\text{P}\times\text{Kt}}{\text{K}-\text{Q 2}}$	$\dfrac{\text{Q R}-\text{K 1 } (a)}{\text{Resigns}}$	$\dfrac{\text{Q}-\text{B 3 ch.}}{\text{Kt}-\text{Q 4}}$
21.	$\dfrac{\text{R}-\text{Q 1 ch.}}{\text{K}-\text{B 3}}$		$\dfrac{\text{Q R}-\text{Kt 1}}{\text{Resigns}}$
22.	$\dfrac{\text{Kt}-\text{K 6}}{\text{P}-\text{Q Kt 3}}$		
23.	$\dfrac{\text{R}-\text{Q B 1}}{\text{K}-\text{Kt 2}}$		
24.	$\dfrac{\text{Kt}-\text{Kt 5}}{\text{P}-\text{Q B 4}}$		
25.	$\dfrac{\text{P}-\text{Kt 4}}{\text{K}-\text{B 3}}$		
26.	$\dfrac{\text{Kt (Kt 5)}-\text{B 7}}{\text{Q R}-\text{Q B 1}}$		
27.	$\dfrac{\text{P}\times\text{P}}{\text{P}-\text{Q Kt 4}}$		
28.	Kt—R 6 and wins		

	(4)	(5)	(6)
	$\dfrac{\text{Morphy}}{\text{De Riviere}}$	$\dfrac{\text{Anderssen}}{\text{Lowenthal}}$	$\dfrac{\text{Anderssen}}{\text{Dufresne}}$
1.	$\dfrac{\text{P}-\text{K 4}}{\text{P}-\text{K 4}}$	$\dfrac{\text{P}-\text{K 4}}{\text{P}-\text{K 4}}$	$\dfrac{\text{P}-\text{K 4}}{\text{P}-\text{K 4}}$
2.	$\dfrac{\text{Kt}-\text{K B 3}}{\text{Kt}-\text{Q B 3}}$	$\dfrac{\text{Kt}-\text{K B 3}}{\text{Kt}-\text{Q B 3}}$	$\dfrac{\text{Kt}-\text{K B 3}}{\text{Kt}-\text{Q B 3}}$
3.	$\dfrac{\text{B}-\text{B 4}}{\text{B}-\text{B 4}}$	$\dfrac{\text{B}-\text{B 4}}{\text{B}-\text{B 4}}$	$\dfrac{\text{B}-\text{B 4}}{\text{B}-\text{B 4}}$
4.	$\dfrac{\text{P}-\text{Q Kt 4}}{\text{B}\times\text{Kt P}}$	$\dfrac{\text{P}-\text{Q Kt 4}}{\text{B}\times\text{Kt P}}$	$\dfrac{\text{P}-\text{Q Kt 4}}{\text{B}\times\text{Kt P}}$
5.	$\dfrac{\text{P}-\text{B 3}}{\text{B}-\text{B 4}}$	$\dfrac{\text{P}-\text{B 3}}{\text{B}-\text{R 4}}$	$\dfrac{\text{P}-\text{B 3}}{\text{B}-\text{R 4}}$
6.	$\dfrac{0-0}{\text{P}-\text{Q 3}}$	$\dfrac{\text{P}-\text{Q 4}}{\text{P}\times\text{P}}$	$\dfrac{\text{P}-\text{Q 4}}{\text{P}\times\text{P}}$
7.	$\dfrac{\text{P}-\text{Q 4}}{\text{P}\times\text{P}}$	$\dfrac{0-0}{\text{P}-\text{Q 3}}$	$\dfrac{0-0}{\text{P}-\text{Q 6}}$

(a) A lively well-played game, on the part of Mr. Horwitz.
(b) B—B 6 checking, would have been still better.

	(4)	(5)	(6)
8.	P × P / B—Kt 3	P × P / B—Kt 3	Q—Kt 3 / Q—B 3
9.	Kt—B 3 / Kt—B 3	P—K R 3 / Kt—B 3	P—K 5 / Q—Kt 3
10.	P—K 5 / P—Q 4	Kt—B 3 / 0—0	R—K 1 / K Kt—K 2
11.	P × Kt / P × B	B—K Kt 5 / P—K R 3	B—R 3 / P—Q Kt 4
12.	P × P / R—K Kt 1	B—R 4 / P—Kt 4	Q × Kt P / R—Q Kt 1
13.	R—K1 ch. / B—K 3	Kt × P (a) / P × Kt	Q—R 4 / B—Kt 3
14.	P—Q 5 / Q—B 3	B × P / B × Q P	Q Kt—Q 2 / B—Kt 2
15.	B—Kt 5 / Q × Kt	Kt—Q 5 / B—K 3	Kt—K 4 / Q—B 4
16.	P × B / Q—Q 6	R—Kt 1 / R—Kt 1	B × Q P / Q—R 4
17.	P × P d. ch. / K × P	R—Kt 3 (b) / K—R 2	Kt—B 6 ch. / P × Kt
18.	R—K 7 ch. / K—Kt 3	B × Kt / B × B	P × P / R—K Kt 1 (see diagram)
19.	Q—K 1 / Q—Q 4	Q—R 5 ch. / K—Kt 1	Q R—Q 1 / Q × Kt
20.	R—Q 1 / Kt—Q 5	R—Kt 3 ch. / Resigns.	R × Kt ch. / Kt × R
21.	R × Kt / B × R		Q × P ch. / K × Q
22.	Q—Kt 1 ch. / Resigns.		B—B 5 d. ch. / K—K 1
23.			B—Q 7 ch. / K—B 1
24.			B × Kt mate (c)

(a) Finely conceived, and accurately calculated to the final *coup*.
(b) Well played. The attack is now irresistible.
(c) One of the finest games ever played.

No. 6. Position after Black's 18th move.

BLACK.

WHITE.

(7)	(8)	(9)
De Riviere & Journaud	Anderssen	Anderssen
Morphy	Mayer	Saalbach
1. P—K 4 / P—K 4	P—K 4 / P—K 4	P—K 4 / P—K 4
2. Kt—K B 3 / Kt—Q B 3	Kt—K B 3 / Kt—Q B 3	Kt—K B 3 / Kt—Q B 3
3. B—B 4 / B—B 4	B—B 4 / B—B 4	B—B 4 / B—B 4
4. P—Q Kt 4 / B×Kt P	P—Q Kt 4 / B×Kt P	P—Q Kt 4 / B×Kt P
5. P—B 3 / B—B 4	P—B 3 / B—R 4	P—B 3 / B—R 4
6. 0—0 / P—Q 3	P—Q 4 / P×P	P—Q 4 (a) / P×P

(a) In his observations upon the present game, the editor of the Vienna "Schachzeitung" attributes the merit of this variation to Mr. Anderssen. I believe this to be an error. The move of 6. P—Q 4 was known and practised here some years before Mr. Anderssen introduced it in his ingenious variations on the Evans' Gambit in 1851.

	(7)	(8)	(9)
7.	P—Q 4 / P×P	0—0 / P—Q 6	0—0 / P—Q 3
8.	P×P / B—Kt 3	Kt—Kt 5 / Kt—R 3	P×P / Kt—B 3 (d)
9.	B—Kt 2 / Kt—B 3	P—K 5 / Kt×P	Q—R 4 / B—Q 2
10.	Q Kt—Q 2 / 0—0	R—K 1 / Q—K 2	B—Q Kt 5 / B—Q Kt 3
11.	P—K 5 / P×P	P—K B 4 / B—Kt 3 ch.	P—K 5 (e) / P—Q R 3
12.	P×P / Kt—Q 4	K—R 1 / Kt—K Kt 5	P×Kt / P×B
13.	Kt—K 4 / B—K 3	Kt—K R 3 / P—Q 3	R—K 1 ch. / B—K 3
14.	K Kt—Kt 5 / P—K R 3	B×P / 0—0	P×P / K R—Kt 1
15.	Kt×B / P×Kt	P×Kt / Kt×K P	Q—Q 1 / P—Q 4
16.	Q—Kt 4 (a) / K—R 1	Kt—B 4 / P—Q B 3	B—Kt 5 / Q—Q 2 (f)
17.	Q R—Q 1 / R—B 5	Kt—Q 2 / P—Kt 4	B—B 6 / B—R 4
18.	Q×K P / R×Kt	Q—R 5 / P—K B 4 (b)	Q Kt—Q 2 / B—Q Kt 5
19.	B×Kt / Kt—Q 5	B—B 4 ch. / K—Kt 2	Kt—Kt 5 / B—K 2
20.	R×Kt / R×R	Kt—B 3 / P—K R 3 (c)	Kt×B / P×Kt

(a) Very well played.

(b) P—K B 3 would have been better, but in any case White must win.

(c) Had he taken the K Kt, the game would have proceeded thus:—

20.		P×Kt
21.	B×P	B—B 2
22.	Kt×Kt	P×Kt
23.	R×P	B×R
24.	Q—R 6 ch.	K—R 1
25.	B×B ch. and wins.	

(d) B—Kt 3 is considered to be a better move.

(e) He might also have played B—Kt 5 advantageously, but the move made is probably more attacking.

(f) He should have played Q—Q 3, with the view of afterwards moving K—Q 2. Even then, however, he must have had a very up-hill battle to fight.

	(7)	(8)	(9)
21.	$\frac{\text{B}\times\text{R}}{\text{B}\times\text{B}}$	$\frac{\text{Kt}\times\text{Kt}}{\text{Q}-\text{K B 3 }(b)}$	$\frac{\text{Q}-\text{R 5 ch.}}{\text{K}-\text{Q 1}}$
22.	$\frac{\text{R}-\text{K 1}}{\text{Q}-\text{Kt 4}}$	$\frac{\text{Kt}-\text{Kt 4}}{\text{B P}\times\text{Kt}}$	$\frac{\text{Q}-\text{B 7}}{\text{Resigns}}$
23.	$\frac{\text{B}-\text{B 3}}{\text{R}-\text{K B 1}}$	$\frac{\text{R}-\text{K 7 ch.}}{\text{Resigns}}$	

	(7)		(7) (contd.)		(7) (contd.)
24.	$\frac{\text{Q}-\text{B 4}}{\text{P}-\text{B 4}}$				
25.	$\frac{\text{P}-\text{K 6 }(a)}{\text{Q}-\text{K 2}}$	34.	$\frac{\text{Q}-\text{B 2}}{\text{R}-\text{R 1}}$	43.	$\frac{\text{Q}-\text{Kt 6 ch.}}{\text{B}-\text{Kt 2}}$
26.	$\frac{\text{Q}-\text{R 4}}{\text{Q}-\text{R 5}}$	35.	$\frac{\text{Q}-\text{K 4}}{\text{R}-\text{Q Kt 1}}$	44.	$\frac{\text{Q}-\text{R 7 ch.}}{\text{K}-\text{B 1}}$
27.	$\frac{\text{Q}-\text{B 2}}{\text{Q}-\text{K 2}}$	36.	$\frac{\text{Q}-\text{Q 5}}{\text{P}-\text{Kt 6}}$	45.	$\frac{\text{P}-\text{R 4}}{\text{R}-\text{Q 8 ch.}}$
28.	$\frac{\text{Q}-\text{Kt 6}}{\text{R}-\text{B 3}}$	37.	$\frac{\text{P}\times\text{P}}{\text{P}\times\text{P}}$	46.	$\frac{\text{K}-\text{Kt 2}}{\text{B}-\text{B 3}}$
29.	$\frac{\text{Q}-\text{K 4}}{\text{R}-\text{B 1}}$	38.	$\frac{\text{B}-\text{Kt 6}}{\text{P}-\text{Kt 7}}$	47.	$\frac{\text{P}\times\text{P}}{\text{B}-\text{Q 5}}$
30.	$\frac{\text{P}-\text{Kt 3}}{\text{P}-\text{Q Kt 4}}$	39.	$\frac{\text{B}-\text{Kt 1}}{\text{R}-\text{Q 1}}$	48.	$\frac{\text{Q}-\text{B 5 ch.}}{\text{K}-\text{Kt 1}}$
31.	$\frac{\text{R}-\text{K 2}}{\text{P}-\text{Kt 5}}$	40.	$\frac{\text{Q}-\text{B 5}}{\text{P}-\text{Kt 4}}$	49.	$\frac{\text{Q}-\text{Kt 6 ch.}}{\text{K}-\text{R 1}}$
32.	$\frac{\text{B}-\text{R 5}}{\text{P}-\text{R 4}}$	41.	$\frac{\text{Q}-\text{Kt 6}}{\text{B}-\text{B 3}}$	50.	$\frac{\text{R}-\text{K 4}}{\text{Q}-\text{Q Kt 2}}$
33.	$\frac{\text{B}-\text{B 7}}{\text{P}-\text{Q R 5}}$	42.	$\frac{\text{Q}\times\text{P ch.}}{\text{K}-\text{Kt 1}}$	51.	$\frac{\text{P}-\text{K 7}}{\text{Resigns.}}$

	(10)	(11)	(12)
	Prince Ouroussoff	Fritz	Mackenzie
	Jaenisch	Zukertort	Delmar
1.	$\frac{\text{P}-\text{K 4}}{\text{P}-\text{K 4}}$	$\frac{\text{P}-\text{K 4}}{\text{P}-\text{K 4}}$	$\frac{\text{P}-\text{K 4}}{\text{P}-\text{K 4}}$
2.	$\frac{\text{Kt}-\text{K B 3}}{\text{Kt}-\text{Q B 3}}$	$\frac{\text{Kt}-\text{K B 3}}{\text{Kt}-\text{Q B 3}}$	$\frac{\text{Kt}-\text{K B 3}}{\text{Kt}-\text{Q B 3}}$

(a) Cleverly conceived. If Black venture to take the Bishop he must infallibly lose.

(b) He could have been mated in three moves if he had taken either Knight.

	(10)	(11)	(12)
3.	B—B 4 / B—B 4	B—B 4 / B—B 4	B—B 4 / B—B 4
4.	P—Q Kt 4 / P—Q 4 (a)	P—Q Kt 4 / B×Kt P	P—Q Kt 4 / B×Kt P
5.	B×P / Kt×P	P—B 3 / B—R 4	P—B 3 / B—R 4
6.	B—Kt 3 / Q—K 2	P—Q 4 / P×P	P—Q 4 / P×P
7.	P—K R 3 / B—Q 2	0—0 / P×P	0—0 / P×P
8.	B—Kt 2 / Kt—Q B 3	Q—Kt 3 / Q—B 3	Q—Kt 3 / Q—B 3
9.	P—Q 3 / 0—0—0	P—K 5 / Q—Kt 3	P—K 5 / Q—Kt 3
10.	B—Q 5 / P—B 4	Kt×P / K Kt—K 2	Kt×P / K Kt—K 2
11.	B×Kt / B×B	Kt—K 2 / P—Kt 4	B—R 3 / 0—0
12.	Kt×P / B×K P	B—Q 3 / Q—K 3	Kt—Q 5 / Kt×Kt
13.	0—0 / Q—Kt 4	Q—Kt 2 / Kt—Kt 3	B×Kt / P—Q 3
14.	Kt—K B 3 / B×Kt	Kt—B 4 / Kt×Kt	P×P / P×P
15.	Q×B / Kt—B 3	B×Kt / P—Q R 3	Q R—Q 1 / B—B 2
16.	Kt—B 3 / P—K R 4	Kt—Kt 5 / Q×K 2	K R—K 1 / Kt—Q 1
17.	Kt—R 4 (b) / B—Q 3	P—K 6 / Q P×P	R—K 7 / Kt—K 3
18.	Q R—Kt 1 / P—B 3	Q×K Kt P / Q—B 1	B×Kt / B×B
19.	B—B 1 / P—B 5	Q—B 6 / B—Kt 3	Q×Kt P / B—Kt 3
20.	B—Q 2 / Kt—Kt 5	B—K 4 / B—Q 2	B×Q P / B—R 6

(a) I should like to see this defence fairly tested in a long series of games between these two accomplished players.

(b) The attack on the one side, and the counter-attack on the other, now render the game very animated and amusing.

	(10)	(11)	(12)
21.	P—Q 4 (a) / Kt—R 3	K R—Q 1 / B—B 4	Kt—K 5 / B×P ch.
22.	Kt—B 3 / Q—K B 4	Q R—B 1 / B—K 2	K×B / Q—B 7 ch.
23.	Kt—K 4 / P—K Kt 4	R×B / K×R	K—Kt 3 / Q×R
24.	R—Kt 3 / B—Kt 1	B×Kt ch. / K—B 1	R×B P / B—K B 4
25.	Q—Q 3 / P—Kt 5	Q—Q 4 / Resigns	R×Kt P ch. / K—R 1
26.	K R—Q Kt 1 / R—R 2		Kt—Kt 6 ch. / B×Kt
27.	R×P (b) / R×R		R×R P ch. / B×R
28.	Q—R 6 / Q—K B 2		B—K 5 ch. / K—Kt 1
29.	Kt—B 5 / Q R—Q 2		Q mates
30.	Kt×K R / R×Kt		
31.	Q×P ch. / R—B 2		
32.	Q×Kt / R—Kt 2		
33.	Q—R 8 ch. / K—B 2		
34.	B×P ch. / Q×B		
35.	Q—R 7 ch / Resigns		

(13)

Tchigorin / Lasker

1.	P—K 4 / P—K 4	2.	Kt—K B 3 / Kt—Q B 3	3.	B—B 4 / B—B 4

(a) Well played. Had he taken the Kt, it is needless to say he must have lost the battle.

(b) Well played again. From this moment White has the game in his hands.

(13) (contd.)

4. $\dfrac{\text{P}-\text{Q Kt 4}}{\text{B}\times\text{Kt P}}$.

5. $\dfrac{\text{P}-\text{B 3}}{\text{B}-\text{R 4}}$

6. $\dfrac{0-0}{\text{P}-\text{Q 3}}$

7. $\dfrac{\text{P}-\text{Q 4}}{\text{B}-\text{Kt 3 ! }(a)}$

8. $\dfrac{\text{P}-\text{Q R 4}}{\text{Kt}-\text{B 3}}$

9. $\dfrac{\text{B}-\text{Q Kt 5}}{\text{P}-\text{Q R 3}}$

10. $\dfrac{\text{B}\times\text{Kt ch.}}{\text{P}\times\text{B}}$

11. $\dfrac{\text{P}-\text{R 5}}{\text{B}-\text{R 2}}$

12. $\dfrac{\text{P}\times\text{P}}{\text{Kt}\times\text{P}}$

13. $\dfrac{\text{Q}-\text{K 2 ?}}{\text{P}-\text{Q 4}}$

14. $\dfrac{\text{Kt}-\text{Q 4 ?}}{\text{Kt}\times\text{Q B P}}$

15. $\dfrac{\text{Kt}\times\text{Kt}}{\text{B}\times\text{Kt}}$

16. $\dfrac{\text{Q}-\text{Q 3}}{\text{P}-\text{Q B 4}}$

17. $\dfrac{\text{Q}-\text{Kt 3}}{\text{B}-\text{K 3}}$

18. $\dfrac{\text{B}-\text{Kt 5}}{\text{Q}-\text{Q 2}}$

19. $\dfrac{\text{Q Q}-\text{B 1}}{\text{P}-\text{K B 3}}$

20. $\dfrac{\text{P}\times\text{P}}{\text{P}\times\text{P}}$

21. $\dfrac{\text{B}-\text{B 4}}{\text{R}-\text{K Kt 1}}$.

22. $\dfrac{\text{Q}-\text{B 3}}{0-0-0}$

23. $\dfrac{\text{K R}-\text{K 1}}{\text{P}-\text{B 5}}$

24. $\dfrac{\text{Q}-\text{K 2}}{\text{B}-\text{K B 4}}$

25. $\dfrac{\text{Q}-\text{R 2}}{\text{R}\times\text{P ch.}}$

26. $\dfrac{\text{K}-\text{R 1 }(b)}{\text{R}\times\text{B P}}$

27. $\dfrac{\text{Resigns}}{}$

Chapter VIII.

EVANS' GAMBIT DECLINED—ANALYSIS.

	(1)	(2)	(3)
1.	$\dfrac{\text{P}-\text{K 4}}{\text{P}-\text{K 4}}$	—	—
2.	$\dfrac{\text{Kt}-\text{K B 3}}{\text{Kt}-\text{Q B 3}}$	—	—
3.	$\dfrac{\text{B}-\text{B 4}}{\text{B}-\text{B 4}}$	—	—
4	$\dfrac{\text{P Q Kt 4}}{\text{B}-\text{Kt 3}}$	—	$\dfrac{}{\text{P}-\text{Q 4}}$
5.	$\dfrac{\text{P}-\text{Q R 4 !}}{\text{P}-\text{Q R 4}}$	$\dfrac{\text{P}-\text{Kt 5}}{\text{Kt}-\text{R 4}}$	$\dfrac{\text{P}\times\text{P}}{\text{Kt}\times\text{Kt P}}$
6.	$\dfrac{\text{P}-\text{Kt 5}}{\text{Kt}-\text{Q 5}}$	$\dfrac{\text{Kt}\times\text{P}}{\text{Q}-\text{B 3 !}}$	$\dfrac{\text{Kt}\times\text{P}}{\text{Q Kt}\times\text{P}}$

(a) Lasker's defence.
(b) If 26. K×R   B—R 6 ch.
     27. K—R 1   Q—Kt 5, and wins.

M

	(1)	(2)	(3)
7.	Kt×P / Q—B 3	B×P ch. / K—B 1	P—Q 4 / B—Kt 5 ch.
8.	Kt—K B 3 / Kt—K 3	P—Q 4 / P—Q 3	B—Q 2 / B×B ch.
9.	P—K 5 / Q—Kt 3	B—R 3 / K Kt—K 2	Kt×B = / B—K 3
10.	0—0 / —	P—K B 4 / P×Kt	
11.		P×P / Q×B P	
12.		R—K B 1 / Q×P ch.	
13.		Q—K 2 / Q×Q ch.	
14.		K×Q / P—K Kt 3	
15.		B—Kt 3 d. ch.	

	(4)	(5)	(6)
1.	—	—	—
2.	—	—	—
3.	—	—	—
4.	—	B—Kt 3	—
5.	—	P—Kt 5 / Kt—R 4	—
6.	—	Kt×P / Kt—K R 3	—
7.	B—Kt 5 ch. / P—B 3	P—Q 4 / P—Q 3	—
8.	Kt×B P / Q—Kt 3	B×Kt / P×Kt	P×B
9.	Q—K 2 ch. / K—B 1	B×Kt P / R—K Kt 1	B×P ch. / K—K 2

	(4)	(5)	(6)
10.	$\dfrac{\text{Kt}-\text{Kt 4}}{\text{B}-\text{K 3}}$	$\dfrac{\text{B} \times \text{P ch}}{\text{K} \times \text{B}}$	$\dfrac{\text{B}-\text{R 5}}{\text{P} \times \text{Kt}}$
11.	$\dfrac{\text{Kt} \times \text{Kt}}{\text{B} \times \text{Kt}}$	$\dfrac{\text{B} \times \text{P}}{\text{B}-\text{K Kt 5}}$	$\dfrac{\text{P}-\text{Q5}}{\text{Q}-\text{K Kt 1}}$
12.	$\dfrac{0-0}{\text{Q}-\text{Kt 3}}$	$\dfrac{\text{Q}-\text{Q 3}}{}$	$\dfrac{\text{B}-\text{B 3}}{\text{Kt}-\text{B 5}}$

Nos. 5 to 9.   Position after Black's 4th move.

BLACK.

WHITE.

	(7)	(8)	(9)
1.	—	—	—
2.	—	—	—
3.	—	—	—
4.	—	—	—
5.	—	$\dfrac{\text{P}-\text{Q R 4}}{\text{P}-\text{Q R 3}}$	$\dfrac{0-0}{\text{P}-\text{Q 3}}$
6.	$\dfrac{}{\text{Q}-\text{Kt 4}}$	$\dfrac{\text{P}-\text{B 3}}{\text{Kt}-\text{B 3}}$	$\dfrac{\text{P}-\text{Q R 4}}{\text{P}-\text{Q R 3}}$

	(7)	(8)	(9)
7.	B×P ch. / K—B 1	Q—K 2 / P—Q 3	P—R 5 / B—R 2
8.	B×Kt / Q×Kt	P—Q 3 / B—K 3	P—Kt 5 / P×P
9.	B—Q 5 / P—B 3	Kt—R 3 / Kt—K 2	B×Kt P / K Kt—K2
10.	Q—B 3 ch. / K—K 1	0—0 / P—B 3	P—Q 4 / P×P
11.	Q—B 7 ch. / K—Q 1	—	—

EVANS' GAMBIT DECLINED—GAMES.

	(1) Schiffers / Pillsbury	(2) Pollock / Mason	(3) Charousek / Lehner
1.	P—K 4 / P—K 4	P—K 4 / P—K 4	P—K 4 / P—K 4
2.	Kt—K B 3 / Kt—Q B 3	Kt—K B 3 / Kt—Q B 3	Kt—K B 3 / Kt—Q B 3
3.	B—B 4 / B—B 4	B—B 4 / B—B 4	B—B 4 / B—B 4
4.	P—Q Kt 4 / P—Q 4	P—Q Kt 4 / B—Kt 3	P—Q Kt 4 / B—Kt 3
5.	P×P / Kt×P	P—B 3 / Kt—B 3	P—Q R 4 / P—Q R 4
6.	0—0 / Kt—K B 3	P—Q 3 / P—Q 3	P—Kt 5 / Kt—Q 5
7.	Kt×P / Q Kt×Q P	B—K Kt 5 / P—K R 3	Kt×Kt ch / Q×Kt
8.	P—Q 4 / B—Q 3	B—R 4 / P—Kt 4	Q—K 2 / 0—0
9.	B—K Kt 5 / P—B 3	B—K Kt 3 / B—K 2	P—Q 3 / P—Q 3
10.	Kt—Q 2 / 0—0	Q—Kt 3 / 0—0	P—R 3 / Kt—R 3
11.	Q—B 3 / P—K R 3	Q Kt—Q 2 / Kt—Kt 3	Kt—R 3 / Kt—B 3

	(1)	(2)	(3)
12.	B—R 4 / B—K 3	P—K R 4 / P—Kt 5	B—Kt 3 / B—Kt 5
13.	Q R—Kt 1 ! / R—Kt 1	P—R 5 ! / Kt—B 5 (c)	Q—Kt 3 / P—Kt 4
14.	Kt—K 4 / B—K 2	B×Kt / P×B	Kt—B 4 / B—R 2
15.	Kt×Kt ch. / B×Kt	Kt—R 4 / P—B 3	Kt—K 3 / B—Q 2
16.	B—K Kt 3 ! / Q—B 1	Q—B 2 / P—Q 4	R—Kt 1 / Kt—R 4
17.	B—Q 3 / Kt—K 2 (a)	B—Kt 3 / P—R 4	Q—B 3 / Kt—B 5
18.	P—B 3 / R—R 1	P×P / B×P	Kt—Q 5 / Q—Q 1
19.	Kt—B 4 ! / B—Q 4	0—0—0 / B—K 3	P—Kt 6 / B×P
20.	Q—K 2 / P—Q Kt 4	P—Q 4 / R—B 1	Kt×B / P—Kt 5
21.	Kt—Q 6 / Q—K 3	P—K 5 / Kt—R 2	Q—Q 1 / P×Kt
22.	Q—Q 2 ! / P—Q R 4 (b)	Kt—B 5 (d) / Q—Kt 4 and wins.	B—R 3 / Q—B 3
23.	K R—K 1 / Q—Q 2		B—B 4 and wins.
24.	P—Q R 4 / P—Kt 5		
25.	P×P / P×P		
26.	R×P / R—R 2		
27.	K R—Kt 1 / B—Kt 4		

(1) (contd.)

28.	Q—K 2 / P—K B 4	
29.	B—K 5 / P—B 5	
30.	P—B 3 / Q—K 3	
31.	R—Kt 8 and wins.	

(a) If 17.   Kt—B 6
       18. Q R—K 1   B×P
       19. B—B 5 !
(b) If 22.   B×R P
       23. K R—K 1, and B—K 4 wins B.
(c) If 13.   P×Kt
       14. P×Kt !
(d) 22. Kt—Kt 6 would have prolonged the game.

CHAPTER IX.

THE TWO KNIGHTS' DEFENCE— ANALYSIS

	(1)	(2)	(3)
1.	P—K 4 / P—K 4	—	—
2.	Kt—K B 3 / Kt—Q B 3	—	—
3.	B—B 4 / Kt—B 3	—	—
4.	Kt—Kt 5 / P—Q 4	—	—
5.	P×P / K Kt×P	—	—
6.	Kt×B P / K×Kt	—	—
7.	Q—B 3 ch. / K—K 3	—	—
8.	Kt—B 3 / Q Kt—K 2	Kt—Kt 5	Kt—Q Kt 5
9.	P—Q 4 / P—B 3	Q—K 4 / P—Q Kt 4 !	Q—K 4 / P—B 3
10.	B—K Kt 5 / P—K R 3	B—Kt 3 / P—B 4	P—Q 4 / Q—Q 3
11.	B×Kt (K 2) / B×B	P—Q 3 / B—Kt 2	P—B 4 / P—Q Kt 4
12.	O—O—O / R—B 1	P—K B 4 / P—B 5	B P×P / Q—Q 2
13.	Q—K 4 / Q—Q 3	P×B P / Kt×Kt	O—O / P×B
14.	K R—K 1 / R—B 4	Q×P ch. / K—Q 2	W mates in 7.
15.	P—K Kt 4 / B—Kt 4 ch.	P×Kt / B×P	
16.	K—Kt 1 / R—B 5	Q—Q 4 ch. / K—B 2	

	(1)	(2)	(3)
17.	$\dfrac{\text{Q}-\text{R }7}{\text{B}-\text{B }3}$		
18.	$\dfrac{\text{P}\times\text{P}}{\text{B}\times\text{P}}$		
19.	$\dfrac{\text{B}\times\text{Kt ch.}}{\text{P}\times\text{B}}$		
20.	$\underline{\text{Kt}\times\text{P and wins.}}$		

	(4)	(5)	(6)
1.	—	—	—
2.	—	—	—
3.	—	—	—
4.	—	—	—
5.	$\overline{\text{Kt}-\text{Q R }4}$	—	—
6.	$\dfrac{\text{B}-\text{Kt }5\text{ ch.}}{\text{P}-\text{B }3}$	—	—
7.	$\dfrac{\text{P}\times\text{P}}{\text{P}\times\text{P}}$	—	—
8.	$\dfrac{\text{Q}-\text{B }3}{\text{Q}-\text{Kt }3}$	$\dfrac{\text{B}-\text{K }2}{\text{P}-\text{K R }3}$	—
9.	$\dfrac{\text{B}-\text{R }4}{\text{B}-\text{K Kt }5}$	$\dfrac{\text{Kt}-\text{K B }3}{\text{P}-\text{K }5}$	—
10.	$\dfrac{\text{Q}-\text{K Kt }3}{\text{P}-\text{K R }3}$	$\dfrac{\text{Kt}-\text{K }5}{\text{B}-\text{Q }3}$	$\text{Q}-\text{Q }5$
11.	$\dfrac{\text{Kt}-\text{K B }3}{0-0-0}$	$\dfrac{\text{P}-\text{K B }4}{\text{Q}-\text{B }2}$	$\dfrac{\text{P}-\text{K B }4}{\text{B}-\text{Q B }4}$
12.		$\dfrac{\text{P}-\text{Q }4}{\text{P}-\text{K Kt }4}$	$\dfrac{\text{R}-\text{B }1}{\text{Q}-\text{Q }1}$
13.		$\dfrac{0-0}{\text{Kt}-\text{Q }4}$	$\dfrac{\text{P}-\text{B }3}{\text{Kt}-\text{Q }4}$
14.		$\dfrac{\text{B}-\text{R }5}{\text{R}-\text{R }2}$	$\dfrac{\text{P}-\text{Q }4}{\text{Q}-\text{R }5\text{ ch.}}$
15.		$\underline{\text{Q}-\text{K }1}$	

	(7)	(8)	(9)
1.	—	—	—
2.	—	—	—
3.	—	—	—
4.	—	$\dfrac{\text{Kt} \times \text{P}}{}$	—
5.	—	$\dfrac{\text{B} \times \text{P ch.}}{\text{K} - \text{K2}}$	$\dfrac{\text{Kt} \times \text{B P}}{\text{Q} - \text{R 5}}$
6.	$\dfrac{\text{P} - \text{Q 3}}{\text{B} - \text{Q B 4}}$	$\dfrac{\text{P} - \text{Q 3}}{\text{Kt} - \text{K B 3}}$	$\dfrac{\text{0} - \text{0}}{\text{B} - \text{B 4}}$
7.	$\dfrac{\text{0} - \text{0}}{\text{0} - \text{0}}$	$\dfrac{\text{B} - \text{Kt 3}}{\text{P} - \text{Q 4}}$	$\dfrac{\text{P} - \text{Q 4}}{\text{B} \times \text{P}}$
8.	$\dfrac{\text{P} - \text{Q B 3}}{\text{P} - \text{K R 3}}$	$\dfrac{\text{P} - \text{K B 4}}{\text{B} - \text{Kt 5}}$	$\dfrac{\text{Kt} \times \text{R}}{\text{Kt} \times \text{B P}}$
9.	$\dfrac{\text{P} - \text{Q Kt 4}}{\text{P} \times \text{Kt}}$	$\dfrac{\text{Q} - \text{Q 2}}{\text{P} - \text{K R 3}}$	$\dfrac{\text{B} - \text{B 7 ch.}}{\text{K} - \text{B 1}}$
10.	$\dfrac{\text{P} \times \text{B}}{\text{Kt} \times \text{Q P}}$	$\dfrac{\text{P} \times \text{P}}{\text{Kt} \times \text{P}}$	$\dfrac{\text{R} \times \text{Kt}}{\text{Q} \times \text{R ch.}}$
11.	$\dfrac{\text{B} \times \text{Kt P}}{\text{P} \times \text{K B 3}}$	$\dfrac{\text{Q} - \text{K 3}}{\text{P} \times \text{Kt}}$	$\dfrac{\text{K} - \text{R 1}}{\text{P} - \text{Q 3}}$
12.	$\dfrac{\text{B} \times \text{Kt ch.}}{\text{Q} \times \text{B}}$	$\dfrac{\text{Q} \times \text{Kt ch.}}{\text{K} - \text{B 2}}$	$\dfrac{\text{B} - \text{Q 5}}{\text{B} - \text{K Kt 5}}$
13.	$\dfrac{\text{B} - \text{K 3} =}{\text{B} - \text{K B 4}}$	$\dfrac{\text{0} - \text{0}}{\text{B} - \text{Q 3}}$	$\dfrac{\text{B} - \text{B 3}}{\text{B} \times \text{B}}$
14.		$\dfrac{\text{Q} \times \text{P ch.} +}{}$	$\dfrac{\text{P} \times \text{B}}{\text{K} - \text{Kt 1} +}$

THE TWO KNIGHTS' DEFENCE—GAMES.

	(1)	(2)	(3)
	Von der Laza	Staunton	Wayte
	Mr. M.	Von der Laza	Williams
1.	$\dfrac{\text{P} - \text{K 4}}{\text{P} - \text{K 4}}$	$\dfrac{\text{P} - \text{K 4}}{\text{P} - \text{K 4}}$	$\dfrac{\text{P} - \text{K 4}}{\text{P} - \text{K 4}}$
2	$\dfrac{\text{K Kt} - \text{B 3}}{\text{Kt} - \text{Q B 3}}$	$\dfrac{\text{Kt} - \text{K B 3}}{\text{Kt} - \text{Q B 3}}$	$\dfrac{\text{Kt} - \text{K B 3}}{\text{Kt} - \text{Q B 3}}$

	(1)	(2)	(3)
3.	B—B 4 / Kt—B 3	B—B 4 / Kt—B 3	B—B 4 / Kt—B 3
4.	Kt—Kt 5 / P—Q 4	Kt—B 3 (a) / B—Kt 5	Kt—Kt 5 / P—Q 4
5.	P×P / Kt×P	0—0 / 0—0	P×P / Kt—Q R 4
6.	Kt×B P / K×Kt	P—Q 3 / P—Q 3	B—Kt 5 ch. / P—B 3
7.	Q—B 3 ch. / K—K 3	B—K Kt 5 / B×Kt	P×P / P×P
8.	Kt—B 3 / Kt (B 3)—K 2	P×B / B—K 3	Q—B 3 / Q—Kt 3
9.	P—Q 4 / P—Q Kt 4	B—Kt 3 / P—Q R 4	B—R 4 / B—K Kt 5
10.	Kt×P / P—B 3	P—Q 4 / P—K R 3	Q—Kt 3 / B—Q B 4
11.	Kt—B 3 / Q—Kt 3	B—R 4 / B×B	0—0 / 0—0
12.	P×P / Q B—Kt 2	P×B / Q—K 2	B—Kt 3 / P—K R 3
13.	Kt—K 4 / Q—Kt 5 ch.	Kt—K1 / P—K Kt 4	Kt—K B 3 / Kt×B
14.	B—Q 2 / Q×B (B 4)	B—Kt 3 / Q R—Q 1	R P×Kt / P—K 5
15.	Q—Kt 4 ch. / K×P	P—R 4 / P—Q 4	Kt—K 5 / B—K 7
16.	P—B 4 ch. / K—Q 5	P×Kt P / R P×P	R—K 1 / Kt—R 4
17.	P—B 3 ch. / Kt×B P	Q—B 3 / P—Q 5 (b)	Kt—Q 7 / Q—Q 1
18.	B×Kt ch. / K×Kt	P—Q B 4 / K—Kt 2 (c)	Q—K 5 / Q×Kt

(a) The move Kt—K Kt 5 was formerly recommended for the first player at this point; that mode of attack, however, is now thought by many players hazardous and superficial.

(b) Well played, as it enables Black to bring his Q Kt into speedy action.

(c) The command Black has of the K R file is all important to him at this juncture.

	(1)	(2)	(3)
19.	$\dfrac{\text{P—B 5 d. ch.}}{\text{K—Q 4}}$	$\dfrac{\text{Q—B 5}}{\text{Kt—R 4}}$	$\dfrac{\text{R} \times \text{B}}{\text{Q—Kt 5}}$
20.	$\dfrac{\text{0—0—0 ch.}}{\text{K—B 4}}$	$\dfrac{\text{Kt—B 3}}{\text{P—B 3}}$	$\dfrac{\text{R} \times \text{K P}}{}$ (g)
21.	$\dfrac{\text{P—Kt 4 ch.}}{\text{K—Kt 4}}$	$\dfrac{\text{Q—Kt 4}}{\text{R—K R I}}$	
22.	$\dfrac{\text{P—R 4 ch.}}{\text{K} \times \text{P}}$	$\dfrac{\text{Kt—R 4}}{\text{K—B 2}}$ (a)	
23.	$\dfrac{\text{Q} \times \text{Q}}{\text{Kt—Q 4}}$	$\dfrac{\text{Kt—B 5}}{\text{Q—K 3}}$	
24.	K—Kt 2 and wins.	$\dfrac{\text{B—R 2}}{\text{Q R—K Kt I}}$	

(2) (contd.)

25.	$\dfrac{\text{Q—Q 1}}{\text{Kt—B 5}}$ (b)		30.	$\dfrac{\text{Q—Q 2}}{\text{Q—Kt 3}}$		35.	$\dfrac{\text{R} \times \text{R}}{\text{R} \times \text{R}}$	
26.	$\dfrac{\text{P—Kt 3}}{\text{Kt—R 6 ch.}}$		31.	$\dfrac{\text{Q—B 2}}{\text{Kt—Kt 3}}$ (c)		36.	$\dfrac{\text{B—Q 2}}{\text{Kt—K B 5}}$	
27.	$\dfrac{\text{K—Kt 2}}{\text{Kt—K 2}}$		32.	$\dfrac{\text{K—B 3}}{\text{Kt (R 6)—B 5}}$ (d)		37.	$\dfrac{\text{B} \times \text{Kt}}{\text{Kt P} \times \text{B}}$	
28.	$\dfrac{\text{P—K Kt 4}}{\text{R—R 2}}$		33.	$\dfrac{\text{P—B 5}}{\text{Q—R 3}}$ (e)		38.	$\dfrac{\text{K—Kt 2}}{\text{R—R 2}}$	
29.	$\dfrac{\text{R—R 1}}{\text{R—K R I}}$		34.	$\dfrac{\text{B} \times \text{Kt}}{\text{R} \times \text{R}}$		39.	$\dfrac{\text{P—Kt 4}}{\text{P} \times \text{P}}$ (f)	

(a) This also is well played.

(b) To give freedom to his Knight, which at present has no escape.

(c) The oncoming of this second Knight renders White's game hopeless.

(d) He had two or three other modes of play, but none which could long ward off the impending blow.

(e) This attempt to divert the attack might have succeeded against a less wary and experienced opponent, but Mr. Heydebrand knows too well the value of a good position, ever to give it up while he can possibly maintain his ground.

(f) By this move White gains a short-lived attack, but he has not force enough to sustain it long.

(g) In this situation, which is remarkably interesting, Black by his next two moves acquired so decisive an advantage that his opponent resigned the game. The discovery of these moves we leave as an instructive exercise, to the ingenuity of our young readers.

(2) (contd.)

40. $\dfrac{\text{Q—Kt 3 ch.}}{\text{Q—K 3}}$ 42. $\dfrac{\text{Q} \times \text{Kt P}}{\text{K—Kt 4}}$ 44. $\dfrac{\text{P—Q R 6}}{\text{P—B 6 ch.}}$

41. $\dfrac{\text{Q} \times \text{P}}{\text{K—Kt 3}}$ 43. $\dfrac{\text{P—R 5 } (a)}{\text{K} \times \text{P}}$ 45. $\dfrac{\text{K—Kt 1}}{\text{Q—R 7 and wins.}}$

(4)	(5)
Taubenhaus	Tchigorin
Schallopp	Charousek
1. $\dfrac{\text{P—K 4}}{\text{P—K 4}}$	$\dfrac{\text{P—K 4}}{\text{P—K 4}}$
2. $\dfrac{\text{Kt—K B 3}}{\text{Kt—Q B 3}}$	$\dfrac{\text{Kt—K B 3}}{\text{Kt—Q B 3}}$
3. $\dfrac{\text{B—B 4}}{\text{Kt—B 3}}$	$\dfrac{\text{B—B 4}}{\text{Kt—B 3}}$
4. $\dfrac{\text{P—Q 4 } (b)}{\text{P} \times \text{P}}$	$\dfrac{\text{P—Q 3 ! } (c)}{\text{B—B 4}}$
5. $\dfrac{\text{Kt—Kt 5}}{\text{Kt—K 4}}$	$\dfrac{\text{P—B 3}}{\text{P—Q 3}}$
6. $\dfrac{\text{B—Kt 3}}{\text{P—K R 3}}$	$\dfrac{\text{Q Kt—Q 2}}{\text{0—0}}$
7. $\dfrac{\text{P—K B 4}}{\text{P} \times \text{Kt}}$	$\dfrac{\text{Kt—B 1}}{\text{P—Q 4}}$
8. $\dfrac{\text{P} \times \text{Kt}}{\text{Kt} \times \text{P}}$	$\dfrac{\text{P} \times \text{P}}{\text{Kt} \times \text{P}}$
9. $\dfrac{\text{0—0}}{\text{P—Q 4}}$	$\dfrac{\text{B—K 3}}{\text{Kt} \times \text{B}}$
10. $\dfrac{\text{P} \times \text{P } e.p.}{\text{Q} \times \text{P}}$	$\dfrac{\text{Kt} \times \text{Kt}}{\text{Q—Q 3}}$

(a) Better, perhaps, to have played K—B 3, in which case the following variation was a probable one :—

43. K—B 3	R—R 6 ch.
44. K—Kt 2	K × P
45. P—B 3 ch.	R × P
46. Kt—R 6 ch.	K—Kt 4
47. K × R, &c.	

Yet even here Black has the advantage.

(b) Turning the game into a Scotch Gambit.

(c) Leading to a quieter, and perhaps sounder, game than 4. Kt—Kt 5.

	(4)	(5)
11.	$\dfrac{\text{B} \times \text{P ch.}}{\text{K} - \text{Q 1}}$	$\dfrac{\text{Q} - \text{K 2}}{\text{B} - \text{K 3}}$
12.	$\dfrac{\text{P} - \text{K Kt 3}}{\text{B} - \text{Q 2}}$	$\dfrac{\text{Kt} - \text{Kt 5}}{\text{B} \times \text{B}}$
13.	$\dfrac{\text{Q} - \text{Q 3}}{\text{B} - \text{B 3}}$	$\dfrac{\text{Kt} \times \text{B}}{\text{Q} - \text{Kt 3}}$
14.	$\dfrac{\text{Kt} - \text{Q 2}}{\text{Kt} \times \text{Kt}}$	$\dfrac{\text{Kt} - \text{K 4}}{\text{B} - \text{K 2}}$
15	$\dfrac{\text{B} \times \text{Kt}}{\text{B} - \text{K 2}}$	$\dfrac{\text{P} - \text{K Kt 4}}{\text{K R} - \text{Q 1}}$
16.	$\dfrac{\text{Q R} - \text{K 1}}{\text{R} \times \text{P (a)}}$	$\dfrac{\text{Kt} - \text{K 3 !}}{\text{P} - \text{Kt 4}}$
17.	$\dfrac{\text{R} - \text{B 5}}{\text{R} \times \text{B}}$	$\dfrac{\text{Kt} - \text{B 5}}{\text{B} - \text{B 1}}$
18.	$\dfrac{\text{Q} \times \text{R}}{\text{Q} \times \text{P ch.}}$	$\dfrac{\text{P} - \text{K R 4 !}}{\text{Q} - \text{K 3}}$
19.	$\dfrac{\text{K} - \text{B 1}}{\text{Q} - \text{R 6 ch.}}$	$\dfrac{\text{Q} - \text{B 3}}{\text{Kt} - \text{K 2}}$
20.	$\dfrac{\text{K} - \text{K 2}}{\text{Q} \times \text{Kt ch.}}$	$\dfrac{\text{P} - \text{R 5}}{\text{R} - \text{Q 2}}$
21.	$\dfrac{\text{K} - \text{B 1}}{\text{Q} \times \text{R ch.}}$	$\dfrac{\text{P} - \text{R 6}}{\text{P} - \text{Kt 3}}$
22.	Resigns.	$\dfrac{\text{Kt} - \text{Kt 7}}{\text{B} \times \text{Kt}}$
23.		P × B and wins.

(a) A very pretty termination by Schallopp.

Chapter X.

RUY LOPEZ—ANALYSIS.

	(1)	(2)	(3)
1.	$\dfrac{\text{P—K 4}}{\text{P—K 4}}$	—	—
2.	$\dfrac{\text{Kt—K B 3}}{\text{Kt—Q B 3}}$	—	—
3.	$\dfrac{\text{B—Kt 5}}{\text{Kt—B 3}}$	—	—
4.	$\dfrac{\text{Q—K 2}}{\text{B—K 2}}$	$\overline{\text{P—Q R 3}}$	$\dfrac{\text{P—Q 4}}{\text{Q Kt} \times \text{P}}$
5.	$\dfrac{\text{P—B 3}}{\text{P—Q 3}}$	$\dfrac{\text{B—R 4}}{\text{P—Q Kt 4}}$	$\dfrac{\text{Kt} \times \text{Kt}}{\text{P} \times \text{Kt}}$
6.	$\dfrac{\text{P—Q 4}}{\text{P} \times \text{P}}$	$\dfrac{\text{B—Kt 3}}{\text{B—B 4}}$	$\dfrac{\text{Q} \times \text{P}}{\text{P—Q B 3}}$
7.	$\dfrac{\text{Kt} \times \text{P}}{\text{B—Q 2}}$	$\dfrac{\text{P—Q R 4}}{\text{R—Q Kt 1}}$	$\dfrac{\text{B—B 4}}{\text{P—Q 4}}$
8.	$\dfrac{\text{Kt} \times \text{Kt}}{\text{B} \times \text{Kt}}$	$\dfrac{\text{P} \times \text{P}}{\text{P} \times \text{P}}$	$\dfrac{\text{P} \times \text{P}}{\text{Kt} \times \text{P}}$
9.	$\dfrac{\text{B} \times \text{B ch.} +}{\text{P} \times \text{B}}$	$\dfrac{\text{Kt—B 3}}{\text{P—Kt 5}}$	$\dfrac{\text{Kt—B 3}}{\text{B—K 3}}$
10.		$\dfrac{\text{Kt—Q 5}}{\text{0—0}}$	$\dfrac{\text{B} \times \text{Kt}}{\text{B} \times \text{B}}$
11.		$\dfrac{\text{0—0}}{\text{P—Q 3}}$	$\dfrac{\text{Kt} \times \text{B}}{\text{Q} \times \text{Kt}}$
12.		$\dfrac{\text{P—K R 3}}{\text{B—K 3}}$	$\dfrac{\text{Q} \times \text{Q} +}{\text{P} \times \text{Q}}$

	(4)	(5)	(6)
1.	—	—	—
2.	—	—	—
3.	—	—	—

	(4)	(5)	(6)
4.	$\dfrac{\text{P—Q 3}}{\text{B—B 4}}$	$\dfrac{\text{Kt—B 3}}{\text{B—Kt 5}}$	$\dfrac{\text{0—0}}{\text{Kt} \times \text{P}}$
5.	$\dfrac{\text{P—B 3}}{\text{Q—K 2}}$	$\dfrac{\text{B} \times \text{Kt}}{\text{Q P} \times \text{B}}$	$\dfrac{\text{R—K 1}}{\text{Kt—K B 3}}$
6.	$\dfrac{\text{0—0}}{\text{0—0}}$	$\dfrac{\text{Kt} \times \text{P}}{\text{B} \times \text{Kt}}$	$\dfrac{\text{Kt} \times \text{P}}{\text{Kt} \times \text{Kt}}$
7.	$\dfrac{\text{P—Q 4}}{\text{B—Kt 3}}$	$\dfrac{\text{Kt P} \times \text{B}}{\text{Kt} \times \text{K P}}$	$\dfrac{\text{R} \times \text{Kt ch.}}{\text{B—K 2}}$
8.	$\dfrac{\text{B—K Kt 5}}{\text{P—Q 3}}$	$\dfrac{\text{Q—K 2}}{\text{Q—Q 4}}$	$\dfrac{\text{Q—K 1}}{\text{P—B 3}}$
9.	$\dfrac{\text{B} \times \text{Q Kt}}{\text{P} \times \text{B}}$	$\dfrac{\text{P—K B 4}}{\text{0—0}}$	$\dfrac{\text{B—R 4}}{\text{P—Q 3}}$
10.	$\dfrac{\text{P} \times \text{P}}{\text{P} \times \text{P}}$	$\dfrac{\text{P—B 4}}{\text{Q—Q 5}}$	$\dfrac{\text{R—K 3}}{\text{B—K 3}} =$
11.	$\dfrac{\text{Q—R 4}}{\text{P—K R 3}}$	$\dfrac{\text{Q R—Kt 1}}{\text{Kt—Q 3}}$	
12.	$\dfrac{\text{B—R 4}}{\text{B—Kt 2}}$	$\dfrac{\text{P—Q 3}}{\text{P—B 3}}$	
13.	$\dfrac{\text{Q Kt—Q 2}}{\text{P—K Kt 4}}$	$\dfrac{\text{Kt—K B 3}}{\text{Q—B 4}}$	
14.	$\dfrac{\text{B—Kt 3}}{\text{Kt—Q 2}}$	$\dfrac{\text{B—K 3}}{\text{Q—R 4 ch.}}$	
15.	$\dfrac{\text{Kt—B 4}}{\text{P—K B 3}} =$	$\dfrac{\text{B—Q 2}}{\text{Q—K R 4}}$	
16.		$\dfrac{\text{0—0}}{\text{K R—K 1}}$	
17.		$\dfrac{\text{Q—B 2}}{\text{P—Q B 4}} =$	

	(7)	(8)	(9)
1.	$\dfrac{\text{P—K 4}}{\text{P—K 4}}$	—	—
2.	$\dfrac{\text{Kt—K B 3}}{\text{Kt—Q B 3}}$	—	—
3.	$\dfrac{\text{B—Kt 5}}{\text{B—B 4}}$	—	—
4.	$\dfrac{\text{P—B 3}}{\text{Q—B 3}}$	—	$\dfrac{}{\text{P—Q 3}}$
5.	$\dfrac{\text{0—0}}{\text{K Kt—K 2}}$	$\dfrac{\text{P—Q 4}}{\text{P} \times \text{P}}$	$\dfrac{\text{P—Q 4}}{\text{P} \times \text{P}}$

	(7)	(8)	(9)
6.	$\dfrac{\text{P—Q 4}}{\text{P}\times\text{P}}$	$\dfrac{\text{P—K 5}}{\text{Q—Kt 3}}$	$\dfrac{\text{P}\times\text{P}}{\text{B—Kt 5 ch.}}$
7.	$\dfrac{\text{B—Kt 5}}{\text{Q—Kt 3}}$	$\dfrac{\text{P}\times\text{P} \mid}{\text{Kt}\times\text{Q P}}$	$\dfrac{\text{K—K 2}}{\text{P—Q 4}}$
8.	$\dfrac{\text{B}\times\text{Kt (K 2)}}{\text{Kt}\times\text{B}}$	$\dfrac{\text{Kt}\times\text{Kt}}{\text{Q—Kt 3}}$	$\dfrac{\text{Q—R 4}}{\text{P}\times\text{P}}$
9.	$\dfrac{\text{P}\times\text{P}}{\text{B—Kt 3}}$	$\dfrac{\text{B—K 3}}{\text{B}\times\text{Kt}}$	$\dfrac{\text{B}\times\text{Kt ch.}}{\text{P}\times\text{B}}$
10.	$\dfrac{\text{Kt—B 3}}{\text{0—0}}$	$\dfrac{\text{Q B}\times\text{B}}{\text{Q}\times\text{B (Kt 5)}}$	$\dfrac{\text{Q}\times\text{P ch.}}{\text{B—Q 2}}$
11.		$\dfrac{\text{P—K 6}}{\text{Q—K Kt 4}}$	$\underline{\text{Q}\times\text{P ch.} +}$
12.		$\dfrac{\text{P}\times\text{B P ch.}}{\text{K}\times\text{P}+}$	

	(10)	(11)	(12)
1.	$\dfrac{\text{P—K 4}}{\text{P—K 4}}$	—	—
2.	$\dfrac{\text{Kt—K B 3}}{\text{Kt—Q B 3}}$	—	—
3.	$\dfrac{\text{B—Kt 5}}{\text{P—Q 3}}$	—	—
4.	$\dfrac{\text{P—B 3}}{\text{P—B 4}}$	—	$\dfrac{\text{P—Q 4}}{\text{B—Q 2}}$
5.	$\dfrac{\text{P—Q 4}}{\text{B P}\times\text{P}}$	$\dfrac{\text{P}\times\text{P}}{\text{B}\times\text{P}}$	$\dfrac{\text{B}\times\text{Kt}}{\text{B}\times\text{B}}$
6.	$\dfrac{\text{Kt}\times\text{P}}{\text{P}\times\text{Kt}}$	$\dfrac{\text{P—Q 4}}{\text{P}\times\text{P}}$	$\dfrac{\text{Kt—B 3}}{\text{P—B 3}}$
7.	$\dfrac{\text{Q—R 5 ch.}}{\text{K—K 2}}$	$\dfrac{\text{P}\times\text{P}}{\text{B—Q 2}}$	$\dfrac{\text{Kt—K R 4}}{\text{Kt—K 2}}$
8.	$\dfrac{\text{B—Kt 5 ch.}}{\text{Kt—B 3}}$	$\dfrac{\text{P—Q 5}}{\text{Q Kt—K 2}}$	$\dfrac{\text{0—0}}{\text{P}\times\text{P}}$
9.	$\dfrac{\text{K B}\times\text{Kt}}{\text{P}\times\text{B}}$	$\dfrac{\text{B}\times\text{B ch.}}{\text{Q}\times\text{B}}$	$\dfrac{\text{Q}\times\text{P}}{\text{Kt—Kt 3}}$
10.	$\dfrac{\text{P}\times\text{P}}{\text{Q—Q 4}}$	$\dfrac{\text{Kt—B 3}}{\text{Kt—B 3}}$	$\dfrac{\text{Kt—B 5}}{\text{Kt—K 4}}$
11.	$\dfrac{\text{B—R 4}}{\text{B—R 3}}$	$\dfrac{\text{B—Kt 5}}{\text{0—0—0}}$	

	(13)	**(14)**	**(15)**
1.	—	—	—
2.	—	—	—
3.	—	—	—
4.	$\dfrac{Kt-B\,3}{Kt-B\,3}$	$\dfrac{P-Q\,4}{P\times P}$	
5.	$\dfrac{P-Q\,4}{P\times P}$	$\dfrac{Kt\times P}{B-Q\,2}$	$\dfrac{B-Q\,2}{Kt-B\,3}$
6.	$\dfrac{Kt\times P}{B-Q\,2}$	$\dfrac{B\times Kt}{P\times B}$	$\dfrac{K\,Kt-K\,2}{P\times P}$
7.	$\dfrac{B-Kt\,5}{B-K\,2}$	$\dfrac{0-0}{P-Kt\,3}$	$\dfrac{P\times P}{B-Kt\,5}$
8.	$\dfrac{0-0}{0-0}$	$\dfrac{P-K\,B\,4}{B-Kt\,2}$	$\dfrac{P-B\,3}{B-K\,3}$
9.		$\dfrac{Kt-Q\,B\,3}{P-B\,4}$	$\dfrac{Kt-B\,1}{}$
10.		$\dfrac{Kt-B\,3}{Kt-K\,2}$	

	(16)	**(17)**	**(18)**
1.	—	—	—
2.	—	—	—
3.	$\dfrac{}{Kt-B\,3}$	—	--
4.	$\dfrac{P-Q\,3}{P-Q\,3}$	—	—
5.	$\dfrac{P-B\,3}{B-Q\,2}$	—	--
6.	$\dfrac{Q\,Kt-Q\,2}{P-K\,Kt\,3}$	—	--
7.	$\dfrac{B-R\,4}{B-Kt\,2}$	$\dfrac{P-Q\,4}{P\times P}$	—
8.	$\dfrac{Kt-B\,1\ (or\ B\,4)}{0-0}$	$\dfrac{P\times P}{P-Q\,4}$	—
9.	$\dfrac{Kt-K\,3}{Kt-K\,2}$	$\dfrac{P\times P}{Kt\times P}$	$\dfrac{P-K\,5}{Kt-K\,5}$

	(16)	(17)	(18)
10.	B—Kt 3 / P—B 3	Q—Kt 3 / Kt—B 3	Q—Kt 3 / Kt—Kt 5
11.	P—K R 4 / Q—B 2	B—B 4 / Q—K 2 ch.	B×B ch. / Q×B
12.		K—Q 1 / Kt—K Kt 5	P—Q R 3 / Kt×Kt
13.		R—K 1 / Kt×P ch.	Kt×Kt / Kt—B 3
14.		K—B 2 / Q×R +	Q×Kt P / Q R—Kt 1
15.			Q—R 6 / R—Kt 3
16.			Q—Q 3 / Q—Kt 5

	(19)	(20)	(21)
1.	—	—	—
2.	—	—	—
3.	—	—	—
4.	Kt—K 2 ? (a)	—	B—B 4
5.	B—Q B 4 / Kt—B 3	Kt—B 3 / Kt—Kt 3	P—B 3 / Q—K 2
6.	Kt—Kt 5 / P—Q 4	O—O / B—K 2	O—O / O—O
7.	P×P / Kt×P	P—Q 4 / P×P	P—Q 4 / B—Kt 3
8.	Q—B 3 / B—K 3	Q×P / O—O	B×Kt / Kt P×B
9.	Kt×B / P×Kt		Kt×P / P—Q 3
10.	Kt—B 3 / B—Kt 5		Kt×Q B P / Q×P
11.	B—Q 2		Kt—Kt 4 / P—B 4
12.			Kt—B 2

(a) A trap, for if White plays 5. Kt×P, Black plays 5. P—B 3, followed by Q—R 4 ch., winning a piece.

	(22)	(23)	(24)
1.	—	—	—
2.	—	—	—
3.	—	—	—
4.	$\dfrac{0-0}{Kt \times P}$	—	—
5.	$\dfrac{P-Q\,4}{B-K\,2}$	—	$\overline{P-Q\,R\,3}$

Nos. 22 to 28.   Position after Black's 4th move.

BLACK.

WHITE.

	(22)	(23)	(24)
6.	$\dfrac{Q-K\,2}{Kt-Q\,3}$	$\dfrac{R-K\,1}{Kt-Q\,3}$	$\dfrac{B \times Kt}{Q\,P \times B}$
7.	$\dfrac{B \times Kt}{Kt\,P \times B}$	$\dfrac{P \times P}{Kt \times B}$	$\dfrac{R-K\,1}{Kt-Q\,3}$
8.	$\dfrac{P \times P}{Kt-Kt\,2}$	$\dfrac{P-Q\,R\,4}{K\,Kt-Q\,5}$	$\dfrac{Kt \times P}{B-K\,2}$
9.	$\dfrac{Kt-Q\,4}{0-0}$	$\dfrac{Kt \times Kt}{0-0}$	$\dfrac{Q-K\,2}{B-K\,3}$
10.	$\dfrac{R-Q\,1}{Q-K\,1}$	$\dfrac{Kt-Q\,B\,3}{P-B\,3}$	$\dfrac{P-Q\,B\,3}{Kt-B\,4}$
11.	$\dfrac{Kt-Q\,B\,3}{P-B\,3}$		$\dfrac{Q\,Kt-Q\,2}{}$

	(25)	(26)	(27)
1.	—	—	—
2.	—	—	—
3.	—	—	—
4.	—	—	—
5.	$\dfrac{\text{R}-\text{K 1}}{\text{Kt}-\text{Q 3}}$	—	$\dfrac{\text{P}-\text{Q 4}}{\text{Kt}-\text{Q 3}}$
6.	$\dfrac{\text{Kt}\times\text{P}}{\text{K}\times\text{Kt}}$	$\dfrac{}{\text{B}-\text{K 2}}$	$\dfrac{\text{B}\times\text{Kt}}{\text{Kt P}\times\text{B}}$
7.	$\dfrac{\text{R}\times\text{Kt ch.}}{\text{B}-\text{K 2}}$	$\dfrac{\text{B}\times\text{Kt}}{\text{Q P}\times\text{B}}$	$\dfrac{\text{P}\times\text{P}}{\text{Kt}-\text{Kt 2}}$
8.	$\dfrac{\text{Kt}-\text{B 3}}{\text{Kt}\times\text{B}}$	$\dfrac{\text{Q}-\text{K 2}}{\text{B}-\text{K 3}}$	$\dfrac{\text{R}-\text{K 1}}{\text{B}-\text{K 2}}$
9.	$\dfrac{\text{Kt}-\text{Q 5}}{\text{0}-\text{0}}$	$\dfrac{\text{P}-\text{Q 3}}{\text{Kt}-\text{B 4}}$	$\dfrac{\text{Kt}-\text{Q 4}}{\text{0}-\text{0}}$
10.	$\dfrac{\text{Kt}\times\text{B ch.}}{\text{K.}-\text{R 1}}$	$\dfrac{\text{Kt}-\text{Q 2}}{\text{0}-\text{0}}$	$\dfrac{\text{Kt}-\text{Q B 3}}{\text{Kt}-\text{B 4}}$
11.	$\dfrac{\text{Q}-\text{R 5}}{\text{P}-\text{K Kt 3}}$	$\dfrac{\text{P}-\text{Q B 3}}{\text{R}-\text{K 1}}$	$\dfrac{\text{B}-\text{K 3}}{\text{Kt}-\text{K 3}}$
12.	$\dfrac{\text{Q}-\text{R 6}}{\text{P}-\text{K B 3}}$	$\dfrac{\text{Kt}-\text{K4}}{\text{Q}-\text{Q 4}}$	$\dfrac{\text{Q}-\text{K 2}}{}$
13.	$\dfrac{\text{Kt}\times\text{P ch.}}{\text{K}-\text{Kt 1}}$		
14.	$\dfrac{\text{R}\times\text{Kt}}{}$		

	(28)	(29)	(30)
1	—	—	—
2.	—	—	—
3.	—	—	—
4.	—	$\dfrac{}{\text{B}-\text{B 4}}$	$\dfrac{\text{P}-\text{Q 4}}{\text{P}\times\text{P}}$
5.	—	$\dfrac{\text{P}-\text{Q B 3}}{\text{Kt}\times\text{P}}$	$\dfrac{\text{P}-\text{K 5}}{\text{Kt}-\text{K 5}}$

	(28)	(29)	(30)
6.	P×P / Kt×B	Q—K 2 / Kt—B 3	0—0 / B—K 2
7.	P—Q R 4 / K Kt—Q 5	P—Q 4 / B—K 2	Kt×P / 0—0
8.	Kt×Kt / Kt×Kt	P×P / Kt—Q 4	Kt—B 5 / P—Q 4
9.	Q×Kt / B—K 2	R—Q 1 / Kt—Kt 3	Kt×B ch. / Kt×Kt
10.		B×Kt / Kt P×B	P—K B 3 / P—Q B 3
11.		Kt—Q 4 / B—Kt 2	P×Kt / Q—Kt 3 ch.
12.		Q—Kt 4	K—R 1 / Q×B
13.			Kt—B 3 / Q—B 4
14.			B—Kt 5 / P—Q 5
15.			B×Kt / Q×B
16.			Q×P / R—K 1

	(31)	(32)	(33)
1.	—	—	—
2.	—	—	—
3.	—	—	K Kt—K 2 / P—B 3
4.	Kt×K P	Q Kt×P ?	P—Q 4
5.	P—Q 5 / Kt—Q 3	Kt×Kt / P×Kt	Kt×P / P×P
6.	B×Kt / Kt P×B	P—K 5 / P—Q B 3	Q—K2 / Q—Q 4
7.	P×P / P—K 5	0—0 / P×B	Kt×Kt / Kt×Kt
8.	Kt—Q 4 / P×P	B—Kt 5 / B—K 2	P—Q 4 / B—K B 4

	(31)	(32)	(33)
9.	$\dfrac{Kt \times P}{Q - Q\,2}$	$\dfrac{P \times Kt}{B \times P}$	$\dfrac{K - Q\,2}{0 - 0 - 0}$
10.		$\dfrac{R - K\,1 \text{ ch.}}{K - B\,1}$	$\dfrac{Kt - B\,4}{B - Kt\,3}$
11.		$\dfrac{B \times B}{Q \times B}$	$\dfrac{B - K\,B\,4}{}$
12.		$\dfrac{P - Q\,B\,3}{P - Q\,4}$	
13.		$\dfrac{P \times P}{B - K\,3}$	
14.		$\dfrac{Kt - B\,3}{P - Q\,R\,3}$	
15.		$\dfrac{R - K\,5}{R - Q\,1}$	
16.		$\dfrac{Q - Kt\,3}{P - K\,Kt\,3}$	

	(34)	(35)	(36)
1.	—	—	—
2.	—	—	—
3.	$\dfrac{Kt - Q\,5}{}$	—	$\dfrac{P - Q\,R\,3}{}$
4.	$\dfrac{Kt \times Kt}{P \times Kt}$	—	$\dfrac{B - R\,4}{Kt - B\,3}$
5.	$\dfrac{P - Q\,3}{P - Q\,B\,3}$	$\dfrac{0 - 0}{P - Q\,B\,3}$	$\dfrac{P - Q\,3}{B - B\,4}$
6.	$\dfrac{B - R\,4}{Kt - B\,3}$	$\dfrac{B - R\,4}{P - Q\,Kt\,4}$	$\dfrac{P - B\,3}{P - Q\,Kt\,4}$
7.	$\dfrac{0 - 0}{P - Q\,4}$	$\dfrac{B - Kt\,3}{P - Q\,R\,4}$	$\dfrac{B - B\,2}{P - Q\,4}$
8.	$\dfrac{P - K\,5}{Kt - Q\,2}$	$\dfrac{P - Q\,B\,3}{P - R\,5}$	$\dfrac{P \times P}{Kt \times P}$
9.	$\dfrac{P - Q\,B\,3}{}$	$\dfrac{B - B\,2}{}$	$\dfrac{0 - 0}{0 - 0}$
10.			$\dfrac{Kt \times P}{Kt \times Kt}$
11.			$\dfrac{P - Q\,4}{B - Q\,3}$

	(34)	(35)	(36)
12	—	—	$\dfrac{P \times Kt}{B \times P}$
13			$B \times P$ ch.

Nos. 36 to 43.   Position after Black's 4th move.

BLACK.

WHITE.

	(37)	(38)	(39)
1.	—	—	—
2.	—	—	--
3.	—	—	—
4.	—	—	—
5.	$\dfrac{Kt-B3}{B-K2}$	$\dfrac{0-0}{Kt \times P}$	—
6.	$\dfrac{B-Kt3}{P-Q3}$	$\dfrac{P-Q4}{P-Q\ Kt\ 4}$	—
7.	$\dfrac{P-Q4}{B-Kt5}$	$\dfrac{B-Kt3}{P-Q4}$	—

	(37)	(38)	(39)
8.	B—K 3 / B×Kt	P×P / Kt—K 2	—— / B—K 3
9.	P×B / P×P	R—K 1 / K Kt—Q B 4	P—B 3 / B—K 2
10.	B×P / Kt×B	Kt—Q 4 / Kt—K 3	R—K 1 / Q—Q 2
11.	Q×Kt / 0—0	P—Q B 3 / P—Q B 4	
12.	Kt—K 2 / Kt—Q 2		
13.	P—Q B 3		

	(40)	(41)	(42)
1.	—	—	—
2.	—	—	—
3.	—	—	—
4.	—	—	—
5.	P—Q 4 / P×P	—	Q—K 2 / P—Q 3
6.	0—0 / B—K 2	—	P—Q 3 / P—K Kt 3
7.	P—K 5 / Kt—K 5	—	P—Q B 3 / B—Kt 2
8.	Kt×P / 0—0 (a)	R—K 1 / Kt—B 4	Q Kt—Q 2 / 0—0
9.	Kt—B 5 / P—Q 4	B×Kt / Q P×B	Kt—B 1 / R—K 1
10.	P×P e.p. / B×Kt	Kt×P / 0—0	
11.	B×Kt / Kt×Q P	Kt—Q B 3 / Kt—K 3	
12.		Kt—B 5 / P—B 3	

(a) If 8. —— / Kt×Kt ; 9. Q×Kt / Kt—Q B 4

	(40)	(41)	(42)
13.		$\dfrac{\text{Kt}\times\text{B ch.}}{\text{Q}\times\text{Kt}}$	
14.		$\dfrac{\text{Q—K 2}}{\text{P}\times\text{P}}$	
15.		$\dfrac{\text{Q}\times\text{P}}{\text{Q—B 2}}$	
16.		$\dfrac{\text{B—K 3}}{\text{B—Q 2}}$	
17.		$\dfrac{\text{Q R—Q 1}}{\text{Q R—K 1}}$	
18.		$\underline{\text{Kt— K 2}}$	

	(43)	(44)	(45)
1.	—	—	—
2.	—	—	—
3.	—	$\overline{\text{P—B 4}}$	—
4.	—	$\dfrac{\text{P—Q 4}}{\text{P}\times\text{Q P}}$	$\dfrac{\text{Kt—Q B 3}}{\text{P}\times\text{P}}$
5.	$\dfrac{\text{P—Q 3}}{\text{P—Q 3}}$	$\dfrac{\text{P—K 5}}{\text{B—B 4}}$	$\dfrac{\text{Q Kt}\times\text{P}}{\text{P—Q 4}}$
6.	$\dfrac{\text{B}\times\text{Kt ch.}}{\text{P}\times\text{B}}$	$\dfrac{\text{0—0}}{\text{K Kt—K 2}}$	$\dfrac{\text{Kt}\times\text{P}}{\text{Q—K 2}}$
7.	$\dfrac{\text{P—K R 3}}{\text{P—K Kt 3}}$	$\dfrac{\text{P—B 3}}{\text{P}\times\text{P}}$	$\dfrac{\text{P—Q 4}}{\text{B—Q 2}}$
8.	$\dfrac{\text{Kt—B 3}}{\text{P—Q B 4}}$	$\dfrac{\text{Q—Kt 3}}{\text{P}\times\text{P}}$	$\dfrac{\text{B}\times\text{Kt}}{\text{B}\times\text{B}}$
9.		$\dfrac{\text{B}\times\text{P}}{\text{P—Q R 3}}$	$\dfrac{\text{Kt—Kt 5}}{\text{Kt—B 3}}$
10.		$\dfrac{\text{Kt—Kt 5}}{\text{R—B 1}}$	$\underline{\text{0—0}}$
11.		$\underline{\text{B—B 4}}$	

	(46)	(47)
1.	—	—
2.	—	—
3.	—	$\dfrac{\text{P—K Kt 3}}{}$
4.	$\dfrac{\text{P—Q 3}}{\text{P}\times\text{P}}$	$\dfrac{\text{P—Q B 3}}{\text{B—Kt 2}}$
5.	$\dfrac{\text{P}\times\text{P}}{\text{P—Q 3}}$	$\dfrac{\text{P—Q 4}}{\text{P}\times\text{P}}$
6.	$\dfrac{\text{B—B 4}}{\text{B—Kt 5}}$	$\dfrac{\text{P}\times\text{P}}{\text{Q Kt—Q 2}}$
7.	$\dfrac{\text{Kt—B 3}}{\text{Kt—B 3}}$	$\dfrac{\text{0—0}}{\text{P—Q B 3}}$
8.	$\dfrac{\text{B—K 3}}{\text{Q—Q 2}}$	$\dfrac{\text{B—B 4}}{\text{P—Q 4}}$
9.	$\dfrac{\text{P—Q R 3}}{\text{P—Q R 3}}$	$\dfrac{\text{P}\times\text{P}}{\text{P}\times\text{P}}$
10.	$\dfrac{\text{Q—Q 2}}{\text{B—K 3}}$	$\dfrac{\text{B—Kt 5 ch.}}{\text{B—Q 2}}$
11.		$\dfrac{\text{B}\times\text{B ch.}}{\text{Q}\times\text{B}}$
12.		$\dfrac{\text{Kt—K 5}}{}$

RUY LOPEZ—GAMES.

	(1) Bird / Anderssen	(2) Captain Kennedy / Major Jaenisch	(3) Gunsberg / Schallopp
1.	$\dfrac{\text{P—K 4}}{\text{P—K 4}}$	$\dfrac{\text{P—K 4}}{\text{P—K 4}}$	$\dfrac{\text{P—K 4}}{\text{P—K 4}}$
2.	$\dfrac{\text{Kt—K B 3}}{\text{Kt—Q B 3}}$	$\dfrac{\text{Kt—K B 3}}{\text{Kt—Q B 3}}$	$\dfrac{\text{Kt—K B 3}}{\text{Kt—Q B 3}}$
3.	$\dfrac{\text{B—Kt 5}}{\text{Kt—B 3}}$	$\dfrac{\text{B—Kt 5}}{\text{P—Q R 3}}$	$\dfrac{\text{B—Kt 5}}{\text{Kt B 3}}$

	(1)	(2)	(3)
4.	$\dfrac{\text{P—Q 4}}{\text{Q Kt}\times\text{P}}$	$\dfrac{\text{B—R 4}}{\text{Kt—B 3}}$	$\dfrac{\text{P—Q 3}}{\text{Kt—K 2}}$
5.	$\dfrac{\text{Kt}\times\text{Kt}}{\text{P}\times\text{Kt}}$	$\dfrac{\text{0—0}}{\text{P—Q Kt 4}}$	$\dfrac{\text{P—B 3}}{\text{P—B 3}}$
6.	$\dfrac{\text{P—K 5}}{\text{Kt—K 5}}$	$\dfrac{\text{B—Kt 3}}{\text{B—B 4}}$	$\dfrac{\text{B—R 4}}{\text{Kt—Kt 3}}$
7.	$\dfrac{\text{0—0}}{\text{Q—R 5}}$	$\dfrac{\text{Kt}\times\text{P}}{\text{Kt}\times\text{Kt}}$	$\dfrac{\text{P—R 4}}{\text{P—K R 4}}$
8.	$\dfrac{\text{P—K Kt 3}\ (a)}{\text{Q—R 6}}$	$\dfrac{\text{P—Q 4}}{\text{B}\times\text{P}}$	$\dfrac{\text{B—K Kt 5}}{\text{Q—Kt 3}}$
9.	$\dfrac{\text{B—K 2}}{\text{P—Q 4}}$	$\dfrac{\text{Q}\times\text{B}}{\text{Kt—B 3}}$	$\dfrac{\text{Q—K 2}}{\text{P—Q 4}\ (e)}$
10.	$\dfrac{\text{P}\times\text{P}\ e.p.}{\text{B}\times\text{P}}$	$\dfrac{\text{Q—B 5}}{\text{B—Kt 2}}$	$\dfrac{\text{P}\times\text{P}}{\text{B—K Kt 5}}$
11.	$\dfrac{\text{Q}\times\text{P}}{\text{B—K B 4}}$	$\dfrac{\text{P—K 5}}{\text{P—Q 3}}$	$\dfrac{\text{P}\times\text{P}}{\text{0—0}}$
12.	$\dfrac{\text{Kt—B 3}}{\text{0—0—0}\ (b)}$	$\dfrac{\text{P}\times\text{P}}{\text{P}\times\text{P}}$	$\dfrac{\text{P}\times\text{P ch.}}{\text{K—Kt 1}}$
13.	$\dfrac{\text{Q}\times\text{R P}\ (c)}{\text{Kt}\times\text{Kt}}$	$\dfrac{\text{R—K 1 ch.}}{\text{Kt—K 4}}$	$\dfrac{\text{0—0}}{\text{Q—R 3}}$
14.	$\dfrac{\text{P}\times\text{Kt}}{\text{P—Q B 3}}$	$\dfrac{\text{Q—Q 4}}{\text{0—0}}$	$\dfrac{\text{B—B 2}}{\text{P—K 5}}$
15.	$\dfrac{\text{B—K 3}}{\text{B—K 5}}$	$\dfrac{\text{Kt—B 3}}{\text{Q—B 2}}$	$\dfrac{\text{B}\times\text{Kt}}{\text{P}\times\text{Kt}}$
16.	$\dfrac{\text{Q—R 8 ch.}}{\text{K—Q 2}}$	$\dfrac{\text{Kt—Q 5}}{\text{Kt}\times\text{Kt}}$	$\dfrac{\text{B—K 5 ch.}}{\text{Kt}\times\text{B}}$
17.	$\dfrac{\text{Q}\times\text{P ch.}}{\text{K—K 1}}$	$\dfrac{\text{B}\times\text{Kt}}{\text{K R—K 1}}$	$\dfrac{\text{Q}\times\text{Kt ch.}}{\text{B—Q 3}}$
18.	$\dfrac{\text{P—B 3}}{\text{B}\times\text{K Kt P}}$	$\dfrac{\text{B—K B 4}}{\text{Q R—Q 1}}$	$\dfrac{\text{Q—K 4}}{\text{K R—K 1}}$
19.	$\dfrac{\text{R—B 2}}{\text{B}\times\text{R ch.}\ (d)}$	$\dfrac{\text{B}\times\text{B}}{\text{Q}\times\text{B}}$	$\dfrac{\text{Q—R 4}}{\text{P}\times\text{P}\ (f)}$

(a) If 8. $\dfrac{\text{Q}\times\text{P}}{\text{B—B 4}}$ and White gets into trouble.

(b) In order to win the Queen, if White should be tempted to take the Kt. The springe, however, is too obvious, and Black lays himself open to a formidable attack.

(c) The right move.

(d) He has nothing better, and his attack is now at an end.

(e) Black sacrifices three Pawns for the attack.

(f) A fine finish to a brilliant game.

	(1)	(2)	(3)
20.	B×B / B—Q 4	B×Kt / Q—K 2 (a)	R—B 1 / Q—Kt 3
21.	P—Q B 4 / B—K 3	P—K B 4 / P×B	P—Q 4 / B—B 5
22.	Q×P ch. / K—K 2	Q—K 3 / P—K 5	Kt—R 3 / B—B 6
23.	B—B 5 ch. / K—B 3	P—Q R 4 / Q—Kt 5	R—K 1 / Q—K B 3 and wins.
24.	Q—B 7 / K—Kt 3	P×P / P×P	
25.	K—R 1 / P—K R 3	P—Q Kt 3 / P—B 4 (b)	
26.	R—Kt 1 ch. / K—R 2	R—R 7 / Q—Q 7	
27.	R—Kt 3 / Q—R 4	R—Q B 7 / Q—Q 3	
28.	B—Q 3 ch. / B—B 4	R—B 5 (c) / Q—Q 2	
29.	Q—K 5 / P—K Kt 3	P—Q Kt 4 / R—Q B 1	
30.	Q—B 6 / K R—Kt 1	Q—Kt 3 Ch. / K—R 1	
31.	Q×B P ch. / R—Kt 2	R—Q 5 / Q—R 2 ch.	
32.	Q—B 6 / Q R—Q 2	Q—K 3 / Q×Q ch.	
33.	B—Q 4 / Q R—K 2	R×Q / P—Kt 3	
34.	P—Q B 5 / B×B	R×Kt P / R×P	
35.	P×B / P—Kt 4	R—Kt 7 / R (K 1)—Q 1	

(a) If 20. $\overline{\text{P×B}}$; 21. $\dfrac{\text{R×P}}{}$, &c.

(b) If instead of 25 $\overline{\text{P—B 4}}$, Black had moved 25. $\overline{\text{R—Q 7}}$, White would have played 26. $\dfrac{\text{Q×P}}{}$.

(c) Well played.

	(1)	(2)	(3)
36.	$\dfrac{\text{P}-\text{B 6}}{\text{R}-\text{K 8 ch.}}$	$\dfrac{\text{P}-\text{R 4}}{\text{R (Q 1)}-\text{Q 7}}$	
37.	$\dfrac{\text{B}-\text{Kt 1}}{\text{R}-\text{B 2}}$	$\dfrac{\text{R}-\text{K Kt 3}}{\text{R}-\text{K 7}}$	
38.	$\dfrac{\text{Q}-\text{Q 8}}{\text{R}\times\text{P}}$	$\dfrac{\text{P}-\text{R 5}}{\text{P}-\text{K 6}}$	
39.	$\dfrac{\text{P}-\text{B 7}}{\text{R}\times\text{R}}$	$\dfrac{\text{P}\times\text{P}}{\text{R}-\text{K 8 ch.}}$	
40.	$\dfrac{\text{Q}-\text{Q 7 ch.}}{\text{K}-\text{Kt 3}}$	$\dfrac{\text{K}-\text{R 2}}{\text{P}\times\text{P}}$	
41.	$\dfrac{\text{Q}-\text{Q 6 ch.}}{\text{K}-\text{B 2}}$	$\dfrac{\text{R}\times\text{P}}{\text{R (K 8)}-\text{K 7}}$	
42.	$\dfrac{\text{Q}\times\text{R}}{\text{R}-\text{K 1}}$	$\dfrac{\text{R}-\text{Q Kt 5}}{\text{R}-\text{B 2}}$	
43.	$\dfrac{\text{Q}-\text{B 2 ch.}}{\text{K}-\text{Kt 1}}$	$\dfrac{\text{R}\times\text{P}}{\text{R}-\text{R 2 ch.}}$	
44.	$\dfrac{\text{Q}-\text{Q B 5}}{\text{Resigns }(a).}$	$\dfrac{\text{K}-\text{Kt 3}}{\text{R}-\text{K Kt 2}}$	
45.		$\dfrac{\text{R}\times\text{R}}{\text{K}\times\text{R}}$	
46.		$\dfrac{\text{P}-\text{Kt 5}}{\text{R}-\text{K 8}}$	
47.		R – K 5 and wins.	

	(4)	(5)	(6)
	$\dfrac{\text{Weiss}}{\text{Pollock}}$	$\dfrac{\text{Steinitz}}{\text{Blackburne}}$	$\dfrac{\text{Showalter}}{\text{Judd}}$
1.	$\dfrac{\text{P}-\text{K 4}}{\text{P}-\text{K 4}}$	$\dfrac{\text{P}-\text{K 4}}{\text{P}-\text{K 4}}$	$\dfrac{\text{P}-\text{K 4}}{\text{P}-\text{K 4}}$
2.	$\dfrac{\text{Kt}-\text{K B 3}}{\text{Kt}-\text{Q B 3}}$	$\dfrac{\text{Kt}-\text{K B 3}}{\text{Kt}-\text{Q B 3}}$	$\dfrac{\text{Kt}-\text{K B 3}}{\text{Kt}-\text{Q B 3}}$
3.	$\dfrac{\text{B}-\text{Kt 5}}{\text{P}-\text{Q R 3}}$	$\dfrac{\text{B}-\text{Kt 5}}{\text{P}-\text{Q R 3}}$	$\dfrac{\text{B}-\text{Kt 5}}{\text{P}-\text{Q R 3}}$

(a) If 44. $\dfrac{}{\text{Q}-\text{Kt 5}}$; 45. $\dfrac{\text{Q}-\text{Q 5 ch.}}{}$, and play as Black will White must win.

	(4)	(5)	(6)
4.	B—R 4 / Kt—B 3	B—R 4 / Kt—B 3	B—R 4 / Kt—B 3
5.	P—Q 3 / P—Q Kt 4	P—Q 3 / P—Q 3	0—0 / Kt×P
6.	B—Kt 3 / B—B 4	P—B 3 / B—K 2	P—Q 4 / P—Q Kt 4
7.	P—B 3 / P—Q 4	P—K R 3 / 0—0	B—Kt 3 / P—Q 4
8.	P×P / Kt×P	Q—K 2 / Kt—K 1	P×P / Kt—K 2
9.	Q—K 2 / 0—0	P—K Kt 4 / P—Q Kt 4	Kt—Kt 5 / Kt×Kt
10.	Q—K 4 / B—K 3	B—B 2 / B—Kt 2	B×Kt / B—Kt 2
11.	Kt×P / Kt×Kt	Q Kt—Q 2 / Q—Q 2	Q—B 3 / Q—Q 2
12.	Q×Kt / Kt—Q Kt 5	Kt—B 1 / Kt—Q 1	Kt—B 3 / P—Q B 3
13.	0—0 / Kt×P	Kt—K 3 / Kt—K 3	K R—K 1 / Q—K 3
14.	Q—R 5 / B×B	Kt—B 5 / P—Kt 3	Q R—Q 1 / Q—Kt 3
15.	P×B / R—K 1	Kt×B ch. / Q×Kt	Q—K 3 / 0—0 ?
16.	Kt—Q 2 / Q—K 2	B—K 3 / Kt (K 1)—Kt 2	Q B—B 4 / Kt—B 4
17.	P—Q Kt 4 / B×P ch.	0—0—0 / P—Q B 4	Q—Kt 6 / Q—Kt 5
18.	K—R 1 / Q—K 8 (a)	P—Q 4 / K P×P	R—Q 3 ! / B—Q Kt 5
19.	P—R 3 / Kt×B (b)	P×P / P—B 5	B—Kt 3 / B×Kt
20.	R×Q / R—R ch.	P—Q 5 / Kt—B 2	R×B / Kt×B
21.	K—R 2 / B—Kt 8 ch.	Q—Q 2 / P—Q R 4	R×P ch. ! / B×R
22.	K—Kt 3 / R—K 6 ch.	B—Q 4 / P—B 3	Q×B ch. / K—Kt 1

(a) The beginning of a magnificent combination.
(b) A further sacrifice.

	(4)	(5)	(6)
23.	$\dfrac{\text{K}-\text{Kt 4}}{\text{Kt}-\text{K 7}}$	$\dfrac{\text{Q}-\text{R 6}}{\text{P}-\text{Kt 5}}$	$\dfrac{\text{Q}-\text{Kt 6 ch.}}{\text{K}-\text{B 1}}$
24.	$\dfrac{\text{Kt}-\text{B 1}}{\text{P}-\text{Kt 3}}$	$\dfrac{\text{P}-\text{Kt 5}}{\text{P}-\text{B 4}}$	$\dfrac{\text{Q}-\text{B 6 ch.}}{\text{K}-\text{Kt 1}}$
25.	$\dfrac{\text{Q}-\text{Q 5}}{\text{P}-\text{R 4 ch.}}$	$\dfrac{\text{B}-\text{B 6}}{\text{Q}-\text{B 2}}$	$\dfrac{\text{Q}-\text{Kt 6 ch.}}{\text{K}-\text{B 1}}$
26.	$\dfrac{\text{K}-\text{Kt 5}}{\text{K}-\text{Kt 2 } (a)}$	$\dfrac{\text{P}\times\text{P}}{\text{P}\times\text{P}}$	$\dfrac{\text{Q}-\text{B 6 ch.}}{\text{K}-\text{Kt 1}}$
27.	$\dfrac{\text{Kt}\times\text{R}}{\text{P}-\text{B 3 } (b)}$	$\dfrac{\text{P}-\text{Kt 6 } (c)}{\text{Q}\times\text{Kt P}}$	$\dfrac{\text{Q}-\text{Kt 6 ch.}}{\text{K}-\text{B 1}}$
28.	Resigns.	$\dfrac{\text{B}\times\text{Kt}}{\text{Q}\times\text{Q ch.}}$	$\dfrac{\text{Q}\times\text{P ch.}}{\text{Resigns.}}$
29.		$\dfrac{\text{B}\times\text{Q}}{\text{R}-\text{B 3}}$	
30.		$\dfrac{\text{K R}-\text{Kt 1 ch.}}{\text{R}-\text{Kt 3}}$	
31.		$\dfrac{\text{B}\times\text{P}}{\text{K}-\text{B 2}}$	
32.		$\dfrac{\text{B}\times\text{R ch.}}{\text{P}\times\text{B}}$	
33.		$\dfrac{\text{Kt}-\text{Kt 5 ch}}{\text{K}-\text{Kt 1}}$	
34.		$\dfrac{\text{K R}-\text{K 1}}{\text{Resigns.}}$	

	(7)	(8)	(9)
	$\dfrac{\text{Steinitz}}{\text{Lasker}}$	$\dfrac{\text{Lasker}}{\text{Steinitz}}$	$\dfrac{\text{Capablanca}}{\text{Janowski}}$
1.	$\dfrac{\text{P}-\text{K 4}}{\text{P}-\text{K 4}}$	$\dfrac{\text{P}-\text{K 4}}{\text{P}-\text{K 4}}$	$\dfrac{\text{P}-\text{K 4}}{\text{P}-\text{K 4}}$
2.	$\dfrac{\text{Kt}-\text{K B 3}}{\text{Kt}-\text{Q B 3}}$	$\dfrac{\text{Kt}-\text{K B 3}}{\text{Kt}-\text{Q B 3}}$	$\dfrac{\text{Kt}-\text{K B 3}}{\text{Kt}-\text{Q B 3}}$

(a) Very finely played.

(b) Black mates in two, thus :—

28. K—R 4	B—B 7 ch.
29. P—Kt 3	B × P mate.

"Mr. Pollock's play from the 17th move renders this game one of the finest monuments of chess ingenuity ; and altogether this game belongs to the most brilliant in the annals of practical play."— Steinitz.

(c) Finely played.   Black cannot play, 27. P × P on account of 28. Kt—Kt 5.

	(7)	(8)	(9)
3.	B–Kt 5 / Kt–B 3	B–Kt 5 / P–Q R 3	B–Kt 5 / P–Q R 3
4.	P–Q 3 / P–Q 3	B–R 4 / P–Q 3	B×Kt / Q P×B
5.	P–B 3 / B–Q 2	P–Q 4 / B–Q 2	Kt–B 3 / B–Q B 4
6.	B–Q 4 / P–K Kt 3	P–B 3 / Kt–B 3	P–Q 3 / B–K Kt 5
7.	Q Kt–Q 2 / B–Kt 2	Q Kt–Q 2 / B–K 2	B–K 3 / B×B
8.	Kt–B 4 (a) / 0–0	0–0 / 0–0	P×B / Q–K 2
9.	Kt–K 3 / Kt–K 2	R–K 1 / R–K 1	0–0 / 0–0–0
10.	B–Kt 3 / P–B 3	Kt–B 1 / B–K B 1	Q–K 1 / Kt–R 3
11.	P–K R 4 ! / Q–B 2	Kt–Kt 3 / P–K Kt 3	R–Kt 1 (c) / P–B 3
12.	Kt–Kt 5 ! / P–Q 4	P–K R 3 ! / B–Kt 2	P–Kt 4 / Kt–B 2
13.	P–B 3 / Q R–Q 1	B–B 2 / B–Q B 1	P–Q R 4 / B×Kt
14.	P–Kt 4 / P×P ?	P–Q 5 / Kt–K 2	R×B / P–Q Kt 3
15.	B P×P / P–K R 3	B–K 3 / R–B 1	B P×P / P×P
16.	Q–B 3 (b) / B–K 1	Q–Q 2 / Kt–K 1	P–Q R 4 / Kt–Q 5
17.	B–B 2 / Kt–Q 2	B–R 6 ! / K–R 1	Q–B 4 /

(a) If 8.   Kt–B 1
      9. Q Kt×P   Kt×Kt
    10. Kt×Kt   B×B
    11. Q×B ch.   P–B 3
    12. P–B 3 (!)
(b) Well played, for if—
    16.   P×Kt
    17. P×P   Kt–R 2
    18. Kt–B 5
(c) The beginning of a characteristic attack by Capablanca.

	(7)	(8)	(9)
18.	Kt—R 3 / Kt—Q B 4	Q R—Q 1 / Kt—Kt 1	P—B 4 / Kt—Kt 4
19.	Kt—B 2 / P—Q Kt 4 ?	B×B ch. / Kt×B	R—B 2 / Kt—K 3
20.	P—Kt 5 / P—K R 4	P—B 4 ! / P—K B 4	Q—B 3 / R—Q 2
21.	Kt—B 5 ! / P×Kt	Q—B 3 / P×P	R—Q 1 / K—Kt 2
22.	P×P / P—B 3	B×P / Kt—B 3	P—Q 4 (a) / Q—Q 3
23.	P—Kt 6 and wins.	Q—K 3 / Kt×B	R—B 2 / P×P
24.		Kt×Kt / R—B 5	P×P / Kt—B 5
25.		P—B 5 / B—B 4 ?	P—B 5 ! / Kt×Kt
26.		Kt (B 3)—Kt 5 and wins.	P×Kt / Q×Q P
27.			P—B 6 ch. / K—Kt 1
28.			P×R and wins (b).

	(10) Alechin / Capablanca	(11) Lasker / Capablanca	(12) Tarrasch / Capablanca
1.	P—K 4 / P—K 4	P—K 4 / P—K 4	P—K 4 / P—K 4
2.	Kt—K B 3 / Kt—Q B 3	Kt—K B 3 / Kt—Q B 3	Kt—K B 3 / Kt—Q B 3
3.	B—Kt 5 / P—Q 3	B—Kt 5 / P—Q R 3	B—Kt 5 / P—Q R 3
4.	P—Q 4 / P×P	B×Kt / Q P×B	B—R 4 / Kt—B 3
5.	Kt×P / B—Q 2	P—Q 4 / P×P	Kt—B 3 / B—K 2

(a) The fight for the Queen's file, culminating in this move, decides the game in White's favour.

(b) Played in the St. Petersburg Tournament, 1914.

	(10)	(11)	(12)
6.	$\dfrac{\text{Q Kt}-\text{B 3}}{\text{Kt}-\text{B 3}}$	$\dfrac{\text{Q}\times\text{P}}{\text{Q}\times\text{Q}}$	$\dfrac{0-0}{\text{P}-\text{Q Kt 4}}$
7.	$\dfrac{0-0}{\text{B}-\text{K 2}}$	$\dfrac{\text{Kt}\times\text{Q}}{\text{B}-\text{Q 3 }(c)}$	$\dfrac{\text{B}-\text{Kt 3}}{\text{P}-\text{Q 3}}$
8.	$\dfrac{\text{Kt}-\text{B 5 }(a)}{\text{B}\times\text{Kt}}$	$\dfrac{\text{Q Kt}-\text{B 3}}{\text{Kt}-\text{K 2}}$	$\dfrac{\text{P}-\text{Q R 4}}{\text{P}-\text{Kt 5}}$
9.	$\dfrac{\text{P}\times\text{B}}{0-0}$	$\dfrac{0-0}{0-0}$	$\dfrac{\text{Kt}-\text{Q 5}}{\text{B}-\text{Kt 5}}$
10.	$\dfrac{\text{R}-\text{K 1}}{\text{Kt}-\text{Q 2}}$	$\dfrac{\text{P}-\text{B 4}}{\text{R}-\text{K 1 }(d)}$	$\dfrac{\text{P}-\text{B 3}}{\text{R}-\text{Q Kt 1}}$
11.	$\dfrac{\text{Kt}-\text{Q 5}}{\text{B}-\text{B 3}}$	$\dfrac{\text{Kt}-\text{Kt 3}}{\text{P}-\text{B 3}}$	$\dfrac{\text{B}-\text{B 4}}{\text{Kt}\times\text{P}}$
12.	$\dfrac{\text{P}-\text{Q B 3}}{\text{Kt}-\text{Kt 3}}$	$\dfrac{\text{P}-\text{B 5 ! }(e)}{\text{P}-\text{Q Kt 3}}$	$\dfrac{\text{P}-\text{Q 4}}{\text{P}\times\text{B P}}$
13.	$\dfrac{\text{Kt}\times\text{B ch.}}{\text{Q}\times\text{Kt}}$	$\dfrac{\text{B}-\text{B 4}}{\text{B}-\text{Kt 2}}$	$\dfrac{\text{P}\times\text{B P}}{0-0}$
14.	$\dfrac{\text{B}\times\text{Kt}}{\text{P}\times\text{B}}$	$\dfrac{\text{B}\times\text{B }(f)}{\text{P}\times\text{B}}$	$\dfrac{\text{B}\times\text{P}}{\text{P}\times\text{P}}$
15.	$\dfrac{\text{Q}-\text{B 3}}{\text{K R}-\text{K 1}}$	$\dfrac{\text{Kt}-\text{Q 4}}{\text{Q R}-\text{Q 1}}$	$\dfrac{\text{P}\times\text{P}}{\text{Kt}-\text{Kt 5}}$
16.	$\dfrac{\text{B}-\text{K 3}}{\text{P}-\text{B 4}}$	$\dfrac{\text{Kt}-\text{K 6}}{\text{R}-\text{Q 2}}$	$\dfrac{\text{Kt}\times\text{Kt}}{\text{R}\times\text{Kt}}$
17.	$\dfrac{\text{R}-\text{K 2}}{\text{R}-\text{K 4}}$	$\dfrac{\text{Q R}-\text{Q 1}}{\text{Kt}-\text{B 1}}$	$\dfrac{\text{B}-\text{Q Kt 5}}{\text{B}\times\text{Kt}}$
18.	$\dfrac{\text{Q R}-\text{K 1}}{\text{Q R}-\text{K 1}}$	$\dfrac{\text{R}-\text{B 2}}{\text{P}-\text{Q Kt 4}}$	$\dfrac{\text{P}\times\text{B}}{\text{Kt}-\text{Kt 4}}$
19.	$\dfrac{\text{Q}-\text{Kt 7 }(b)}{\text{Q}\times\text{P}}$	$\dfrac{\text{K R}-\text{Q 2 }(g)}{\text{R (Q 2)}-\text{K 2}}$	$\dfrac{\text{R}-\text{R 3}}{\text{B}-\text{B 3}}$
20.	$\dfrac{\text{Q}\times\text{B P}}{\text{Q}-\text{K 3}}$	$\dfrac{\text{P}-\text{Q Kt 4}}{\text{K}-\text{B 2}}$	$\dfrac{\text{P}-\text{B 4}}{\text{Kt}-\text{K 3}}$
21.	$\dfrac{\text{Q}\times\text{R P}}{\text{Kt}-\text{Q 4}}$	$\dfrac{\text{P}-\text{Q R 3}}{\text{B}-\text{R 1}}$	$\dfrac{\text{R}-\text{R 3}}{\text{R}\times\text{Q P}}$
22.	$\dfrac{\text{K}-\text{B 1}}{\text{Kt}-\text{B 5}}$	$\dfrac{\text{K}-\text{B 2}}{\text{R}-\text{R 2}}$	$\dfrac{\text{Q}-\text{R 5}}{\text{P}-\text{R 3}}$

(a) Not good, since the Pawn becomes a source of weakness.
(b) Putting the Queen out of action.
(c) 7. B—Q 2 and 0—0—0 gives Black a good game.
(d) 10. B—Q B 4 is better.
(e) A fine move, hampering Black's position badly.
(f) Disposing of Black's only active piece.
(g) To stop Kt—Kt 3.

	(10)	(11)	(12)
23.	$\dfrac{\text{R}-\text{Q 2}}{\text{Kt}\times\text{P !}}$	$\dfrac{\text{P}-\text{Kt 4}}{\text{P}-\text{R 3}}$	$\dfrac{\text{R}-\text{K Kt 3}}{\text{K}-\text{R 1}}$
24.	$\dfrac{\text{K}\times\text{Kt}}{\text{Q}-\text{Kt 5 ch.}}$	$\dfrac{\text{R}-\text{Q 3}}{\text{P}-\text{Q R 4 }(a)}$	$\dfrac{\text{Q}-\text{B 5}}{\text{B}-\text{R 5}}$
25.	$\dfrac{\text{K}-\text{B 1}}{\text{Q}-\text{R 6 ch.}}$	$\dfrac{\text{P}-\text{K R 4}}{\text{P}\times\text{P}}$	$\dfrac{\text{R}-\text{K R 3}}{\text{Q}-\text{B 3}}$
26.	$\dfrac{\text{K}-\text{K 2}}{\text{R}\times\text{B ch.}}$	$\dfrac{\text{P}\times\text{P}}{\text{R (R 2)}-\text{K 2}}$	$\dfrac{\text{Q}-\text{Kt 4}}{\text{B}-\text{Kt 4}}$

Position after Black's 24th move.

BLACK.—Capablanca.

WHITE.—Lasker.

	(10)	(11)	(12)
27.	$\dfrac{\text{P}\times\text{R}}{\text{Q}\times\text{K P ch.}}$	$\dfrac{\text{K}-\text{B 3}}{\text{R}-\text{K Kt 1}}$	$\dfrac{\text{B}-\text{K 3}}{\text{Kt}\times\text{P}}$
28.	$\dfrac{\text{K}-\text{Q 1}}{\text{Q}\times\text{R ch.}}$	$\dfrac{\text{K}-\text{B 4}}{\text{P}-\text{Kt 3}}$	$\dfrac{\text{B}\times\text{R}}{\text{Kt}\times\text{R ch.}}$
29.	$\dfrac{\text{K}-\text{B 2}}{\text{Q}-\text{K 5 ch.}}$	$\dfrac{\text{R}-\text{Kt 3}}{\text{P}-\text{Kt 4 ch.}}$	$\dfrac{\text{K}-\text{R 1}}{\text{Q}-\text{K 3}}$
30.	$\dfrac{\text{K}-\text{Kt 3}}{\text{Q}-\text{B 3}}$	$\dfrac{\text{K}-\text{B 3}}{\text{Kt}-\text{Kt 3 }(b)}$	$\dfrac{\text{Q}-\text{B 3}}{\text{B}-\text{Q 7}}$

(a) An effort to free his position and relieve the pressure on the centre. See Diagram.

(b) If 31. R×P   Kt—B 5

      32. R—Q 8   Kt—K 4 (ch.), and P×P, &c.

	(10)	(11)	(12)
31.	$\dfrac{\text{P—Q R 4}}{\text{P—Q 4}}$	$\dfrac{\text{P}\times\text{P}}{\text{R P}\times\text{P}}$	$\dfrac{\text{Q—Q 3}}{\text{B—R 4}}$
32.	$\dfrac{\text{P—R 5}}{\text{Q—Kt 4 ch.}}$	$\dfrac{\text{R—R 3}}{\text{R—Q 2}}$	$\dfrac{\text{B—B 6}}{\text{P—Q 4}}$
33.	$\dfrac{\text{K—R 3}}{\text{R—Kt 1}}$	$\dfrac{\text{K—Kt 3}}{\text{K—K 1}}$	$\dfrac{\text{R—Q B 1}}{\text{Kt—B 5}}$
34.	$\dfrac{\text{K—R 2}}{\text{P—R 3}}$	$\dfrac{\text{R (Q 1)—K R 1}}{\text{B—Kt 2}}$	$\dfrac{\text{Q—K 3}}{\text{B—Q 7}}$
35.	$\dfrac{\text{P—R 6}}{\text{Q—Kt 6}}$	$\dfrac{\text{P—K 5 }(b)}{\text{Q P}\times\text{P}}$	$\dfrac{\text{Q—Q R 3}}{\text{R—Q Kt 1}}$
36.	Resigns (a)	$\dfrac{\text{Kt—K 4}}{\text{Kt—Q 4 }(c)}$	Resigns.
37.		$\dfrac{\text{Kt (K 6)—B 5}}{\text{B—B 1 }(d)}$	
38.		$\dfrac{\text{Kt}\times\text{R}}{\text{B}\times\text{Kt}}$	
39.		$\dfrac{\text{R—R 7}}{\text{R—B 1}}$	
40.		$\dfrac{\text{R—Q R 1}}{\text{K—Q 1}}$	
41.		$\dfrac{\text{R—R 8 ch.}}{\text{B—B 1}}$	
42.		$\dfrac{\text{Kt—B 5}}{\text{Resigns.}}$	

(a) For if—

36. K—Kt 1	R—K 1
37. R—Q B 2	R—K 8 ch.
38. R—B 1	R—K 7

and mate follows. Played in the St. Petersburg Tournament, 1914.

(b) The beginning of a splendid combination, quite in Lasker's best style.

(c) If 35.   R×R

     36. R—R 7 ch.   K—K 1

     37. Kt×P mate.

(d) If 36.   R—B 2

     37. Kt×B, and Kt—Q 6 ch. wins.

Lasker's conduct of the whole game is an admirable example of the modern school.

	(13)	(14)
	Capablanca	Alechin
	Blackburne	Capablanca
	P—K 4	P—K 4
	P—K 4	P—K 4
	Kt—K B 3	Kt—K B 3
2.	Kt—Q B 3	Kt—Q B 3
	B—Kt 5	B—Kt 5
3.	Kt—Q 5	P—Q 3
	Kt×Kt	P—Q 4
4.	P×Kt	P×P
	0—0	Kt×P
5.	P—K Kt 3	B—Q 2
	P—Q 3	Kt—Q B 3
6.	B—Kt 2	Kt—B 3
	Kt—Q 2	0—0
7.	Kt—K 2	B—K 2
	P—K B 4	Kt—B 5
8.	P—Q B 3	B×Kt
	B—B 4	P×B
9.	P—Q 4	0—0
	B—Kt 3	R—K 1
10.	0—0	Kt—Q 2
	Kt—B 3	Kt—Q 5
11.	P—Q B 4	B—B 3
	P—K 5	P—Q B 3
12.	P—Q Kt 4	Kt—Kt 3
	P—B 3	Kt×B ch.
13.	P—B 5	Q×Kt
	B—B 2	B×Kt
14.	P×Q B P	P×B
	Kt P×P	Q—B 3
15.	Q—R 4	K R—K 1
	B—Q 2	B—K 3
16.	B—Kt 5	P—B 4
	P—Q 4	R—K 2
17.	Q—Kt 3	R—K 4
	R—Kt 1	Q R—K 1
18.	P—Q R 3	Q R—K 1 (a)

(a) If 18.   R×P
    19. B—Q 4 wins the exchange.

	(13)	(14)
19.	$\dfrac{\text{P—K R 3}}{\text{B—B 4}}$	$\dfrac{\text{Q—Kt 7}}{\text{Q} \times \text{P}}$
20.	$\dfrac{\text{P—Kt 4}}{\text{B} \times \text{B}}$	$\dfrac{\text{Q} \times \text{B P}}{\text{Q—K 3}}$
21.	$\dfrac{\text{Q} \times \text{B}}{\text{P—B 4}}$	$\dfrac{\text{Q} \times \text{R P}}{\text{Kt—Q 4}}$
22.	$\dfrac{\text{K—R 2}}{\text{Kt—B 3}}$	$\dfrac{\text{K—B 1}}{\text{Kt—B 5}}$

Position after Black's 25th move.

BLACK.—Blackburne.

WHITE.—Capablanca.

	(13)	(14)
23.	$\dfrac{\text{R—Kt 1}}{\text{Kt—Q 1}}$	$\dfrac{\text{R—Q 2}}{\text{Kt} \times \text{P} \,(c)}$
24.	$\dfrac{\text{P} \times \text{P}}{\text{R} \times \text{P}}$	$\dfrac{\text{K} \times \text{Kt}}{\text{Q—Kt 5 ch.}}$
25.	$\dfrac{\text{Kt—R 4}}{\text{R—R 4}}$	$\dfrac{\text{K—B 1}}{\text{Q—R 6 ch.}}$
26.	$\dfrac{\text{Kt} \times \text{P} \,(a)}{\text{P} \times \text{Kt} \,(b)}$	$\dfrac{\text{K—K 2}}{\text{R} \times \text{B ch.}}$

(a) An elegant and sound sacrifice. See Diagram.
(b) There is nothing better.
(c) Admirable!

	(13)	(14)
27.	$\dfrac{\text{R} \times \text{K Kt P}}{\text{Q}-\text{Kt 1 }(a)}$	$\dfrac{\text{P} \times \text{R}}{\text{Q} \times \text{K P ch.}}$
28.	$\dfrac{\text{R} \times \text{B ch.}}{\text{K} \times \text{R}}$	$\dfrac{\text{K}-\text{Q 1}}{\text{Q} \times \text{R ch.}}$
29.	$\dfrac{\text{R}-\text{Kt 1 ch.}}{\text{K}-\text{B 1}}$	$\dfrac{\text{K}-\text{B 2}}{\text{Q}-\text{K 5 ch.}}$
30.	$\dfrac{\text{Q}-\text{Kt 6}}{\text{R} \times \text{P ch.}}$	$\dfrac{\text{K}-\text{Kt 3}}{\text{Q}-\text{B 3}}$
31.	$\dfrac{\text{K} \times \text{R}}{\text{Resigns }(b)}$	$\dfrac{\text{P}-\text{Q R 4}}{\text{P}-\text{Q 4}}$
32.		$\dfrac{\text{P}-\text{R 5}}{\text{Q}-\text{Kt 4 ch.}}$
33.		$\dfrac{\text{K}-\text{R 3 }(c)}{\text{R}-\text{Kt 1}}$
34.		$\dfrac{\text{K}-\text{R 2}}{\text{P}-\text{R 3}}$
35.		$\dfrac{\text{P}-\text{R 6}}{\text{Q}-\text{Kt 6 ch.}}$
36.		Resigns (d).

(a) Here, however, he might have played Q—B 2. But his game is gone.

(b) A good specimen of the Cuban master's attacking style.

(c) If 33 K—R 2   Q—R 5 ch., and R—K 8 ch., &c.

(d) For if—

36.	K—Kt 1	R—K 1
37.	R—Q B 2	R—K 8 ch.
38.	R—B 1	R—K 7
39.	Q—Kt 7	R × P ch., and mates next move.

Another example of the Cuban's forcible style.

CHAPTER XI.

THE DOUBLE RUY LOPEZ, AND FOUR KNIGHTS' GAME—ANALYSIS.

	(1)	(2)	(3)
1.	P—K 4 / P—K 4	—	—
2.	Kt—K B 3 / Kt—Q B 3	—	—
3.	Kt—B 3 / Kt—B 3	—	—
4.	B—Kt 5 / B—Kt 5	—	—
5.	O—O / O—O	—	Kt—Q 5 / Kt×Kt
6.	Kt—Q 5 / Kt×Kt	P—Q 3 / P—Q 3	P×Kt / P×K 5
7.	P×Kt / P—K 5	B×Kt / P×B	P×Kt / Q P×P
8.	P×Kt / Q P×P	Kt—K 2	B—K 2
9.	B—K 2 / P×Kt		
10.	B×P		

	(4)	(5)	(6)	(7)
1.	—	—	—	—
2.	—	—	—	—
3.	—	—	—	—
4.	—	P—Q R 3	B—B 4	Kt—Q 5

	(4)	(5)	(6)	(7)
5.	—	B×Kt / QP×B	Kt×P / Kt×Kt	Kt×P / K Kt×P
6.	Kt—Q 5	Kt×P / Kt×P	P—Q 4 / B—Q 3	Kt×Kt / Q—K 2
7.	Kt×Kt / P×Kt	Kt×Kt / Q—Q 5	P×Kt / B×P	0—0 / Q×Kt
8.	Q—Kt 4 / Q—B 3	0—0 / Q×K Kt	Kt—K 2 / Q—K 2	R—K 1 / B—K 2
9.	0—0 / P—B 3	P—Q 4 / Q—K B 4	B—Q 3 / Kt×P	Kt—B 3 / Q—Q 3
10.	R—K 1 ch. / K—Q 1	R—K 1 / B—K 3	0—0 / P—Q 4	B—B 4
11.	B—B 4 / P—Q B	B—Kt 5 / P—R 3	R—K 1 / 0—0	
12.	Q—Kt 3 / B—K B 4	Q—Q 3	Kt—B 4	
13.	P—Q B 3 / B—B 4			

THE DOUBLE RUY LOPEZ AND FOUR KNIGHTS' GAME —GAMES.

	(1) L. Paulson / Morphy	(2) Gunsberg / Pollock	(3) Bardeleben / Mackenzie
1.	P—K 4 / P—K 4	P—K 4 / P—K 4	P—K 4 / P—K 4
2.	Kt—K B 3 / Kt—Q B 3	Kt—K B 3 / Kt—Q B 3	Kt—K B 3 / Kt—Q B 3
3.	Kt—B 3 / Kt—B 3	Kt—B 3 / Kt—B 3	Kt—B 3 / Kt—B 3
4.	B—Kt 5 / B—B 4	P—Q R 3 / P—Q 4	B—Kt 5 / B—Kt 5
5.	0—0 / 0—0	B—Kt 5 / P—Q 5	0—0 / 0—0

	(1)	(2)	(3)
6.	$\dfrac{\text{Kt}\times\text{P}}{\text{R}-\text{K 1}}$	$\dfrac{\text{Kt}-\text{K 2}}{\text{B}-\text{Q 3}}$	$\dfrac{\text{P}-\text{Q 3}}{\text{P}-\text{Q 3}}$
7.	$\dfrac{\text{Kt}\times\text{Kt}}{\text{Q P}\times\text{Kt}}$	$\dfrac{\text{P}-\text{Q 3}}{\text{P}-\text{K R 3}}$	$\dfrac{\text{B}\times\text{Kt}}{\text{P}\times\text{B}}$
8.	$\dfrac{\text{B}-\text{B 4}}{\text{P}-\text{Q Kt 4}}$	$\dfrac{0-0}{0-0}$	$\dfrac{\text{Kt}-\text{K 2}}{\text{P}-\text{K R 3}}$
9.	$\dfrac{\text{B}-\text{K 2}}{\text{Kt}\times\text{P}}$	$\dfrac{\text{Kt}-\text{Kt 3}}{\text{Kt}-\text{K 2}}$	$\dfrac{\text{Kt}-\text{Kt 3}}{\text{B}-\text{Q B 4}}$
10.	$\dfrac{\text{Kt}\times\text{Kt}}{\text{R}\times\text{Kt}}$	$\dfrac{\text{Kt}-\text{R 4}}{\text{P}-\text{K Kt 4}}$	$\dfrac{\text{P}-\text{B 3}}{\text{B}-\text{Kt 3}}$
11.	$\dfrac{\text{B}-\text{B 3}}{\text{R}-\text{K 3}}$	$\dfrac{\text{K Kt}-\text{B 5}}{\text{B}\times\text{Kt}}$	$\dfrac{\text{P}-\text{Q 4}}{\text{P}\times\text{P}}$
12.	$\dfrac{\text{P}-\text{B 3}}{\text{Q}-\text{Q 6}}$	$\dfrac{\text{P}\times\text{B}}{\text{Q}-\text{B 1}}$	$\dfrac{\text{Kt}\times\text{P}}{\text{B}\times\text{Kt}}$
13.	$\dfrac{\text{P}-\text{Q Kt 4}}{\text{B}-\text{Kt 3}}$	$\dfrac{\text{Q}-\text{B 3}}{\text{P}-\text{Kt 5}}$	$\dfrac{\text{P}\times\text{B}}{\text{P}-\text{Q 4}}$
14.	$\dfrac{\text{P}-\text{Q R 4}}{\text{P}\times\text{P}}$	$\dfrac{\text{Q}-\text{K 2}}{\text{Kt}\times\text{P}}$	$\dfrac{\text{P}-\text{K 5}}{\text{Kt}-\text{K 5}}$
15.	$\dfrac{\text{Q}\times\text{P}}{\text{B}-\text{Q 2}}$	$\dfrac{\text{Kt}\times\text{Kt}}{\text{Q}\times\text{Kt}}$	$\dfrac{\text{Q}-\text{B 2}\,!}{\text{Kt}\times\text{Kt}}$
16.	$\dfrac{\text{R}-\text{R 2}}{\text{Q R}-\text{K 1}}$	$\dfrac{\text{B}\times\text{P}}{\text{K R}-\text{Q 1}}$	$\dfrac{\text{R P}\times\text{Kt}}{\text{Q}-\text{K 1}}$
17.	$\dfrac{\text{Q}-\text{R 6 }(a)}{\text{Q}\times\text{B }(b)}$	$\dfrac{\text{P}-\text{K B 3}}{\text{Q}-\text{R 4}}$	$\dfrac{\text{B}-\text{Q 2}}{\text{P}-\text{K B 4}}$
18.	$\dfrac{\text{P}\times\text{Q}}{\text{R}-\text{Kt 3 ch.}}$	$\dfrac{\text{Q}-\text{Q 2}}{\text{K}-\text{R 2}}$	$\dfrac{\text{Q R}-\text{B 1 }!}{\text{B}-\text{Q 2}}$
19.	$\dfrac{\text{K}-\text{R 1}}{\text{B}-\text{R 6}}$	$\dfrac{\text{B}-\text{Kt 5}}{\text{P}-\text{K 5}}$	$\dfrac{\text{P}-\text{B 4}}{\text{Q}-\text{K 3}}$
20.	$\dfrac{\text{R}-\text{Q 1}}{\text{B}-\text{Kt 7 ch.}}$	$\dfrac{\text{P}-\text{K B 4 }(c)}{\text{P}-\text{K 6}}$	$\dfrac{\text{B}-\text{R 5}}{\text{K R}-\text{B 1}}$
21.	$\dfrac{\text{K}-\text{Kt 1}}{\text{B}\times\text{P d. ch.}}$	$\dfrac{\text{Q}-\text{K 2}}{\text{P}-\text{Kt 6 }(d)}$	$\dfrac{\text{R}-\text{B 3}}{\text{P}-\text{R 4}}$

(a) White cannot be blamed for not seeing the most wonderful combination that his opponent had prepared.

(b) One of the most charming poetical chess combinations that has ever been devised in practical play.

(c) If 20. Q P×P   Q×P ch.
     21. K—B 2   P×P
     22. K×P   Q—R 4 ch. and wins.

(d) Very fine play.

	(1)	(2)	(3)
22.	K—B 1 / B—Kt 7 ch. (a)	Q×Q ch. / Kt×Q	R—R 3 / K—B 2
23.	K—Kt 1 / B—R 6 d. ch.	B×R / P×P ch.	K—B 2 / Q—K 2
24.	K—R 1 / B×P	K×P / R×B	Q—B 5 / Q×Q
25.	Q—B 1 / B×Q	K—Kt 1 / B×P	R×Q / K R—Q Kt 1
26.	R×B / R—K 7	Q R—K 1 / R—Q 3 (c)	P—Kt 3 / R—Kt 2
27.	R—R 1 / R—R 3	B—B 4 / Kt—Kt 6 (d)	B—Q 2 / R—Kt 4
28.	P—Q 4 / B—K 6 and wins (b)	Resigns.	R×R / P×R

(3) (contd.)

29.	R—R 6 / P—B 3	35.	K—Q 3 / K—Q 2	41.	K—B 3 / B—R 3
30.	B—Kt 4 / K—K 3	36.	B—Kt 6 / P—Kt 5	42.	K—Kt 4 / P—Kt 3
31.	B—B 5 / B—K 1	37.	B—B 5 / B—R 3 ch.	43.	K—B 5 / B—Q 6
32.	R×P / R×R	38.	K—B 2 / B—B 8	44.	K—Kt 6 / B—B 7
33.	B×R / B—Q 2	39.	B×P / B×P	45.	P—R 4 / K—B 1
34.	K—K 3 / B—B 1	40.	B—K 1 / B—B 8	46.	P—R 5 / B×P

(a) Black would have won more elegantly by—

22.	R—Kt 7 (threatening R×R P)
23. Q—Q 3	R×B P ch.
24. K—Kt 1	R—Kt 7 ch.
25. K moves	R—Kt 8 mate.

(b) And wins for if 29. B×B, R (R 3)×P ch., and the other Rook mates next move. (Bauer subsequently pointed out another pretty mate overlooked by Morphy, as follows:—

23.	B—K 5 d. ch.
24. K—B 1	B—K B 4
25. Q—K 2	B—R 6 ch.
26. K—K 1	R—Kt 8, mate.)

(c) Again very well played.
(d) Neat finish.

(3) (*contd.*)

47. $\dfrac{\text{P} - \text{R } 6}{\text{K} - \text{Kt } 1}$

48. $\dfrac{\text{P} - \text{K } 6}{\text{P} - \text{B } 4}$

49. $\dfrac{\text{P} \times \text{P}}{\text{P} - \text{Q } 5}$

50. $\dfrac{\text{P} - \text{K } 7}{\text{Resigns.}}$

(4)

Capablanca
Lasker

1. $\dfrac{\text{P} - \text{K } 4}{\text{P} - \text{K } 4}$

2. $\dfrac{\text{Kt} - \text{K B } 3}{\text{Kt} - \text{Q B } 3}$

3. $\dfrac{\text{Kt} - \text{B } 3}{\text{Kt} - \text{B } 3}$

4. $\dfrac{\text{B} - \text{Kt } 5}{\text{B} - \text{Kt } 5}$

5. $\dfrac{0 - 0}{0 - 0}$

6. $\dfrac{\text{P} - \text{Q } 3}{\text{P} - \text{Q } 3}$

7. $\dfrac{\text{B} - \text{Kt } 5}{\text{B} \times \text{Kt}}$

8. $\dfrac{\text{P} \times \text{B}}{\text{P} - \text{K R } 3}$

9. $\dfrac{\text{B} - \text{R } 4}{\text{B} - \text{Kt } 5}$

10. $\dfrac{\text{P} - \text{K R } 3}{\text{B} \times \text{Kt}}$

11. $\dfrac{\text{Q} \times \text{B}}{\text{P} - \text{Kt } 4}$

12. $\dfrac{\text{B} - \text{Kt } 3}{\text{Kt} - \text{Q } 2}$

13. $\dfrac{\text{P} - \text{Q } 4}{\text{P} - \text{K B } 3}$

14. $\dfrac{\text{Q} - \text{Kt } 4}{\text{K} - \text{R } 1}$

15. $\dfrac{\text{P} - \text{K R } 4}{\text{R} - \text{B } 2}$

16. $\dfrac{\text{P} \times \text{P}}{\text{R P} \times \text{P}}$

17. $\dfrac{\text{P} - \text{B } 3}{\text{Kt} - \text{B } 1}$

18. $\dfrac{\text{K} - \text{B } 2}{\text{R} - \text{R } 2}$

19. $\dfrac{\text{R} - \text{R } 1}{\text{Q} - \text{K } 2}$

20. $\dfrac{\text{Q} - \text{B } 5}{\text{R} - \text{Q } 1}$

21. $\dfrac{\text{R} \times \text{R ch.}}{\text{Kt} \times \text{R}}$

22. $\dfrac{\text{R} - \text{R } 1}{\text{R} - \text{K Kt } 1}$

23. $\dfrac{\text{B} \times \text{Kt}}{\text{P} \times \text{B}}$

24. $\dfrac{\text{R} - \text{Q Kt } 1}{\text{K} - \text{Kt } 2}$

25. $\dfrac{\text{R} - \text{Kt } 7}{\text{R} - \text{Q R } 1}$

26. $\dfrac{\text{K} - \text{K } 2}{\text{Kt} - \text{B } 1}$

27. $\dfrac{\text{P} - \text{Q } 5}{\text{P} - \text{B } 4}$

28. $\dfrac{\text{B} - \text{B } 2}{\text{Q} - \text{Q } 1}$

29. $\dfrac{\text{P} - \text{Kt } 3}{\text{R} - \text{Kt } 1}$

30. $\dfrac{\text{R} - \text{Kt } 3}{\text{R} \times \text{R}}$

31. $\dfrac{\text{B P} \times \text{R}}{\text{Q} - \text{Q } 2}$

32. $\dfrac{\text{Q} \times \text{Q}}{\text{Kt} \times \text{Q}}$

Drawn (*a*)

(*a*) Played in the St. Petersburg Tournament, 1914. This is the first game in which these two great masters met.

CHAPTER XII.

SCOTCH GAMBIT—ANALYSIS.

	(1)	(2)	(3)
1.	P—K 4 / P—K 4	—	—
2.	Kt—K B 3 / Kt—Q B 3	—	—
3.	P—Q 4 / Kt×P	—	—
4.	Kt×Kt / P×Kt	—	Kt×P / Kt—K 3
5.	Q×P / Kt—K 2	Q—B 3	B—Q B 4 / Kt—B 3
6.	B—Q B 4 (or Kt 5) / Kt—B 3	P—K 5 / Q—K Kt 3	0—0 / P—Q 3
7.	Q—Q 5 / Q—B 3	Kt—B 3 / Q×B P	Kt—Kt 4 / B—K 2
8.	0—0 / B—K 2	B—Q 3 / B—B 4	
9.		Q×B / Q×B	
10.		Kt—Kt 5 / Q—K 5 ch.	
11.		B—K 3 / Q×Kt P	
12.		Kt×P ch. / K—Q 1	
13.		Q—B 8 ch. / K×Kt	
14.		R—B 1 ch. and wins	

	(4)	(5)	(6)
1.	—	—	P—K 4 / P—K 4
2.	—	—	Kt—K B 3 / Kt—Q B 3
3.	—	—	P—Q 4 / P×P
4.	—	—	B—Q B 4 / B—B4
5.	P—K B 4 / B—B 4 (a)	Q—B 3	P—B3 / P—Q 6
6.	Kt—K B 3 / Q—B 3	Kt—Kt 4 / Q—R 5 ch.	P—Q Kt 4 / B—Kt 3
7.	P—K 5 / Q—Kt 3	P—Kt 3 / Q—R 4	P—Kt 5 / Q—K 2
8.	Kt—B 3 / B—Kt 5	B—K 2 / Q—R 6	0—0 / Kt—K 4
9.	B—Q 3 / Q×Kt P	Kt—B 2 / Q—R 3	Kt×Kt / Q×Kt
10.	R—K Kt 1+	P—B 5 / Kt—Kt 4	Q—Kt 3 / Q—B 3 or K 2
11.		P—K R 4 and wins a piece.	P—K 4+

	(7)	(8)	(9)
1.	—	—	—
2.	—	—	—
3.	—	—	—
4.	—	—	—
5.	—	Kt—Kt 5 / Kt—R 3 !	—
6.	—	Kt×B P / Kt×Kt	—
7.	Q—Kt 3 / Q—B 3	B×Kt ch. / K×B	—

(a) If 5. P—Q 3 ; 6. B—Kt 5 ch. / P—B 3 ; 7. Kt×Q B P / Q—Kt 3 ; 8. Kt—Q 4 d. ch.+

	(7)	**(8)**	**(9)**
8.	$\dfrac{0-0}{P-Q\,3}$	$\dfrac{Q-R\,5\ ch.}{P-Kt\,3}$	—
9.	$\dfrac{B\times P\ (Q\,6)}{B-K\,3}$	$\dfrac{Q\times B}{P-Q\,3}$	$\dfrac{}{P-Q\,4}$
10.	$\dfrac{Q-B\,2}{Kt-K\,2}$	$\dfrac{Q-Q\,Kt\,5}{P-Q\,R\,3}$	$\dfrac{Q\times P\ ch.}{Q\times Q}$
11.	$\dfrac{B-K\,Kt\,5}{Q-Kt\,3}$	$\dfrac{Q-Q\,3}{K-Kt\,2}$	$\dfrac{P\times Q}{R-K\,I\ ch.}$

Nos. 8, 9, 10, and 11. Position after White's 9th move.

BLACK.

WHITE.

(Cochrane-Schumoff Defence.)

12.	$\dfrac{P-Kt\,5}{Kt-K\,4}$	$\dfrac{0-0}{B-K\,3}$	$\dfrac{K-Q\,1}{Kt-Kt\,5}$
13.	$\dfrac{Kt\times Kt}{P\times Kt}$	$\dfrac{P-Q\,B\,3}{Q-B\,3}$	$\dfrac{B-Q\,2}{Kt\times P\ (Q\,5)}$
14.	$\dfrac{B\times Kt+}{K\times B}$	$\dfrac{B-Q\,2+}{}$	$\dfrac{Kt-R\,3}{B-B\,4}$
15.			$\dfrac{Kt-Kt\,5}{Q\,R-Q\,1}$
16.			$\dfrac{Kt\times P\ (Q\,5)}{Kt-B\,5\ and\ wins.}$

	(10)	(11)	(12)
1.	—	—	$\dfrac{\text{P—K 4}}{\text{P—K 4}}$
2.	—	—	$\dfrac{\text{Kt—K B 3}}{\text{Kt—Q B 3}}$
3.	—	...	$\dfrac{\text{P—Q 4}}{\text{P}\times\text{P}}$
4.	—	—	$\dfrac{\text{B—Q B 4}}{\text{B—B 4}}$
5.	—	—	$\dfrac{\text{0—0}}{\text{P—Q 3}}$
6.	—	—	$\dfrac{\text{P—B 3}}{\text{P}\times\text{P}}$
7.	—	—	$\dfrac{\text{Kt}\times\text{P}}{\text{K Kt—K 2}}$ (a)
8.	—	—	$\dfrac{\text{Kt—K Kt 5}}{\text{Kt—K 4}}$
9.	—		
10.	$\dfrac{\text{P}\times\text{P}}{\text{R—K 1}}$ ch.	$\dfrac{\text{0—0}}{\text{P}\times\text{P}}$	
11.	$\dfrac{\text{K—Q 1}}{\text{R—K 4}}$	$\dfrac{\text{P—Q B 3}}{\text{B—K 3}}$	
12.	$\dfrac{\text{P—Q B 4}}{\text{Q—R 5}}$	$\dfrac{\text{P—B 3 ?}}{\text{P—K 6}}$	
13.	$\dfrac{\text{Q—Q R 3}}{\text{B—Kt 5}}$ ch.	$\dfrac{\text{P}\times\text{P}}{\text{P}\times\text{K 7}}$	
14.	$\dfrac{\text{P—B 3}}{\text{Q—B 7}}$	$\dfrac{\text{R—K 1}}{\text{Q}\times\text{P}}$ ch.	
15.	$\dfrac{\text{B—Q 2}}{\text{Q}\times\text{Kt P}}$ and wins.	$\dfrac{\text{Q}\times\text{Q}}{\text{Kt}\times\text{Q}}$	
16.		$\dfrac{\text{Kt—R 3}}{\text{K R—K 1}}$	
17.		$\dfrac{\text{B—K 3}}{\text{Kt—K B 4}}$	
18.		$\dfrac{\text{R}\times\text{P}}{\text{B}\times\text{P}}$	

(a) If 7. $\dfrac{}{\text{B—K 3}}$; 8. $\dfrac{\text{B}\times\text{B}}{\text{P}\times\text{P}}$; 9. $\dfrac{\text{Kt—Kt 5}}{\text{Q—B 1}}$.

	(13)	(14)	(15)
1.	—	—	—
2.	—	—	—
3.	—	—	—
4.	—	—	Kt—B 3 (a)
5.	Q—B 3	—	Kt×P / Kt×P
6.	P—B 3 / P—Q 3	—	B×P ch. / K×B
7.	P—Q Kt 4 / B—Kt 3	B—K 3	Q—R 5 ch. / P—Kt 3
8.	B—Kt 2 / Kt—K 4	B×B / P×B	Q—Q 5 ch. / K—Kt 2
9.	Kt×Kt / P×Kt	Kt—K Kt 5 / Q—B 1	Kt×Kt / Q—R 5
10.	P×P / B×P	Q—R 5 ch. / P—Kt 3	Q—Q 4 ch. / K—Kt 1
11.	B×B / P×B	Q—Kt 4 / P—K 4	Kt—K 5+
12.	P—K 5 / Q—Kt 3	Kt—K 6 / Kt—B 3	
13.	P—Q R 4 / P—Q R 4	Q—R 3 / K—K 2	
14.	P×P / R×P	Kt—Q 5 ch. / Kt×Kt	
15.	Kt—R 3+	P×Kt	

	(16)	(17)	(18)
1.	—	—	—
2.	—	—	—

(a) If 4. P—Q 3; 5. P—B 3 / P×P ; 6. Kt×P +

	(16)	(17)	(18)
3.	—	—	—
4.	—	—	—
5.	$\dfrac{\text{P—K 5}}{\text{Kt—K Kt 5}}$	$\dfrac{\text{Kt—Kt 5}}{\text{P—Q 4}}$	
6.	$\dfrac{\text{B} \times \text{P ch.}}{\text{K} \times \text{B}}$	$\dfrac{\text{P} \times \text{P}}{\text{Q—K 2 ch.}}$	$\dfrac{\text{Kt—K 4}}{\text{B—Kt 3}}$
7.	$\dfrac{\text{Kt} \times \text{Kt ch.}}{\text{K—Kt 1}}$	$\dfrac{\text{K—B 1}}{\text{Kt—K 4}}$	$\dfrac{\text{P—K R 3}}{\text{Q} \times \text{P}}$
8.	$\dfrac{\text{Q} \times \text{Kt}}{\text{P—K R 3}}$	$\dfrac{\text{Q} \times \text{P}}{\text{P—K R 3}}$	$\dfrac{\text{P} \times \text{Kt}}{\text{Q} \times \text{Kt ch.}}$
9.	$\dfrac{\text{Kt—K B 3}}{\text{P—Q 3}}$	$\dfrac{\text{Kt—K 4}+}{}$	$\dfrac{\text{Q—K 2}}{\text{Q} \times \text{Q ch.}}$
10.	$\dfrac{\text{Q—K 4}}{\text{P} \times \text{P}}$		$\dfrac{\text{B} \times \text{Q}}{\text{B} \times \text{P (K 4)}}$
11.	$\dfrac{\text{Kt} \times \text{K P}}{\text{Kt} \times \text{Kt}}$		$\dfrac{\text{Kt} \times \text{P}}{\text{B} \times \text{B}+}$
12.	$\dfrac{\text{Q} \times \text{Kt}}{\text{K—R 2}}$		$\dfrac{\text{K} \times \text{B}}{}$
13.	$\dfrac{\text{0—0}}{\text{P—K Kt 3}}$		
14.	$\dfrac{\text{R—Q 1}}{\text{B—Kt 2}}$		
15.	$\dfrac{\text{Q—Kt 3}}{\text{P—Q B 3}}$		
16.	$\dfrac{\text{P—Q B 3}}{\text{Q—K 2}}$		

	(19)	(20)	(21)
1.	$\dfrac{\text{P—K 4}}{\text{P—K 4}}$	—	—
2.	$\dfrac{\text{Kt—K B 3}}{\text{Kt—Q B 3}}$	—	—
3.	$\dfrac{\text{P—Q 4}}{\text{P} \times \text{P}}$	—	—
4.	$\dfrac{\text{B—Q B 4}}{\text{Q—B 3}}$	$\dfrac{}{\text{B—Kt 5 ch.}}$	—

	(19)	(20)	(21)
5.	$\dfrac{0-0}{P-Q\,3}$	$\dfrac{P-B\,3}{P\times P}$	—
6.	$\dfrac{P-B\,3}{P-Q\,6}$	$\dfrac{0-0}{P-B\,7}$	$\dfrac{P\times P}{B-R\,4}$
7.	$\dfrac{Q\times P}{Q-Kt\,3}$	$\dfrac{Q\times P}{P-Q\,3}$	$\dfrac{P-K\,5}{P-Q\,4}$
8.	$\dfrac{B-B\,4}{B-K\,2}$	$\dfrac{P-Q\,R\,3}{B-Q\,B\,4}$	$\dfrac{Q\times P}{Q\times Q}$
9.	$\dfrac{Kt-R\,3}{P-Q\,R\,3}$	$\dfrac{P-Q\,Kt\,4\ (a)}{B-Kt\,3}$	$\dfrac{B\times Q}{K\,Kt-K\,2}$

No. 21.   Position after Black's 6th move.

BLACK.

WHITE.

10.	$\dfrac{Kt-B\,2}{Kt-R\,3}$	$\dfrac{B-Kt\,2}{Kt-B\,3}$ =	$\dfrac{B\times Kt\ ch.}{Kt\times B}$
11.			$\dfrac{B-B\,4}{0-0}$
12.			$\dfrac{0-0}{K\,R-K\,1}$
13.			$\dfrac{P-K\,R\,3}{}$ =

(a) If 9. $\dfrac{\ }{Q\,Kt-Q\,5}$; 10. $\dfrac{B\times P\ ch.}{K-B\,1}$; 11. $\dfrac{Q-Q\,3}{Q-K\,B\,3}$; 12. $\dfrac{B-R\,5}{}$

	(22)	(23)	(24)
1.	—	—	—
2.	—	—	—
3.	—	—	—
4.	—	—	—
5.	—	—	—

No. 24. Position after White's 7th move.

BLACK.

WHIT_.

	(22)	(23)	(24)
6.	—	—	$\dfrac{0-0}{P \times P}$
7.	$\dfrac{\text{K Kt}-\text{K 2}}{}$	$\dfrac{0-0}{P-Q 3}$	$\dfrac{Q B \times P}{B - B 1}$
8.	$\dfrac{B-R 3}{0-0}$	$\dfrac{P-K 5}{B-K 3}$	$\dfrac{Kt-Q B 3}{Kt-R 3}$
9.	$\dfrac{0-0}{K-R 1}$	$\dfrac{B \times B}{P \times B}$	$\dfrac{P-K 5}{B-K 2}$
10.	$\dfrac{Kt-Kt 5}{Kt \times P}$	$\dfrac{Q-Kt 3}{Q-B 1}$	$\dfrac{Kt-K 4}{0-0}$

	(22)	(23)	(24)
11.	Kt×R P / K×Kt !	P×P / P×P	Q-Q 2 / P-Q 3
12.	Q-R 5 ch. / K-Kt 1	Kt-Kt 5+	Kt-B 6 ch.+
13.	Q×Kt / Kt-B 3		
14.	Q-R 5 / P-Q 3		
15.	B-Q 3 / P-K Kt 3		
16.	B×Kt P / P×B		
17.	Q×P h., &c.		

	(25)	(26)	(27)	(28)
1.	—	P-K 4 / P-K 4	—	—
2.	—	Kt-B 3 / Kt-Q B 3	—	—
3.	—	P-Q 4 / P×P	—	—
4.	—	Kt×P / Q-R 5	—	B-B 4
5.	—	Kt-Kt 5 / B-B 4	Q×P ch.	Kt×Kt / Q-B 3
6.	—	Q-B 3 / Kt-Q 5	B-K 2 / K-Q 1	Q-K B 3 / Q×Q
7.	K-B 1	Kt×P ch. / K-Q 1	0-0 / P-Q R 3	P×Q / Kt P×Kt
8.	P-K 5 / Q-K 2	Q-K B 4 / Kt×P ch.	Q Kt-B 3 / Q-K 1	B-K B 4 / P-Q 3
9.	P-Q R 3 / B-B 4	K-Q 1 / Q×Q	Kt-Q 4+	B-B 4 / B-K 3
10.	Kt-B 3 / P-Q 3	B×Q / Kt×R		Kt-Q 2—
11.	Kt-Q 5 / Q-Q 2	Kt×R		
12.	R-K 1 / P×P			

(25)	(26)	(27)	(28)

13. $\dfrac{\text{B} \times \text{P}}{\text{Kt} \times \text{B}}$

14. $\dfrac{\text{Kt} \times \text{Kt}}{\text{Q} - \text{Q 1}}$

15. $\dfrac{\text{Kt} \times \text{P}}{}$ and wins.

SCOTCH GAMBIT—GAMES.

	(1)	(2)	(3)
	Edinburgh (Match 1826)	Cochrane	Cochrane
	London	Walker	Deschappelles
1.	$\dfrac{\text{P} - \text{K 4}}{\text{P} - \text{K 4}}$	$\dfrac{\text{P} - \text{K 4}}{\text{P} - \text{K 4}}$	$\dfrac{\text{P} - \text{K 4}}{\text{P} - \text{K 4}}$
2.	$\dfrac{\text{Kt} - \text{K B 3}}{\text{Kt} - \text{Q B 3}}$	$\dfrac{\text{Kt} - \text{K B 3}}{\text{Kt} - \text{Q B 3}}$	$\dfrac{\text{Kt} - \text{K B 3}}{\text{Kt} - \text{Q B 3}}$
3.	$\dfrac{\text{P} - \text{Q 4}}{\text{Kt} \times \text{P}}$	$\dfrac{\text{P} - \text{Q 4}}{\text{Kt} \times \text{P}}$	$\dfrac{\text{P} - \text{Q 4}}{\text{P} \times \text{P}}$
4.	$\dfrac{\text{Kt} \times \text{Kt}}{\text{P} \times \text{Kt}}$	$\dfrac{\text{Kt} \times \text{P}}{\text{Kt} - \text{K 3}}$	$\dfrac{\text{B} - \text{Q B 4}}{\text{B} - \text{B 4}}$
5.	$\dfrac{\text{Q} \times \text{P}}{\text{Kt} - \text{K 2}}$	$\dfrac{\text{B} - \text{Q B 4}}{\text{P} - \text{Q B 3}}$	$\dfrac{\text{Kt} - \text{Kt 5}}{\text{Kt} - \text{K 4}}$ (c)
6.	$\dfrac{\text{B} - \text{B 4}}{\text{Kt} - \text{B 3}}$	$\dfrac{0 - 0}{\text{Kt} - \text{B 3}}$	$\dfrac{\text{B} \times \text{P ch.}}{\text{Kt} \times \text{B}}$
7.	$\dfrac{\text{Q} - \text{Q 5}}{\text{Q} - \text{B 3}}$	$\dfrac{\text{Kt} \times \text{K B P}}{\text{K} \times \text{Kt}}$ (b)	$\dfrac{\text{Kt} \times \text{Kt}}{\text{B} - \text{Kt 5 ch.}}$
8.	$\dfrac{\text{Kt} - \text{B 3}}{\text{B} - \text{Kt 5}}$ (a)	$\dfrac{\text{B} \times \text{Kt ch.}}{\text{K} \times \text{B}}$	$\dfrac{\text{P} - \text{Q B 3}}{\text{P} \times \text{P}}$
9.	$\dfrac{\text{B} - \text{Q 2}}{\text{P} - \text{Q 3}}$	$\dfrac{\text{P} - \text{K 5}}{\text{Kt} - \text{Q 4}}$	$\dfrac{\text{P} \times \text{P}}{\text{B} \times \text{P ch.}}$
10.	$\dfrac{\text{B} - \text{Q Kt 5}}{\text{B} - \text{Q 2}}$	$\dfrac{\text{P} - \text{Q B 4}}{\text{Kt} - \text{Kt 3}}$	$\dfrac{\text{Kt} \times \text{B}}{\text{K} \times \text{Kt}}$

(a) Castling would have been better play, because Black would then have had no favourable opportunity of bringing their K B into the field.

(b) We are indebted to Mr. Cochrane for this ingenious variation from the ordinary opening.

(c) This is not the correct move, he should have played Kt—R 3.

	(1)	(2)	(3)
11.	Q – B 4 / B – Q B 4	K – R 1 / P – K R 4	Q – Q 5 ch. / K – B 1
12.	0 – 0 / 0 – 0	P – B 4 / P – Kt 3	B – R 3 ch. / P – Q 3
13.	Q – Q 3 (a) / Kt – K 4	P – B 5 ch. / K × K P	P – K 5 / Q – Kt 4
14.	Q – Kt 3 / B × B	B – B 4 ch. / Resigns.	P × P (b) / Q × Q
15.	Kt × B / P – Q B 3		P × P d. ch. / K – B 2
16.	Kt – B 3 / Kt – B 5		Kt × Q / B – Q 2
17.	B – Kt 5 / Q – Kt 3		0 – 0 / R – B 1
18.	P – Kt 3 / P – B 3		B – Q 6 / K – K 3
19.	B – B 1 / Q × Q		B – Kt 3 / B – B 3
20.	P × Q / B – Q 5		Q R – Q 1 / B × Kt
21.	P × Kt / B × Kt		K R – K 1 ch. / K – B 3
22.	R – Kt 1 / P – Q Kt 3		R × B / K 1 – K 3
23.	R – Q 1 / Q R – K 1		R – R 5 / Kt – B 4
24.	R – Q Kt 3 / B – R 4		R – B 5 / Kt × B
25.	P – K B 3 / P – K B 4		R P × Kt / K – B 2

(a) Kt – Q 5 looks a tempting move, but it would have been a very bad one for them (e.g.)—

13.	Kt – Q 5	Q – R 5
14.	Kt × P	R – B 1
15.	Kt – Q 5	Kt – K 4
16.	Q – K 2	B – K Kt 5
17.	Q – K	Kt – B 6 ch.

And Black win.

(b) The termination of this game is very ingeniously played by Mr. Cochrane.

	(1)	(2)	(3)
26.	P×P / R—K 7 (a)		R—Q 1 / K R—K 1
27.	P—K Kt 4 / R×B P		R—Q 3 / K R—K 2
28.	B—B 4 / R×B P		R—B 5 ch. / K—K 1 (d)
29.	B×P / R—K 1		R—Q 8 ch. / R×R
30.	R—R 3 / P—K R 3		R—B 8 ch. / K×R
31.	B—B 7 / R—K 2		P × R(Q) ch. and wins.
32.	R—Q 8 ch. / K—R 2		

	(1)		(1) (contd.)		(1) (contd.)
33.	R—Q B 8 / R—B 8 ch.	37.	P—B 4 / B—Q 7	41.	K—Kt 4 / P—R 4 ch.
34.	K—R 2 / R (K 2)—K 8	38.	P—Kt 3 / B—R 4 (c)	42.	K—B 3 / R (R 7)—B 7 ch.
35.	K—R 3 / R—R 8 ch.	39.	R—K 3 / R—B 7	43.	K—K 4 / P—Kt 3
36.	B—R 2 / B—B 6 (b)	40.	P—Kt 5 / R (R 8)×B ch.	44.	R—B 7 ch. / K—Kt 1

(a) They should have taken the P with K R.

(b) From the subjoined variation it appears that they would **not** have improved their game by the move of B—Q 7.

36.		B—Q 7
37.	R—R 4	B—K 6
38.	R—K 4	B—Kt 8
39.	R (K 4)—K 8	R×B
40.	K—Kt 3	

And White must win.

(c) If Black had played R—Q B 7, the opposing party would have moved P—K Kt 5 (e.g.)—

38.		R—Q B 7
39.	P—Kt 5	P×P (or A)
40	R×P	

And White wins.

(A.)

39.		R (R 8)×B
40.	K—Kt 4	

Black cannot save the game.

(d) K—K 3 would have saved the game.

(1) (contd.)

45. $\dfrac{\text{K—K 5}}{\text{R—B 4 ch.}}$

46. $\dfrac{\text{K—B 6}}{\text{Q R} \times \text{P ch.}}$

47. $\dfrac{\text{K} \times \text{P}}{\text{R—B 1}}$

48. $\dfrac{\text{K R—K Kt 7 ch.}}{\text{K—R 1}}$

49. $\dfrac{\text{K—R 6}}{\text{B—Kt 5}}$

50. $\dfrac{\text{R—K 6}}{\text{R—B 4}}$

51. $\dfrac{\text{R—R 7 ch.}}{\text{K—Kt 1}}$

52. $\dfrac{\text{R—Kt 6 ch.}}{\text{K—B 1}}$

53. $\dfrac{\text{R} \times \text{B P}}{\text{R—B 4}}$

54. $\dfrac{\text{R—B 6 ch.}}{\text{K—K 1}}$

55. $\dfrac{\text{P—Kt 6}}{\text{R—Q B 6}}$

56. $\dfrac{\text{P—Kt 4}}{\text{B—B1 ch.}}$

57. $\dfrac{\text{R} \times \text{B ch.}}{\text{K} \times \text{R}}$

58. $\dfrac{\text{P—Kt 7 ch.}}{\text{K—B 2}}$

59. $\dfrac{\text{R—R 8}}{\text{R—B 3 ch.}}$

60. $\dfrac{\text{K—R 7}}{\text{Resigns.}}$

	(4)	(5)	(6)
	Staunton	Cochrane	Capt. Kennedy
	Popert	Popert	Greville
1.	$\dfrac{\text{P—K 4}}{\text{P—K 4}}$	$\dfrac{\text{P—K 4}}{\text{P—K 4}}$	$\dfrac{\text{P—K 4}}{\text{P—K 4}}$
2.	$\dfrac{\text{Kt—K B 3}}{\text{Kt—Q B 3}}$	$\dfrac{\text{Kt—K B 3}}{\text{Kt—Q B 3}}$	$\dfrac{\text{Kt—K B 3}}{\text{Kt—Q B 3}}$
3.	$\dfrac{\text{P—Q 4}}{\text{P} \times \text{P}}$	$\dfrac{\text{P—Q 4}}{\text{P} \times \text{P}}$	$\dfrac{\text{P—Q 4}}{\text{P} \times \text{P}}$
4.	$\dfrac{\text{B—Q B 4}}{\text{B—Kt 5 ch.}}$	$\dfrac{\text{B—Q B 4}}{\text{B—Kt 5 ch.}}$	$\dfrac{\text{Kt} \times \text{P}}{\text{B—B 4 } (b)}$
5.	$\dfrac{\text{P—B 3}}{\text{P} \times \text{P}}$	$\dfrac{\text{P—B 3}}{\text{P} \times \text{P}}$	$\dfrac{\text{Kt} \times \text{Kt}}{\text{Q—B 3}}$
6.	$\dfrac{\text{0—0}}{\text{P—B 7}}$	$\dfrac{\text{P} \times \text{P}}{\text{B—R 4}}$	$\dfrac{\text{Q—K 2}}{\text{Q P} \times \text{Kt}}$
7.	$\dfrac{\text{Q} \times \text{P}}{\text{P—Q 3}}$	$\dfrac{\text{P—K 5}}{\text{P—Q 3 } (a)}$	$\dfrac{\text{Kt—B 3}}{\text{B—K 3}}$
8.	$\dfrac{\text{P—Q R 3}}{\text{B—R 4}}$	$\dfrac{\text{Q—Kt 3}}{\text{Q—K 2}}$	$\dfrac{\text{B—Q 3}}{\text{0—0—0}}$
9.	$\dfrac{\text{P—Q Kt 4}}{\text{B—Kt 3}}$	$\dfrac{\text{0—0}}{\text{P} \times \text{P}}$	$\dfrac{\text{Q—B 4}}{\text{P—K R 3}}$

(a) In the analysis of this opening it is shown that the better move is—7. P—Q 4.

(b) This perhaps is the strongest way of replying to White's move of Kt × P.

	(4)	(5)	(6)
10.	B--Kt 2 / Kt—B 3	B—R 3 / Q—B 3	Q×Q / Kt×Q
11.	P—K 5 / P×P	Q Kt—Q 2 / B—B 4	0—0 / P—K Kt 4
12.	Kt×P / Kt×Kt	Kt×P / Kt×Kt	Kt—K 2 / P—Kt 5
13.	B×Kt / 0-0	Q—Kt 5 ch. / Kt—B 3	P—Q Kt 3 / K R—Kt 1 (f)
14.	Kt—Q B 3 / Kt—Kt 5	K R—K 1 ch. / B—K 3	B×P / Kt—R 4
15.	B—K Kt 3 / Q—K Kt 4	B×B / P×B	Kt—B 4 / P—Kt 6 (g)
16.	Q R—K 1 / B—K B 4	Q×P (e) / R—Q 1	Kt×Kt / P×B P ch.
17.	Q—Kt 3 / P—Q B 3 (a)	Q×Kt ch. / K—B 2	K—R 1 / R—R 1
18.	B—Q 6 / Kt×B P	Kt—K4 / Kt—K 2	B—K Kt 5 / Q R—K Kt 1
19.	B×R (b) / B—R 6 (c)	Kt—Kt 5 ch. / Q×Kt	Kt—Kt 7 (h) / B—Q 3
20.	B×P ch. / K—B 1	Q×P ch. and wins.	P—K R 3 / B×P
21.	B—Q 5 (d) / P×B		P×B / R×Kt
22.	Q×P / Q—B 3		R×P / R×P ch.
23.	P×B / Kt×P db. ch.		K—Kt 1 / R×B ch.

(a) Highly ingenious, the object being to tempt White to attack the Rook, that Black might be enabled to take the K B P.

(b) If he had taken the Knight, Black would have had a fine position of offence.

(c) This is very skilful, nothing but the nicest care can save White's game.

(d) The only move apparently to avert the threatened defeat.

(e) This game is admirably played by Mr. Cochrane.

(f) The sacrifice of the P here to gain an opening on the adverse K R's file, is the conception of an adept in chess strategy.

(g) This and the subsequent moves of Mr. Greville are of the very first order of fine play.

(h) With the view to play B—B 6 if Black took the Knight.

	(4)	**(5)**	**(6)**
24.	$\dfrac{\text{K—Kt 2}}{\text{Kt—B 7}}$		$\dfrac{\text{R—Kt 2}}{\text{B—B 4 ch.}}$
25.	$\dfrac{\text{Kt—K 4}}{\text{Q—Kt 3 ch.}}$		$\dfrac{\text{K—B 1}}{\text{R—R 8 ch.}}$
26.	$\dfrac{\text{Q—Kt 5}}{\text{Q—Q B 3}}$		$\dfrac{\text{K—K 2}}{\text{R×R ch.}}$
27.	$\dfrac{\text{R×Kt ch.}}{\text{B×R}}$		$\dfrac{\text{K—B 3}}{\text{R—B 7 ch.}}$
28.	$\dfrac{\text{K×B}}{\text{K—Kt 1}}$		$\dfrac{\text{K—Kt 3}}{\text{R×R and wins.}}$
	White wins.		

	(7)	**(8)**	**(9)**
	Greville	Laroche	Schumoff
	Kieseritsky	De Riviere	Jaenisch
1.	$\dfrac{\text{P—K 4}}{\text{P—K 4}}$	$\dfrac{\text{P—K 4}}{\text{P—K 4}}$	$\dfrac{\text{P—K 4}}{\text{P—K 4}}$
2.	$\dfrac{\text{Kt—K B 3}}{\text{Kt—Q B 3}}$	$\dfrac{\text{Kt—K B 3}}{\text{Kt—Q B 3}}$	$\dfrac{\text{Kt—K B 3}}{\text{Kt—Q B 3}}$
3.	$\dfrac{\text{P—Q 4}}{\text{P×P}}$	$\dfrac{\text{P—Q 4}}{\text{Kt×P}}$	$\dfrac{\text{P—Q 4}}{\text{P×P}}$
4.	$\dfrac{\text{B—Q B 4}}{\text{B—Kt 5 ch.}}$	$\dfrac{\text{Kt×P}}{\text{Kt—K 3}}$	$\dfrac{\text{B—Q B 4}}{\text{B—B 4}}$
5.	$\dfrac{\text{P—B 3}}{\text{P×P}}$	$\dfrac{\text{P—K B 4}}{\text{B—B 4}}$	$\dfrac{\text{Kt—Kt 5}}{\text{Kt—R 3}}$
6.	$\dfrac{\text{0—0}}{\text{P×P}}$	$\dfrac{\text{B—Q B 4}}{\text{P—Q 3}}$	$\dfrac{\text{Kt×B P}}{\text{Kt×Kt}}$
7.	$\dfrac{\text{B×P}}{\text{K—B 1 (a)}}$	$\dfrac{\text{Kt—Q 3 (b)}}{\text{Kt—B 3}}$	$\dfrac{\text{B×Kt ch.}}{\text{K×B}}$
8.	$\dfrac{\text{P—K 5}}{\text{P—Q 3}}$	$\dfrac{\text{P—K 5}}{\text{Kt—K 5}}$	$\dfrac{\text{Q—R 5 ch.}}{\text{P—Kt 3}}$
9.	$\dfrac{\text{Q—Kt 3}}{\text{Kt—R 3}}$	$\dfrac{\text{Q—B 3}}{\text{P—Q 4}}$	$\dfrac{\text{Q×B}}{\text{P—Q 3 (c)}}$

(a) This is inferior, we think, to returning the Bishop home again.
(b) Checking with the Bishop at Kt 5 would not have been **bad** play.
(c) It was subsequent to playing this game that Mr. Schumoff discovered that the move 9. $\dfrac{\text{P—Q 4}}{}$ was far preferable to 9. $\dfrac{}{\text{P—Q 3}}$.

	(7)	(8)	(9)
10.	$\dfrac{\text{P}\times\text{P}}{\text{P}\times\text{P}}$	$\dfrac{\text{Kt}\times\text{B}}{\text{Q Kt}\times\text{Kt}}$	$\dfrac{\text{Q}-\text{Q Kt 5}}{\text{R}-\text{K 1}}$
11.	$\dfrac{\text{P}-\text{Q R 3}}{\text{B}-\text{R 4}}$	$\dfrac{\text{B}-\text{Q 3}}{\text{Kt}\times\text{B ch.}}$	$\dfrac{\text{0}-\text{0}}{\text{R}\times\text{P }(f)}$
12.	$\dfrac{\text{Kt}-\text{B 3}}{\text{B}-\text{Kt 3}}$	$\dfrac{\text{P}\times\text{Kt}}{\text{Kt}-\text{B 4}}$	$\dfrac{\text{Q}-\text{Q 5 ch.}}{\text{R}-\text{K 3}}$
13.	$\dfrac{\text{Kt}-\text{Q 5}}{\text{Kt}-\text{R 4}}$	$\dfrac{\text{P}-\text{Q Kt 4}}{\text{Kt}-\text{K 3}}$	$\dfrac{\text{B}-\text{Kt 5}}{\text{Q}-\text{K 1}}$
14.	$\dfrac{\text{Q}-\text{B 3 }(a)}{\text{Kt}-\text{B 4}}$	$\dfrac{\text{B}-\text{Kt 2}}{\text{P}-\text{Q B 3}}$	$\dfrac{\text{P}-\text{K B 4}}{\text{K}-\text{Kt 2}}$
15.	$\dfrac{\text{B}-\text{Q 3}}{\text{P}-\text{B 3}}$	$\dfrac{\text{0}-\text{0}}{\text{Q}-\text{Kt 3 ch.}}$	$\dfrac{\text{P}-\text{B 5}}{\text{R}-\text{K 4 }(g)}$
16.	$\dfrac{\text{Q R}-\text{K 1 }(b)}{\text{Kt}-\text{B 3}}$	$\dfrac{\text{K}-\text{R 1}}{\text{0}-\text{0}}$	$\dfrac{\text{P}-\text{B 6 ch.}}{\text{K}-\text{R 1}}$
17.	$\dfrac{\text{Kt}\times\text{B}}{\text{P}\times\text{Kt}}$	$\dfrac{\text{P}-\text{B 5 }(d)}{\text{Kt}-\text{Q 5}}$	$\dfrac{\text{P}-\text{B 7}}{\text{K}-\text{Kt 2}}$
18.	$\dfrac{\text{Kt}-\text{Kt 5 }(c)}{\text{R}-\text{R 4}}$	$\dfrac{\text{Q}-\text{R 5 }(e)}{\text{Kt}\times\text{P}}$	$\dfrac{\text{P}\times\text{Q (Kt) ch.}}{\text{R}\times\text{Kt}}$
19.	$\dfrac{\text{B}\times\text{Kt}}{\text{R}\times\text{B}}$	$\dfrac{\text{R}\times\text{Kt}}{\text{P}-\text{Kt 3}}$	$\dfrac{\text{Q}-\text{B 7 ch.}}{\text{K}-\text{R 1}}$

(a) The attack is sustained with a good deal of vigour and in-genuity.

(b) Threatening to take off the K Kt, and then plant the Rook at K 7. The young player will comprehend the importance of the Rook being so placed from the annexed moves, which are probable when the Rook is played thus. Let us suppose White had now to move :—

B×Kt	B×B
R—K 7	R—B 1
Q—Q 2	Kt—B 5, or R—B 7
R×P	Kt or R×Q
B×P ch.	

and then White mates with the Knight's next move.

(c) Well played. Black dare not capture the Knight.

(d) White has now an excellent game.

(e) Better perhaps to have taken the Knight. For suppose :—

18. $\dfrac{\text{B}\times\text{Kt}}{\text{Q}\times\text{B}}$; 19. $\dfrac{\text{Q}-\text{Kt 3}}{\text{Q}\times\text{R}}$; 20. $\dfrac{\text{P}-\text{B 6}}{\text{P}-\text{K Kt 3}}$; 21. $\dfrac{\text{Q}-\text{K 3}}{\text{K}-\text{R 1}}$;

22. $\dfrac{\text{Kt}-\text{Q 2}}{\text{Q}\times\text{P}}$; 23. $\dfrac{\text{Q}-\text{R 6}}{\text{R}-\text{K Kt}}$; 24. $\dfrac{\text{Kt}-\text{B 3}}{}$, and wins.

(f) This was an error.

(g) Fatal.

	(7)	**(8)**	**(9)**
20.	$\dfrac{\text{Kt}-\text{K 6 ch.}}{\text{B}\times\text{Kt}}$	$\dfrac{\text{R}-\text{Kt 5}}{\text{Q}-\text{B 7}}$	B−B 6 mate.
21.	$\dfrac{\text{R}\times\text{B}}{\text{R}-\text{K 4}}$	$\dfrac{\text{Kt}-\text{Q 2}}{\text{Q}\times\text{Kt}}$	
22.	$\dfrac{\text{Q}-\text{R 3}}{\text{R}-\text{Q Kt 4}}$	$\dfrac{\text{B}-\text{Q 4}}{\text{Q}\times\text{Q Kt P}}$	
23.	$\dfrac{\text{B}-\text{R 1}}{\text{K}-\text{B 2}}$	$\dfrac{\text{B}-\text{Kt 1}}{\text{Q}-\text{K 2}}$	**(8) (cont.)**
24.	$\dfrac{\text{P}-\text{B 4}}{\text{P}-\text{R 3}}$	$\dfrac{\text{Q}-\text{R 4 }(b)}{\text{K}-\text{R 1}}$	30. $\dfrac{\text{R (Q 5)}-\text{K 5}}{\text{Q}-\text{Q 2}}$
25.	$\dfrac{\text{K R}-\text{K 1}}{\text{P}-\text{Q 4 }(a)}$	$\dfrac{\text{P}-\text{K 6 }(c)}{\text{P}-\text{Q B 4}}$	31. $\dfrac{\text{P}-\text{Q 4 }(d)}{\text{P}\times\text{P}}$
26.	$\dfrac{\text{Q}-\text{R 5 ch.}}{\text{P}-\text{Kt 3}}$	$\dfrac{\text{P}\times\text{P}}{\text{R}\times\text{P}}$	32. $\dfrac{\text{R}\times\text{B}}{\text{R}\times\text{R}}$
27.	$\dfrac{\text{Q}-\text{K 2}}{\text{Kt}-\text{K 4}}$	$\dfrac{\text{R}-\text{K 1}}{\text{B}-\text{K 3}}$	33. $\dfrac{\text{R}\times\text{R}}{\text{P}-\text{Q 6 }(e)}$
28.	$\dfrac{\text{P}\times\text{Kt}}{\text{Kt}\times\text{R}}$	$\dfrac{\text{Q}-\text{R 6}}{\text{R}-\text{B 3}}$	34. $\dfrac{\text{B}-\text{K 3}}{\text{Q}-\text{R 5}}$
29.	$\dfrac{\text{P}\times\text{P d. ch.}}{\text{Resigns.}}$	$\dfrac{\text{R}\times\text{Q P}}{\text{P}-\text{Kt 3}}$	35. $\dfrac{\text{R}-\text{K 7}}{\text{Resigns.}}$

	(10)	**(11)**	**(12)**
	Schumoff	Millard	Morphy (f)
	Prince Ouroussoff	Wilkinson	Kipping
1.	$\dfrac{\text{P}-\text{K 4}}{\text{P}-\text{K 4}}$	$\dfrac{\text{P}-\text{K 4}}{\text{P}-\text{K 4}}$	$\dfrac{\text{P}-\text{K 4}}{\text{P}-\text{K 4}}$
2.	$\dfrac{\text{Kt}-\text{K B 3}}{\text{Kt}-\text{Q B 3}}$	$\dfrac{\text{Kt}-\text{K B 3}}{\text{Kt}-\text{Q B 3}}$	$\dfrac{\text{Kt}-\text{K B 3}}{\text{Kt}-\text{Q B 3}}$
3.	$\dfrac{\text{P}-\text{Q 4}}{\text{P}\times\text{P}}$	$\dfrac{\text{P}-\text{Q 4}}{\text{P}\times\text{P}}$	$\dfrac{\text{P}-\text{Q 4}}{\text{P}\times\text{P}}$
4.	$\dfrac{\text{B}-\text{Q B 4}}{\text{B}\times\text{B 4}}$	$\dfrac{\text{B}-\text{Q B 4}}{\text{B}-\text{B 4}}$	$\dfrac{\text{B}-\text{Q B 4}}{\text{B}-\text{B 4}}$

(a) After this move the game is quite irretrievable.
(b) Threatening to win the Queen.
(c) White plays very cleverly from this point to the finish.
(d) Finely played.
(e) Taking the Rook would be immediately fatal.
(f) Morphy playing eight simultaneous games without sight of the boards.

	(1C)	(11)	(12)
5.	Kt—Kt 5 / Kt—R 3	Kt—Kt 5 / Kt—R 3	0—0 / P—Q 3
6.	Kt×B P / Kt×Kt	Kt×B P / Kt×Kt	P—B 3 / Q—B 3
7.	B×Kt ch. / K×B	B×Kt ch. / K×B	B—K Kt 5 / Q—Kt 3
8.	Q—R 5 ch. / P—Kt 3	Q—R 5 ch. / P—Kt 3	P×P / Kt×P
9.	Q×B / P—Q 4 (a)	Q×B / P—Q 4 (e)	Kt×Kt / Q×B
10.	0—0 / P×P	0—0 / P×P	P—B 4 / Q—Kt 3
11.	P—Q B 3 (b) / R—K 1 (c)	Kt—Q 2 / R—K 1	K—R 1 / Kt—R 3
12.	P×P / Q×P	Kt—Kt 3 / R—K 4	P—K R 3 (f) / B×P
13.	Q—K Kt 5 / B—B 4	Q—B 4 ch. / B—K 3	P×B / Q×P ch.
14.	B—Q 2 / Kt—K 4	Q—K 2 / Q—R 5	Q—B 3 / Q×K Kt
15.	B—B 3 / Q—Q 3	B—Q 2 / R—R 4	R—K 1 ch. / K—Q 2
16.	Q—R 6 / Kt—Kt 5 (d)	P—K R 3 / B×P	Kt—R 3 / B×Kt
17.	Q×R P ch. / K—K 3	P×B / Q×P (R 3)	B—Kt 5 ch. / P—B 3

(a) Mr. Schumoff has in this instance to defend himself against his own variation.

(b) I believe this to be the best possible move, and one which effectually prevents the second player from establishing his Pawns in the centre.

(c) If P—Q 6, White, as was shown before, would have checked with Q—B 4, and then have taken the K P.

(d) The safer game was to retreat the King to Kt 1, yet by opening the Rook's file there is promise of a fine attack.

(e) This game is a good example of the vigorous attack obtained by the second player in the Schumoff-Cochrane defence of the " Scotch Gambit."

(f) A slip. The only one Mr. Morphy was guilty of throughout the whole of this prodigious exploit.

	(10)	(11)	(12)
18.	Kt—R 3 / R—K 2 (a)	P—K B 3 / P—K 6	P×B (d) / K R—K 1
19.	Q—R 4 / R—Q 1 (b)	Resigns.	Q R—B 1 / P—Q 4
20.	Kt—B 4 / Q—B 4 (c)		Q—Q Kt 3 / K—B 2
21.	P—K R 3 / Kt×P		B—Q 3 / R—K 6
22.	R×Kt / R—Q 4		R×R / Q×R
23.	P—K Kt 4 / R—B 2		R—Q Kt 1 / Q×P ch.
24.	P×B ch. / R (B 2)×P		K—Kt 1 / P—Q Kt 3
25.	Q×P ch. / K—B 2		R—K 1 / Q—Kt 6 ch.
26.	Kt—K 3 / R×R		K—B 1 / Q×P ch.
27.	Q×R ch. / Q×Q		K—Kt 2 / Q—Kt 4 ch.
28.	Kt×Q and wins.		K—B 1 / Kt—Kt 5
29.			R—K 2 / Kt—K 6 ch.
30.			Resigns.

(a) P—K Kt 4 looks a good move, but White may escape all danger to his Queen by playing her boldly to R 3.

(b) I should have been inclined to move P—K Kt 4, following it with R—R 2, leaving White to exchange Queens if he thought proper. By this line of operation, Black would have been enabled to force an opening on the adverse King's side.

(c) This fatal error costs a piece. He should have played P—K Kt 4; in any case, however, his game would have been inferior to his adversary's.

(d) All this is very ingenious, but the loss of Pawns and exposure of his King, entailed by the slip at move 12 are irreparable.

(13)

Morphy
——————
Boden

1.	$\dfrac{\text{P—K 4}}{\text{P—K 4}}$	13.	$\dfrac{\text{P—K R 3}}{\text{B—R 4}}$	25.	$\dfrac{\text{B—Kt 1}}{\text{K—B 2}}$
2.	$\dfrac{\text{Kt—K B 3}}{\text{Kt—Q B 3}}$	14.	$\dfrac{\text{P—K Kt 4}}{\text{B—Kt 3 }(c)}$	26.	$\dfrac{\text{P—K 6 ch.}}{\text{K—Kt 2}}$
3	$\dfrac{\text{P—Q 4}}{\text{P} \times \text{P}}$	15.	$\dfrac{\text{Q—Q 2}}{\text{R—K 1}}$	27.	$\dfrac{\text{Q—Q 3}}{\text{P—B 4}}$
4.	$\dfrac{\text{B—Q B 4}}{\text{B—B 4}}$	16.	$\dfrac{\text{Q R—K 1}}{\text{B—B 2}}$	28.	$\dfrac{\text{P} \times \text{P}}{\text{Q—B 3}}$
5.	$\dfrac{\text{0—0}}{\text{P—Q 3}}$	17.	$\dfrac{\text{Kt—Q Kt 5}}{\text{K—R 2}}$	29.	$\dfrac{\text{P} \times \text{P}}{\text{Q} \times \text{Q Kt P }(e)}$
6.	$\dfrac{\text{P—B 3}}{\text{Kt—B 3}}$	18.	$\dfrac{\text{B} \times \text{Kt }(d)}{\text{P} \times \text{B}}$	30.	$\dfrac{\text{P—B 5}}{\text{Q—B 3}}$
7.	$\dfrac{\text{P} \times \text{P}}{\text{B—Kt 3}}$	19.	$\dfrac{\text{Kt} \times \text{B}}{\text{Q} \times \text{Kt}}$	31.	$\dfrac{\text{P—K 7}}{\text{P—B 5}}$
8.	$\dfrac{\text{Kt—B 3}}{\text{0—0}}$	20.	$\dfrac{\text{Q—B 3}}{\text{Q—Q 1}}$	32.	$\dfrac{\text{Q—K Kt 3}}{\text{P—B 6}}$
9.	$\dfrac{\text{P—Q 5}}{\text{Kt—R 4 }(a)}$	21.	$\dfrac{\text{Kt—R 4}}{\text{P—Kt 3}}$	33.	$\dfrac{\text{R—K 6}}{\text{Q—Q 5 ch.}}$
10.	$\dfrac{\text{B—Q 3}}{\text{P—Q B 4}}$	22.	$\dfrac{\text{P—B 4}}{\text{K—Kt 2}}$	34.	$\dfrac{\text{Q—B 2}}{\text{Q} \times \text{P}}$
11.	$\dfrac{\text{B—K Kt 5 }(b)}{\text{P—K R 3}}$	23.	$\dfrac{\text{Kt} \times \text{B}}{\text{P} \times \text{Kt}}$	35.	$\dfrac{\text{P—B 6 ch.}}{\text{Resigns.}}$
12.	$\dfrac{\text{B—R 4}}{\text{B—Kt 5}}$	24.	$\dfrac{\text{P—K 5}}{\text{R—Q B 1}}$		

(a) This is rarely a good place for the Knight. In the present instance it necessitates P—Q B 4, thereby depriving Black of all hope of breaking his opponent's centre.

(b) Had White played P—Q R 3 to win the Knight, Black would have replied with P—B 5.

(c) Black's game is brought to a deadlock through his unfortunate 9th move.

(d) White being certain of breaking through with his Pawns does not object to exchanges.

(e) As good as anything else. The game is gone.

CHAPTER XIII.

PONZIANI'S OR STAUNTON'S OPENING— ANALYSIS.

	(1)	(2)	(3)
1.	$\dfrac{\text{P—K 4}}{\text{P—K 4}}$	—	—
2.	$\dfrac{\text{Kt—K B 3}}{\text{Kt—Q B 3}}$	—	—
3.	$\dfrac{\text{P—B 3}}{\text{P—B 4 } (a)}$	—	$\overline{\text{P—Q 4}}$
4.	$\dfrac{\text{P—Q 4}}{\text{P}\times\text{K P}}$	$\overline{\text{P—Q 3 !}}$	$\dfrac{\text{B—Kt 5}}{\text{P}\times\text{P}}$
5.	$\dfrac{\text{Kt}\times\text{P}}{\text{Kt—B 3}}$	$\dfrac{\text{Q P}\times\text{P}}{\text{B P}\times\text{P}}$	$\dfrac{\text{Kt}\times\text{P}}{\text{Q—Kt 4 (or Q 4 !)}}$
6.	$\dfrac{\text{B—Q Kt 5}}{\text{P—Q R 3}}$	$\dfrac{\text{Kt—Kt 5}}{\text{P—Q 4}}$	$\dfrac{\text{Q—R 4}}{\text{Q}\times\text{Kt}}$
7.	$\dfrac{\text{B}\times\text{Kt}}{\text{Kt P}\times\text{B}}$	$\dfrac{\text{P—K 6}}{\text{Kt—K 4}}$	$\dfrac{\text{B}\times\text{Kt ch.}}{\text{K—Q 1}}$
8.	$\dfrac{\text{B—Kt 5}}{\text{R—Kt 1}}$	$\dfrac{\text{Q—Q 4}}{\text{Q—Q 3}}$	$\overline{\text{Q}\times\text{K P}+}$
9.	$\overline{\dfrac{\text{P—Q Kt 4}}{\text{B—Kt 2}}}$	$\overline{\text{Kt—Q R 3}+}$	
10.	$\dfrac{\text{0—0}}{\text{P—Q 4}}$		
11.	$\dfrac{\text{P—B 3}}{\text{B—K 2}}$		
12.	$\dfrac{\text{P}\times\text{P}}{\text{0—0}}$		
13.	$\overline{\text{Kt—Q 2}+}$		

(a) Ponziani Counter Gambit.

	(4)	(5)	(6)
1.	—	—	—
2.	—	—	—
3.	$\dfrac{\text{Kt—K B 3}}{}$	—	$\dfrac{\text{B—B 4}}{}$
4.	$\dfrac{\text{P—Q 4}}{\text{Kt} \times \text{K P}}$	—	$\dfrac{\text{P—Q Kt 4}}{\text{B—Kt 3}}$
5.	$\dfrac{\text{P} \times \text{P}}{\text{P—Q 4}}$	$\dfrac{\text{P—Q 5}}{\text{B—B 4}}$	$\dfrac{\text{P—Kt 5}}{\text{Kt—R 4}}$
6.	$\dfrac{\text{B—Q Kt 5}}{\text{B—Q B 4}}$	$\dfrac{\text{P} \times \text{Kt}}{\text{B} \times \text{P ch.}}$	$\dfrac{\text{Kt} \times \text{P}}{\text{Q—K 2}}$
7.	$\dfrac{\text{Kt—Q 4}}{\text{B} \times \text{Kt (or 0—0)}}$	$\dfrac{\text{K—K 2}}{\text{Kt P} \times \text{P}}$	$\dfrac{\text{P—Q 4}}{\text{P—Q 3}}$
8.	$\dfrac{\text{P} \times \text{B}}{\text{0—0}}$	$\dfrac{\text{Q—R 4}}{\text{P—K B 4}}$	$\dfrac{\text{B—R 3}}{\text{P—K B 3}}$ (a)
9.	$\dfrac{\text{B} \times \text{Kt}}{\text{P} \times \text{B}}$	$\dfrac{\text{Q Kt—Q 2}}{\text{0—0}}$	$\dfrac{\text{Kt—B 3}}{\text{Q} \times \text{P ch.}}$
10.	$\dfrac{\text{0—0}}{\text{B—R 3}}$	$\dfrac{\text{Kt} \times \text{Kt}}{\text{P} \times \text{Kt}}$	$\dfrac{\text{B—K 2}}{\text{Kt—R 3}}$
11.	$\dfrac{\text{R—K 1}}{\text{Q—R 5}}$	$\dfrac{\text{Q} \times \text{P (K 5)}}{\text{B—Kt 3}}$	$\dfrac{\text{0—0}}{\text{0—0}}$
12.	$\dfrac{\text{P—K Kt 3}}{\text{Q—R 6}}$	$\dfrac{\text{B—Kt 5}}{\text{Q—K 1}}$	$\text{B—Q 3}+$
13.		$\dfrac{\text{R—K 1}}{\text{P—Q 3}}$	

PONZIANI'S OR STAUNTON'S OPENING—GAMES

	(1)	(2)	(3)
	$\dfrac{\text{Staunton}}{\text{Harrwitz}}$	$\dfrac{\text{Capt. Evans}}{\text{Horwitz}}$	$\dfrac{\text{Horwitz}}{\text{Harrwitz}}$
1.	$\dfrac{\text{P—K 4}}{\text{P—K 4}}$	$\dfrac{\text{P—K 4}}{\text{P—K 4}}$	$\dfrac{\text{P—K 4}}{\text{P—K 4}}$
2.	$\dfrac{\text{Kt—K B 3}}{\text{Kt—Q B 3}}$	$\dfrac{\text{Kt—K B 3}}{\text{Kt—Q B 3}}$	$\dfrac{\text{Kt—K B 3}}{\text{Kt—Q B 3}}$

(a) Or 8. $\dfrac{}{\text{Q—R 5}}$; 9. $\dfrac{\text{Kt—B 3}}{\text{Q} \times \text{P ch.}}$; 10 $\dfrac{\text{B—K 2}}{\text{Kt—K 2}}$; 11. $\dfrac{\text{Q Kt—Q 2}}{}+$

	(1)	(2)	(3)
3.	$\dfrac{\text{P—B 3}}{\text{P—B 4}}$	$\dfrac{\text{P—B 3}}{\text{P—B 4}}$	$\dfrac{\text{P—B 3}}{\text{B—B 4}}$
4.	$\dfrac{\text{P—Q 4}}{\text{P×K P}}$	$\dfrac{\text{P—Q 4}}{\text{P×Q P } (c)}$	$\dfrac{\text{P—Q Kt 4}}{\text{B—Kt 3}}$
5.	$\dfrac{\text{Kt×P}}{\text{Kt—B 3}}$	$\dfrac{\text{P—K 5}}{\text{P×P}}$	$\dfrac{\text{P—Kt 5}}{\text{Kt—R 4}}$
6.	$\dfrac{\text{B—Q Kt 5}}{\text{P—Q R 3}}$	$\dfrac{\text{Kt×P}}{\text{B—Kt 5}}$	$\dfrac{\text{Kt×P}}{\text{Q—K 2}}$
7.	$\dfrac{\text{B×Kt}}{\text{Kt P×B}}$	$\dfrac{\text{B—K Kt 5}}{\text{K Kt—K 2}}$	$\dfrac{\text{P—Q 4}}{\text{P—Q 3}}$
8.	$\dfrac{\text{B—K Kt 5}}{\text{R—Q Kt 1}}$	$\dfrac{\text{B—B 4}}{\text{P—Q 4}}$	$\dfrac{\text{B—R 3}}{\text{P—K B 3}}$
9.	$\dfrac{\text{P—Q Kt 4}}{\text{B—Kt 2}}$	$\dfrac{\text{P×P } e.p.}{\text{Q×P}}$	$\dfrac{\text{Kt—B 3}}{\text{Q×P ch.}}$
10.	$\dfrac{\text{Q—R 4}}{\text{P—Q 4}}$	$\dfrac{\text{Q—K 2}}{\text{Kt—Q 5}}$	$\dfrac{\text{B—K 2}}{\text{Kt—R 3}}$
11.	$\dfrac{\text{0—0 } (a)}{\text{P—K R 3}}$	$\dfrac{\text{Kt×Kt}}{\text{Q×Kt}}$	$\dfrac{\text{0—0}}{\text{0—0}}$
12.	$\dfrac{\text{B—R 4}}{\text{Q—Q 3}}$	$\dfrac{\text{0—0 } (d)}{\text{B—Q 2}}$	$\dfrac{\text{B—Q 3}}{\text{Q—Kt 5}}$
13.	$\dfrac{\text{B—Kt 3 } (b)}{\text{R—Kt 1}}$	$\dfrac{\text{Kt—Q 5}}{\text{0—0—0 } (e)}$	$\dfrac{\text{B—Kt 4}}{\text{Q—K 3}}$
14.	$\dfrac{\text{Kt—Q 2}}{\text{R—B 1}}$	$\dfrac{\text{B×Kt}}{\text{B×B}}$	$\dfrac{\text{R—K 1}}{\text{Q—B 2}}$
15.	$\dfrac{\text{Kt×Kt}}{\text{Kt—Q 2}}$	$\dfrac{\text{Kt×B ch.}}{\text{K—Kt 1}}$	$\dfrac{\text{P—Q 5}}{\text{Kt—Kt 5}}$
16.	$\dfrac{\text{Kt—R 5}}{\text{Kt—Kt 3}}$	$\dfrac{\text{K R—Q 1}}{\text{Q—R 5}}$	$\dfrac{\text{R—B 1}}{\text{Kt—K 4}}$
17.	$\dfrac{\text{Q—B 2}}{\text{B—R 1}}$	$\dfrac{\text{B—Kt 3}}{\text{Q—R 3}}$	$\dfrac{\text{Kt×Kt}}{\text{B P×Kt}}$

(a) The following moves will show the probable result of taking the Pawn with Knight :—

| 11. Kt×P | Q—Q 2 |
| 12. P—Kt 5 | R—R 1 |

(His best move ; if P×P, then White plays Q—R 7).

| 13. Q—Q 1 | P×P, or B×Kt |

And White has little, if any, advantage.

(b) Threatening to win the Rook by Kt—B 7, or Kt 6.

(c) In the previous game the King's Pawn was taken.

(d) White has now an overwhelming attack.

(e) The loss of a Piece eventually was inevitable, and Black did wisely in giving it up at once, to bring his other forces into action.

	(1)	(2)	(3)
18.	$\dfrac{\text{P}-\text{B }3\ (a)}{\text{P}\times\text{P}}$	$\dfrac{\text{R}-\text{Q }2}{\text{P}-\text{B }5}$	$\dfrac{\text{Kt}-\text{Q }2}{\text{Q}\times\text{Q P}}$
19.	$\dfrac{\text{R}\times\text{P}}{\text{Q}-\text{K }3}$	$\dfrac{\text{Q R}-\text{Q }1}{\text{P}-\text{B }6}$	$\dfrac{\text{Kt}-\text{B }4}{\text{P}\times\text{K }5}$
20.	$\dfrac{\text{Q R}-\text{K }1}{\text{B}-\text{K }2}$	$\dfrac{\text{Q}\times\text{P}}{\text{P}-\text{R }3}$	$\dfrac{\text{Kt}\times\text{B}}{\text{R P}\times\text{Kt}}$
21.	$\dfrac{\text{Kt (K }5)\times\text{P}}{\text{Q}\times\text{R }(b)}$	$\dfrac{\text{R}\times\text{B}}{\text{R}\times\text{R}}$	$\dfrac{\text{B}-\text{B }2}{\text{Q}\times\text{Q}}$
22.	$\dfrac{\text{B}\times\text{Q}}{\text{B}\times\text{Kt}}$	$\dfrac{\text{R}\times\text{R}}{\text{Q}-\text{B }8\text{ ch.}}$	$\dfrac{\text{B}\times\text{Q}}{\text{B}-\text{K }3}$
23.	$\dfrac{\text{Q}-\text{Kt }6\text{ ch.}}{\text{K}-\text{Q }1}$	$\dfrac{\text{Q}-\text{Q }1}{\text{Q}\times\text{P}}$	$\dfrac{\text{B}-\text{B }2}{\text{K R}-\text{K }1}$
24.	Kt$\times$B ch. and wins.	$\dfrac{\text{R}-\text{Q }8\text{ ch.}}{\text{R}\times\text{R}}$	$\dfrac{\text{B}\times\text{K P}}{\text{B}-\text{B }5}$
25.		$\dfrac{\text{Q}\times\text{R ch.}}{\text{K}-\text{R }2}$	$\dfrac{\text{K R}-\text{K }1}{\text{P}-\text{Q }4}$
26.		Kt$-$B 6 ch. and mate in four.	$\dfrac{\text{B}-\text{B }3}{\text{B}\times\text{P}}$

(3) (contd.)

27.	$\dfrac{\text{K R}-\text{Q }1}{\text{B}-\text{Kt }6}$	33.	$\dfrac{\text{R}\times\text{P}}{\text{P}-\text{R }3}$	39.	$\dfrac{\text{R}-\text{Kt }5}{\text{P}-\text{R }5}$
28.	$\dfrac{\text{B}\times\text{P ch.}}{\text{B}\times\text{B}}$	34.	$\dfrac{\text{R}-\text{Q }8\text{ ch.}}{\text{K}-\text{R }2}$	40.	$\dfrac{\text{R}\times\text{P}}{\text{K}-\text{R }2}$
29.	$\dfrac{\text{R}\times\text{B}}{\text{Kt}-\text{B }3}$	35.	$\dfrac{\text{R (Q }5)-\text{Q }7}{\text{R}\times\text{P}}$	41.	$\dfrac{\text{R}-\text{Kt }4}{\text{R}-\text{R }8\text{ ch.}}$
30.	$\dfrac{\text{R}-\text{Q B }1}{\text{Kt}\times\text{B}}$	36.	$\dfrac{\text{R}\times\text{P ch.}}{\text{K}-\text{R }1}$	42.	$\dfrac{\text{K}-\text{R }2}{\text{R}-\text{R }5}$
31.	$\dfrac{\text{P}\times\text{Kt}}{\text{R}-\text{R }7}$	37.	$\dfrac{\text{R}\times\text{P}}{\text{R}-\text{Kt }7}$	43.	$\dfrac{\text{R}\times\text{P ch.}}{\text{K}-\text{Kt }2}$
32.	$\dfrac{\text{P}-\text{R }3}{\text{K R}-\text{K }7}$	38.	$\dfrac{\text{R}-\text{Kt }6}{\text{P}-\text{R }4}$	44.	$\dfrac{\text{R}-\text{B }4\text{ and wins}}{}$

(a) This is much stronger than Kt (Kt 5)$\times$P.
(b) He has no better move—the game is beyond hope.

	(4)	(5)
	Brien	Janssens
	Falkbeer	Brien
1.	P—K 4 / P—K 4	P—K 4 / P—K 4
2.	Kt—K B 3 / Kt—Q B 3	Kt—K B 3 / Kt—Q B ?
3.	P—B 3 / Kt—B 3	P—B 3 / P—Q 4
4.	P—Q 4 / Kt×P	Q—R 4 (a) / P×P (b)
5.	P—Q 5 / B—B 4	Kt×P / Q—Q 4
6.	P×Kt / Kt×K B P	Kt×Kt / P×Kt
7.	Q—Q 5 / P—Q 3	B—B 4 / Q—Q 2
8.	P×Q Kt P / B×P	0—0 / B—Q 3
9.	Q×B / Kt×R	B—Kt 5 (c) / P×B
10	Q—B 6 ch / K—B 1	Q×P ch. / Kt—K 2
11.	B—K 2 / P—B 3	Q×R / P—Q B 3 (d)

(a) The usual course here is to play B—Kt 5. Mr. Janssen's deviation, as bold as it is original, seems calculated to ensure the opening player at least as much attack as the old move, and to involve his adversary in a more complex and dangerous line of defence.

(b) Among the few players who have looked with attention at the opening as newly shaped, it is agreed that Q—Q 3 is sounder play at this moment than taking the King's Pawn.

(c) This is so ingenious that one is grieved to find it turn out badly, and to discover that the homely plodding move of R—K 1 would have answered better.

(d) Now comes the pinch for which White had evidently not provided when he manœuvred so cleverly to win the exchange. The Queen is in jeopardy. How is she to be saved? And if preserved, how can she again be brought into co-operation with the rest of the forces? White solves the first of these problems satisfactorily. He saves his Queen. But the second is beyond his skill, and she remains isolated and helpless for the rest of the battle.

	(4)	(5)
12.	$\dfrac{\text{P—Q Kt 4}}{\text{B—Kt 3}}$	$\dfrac{\text{P—Q 3 } (b)}{\text{0—0}}$
13.	$\dfrac{\text{B—Q B 4}}{\text{Kt—B 7}}$	$\dfrac{\text{B—K 3}}{\text{B—Kt 2}}$
14.	$\dfrac{\text{Q—Q 5}}{\text{Q—K 1}}$	$\dfrac{\text{Q} \times \text{P}}{\text{P—Q B 4 } (c)}$
15.	$\dfrac{\text{Kt—R 4}}{\text{R—Q 1}}$	$\dfrac{\text{Q—R 3 } (d)}{\text{Q—Kt 5 } (e)}$
16.	$\dfrac{\text{P—Kt 5}}{\text{Kt—Kt 5}}$	$\dfrac{\text{P—B 3}}{\text{Q—R 5}}$
17.	$\dfrac{\text{Kt—B 5}}{\text{P—K 5}}$	$\dfrac{\text{P—K B 4}}{\text{Q—Kt 5}}$
18.	$\dfrac{\text{Kt—Q 4}}{\text{B} \times \text{Kt}}$	$\dfrac{\text{R—B 2}}{\text{Q—Q 8 ch}}$
19.	$\dfrac{\text{P} \times \text{B}}{\text{Kt} \times \text{P}}$	$\dfrac{\text{R—B 1}}{\text{Q—K 7}}$
20.	$\dfrac{\text{B—B 4}}{\text{Kt—Kt 5}}$	$\dfrac{\text{B—B 2}}{\text{Kt—B 4}}$
21.	$\dfrac{\text{Kt—Q B 3}}{\text{P—Kt 4 } (a)}$	$\dfrac{\text{Q—Kt 3}}{\text{B} \times \text{Kt P } (f)}$

(a) An unsound combination. Black evidently overlooked the fatal consequences of the move with which he intended to follow it up, R—Q 2 is perhaps his best play at this point, and then R—K 2, if the Knight ventured to capture the King's Pawn.

(b) It was suggested afterwards that White might have saved his Queen equally, by playing P—Q R 4.

(c) *Coup juste.* Compelling White to sacrifice his Queen for a minor piece, or to consign her to ruinous inactivity.

(d) Imperative, or Black would have won her by R—R 1.

(e) Black appears to have overlooked the surest, and at the same time the most expeditious mode of winning. He should, if I mistake not, have taken the K Kt P at once. For example—

15.	B × Kt P
16. K × B	

(If he does not take the Bishop his game is equally lost.)

16.	Q—Kt 5 ch.
17. K—R 1	Q—R 6

And White has no resource.

(f) The young player must observe that if White take this Bishop he subjects himself to immediate mate.

	(4)	(5)
22.	$\dfrac{\text{B} \times \text{Kt P}}{\text{Q} - \text{R } 4}$	$\dfrac{\text{Kt} - \text{R } 3}{\text{Q} - \text{Kt } 5}$
23.	$\dfrac{\text{B} - \text{R } 6 \text{ ch. and wins}}{}$	$\dfrac{\text{B} - \text{Kt } 3}{\text{Kt} \times \text{B}}$
24.		$\dfrac{\text{P} \times \text{Kt}}{\text{Q} \times \text{Kt P}}$
25.		Resigns.

BOOK III.

CHAPTER I.

KING'S BISHOP'S OPENING—ANALYSIS.

	(1)	(2)	(3)
1.	$\frac{\text{P}-\text{K 4}}{\text{P}-\text{K 4}}$	—	—
2.	$\frac{\text{B}-\text{B 4}}{\text{B}-\text{B 4}}$	—	—
3.	$\frac{\text{P}-\text{Q B 3}}{\text{Kt}-\text{K B 3}}$	$\overline{\text{Q}-\text{K 2}}$	—
4.	$\frac{\text{P}-\text{Q 4}}{\text{P}\times\text{P}}$	$\frac{\text{Kt}-\text{B 3}}{\text{P}-\text{Q 3 !}\,(b)}$	—
5.	$\frac{\text{P}-\text{K 5}}{\text{P}-\text{Q 4}}$	$\frac{\text{P}-\text{Q 4}}{\text{P}\times\text{P}}$	—
6.	$\frac{\text{P}\times\text{Kt}(\text{B}-\text{Q Kt. 5 !})}{\text{P}\times\text{B}}$	$\frac{0-0}{\text{P}\times\text{P}}$	—
7.	$\frac{\text{P}\times\text{Kt P}\,(a)}{\text{R}-\text{Kt 1}}$	$\frac{\text{P}-\text{Q Kt 4}}{\text{B}-\text{Kt 3}}$	$\overline{\text{B}\times\text{P}}$
8	$\frac{\text{Q}-\text{R 5}}{\text{Q}-\text{K 2 ch.}}$	$\frac{\text{Kt}\times\text{P}}{\text{K Kt}-\text{B 3}}$	$\frac{\text{Q}-\text{R 4 ch.}}{\text{Kt}-\text{B 3}}$

(a) If 7. $\frac{\text{Q}-\text{R 5}}{0-0\,!}$; 8. $\frac{\text{Q}\times\text{B}}{\text{R}-\text{K 1 ch.}}$; 9. $\frac{\text{Kt}-\text{K 2}}{\text{P}-\text{Q 6}}$; 10. $\frac{\text{B}-\text{K 3}}{\text{P}\times\text{Kt}}$; 11. $\frac{\text{Kt}-\text{Q 2}}{\text{Kt}-\text{R 3}}$; 12. $\frac{\text{Q}\times\text{P}}{\text{Q}\times\text{P}}$; 13. $\underline{\text{Q}\times\text{P (K 2)}}=$

(b) If 4. $\frac{}{\text{B}\times\text{P ch.}}$; 5. $\frac{\text{K}\times\text{B}}{\text{Q}-\text{B 4 ch.}}$; 6. $\frac{\text{P}-\text{Q 4}}{\text{Q}\times\text{B}}$; 7. $\frac{\text{Kt}\times\text{P}}{\text{Q}-\text{K 3}}$; 8. $\frac{\text{R}-\text{K 1}}{}$, or 4. $\frac{\text{P}-\text{Q 4}}{\text{P}\times\text{P}}$; 5. $\frac{}{\text{Q}\times\text{P ch.}}$; 6. $\frac{\text{Kt}-\text{K 2}}{\text{B}-\text{Kt 5 ch.}}$; 7. $\frac{\text{B}-\text{Q 2}}{\text{B}\times\text{B ch.}}$; 8. $\frac{\text{Kt}\times\text{B}}{\text{Q}-\text{K 2}}$; 9. $\frac{0-0}{\text{Q}-\text{Q}}$ (or Kt$-$B 3); 10. $\frac{\text{R}-\text{K 1}}{\text{Kt}-\text{K 2}}$.

	(1)	(2)	(3)
9.	$\dfrac{\text{K}-\text{Q 1}}{\text{R}\times\text{P}}$	$\dfrac{\text{Kt}-\text{Q 5}}{\text{Kt}\times\text{Kt}}$	$\dfrac{\text{B}-\text{Q Kt 5}}{\text{P}-\text{B 7 !}}$
10.	$\dfrac{\text{Kt}-\text{B 3}}{\text{Kt}-\text{B 3}}$	$\dfrac{\text{P}\times\text{Kt}}{\text{0}-\text{0}}$	$\dfrac{\text{B}\times\text{Kt ch.}}{\text{K}-\text{B 1 !}}$
11.	$\dfrac{\text{R}-\text{K 1}}{\text{B}-\text{K 3}}$	$\dfrac{\text{B}-\text{Kt 2}}{\text{B}-\text{Kt 5}}$	$\dfrac{\text{B}\times\text{P}}{\text{B}\times\text{B}}$
12.	$\dfrac{\text{R}\times\text{B}}{\text{Q}\times\text{R}}$	$\dfrac{\text{R}-\text{K 1}}{\text{Q}-\text{Q 1}}$	$\dfrac{\text{Q}\times\text{B}}{\text{P}\times\overline{\text{Kt}}\ (\text{Q})}$
13.	$\dfrac{\text{Q}\times\text{B}}{\text{P}-\text{Kt 3}}$		$\dfrac{\text{R}\times\text{Q}}{\text{B}\times\text{P}}$
14.	$\dfrac{\text{Q}-\text{Q Kt 5}}{\text{R}\times\text{P}}$		$\dfrac{\text{R}-\text{K 1}}{\text{P}-\text{K B 4 !}}$
15.	$\dfrac{\text{P}\times\text{P}}{\text{P}-\text{Q R 3}}$		$\dfrac{\text{Kt}-\text{Kt 5}}{\text{Q}-\text{Q 2}}$
16.	$\dfrac{\text{Q}-\text{R 4}}{\text{R}\times\text{B P}}$		$\dfrac{\text{Kt}\times\text{B}}{\text{P}\times\text{Kt}}$
17.	$\dfrac{\text{Kt}-\text{K 5}}{\text{P}-\text{Kt 4 and wins.}}$		$\dfrac{\text{Q}\times\text{K P}}{}$

	(4)	(5)	(6)
	—	—	—
	—	—	—
3.	$\dfrac{}{\text{Q}-\text{Kt 4}}$	$\dfrac{}{\text{P}-\text{Q 4}}$	—
4.	$\dfrac{\text{Q}-\text{B 3}}{\text{Q}-\text{Kt 3 !}}$	$\dfrac{\text{B}\times\text{P}}{\text{K Kt}-\text{B 3}}$	—
5.	$\dfrac{\text{Kt}-\text{K 2}}{\text{P}-\text{Q 3}}$	$\dfrac{\text{Q}-\text{B 3}}{\text{0}-\text{0 (see diagram)}}$	$\dfrac{\text{Q}-\text{Kt 3}}{\text{0}-\text{0}}$
6.	$\dfrac{\text{P}-\text{Q 4}}{\text{B}-\text{Kt 3}}$	$\dfrac{\text{P}-\text{Q 4}}{\text{P}\times\text{P}}$	$\dfrac{\text{B}\times\text{Kt P}}{\text{B}\times\text{B}}$
7.	$\dfrac{\text{P}\times\text{P}}{\text{P}\times\text{P}}$	$\dfrac{\text{B}-\text{Kt 5}}{\text{P}\times\text{P}}$	$\dfrac{\text{Q}\times\text{B}}{\text{Q}-\text{Q 6}}$
8.	$\dfrac{\text{Kt}-\text{Kt 3}}{\text{Kt}-\text{B 3}}$	$\dfrac{\text{Kt}\times\text{P}}{\text{Q Kt}-\text{Q 2}}$	$\dfrac{\text{Q}\times\text{R}}{\text{Q}-\text{R 3}}$
9.	$\dfrac{\text{P}-\text{K R 3}=}{}$	$\dfrac{\text{0}-\text{0}}{\text{P}-\text{B 3}}$	$\dfrac{\text{P}-\text{Q 4}}{\text{Q Kt}-\text{Q 2}}$

	(4)	(5)	(6)
10.		$\dfrac{\text{B—Kt 3}}{\text{Q—K 2}}$	$\dfrac{\text{Q} \times \text{R ch.}}{\text{B} \times \text{Q}}$
11.			$\dfrac{\text{P—B 3}}{\text{P} \times \text{Q P}}$
12			$\dfrac{\text{P} \times \text{P}}{\text{Q—Q 6}} +$

No. 5.   Position after White's 5th move.

BLACK.

WHITE.

	(7)	(8	(9)
1.	—	—	—
2.	—	—	—
3.	—	—	—
4.	—	—	—
5.	—	—	—
6.	$\dfrac{\text{Kt—B 3}}{\text{P—B 3}}$	—	—

(7)	(8)	(9)
7. $\frac{B \times P \text{ ch.}}{R \times B}$	—	—
8. $\frac{Kt \times P}{B \times P \text{ ch.}}$	—	—
9. $\frac{K - B\ 1}{Kt - Q\ 4}$	—	—
10. $\frac{Kt \times R}{Q - B\ 3}$	$\frac{P \times Kt}{B - R\ 5 \text{ d. ch.}}$	$\frac{P - Q\ B\ 4}{Kt - K\ 6 \text{ ch.}}$
11. $\frac{Kt - K\ 5}{Q \times Kt}$	$\frac{K\ Kt - B\ 3}{B - Kt\ 5}$	$\frac{Q\ P \times Kt}{B - R\ 5 \text{ d. ch.}}$
12. $\frac{K \times B}{Q - B\ 5 \text{ ch.}}$	$\frac{P - Q\ 4}{R \times Kt \text{ ch.}}$	$\frac{Kt \times R}{Q - B\ 3 \text{ ch.}}$
13. $\frac{K - Kt\ 1\ !}{Q \times K\ P}$	$\frac{P \times R}{B \times P}$	$\frac{K - K\ 2}{Q - B\ 7 \text{ ch.}}$
14. $\frac{P - K\ R\ 3}{B - K\ 3}$	$\frac{P - Q\ B\ 4}{Q - B\ 3 \text{ and wins.}}$	$\frac{K - Q\ 3}{Kt - R\ 3}$
15. $\frac{Q - Q\ 1}{Kt - Q\ 2}$		$\frac{Q - R\ 3}{B - Kt\ 5}$
16. $\frac{Q - B\ 3}{Q - Kt\ 3}$		$\frac{Kt - B\ 3}{K \times Kt \text{ and wins.}}$
17. $\frac{P - Q\ 4}{R - K\ B\ 1}$		
18. $\frac{Q - K\ 2}{B - B\ 4}$		
19. $\frac{Kt - Q\ 2}{B - Q\ 6}$		
20. $\frac{Q - K\ 1}{Kt - B\ 5 \text{ and wins.}}$		

(10)	(11)	(12)
1. $\frac{P - K\ 4}{P - K\ 4}$	—	—
2. $\frac{B - B\ 4}{B - B\ 4}$	—	—
3. $\frac{P - Q\ B\ 3}{Kt - Q\ B\ 3}$	$\frac{Kt - K\ B\ 3}{P - Q\ 3}$	$\overline{Kt - K\ B\ 3}$

	(10)	(11)	(12)
4.	$\dfrac{\text{P}-\text{Q 4}}{\text{B}-\text{Kt 3 !}}$	$\dfrac{\text{P}-\text{B 3}\ (a)}{\text{Kt}-\text{K B 3}}$	$\dfrac{\text{Kt}\times\text{P}}{\text{Kt}\times\text{P}}$
5.	$\dfrac{\text{Kt}-\text{K 2}}{\text{Kt}-\text{B 3}}$	$\dfrac{\text{P}-\text{Q 4}}{\text{P}\times\text{P}}$	$\dfrac{\text{B}\times\text{P ch.}}{\text{K}-\text{B 1}}$
6.	$\dfrac{\text{Q}-\text{Q 3}}{0-0}$	$\dfrac{\text{P}\times\text{P}}{\text{B}-\text{Kt 5 ch.}}$	$\dfrac{\text{Q}-\text{B 3}}{\text{B}\times\text{P ch.}}$
7.	$\dfrac{\text{P}-\text{B 4}}{\text{P}\times\text{Q P}}$	$\dfrac{\text{B}-\text{Q 2}}{\text{B}\times\text{B ch.}}$	$\dfrac{\text{K}-\text{K 2}}{\text{P}-\text{Q 3}}$
8.	$\dfrac{\text{P}-\text{K 5}}{\text{P}-\text{Q 4}}$	$\dfrac{\text{Kt}\times\text{B}}{\text{P}-\text{Q 4}}$	$\dfrac{\text{Q}\times\text{Kt}}{\text{P}\times\text{Kt}}$
9.	$\dfrac{\text{B}-\text{Kt 3}}{\text{Kt}-\text{K 5}}$	$\dfrac{\text{P}\times\text{P}}{\text{Kt}\times\text{P}}$	$\dfrac{\text{R}-\text{B 1}\ +}{}$
10.	$\dfrac{\text{P}\times\text{P}}{\text{P}-\text{B 4}}$	$\dfrac{\text{Q}-\text{Kt 3}}{\text{P}-\text{Q B 3}}$	
11.	$\dfrac{\text{Q Kt}-\text{B 3}}{\text{B}-\text{K 3}}$ =	$\dfrac{0-0\ +}{0-0}$	

	(13)	(14)	(15)
1.	—	—	—
2.	—	—	—
3.	$\dfrac{\text{Q}-\text{B 3}}{\text{Kt}-\text{K B 3}}$	$\dfrac{\text{Q}-\text{Kt 4}}{\text{Q}-\text{B 3}}$	$\dfrac{\text{Q}-\text{R 5}}{\text{Q}-\text{K 2}}$
4.	$\dfrac{\text{P}-\text{K Kt 4}}{\text{P}-\text{Q 4}}$	$\dfrac{\text{P}-\text{Q 4 (Q}-\text{Kt 3 !)}}{\text{B}\times\text{P}}$	$\dfrac{\text{Kt}-\text{K B 3}}{\text{P}-\text{Q 3}}$
5.	$\dfrac{\text{B}\times\text{P}}{\text{B}\times\text{P (K 4)}}$	$\dfrac{\text{Kt}-\text{K B 3}}{\text{Kt}-\text{B 3}}$	$\dfrac{\text{Kt}-\text{Kt 5}}{\text{Kt}-\text{K B 3}}$
6.	$\dfrac{\text{Q}-\text{Q Kt 3}}{\text{Kt}\times\text{B}}$	$\dfrac{\text{Q}-\text{Kt 3}}{\text{P}-\text{Q 3}}$	$\dfrac{\text{Q}\times\text{P ch. !}}{\text{Q}\times\text{Q}}$
7.	$\dfrac{\text{P}\times\text{Kt}}{\text{B}-\text{Kt 3}}$	$\dfrac{\text{B}-\text{K Kt 5}}{\text{Q}-\text{K Kt 3}}$	$\dfrac{\text{B}\times\text{Q ch. }(b)}{\text{K}-\text{K 2}}$
8.	$\dfrac{\text{Q}-\text{Kt 3}}{\text{Q}-\text{B 3}\ +}$	$\dfrac{\text{Kt}-\text{Q 2}}{\text{P}-\text{K R 3}\ +}$	$\dfrac{\text{B}-\text{Q B 4}}{\text{P}-\text{K R 3}}$
9.			$\dfrac{\text{Kt}-\text{K B 3}}{\text{Kt}\times\text{K P}}$ =

(a) If 4. $\dfrac{\text{P}-\text{B 4}}{\text{P}\times\text{P}}$; 5. $\dfrac{\text{Kt}\times\text{P}}{\text{Kt}-\text{K 2}}$, &c.

(b) If 7. $\dfrac{\text{Kt}\times\text{Q}}{\text{R}-\text{B 1}}$; 8. $\dfrac{\text{Kt}-\text{Kt 5}}{\text{P}-\text{K R 3}}$; 9. $\dfrac{\text{Kt}-\text{K B 3}}{\text{Kt}\times\text{P}}$; 10. $\dfrac{0-0}{\text{Kt}\times\text{B P}}$; 11. $\dfrac{\text{R}\times\text{Kt}}{\text{B}\times\text{R ch.}}$; 12. $\dfrac{\text{K}\times\text{B}}{\text{P}-\text{K 5}\ +}$

	(16)	(17)	(18)
		McDonnell's Double Gambit.	
1.	P—K 4 / P—K 4	—	—
2.	B—B 4 / B—B 4	—	—
3.	P—Q 4 / B×P	P—Q Kt 4 ! / B×Kt P	—
4.	Kt—K B 3 / Kt—Q B 3	P—K B 4 (a) / P—Q 4	P×P
5.	P—B 3 / B—Kt 3	P×Q P / P—K 5	Kt—K B 3 / Q—K 2
6.	Kt—Kt 5 / Kt—R 3	Kt—K 2 / Kt—K B 3	Q—K 2 / Kt—K B 3
7.	R—R 5 / 0—0	0—0 / 0—0	P—K 5 / Kt—R 4
8.		Kt—Q B 3 / P—B 3	P—B 3 / B—R 4
9.		P×P / Kt×P	P—Q 4 / B—Kt 3
10.		K—R 1 / B—Kt 5 +	P—Kt 4 + / P×P *e.p.* (or P—Q 4)

	(19)	(20)	(21)
		Lopez Gambit.	
1.	—	—	—
2.	—	—	—
3.	P—B 4 / B×Kt	Q—K 2 / P—Q 3	—
4.	Q—R 5 / Q—K 2	P—B 4 / Kt—K B 3	B×Kt / R×B
5.	R×B / P—Q 3	Kt—K B 3 / Q—K 2	R×B / Kt—K B 3
6.	P—B 5 / Kt—K B B	P—Q 3 / B—K Kt 5	P—Q 3 / Q—K 2

(a) Or 4. P—Q B 3 / B—R 4 ; 5. Kt—K B 3 / Kt—Q B 3 Evans' Gambit.

	(19)	(20)	(21)
7.	Q–Kt 5 / Kt×P	P×P / P×P	Kt–Q B 3 / Kt–B 3
8.	Q×Kt P / Q–B 3	B–K Kt 5 / Q Kt–Q 2	B–K 3 / P×P
9.	B×P ch. / K–K 2	Q Kt–Q 2 / 0-0-0	Q B×P / Kt–Q 5
10.	Q×Q ch. / Kt×Q	0-0-0	Q–B 2 / Kt–K 3
11.	B–Kt 3 / B×P +	—	P–K Kt 4 +

	(22) Lopez Gambit.	(23)	(24)
1.	—	P–K 4 / P–K 4	—
2.	—	B–B 4 / B–B 4	—
3.	—	Q–K 2 / Q–K 2	Kt–Q B 3 / P–Q B 3
4.	P×P	P–B 4 / Kt–K B 3	Kt–B 3 / P–B 4
5.	Kt–K B 3 / P–K Kt 4	Kt–K B 3 / P–Q 3	B×Kt / R×B
6.	P–Q 4 / B–Kt 3	Kt–B 3 / P–B 3	0-0 / P–Q B
7.	P–K R 4 / P–Kt 5	P–Q 3 / B–K Kt 5	P–Q 4 / B×P
8.	Kt–Kt 5 / Kt–K R 3	P–B 5 / Q Kt–Q 2	Kt×B / P×Kt
9.	B×P (B 5) +	B–K Kt 5 / P–K R 3	P×P / B×P
10.		B–R 4 / P–K Kt 4 =	R–K 1 / B–K 3
11.			Kt–K 4 / P–K R 3
12.			P–K R 3 / B–B 4
13.			P–Q 4 / B–Q 6 +

	(25)	(26)	(27)
1	—	—	—
2	—	Kt—K B 3 (b)	—
3	—	P—Q 4 / P×P	P—Q 3 / B—B 4
4	B×P ch. / K×B	P—K 5 / P—Q 4	Kt—K B 3 / P—Q 3
5	Q—B 4 ch. / P—Q 4	B—Kt 3 / Kt—K 5	P—B 3 / 0—0
6	Q×B / P×P	Kt—K 2 / P—Q B 4	P—Q R 4 / P—Q R 4 =
7	Q—B 4 ch. (a) / B—K 3	P—K B 3 / Kt—Kt 4	
8	Q×P / Kt—B 3 +	Kt—B 4 / P—P 5	
9		B—R 4 ch. / Kt—B 3	
10		B×Kt ch. / P×B	
11		Q×P / Kt—K 3	
12		Kt×Kt / P×Kt	
13		0—0 / P—B 4	

	(28)	(29)	30)
1.	—	—	—
2.	—	—	—
3.	P—B 4 / P—Q 4	Kt×P	Kt—K B 3 / Kt×P
4.	P×Q P / P×P	P—Q 3 / Q—R 5 ch.	P—Q 3 / Kt—Q 3
5.	P—Q 4 / B—K Kt 5	P—Kt 3 / Kt×Kt P	Kt×P / Kt×B

(a) Or 7. $\dfrac{\text{Kt—K 2}}{\text{———}}$, or 7. $\dfrac{\text{Kt—Q B 3}}{\text{———}}$

(b) The King's Knight's defence in the King's Bishop's opening.

	(28)	(29)	(30)
6.	$\dfrac{\text{Kt} - \text{K B 3}}{}$ ▬	$\dfrac{\text{Kt} - \text{K B 3}}{\text{Q} - \text{R 4}}$	$\dfrac{\text{Kt} \times \text{Kt}}{\text{P} - \text{Q 4}}$
7.		$\dfrac{\text{R} - \text{Kt 1}}{\text{Kt} - \text{B 4}}$	$\dfrac{\text{Kt} - \text{K 5}}{\text{B} - \text{Q 3}}$
8.		$\dfrac{\text{R} - \text{Kt 5}}{\text{Q} - \text{R 6}}$	$\dfrac{\text{P} - \text{Q 4}}{0 - 0}$
9.		$\dfrac{\text{B} \times \text{P ch.}}{\text{K} \times \text{B}}$	$\dfrac{0 - 0}{\text{P} - \text{K B 3}}$
10.		$\dfrac{\text{R} - \text{R 5}}{\text{Q} - \text{Kt 7}}$	$\dfrac{\text{Kt} - \text{K B 3}}{}$ ▬
11.		$\dfrac{\text{R} \times \text{Kt ch.}}{\text{K} - \text{K 1}}$	
12		$\dfrac{\text{R} - \text{Kt 5}}{\text{Q} - \text{R 6 !}}$	
13		$\dfrac{\text{R} - \text{Kt 3}}{\text{Q} - \text{R 4 !}}$	
14.		$\text{Q} - \text{K 2}$	

	(31)	(32)	(33)
1.	$\dfrac{\text{P} - \text{K 4}}{\text{P} - \text{K 4}}$	—	—
2.	$\dfrac{\text{B} - \text{B 4}}{\text{P} - \text{K B 4}}$ (a)	—	—
3.	$\dfrac{\text{P} - \text{Q 3}}{\text{Kt} - \text{K B 3}}$	$\dfrac{\text{P} - \text{Q 4}}{\text{P} \times \text{Q P !}}$	$\dfrac{\text{B} \times \text{Kt}}{\text{R} \times \text{B}}$
4.	$\dfrac{\text{P} - \text{B 4}}{\text{K P} \times \text{P}}$	$\dfrac{\text{Q} \times \text{P}}{\text{Kt} \times \text{Q B 3}}$	$\dfrac{\text{P} \times \text{P}}{\text{P} - \text{Q 4}}$
5.	$\dfrac{\text{B} \times \text{P}}{\text{P} \times \text{P}}$	$\dfrac{\text{Q} - \text{K 3}}{\text{P} \times \text{P}}$	$\dfrac{\text{Q} - \text{R 5 ch.}}{\text{P} - \text{Kt 3}}$
6.	$\dfrac{\text{P} \times \text{P}}{\text{Q} - \text{K 2}}$	$\dfrac{\text{Q} \times \text{P ch.}}{\text{Q} - \text{K 2}}$ =	$\dfrac{\text{P} \times \text{P}}{\text{R} \times \text{P}}$
7.	$\dfrac{\text{P} - \text{K 5}}{\text{P} - \text{Q 3}}$		$\dfrac{\text{Kt} - \text{K B 3}}{\text{Kt} - \text{Q B 3}}$
8.	$\dfrac{\text{Q} - \text{K 2}}{\text{I} \times \text{P}}$		$\dfrac{\text{Q} \times \text{R P}}{\text{Q} - \text{B 3}}$
9.	$\dfrac{\text{B} \times \text{P}}{\text{P} - \text{B 3}}$		$\dfrac{\text{P} - \text{Q 3}}{\text{B} - \text{Q B 4}}$

(a) Counter Gambit in the King's Bishop's opening.

	(31)	(32)	(33)
10.	Kt−K B 3 +		B−K 3 / B×B
11.			P×B = / R×P

	(34)	(35)	(36)	(37)
1.	—	—	—	—
2.	---	P−Q B 3	---	—
3.	P×P / Kt−K B 3	Q−K 2 / Kt−B 3	P−Q 4 / Kt−K B 3	P−Q 4
4.	P−Q 4 / P×P	P−B 4 / P−Q 3	P×P / Q−R 4 ch.	P×Q P / B P×P
5.	Q×P / P−Q 4	P×P / P×P	P−B 3 / Q×P (K 5)	B−Kt 5 ch. / B−Q 2
6.	B−Q 3 / Kt−B 3	Kt−K B 3 / B−Q 3	B−Q 3 / B−B 4	B×B ch. / Kt×B
7.	Q−K 3 ch. / K−B 2	P−Q 4 / P×P	P−K B 4 / Q−K 2	P×P / Kt×P
8.	Kt−K 2 / B−Kt 5 ch.	P−K 5 / 0−0	P−K 5 +	Q −K 2 / Q−K 2
9.	P−Q B 3 / R−K 1	0−0 / B−Q B 4 (a)		Kt−Q B 3 / 0−0−0
10.	Q−Kt 3 / B−Q 3 +	Q−Q 3 / Kt−Q 4		B−B 4 / Kt−Q B 3
11		Kt−Kt 5 / P−K Kt 3		0−0−0 +
12.		Kt−K 4 / B−K 2		
13.		B×Kt / P×P		
14.		Kt−B 6 ch. / B×Kt		
15.		P×B +		

(a) If 9. —/R−K 1 ; 10. Kt−Kt 5 / R×P ; 11. Kt×B P / R×Q ; 12. Kt×Q d. ch. / K−R 1 ; 13. B×R+

KING'S BISHOP'S OPENING—GAMES.

	(1) Staunton / Popert	(2) La Bourdonnais / McDonnell	(3) Staunton / Cochrane
1.	P—K 4 / P—K 4	P—K 4 / P—K 4	P—K 4 / P—K 4
2.	B—B 4 / B—B 4	B—B 4 / B—B 4	B—B 4 / B—B 4
3.	P—Q B 3 / P—Q 3 (a)	Q—K 2 / Kt—K B 3	Kt—K B 3 / Kt—Q B 3
4.	Kt—B 3 (b) / Kt—K B 3	P—Q 3 / Kt—B 3	P—Q Kt 4 (e) / B×Kt P
5.	P—Q 4 / P×P	P—Q B 3 / Kt—K 2	P—B 3 / B—R 4
6.	P×P / B—Kt 5 ch.	P—B 4 / P×P (d)	0—0 / B—Kt 3
7.	B—Q 2 / B×B ch.	P—Q 4 / B—Kt 3	P—Q 4 / P×P
8.	Q Kt×B / 0—0 (c)	B×P (B 4) / P—Q 3	Kt×P / Kt×Kt
9.	B—Q 3 / Kt—B 3	B—Q 3 / Kt—Kt 3	P×Kt / P—Q 3
10.	P—Q R 3 / B—Kt 5	B—K 3 / 0—0	P—Q R 4 / P—Q B 3
11.	Q—B 2 / P—K R 3	P—K R 3 / R—K 1	P—R 5 / B—B 2 (f)
12.	R—Q B 1 / P—Q 4	Kt—Q 2 / Q—K 2	Q—Kt 3 / Q—K 2

(a) Not so good a move as Kt—B 3, or Q—Kt 4.

(b) P—Q 4 would perhaps have been stronger play.

(c) P—Q 4 is a better move at this point.

(d) In this opening it is not advisable for the second player to take the gambit Pawn with his K P.

(e) We have now the same position brought about which occurs in the Evans' Gambit.

(f) If he had taken the Pawn, Black, by B×P ch., and, after the Knight had taken Bishop, Q—R 5 ch. would have gained a more valuable Pawn in return, and have deprived his opponent of the privilege of castling.

	(1)	(2)	(3)
13.	$\dfrac{\text{P}-\text{K 5}}{\text{B}\times\text{Kt}}$	$\dfrac{\text{0}-\text{0}-\text{0}}{\text{P}-\text{B 4}}$	$\dfrac{\text{B}-\text{R 3}}{\text{Q}-\text{B 3}}$
14.	$\dfrac{\text{Kt}\times\text{B}}{\text{Kt}-\text{K R 4}}$	$\dfrac{\text{K}-\text{Kt 1}}{\text{P}\times\text{P}}$	$\dfrac{\text{Kt}-\text{B 3}}{\text{Q}-\text{Kt 3}}$
15.	$\dfrac{\text{P}-\text{K Kt 3}}{\text{P}-\text{K Kt 3}}$	$\dfrac{\text{P}\times\text{P}}{\text{P}-\text{Q R 4}}$	$\dfrac{\text{Kt}-\text{K 2}}{\text{Kt}-\text{R 3}}$
16.	$\dfrac{\text{P}-\text{Q Kt 4}}{\text{Q}-\text{Q 2 }(a)}$	$\dfrac{\text{K Kt}-\text{B 3}}{\text{B}-\text{Q 2}}$	$\dfrac{\text{P}-\text{K 5}}{\text{P}-\text{Q 4}}$
17.	$\dfrac{\text{Q}-\text{Q 2}}{\text{K}-\text{R 2}}$	$\dfrac{\text{P}-\text{K Kt 4}}{\text{P}-\text{R 3}}$	$\dfrac{\text{B}-\text{Q 3}}{\text{Kt}-\text{B 4}}$
18.	$\dfrac{\text{0}-\text{0}}{\text{Q R}-\text{K 1}}$	$\dfrac{\text{Q R}-\text{Kt 1}}{\text{P}-\text{Q R 5}}$	$\dfrac{\text{Q}-\text{Kt 4}}{\text{B}-\text{Q 1}}$
19.	$\dfrac{\text{R}-\text{B 3}}{\text{Kt}-\text{Q 1}}$	$\dfrac{\text{P}-\text{Kt 5}}{\text{P}\times\text{P}}$	$\dfrac{\text{Q}-\text{Kt 1}}{\text{Q}-\text{R 4}}$
20.	$\dfrac{\text{Kt}-\text{R 4}}{\text{P}-\text{Q B 3}}$	$\dfrac{\text{B}\times\text{P}}{\text{P}-\text{R 6}}$	$\dfrac{\text{Kt}-\text{Kt 3}}{\text{Kt}\times\text{Kt}}$
21.	$\dfrac{\text{P}-\text{B 4}}{\text{P}-\text{K B 4}}$	$\dfrac{\text{P}-\text{Kt 3}}{\text{B}-\text{B 3}}$	$\dfrac{\text{P}\times\text{Kt}}{\text{B}\times\text{P}}$
22.	$\dfrac{\text{P}-\text{Kt 4}}{\text{Kt}-\text{Kt 2}}$	$\dfrac{\text{R}-\text{Kt 4}}{\text{B}-\text{R 4}}$	$\dfrac{\text{B}-\text{B 5}}{\text{B}-\text{Kt 3}}$
23.	$\dfrac{\text{P}\times\text{P}}{\text{Kt}\times\text{P}}$	$\dfrac{\text{P}-\text{R 4}}{\text{B}\times\text{Kt}}$	$\dfrac{\text{Q}-\text{Kt 4}}{\text{Q}-\text{Kt 4}}$
24.	$\dfrac{\text{Kt}\times\text{Kt}}{\text{P}\times\text{Kt}}$	$\dfrac{\text{Kt}\times\text{B}}{\text{R}-\text{R 4}}$	$\dfrac{\text{B}\times\text{B}}{\text{R}\times\text{B}}$
25.	$\dfrac{\text{K}-\text{R 1}}{\text{R}-\text{Kt 1}}$	$\dfrac{\text{P}-\text{R 5}}{\text{R}\times\text{B}}$	$\dfrac{\text{P}-\text{K 6}}{\text{P}\times\text{P}}$
26.	$\dfrac{\text{R (B 3)}-\text{B 1}}{\text{Q}-\text{K B 2}}$	$\dfrac{\text{R}\times\text{R}}{\text{Kt}-\text{B 5}}$	and white announced mate in 8 moves.
27.	$\dfrac{\text{Q}-\text{Q B 2}}{\text{Q R}-\text{B 1}}$	$\dfrac{\text{Q}-\text{B 3}}{\text{Kt}\times\text{B}}$	
28.	$\dfrac{\text{R}-\text{K Kt 1}}{\text{Kt}-\text{K 3}}$	$\dfrac{\text{P}\times\text{Q 5}}{\text{Kt}\times\text{Q P}}$	
29.	$\dfrac{\text{R}\times\text{R}}{\text{K}\times\text{R}}$	$\dfrac{\text{R}-\text{Kt 1 }(b)}{\text{Kt}-\text{B 6 ch.}}$	
30.	$\dfrac{\text{R}-\text{Kt 1 ch.}}{\text{K}-\text{R 1}}$	$\dfrac{\text{K}-\text{R 1}}{\text{B}\times\text{P}}$	

(a) Intending, if P—Kt 5, to move Q—Kt 5.

(b) This portion of the game is full of interest and instruction, and is remarkably well played.

	(1)	(2)	(3)
31.	Q—B 2 / Q—R 4 (a)	R × P / K—R 1	
32.	B—K 2 / Q—B 2	Q—Kt 3 / B—Kt 3	
33.	Q—R 4 / Q—R 2	P × B / Q—K 8 ch.	
34.	B—R 5 / Kt × Q P	R × Q (d) / R × R ch.	
35.	R—Kt 3 / P—Kt 3	Q × R / Kt × Q	
36.	B—Kt 6 (b) / Q—Kt 2	R—R 7 ch. / K—Kt 1	
37.	B—B 7 / R × B (c)	P × P ch. / K × R	
38.	R × R / K × R	P—B 8 (Q) / Kt—B 7 mate.	
39.	K—Kt 2 and wins.		

	(4)	(5)	(6)
	Walker / Daniels	Posen / Berlin (Played by correspondence)	Dr. B / V. H. Der Laza
1.	P—K 4 / P—K 4	P—K 4 / P—K 4	P—K 4 / P—K 4
2.	B—B 4 / B—B 4	B—B 4 / Kt—K B 3	B—B 4 / Kt—K B 3

(a) A lost move.

(b) It would have been more decisive if played to K B 7 at once.

(c) If Q × B, mate follows in three moves.

(d) White loses the game by this move. The following variation by the writer, was published some years since, and seems to prove that White might have won easily from this point:—

33.		Q—K 8 ch.
34.	Kt—Kt 1	Q × Q
35.	R—R 7 ch.	K—Kt 1

(If White take the Queen instead of checking with his Rook, he loses the game.)

36.	P × P ch.	K × R
37.	R—R 1 ch.	K—Kt 2
38.	P × R (Q) and wins.	

	(4)	(5)	(6)
3.	P—Q B 3 / P—Q 4	Kt—K B 3 / Kt×P	P—Q 4 / P×P
4.	B×P / Kt—K B 3	Kt×P / P—Q 4	P—K 5 / P—Q 4
5.	Q—Kt 3 / 0—0	B—Kt 3 / Q—Kt 4	B—Kt 3 / Kt—K 5
6.	Kt—B 3 / P—B 3 (a)	Kt×P / Q×Kt P	Kt—K B 3 / B—Kt 5 ch.
7.	B×P ch. (b) / R×B	R—B 1 / Q Kt—B 3	P—B 3 / P×P
8.	Kt×P / Q—K 2	P—Q B 3 / Kt—B 4	0—0 / P×P
9.	Q×R ch. / Q×Q	P—Q 4 / Kt×B	Q B×P / B—K 3
10.	Kt×Q / K×Kt	Kt×R / Q—K 5 ch.	Kt—Q 4 / P—Q B 4
11.	P—Q 4 / B—Kt 3	Q—K 2 / Q×Q	Kt×B / P×Kt
12.	P—B 3 / B—K 3	K×Q / Kt×R	P—B 3 / Kt—Kt 4
13.	B—K 3 / Kt—R 3	R—Kt 1 / B—K B 4	P—B 4 / Kt—K 5
14.	K—B 2 / Kt—B 2	Kt—Q 2 / 0—0—0	P—B 5 / P—B 5
15.	Kt—Q 2 / P—Kt 3	Kt—B 3 / R—K 1 ch.	B—R 4 ch. (c) / Kt—B 3
16.	P—K Kt 4 / K—Kt 2	B—K 3 / Kt—B 7	P×P (d) / B—B 4 ch.
17.	P—K R 4 / R—K 1	Kt—B 7 / Kt×B	B—Q 4 / Q—Kt 3
18.	P—R 5 / B—B 2	P×Kt / P—K Kt 3	B×B / Q×B ch.
19.	P×P / B×P	P—K R 4 / R—K 2	K—R 1 / Kt—B 7 ch.

(a) This is not advisable.   It would be better to play Kt×B.

(b) The notion of this sacrifice originated with Messrs. Henderson and Williams, of Bristol, during an examination of the present opening.

(c) Q—R 5 ch., appears a stronger move.

(d) Again, checking with the Queen seems preferable.

	(4)	(5)	(6)
20.	Q R—K Kt 1 / Kt—K 3	Kt—K 5 / Kt×Kt	R×Kt / Q×R
21.	Kt—B 4 / B—B2	Kt×Kt / B—Kt 2	Kt—B 3 / 0—0
22.	P—K 5 / Kt—Q 4	Kt—B 3 / R—K 5	Kt×P / Q R—K 1
23.	B—R 6 ch. / K—B 2	P—R 5 / B—R 3 and wins.	P—K 7 / R—B 4
24.	K—Kt 3 / P—Q Kt 4		B—B 2 / R×P (K 4)
25.	Kt—K 3 / Kt×Kt		P—K R 3 / Kt×P
26.	B×Kt / P—B 4		Kt×Kt ch. / Q R×Kt
27.	P—K B 4 / P×P		Resigns.
28.	P×P / B—Q 6		
29.	P—K B 5 / Resigns.		

	(7) Bledow / Heydebrand	(8) Bledow / Heydebrand	(9) Discart / Bonetti
1.	P—K 4 / P—K 4	P—K 4 / P—K 4	P—K 4 / P—K 4
2.	B—B 4 / B—B4	B—B 4 / Kt—K B 3	P—Q 4 / P×P
3.	P—Q B 3 / Q—K 2	P—Q 4 / P×P	B—Q B 4 / B—Kt 5 ch.
4.	Kt—K B 3 / Kt—Q B 3	P—K 5 / P—Q 4	P—B 3 / P×P
5.	P—Q 4 / B—Kt 3	B—Kt 3 / Kt—K 5	P×P / Q—B 3
6.	0—0 / P—Q 3	Kt—K B 3 / B—Kt 5 ch.	P×B (a) / Q×R
7.	P—Q R 4 / P—Q R 4	P—B 3 / P×P	Q—Kt 3 / Q—B 3

(a) By this sacrifice White obtains a strong attack.

	(7)	(8)	(9)
8.	$\dfrac{\text{B}-\text{K }3}{\text{Kt}-\text{B }3}$	$\dfrac{0-0}{\text{P}\times\text{P}}$	$\dfrac{\text{B}-\text{Kt }2}{\text{Q}-\text{Kt }3}$
9.	$\dfrac{\text{P}\times\text{P}}{\text{Kt}\times\text{P}}$	$\dfrac{\text{B}\times\text{P}}{\text{B}-\text{K }3}$	$\dfrac{\text{Kt}-\text{K }2}{\text{Kt}-\text{K R }3\ (a)}$
10.	$\dfrac{\text{Kt}\times\text{Kt}}{\text{P}\times\text{Kt}}$	$\dfrac{\text{Kt}-\text{Q }4}{\text{P}-\text{Q B }4}$	$\dfrac{\text{Q Kt}-\text{B }3}{\text{P}-\text{Q B }3}$
11.	$\dfrac{\text{B}\times\text{B}}{\text{P}\times\text{B}}$	$\dfrac{\text{Kt}\times\text{B}}{\text{P}\times\text{Kt}}$	$\dfrac{\text{Kt}-\text{B }4}{\text{Q}-\text{Kt }4}$
12.	$\dfrac{\text{Kt}-\text{Q }2}{0-0}$	$\dfrac{\text{P}-\text{B }3}{\text{Kt}-\text{Kt }4}$	$\dfrac{\text{Q Kt}-\text{K }2}{0-0}$
13.	$\dfrac{\text{Q}-\text{K }2}{\text{B}-\text{Q }2}$	$\dfrac{\text{P}-\text{B }4}{\text{Kt}-\text{K }5}$	$\dfrac{\text{P}-\text{K R }4}{\text{Q}-\text{K }2}$
14.	$\dfrac{\text{Q R}-\text{Q }1}{\text{B}\times\text{P}}$	$\dfrac{\text{P}-\text{B }5}{\text{P}-\text{B }5}$	$\dfrac{\text{Q}-\text{Kt }3}{\text{P}-\text{K Kt }3}$
15.	$\dfrac{\text{P}-\text{Q Kt }3}{\text{B}-\text{B }3}$	$\dfrac{\text{B}-\text{R }4\text{ ch.}}{\text{Kt}-\text{B }3}$	$\dfrac{\text{Kt}\times\text{P}}{\text{Q}\times\text{Kt P ch}}$
16.	$\dfrac{\text{P}-\text{B }4}{\text{Q R}-\text{Q }1}$	$\dfrac{\text{P}\times\text{P}}{\text{B}-\text{B }4\text{ ch.}}$	$\dfrac{\text{B}-\text{B }3}{\text{Q}-\text{Kt }8\text{ ch.}}$
17.	$\dfrac{\text{P}\times\text{K P}}{\text{Q}\times\text{P}}$	$\dfrac{\text{B}-\text{Q }4}{\text{Q}-\text{Kt }3}$	$\overline{\text{K}-\text{Q }2\text{ and wins.}}$
18.	$\dfrac{\text{R}-\text{B }5}{\text{Q}-\text{Q }3}$	$\dfrac{\text{B}\times\text{B}}{\text{Q}\times\text{B ch.}}$	
19.	$\dfrac{\text{P}-\text{K }5}{\text{Q}-\text{B }4\text{ ch.}}$	$\dfrac{\text{K}-\text{R }1}{\text{Kt}-\text{B }7\text{ ch.}}$	
20.	$\dfrac{\text{K}-\text{R }1}{\text{Kt}-\text{K }5}$	$\dfrac{\text{R}\times\text{Kt}}{\text{Q}\times\text{R}}$	
21.	$\dfrac{\text{Kt}\times\text{Kt}}{\text{R}\times\text{R ch.}}$	$\dfrac{\text{Kt}-\text{B }3}{0-0}$	
22.	$\dfrac{\text{Q}\times\text{R}}{\text{B}\times\text{Kt}}$	$\dfrac{\text{Kt}\times\text{P}}{\text{Q R}-\text{K }1}$	
23.	$\dfrac{\text{R}\times\text{P}}{\text{R}\times\text{R}}$	$\dfrac{\text{P}-\text{K }7}{\text{R}-\text{B }4}$	
24.	$\dfrac{\text{Q}-\text{Q }8\text{ ch.}}{\text{Q}-\text{K B }1}$	$\dfrac{\text{B}-\text{B }2}{\text{R}\times\text{P}}$	
25.	$\dfrac{\text{B}\times\text{R ch.}}{\text{K}\times\text{B}}$	$\dfrac{\text{P}-\text{K R }3}{\text{Kt}\times\text{P}}$	

(a) He dared not take the Kt P.

	(7)	**(8)**	**(9)**
26.	P—K 6 ch. / K—Kt 1	Kt×Kt / R×Kt	
27.	P—K 7 / Resigns.	Resigns.	

	(10) Lowenthal & Falkbeer / Staunton & Ranken	**(11)** Journoud / Kieseritsky	**(12)** Stanley / Rousseau
1.	P—K 4 / P—K 4	P—K 4 / P—K 4	P—K 4 / P—K 4
2.	P—Q 4 / P×P	P—Q 4 / P×P	B—B 4 / Kt—K B 3
3.	Kt—K B 3 (a) / Kt—Q B 3	Kt—K B 3 / P—Q B 4	Kt—Q B 3 / B—B 4
4.	B—Q B 4 / B—B 4	B—Q B 4 / P—Q Kt 4	Kt—B 3 / P—Q 3
5.	0—0 / P—Q 3	B—Q 5 (f) / P—Q B 3	P—K R 3 / 0—0
6.	P—B 3 / Q—B 3 (b)	0—0 / R—Kt 1	P—Q 3 / B—K 3
7.	B—Q Kt 5 / B—K Kt 5	B—K B 4 / R—Kt 3	B—Kt 3 / Kt—B 3
8.	Q—R 4 / K Kt—K 2	Q Kt—Q 2 / P—Q 3	Kt—K 2 / Q—K 2
9.	Kt×P / 0—0 (c)	P—B 4 / Kt—Kt 5	Kt—Kt 3 / Kt—Q 5
10.	B—K 3 (d) / Q—Kt 3 (e)	P×P / Kt×B	Kt×Kt / B—Kt

(a) This resolves the opening into a position of the " Scotch " game.

(b) A defence much in favour with our great player McDonnell, and which people are beginning to estimate more highly than they did formerly.

(c) White dare not avail themselves of the gratuity in the shape of a Pawn now offered, as it would involve the certain loss of the game.

(d) The best move undoubtedly.

(e) Threatening B—R 6, &c.

(f) The youngest player will perceive that he would have lost his Bishop if he had taken the Pawn by 5. Q—R 5 ch.

	(10)	(11)	(12)
11.	K—R 1 / B×Kt	P×Kt / Kt—B 3	P—Q B 3 (g) / B—Kt 3
12.	B×B (a) / B—Q 2 (b)	Kt—B 4 / Kt×P (e)	0—0 / P—Q 4 (h)
13.	Kt—Q 2 / P—B 4	Kt×R / Q×Kt	B—Kt 5 / P—B 3
14.	Q R—K 1 / P×P	Q—K 2 ch. / B—K 3	Kt—R 5 / P×P
15.	Kt×P / P—Q R 3	B—Kt 3 / B—K 2	P×P / B×B
16.	B×Kt (c) / B×B	P—Q R 4 / 0—0	Q—B 3 (i) / B—B 5
17.	Q—B 4 ch. / B—Q 4	Kt—Q 2 / Kt—Kt 5	B×Kt / Q—K 3
18.	Q—K 2 / Kt—B 4 (d)	Q R—Q B 1 / P—Q 4 (f)	K—P 1 / B—K 7

(a) Had they taken with the Pawn, Black could safely have won their K P.

(b) Probably the best move, as it leaves them free to take the K P, or, after playing P—Q R 3, to gain an awkward attack upon the adverse Queen.

(c) White might now have made a desperate effort to recover themselves by Kt—B 6 ch., but properly answered that move would have cost them the exchange, and left their game in other respects no better than it was before.

(d) Now Black have fairly got the attack into their own hands, and they never offer the enemy a chance of retrieving their position.

(e) If he had taken the Pawn with his Rook, the following would have been probably the consequence:—

12.		R×P
13.	Q—K 2 ch.	K—Q 2 !
14.	Q Kt—K 5 ch.	K—B 2 !
15.	Q×R and wins.	

(f) Black's cluster of centre Pawns begins to assume a dangerous aspect, and will certainly give the adversary trouble, unless he exercises all his vigilance.

(g) White gains a move by this exchange of Pieces.

(h) P—K R 3 would have been better play.

(i) This is very finely played, and is an example to young players of the importance of gaining time at chess. Had White paused in his attack to recover the lost Bishop, the adversary might have succeeded in dislodging one or other of the Pieces by which he is beleaguered, or in bringing his own forces to the rescue, and then have ultimately retrieved the game.

	(10)	(11)	(12)
19.	P—B 3	K—R 1	Kt×Q
	Q R—K 1	P—B 5	B×Q
20.	B—B 2	P—B 4	Kt×R
	B×P	P—Q 6	Resigns
21.	P—Q B 4	Q—B 3	
	P—Q 4	B—K B 4	
22.	P×P	K R—K 1	
	Kt—Q 3	B—B 3	
23.	Q—Q 2	B—B 2	
	B—B 5	B—Q 5 (a)	
24.	R—K Kt 1	K—Kt 1	
	R×Kt	Kt—B 7	
25.	R×R	R—K 5	
	Q×R	B—Kt 5 (b)	
26.	P×Q	Q×B (c)	
	Kt×P	B×B ch.	
27.	B—K 3	K—R 1	
	Kt×Q	B—K 6	
28.	B×Kt	R—Q 1	
	R—B 7	B—Q 5	
29.	B—B 3	R×P (d)	
	B×P	Kt—K 6	
30.	P—R 3	Q—B 3	
	P—K R 4	B×P	
31.	P—R 4	Kt×P	
	K—B 2	Kt×Kt	
32.	R—Q 1	Q×P (e)	
	P—Q B 3	Kt—K 6	
33.	R—Q 2	P—R 5	
	B×P ch.	Kt×R (Q 1) (f)	

(a) This appears at first view to relieve White a little, but his position is one of extreme peril, nevertheless.

(b) Well played.

(c) It would have been better, perhaps, to have played the Queen to K Kt 3, instead of taking the Bishop at this moment.

(d) It was impossible to avoid the loss of a Rook for the Knight or Bishop, if Black chose to take it.

(e) He should have taken the Pawn with the K R, and he would then have stood a fair chance of drawing the game, we believe.

(f) M. Journoud omitted to take this into account when he attacked the Queen.

	(10)	(11)		(10) (*contd.*)
34.	$\dfrac{\text{K}-\text{Kt 1}}{\text{R}\times\text{R}}$	$\dfrac{\text{P}\times\text{Q}}{\text{Kt}-\text{B 7 ch.}}$		
35.	$\dfrac{\text{B}\times\text{R}}{\text{B}-\text{K 5}}$	$\dfrac{\text{K}-\text{Kt 1}}{\text{Kt}\times\text{Q}}$		
36.	$\dfrac{\text{K}-\text{B 2}}{\text{K}-\text{K 3}}$	$\dfrac{\text{P}\times\text{P}}{\text{Kt}\times\text{P}}$		
37.	$\dfrac{\text{B}-\text{B 3}}{\text{P}-\text{K Kt 3}}$	$\dfrac{\text{R}-\text{Q 7}}{\text{B}-\text{Q 5 ch.}\ (a)}$	44.	$\dfrac{\text{K}-\text{Q 2}}{\text{P}-\text{Kt 5}}$
38.	$\dfrac{\text{B}-\text{Q 4}}{\text{P}-\text{Q Kt 4}}$	$\dfrac{\text{K}-\text{B 1}}{\text{B}-\text{Kt 3}}$	45.	$\dfrac{\text{B}-\text{Q 8}}{\text{K.}-\text{Kt 4}}$
39.	$\dfrac{\text{P}-\text{Q Kt 4}}{\text{K}-\text{Q 4}}$	$\dfrac{\text{R}-\text{Kt 7}}{\text{Kt}-\text{Q 4}}$	46.	$\dfrac{\text{K}-\text{B 1}}{\text{P}-\text{R 4}}$
40.	$\dfrac{\text{K}-\text{K 3}}{\text{B}-\text{B 4}}$	$\dfrac{\text{K}-\text{K 2}}{\text{B}\times\text{P}}$	47.	$\dfrac{\text{K}-\text{Kt 2}}{\text{P}-\text{R 5}}$
41.	$\dfrac{\text{B}-\text{Kt 6}}{\text{K}-\text{B 5}}$	$\dfrac{\text{R}\times\text{B}}{\text{Kt}-\text{B 6 ch.}}$	48.	$\dfrac{\text{B}-\text{B 6}}{\text{P}-\text{R 6 ch.}}$
42.	$\dfrac{\text{B}-\text{R 5}}{\text{P}-\text{B 4}}$	$\dfrac{\text{K}-\text{Q 3}}{\text{Kt}\times\text{P}}$	49.	$\dfrac{\text{K}-\text{R 1}}{\text{P}-\text{Q Kt 6}}$
43.	$\dfrac{\text{P}\times\text{P}}{\text{K}\times\text{P}}$	Resigns	50.	Resigns.

	(13) Schulten / Horwitz	(14) Kieseritzky / Horwitz	(15) Dr. Bledow / Van Bilguer
1.	$\dfrac{\text{P}-\text{K 4}}{\text{P}-\text{K 4}}$	$\dfrac{\text{P}-\text{K 4}}{\text{P}-\text{K 4}}$	$\dfrac{\text{P}-\text{K 4}}{\text{P}-\text{K 4}}$
2.	$\dfrac{\text{B}-\text{B 4}}{\text{Kt}-\text{K B 3}}$	$\dfrac{\text{B}-\text{B 4}}{\text{Kt}-\text{K B 3}}$	$\dfrac{\text{B}-\text{B 4}}{\text{P}-\text{K B 4}}$
3.	$\dfrac{\text{Kt}-\text{Q B 3}}{\text{P}-\text{Q Kt 4}}$	$\dfrac{\text{Kt}-\text{K B 3}}{\text{Kt}\times\text{P}}$	$\dfrac{\text{P}-\text{Q 3}}{\text{Kt}-\text{K B 3}}$
4.	$\dfrac{\text{B}\times\text{Kt P}}{\text{B}-\text{B 4}}$	$\dfrac{\text{P}-\text{Q 3}}{\text{Kt}-\text{K B 3}}$	$\dfrac{\text{Kt}-\text{K B 3}}{\text{P}\times\text{P}}$
5.	$\dfrac{\text{P}-\text{Q 3}}{\text{P}-\text{B 3}}$	$\dfrac{\text{Kt}\times\text{P}}{\text{P}-\text{Q 4}}$	$\dfrac{\text{P}\times\text{P}}{\text{Kt}\times\text{P}}$
6.	$\dfrac{\text{B}-\text{Q B 4}}{\text{Q}-\text{Kt 3}}$	$\dfrac{\text{Q}-\text{K 2}}{\text{B}-\text{K 3}}$	$\dfrac{\text{Q}-\text{Q 5}}{\text{Kt}-\text{Q 3}}$

(*a*) The latter portion of this game is capitally played by M. Kieseritzky.

(13)	(14)	(15)
7. $\dfrac{Q-K\ 2}{P-Q\ 4}$	$\dfrac{B-Kt\ 3}{B-Q\ 3}$	$\dfrac{Kt \times K\ P}{P-B\ 3}$
8 $\dfrac{P \times P}{0-0}$	$\dfrac{P-K\ B\ 4}{0-0}$	$\dfrac{Q-B\ 7\ \text{ch.}}{Kt \times Q}$
9. $\dfrac{Kt-K\ 4}{Kt \times Kt}$	$\dfrac{0-0}{Q\ Kt-Q\ 2}$	$\dfrac{B \times Kt\ \text{ch.}}{K-K\ 2}$
10. $\dfrac{P \times Kt}{B \times P\ \text{ch. } (a)}$	$\dfrac{Kt-Q\ B\ 3}{B-B\ 4\ \text{ch.}}$	$\dfrac{B-Kt\ 5\ \text{ch.}}{K-Q\ 3}$
11. $\dfrac{Q \times B}{Q-Kt\ 5\ \text{ch.}}$	$\dfrac{K-R\ 1}{Kt \times Kt}$	$\dfrac{B \times Q}{K \times Kt}$
12. $\dfrac{B-Q\ 2}{Q \times K\ B}$	$\dfrac{P \times Kt}{Kt \times Kt\ 5}$	$\dfrac{P-K\ B\ 4\ \text{ch.}}{K-B\ 4}$
13. $\dfrac{Q-B\ 3}{P-K\ B\ 4}$	$\dfrac{B-K\ B\ 4}{P-Q\ B\ 3}$	$\dfrac{B-Kt\ 5}{B-Kt\ 5\ \text{ch.}}$
14. $\dfrac{P \times K\ B\ P}{B \times P}$	$\dfrac{Kt-K\ 4\ (c)}{P \times Kt}$	$\dfrac{P-B\ 3}{R-B\ 1}$
15. $\dfrac{Q-Kt\ 3}{}$	$\dfrac{B \times B}{Kt-B\ 7\ \text{ch.}}$	$\dfrac{B-Kt\ 3}{P-K\ R\ 3}$
16. Black mates in 3 (b)	$\dfrac{R \times Kt}{B \times R}$	$\dfrac{B-B\ 2\ \text{ch.}}{K-Kt\ 5}$
17	$\dfrac{B-Q\ Kt\ 3}{Q-Q\ 5\ (d)}$	$\dfrac{B-Q\ 1\ \text{ch.}}{K-B\ 4}$
18.	$\dfrac{R-K\ B\ 1}{P-K\ 6}$	$\dfrac{P-Kt\ 4\ \text{ch.}}{K-Kt\ 3}$
19.	$\dfrac{P-K\ Kt\ 3}{Q\ R-Q\ 1}$	$\dfrac{B-B\ 2\ \text{ch.}}{K-B\ 2}$
20.	$\dfrac{B-Kt\ 5}{R-Q\ 2}$	$\dfrac{B-K\ R\ 4}{B-K\ 2}$
21.	$\dfrac{P-K\ 6}{P \times P}$	$\dfrac{B-Kt\ 3}{P-Q\ 4}$
22.	$\dfrac{B \times P\ \text{ch.}}{K-R\ 1}$	$\dfrac{P-K\ B\ 5}{Kt-Q\ 2}$
23.	$\dfrac{Q \times P\ (e)}{Q \times Q}$	$\dfrac{Kt-Q\ 2}{B-B\ 3}$

(a) Black plays capitally now to the end.

(b) It is rarely in actual play one sees so pretty a mate.

(c) This is pretty, but not sound.

(d) A good move.　If White plays P—B 3, Black plays P × P.

(e) He would have been mated in two moves, on taking the Rook with his Bishop.

	(13)	(14)	(15)
24.		B×Q / R—K 2	Kt—B 3 / R—K 1 ch.
25.		B×B 5 / R×B	K—B 2 / Kt—B 4
26.		B×R / R—K 7	K R—K 1 / B—Q 2
27.		K—Kt 2 / B—Q 5 d. ch.	P—Kt 4 / Kt—K 5 ch.
28.		K—R 3 / R×B P	R×Kt (a) / P×R
29.		B—R 3 / P—K R 3	B—Kt 3 ch. / K—B 1
30.		K—Kt 4 / B×P	B—Q 6 ch. / B—K 2
31.		B—Q 6 / B—B 3	Kt—K 5 / P—K Kt 4 (b)
32.		P—K R 4 / R×P	P—B 6 (c) / P—K 6 ch.
33.		K—B 5 / K—R 2	K—Kt 1 / Resigns.
34.		K—K 6 / R—Q 7	
35.		R—B 3 / P—Q R 4	
36.		K—Q 7 / R—Q B 7	
37.		P—Q 4 / B×P	
38.		Resigns.	

	(16)	(17)	(18)
	Schlechter / Marshall	Teichmann / Morco	Leonhardt / Maroczy
1.	P—K 4 / P—K 4	P—K 4 / P—K 4	P—K 4 / P—K 4
2.	B—B 4 / Kt—K B 3	B—B 4 / Kt—K B 3	B—B 4 / Kt—K B 3

(a) The terminating moves are admirably played by Dr. Bledow.
(b) It is quite evident that on taking the Bishop, mate would have followed next move.
(c) Beautifully played.

	(16)	(17)	(18)
3.	$\dfrac{\text{P—Q 4}}{\text{P} \times \text{P}}$	$\dfrac{\text{P—Q 3}}{\text{P—Q 4 ?}}$	$\dfrac{\text{P—Q 3}}{\text{B—B 4}}$
4.	$\dfrac{\text{Kt—K B 3}}{\text{B—B 4}}$	$\dfrac{\text{P} \times \text{P}}{\text{Kt} \times \text{P}}$	$\dfrac{\text{Kt—Q B 3}}{\text{P—Q 3}}$
5.	$\dfrac{0-0}{\text{P—Q 3}}$	$\dfrac{\text{Q—K 2}}{\text{Q Kt—B 3}}$	$\dfrac{\text{P—B 4}}{\text{P—B 3}}$
6.	$\dfrac{\text{P—B 3}}{\text{P} \times \text{P}}$	$\dfrac{\text{Kt—K B 3}}{\text{B—K Kt 5}}$	$\dfrac{\text{Kt—B 3}}{\text{P—Q Kt 4 ?}}$
7.	$\dfrac{\text{Kt} \times \text{P}}{0-0}$	$\dfrac{\text{P—K R 3}}{\text{B} \times \text{Kt}}$	$\dfrac{\text{B—Kt 3}}{\text{P—Q R 4}}$
8.	$\dfrac{\text{B—K Kt 5}}{\text{B—K 3}}$	$\dfrac{\text{Q} \times \text{B}}{\text{Kt—B 3}}$	$\dfrac{\text{P—Q R 4}}{\text{P—Kt 5}}$
9.	$\dfrac{\text{Q—Kt 3}}{\text{B—B}}$	$\dfrac{0-0}{\text{P—Q R 3}}$	$\dfrac{\text{Kt—K 2}}{\text{Q—B 2}}$
10.	$\dfrac{\text{Q} \times \text{B}}{\text{P—K R 3}}$	$\dfrac{\text{Kt—B 3}}{\text{B—K 2}}$	$\dfrac{\text{P} \times \text{P}}{\text{P} \times \text{P}}$
11.	$\dfrac{\text{B—R 4}}{\text{Q Kt—Q 2}}$	$\dfrac{\text{Kt—K 4}}{0-0 \; (a)}$	$\dfrac{\text{R—B 1}}{0-0}$
12.	$\dfrac{\text{P—Q Kt 4}}{\text{B—Kt 3}}$	$\dfrac{\text{P—B 3}}{\text{Q—Q 2} \; (b)}$	$\dfrac{\text{Kt—Kt 3}}{\text{B—K 3}}$
13.	$\dfrac{\text{P—K 5}}{\text{P} \times \text{P}}$	$\dfrac{\text{B—K 3}}{\text{Q R—Q 1}}$	$\dfrac{\text{Kt—Kt 5}}{\text{B} \times \text{B}}$
14.	$\dfrac{\text{Q R—Q 1}}{\text{Q—K 2}}$	$\dfrac{\text{Q R—Q 1}}{\text{Kt—Q 4 ?}}$	$\dfrac{\text{R} \times \text{Kt !}}{\text{Kt—Q 2} \; (c)}$
15.	$\dfrac{\text{R} \times \text{Kt !}}{\text{Q} \times \text{R}}$	$\dfrac{\text{Kt—Kt 3}}{\text{Q—B 3}}$	$\dfrac{\text{R—B 1} \; (d)}{\text{P—R 3}}$
16.	$\dfrac{\text{B} \times \text{Kt}}{\text{P} \times \text{B}}$	$\dfrac{\text{Kt—B 5 !}}{\text{K R—K 1}}$	$\dfrac{\text{P} \times \text{B}}{\text{P} \times \text{Kt}}$
17.	$\dfrac{\text{Kt—Q 5}}{\text{Q—K 3}}$	$\dfrac{\text{Q—Kt 3}}{\text{Kt—R 4}}$	$\dfrac{\text{B} \times \text{P}}{\text{P—B 3}}$

(a) If 11.   Kt—Q 5
      12. Kt × Kt ch.   B × Kt
      13. Q × P   Kt × P
      14. Q—B 6 ch. !
(b) He should have played Kt × Kt.
(c) If 14.   P × R
      15. Q—R 5   P × Kt
      16. Q × Kt P ch. &c.
(d) If 15. Kt × R P !   P × R
      16. Q—Kt 4 ch.   K—R 1
      17. Kt—B 5 !

	(16)	(17)	(18)
18.	$\dfrac{\text{Kt}-\text{R 4 !}}{\text{K R}-\text{Q 1}}$	$\dfrac{\text{Q}\times\text{K P}}{\text{Kt}\times\text{B}}$	$\dfrac{\text{B}-\text{Q 2}}{\text{B}-\text{Q 5}}$
19.	$\dfrac{\text{Kt}-\text{B 5}}{\text{R}\times\text{Kt}}$	$\dfrac{\text{Kt}\times\text{B ch.}}{\text{K}-\text{B 1}}$	$\dfrac{\text{Q}-\text{B 2}}{\text{P}-\text{Kt 3}}$
20.	$\dfrac{\text{Q}-\text{Kt 4 ch.}}{\text{K}-\text{B 1}}$	$\dfrac{\text{P}\times\text{Kt}}{\text{R}\times\text{R}}$	$\dfrac{\text{P}-\text{R 4}}{\text{Kt}-\text{B 4}}$
21.	$\dfrac{\text{Q}-\text{R 3}}{\text{B}\times\text{P ch. !}}$	$\dfrac{\text{R}\times\text{R}}{\text{Resigns.}}$	$\dfrac{\text{Kt}-\text{K 2}}{\text{B}\times\text{P}}$
22.	$\dfrac{\text{K}\times\text{B}}{\text{Q}-\text{Kt 3 ch.}}$		$\dfrac{\text{R}-\text{R 2}}{\text{Q}-\text{Q 3 ! and wins}}$
23.	$\dfrac{\text{K}-\text{K 2}}{\text{Q R}-\text{Q 1}}$		
24.	$\dfrac{\text{Q}\times\text{P ch.}}{\text{K}-\text{K 1}}$		
25.	$\dfrac{\text{Kt}-\text{Kt 7 ch.}}{\text{K}-\text{K 2}}$		
26.	$\dfrac{\text{Kt}-\text{B 5 ch.}}{\text{K}-\text{Q 2}}$		
27.	$\dfrac{\text{Q}-\text{R 3}}{\text{Q}-\text{R 3 ch.}}$		
28.	$\dfrac{\text{K}-\text{B 2}}{\text{R}-\text{Q 7 ch. and win}}$		

Chapter II.

THE CENTRE GAMBIT—ANALYSIS.

	(1)	(2)	(3)
1.	$\dfrac{\text{P}-\text{K 4}}{\text{P}-\text{K 4}}$	—	—
2.	$\dfrac{\text{P}-\text{Q 4}}{\text{P}\times\text{P}}$	—	—

	(1)	(2)	(3)
3.	$\dfrac{Q \times P}{Kt - Q B 3}$	—	—
4.	$\dfrac{Q - K 3}{Kt - B 3}$	—	$\dfrac{}{P - K Kt 3}$
5.	$\dfrac{B - K 2}{B - K 2}$	$\dfrac{Kt - Q B 3}{B - Q Kt 5}$	$\dfrac{Kt - Q B 3}{B - Kt 2}$
6.	$\dfrac{P - K 5}{Kt - Q 4}$	$\dfrac{B - Q 2}{0 - 0}$	$\dfrac{B - Q 2}{Kt - B 3}$

Nos. 1 to 6.   Position after White's 3rd move.

BLACK.

WHITE.

	(1)	(2)	(3)
7.	$\dfrac{Q - K Kt 3}{}$	$\dfrac{0 - 0 - 0}{R - K 1}$	$\dfrac{0 - 0 - 0}{0 - 0}$
8.		$\dfrac{B - Q B 4}{B \times Kt}$	$\dfrac{B - K 2}{R - K 1}$
9.		$\dfrac{B \times B}{Kt \times P}$	$\dfrac{P - B 3}{P - Q 4}$
10.		$\dfrac{Q - B 4}{Kt - Kt 4}$	
11.		$\dfrac{Kt - B 3}{Kt - K 3}$	
12.		$\dfrac{Q - Kt 3}{P - B 3}$	

	(4)	(5)	(6)
1.	—	—	—
2	—	—	—
3.	—	—	—
4	Kt—B 3	Q—R 4 / B—B 4	Q—Q 1 / Kt—B 3
5.	B—Q 2 / P—K Kt 3	Kt—K B 3 / P—Q 3	B—Q 3 / P—Q 4
6.	Kt—Q B 3 / B—Kt 2	B—Q B 4 / Kt—B 3	P×P / Q×P
7.	0-0-0 / P—Q 3	0-0 / B—Q 2	Kt—K B 3 / B—K Kt 5
8.	Kt—Q 5 / B—K 3		Q Kt—Q 2 / 0-0-0
9.	Kt×Kt / B×Kt		0-0 / B—Kt 5
10.	P—K B 4		B—K 2 / K R—K 1

	(7)	.(8)
1.	—	—
2.	—	—
3.	B—Q B 4 / Kt—KB 3	B—Kt 5 ch.
4.	P—K 5 / P—Q 4	P—B 3 / P×P
5.	B—Kt 5 ch. / B—Q 2	P×P / Q—B 3
6.	B×B ch. / K Kt×B	P×B / Q×R
7.	Q×P / Kt—Q B 3	Q—Kt 3 / P—Q 4
8.	Q×P / K Kt×P	B×P / B—K 3

	(7)	(8)
9.	$\dfrac{Q \times Q}{R \times Q}$	$\dfrac{B \times B}{P \times B}$
10.	$\dfrac{B-Q\,2}{B-Q\,3}$	$\dfrac{Q \times P \text{ ch.}}{Kt-K\,2}$
11.		$\dfrac{Q-Kt\,3}{Q\,Kt-B\,3}$
12.		$\dfrac{Kt-K\,2}{0-0-0}$

THE CENTRE GAMBIT—GAMES.

	(1) Potter —	(2) Mieses Schlechter
1.	$\dfrac{P-K\,4}{P-K\,4}$	$\dfrac{P-K\,4}{P-K\,4}$
2.	$\dfrac{P-Q\,4}{P \times P}$	$\dfrac{P-Q\,4}{Kt-Q\,B\,3}$
3.	$\dfrac{B-Q\,B\,4}{P-Q\,B\,4}$	$\dfrac{P \times P}{Kt \times P}$
4.	$\dfrac{Kt-K\,B\,3}{P-Q\,3}$	$\dfrac{Kt-Q\,B\,3}{B-B\,4}$
5.	$\dfrac{0-0}{Kt-Q\,B\,3}$	$\dfrac{P-B\,4}{Kt-Kt\,3}$
6.	$\dfrac{P-B\,3}{P-Q\,6}$	$\dfrac{Kt-B\,3}{P-Q\,3}$
7.	$\dfrac{R-K\,1}{B-Kt\,5}$	$\dfrac{Kt-Q\,R\,4}{B-Kt\,3}$
8.	$\dfrac{P-K\,5}{Kt \times P}$	$\dfrac{Kt \times B}{R\,P \times Kt}$
9.	$\dfrac{Kt \times Kt}{B \times Q}$	$\dfrac{B-B\,4}{Q-K\,2}$
10.	$\dfrac{B-Q\,Kt\,5 \text{ ch.}}{K-K\,2}$	$\dfrac{0-0}{Kt-B\,3}$
11.	$\dfrac{B-Kt\,5 \text{ ch.}}{P-B\,3}$	$\dfrac{P-K\,5}{P \times P}$
12.	$\dfrac{Kt-Kt\,6 \text{ db. ch.}}{K-B\,2}$	$\dfrac{P \times P}{Kt \times P}$
13.	$Kt \times R$ mate.	$\dfrac{Kt \times Kt}{Q \times Kt}$

(2) (contd.)

14. $\dfrac{R-K\,1}{Kt-K\,5}$

15. $\dfrac{B-Q\,5}{P-K\,B\,4}$

16. $\dfrac{Q-Q\,3}{B-K\,3\,!}$

17. $\dfrac{B\times Kt}{0-0}$

18. $\dfrac{B-B\,4}{P\times B}$

19. $\dfrac{B\times Q}{P\times Q}$

20. $\dfrac{B\times Kt\,P}{K\times B}$

21. $\dfrac{R\times B}{P\times P}$

22. $\dfrac{R-K\,2}{R\times P}$ and wins.

Chapter III.

DANISH GAMBIT—ANALYSIS.

(1)   (2)   (3)

1. $\dfrac{P-K\,4}{P-K\,4}$ —   —

2. $\dfrac{P-Q\,4}{P\times P}$ —   —

Nos. 1 to 7.   Position after White's 4th move.

BLACK.

WHITE.

	(1)	(2)	(3)
3.	$\dfrac{\text{P—Q B 3}}{\text{P} \times \text{P}}$	—	—
4.	$\dfrac{\text{B—Q B 4}}{\text{Kt—K B 3}}$	—	—
5.	$\dfrac{\text{Kt} \times \text{P}}{\text{B—Kt 5}}$	—	—
6.	$\dfrac{\text{Kt—K 2}}{\text{0—0}}$	—	$\dfrac{\text{B} \times \text{P ch.}}{\text{K} \times \text{B}}$
7.	$\dfrac{\text{P—K 5}}{\text{P—Q 4}}$	$\overline{\text{Kt—K 5}}$	$\dfrac{\text{Q—Kt 3 ch.}}{\text{P} \times \text{Q 4}}$
8.	$\dfrac{\text{P} \times \text{Kt}}{\text{P} \times \text{B}}$	$\dfrac{\text{0—0}}{\text{Kt} \times \text{Kt}}$	$\dfrac{\text{Q} \times \text{B}}{\text{Kt} \times \text{P}}$
9.	$\dfrac{\text{0—0}}{\text{Q} \times \text{P}}$	$\dfrac{\text{P} \times \text{Kt}}{\text{B—B 4}}$	$\dfrac{\text{K Kt—K 2}}{\text{R—K 1}}$
10.		$\dfrac{\text{Kt} \times \text{Kt 3}}{\text{Q—R 5}}$	$\dfrac{\text{0—0}}{\text{K—Kt 1}}$
11.		$\dfrac{\text{Q—K 2}}{\text{P—Q 3}}$	

	(4)	(5)	(6)	(7)
1.	—	—	—	—
2.	—	—	—	—
3.	—	—	—	—
4.	—	$\overline{\text{P} \times \text{P}}$	—	—
5.	$\dfrac{\text{P—K 5}}{\text{P—Q 4}}$	$\dfrac{\text{Q B} \times \text{P}}{\text{Kt—K B 3}}$	—	—
6.	$\dfrac{\text{Kt} \times \text{P}}{\text{P} \times \text{B}}$	$\dfrac{\text{Kt—Q B 3}}{\text{Kt—B 3}}$	$\overline{\text{B—Kt 5}}$	$\dfrac{\text{P—K 5}}{\text{B—Kt 5 ch.}}$
7.	$\dfrac{\text{Q} \times \text{Q ch.}}{\text{K} \times \text{Q}}$	$\dfrac{\text{Kt—B 3}}{\text{B—Kt 5}}$	$\dfrac{\text{Kt—K 2}}{\text{Kt} \times \text{P}}$	$\dfrac{\text{K—B 1}}{\text{P—Q 4}}$
8.	$\dfrac{\text{P} \times \text{Kt}}{\text{P} \times \text{P}}$	$\dfrac{\text{Q—B 2}}{\text{P—Q 3}}$	$\dfrac{\text{0—0}}{\text{Kt} \times \text{Kt}}$	$\dfrac{\text{P} \times \text{Kt}}{\text{P} \times \text{B}}$
9.	$\dfrac{\text{B—B 4}}{\text{B—K B 4}}$	$\dfrac{\text{0—0—0}}{\text{B} \times \text{Kt}}$	$\dfrac{\text{Kt} \times \text{Kt}}{\text{B} \times \text{Kt}}$	$\dfrac{\text{Q—R 4 ch.}}{\text{Kt—B 3}}$
10.	$\dfrac{\text{0—0—0 ch}}{\text{B—Q 6}}$	$\dfrac{\text{Q} \times \text{B}}{\text{B} \times \text{K 3}}$	$\dfrac{\text{B} \times \text{B}}{\text{Q—Kt 4}}$	$\dfrac{\text{P} \times \text{P}}{\text{R—Kt 1}}$
11.		$\overline{\text{P—K 5}}$	$\overline{\text{R—K 1 ch.}}$	$\dfrac{\text{Kt—Q B 3}}{\text{B} \times \text{Kt}}$

DANISH GAMBIT—GAMES.

	(1) Lindehn / Maczuski	(2) Mieses / Marshall
1.	P—K 4 / P—K 4	P—K 4 / P—K 4
2.	P—Q 4 / P×P	P—Q 4 / P×P
3.	P—Q B 3 / P×P	P—Q B 3 / P×P
4.	B—Q B 4 / P×P	B—Q B 4 / P×P
5.	Q B×P / Kt—K B 3	Q B×P / P—Q 3
6.	Kt—Q B 3 / B—Kt 5	Kt—K 2 / Kt—Q B 3 (b
7.	Kt—K 2 / Kt×P	0—0 / B—K 3
8.	0—0 / Kt×Kt	B—Q 5 / Kt—B 3
9.	Kt×Kt / B×Kt	Q—Kt 3 / Q—B 1
10.	B×B / Q—Kt 4	Kt—B 4 / Kt—Q 1
11.	R—Kt ch. / K—Q 1	B×Kt / P×B
12.	P—K B 4 / Q×P	Kt—R 5 / P—B 3
13.	B×Kt P / R—Kt 1	R—K 1 ! / B—K 2
14.	Q—Kt 4 / Resigns (a)	Q—K B 3 / R—K Kt 1
15.		Kt×P ch. / B×Kt
16.		Q×B / P×B

(a) A neat finish.
(b) Or Kt—Q 2.

(2) (*contd.*)

17. $\dfrac{P \times P}{R - Kt\,3}$ (a)

18. $\dfrac{Q - R\,8 \text{ ch.}}{K - Q\,2}$

19. $\dfrac{Kt - B\,3}{B \times P}$ (b)

20. $\dfrac{Q - K\,8 \text{ ch.}}{K - B\,2}$

21. $\dfrac{Kt \times B \text{ ch.}}{K - Kt\,1}$

22. $\dfrac{Q\,R - B\,1}{Kt - B\,3}$

23. $\dfrac{R \times Kt\,!}{P \times R}$

24. $\dfrac{R - Kt\,1 \text{ mate.}}{}$

Chapter IV.

QUEEN'S BISHOP'S PAWN OPENING— ANALYSIS.

	(1)	(2)	(3)	(4)
1.	$\dfrac{P-K\,4}{P-K\,4}$	—	—	—
2.	$\dfrac{P-Q\,B\,3}{P-Q\,4\,!}$ (c)	—	—	—
3.	$\dfrac{Kt-K\,B\,3}{P\times P}$	—	$\dfrac{P\times P}{Q\times P}$	$\dfrac{Kt-K\,B\,3}{}$
4.	$\dfrac{Kt\times P}{B-Q\,3}$	$\dfrac{Q-R\,4 \text{ ch.}}{P-B\,3}$	$\dfrac{P-Q\,4}{Kt-Q\,B\,3}$	$\dfrac{P-Q\,4}{Kt\times P}$
5.	$\dfrac{Kt-B\,4}{B-K\,3}$	$\dfrac{Q\times K\,P}{B-Q\,3}$	$\dfrac{B-K\,3}{B-K\,B\,4}$	$\dfrac{Kt\times P}{B-Q\,3}$
6.	$\dfrac{P-Q\,4}{P\times P \text{ e.p.}}$	$\dfrac{B-Q\,B\,4}{Kt-K\,B\,3}$	$\dfrac{P-B\,4}{Q-R\,4 \text{ ch.}}$	$\dfrac{Kt-Q\,3}{P-Q\,B\,4}$

(a) K — B 1 is better.

(b) Kt — B 3 might have prolonged the defence. The next move facilitates a pretty ending.

(c) If 2. $\dfrac{}{Kt-K\,B\,3}$; 3. $\dfrac{P-Q\,4}{Kt\times P}$; 4. $\dfrac{P\times P}{P-Q\,4\,!}$; 5. $\dfrac{B-K\,3}{}$ =

	(1)	(2)	(3)	(4)
7.	$\dfrac{\text{B} \times \text{P}}{} =$	$\dfrac{\text{Q} - \text{K 2}}{\text{P} - \text{K 5}}$	$\dfrac{\text{B} - \text{Q 2}}{\text{Q} - \text{Kt 3}}$	$\dfrac{\text{P} \times \text{P}}{\text{Kt} \times \text{P}}$
8.		$\dfrac{\text{P} - \text{Q 3}}{\text{0} - \text{0}}$	$\dfrac{\text{P} \times \text{P}}{\text{Kt} - \text{Q 5} +}$	$\dfrac{\text{B} - \text{K 3}}{\text{Kt} \times \text{Kt ch.}}$
9.		$\dfrac{\text{P} \times \text{P}}{\text{Kt} \times \text{P}}$		$\dfrac{\text{B} \times \text{Kt}}{\text{Kt} - \text{B 3}}$
10.		$\dfrac{\text{B} - \text{K 3}}{\text{B} - \text{K B 4}} =$		$\dfrac{\text{0} - \text{0}}{\text{0} - \text{0}} =$

QUEEN'S BISHOP'S PAWN OPENING—GAMES.

	(1) Staunton / Cochrane	(2) Capt. Evans / St. Amant	(3) Walker / St. Amant
1.	$\dfrac{\text{P} - \text{K 4}}{\text{P} - \text{K 4}}$	$\dfrac{\text{P} - \text{K 4}}{\text{P} - \text{K 4}}$	$\dfrac{\text{P} - \text{K 4}}{\text{P} - \text{K 4}}$
2.	$\dfrac{\text{P} - \text{Q B 3}}{\text{P} - \text{Q 4}}$	$\dfrac{\text{P} - \text{Q B 3}}{\text{P} - \text{Q B 4}}$	$\dfrac{\text{P} - \text{Q B 3}}{\text{P} - \text{Q 4}}$
3.	$\dfrac{\text{Kt} - \text{K B 3}}{\text{Kt} - \text{K B 3}}$	$\dfrac{\text{Kt} - \text{K B 3}}{\text{Kt} - \text{Q B 3}}$	$\dfrac{\text{P} \times \text{P}}{\text{Q} \times \text{P}}$
4.	$\dfrac{\text{Kt} \times \text{P}}{\text{Kt} \times \text{P}}$	$\dfrac{\text{B} - \text{B 4}}{\text{Kt} - \text{B 3}}$	$\dfrac{\text{Kt} - \text{K B 3}}{\text{B} - \text{B 4}}$
5.	$\dfrac{\text{P} - \text{Q 4}}{\text{B} - \text{Q 3}}$	$\dfrac{\text{P} - \text{Q 4}}{\text{B P} \times \text{P}}$	$\dfrac{\text{P} - \text{Q Kt 3}}{\text{B} - \text{K Kt 5}}$
6.	$\dfrac{\text{Kt} - \text{Q 2}}{\text{0} - \text{0}}$	$\dfrac{\text{Kt} - \text{Kt 5} \,(a)}{\text{P} - \text{Q 4}}$	$\dfrac{\text{B} - \text{K 2}}{\text{P} - \text{K 5}}$
7.	$\dfrac{\text{Kt} \times \text{Kt}}{\text{P} \times \text{Kt}}$	$\dfrac{\text{P} \times \text{P}}{\text{Kt} \times \text{P}}$	$\dfrac{\text{Kt} - \text{Q 4}}{\text{B} \times \text{B}}$
8.	$\dfrac{\text{B} - \text{K B 4}}{\text{B} \times \text{Kt}}$	$\dfrac{\text{Kt} \times \textbf{B} \text{ P}}{\text{K} \times \text{Kt}}$	$\dfrac{\text{Kt} \times \text{B}}{\text{Kt} - \text{Q B 3}}$
9.	$\dfrac{\text{B} \times \text{B}}{\text{Kt} - \text{B 3}}$	$\dfrac{\text{Q} - \text{B 3 ch.}}{\text{K} - \text{K 3}}$	$\dfrac{\text{0} - \text{0}}{\text{Kt} - \text{K 4}}$
10.	$\dfrac{\text{B} - \text{Q B 4}}{\text{B} - \text{K 3}}$	$\dfrac{\text{0} - \text{0}}{\text{Kt} - \text{R 4}}$	$\dfrac{\text{Kt} - \text{B 4}}{\text{Q} - \text{Q 3}}$
11.	$\dfrac{\text{B} - \text{Q Kt 5}}{\text{Kt} - \text{K 2}}$	$\dfrac{\text{B} - \text{K Kt 5}}{\text{Q} - \text{Q 3}}$	$\dfrac{\text{P} - \text{Q 4}}{\text{P} \times \text{P } e.p.}$

(a) We have here a position almost identical with the leading one of the Two Knights' Game.

	(1)	(2)	(3)
12.	0—0 / P—Q B 3	P—K Kt 4 (c) / Q—Q 2	R—K 1 / 0—0—0
13.	B—R 4 / Kt—Kt 3	B—Q 3 / Q—K B 2	Kt—Q 2 / P—K B 4
14.	B—K Kt 3 / P—K B 4	B—B 5 ch. / K—Q 3	P—Q R 4 / P—Q R 4
15.	P—K B 4 / P×P e.p.	P×P / B×B	P—Q Kt 4 / P×P
16.	R×P / P—B 5	P×P ch. / K×P	P×P / B—Q 5
17.	B—Kt 3 (a) / Q—Q 3	P×B / Kt—Q B 3	R—Kt 1 / Kt—K B 3
18.	B—K B 2 / K—R 1	R—K 1 ch. / K—Q 3	Kt—Kt 3 / K Kt—Kt 5
19.	B×B / Q×B	R—K 6 ch. / K—B 4	Kt×B / Q×Kt
20.	Q—Q 3 / Q R—K 1	B—K 3 ch. / Kt×B	B—K 3 / Q—Q 3
21.	R—R 3 / Q—B 4	Q×Kt ch. / K—Kt 4	B—B 5 / Q—K R 3
22.	Q—B 3 / R—K 5	Q—Q 3 ch. / K—Kt 3	Kt—R 3 / K R—K 1
23.	R—R 5 / Q—K 3	Q—Kt 3 ch. / K—B 2	P—R 5 / P—Q 7
24.	P—B 4 / R—K 1	R×Kt ch. and wins.	R—K B 1 / Kt—Q 6
25.	P—Q Kt 3 / Q—B 3		P—R 6 / P×P
26.	R—K B 1 / R—K 7		Q—B 3 / R—K 5
27.	P—Q R 4 / R—R 7		Q×P ch. / Q—K 3
28.	P—Q 5 / R—R 8		Q×Q ch. / R×Q
29.	B×P (b) / K R—K 8		Kt—Kt 5 / R—K 8

(a) But for this move of resource, Black would evidently have gained the exchange at least.

(b) An important outlet for his King.

(c) White plays extremely well in this game.

	(1)	(2)	(3)
30.	$\dfrac{\text{R} \times \text{R}}{\text{R} \times \text{R ch.}}$		$\dfrac{\text{B} - \text{K 3}}{\text{Kt} \times \text{B}}$
31.	$\dfrac{\text{K} - \text{B 2}}{\text{Q} - \text{R 8 } (a)}$		$\dfrac{\text{P} \times \text{Kt}}{\text{R} \times \text{R ch.}}$
32.	$\dfrac{\text{Q} - \text{Q 3}}{\text{R} - \text{K Kt 8}}$		$\dfrac{\text{K} \times \text{R}}{\text{Kt} - \text{Q B 8 and wins.}}$
33.	$\dfrac{\text{Q} - \text{K 2}}{\text{Kt} - \text{K 2}}$		
34.	$\overline{\text{P} - \text{Q 6 and wins.}}$		

(a) Black has now a very menacing position.

BOOK IV.

CHAPTER I.

THE KING'S KNIGHT'S GAMBIT—ANALYSIS.

	(1)	(2)	(3)
1.	P—K 4 / P—K 4	—	—
2.	P—K B 4 / P×P	—	—
3.	Kt—K B 3 / P—K Kt 4	—	—
4.	B—B 4 / B—Kt 2 !	—	—
5.	P—Q 4 / P—Q 3	P—K R 4 / P—K R 3 !	—
6.	P—B 3 / P—Kt 5 !	P—Q 4 / P—Q 3	—
7.	Kt—Kt 1 / Q—R 5 ch.	P—B 3 / P—Kt 5	Kt—Q B 3 / P—Q B 3
8.	K—B 1 / B—R 3	B×P (B 4) / P×Kt	P×P / P×P
9.	Q—Kt 3 / Q—R 4 +	Q×P / B—K 3	R×R / B×R
10.		Kt—Q 2 / Kt—K 2	Kt—K 5 / P×Kt
11.		P—R 5 / B×B	Q—R 5 / Q—B 3
12.		Kt×B / P—Kt 4	P×P / Q—Kt 2
13.		Kt—K 3 / Kt—Q B 3 +	P—K 6 / B×P
14.			B×B / Kt—K B 3
15			B×P ch. / K—K 2
16.			Q—Kt 6 / Q×B+

	(4)	(5)	(6)
1.	—	—	—
2.	—		—
3.	—	—	—
4.	—	—	—
5.	$\dfrac{0-0}{P-Q\ 3\ )}$	—	—

Nos. 1 to 8.   Position after Black's 4th move.

BLACK.

WHITE.

	(4)	(5)	(6)
6.	$\dfrac{P-Q\ 4}{P-K\ R\ 3}$	—	—
7.	$\dfrac{P-B\ 3}{B-K\ 3}$	Kt—Q 2	Kt—K 2
8.	$\dfrac{B\times B}{P\times B}$	P—K Kt 3	P—K Kt 3
		P—Kt 5 !	P—Kt 5
9.	$\dfrac{Q-Kt\ 3}{Q-B\ 1}$	Q B×P	Kt—R 4
		P×Kt	P—B 6
10.	$\dfrac{P-K\ R\ 4}{P-Kt\ 5}$	Q×P	P—K R 3
		Kt—Kt 3	P—K R 4

	(4)	(5)	(6)
11.	Kt—R 2 / P—Kt 6	B×P ch. / K×B	Kt×P / P×Kt
12.	Kt—B 3 / P—K 4	B—K 5 d. ch. / Kt—B 3	Q×P / P—B 3
13.	P×P / P×P	B×Kt / B×B	P—K 5 / P—K B 4 !
14.	Kt—R 3 / Kt—K 2	P—K 5 / P×P	P×Q P / P×P
15.	Kt—B 4 / Kt—Q B 3	P×P / P—K R 4	B—K Kt 5 / Q Kt—B 3
16.	Kt (B 4)×P / Kt×Kt	P×B / Kt—B 5	
17.	Kt×Kt / B×Kt	Q—B 4 / B—K 3	
18.	B×P / B—Q 3 !	P—Q Kt 3 / Kt—Q 3 =	
19.	Q—Kt 5 ch. / Q—Q 2 !		
20.	Q—R 5 ch. / K—Q 1		
21.	Q R—Q 1 / Q—K 1		
22.	Q—B 3 / K—B 1		
23.	B×B / P×B		

	(7)	(8)
1.	—	—
2.	—	—
3.	—	—
4.	—	—
5.	—	—
6.	—	—

	(7)	(8)
7.	$\dfrac{}{\text{Q}-\text{K 2}}$	—
8.	$\dfrac{\text{P}-\text{K 5}}{\text{P}\times\text{P}}$	$\dfrac{\text{P}-\text{K Kt 3}}{\text{P}-\text{Kt 5}}$
9.	$\dfrac{\text{Kt}\times\text{P}}{\text{B}\times\text{Kt}}$	$\dfrac{\text{Q B}\times\text{P}}{\text{P}\times\text{Kt}}$
10.	$\dfrac{\text{R}-\text{K 1}}{\text{B}-\text{K 3}}$	$\dfrac{\text{Q}\times\text{P}}{\text{Kt}-\text{Q B 3}}$
11.	$\dfrac{\text{B}\times\text{B}}{\text{P}\times\text{B}}$	$\dfrac{\text{Kt}-\text{Q 2}}{\text{B}-\text{Q 2}}$
12.	$\dfrac{\text{R}\times\text{B}}{\text{Kt}-\text{Q B 3}}$	$\dfrac{\text{Q R}-\text{K 1}}{\text{0}-\text{0}-\text{0}}$
13.	$\dfrac{\text{R}-\text{K 1}}{\text{0}-\text{0}-\text{0}}$	$\dfrac{\text{P}-\text{K 5}}{\text{P}\times\text{P}}$
14.	$\dfrac{\text{Q}-\text{Kt 4}}{\text{R}-\text{K 1}}$	$\dfrac{\text{P}\times\text{P}}{\text{P}-\text{K R 4}}$
15.	$\dfrac{\text{P}-\text{Kt 3}}{\text{Kt}-\text{B 3}}$	

THE KING'S KNIGHT'S GAMBIT—GAMES.

	(1) V. H. der Laza / Dr. Bledow	(2) V. H. der Laza / Mr. H.——	(3) Staunton & Barnes / Lowenthal & Owen
1.	$\dfrac{\text{P}-\text{K 4}}{\text{P}-\text{K 4}}$	$\dfrac{\text{P}-\text{K 4}}{\text{P}-\text{K 4}}$	$\dfrac{\text{P}-\text{K 4}}{\text{P}-\text{K 4}}$
2.	$\dfrac{\text{P}-\text{K B 4}}{\text{P}\times\text{P}}$	$\dfrac{\text{P}-\text{K B 4}}{\text{P}\times\text{P}}$	$\dfrac{\text{P}-\text{K B 4}}{\text{P}\times\text{P}}$
3.	$\dfrac{\text{Kt}-\text{K B 3}}{\text{P}-\text{K Kt 4}}$	$\dfrac{\text{Kt}-\text{K B 3}}{\text{P}-\text{K Kt 4}}$	$\dfrac{\text{Kt}-\text{K B 3}}{\text{P}-\text{K Kt 4}}$
4.	$\dfrac{\text{B}-\text{B 4}}{\text{B}-\text{Kt 2}}$	$\dfrac{\text{B}-\text{B 4}}{\text{B}-\text{Kt 2}}$	$\dfrac{\text{B}-\text{B 4}}{\text{B}-\text{Kt 2}}$
5.	$\dfrac{\text{P}-\text{Q 4}}{\text{Q}-\text{K 2 }(a)}$	$\dfrac{\text{0}-\text{0}}{\text{P}-\text{K R 3}}$	$\dfrac{\text{P}-\text{B 3}}{\text{P}-\text{Q 3}}$
6.	$\dfrac{\text{0}-\text{0}}{\text{P}-\text{K R 3}}$	$\dfrac{\text{P}-\text{Q 4}}{\text{P}-\text{Q 3}}$	$\dfrac{\text{0}-\text{0 }(b)}{\text{P}-\text{K R 3}}$

(a) The proper move, as is seen in the foregoing variations, is
5 P—Q 3.

(b) White might also have played 6. $\dfrac{\text{Q}-\text{Kt 3}}{}$.

	(1)	(2)	(3)
7.	Kt—B 3 / P—Q B 3	P—B 3 / P—Q B 3	P—K Kt 3 / P—Kt 5
8.	P—K 5 / Q—Kt 5	Q—Kt 3 (b) / Q—K 2	Kt—R 4 / P—B 6
9.	Kt—K 4 / B—B 1	P—Kt 3 / P—Kt 5	P—Q 4 / P—Q B 3
10.	Q—K 2 (a) / P—K 5	B×P (B 4) / P×Kt	Q—Kt 3 / Q—K 2
11.	Kt—Q 6 ch. / B×Kt	R×P / B—K 3	Kt—R 3 / P—Q R 4
12.	P×B d. ch. / K—Q 1	P—Q 5 / B—Kt 5	B—-B 4 (d) / P—Kt 4
13.	Kt—K 5 / R—R 2	P×P / B×R	Kt×Kt P / P×Kt
14.	P—B 3 / P—B 6	P×P / Q×K P	Q×P ch. (e) / K—Q 1 (f)
15.	Q—K 4 / Kt—B 3	P×R (Q) / Q×Q	B—Q 5 / Q—R 2
16.	Q×R / Kt×Q	B×P ch. / K—B 1	B×R / Q×B
17.	White mates in 6	B×Kt / R×B	Q—Kt 6 ch. / K—K 1
18.		B×P ch. / K—K 1	Q×Q P / Kt—Q B 3
19.		White mates in 3 (c)	Kt—B 5 / B—B 1
20.			Q—Q 5 / Kt—B 3

(a) This little game is excellently played by White.

(b) Having now your Q P protected, and an opening for your Queen, you can advantageously advance the K Kt P, and sacrifice your Kt, as in the Muzio Gambit.

(c) A brilliant and amusing little skirmish.

(d) An indispensable preliminary to the plan of action White contemplate pursuing.

(e) The sacrifice of the Knight, if Black advanced their Q Kt P was resolved on, but it could not have been hazarded before playing B—K B 4.

(f) K—B was thought by some to be the best move, but in that and every other case White's attack would still have proved irresistible.

(3) *(contd.)*

21. $\dfrac{\text{Kt—Q 6 ch.}}{\text{B}\times\text{Kt}}$

22. $\dfrac{\text{Q}\times\text{B}}{\text{Kt}\times\text{K P}}$

23. $\dfrac{\text{Q R—K 1}}{\text{P—B 4}}$

24. $\dfrac{\text{Q—Kt 6 ch.}}{\text{K—B 1}}$

25. $\dfrac{\text{B—Q 6 ch.}}{\text{Kt}\times\text{B}}$

26. $\dfrac{\text{Q}\times\text{Kt ch.}}{\text{K—Kt 2}}$

27. $\dfrac{\text{P—Q 5}}{\text{Kt—Q 1}}$

28. $\dfrac{\text{R—K 7 ch.}}{\text{Kt—B 2}}$

29. $\dfrac{\text{Q—K 5 ch.}}{\text{K—Kt 3}}$

30. $\dfrac{\text{R}\times\text{Kt}}{\text{K}\times\text{R}}$

31. $\dfrac{}{\text{Q}\times\text{R and wins.}}$

	(4) Morphy / Anderssen	(5) Dubois / De Riviere	(6) Stanley / Lowenthal
1.	P—K 4 / P—K 4	P—K 4 / P—K 4	P—K 4 / P—K 4
2.	P—K B 4 / P×P	P—K B 4 / P×P	P—K B 4 / P×P
3.	Kt—K B 3 / P—K B 4	Kt—K B 3 / K Kt 4	Kt—K B 3 / P—K Kt 4
4.	B—B 4 / B—Kt 2	B—B 4 / B—Kt 2	B—B 4 / B—Kt 2
5.	0—0 / P—Q 3	P—Q 4 / P—Q 3	0—0 / P—Q 3
6.	P—B 3 / Kt—Q B 3	Kt—B 3 (b) / P—Q B 3 (c)	P—B 3 / P—K R 3
7.	Q—Kt 3 / Q—K 2	0—0 / B—Kt 5	P—Q 4 / P—Q B 3
8.	P—Q 4 / P—Q R 3	P—K Kt 3 / B—R 6	P—K Kt 3 / P—Kt 5
9.	Kt×P (a) / Q×Kt	R—B 2 / P—Kt 5	Q B×P / P×Kt
10.	B×P ch. / K—Q 1	Kt—R 4 / P—B 6	Q×P / Kt—B 3 (d)

(a) It is to prevent this attack that Black is always recommended to play P—K R 3 as soon as White throws up his Q P. Black's 8th move was very weak and inefficient.

(b) This is a favourite mode of continuing the attack in Italy.

(c) Far from good.

(d) 10. $\dfrac{}{\text{Q—B 3}}$ is better.

	(4)	(5)	(6)
11.	$\dfrac{\text{B} \times \text{P}}{\text{Q}-\text{K} 2}$	$\dfrac{\text{Kt}-\text{B} 5}{\text{K}-\text{B} 1}$	$\dfrac{\text{B} \times \text{Q P}}{\text{B}-\text{Kt} 5}$
12.	$\dfrac{\text{B} \times \text{Kt}}{\text{B}-\text{Kt} 5}$	$\dfrac{\text{B}-\text{B} 4}{\text{B}-\text{B} 3}$	$\dfrac{\text{Q}-\text{B} 4}{\text{B}-\text{R} 4}$
13.	$\dfrac{\text{Kt}-\text{Q} 2}{\text{K}-\text{Q} 2}$	$\dfrac{\text{B} \times \text{Q P ch.}}{\text{B}-\text{K} 2}$	$\dfrac{\text{Q}-\text{K} 5 \text{ ch.}}{\text{K}-\text{Q} 2}$
14.	$\dfrac{\text{B}-\text{Q} 5}{\text{Kt}-\text{Q} 1}$	$\dfrac{\text{B}-\text{B} 4}{\text{Resigns.}}$	$\dfrac{\text{Q}-\text{B} 5 \text{ ch.}}{\text{K}-\text{K} 1}$
15.	$\dfrac{\text{B} \times \text{Kt P}}{\text{Kt} \times \text{B}}$		$\dfrac{\text{P}-\text{K} 5}{\text{B}-\text{Kt} 3}$
16.	$\dfrac{\text{Q} \times \text{Kt}}{\text{P}-\text{Q R} 4 \ (a)}$		$\dfrac{\text{Q}-\text{B} 3}{\text{Kt}-\text{Q} 4}$
17.	$\dfrac{\text{B} \times \text{P} \ (b)}{\text{B} \times \text{Q P ch.}}$		$\dfrac{\text{B} \times \text{Kt}}{\text{P} \times \text{B}}$
18.	$\dfrac{\text{P} \times \text{B}}{\text{Q} \times \text{B}}$		$\dfrac{\text{Q} \times \text{Q P}}{\text{Q}-\text{Q} 2}$
19.	$\dfrac{\text{R}-\text{B} 7 \text{ ch. and wins.}}{}$		$\dfrac{\text{Kt}-\text{R} 3}{\text{Kt}-\text{B} 3}$
20.			$\dfrac{\text{Q R}-\text{K} 1}{\text{B}-\text{B} 1}$
21.			$\dfrac{\text{Kt}-\text{Kt} 5}{\text{B} \times \text{B}}$
22.			$\dfrac{\text{Kt} \times \text{B ch.} \ (c)}{\text{K}-\text{Q} 1}$
23.			$\dfrac{\text{Kt} \times \text{P ch.} \ (d)}{\text{B} \times \text{Kt}}$

(a) Quite useless. Surely it would have been better to have played 16. $\dfrac{}{\text{K R}-\text{Q Kt} 1}$; 17. $\dfrac{\text{Q}-\text{Q} 5}{\text{R}-\text{Kt} 4}$, or perhaps, 17. $\dfrac{}{\text{B}-\text{K} 3}$

(b) Clever and decisive.

(c) 22. $\dfrac{\text{P}-\text{K} 6}{}$ looks better, but in reality is not so good.

(d) I rather prefer the following:—23. $\dfrac{\text{P}-\text{K} 6}{\text{P} \times \text{P!}}$; 24. $\dfrac{\text{R} \times \text{P}}{\text{B}-\text{R} 4}$

$\left(\text{If } 24. \ \dfrac{}{\text{Kt}-\text{K} 2}; 25. \ \dfrac{\text{Kt} \times \text{P ch.}}{} \text{ wins.} \quad \text{If } 24. \ \dfrac{}{\text{R}-\text{K Kt} 1};\right.$

25. $\dfrac{\text{K R}-\text{B} 6}{}$); 25. $\dfrac{\text{K R}-\text{K} 1}{\text{B}-\text{Kt} 5}$; 26. $\dfrac{\text{Kt} \times \text{P ch.}}{\text{K}-\text{B} 2!}$; 27. $\dfrac{\text{R}-\text{Q} 6}{}$

and wins.

(6) (*contd.*)

24. $\dfrac{Q \times Q \text{ ch.}}{K \times Q}$ 27. $\dfrac{P-B 4}{R-K B 1}$ 30. $\dfrac{P-Kt 3}{P \times P}$

25. $\dfrac{R \times B \text{ ch.}}{Kt-K 2}$ 28. $\dfrac{R-R 7}{R-Q 1}$ 31. $\dfrac{P \times P \text{ and wins}}{}$

26. $\dfrac{P-K 6 \text{ ch.}}{K-K 1}$ 29. $\dfrac{P-Q 5}{P-Kt 4}$

	(7)	**(8)**
	Heydebrand	Bird
	Der Goltz	Smith
1.	$\dfrac{P-K 4}{P-K 4}$	$\dfrac{P-K 4}{P-K 4}$
2.	$\dfrac{P-K B 4}{P \times P}$	$\dfrac{P-K B 4}{P \times P}$
3.	$\dfrac{Kt-K B 3}{P-K Kt 4}$	$\dfrac{Kt-K B 3}{P-K Kt 4}$
4.	$\dfrac{B-B 4}{B-Kt 2}$	$\dfrac{B-B 4}{B-Kt 2}$
5.	$\dfrac{P-B 3}{P-K R 3}$	$\dfrac{0-0}{P-Q 3}$
6.	$\dfrac{P-Q 4}{P-Q 3}$	$\dfrac{P-Q 4}{P-K R 3}$
7.	$\dfrac{0-0}{Kt-Q 2}$	$\dfrac{P-B 3}{Kt-Q 2}$
8.	$\dfrac{P-Q R 4 \; (a)}{Kt-K 2}$	$\dfrac{P-K Kt 3}{P-Kt 5}$
9.	$\dfrac{Q-Kt 3 \; (b)}{0-0}$	$\dfrac{Kt-R 4}{P-B 6}$
10.	$\dfrac{P-K Kt 3}{P-Kt 5}$	$\dfrac{Kt-B 5}{Q-B 3}$

(*a*) Surely this is giving Black too much time.   8. $\dfrac{P-K Kt 3}{}$
seems better.

(*b*) If White resolved on setting up this attack it would have been better made on the preceding move, as Black must have replied with $\dfrac{}{Q-K 2}$, and his game would have been hampered for some time.

	(7)	(8)
11.	Kt—R 4 / P—B 6	B—B 4 / Kt—Kt 3
12.	P—R 3 / P—K R 4	B—Kt 5 ch. / K—B 1
13.	B—K Kt 5 / Kt—K B 3	Kt—K 3 / Q—K 2
14.	B—Q 3 / K—R 1	R—K 1 / P—K R 4
15.	Kt—Q 2 / Kt—R 2	Kt—Q 5 / Q—Q 1
16.	B×Kt / Q×B	Kt— Q 2 / P—R 5
17.	P×P / P×P	Kt—B 4 / Kt×Kt (B 4)
18.	K—B 2 / Kt—Kt 4	B×Kt / P×P
19.	Q Kt×P (a) / P×Kt	B×P / P—Q B 3
20.	R—R 1 / Kt×P ch. (b)	Kt—K 3 / Q—K 2
21.	B×Kt / Q×B	P—K 5 / P×P
22.	Q R—K 1 / B—K 3 (c)	P×P / B×P
23.	Kt—Kt 6 db. ch. / K—Kt 1	Kt×P / Q—B 4 ch.
24.	Kt—K 7 mate.	B—B 2 / B×P ch.
25.		K—R 1 / B—Q 3 d. ch.
26.		K—Kt 1 / R—R 8 ch. and wins.

(a) This and the previous move of White are extremely well played.

(b) This is ill judged, as it compels Black to give up again almost immediately the piece he has won.

(c) This throws away the game at once. The only move to avert instant defeat is 22. B×P ch.

Chapter II.

CUNNINGHAM GAMBIT—ANALYSIS.

	(1)	(2)	(3)
1.	$\dfrac{\text{P}-\text{K }4}{\text{P}-\text{K }4}$	—	—
2.	$\dfrac{\text{P}-\text{K B }4}{\text{P}\times\text{P}}$	—	—
3.	$\dfrac{\text{Kt}-\text{K B }3}{\text{B}-\text{K }2}$	—	—
4.	$\dfrac{\text{B}-\text{B }4}{\text{B}-\text{R }5\text{ ch.}}$	—	—
5.	$\dfrac{\text{K}-\text{B }1}{\text{B}-\text{B }3}$	$\overline{\text{Kt}-\text{K Kt }3}$	$\dfrac{\text{P}-\text{Kt }3}{\text{P}\times\text{P}}$
6.	$\dfrac{\text{P}-\text{K }5}{\text{B}-\text{K }2}$	$\dfrac{\text{P}-\text{Q }4}{\text{Kt}-\text{Kt }5}$	$\dfrac{0-0}{\text{P}\times\text{P ch.}}$
7.	$\dfrac{\text{P}-\text{Q }4}{\text{P}-\text{Q }4}$	$\dfrac{\text{Q}-\text{K }2}{\text{Kt}-\text{B }7}$	$\dfrac{\text{K}-\text{R }1}{\text{B}-\text{B }3}$
8.	$\dfrac{\text{B}-\text{K }2}{\text{P}-\text{K Kt }4}$	$\dfrac{\text{Kt}\times\text{B}}{\text{Kt}\times\text{R}}$	$\dfrac{\text{Kt}-\text{K }5}{\text{B}\times\text{Kt !}}$
9.	$\dfrac{\text{P}-\text{K R }4}{\text{P}-\text{Kt }5}$	$\dfrac{\text{Kt}-\text{K B }3}{\text{Kt}-\text{Kt }6\text{ ch.}}$	$\dfrac{\text{Q}-\text{R }5}{\text{Q}-\text{K }2 !}$
10.	$\dfrac{\text{Kt}-\text{R }2}{\text{P}-\text{K R }4}$	$\dfrac{\text{P}\times\text{Kt}}{\text{P}\times\text{P}}$	$\dfrac{\text{R}\times\text{P}}{\text{Q}-\text{B }4}$
11.	$\dfrac{\text{B}\times\text{P (B }4)}{\text{B}\times\text{P}}$	$\underline{\text{B}-\text{B }4 \ +}$	$\dfrac{\text{R}-\text{B }8\text{ d. ch.}}{\text{K}-\text{K }2}$
12.	$\dfrac{\text{P}-\text{K Kt }3}{\text{B}-\text{Kt }4}$		$\dfrac{\text{P}-\text{Q }4}{\text{Q}\times\text{P !}}$
13.	$\overline{\text{Kt}\times\text{P}}$		$\dfrac{\text{B}-\text{Kt }5\text{ ch.}}{\text{K}-\text{Q }3 !}$
14.			$\dfrac{\text{Kt}-\text{Q }2}{\text{Kt}-\text{K B }3}$
15.			$\dfrac{\text{Q}-\text{B }7}{\text{Kt}\times\text{P}}$
16.			$\dfrac{\text{B}-\text{K }3}{\text{Kt}-\text{Kt }6\text{ ch.}}$

	(1)	(2)	(3)
17.			K—Kt 2
			$\overline{Q \times B}$
18.			Q—Q 5 ch.
			$\overline{K-K\,2}$
19.			Q—B 7 ch.
			$\overline{K-Q\,3}$
			Drawn.

Nos. 3, 4, 5, 6, and 7. Position after White's 7th move.

BLACK.

WHITE.

	(4)	(5)	(6)	(7)
1.	—	—	—	—
2.	—	—	—	—
3.	—	—	—	—
4.	—	—	—	—
5.	—	—	—	—

	(4)	(5)	(6)	(7)
6.	—	—	—	—
7.	—	$\overline{P-Q\,4}$	$\overline{B-K\,2}$	$\overline{P-Q\,4}$
8.	$\dfrac{P-K\,5}{P-Q\,4}$	$\dfrac{B\times P}{Kt-K\,B\,3}$	$\dfrac{B\times P\ ch.}{K\times B}$	$\dfrac{B\times P}{Kt-K\,B\,3}$
9.	$\dfrac{P\times B}{Kt\times P}$	$\dfrac{B\times P\ ch.}{K\times B}$	$\dfrac{Kt-K\,5\ db.ch.}{K-K\,3\,!}$	$\dfrac{B-Kt\,3}{Kt\times P}$
10.	$\dfrac{B-Kt\,3}{B-K\,3}$	$\dfrac{Kt\times B}{R-B\,1}$	$\dfrac{Q-Kt\,4\ ch.}{K\times Kt}$	$\dfrac{Q-K\,2}{Q-K\,2}$
11.	$\dfrac{P-Q\,4}{Kt-K\,5}$	$\dfrac{P-Q\,4}{K-Kt\,1}$	$\dfrac{Q-B\,5\ ch.}{K-Q\,3}$	$\dfrac{B\times P\ ch.}{K-B\,1}$
12.	$\dfrac{B-K\,B\,4}{P-K\,B\,4}$	$\dfrac{B-Kt\,5}{Kt\times P}$	$Q-Q\,5\ +$	$\dfrac{Q\times P}{Kt-Kt\,6\ ch.}$
13.	$\dfrac{Q\ Kt-Q\,2}{Q-K\,2}$	$\dfrac{B\times Q}{R\times R\ ch.}$		$\dfrac{K-Kt\,2}{Kt\times R}$
14.	$\dfrac{P-B\,4}{P-Q\,B\,3}$	$\dfrac{Q\times R}{Kt-Kt\,6\ ch.}$		$\dfrac{Q\times B}{Q\times Q}$
15.	$\dfrac{P\times Q\,P}{P\times P}$	$\dfrac{K\times P}{Kt\times Q\ ch.\ +}$		$\dfrac{Kt\times Q}{K\times B}$
16.	$\dfrac{R-B\,1}{Kt-Q\,B\,3}$			$K\times Kt\ +$
17.	$\dfrac{Kt\times Kt}{B\,P\times Kt}$			
18.	$\dfrac{Kt\times P}{O-O}$			
19.	$Q-Q\,2\ +$			

CUNNINGHAM GAMBIT—GAMES.

	(1)	(2)
	V. H. de L.	Bilguer
	$\overline{M.\ G.}$	$\overline{M\text{——}t}$
1.	$\dfrac{P-K\,4}{P-K\,4}$	$\dfrac{P-K\,4}{P-K\,4}$
2.	$\dfrac{P-K\,B\,4}{P\times P}$	$\dfrac{P-K\,B\,4}{P\times P}$
3.	$\dfrac{Kt-K\,B\,3}{B-K\,2}$	$\dfrac{Kt-K\,B\,3}{B-K\,2}$
4.	$\dfrac{B-B\,4}{B-R\,5\ ch.}$	$\dfrac{B-B\,4}{B-R\,5\ ch.}$

	(1)	(2)
5.	$\dfrac{\text{P—Kt 3 }(a)}{\text{P}\times\text{P}}$	$\dfrac{\text{P—Kt 3}}{\text{P}\times\text{P}}$
6.	$\dfrac{\text{0—0}}{\text{P}\times\text{P ch.}}$	$\dfrac{\text{0—0}}{\text{P}\times\text{P ch.}}$
7.	$\dfrac{\text{K—R 1}}{\text{B—B 3}}$	$\dfrac{\text{K—R 1}}{\text{P—Q 3 }(d)}$
8.	$\dfrac{\text{Kt—K 5}}{\text{B}\times\text{Kt}}$	$\dfrac{\text{B}\times\text{P ch.}}{\text{K}\times\text{B}}$
9.	$\dfrac{\text{Q—R 5}}{\text{Q—K 2}}$	$\dfrac{\text{Kt}\times\text{B d. ch.}}{\text{Kt—B 3}}$
10.	$\dfrac{\text{R}\times\text{P}}{\text{Q—B 4}}$	$\dfrac{\text{P—Q 4 }(e)}{\text{B—R 6}}$
11.	$\dfrac{\text{R—B 8 db. ch.}}{\text{K—K 2}}$	$\dfrac{\text{R—B 3}}{\text{B—Kt 5 }(f)}$
12.	$\dfrac{\text{P—Q 4}}{\text{Q}\times\text{P }(b)}$	$\dfrac{\text{R}\times\text{Kt ch.}}{\text{Q}\times\text{R}}$
13.	$\dfrac{\text{B—Kt 5 ch.}}{\text{Kt—B 3 }(c)}$	$\dfrac{\text{Q}\times\text{B}}{\text{Q—B 8 ch.}}$
14.	$\dfrac{\text{B}\times\text{Kt ch.}}{\text{P}\times\text{B}}$	$\dfrac{\text{K}\times\text{P}}{\text{Q}\times\text{B}}$
15.	$\dfrac{\text{Q—B 7 ch.}}{\text{K—Q 3}}$	$\dfrac{\text{Kt—B 3}}{\text{Q}\times\text{R}}$
16.	$\dfrac{\text{Kt—B 3}}{\text{R}\times\text{R}}$	$\dfrac{\text{Q—B 5 ch.}}{\text{K—K 1}}$
17.	$\dfrac{\text{Q}\times\text{R ch.}}{\text{K—B 3}}$	$\dfrac{\text{Q—Q B 8 ch.}}{\text{K—K 2}}$
18.	$\dfrac{\text{Q—Kt 4}}{\text{P—Q 4}}$	$\dfrac{\text{Q}\times\text{P ch.}}{\text{K—K 1}}$
19.	$\dfrac{\text{B—Kt 5 ch.}}{\text{K—Kt 3}}$	$\dfrac{\text{Q—B 8 ch.}}{\text{K—B 2}}$
20.	$\dfrac{\text{Kt—R 4 mate}}{\ }$	$\dfrac{\text{Q}\times\text{P ch.}}{\text{K—K 1}}$
21.		Kt—B 5 and wins.

(a) The correct reply is 5. K—B 1, as shown in the preceding variations.

(b) The best move.

(c) K—Q 3 is the proper play.

(d) P—Q 4 is far better.

(e) If Q—R 5 ch., Black's answer is K—Kt 1.

(f) Q—Q 2 is a better move.

CHAPTER III.

THE SALVIO GAMBIT—ANALYSIS.

(For Games, see p. 285.)

(For Games, see p. 285.)

	(1)	(2)	(3)
1.	$\dfrac{\text{P—K 4}}{\text{P—K 4}}$	—	—
2.	$\dfrac{\text{P—K B 4}}{\text{P} \times \text{P}}$	—	—
3.	$\dfrac{\text{Kt—K B 3}}{\text{P—K Kt 4}}$	—	—
4.	$\dfrac{\text{B—B 4}}{\text{P—Kt 5}}$	—	—
5.	$\dfrac{\text{Kt—K 5}}{\text{Q—R 5 ch.}}$	—	—
6.	$\dfrac{\text{K—B 1}}{\text{Kt—K B 3}}$	—	$\dfrac{}{\text{Kt—K R 3}}$
7.	$\dfrac{\text{Q—K 1 !}}{\text{Q} \times \text{Q ch. !}}$	$\dfrac{\text{B} \times \text{P ch.}}{\text{K—K 2 !}}$	$\dfrac{\text{P—Q 4}}{\text{P—B 6}}$
8.	$\dfrac{\text{K} \times \text{Q}}{\text{Kt} \times \text{P}}$	$\dfrac{\text{B—Kt 3}}{\text{P—Q 3}}$	$\dfrac{\text{P} \times \text{P } (a)}{\text{P—Q 3}}$
9.	$\dfrac{\text{B} \times \text{P ch.}}{\text{K—K 2 !}}$	$\dfrac{\text{Kt—Q 3}}{\text{Kt—R 4}}$	$\dfrac{\text{Kt—Q 3}}{\text{P} \times \text{P}}$
10.	$\dfrac{\text{B—R 5}}{\text{P—Kt 6}}$	$\dfrac{\text{Q—K 1}}{\text{P—Kt 6}}$	$\dfrac{\text{Kt—B 2}}{\text{B—R 6 ch.}}$
11.	$\dfrac{\text{P—K R 3}}{\text{P—Q 3}}$	$\dfrac{\text{K—Kt 1}}{\text{B—Kt 2}}$	$\dfrac{\text{Kt} \times \text{B}}{\text{Q} \times \text{Kt ch.}}$
12.	$\dfrac{\text{Kt—Q 3}}{\text{B—R 3}}$	$\dfrac{\text{P—B 3}}{\text{Q—Kt 4 +}}$	$\dfrac{\text{K—B 2}}{\text{Q—Kt 7 ch.}}$
13.	$\dfrac{\text{Kt—B 3}}{\text{Kt} \times \text{Kt}}$		$\dfrac{\text{K—K 3}}{\text{Kt—Kt 5 ch.}}$

(a) If 8. $\dfrac{\text{Q—K 1}}{\text{Q} \times \text{Q ch.}}$; 9. $\dfrac{\text{K} \times \text{Q}}{\text{P} \times \text{Kt P}}$; 10. $\dfrac{\text{R—Kt 1}}{\text{P—Q 3}}$; 11. $\dfrac{\text{Kt—Q 3}}{\text{Kt—Kt 1}}$; 12. $\dfrac{\text{P} \times \text{P}}{\text{P—K R 4 +}}$

	(1)	(2)	(3)
14.	$\dfrac{\text{Q P} \times \text{Kt}}{\text{R} - \text{B 1}}$		$\dfrac{\text{K} - \text{B 4}}{\text{B} - \text{R 3} \text{ ch. and mate}}$
15.	$\dfrac{\text{R} - \text{B 1}}{\text{B} - \text{B 4}}$		in 2.
16.	$\dfrac{\text{Kt} \times \text{P}}{\text{B} \times \text{Kt}}$		
17.	$\dfrac{\text{B} \times \text{B}}{\text{R} - \text{Kt 1}}$		
18.	$\dfrac{\text{B} \times \text{Q P ch.}}{\text{P} \times \text{B}}$		
19.	$\dfrac{\text{R} \times \text{B}}{\text{R} - \text{Kt 2}} +$		

No. 3.   Position after Black's 7th move.

BLACK.

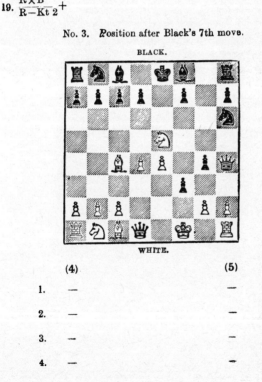

WHITE.

	(4)	(5)
1.	—	—
2.	—	—
3.	—	—
4.	—	—

	(4)	(5)
5.	—	—
6.	—	—
7.	$\dfrac{}{P-Q\,3}$	—
8.	$\dfrac{Kt-Q\,3}{P-B\,6}$	$\dfrac{B-B\,4}{P\times P\ \text{ch.}}$
9.	$\dfrac{P-K\,Kt\,3}{Q-K\,2\,!}$	$\dfrac{K\times P}{P-Q\,3}$
10.	$\dfrac{Kt-B\,3}{P-Q\,B\,3}$	$\dfrac{B\times Kt}{B\times B}$
11.	$\dfrac{P-K\,R\,3}{P-K\,B\,4}$	$\dfrac{Kt-Q\,3}{Q-R\,6\ \text{ch.}}$
12.	$\dfrac{B\times Kt}{B\times B}$	$\dfrac{K-B\,2}{Q-K\,6\ \text{ch.}}$
13.	$\dfrac{P\times P\ (B\,4)}{B\times P}$	$\dfrac{K-B\,1}{P-Kt\,6\ +}$
14.	$\dfrac{P\times Kt\,P}{B\times Kt\ \text{ch.}}$	
15.	$\dfrac{Q\times B}{}\ +$	

Chapter IV.

THE COCHRANE GAMBIT—ANALYSIS.

	(1)	(2)	(3)
1.	$\dfrac{P-K\,4}{P-K\,4}$	—	—
2.	$\dfrac{P-K\,B\,4}{P\times P}$	—	—
3.	$\dfrac{Kt-KB\,3}{P-K\,Kt\,4}$	—	—
4.	$\dfrac{B-B\,4}{P-Kt\,5}$	—	—
5.	$\dfrac{Kt-K\,5}{Q-R\,5\ \text{ch.}}$	—	—

	(1)	(2)	(3)
6.	K—B 1 / P—B 6 (a)	—	—
7.	P—Q 4 ! / P×P ch. !	B×P ch. / K—K 2	—
8.	K×P / Q—R 6 ch.	P×P / P—Q 3	B×Kt / R×B !
9.	K—Kt 1 / Kt—K R 3	B×Kt / P×Kt	P×P / P—Q 3

Nos. 1 to 13.   Position after Black's 6th move.

BLACK.

WHITE.

	(1)	(2)	(3)
10.	Q—Q 3 / Q×Q	B—B 4 / P×P	Kt×P / B×Kt
11.	P×Q / P—Q 3	Q×P / B—R 6 ch.	P×B / R×P +
12.	B×Kt / B×B	K—Kt 1 / Q—K8 ch.	
13.	Kt×P / B—K 6 ch.	B—B 1 / R—Kt 1 ch. and wins.	
14.	K—Kt 2 / R—B 1		
15.	R—B 1 / B×P +		

(a) This move constitutes the Cochrane Gambit.

	(4)	(5)	(6)
1.	—	—	—
2.	—	—	—
3.	—	—	—
4.	—	—	—
5.	—	—	—
6.	—	—	—
7.	$\dfrac{\text{P—K Kt 3}}{\text{Q—R 6 ch.}}$	—	—
8.	$\dfrac{\text{K—B 2 !}}{\text{Kt—K B 3}}$	—	—
9.	$\dfrac{\text{P—Q 3}}{\text{P—Q 3}}$	$\dfrac{\text{K—K 3}}{\text{B—R 3 ch.}}$	$\dfrac{\text{Kt—B 3}}{\text{Q—Kt 7 ch.}}$
10.	$\dfrac{\text{Kt×B P}}{\text{P—Q 4}}$	$\dfrac{\text{K—Q 3}}{\text{P—Q 3}}$	$\dfrac{\text{K—K 3}}{\text{B—R 3 ch.}}$
11.	$\dfrac{\text{Kt×R}}{\text{Q—Kt 7 Ch.}}$	$\dfrac{\text{Kt×B P}}{\text{P—Q 4}}$	$\dfrac{\text{K—Q 3}}{\text{Kt—B 3}}$
12.	$\dfrac{\text{K—K 3}}{\text{Kt—Q B 3}}$	$\dfrac{\text{B×Q P}}{\text{Kt×B}}$	$\dfrac{\text{Kt×B P}}{\text{Kt—Kt 5 ch.}}$
13.	$\dfrac{\text{Kt—B 7}}{\text{K×Kt}}$	$\dfrac{\text{Kt×B}}{\text{Kt—Kt 5 ch}}$	$\dfrac{\text{K—Q 4}}{\text{Q—B 7 ch.}}$
14.	$\dfrac{\text{B×P ch.}}{\text{Kt×B}}$	$\dfrac{\text{K—B 4}}{\text{Q×Kt}}$	$\dfrac{\text{K—K 5}}{\text{P—Q 3 ch.}}$
15.	$\dfrac{\text{P×Kt}}{\text{B—R 3 ch. and wins.}}$	$\dfrac{\text{K×Kt}}{\text{Kt—R 3 ch.}}$	$\dfrac{\text{K×Kt}}{\text{Q—Q 5 ch. and wins.}}$
16.	—	$\dfrac{\text{K—B 3}}{\text{Q—B 3 ch.}}$	—
17.	—	$\dfrac{\text{K—Q 3}}{\text{Kt—Kt 5 ch.}}$	—
18.	—	$\dfrac{\text{K—K 3}}{\text{Kt×P ch. and wins.}}$	—

	(7)	(8)	(9)
1.	—	—	—
2.	—	—	—
3.	—	—	—
4.	—	—	—
5.	—	—	—

Nos. 7 to 13.   Position after Black's 7th move.

BLACK.

WHITE.

6.	—	—	—
7.	$\dfrac{P \times P}{Kt-K\,B\,3}$	—	—
8.	$\dfrac{P-Q\,4}{P-Q\,3}$	$\dfrac{B \times P\ ch.}{K-K\,2}$	$\dfrac{Kt \times Kt\ P}{Kt \times Kt}$
9.	$\dfrac{Kt \times Kt\ P}{Q-R\,6\ ch.}$	$\dfrac{B-B\,4}{P-Q\,3}$	$\dfrac{P \times Kt}{Q-R\,6\ ch.}$
10.	$\dfrac{K-K\,1}{Kt \times Kt}$	$\dfrac{Kt-Q\,3}{P \times P}$	$\dfrac{K-K\,1}{P-Q\,4}$

	(7)	(8)	(9)
11.	$\dfrac{\text{P}\times\text{Kt}}{\text{B—K 2}}$	$\dfrac{\text{Kt—B 2}}{\text{B—R 6 ch.}}$	$\dfrac{\text{B—K 2}}{\text{Q—R 5 ch.}}$
12.	$\dfrac{\text{R—B 1}}{\text{B—R 5 ch.}}$	$\dfrac{\text{Kt}\times\text{B}}{\text{Q}\times\text{Kt ch.}}$	$\dfrac{\text{K—B 1}}{\text{P—K R 4}}$
13.	$\dfrac{\text{K—Q 2}}{\text{B}\times\text{P}}$	$\dfrac{\text{K—K 1}}{\text{Kt}\times\text{P} +}$	
14.	$\dfrac{\text{B—K 2}}{\text{B—Kt 4 ch.}}$		
15.	$\dfrac{\text{K—K 1}}{\text{Q—R 5 ch.}}$		
16.	$\dfrac{\text{R—B 2}}{\text{B}\times\text{B (B 1)}}$		
17.	$\dfrac{\text{Q}\times\text{B}}{\text{B}\times\text{B}}$		
18.	$\dfrac{\text{K}\times\text{B}}{\text{Q}\times\text{P ch.}}$		
19.	$\dfrac{\text{Q—K 3}}{\text{Q}\times\text{Q ch.} +}$		

	(10)	(11)	(12)	(13)
1.	—	—	—	—
2.	—	—	—	—
3.	—	—	—	—
4.	—	—	—	—
5.	—	—	—	—
6.	—	—	—	—
7.	—	—	—	—
8.	$\dfrac{\text{Q—K 2}}{\text{P—Q 3}}$	$\dfrac{\text{Q—K 1}}{\text{Q—R 6 ch.}}$	$\dfrac{\text{P—K R 3}}{\text{P}\times\text{R P}}$	—
9.	$\dfrac{\text{Kt}\times\text{B P}}{\text{P}\times\text{P}}$	$\dfrac{\text{K—K 2}}{\text{P—Q 3}}$	$\dfrac{\text{Q—K 1}}{\text{Q—Kt 4}}$	$\dfrac{\text{P—Q 4}}{\text{P—Q 3}}$

	(10)	(11)	(12)	(13)
10.	Q—B 2	Kt×Kt P	Kt—Kt 4	Kt—Q 3
	B—R 6 ch.	Kt×Kt	Kt×Kt	Kt—R 4
11.	K—K 1	P×Kt	P×Kt	Q—K 1
	Q×K P ch.	B×P ch.	Q×P	Kt—Kt 6 ch.
12.	K—Q 1	K—B 2	Q—K 2	K—Kt 1
	Q×B and wins.	B—K 2	P—K R 4	R—Kt 1
13.		Q—K 3	Kt—B 3	K—R 2
		B—R 5 ch.	R—Kt 1	Kt—K 7 and
14.		K—Kt 1	K—K 1	wins
		B—B 6 +	B—K 2	
15.			Kt—Q 5	
			Q—R 5 ch.	
16.			K—Q 1	
			P—Q B 3	
17.			Kt—B 7 ch.	
			K—Q 1	
18.			Kt×R	
			P—Q 4	
19.			Q—K 1	
			P×B and wins.	

THE SALVIO AND COCHRANE GAMBITS—GAMES.

	(1)	(2)	(3)
	Mr. H.	La Bourdonnais	
	V. H. der Laza	Cochrane	
1.	P—K 4	P—K 4	P—K 4
	P—K 4	P—K 4	P—K 4
2.	P—K B 4	P—K B 4	P—KB 4
	P×P	P×P	P×P
3.	Kt—K B 3	Kt—K B 3	Kt—KB 3
	P—K Kt 4	P—K Kt 4	P—KKt 4
4.	B—B 4	B—B 4	B—B 4
	P—Kt 5	P—Kt 5	P—Kt 5
5.	Kt—K 5	Kt—K 5	Kt—K 5
	Q—R 5 ch.	Q—R 5 ch.	Q—R 5 ch.
6.	K—B 1	K—B 1	K—B 1
	Kt—K R 3	P—B 6	P—B 6

	(1)	(2)	(3)
7.	P—Q 4 / P—B 6	P—K Kt 3 (b) / Q—R 6 ch.	Q—K 1 / P×P ch.
8.	P—K Kt 3 / Q—R 6 ch.	K—B 2 / Q—Kt 7 ch.	K×P / Q—R 6 ch.
9.	K—B 2 / Q—Kt 7 ch.	K—K 3 / B—R 3 ch.	K—B 2 / B—Kt 2
10.	K—K 3 / P—K B 3 (a)	K—Q 3 / P—Q 4	P—Q 4 / P—Q 3
11.	Kt—Q 3 / Kt—B 2	B×P / Kt—R 3	B×P ch. / K—K 2
12.	Kt—B 4 / B—R 3	P—B 3 / P—Q B 3	B×K Kt (c) / R×B
13.	K—Q 3 / B×Kt	B×B P ch. / K—K 2	Kt—B 4 / Q—B 6 ch.
14.	B×B / P—B 3	B—Kt 3 / Kt—B 4 ch.	K—Kt 1 / B×P ch.
15.	Kt—B 3 / 0—0	K—B 2 / Kt×P	B—K 3 / P—Kt 6
16.	B—Q 6 / P—Kt 4	Q—B 1 / B—B 4	P—K R 3 (d) / P—Kt 7
17.	B×Kt ch. / R×B	Q×Q / Kt—B 7 d. ch.	R—R 2 / B×R P
18.	P—K R 3 / P—Kt 5	P—Q 3 / P×Q	Q Kt—Q 2 (e) / Q—B 8 ch.
19.	B×P / B—R 3 ch.	R—K Kt 1 / R—Q 1	Kt×Q / P×Kt (Q) mate.
20.	K—K 3 / Q×Kt P	B×B / Kt×B	(2) (contd.)
21.	Q—K Kt 1 / Q—Q B 2	R×P / Kt×P	24. Kt—Q 2 / Kt—B 4
22.	Q×P ch. / R—K Kt 2	Kt×Kt / B×Kt ch.	25. B—Q 1 / Kt—K 6
23.	Q×P (B 6) and wins	K—B 1 / K R—B 1	26. K R—Kt 1 / B—B 8

(a) The proper move is that given by Silberschmidt, of P—K B 4.

(b) P—Q 4 is now considered to be the best move.

(c) If White plays B—Kt 5 ch., Black interposes Bishop and wins a Piece.

(d) He has no better move.

(e) If R×B, Black takes Rook with Queen, and presently wins the adverse Queen.   Or if, instead of taking Bishop, White check with his Q at R 4, Black moves King to his square, and wins in a few moves.

(2) (contd.)

27. P—Kt 3 / R—B 7   28. R×B / Kt×R   29. Kt×Kt / R×B ch.   30. K×R / R×Kt ch. (a) and wins

	(4) Michelet / Kilsevetsky	(5) Tchigorin / Winawer	(6) Blackburne, Winawer, Bird / V. Paulsen, W. Paulsen, Zukertort
1.	P—K 4 / P—K 4	P—K 4 / P—K 4	P—K 4 / P—K 4
2.	P—K B 4 / P×P	P—K B 4 / P×P	P— K B 4 / P×P
3.	Kt—K B 3 / P—K Kt 4	Kt—K B 3 / P—K Kt 4	Kt—K B 3 / P—K Kt 4
4.	B—B 4 / P—Kt 5	B—B 4 / P—Kt 5	B—B 4 / P—Kt 5
5.	Kt—K 5 / Q—R 5 ch.	Kt—K 5 / Q—R 5 ch.	Kt—K 5 / Q—R 5 ch.
6.	K—B 1 / P—B 6	K—B 1 / P—B 6 (b)	K—B 1 / Kt—K R 3
7.	P—Q 4 / K Kt—B 3	P—Q 4 / Kt—K B 3	P—Q 4 / P—B 6 !
8.	Kt—B 3 / B—Kt 2	Kt—B 3 / P×P ch.	B—B 4 / P—Q 3
9.	P—K Kt 3 / Q—R 6 ch.	K×P / Q—R 6 ch.	Kt—Q 3 / P×P ch.
10.	K—B 2 / P—Q 3	K—Kt 1 / P—Q 4	K×P / Kt—B 3
11.	Kt×B 1 / R—B 1	B×P / Kt×B	B—K Kt 3 / Q—K 2
12.	Kt—K Kt 5 / Q—Kt 7 ch.	Kt×Kt / B—Q 3	Kt—B 2 / B—Kt 2
13.	K—K 3 / B—R 3	Q—K 1 / Kt—Q 2	P—B 3 / B—Q 2
14.	K—Q 3 / Kt—B 3	Kt—Kt / B×Kt	Kt—Q 2 / 0—0—0

(a) The termination is played with Mr. Cochrane's characteristic brilliancy.

(b) This move constitutes the Cochrane Gambit.

	(4)	(5)	(6)
15.	P—Q R 3 / B×Kt	P—K 5 / 0—0—0	P—Kt 4 / P—B 4
16.	B×B / Kt×K P	P×B / Q R—K 1	P—Kt 5 / Kt—R 4
17.	Q—K 1 / B—B 4	Q—R 5 / Resigns.	R—K 1 / Kt×B
18.	Kt×Kt / P—B 7		Kt×Kt / B×Kt P
19.	Q—K 3 / K—Q 2		P×P / Q—B 2
20.	B—Q 5 / Q R—K 1		Kt—K 3 / Kt×P
21.	Q R—K B 1 / B×Kt ch.		Kt×Kt / Q×Kt
22.	B×B / R×B 6		Q×P / Q×Q
23.	Q×R / P×Q		Kt×Q / P—K R 4
24.	B—B 5 ch. / R—K 3		Kt—K 3 / P—R 5
25.	P—Q 5 / Kt—K 4 ch.		B—B 2 / Q R—Kt 1
26.	K—Q 4 / P—K R 4		K—R 1 / R—B 1
27.	P×R ch. / K—K 1		B—Kt 1 / K R—Kt 1
28.	B—B 6 / P—R 5		Q R—Q 1 / B—K R 3
29.	B×Kt / P×B ch.		P—Q 5 / R—B 6
30.	K×P / P×P		R—Q 4 / R×B ch.
31.	K—B 6 and wins.		R×R / B×Kt
32.			R—Kt 8 ch. / K—Q 2
33.			Q R—K Kt 4 / R—B 8 ch.
34.			K—Kt 2 / R—B 7 ch. and wins.

Chapter V.

THE MUZIO GAMBIT—ANALYSIS.

	(1)	(2)	(3)
1.	$\dfrac{\text{P—K 4}}{\text{P—K 4}}$	—	—
2.	$\dfrac{\text{P—K B 4}}{\text{P}\times\text{P}}$	—	—

Position after White's 5th move.

BLACK.

WHITE.

	(1)	(2)	(3)
3.	$\dfrac{\text{Kt—K B 3}}{\text{P—K Kt 4}}$	—	—
4.	$\dfrac{\text{B—B 4}}{\text{P—Kt 5}}$	—	—
5.	$\dfrac{\text{0—0}}{\text{P}\times\text{Kt}}$ (a)	—	—

(a) If 5. $\dfrac{}{\text{Q—K 2}}$; 6. $\dfrac{\text{P—Q 4}}{\text{P}\times\text{Kt}}$; 7. $\dfrac{\text{Q}\times\text{P}}{}$

	(1)	(2)	(3)
6.	$\dfrac{Q \times P}{Q - B\,3}$	—	—
7.	$\dfrac{P - K\,5}{Q \times P}$	—	—
8.	$\dfrac{P - Q\,3}{B - R\,3}$	—	—
9.	$\dfrac{B - Q\,2}{Kt - K\,2}$	—	—
10.	$\dfrac{Kt - B\,3}{Q\,Kt - B\,3}$	—	$\overline{P - Q\,B\,3}$

Position after White's 10th move.

BLACK.

WHITE.

	(1)	(2)	(3)
11.	$\dfrac{Q\,R - K\,1}{Q - B\,4\,\text{ch.}}$	—	$\dfrac{Q\,R - K\,1}{Q - B\,4\,\text{ch.}}$
12.	$\dfrac{K - R\,1}{Kt - Q\,5}$	—	$\dfrac{K - R\,1}{P - Q\,4}$
13.	$\dfrac{R \times Kt\,\text{ch.}}{K \times R}$	$\dfrac{Q - R\,3}{B - Kt\,4}$	$\dfrac{Q - R\,5}{Q - Q\,3}$
14.	$\dfrac{Kt - Q\,5\,\text{ch.}}{K - Q\,1}$	$\dfrac{Q - R\,5}{Q - B\,4}$	$\dfrac{B \times Q\,P}{P \times B}$
15.	$\dfrac{Q - R\,5}{Q - B\,1}$	$\dfrac{Kt - K\,4}{P - K\,R\,3}$	$\dfrac{Kt \times P}{Q\,Kt - B\,3}$

	(1)	(2)	(3)
16.	Q–R 4 ch. / P–B 3	B–B 3 / Kt×P	B–B 3 / Q–Kt 3
17.	B×P / B×B	Kt–B 6 ch. / K–Q 1	R×Kt ch. / K–B 1
18.	R×B / Kt–B 3	Q×B P / Kt×R	R–K 8 ch. / K×R
19.	R×P / Q–K 1	R×Kt / Q–B 4	Kt–B 6 ch. / K–B 1
20.	R–B 8 d. ch / Kt–K 2	P–Q Kt 4 / Q–Q 3	Q–B 5 ch. / Kt–K 2 !
21.	Q×Kt mate	Kt–K 4 / Q–K Kt 3	R–K 1 / B–K 3
22.		Kt×B and wins	Kt–Q 7 ch. / B×Kt
23.			Q×Kt ch. / K–Kt 1
24.			Q×B / Q R–K B 1
25.			Q×Q Kt P

	(4)	(5)	(6)
1.	—	—	—
2.	—	—	—
3.	—	—	—
4.	—	—	—
5.	—	—	—
6.	—	—	—
7.	—	—	—
8.	—	—	—

	(4)	(5)	(6)
9.	—	—	—
10.	—	$\overline{0-0}$	—
11.	—	$\dfrac{\text{Q R}-\text{K 1}}{\text{Q}-\text{B 4 ch.}}$	—
12.	—	$\dfrac{\text{K}-\text{R 1}}{\text{Q Kt}-\text{B 3}}$	—
13.	—	$\dfrac{\text{Q B}\times\text{P}}{\text{B}-\text{Kt 2}}$	—
14.	—	$\dfrac{\text{B}-\text{K 3}}{\text{Kt}-\text{Q 5}}$	—
15.	—	$\dfrac{\text{B}\times\text{P ch.}}{\text{K}-\text{R 1}}$	—
16.	—	$\dfrac{\text{B}\times\text{Kt}}{\text{B}\times\text{B}}$	—
17.	—	$\dfrac{\text{Q}-\text{K 4}}{\text{Kt}-\text{Q B 3}}$	—
18.	—	$\dfrac{\text{R}-\text{B 5}}{\text{Kt}-\text{K 4}}$	—
19.	$\overline{\text{K}-\text{Q 1}}$	$\dfrac{\text{Q R}-\text{K B 1}}{\text{P}-\text{Q 4}}$	—
20.	$\dfrac{\text{Q}-\text{Q 5 ch.}}{\text{K}-\text{B 2}}$	$\dfrac{\text{Q}-\text{K R 4}}{\text{Kt}\times\text{B}}$	—
21.	$\dfrac{\text{B}-\text{K 5 ch.}}{\text{Kt}\times\text{B}}$	$\dfrac{\text{R}\times\text{Kt}}{\text{R}\times\text{R}}$	$\dfrac{\text{R}\times\text{P}}{\text{Q}-\text{Kt 3}}$
22.	$\dfrac{\text{Q}\times\text{Kt ch.}}{\text{K}-\text{B 3 !}}$	$\dfrac{\text{R}\times\text{R}}{\text{B}-\text{B 4}}$	$\dfrac{\text{R}\times\text{B}}{\text{Q}-\text{K Kt 3}}$
23.	$\dfrac{\text{Q}-\text{Q 5 ch.}}{\text{K}-\text{Kt 3}}$	$\dfrac{\text{R}\times\text{B}}{\text{B}\times\text{Kt}}$	$\dfrac{\text{R}-\text{B 6}}{\text{Q}-\text{Kt 2}}$
24.	$\dfrac{\text{Q}-\text{Q 6 ch.}}{\text{K}-\text{R 4}}$	$\dfrac{\text{Kt P}\times\text{B}}{\text{Q}\times\text{P}} =$	$\dfrac{\text{R (Q 4)}-\text{K B 4}}{\text{B}-\text{Q 2}}$
25.	$\dfrac{\text{Q}-\text{B 5 ch.}}{\text{K}-\text{R 3}}$		$\dfrac{\text{Q}-\text{B 2}}{\text{B}-\text{K 1}}$
26.	$\dfrac{\text{Q}-\text{B 4 ch.}}{\text{P}-\text{Kt 4}}$		$\text{Kt}-\text{Q 5}+$
27.	$\dfrac{\text{Q}-\text{B 6 ch.}}{\text{K}-\text{R 4}}$		
28.	$\underline{\text{P}-\text{Q R 4 and wins}}$		

	(7)	(8)	(9)
1.	—	—	—
2.	—	—	—
3.	—	—	—
4.	—	—	—
5.	—	—	—
6.	—	—	$\dfrac{B-R\,3}{P-Q\,4}$
7.	—	—	$\dfrac{P-Q\,4}{Kt-Q\,B\,3}$
8.	—	$\dfrac{P-Q\,Kt\,3}{Q \times R\,!}$	$\dfrac{Kt-B\,3}{Kt \times P}$
9.	—	$\dfrac{Kt-B\,3}{B-B\,4\text{ ch.}}$	$\dfrac{Q-R\,5}{Kt-Q\,Kt\,3}$
10.	—	$\dfrac{K-R\,1}{Kt-K\,2}$	$\dfrac{Q\,B \times P}{B \times B}$
11.	—	$\dfrac{P-Q\,4}{B \times P}$	$\dfrac{R \times B}{Q-K\,2}$
12.	—	$\dfrac{B \times P\text{ ch.}}{K-Q\,1}$	$\dfrac{B \times Kt}{Q\,P \times B}$
13.	—	$\dfrac{B-Q\,2}{Q \times R\text{ ch.}}$	Q R—K B 1 and wins
14.	—	$\dfrac{Q \times Q}{R-K\,B\,1}$	
15.	—	$\dfrac{Q \times P}{B \times Kt}$	
16.	—	$\dfrac{B \times B}{P-Q\,3+}$	
17.	—		
18.	—		
19.	—		
20.	—		

(7) *(contd.)*

21. $\dfrac{}{Q \times R}$

22. $\dfrac{Kt \times Q}{B - Kt\,2\,!}$

23. $\dfrac{Kt - B\,6}{P - K\,R\,3}$

24. $\dfrac{Q - K\,4}{Kt - Kt\,4}$

25. $\dfrac{Q - Kt\,6}{R \times Kt}$

26. $\dfrac{R \times R}{B \times R}$

27. $\dfrac{Q \times B\ ch.}{K - R\,2}$

28. $\dfrac{P - K\,R\,4+}{}$

Position after Black's 20th move.

BLACK.

WHITE.

	(10)	(11)	(12)
1.	—	—	—
2.	—	—	—
3.	—	—	—

	(10)	(11)	(12)
4	—	—	—
5.	—	—	—
6.	P—Q 3	Q—K 2	—
7.	P—Q 4 / B—R 3	P—Q 4 / Kt—Q B 3	—
8.	Q B×P / B×B	Q×P / Kt×P	Q B×P / Kt×P
9.	Q×B / Q—K 2	B×P ch. / K—Q 1	Q—R 5 / Kt—K 3 !
10.	B×P ch. / K—Q 1	Kt—B 3 / Kt—R 3	B×Kt / Q P×B
11.	P—K 5+	B—K 3 / Kt—K 3	B—K 5 / Q—B 4 ch.
12.		B×Kt / Q×B	K—R 1 / Kt—R 3
13.		Kt—Q 5 / P—Q 3	P—Q Kt 4 / Q—B 5
14.		Q—R 4 ch. +	Kt—Q 2 / Q×B P
15.			B×R / Q×Kt
16.			Q R—Q 1 / Q—K 6
17.			B—B 6+

	(13)	(14)	(15)
1.	—	—	—
2.	—	—	—
3.	—	—	—
4.	—	—	—
5.	P—Q 4 (a) / P×Kt	—	—

(a) Ghulam Kassim's attack.

	(13)	(14)	(15)
6.	Q×P / P-Q 4	—	—
7.	B×Q P / P-Q B 3	Kt-K B 3	P-Q B 3
8.	B-Kt 3 (a) / Q×Q P	0-0 / K×B	B×P ch. / K×B
9.	Q B×P / Kt-K B 3	P×Kt / Q-B 3	Q×P ch. / Kt-K B 3
10.	Kt-Q 2 / B-K Kt 5	B×P / Q×Q P ch.	P-K 5 / B-Kt 2
11.	Q-Kt 3 / Kt×P	B-K 3 / Q-K R 5	0-0 / R-B 1
12.	Kt×Kt / Q×Kt ch.	Kt-Q 2 / B-Q 3	Q-R 4 / K-Kt 1
13.	K-Q 2+	Q×B P ch. / K-Q 1	B-K Kt 5 / Q Kt-Q 2
14.	—	Kt-B 3 and wins	Kt-B 3 / P-K R 3 and wins

	(16)	(17)	(18)
1.	—	—	—
2.	—	—	—
3.	—	—	—
4.	—	—	—
5.	—	Kt-B 3 (b) / P×Kt	—
6.	P-Q 3	Q×P / P-Q 4	—
7.	0-0 / Q-B 3	B×Q P / P-Q B 3	—

(a) If 8. B×P ch. / K×B ; 9. Q B×P / Kt-K B 3 ; 10. P-B 3 / B-K Kt 5 +

(b) McDonnell's attack.

	(16)	(17)	(18)
8.	Kt−R 3 / Q×P ch.	B−Kt 3 / B−K 3	B×P ch. / K×B
9.	K−R 1 / B−R 3	B×B / P×B	Q−R 5 ch. / K−Kt 2
10.	Q B×P / Q−B 3	Q−R 5 / K−Q 2	P−Q 4 / B−K 3
11.	Q−K 3 / Q−Kt 3	P−Q 4 / Q−B 3	Q B×P / B−B 2
12.	P−K 5 / B×B	P−K 5 / Q−B 4	B−K 5 ch. / Kt−B 3
13.	R×B / B−K 3	Q−B 3 / B−Q Kt 5	Q−Kt 5 ch. / B−Kt 3
14.	P×P + /	Q B×P / K Kt−K 2	
15.	—	0−0 / B×Kt	
16.	—	P×B / Kt−R 3 +	

	(19)	(20)	(21)	(22)
1.	—	—	—	—
2.	—	—	—	—
3.	—	—	—	—
4.	—	—	—	—
5.	—	B×P ch. / K×B	—	—
6.	Q−B 3	Kt−K 5 ch. / K−K 1	—	K−K 3
7.	Kt−Q 5 / Q−K 4	Q×P / Kt−K B 3	Q−B 3	Q×P ch. / K×Kt
8.	P−B 3 / B−R 3	Q×B P / P−Q 3	Q−R 5 ch. / K−K 2	Q−B 5 ch. / K−Q 3
9.	P−Q 4 / Q−Q 3	Kt−B 4 / Kt−B 3	Kt−B 7 / Q×Kt	P−Q 4 / B−Kt 2
10.	P−K 5 / Q−Q B 3	0−0 / B−Kt 2	Q−K 5 ch. / Q−K 3 !	B×P ch. / K−K 2

	(19)	(20)	(21)	(22)
11.	B—Q Kt 5 / Q—K Kt 3	P—Q 3 / B—K 3	Q×R / Kt—K B 3	B—Kt 5 ch. / B—B 3
12.	Kt×P ch. +	Q—K Kt 3 / Q—K 2	0—0 ! / P—Q 3	0—0 / Q—K B 1
13.			Kt—B 3 / P—Q B 3	Q—K 5 ch. / and wins
14.			R×P / Q Kt—Q 2	
15.			P—Q 4 / Q—B 2	
16.			P—K 5 / P×P	
17.			P×P / Q Kt×P	
18.			P—Q Kt 3 / Kt—Kt 3	
19.			B—R 3 ch. / K—K 1	
20.			R×Kt / Kt×Q	
21.			R×Q / Kt×R	
22.			R—K 1 ch.+	

THE MUZIO GAMBIT—GAMES.

	(1)	(2)	(3)
	V. H. der Laza / Szen		Staunton / Amateur
1.	P—K 4 / P—K 4	P—K 4 / P—K 4	P—K 4 / P—K 4
2.	P—K B 4 / P×P	P—K B 4 / P×P	P—K B 4 / P×P
3.	Kt—K B 3 / P—K Kt 4	Kt—K B 3 / P—K Kt 4	Kt—K B 3 / P—K Kt 4
4.	B—B 4 / P—Kt 5	B—B 4 / P—Kt 5	B—B 4 / P—Kt 5
5.	0—0 / P×Kt	0—0 / P×Kt	0—0 / P×Kt

	(1)	(2)	(3)
6.	Q×P / Q—B 3	Q×P / Q—B 3	Q×P / Q—B 3
7.	P—K 5 / Q×K P	P—K 5 / Q×K P	P—K 5 / Q×K P
8.	P—Q 3 / B—R 3	P—Q 3 / B—R 3	P—Q 3 / B—R 3
9.	Kt—B 3 / K Kt—K 2	B—Q 2 / K Kt—K 2	Kt—B 3 / P—Q B 3
10.	B—Q 2 / 0—0 (a)	Kt—B 3 / P—Q B 3	Q B×P / Q—Q 5 ch.
11.	Q R—K 1 / Q—B 4 ch.	Q R—K 1 / Q—B 4 ch.	K—R 1 / B×B
12.	K—R 1 / P—Q B 3	K—R 1 / P—Q 4	Q R—K 1 ch. / K Kt—K 2
13.	Kt—K 4 / Q—B 4	Q—R 5 / Q—Q 3	R—K 4 / Q—Kt 2
14.	B—B 3 / B—Kt 2	B×Q P / 0—0	Q×B / P—Q 4
15.	Kt—Q 6 / Q—K Kt 4	B—Kt 3 / Q—K Kt 3	B×Q P / P×B
16.	R×Kt (b) / B×B (c)	Q—B 5 / Kt—B 4	R×Kt ch. / K×R
17.	R×B P / R×R	Q B×P / B×B	Kt×P ch. / K—K 3
18.	B×R ch. / K—Kt 2	R×B / Kt—Kt 2	Q—K 4 ch. / K—Q 2
19.	P×B / Kt—R 3	Kt—K 4 / Kt—K 3	Q—K 7 ch. / K—B 3
20.	Q×P / Q×Q	B×Kt / B×B	Q—B 7 ch. / K×Kt
21.	R×Q / Kt—B 2	Kt—B 6 ch. / K—Kt 2	P—B 4 ch. / K—Q 5
22.	B—Kt 3 / Kt—Q 4	R×B / P×R	Q—Q 6 ch. / K—K 6
23.	B×Kt / P×B	Kt—R 5 ch. / K—R 3	Q—B 4 ch. / K×Q P

(a) Not considered so strong a move as 10. P—Q B 3.

(b) Well played.

(c) Had he taken Rook with Queen, White would have won a Piece by Kt—K B 5.

	(1)	(2)	(3)
24.	$\dfrac{\text{R—B 7 ch.}}{\text{K—Kt 1}}$	$\dfrac{\text{R} \times \text{R}}{\text{Q} \times \text{Kt}}$	White mates in 2
25.	$\dfrac{\text{R—K 7}}{\text{P—Kt 3}}$	$\dfrac{\text{R—B 6 ch.}}{\text{K—Kt 2}}$	
26.	$\dfrac{\text{R—K 8 ch.}}{\text{K—Kt 2}}$	$\dfrac{\text{Q mates}}{}$	
27.	$\dfrac{\text{R} \times \text{B and wins}}{}$		

	(4) From Ghulam Kassim	(5) McDonnell Labourdonnais	(6) Heydebrand Szen
1.	$\dfrac{\text{P—K 4}}{\text{P—K 4}}$	$\dfrac{\text{P—K 4}}{\text{P—K 4}}$	$\dfrac{\text{P—K 4}}{\text{P—K 4}}$
2.	$\dfrac{\text{P—K B 4}}{\text{P} \times \text{P}}$	$\dfrac{\text{P—K B 4}}{\text{P} \times \text{P}}$	$\dfrac{\text{P—K B 4}}{\text{P} \times \text{P}}$
3.	$\dfrac{\text{Kt—K B 3}}{\text{P—K Kt 4}}$	$\dfrac{\text{Kt—K B 3}}{\text{P—K Kt 4}}$	$\dfrac{\text{Kt—K B 3}}{\text{P—K Kt 4}}$
4.	$\dfrac{\text{B—B 4}}{\text{P—Kt 5}}$	$\dfrac{\text{B—B 4}}{\text{P—Kt 5}}$	$\dfrac{\text{B—B 4}}{\text{P—Kt 5}}$
5.	$\dfrac{\text{P—Q 4}}{\text{P} \times \text{Kt}}$	$\dfrac{\text{Kt—B 3}}{\text{P} \times \text{Kt}}$	$\dfrac{\text{0—0}}{\text{P} \times \text{Kt}}$
6.	$\dfrac{\text{Q} \times \text{P}}{\text{P—Q 4}}$	$\dfrac{\text{Q} \times \text{P}}{\text{B—R 3}}$	$\dfrac{\text{Q} \times \text{P}}{\text{Q—B 3}}$
7.	$\dfrac{\text{B} \times \text{P}}{\text{Kt—K B 3}}$	$\dfrac{\text{P—Q 4}}{\text{Kt—Q B 3}}$	$\dfrac{\text{P—K 5}}{\text{Q} \times \text{P}}$
8.	$\dfrac{\text{0—0}}{\text{Kt} \times \text{B}}$	$\dfrac{\text{0—0}}{\text{Kt} \times \text{P}}$	$\dfrac{\text{P—Q 3}}{\text{B—R 3}}$
9.	$\dfrac{\text{P} \times \text{Kt}}{\text{Q—B 3}}$	$\dfrac{\text{B} \times \text{P ch.}}{\text{K} \times \text{B}}$	$\dfrac{\text{Kt—B 3}}{\text{Kt—K 2}}$
10.	$\dfrac{\text{Q—K 4 ch.}}{\text{K—Q 1}}$	$\dfrac{\text{Q—R 5 ch.}}{\text{K—Kt 2}}$	$\dfrac{\text{B—Q 2}}{\text{0—0}}$
11.	$\dfrac{\text{B} \times \text{P}}{\text{Q—K 2}}$	$\dfrac{\text{Q B} \times \text{P}}{\text{B} \times \text{B}}$	$\dfrac{\text{Q R—K 1}}{\text{Q—B 4 ch.}}$
12.	$\dfrac{\text{Q—B 3}}{\text{R—Kt 1}}$	$\dfrac{\text{R} \times \text{B}}{\text{K Kt—B 3}}$	$\dfrac{\text{K—R 1}}{\text{P—Q B 3 }(a)}$

(a) 12. $\dfrac{}{\text{Kt—Q B 3}}$ is better.

	(4)	(5)	(6)
13.	$\dfrac{\text{Kt}-\text{Q 2}}{\text{B}-\text{K Kt 5}}$	$\dfrac{\text{Q}-\text{Kt 5 ch.}}{\text{K}-\text{B 2}}$	$\dfrac{\text{Kt}-\text{K 4}}{\text{Q}-\text{B 4}}$
14.	$\dfrac{\text{Q}-\text{B 2}}{\text{Kt}-\text{Q 2}}$	$\dfrac{\text{Q R}-\text{K B 1}}{\text{K}-\text{K 1}}$	$\dfrac{\text{B}-\text{B 3}}{\text{B}-\text{Kt 2}}$
15.	$\dfrac{\text{Q R}-\text{K 1}}{\text{Q}-\text{B 3}}$	$\dfrac{\text{R}\times\text{Kt}}{\text{Q}-\text{K 2}}$	$\dfrac{\text{Kt}-\text{Q 6}}{\text{Q}-\text{Kt 4}}$
16.	$\dfrac{\text{Kt}-\text{K 4}}{\text{Q}-\text{Kt 3}}$	$\dfrac{\text{Kt}-\text{Q 5}}{\text{Q}-\text{B 4}}$	$\dfrac{\text{R}\times\text{Kt}}{\text{B}\times\text{B}}$
17.	$\dfrac{\text{P}-\text{B 4}}{\text{B}-\text{Q 3}}$	$\dfrac{\text{K}-\text{R 1}}{\text{Kt}-\text{K 3}}$	$\dfrac{\text{R}\times\text{B P}}{\text{R}\times\text{R}}$
18.	$\dfrac{\text{B}\times\text{B}}{\text{P}\times\text{B}}$	$\dfrac{\text{R}\times\text{Kt}}{\text{P}\times\text{R}}$	$\dfrac{\text{B}\times\text{R ch. } (a)}{\text{K}-\text{Kt 2}}$
19.	$\dfrac{\text{P}-\text{B 5}}{\text{P}\times\text{P}}$	$\dfrac{\text{Kt}-\text{B 6 ch. and wins.}}{}$	$\dfrac{\text{P}\times\text{B}}{\text{Kt}-\text{R 3}}$
20.	$\dfrac{\text{P}\times\text{P}}{\text{K R}-\text{K 1}}$		$\dfrac{\text{Q}\times\text{B P}}{\text{Q}\times\text{Q}}$
21.	$\dfrac{\text{Kt}-\text{Q 6}}{\text{R}\times\text{R}}$		$\dfrac{\text{R}\times\text{Q}}{\text{Kt}-\text{B 2 } (b)}$
22.	$\dfrac{\text{Q}\times\text{R}}{\text{K}-\text{B 2}}$		$\dfrac{\text{B}-\text{Kt 3}}{\text{Kt}-\text{Q 4}}$
23.	$\dfrac{\text{Q}-\text{Kt 4}}{\text{K}-\text{Q 1}}$		$\dfrac{\text{B}\times\text{Kt}}{\text{P}\times\text{B}}$
24.	White wins		$\dfrac{\text{R}-\text{B 7 ch.}}{\text{K}-\text{Kt 1}}$
25.			$\dfrac{\text{R}-\text{K 7}}{\text{P}-\text{Kt 3}}$
26.			$\dfrac{\text{R}-\text{K 8 ch.}}{\text{K}-\text{Kt 2}}$
27.			$\dfrac{\text{R}\times\text{B and wins.}}{}$

(a) Or 18. $\dfrac{\text{Kt}\times\text{R}}{}$.

(b) 21. $\dfrac{}{\text{Kt}-\text{B 4}}$ would have been rather better; as if 22. $\dfrac{\text{B}-\text{Kt 3}}{\text{Kt}\times\text{B}}$;

23. $\dfrac{\text{P}\times\text{Kt}}{\text{P}-\text{Kt 3}}$, and Black has gained a move. If 22. $\dfrac{\text{R}-\text{Kt 4 ch.}}{\text{K}-\text{B 1}}$;

23. $\dfrac{\text{R}-\text{Kt 8 ch.}}{\text{K}-\text{K 2}}$, and White cannot win the Bishop without losing a Piece in return,—though in any case he would have had the advantage.

	(7)	(8)	(9)
	Baron Sternfeld	Staunton	Heydebrand
	Hert	Amateur	Mayet
1.	P—K 4 / P—K 4	P—K 4 / P—K 4	P—K 4 / P—K 4
2.	P—K B 4 / P×P	P—K B 4 / P×P	P—K B 4 / P×P
3.	Kt—K B 3 / P—K Kt 4	Kt—K B 3 / P—K Kt 4	Kt—K B 3 / P—K Kt 4
4.	B—B 4 / P—Kt 5	B—B 4 / P—Kt 5	B—B 4 / P—Kt 5
5.	0—0 / P×Kt	0—0 / P×Kt	Kt—B 3 / P×Kt
6.	Q×P / Q—B 3	Q×P / Q—B 3	Q×P / B—R 3
7.	P—K 5 / Q×P	P—K 5 / Q×P	P—Q 4 / Kt—Q B 3
8.	P—Q 3 / B—R 3	P—Q 3 / B—R 3	B×P ch. (a) / K×B
9.	Kt—B 3 / Kt—K 2	Kt—B 3 / P—Q B 3	Q—R 5 ch. / K—Kt 2
10.	B—Q 2 / P—Q B 3	Q B×P / Q×B	0—0 / Q—Kt 4
11.	Q R—K 1 / Q—B 4 ch.	Q—R 5 / Q—Q 5 ch.	Q—Q 1 / P—Q 3
12.	K—R 1 / P—Q 4	K—R 1 / P—Q 4	B×P / Q×B (b)
13.	Q—R 5 / Q—Q 3	Q×P ch. / K—Q 1	R×Q / B×R
14.	B×Q P / P×B	Q R—K 1 / B—Q 2	Kt—Q 5 / B—Kt 4
15.	Kt×P / Kt—B 3	B×Q P / P×B	Kt×P / R—Kt 1
16.	R×Kt ch. / Kt×R	Kt×P / Q—Kt 2	Q—R 5 / P—K R 3

Notes by Mr. Heydebrand.

(a) 8. $\dfrac{0—0}{}$ would be better.

(b) Black would have got his Queen away, but, as he obtained four Pieces for her, he preferred giving her up for the sake of the attack. The position of White's Pawns, however, was strong enough to prevent the effectual development of the enemy's game.

	(7)	(8)	(9)
17.	R—K 1 / B—B 1	Q—R 5 / Q—Kt 3	Kt—K 8 ch. / K—B 1
18.	B—Kt 4 / Q—K Kt 3	Q—R 4 ch. / K—B 1	R—B 1 ch. / K—K 2
19.	B×Kt / Q×Q	R—B 6 / Q—Kt 2	Q—B 7 ch. / K—Q 1
20.	Kt—B 6 mate.	Q—B 4 ch. / Kt—B 3	Kt×P / K Kt—K 2
21.		R×Kt ch. / B×R	Q—B 2 / R—Kt 1
22.		R—K 8 ch. / K—Q 2	P—K R 4 / K—Q 2
23.		R×R / Q—K 4	P—K 5 / P—Kt 3
24.		Q—Kt 4 ch. / K—Q 3	P×B / B—R 3
25.		R—Q 8 ch. / K—B 4	R—K1 / R×P
26.		Q mates.	Q—B 4 / Kt—Q 4
27.			Q—B 7 ch. / Kt (B 3)—K 2
28.			P—B 4 / Q R—K Kt 1
29.			P×Kt / R×P ch.
30.			K—R 1 / K R—Kt 2
31.			Q—K 6 ch. / K—Q 1
32.			Kt—B 7 ch. / K—K 1
33.			P—Q 6 / R×Kt
34.			P—Q 7 ch. / K—Q 1
35.			Q×R / Resigns.

CHAPTER VI.

THE ALLGAIER GAMBIT—ANALYSIS.

	(1)	(2)	(3)
1.	$\dfrac{\text{P.}-\text{K 4}}{\text{P}-\text{K 4}}$	—	—
2.	$\dfrac{\text{P}-\text{K B 4}}{\text{P}\times\text{P}}$	—	—
3.	$\dfrac{\text{Kt}-\text{K B 3}}{\text{P}-\text{K Kt 4}}$	—	—
4.	$\dfrac{\text{P}-\text{K R 4}}{\text{P}-\text{Kt 5}}$	—	—
5.	$\dfrac{\text{Kt}-\text{Kt 5}}{\text{P}-\text{K R 3}}$	—	—
	(P—K B 3 ?)		
6.	$\dfrac{\text{Kt}\times\text{P}}{\text{K}\times\text{Kt}}$	—	—
7.	$\dfrac{\text{Q}\times\text{P}}{\text{Kt}-\text{K B 3}}$	$\dfrac{\text{B}-\text{B 4 ch.}}{\text{P}-\text{Q 4 !}}$	—
8.	$\dfrac{\text{Q}\times\text{B P}}{\text{B}-\text{Q 3 !}}$	$\dfrac{\text{B}\times\text{P ch.}}{\text{K}-\text{K 1}}$	—
9.	$\dfrac{\text{B}-\text{B 4 ch.}}{\text{K}-\text{Kt 2 !}}$	$\dfrac{\text{P}-\text{Q 4}}{\text{Kt}-\text{K 2}}$	$\overline{\text{P}-\text{B 6}}$
10.	$\dfrac{\text{Q}-\text{B 5}}{\text{B}-\text{Kt 6 ch.}}$	$\dfrac{\text{Kt}-\text{B 3}}{\text{B}-\text{Kt 2}}$	$\dfrac{\text{P}\times\text{P}}{\text{B}-\text{K 2}}$
11.	$\dfrac{\text{K}-\text{B 1}}{\text{R}-\text{B 1}+}$	$\dfrac{\text{Q B}\times\text{P}}{\text{Q Kt}-\text{B 2}}$	$\dfrac{0-0}{\text{P}-\text{Kt 6}}$
12.		$\overline{\text{B}-\text{K 3}}$	$\dfrac{\text{P}-\text{K B 4}}{\text{P}-\text{K R 4}}$
13.			$\dfrac{\text{B}\times\text{Kt}}{\text{R}\times\text{B}}$
14.			$\dfrac{\text{Q}\times\text{P ch.}}{\text{K}-\text{B 1}}$
15.			$\dfrac{\text{Q}-\text{R 6 ch.}}{\text{R}-\text{Kt 2}}$

(3) (contd.)

16. $\dfrac{\text{P—B 3}}{\text{B} \times \text{R P}}$

17. $\dfrac{\text{P—B 5}}{\text{B—K Kt 5}}$

18. $\dfrac{\text{B} \times \text{B}}{\text{Q} \times \text{B}}$

19. $\dfrac{\text{Q} \times \text{Q}}{\text{R} \times \text{Q}}$

20. $\dfrac{\text{Kt—Q 2}}{}$

	(4)	**(5)**	**(6)**	**(7)**
1.	—	—	—	—
2.	—	—	—	—
3.	—	—	—	—
4.	—	—	—	—

Nos. 2, 3, and 4.   Position after White's 8th move.

BLACK.

WHITE.

	(4)	**(5)**	**(6)**	**(7)**
5.	—	—	$\dfrac{\text{P—K R 4}}{}$	$\dfrac{\text{P—Q 4}}{}$
6.	—	—	$\dfrac{\text{B—B 4}}{\text{Kt—K R 3}}$	$\dfrac{\text{P} \times \text{P}}{\text{Q} \times \text{P}}$
7.	—	$\dfrac{\text{Q} \times \text{P}}{\text{Q—B 3}}$	$\dfrac{\text{P—Q 4}}{\text{P—K B 3}}$	$\dfrac{\text{Kt—Q B 3}}{\text{Q—K 4 ch.}}$
8.	$\dfrac{}{\text{K—Kt 2}}$	$\dfrac{\text{P—Q 4}}{\text{Q} \times \text{Q P}}$	$\dfrac{\text{Q B} \times \text{P}}{\text{P} \times \text{Kt}}$	$\dfrac{\text{Q—K 2}}{\text{P—K B 3}}$

	(4)	(5)	(6)	(7)
9.	P—Q 4 / P—B 6	Q×P ch. / Q—B 3	P×P / Kt—B 2	Q×Q ch. / P×Q
10.	P×P / B—K 2	Q—Kt 4 ch. / Q—Kt 3	P—Kt 6 / Kt—Q 3	B—B 4 / Kt—K R 3
11.	0—0 / P—Kt 6 !	B—B 4 ch. / K—Kt 2	B×Kt / P×B	P—Q 4 / P×P
12.	B—B 4	Q—B 3 / Kt—K B 3	B—B 7 ch. / K—K 2	Kt—Kt 5 / Kt—R 3
13.		Kt—B 3 / B—Q Kt 5	0—0 / Q—Q R 4	Q B×P / B—Kt 5 ch.
14.		B—Q 2 / P—Q 3+	B—Q 5 / K—K 1	P—B 3 / P×P
15.			Q—Q B 1 / K—Q 1	P×P / B—R 4
16.			Q—Kt 5 ch. / B—K 2	0—0—0 +
17.			P—Kt 7 ch. and wins.	

THE ALLGAIER GAMBIT—GAMES.

	(1)	(2)	(3)
	Prince Ouroussoff / Mr. Bihn	Prince Ouroussoff / Mr. Bihn	Prince Ouroussoff / Mr. Bihn
1.	P—K 4 / P—K 4	P—K 4 / P—K 4	P—K 4 / P—K 4
2.	P—K B 4 / P×P	P—K B 4 / P×P	P—K B 4 / P×P
3.	Kt—K B 3 / P—K Kt 4	Kt—K B 3 / P—K Kt 4	Kt—K B 3 / P—K Kt 4
4.	P—K R 4 / P—Kt 5	P—K R 4 / P—Kt 5	P—K R 4 / P—Kt 5
5.	Kt—Kt 5 / P—K R 3 (a)	Kt—Kt 5 / P—K R 3	Kt—Kt 5 / P—Q 4 (b)

(a) This move is considered the best by all the authors except the celebrated Ponziani.

(b) Discouraged by his previous defeats at this opening, Mr. Bihn in the present instance essays to maintain that system of defence recommended by Ponziani, who disapproves (erroneously in the opinion of Mr. Jaenisch and other authors) of the move 5. P—K R 3.

	(1)	(2)	(3)
6.	Kt×P / K×Kt	Kt×P / K×Kt	P—Q 4 (f) / P—K R 3
7.	B—B 4 ch (a) / P—Q 4	B—B 4 ch. / P—Q 4	Kt×P / K×Kt
8.	B×P ch. / K—Kt 2 (b)	B×P ch. / K—Kt 2	B×P / P×P
9.	P—Q 4 / Kt—K B 3 (c)	P—Q 4 / P—B 6	B—B 4 ch. / K—Kt 2
10.	Kt—B 3 / B—Kt 5	P×P / Kt—K B 3 (d)	B—K 5 ch. / Kt—B 3
11.	Q B×P / Kt×B	Kt—B 3 / B—Kt 5	0—0 / B—K 2
12.	P×Kt / Q×P	B—K B 4 / P×P (e)	Kt—B 3 / Kt—B 3
13.	0—0 / B×Kt	Q×P / P—B 3	R—B 4 (g) / Kt×B
14.	B—K 5 ch. / K—Kt 1	R—Kt 1 ch. / K—R 2	P×Kt / Q×Q ch.

(a) The usual move is—

| 7. Q×P | Kt—K B 3 |
| 8. Q×B P | B—Q 3 |

And the game is in Black's favour. Allgaier himself, who has proclaimed his Gambit invincible, has not given the move 7 B—B 4 ch., but it has been briefly alluded to by Der Laza, in his "Leitfaden."

(b) K—K 1 is the best retreat; the "Handbuch" then continues:—

9. $\frac{\text{P—Q 4}}{\text{Kt—K 2}}$ (he may also play with advantage 9. $\frac{}{\text{P—B 6}}$),

10. $\frac{\text{Kt—B 3}}{\text{B—Kt 2}}$, and Black has a safe game.

(c) Here also 9. $\frac{}{\text{P—B 6}}$ 10. $\frac{\text{P×P}}{\text{B—K 2}}$, leads to the advantage of Black.

(d) 10. $\frac{}{\text{B—K 2}}$, seems stronger.

(e) Why permit, by taking this Pawn, the entry of White's Queen into the game ?

(f) This move, the invention of the Prince Ouroussoff, has not been foreseen by Ponziani, who mentions only 6. $\frac{\text{P—K 5}}{}$, or 6. $\frac{\text{P×P}}{}$, or 6. $\frac{\text{P—Q 3}}{}$.

(g) White sustains his attack with great ability. From first to last every move tells.

	(1)	(2)	(3)
15.	Q—Q 3 / B×P ch.	B—K 5 / R—B 1	R×Q / B—B 4 ch.
16.	B×B / Q—R 4	Q—Kt 3 / Q—K 2	K—R 2 / Kt—R 4
17.	Q—B 4 ch. / K—R 2	Q—Kt 6 ch. / K—R 1	R—B 7 ch. / K—Kt 3
18.	R—B 7 ch. / K—Kt 3	Q×P ch. / Q—R 2	Kt×P (a) / B—Kt 3
19.	R—Kt 7 ch / K—B 4	B×Kt ch. / R×B	Kt—Q 6 (b) / P—Kt 6 ch.
20.	R—B 1 ch. / K—K 5	R—Kt 8 mate.	K—R 1 / P×Kt
21.	B—B 6 d. ch. / K—K 6		R×P ch. / Kt—B 3
22.	Q—Q 3 mate.		R (Q 6) ×Kt ch. / K—R 4
23.	—		R—Kt 7 / K×P
24.	—		white mates in 3.

CHAPTER VII.

THE KIESERITSKY GAMBIT—ANALYSIS.

	(1)	(2)	(3)
1.	P—K 4 / P—K 4	—	—
2.	P—K B 4 / P×P	—	—
3.	Kt—K B 3 / P—K Kt 4	—	—
4.	P—K R 4 / P—Kt 5	—	—
5.	Kt—K 5 / P—K R 4	Kt—K B 3	P—Q 3

(a) Strong, but not so strong, I apprehend, as R × B P, threatening not only to win the Bishop, but to give mate, by B—B 7 ch., in three or four moves.

(b) Ingenious, since whether Black take it or not, he has no escape.

	(1)	(2)	(3)
6.	$\dfrac{\text{B—B 4}}{\text{Kt—K R 3}}$	$\dfrac{\text{B—B 4}}{\text{Q—K 2}}$	$\dfrac{\text{Kt} \times \text{Kt P}}{\text{B—K 2}}$
7.	$\dfrac{\text{P—Q 4}}{\text{P—Q 3}}$	$\dfrac{\text{P—Q 4}}{\text{P—Q 3}}$	$\dfrac{\text{P—Q 4}}{\text{B} \times \text{R P ch.}}$
8.	$\dfrac{\text{Kt—Q 3}}{\text{P—B 6}}$	$\dfrac{\text{Kt} \times \text{B P}}{\text{Q} \times \text{P ch.}}$	$\dfrac{\text{Kt—B 2}}{\text{Q—Kt 4}}$
9.	$\dfrac{\text{P—K Kt 3 } (a)}{\text{P—Q 4}}$	$\dfrac{\text{Q—K 2}}{\text{Q} \times \text{Q ch.}}$	$\dfrac{\text{Q—B 3}}{\text{P—Kt 6}}$
10.	$\dfrac{\text{B} \times \text{Q P } (b)}{\text{P—Q B 3}}$	$\dfrac{\text{K} \times \text{Q}}{\text{P—Q 4}}$	$\dfrac{\text{Kt—B 3}}{\text{Kt—B 3}}$
11.	$\dfrac{\text{B—Kt 3}}{\text{Q} \times \text{Q P}+}$	$\dfrac{\text{Kt} \times \text{R}}{\text{P} \times \text{B}+}$	$\dfrac{\text{B—Q 2}}{}=$

(a) If 9. $\dfrac{\text{P} \times \text{P}}{\text{B—K 2}}$; 10. $\dfrac{\text{B—K 3}}{\text{B} \times \text{P (ch.)}}$; 11. $\dfrac{\text{K—Q 2}}{\text{P} \times \text{P}}$ (or P—Kt 6);

12. $\dfrac{\text{Q} \times \text{P}}{\text{B—K Kt 5}}$; 13. $\dfrac{\text{Q—B 4}}{}$

(b) If 10. $\dfrac{\text{P} \times \text{P}}{\text{Kt—B 4}}$ (see Diagram); 11. $\dfrac{\text{K—B 2}}{\text{Kt} \times \text{Q P}}$; 12. $\dfrac{\text{B—K Kt 5}+}{}$;

or 11. $\dfrac{}{\text{B—K 2}}$; 12. $\dfrac{\text{K R—K 1}}{\text{K—B 1}}$ (Kt—K 5 !); 13. $\dfrac{\text{B—K B 4}}{\text{Kt} \times \text{R P}}$

14. $\dfrac{\text{R} \times \text{B !}}{\text{Q} \times \text{R}}$; 15. $\dfrac{\text{Q—Q 2 !}}{\text{Kt—B 4}+}$.

Note (b).   Position after White's 10th move.

BLACK.

WHITE.

No. 1.   Position after Black's 8th move.

BLACK.

WHITE.

	(4)	(5)	(6)
1.	—	—	—
2.	—	—	—
3.	—	—	—
4.	—	—	—
5.	$\overline{\text{P—K R 4}}$	—	$\overline{\text{Kt—KB3}}$
6.	$\dfrac{\text{B—B 4}}{\text{R—R 2}}$	—	$\dfrac{\text{Kt×Kt P}}{\text{Kt×P}}$
7.	$\dfrac{\text{P—Q 4 }(a)}{\text{P—B 6}}$	—	$\dfrac{\text{P—Q 3 !}}{\text{Kt—Kt 6}}$
8.	$\dfrac{\text{P—K Kt 3}}{\text{Kt—Q B 3}}$	—	$\dfrac{\text{B×P}}{\text{Kt×R}}$
9.	$\dfrac{\text{Kt×Kt}}{\text{Q P×Kt}}$	$\dfrac{\text{Kt—Kt 6}}{\text{B—Kt 2}}$	$\dfrac{\text{Q—K 2 ch.}}{\text{Q—K 2}}$

(a) If 7. $\dfrac{\text{Kt×P}}{\text{R×Kt}}$; 8. $\dfrac{\text{B×R ch.}}{\text{K×B}}$; 9. $\dfrac{\text{P—Q 4}}{\text{P—B 6}}$; 10. $\dfrac{\text{P×P}}{\text{P—Q 3+}}$.

	(4)	(5)	(6)
10.	B—B 4 Q—K 2	P—B 3 Kt—K B 3	Kt—B 6 ch. K—Q 1
11.	Kt—B 3 B—K 3	B—K Kt 5 P×Kt	B×P ch. K×B
12.	P—Q 5 0—0—0	P—K 5 P—Q 4	Kt— Q 5 ch. K—Q 1
13.		B—Q 3 B—B 4	Kt×Q B×Kt
14.		B×B P×B	Q—Kt 4 R—K 1
15.		Q—Q 3 Q—Q 2	B—K 2 B—Q 3
16.		P×Kt B—R 1	Kt—B 3 Kt—Kt 6
17.			Q—Kt 5 ch. K—B 2
18.			Kt—Kt 5 ch. K—B 3
19.			Kt×B R×B ch.
20.			K—Q 1 R×Kt P
21.			Q—B 6 R—Kt 8 ch
22.			K—Q 2 R×R
23.			Kt—K 8 d. ch. K—Kt 4
24.			Kt—B 7 ch. and wins.

	(7)	(8)	(9)
1.	—	—	—
2.	—	—	—
3.	—	—	—
4.	—	—	—

	(7)	(8)	(9)
5.	—	$\overline{P-K R 4}$	—
6.	—	B—B 4 $\overline{R-R 2}$	—
7.	—	P—Q 4 $\overline{P-B 6}$	$\overline{Q-B 3}$
8.	$\overline{Q-K 2}$ ch.	P×P $\overline{P-Q 3}$	P—B 3 $\overline{P-Q 3}$

Nos. 6 and 7.   Position after White's 8th move.

BLACK.

WHITE.

9.	B—K 2 $\overline{Q-Kt 5}$ ch.	Kt.—Q 3 $\overline{B-K 2}$	Kt—Q 3 $\overline{B-R 3}$
10.	B—Q 2 $\overline{Q-Kt 3}$	B—K 3 $\overline{B \times P}$ ch.	P—K 5 $\overline{P \times P}$
11.	B—B 3 $\overline{Kt \times R}$	K—Q 2 $\overline{P \times P}$	P×P $\overline{Q-K 2}$
12.	B×R $\overline{Q-Kt 8}$ ch.	Q×P $\overline{B-Kt 5}$	0—0 $\overline{Q \times R\ P}$
13.	B—B 1 $\overline{Kt-Kt 6}$	Q—B 4 $\overline{R-Kt 2}$	Kt×P $\overline{B \times Kt}$ (!)

	(7)	(8)	(9)
14.	Q—B 3	Kt—B 3 / B—Kt 4	R × B
15.		Q—B 2 / Kt—Q 2	
16.		Q R—K B 1 / B × B ch.	

Nos. 8 and 9.　Position after White's 7th move.

BLACK.

WHITE.

17.		Q × B / Kt—Kt 3	
18.		B—Kt 3 / Q—K 2	
19.		Kt—B 4 / Kt—K B 3	
20.		Q R—K Kt 1	

KIESERITSKY GAMBIT—GAMES.

	(1) Kieseritsky / Walker	(2) V. H. der Laza / Mr. H.——	(3) Kieseritsky / Calvi
1.	P—K 4 / P—K 4	P—K 4 / P—K 4	P—K 4 / P—K 4
2.	P—K B 4 / P×P	P—K B 4 / P×P	P—K B 4 / P×P
3.	Kt—K B 3 / P—K Kt 4	Kt—K B 3 / P—K Kt 4	Kt—K B 3 / P—K Kt 4
4.	P—K R 4 / P—Kt 5	P—K R 4 / P—Kt 5	P—K R 4 / P—Kt 5
5.	Kt—K 5 / P—K R 4	Kt—K 5 / B—K 2	Kt—K 5 / P—K R 4
6.	B—B 4 / Kt—K R 3	B—B 4 / B×P ch.	B—B 4 / R—R 2
7.	P—Q 4 / P—Q 3	K—B 1 / Kt—K B 3	P—Q 4 / P—Q 3
8.	Kt—Q 3 / P—B 6	Kt×Kt P / Kt×Kt	Kt—Q 3 / P—B 6
9.	P—K Kt 3 / P—Q 4 (a)	Q×Kt / P—Q 4	P×P / P—Q B 3
10.	B×Q P (b) / P—Q B 3	Q×B P / P×B	Kt—B 4 / Kt—K 2
11.	B—Kt 3 / Q×Q P	R×B / B—K 3	Kt—B 3 / Kt—Q 2
12.	Kt—B 3 / B—Q 3	P—Q Kt 3 / Q—Q 5	K—B 2 / R—R 1
13.	Kt—B 4 / Q×Q ch.	Kt—B 3 / Kt—Q 2	Q—Q 3 / B—Kt 2
14.	Kt×Q / B×Kt	B—Kt 2 / P—K B 3	B—Q 2 / K—B 1
15.	B×B / B—K 3	Q×B P / K R—Kt 1	Q R—K 1 / Q—Kt 3

(a) This is the principal feature of the defence, for which we are indebted to Mr. Knight.

(b) If he takes Pawn with Pawn, then Black follows with Kt—B 4, threatening both Q P and K R P.

	(1)	(2)	(3)
16.	Kt—K 3 / Kt—Q 2	R—Q 1 / P×P	B—K 3 / Q—B 2
17.	B×B / P×B	R P×P / B—Kt 5	B—K 6 / P—Kt 4
18.	Kt—B 4 / Kt—B 2	Q—Kt 3 / Kt—K 4	P—Kt 4 / Q Kt—Kt 3
19.	0—0—0 / P—K 4	Kt—R 4 / Q×K P	B—Kt 3 / P—R 4
20.	B—K 3 / K—K 2	Q R—K 1 / B—K 7 ch.	P—Q R 3 / P—Q R 5
21.	R—Q 3 / Kt—B 3	K—B 2 / Q—Q 4	B—R 2 / B—Kt 2
22.	R—Q Kt 3 / P—Q Kt 3	B×Kt / P×B	P—K 5 / P—Q 4
23.	R—K 1 / K R—Q 1	Q—R 2 / 0—0—0	P—K 6 / B—B 1
24.	P—Q R 4 / K—K 3	R×B / P—Kt 4	B—B 1 / Q—Q 3
25.	P—R 5 (a) / Kt×K P	Q—R 3 ch. / K—Kt 1	P×B P / K×P
26.	P×P / P×P	Kt—B 3 / R—B 1 ch.	Kt—K 4 / Q—Q B 2
27.	K—Kt 1 / P—Kt 4	K—Kt 1 / Q—B 2	Kt—Kt 5 ch. / K—Kt 1
28.	Kt—R 3 / Kt—Q 7 ch.	Q—K 3 / R—K 1	R×Kt / Q×R
29.	B×Kt / R×B	Kt×P / R—Kt 3	R—K 1 / Q—B 3
30.	Resigns (b)	White wins.	R—K 8 ch. / B—B 1
31.			Kt—Kt 6 / B—B 4
32.			Q×B (c) / Q×Q

(a) Much better to have protected his K P.

(b) This game is much below the usual standard of M. Kieseritzky's play.

(c) The termination of this game is very beautifully played by M. Kieseritzky.

(3) (contd.)

33. $\dfrac{\text{Kt}-\text{K 7 ch.}}{\text{K}-\text{Kt 2}}$

34. $\dfrac{\text{K} \times \text{Q ch.}}{\text{K}-\text{B 3}}$

35. $\dfrac{\text{R}-\text{K 6 ch}}{\text{K} \times \text{Kt}}$

36. $\dfrac{}{\text{B}-\text{Kt 1 and mates next move.}}$

	(4) Cochrane / Evans	(5) Heydebrand / Staunton	(6) Anderssen / Kieseritzky
1.	$\dfrac{\text{P}-\text{K 4}}{\text{P}-\text{K 4}}$	$\dfrac{\text{P}-\text{K 4}}{\text{P}-\text{K 4}}$	$\dfrac{\text{P}-\text{K 4}}{\text{P}-\text{K 4}}$
2.	$\dfrac{\text{P}-\text{K B 4}}{\text{P} \times \text{P}}$	$\dfrac{\text{P}-\text{K B 4}}{\text{P} \times \text{P}}$	$\dfrac{\text{P}-\text{K B 4}}{\text{P} \times \text{P}}$
3.	$\dfrac{\text{Kt}-\text{K B 3}}{\text{P}-\text{K Kt 4}}$	$\dfrac{\text{Kt}-\text{K B 3}}{\text{P}-\text{K Kt 4}}$	$\dfrac{\text{Kt}-\text{K B 3}}{\text{P}-\text{K Kt 4}}$
4.	$\dfrac{\text{P}-\text{K R 4}}{\text{P}-\text{Kt 5}}$	$\dfrac{\text{P}-\text{K R 4}}{\text{P}-\text{Kt 5}}$	$\dfrac{\text{P}-\text{K R 4}}{\text{P}-\text{Kt 5}}$
5.	$\dfrac{\text{Kt}-\text{K 5}}{\text{P}-\text{K R 4}}$	$\dfrac{\text{Kt}-\text{K 5}}{\text{Kt}-\text{K B 3}}$	$\dfrac{\text{Kt}-\text{K 5}}{\text{P}-\text{K R 4}}$
6.	$\dfrac{\text{B}-\text{B 4}}{\text{R}-\text{R 2}}$	$\dfrac{\text{B}-\text{B 4}}{\text{P}-\text{Q 4} \ (b)}$	$\dfrac{\text{B}-\text{B 4}}{\text{R}-\text{R 2}}$
7.	$\dfrac{\text{Kt} \times \text{B P}}{\text{R} \times \text{Kt}}$	$\dfrac{\text{P} \times \text{P}}{\text{B}-\text{Q 3}}$	$\dfrac{\text{P}-\text{Q 4}}{\text{P}-\text{Q 3}}$
8.	$\dfrac{\text{B} \times \text{R ch.}}{\text{K} \times \text{B}}$	$\dfrac{\text{P}-\text{Q 4}}{\text{Kt}-\text{R 4} \ (c)}$	$\dfrac{\text{Kt} \times \text{B P}}{\text{R} \times \text{Kt}}$
9.	$\dfrac{\text{P}-\text{Q 4}}{\text{B}-\text{R 3} \ (a)}$	$\dfrac{\text{Kt} \times \text{P}}{\text{Kt}-\text{Kt 6}}$	$\dfrac{\text{B} \times \text{R ch.}}{\text{K} \times \text{B}}$
10.	$\dfrac{\text{B} \times \text{P}}{\text{B} \times \text{B}}$	$\dfrac{\text{R}-\text{Kt 1}}{\text{Q} \times \text{P}}$	$\dfrac{\text{B} \times \text{P}}{\text{B}-\text{R 3}}$

(a) This is the error which loses Black's game. The correct move is 9. $\dfrac{}{\text{P}-\text{B 6}}$.

(b) This is a novelty, and followed by Kt—R 4, presently, appears to me a better defence than that of Q—K 2, recommended by the books.

(c) In this consists the main strength of the new defence to Kieseritsky's powerful Gambit. After the Knight is played thus, White's attack seems over, and the advantage of the position to be altogether on the side of his adversary.

	(4)	(5)	(6)
11.	0--0 / Q×P	Kt--B 2 / Q—K 2 ch. (a)	0—0 / B×B
12.	R×B ch. / Kt—B 3	B—K 2 / 0—0	R×B ch. / K—Kt 2
13.	P—K 5 / P—Q 4	Kt—B 3 / R—K 1	Kt--B 3 / Q×P
14.	R×Kt ch. / K—Kt 2	Kt—R 1 / Kt×B	Kt—Q 5 / Kt—Q R 3
15.	Q—Q 2 / Kt—Q 2	Resigns	Q—Q 3 / P—B 3
16.	Q—K R 6 ch. / Resigns.		Q R—K B 1 / B—K 3 (b)

(6) (contd.)

17.	Kt—K 3 / Kt—Kt 5 (c)	20.	R—B 7 ch. (e) / K—R 1 (f)	23.	R×B / Kt— B 3
18.	Q—R 3 / P—B 4	21.	P—Kt 4 / Q—Kt 4 (g)	24.	P—Q 7 / Kt×K P
19.	P×P (d) / Kt×R P	22.	P×P (h) / B×R	25.	Q—Q 3 / Kt—B 6

(a) The best move apparently; for if he had played Q—R 7 White might have escaped by K—Q 2.

(b) If he had ventured to take the Knight, White would have obtained an attack all but irresistible by first checking with the Rook and afterwards taking Pawn with Pawn.

(c) Mr. Kieseritsky justly blames this move. Kt—R 3 would, perhaps, have been more to the purpose.

(d) P—Q 5 looks at least as good as taking the Pawn.

(e) Why not 20. $\dfrac{Q \times Kt}{}$? Black loses his own Queen if the Bishop takes Queen.

(f) 20. $\dfrac{}{B \times R}$ obviously loses the Queen.

(g) To interpose her majesty if White's Queen checks.

(h) Suppose instead of this move White had played 22. $\dfrac{Q\ R—B\ 5}{}$ Black's best reply is,—22. $\dfrac{}{B \times R.}$ 23. $\dfrac{Q—Kt\ 2\ ch.}{Kt—B\ 3}$ 24. $\dfrac{Kt \times B.}{}$ White must now win another Piece, and will afterwards have equal forces, and decidedly the better position.

(6) (contd.)

26. $\dfrac{\text{R}-\text{B }5}{\text{Q}-\text{Q }1}$ 30. $\dfrac{\text{Kt}-\text{B }5 \text{ ch.}}{\text{K}-\text{B }3}$ 34. $\dfrac{\text{Kt}-\text{K R }5}{\text{R}\times\text{Kt ch.}}$

27. $\dfrac{\text{Q}-\text{Q }4 \text{ ch.}}{\text{K}-\text{Kt }1}$ 31. $\dfrac{\text{Kt}-\text{Kt }3}{\text{Q}-\text{Kt }3 \text{ ch.}}$ 35. $\dfrac{\text{R}\times\text{R}}{\text{Q}-\text{Q }3 \text{ ch.}}$

28. $\dfrac{\text{Q}-\text{B }4 \text{ ch.}}{\text{K}-\text{R }1}$ 32. $\dfrac{\text{K}-\text{R }2}{\text{K}-\text{Kt }3}$ 36. $\dfrac{\text{Resigns.}}{\quad}$

29. $\dfrac{\text{R}\times\text{P ch. } (i)}{\text{K}-\text{Kt }2}$ 33. $\dfrac{\text{R}-\text{K }5}{\text{R}-\text{R }1 \text{ ch.}}$

(7)	(8)	(9)
Kieseritsky	Morphy	Anderssen
Szen	Anderssen	Morphy
1. $\dfrac{\text{P}-\text{K }4}{\text{P}-\text{K }4}$	$\dfrac{\text{P}-\text{K }4}{\text{P}-\text{K }4}$	$\dfrac{\text{P}-\text{K }4}{\text{P}-\text{K }4}$
2. $\dfrac{\text{P}-\text{K B }4}{\text{P}\times\text{P}}$	$\dfrac{\text{P}-\text{K B }4}{\text{P}\times\text{P}}$	$\dfrac{\text{P}-\text{K B }4}{\text{P}\times\text{P}}$
3. $\dfrac{\text{Kt}-\text{K B }3}{\text{P}-\text{K Kt }4}$	$\dfrac{\text{Kt}-\text{K B }3}{\text{P}-\text{K Kt }4}$	$\dfrac{\text{Kt}-\text{K B }3}{\text{P}-\text{K Kt }4}$
4. $\dfrac{\text{P}-\text{K R }4}{\text{P}-\text{Kt }5}$	$\dfrac{\text{P}-\text{K R }4}{\text{P}-\text{Kt }5}$	$\dfrac{\text{P}-\text{K R }4}{\text{P}-\text{Kt }5}$
5. $\dfrac{\text{Kt}-\text{K }5}{\text{P}-\text{K R }4}$	$\dfrac{\text{Kt}-\text{K }5}{\text{K Kt}-\text{B }3}$	$\dfrac{\text{Kt}-\text{K }5}{\text{Kt}-\text{K B }3}$
6. $\dfrac{\text{B}-\text{B }4}{\text{R}-\text{R }2}$	$\dfrac{\text{Kt}\times\text{Kt P}}{\text{Kt}\times\text{P}}$	$\dfrac{\text{Kt}\times\text{Kt P}}{\text{P}-\text{Q }4}$
7. $\dfrac{\text{P}-\text{Q }4}{\text{P}-\text{Q }3}$	$\dfrac{\text{P}-\text{Q }3}{\text{Kt}-\text{Kt }6}$	$\dfrac{\text{Kt}\times\text{Kt ch.}}{\text{Q}\times\text{Kt}}$
8. $\dfrac{\text{Kt}-\text{Q }3}{\text{P}-\text{B }6}$	$\dfrac{\text{B}\times\text{P}}{\text{Kt}\times\text{R}}$	$\dfrac{\text{Kt}-\text{B }3}{\text{Q}-\text{Kt }3}$
9. $\dfrac{\text{P}-\text{K Kt }3}{\text{B}-\text{K }3 \,(a)}$	$\dfrac{\text{Q}-\text{K }2 \text{ ch.}}{\text{Q}-\text{K }2}$	$\dfrac{\text{Q}-\text{B }3}{\text{B}-\text{Q }3}$
10. $\dfrac{\text{B}-\text{K Kt }5}{\text{B}-\text{K }2}$	$\dfrac{\text{Kt}-\text{B }6 \text{ ch.}}{\text{K}-\text{Q }1}$	$\dfrac{\text{B}-\text{Q }3 \,(b)}{\text{B}-\text{K Kt }5}$
11. $\dfrac{\text{B}\times\text{B (K }3)}{\text{P}\times\text{B}}$	$\dfrac{\text{B}\times\text{P ch.}}{\text{K}\times\text{B}}$	$\dfrac{\text{Q}-\text{B }2}{\text{Kt}-\text{Q }2}$

(i) Why not rest content with a drawn game ?

(a) The "Handbuch" gives here for Black 9. $\dfrac{\quad}{\text{B}-\text{R }3}$.

(b) Could he have played a more obliging move ? locking up his own game and enabling his opponent to develop his without the slightest difficulty.

	(7)	(8)	(9)
12.	Kt—B 4 / K—Q 2	Kt—Q 5 ch. / K—Q 1	P×P / P—K B 4
13.	P—Q 5 / P—K 4	Kt×Q / B×Kt	B—Kt 5 / P—Q R 3
14.	Kt—K 6 / Q—K 1	Q—Kt 4 (d) / P—Q 3	B×Kt ch. / K×B
15.	Q—Q 3 / P—Q R 3	Q—K B 4 / R—Kt 1	P—Q 3 / Q R—K 1 ch.
16.	Kt—B 3 / K—B 1	Q×B P / B×P ch.	K—B 1 / K R—Kt 1 (f)
17.	Q—B 4 / B×B	K—Q 2 / R—K 1	R—R 2 / P—B 6
18.	P×B / P—Kt 4	Kt—R 3 / Kt—R 3 (e)	P—Kt 3 / B—R 4
19.	Q—Kt 4 / P—B 4 (a)	Q—R 5 / B—B 3	B—Kt 5 (g) / P—R 3
20.	Q—R 5 (b) / Q R—R 2	Q×Kt / B×P	Q—R 7 / P×B
21.	Q—Kt 6 (c) / K R—Q 2	Q—R 4 ch. / K—Q 2	Kt—R 4 / P×P
22.	Kt—Q 1 / Q R—Kt 2	R—Kt 1 / Resigns.	Q×Kt P / P×P and wins.
23.	Q—R 5 / R—K 2		
24.	Kt—K 3 / R×Kt		

(a) This bold advance of the infantry serves as a momentary check to White's attack, but in the end it leaves the Black King too much exposed for safety.

(b) Better than taking the Pawn in passing, because it retards the freedom of the adverse pieces.

(c) 21. $\dfrac{\text{P—Kt 6}}{}$ seems also an embarrassing move.

(d) Up to this point the moves are those given in the " Books." The " Handbuch " dismisses the game with the remark that Black has the best of it, as White cannot win the Knight at R 1.

(e) This move loses the game.

(f) White's game is now hopeless.

(g) B—B 4 would perhaps have been better. It could not be worse.

(7)

25. $\dfrac{P \times R}{Q \times P}$

26. $\dfrac{Kt-Q\,5}{Kt-K\,2}$

27. $\dfrac{R \times P}{Kt \times Kt}$

28. $\dfrac{R-R\,8\ \text{ch.}}{K-Q\,2}$

29. $\dfrac{P \times Kt}{Q \times P}$

30. $\dfrac{Q-Q\,8\ \text{ch.}}{K-B\,3}$

31. $\dfrac{Q-B\,8\ \text{ch.}}{K-Kt\,3}$

(7) *(contd.)*

32. $\dfrac{Q \times Kt\ P}{R-K\,B\,2}$ *(a)*

33. $\dfrac{R \times Kt\ \text{ch.}}{K-R\,2}$

34. $\dfrac{R-K\,R\,8}{P-K\,5}$

35. $\dfrac{P-Kt\,6}{P-K\,6}$ *(b)*

36. $\dfrac{R-R\,2}{R-K\,2}$

37. $\dfrac{R-Q\,1}{P-B\,7\ \text{ch.}}$

38. $\dfrac{K-B\,1}{Q-K\,4}$

39. $\dfrac{K-K\,2}{Q \times Q\ Kt\ P}$

40. $\dfrac{Q-B\,5}{Q-Kt\,5}$

41. $\dfrac{R-R\,4}{Q-Q\,B\,6}$

42. $\dfrac{Q-Q\,3}{Q-Kt\,7}$

43. $\dfrac{R-R\,7}{R \times R}$

44. $P \times R$ and wins.

(10)

Anderssen

Morphy

1. $\dfrac{P-K\,4}{P-K\,4}$

2. $\dfrac{P-K\,B\,4}{P \times P}$

3. $\dfrac{Kt-K\,B\,3}{P-K\,Kt\,4}$

4. $\dfrac{P-K\,R\,4}{P-Kt\,5}$

5. $\dfrac{Kt-K\,5}{Kt-K\,B\,3}$

6. $\dfrac{Kt \times Kt\ P}{P-Q\,4}$

7. $\dfrac{Kt \times Kt\ \text{ch.}}{Q \times Kt}$

8. $\dfrac{Q-K\,2}{B-Q\,3}$

9. $\dfrac{Kt-B\,3}{P-B\,3}$

10. $\dfrac{P-Q\,4}{Q \times Q\ P}$ *(c)*

11. $\dfrac{B-Q\,2}{R-Kt\,1}$

12. $\dfrac{P \times P\ \text{d. ch.}}{K-Q\,1}$

13. $\dfrac{0-0-0}{B-Kt\,5}$ *(d)*

14. $\dfrac{Q-K\,4}{Q \times Q}$

(*a*) An ingenious attempt to open a counter-attack, which, without great care on the part of White, would have wrested the game from him in spite of his superiority of force.

(*b*) Mr. S. plays this disheartening end game admirably.

(*c*) White sacrifices this Pawn to enable him to free his game.

(*d*) Finely played. It is not every player who would have dared risk such a sacrifice against such an opponent.

(10) *(contd.)*

15. $\dfrac{\text{Kt} \times \text{Q}}{\text{B} \times \text{R}}$

16. $\dfrac{\text{Kt} \times \text{B}}{\text{B} - \text{R} \, 4}$

17. $\dfrac{\text{B} \times \text{P}}{\text{P} \times \text{P}}$

18. $\dfrac{\text{Kt} \times \text{Kt P}}{\text{K} - \text{K} \, 2}$

19. $\dfrac{\text{B} - \text{Q Kt 5}}{\text{R} \times \text{P} \, (a)}$

20. $\dfrac{\text{R} - \text{K 1 ch.}}{\text{K} - \text{B} \, 3}$

21. $\dfrac{\text{R} - \text{K 8}}{\text{B} - \text{Kt 3}}$

22. $\dfrac{\text{Kt} - \text{Q 6}}{\text{Kt} - \text{B 3} \, (b)}$

23. $\dfrac{\text{R} \times \text{R}}{\text{R} \times \text{P ch.}}$

24. $\dfrac{\text{K} - \text{Q 1}}{\text{Kt} - \text{Q 5}}$

25. $\dfrac{\text{R} - \text{K 8}}{\text{B} - \text{R 4 ch}}$

26. $\dfrac{\text{K} - \text{K 1}}{\text{Kt} - \text{B 6 ch.}}$

27. $\dfrac{\text{K} - \text{B 1}}{\text{R} \times \text{P}}$

28. $\dfrac{\text{B} - \text{K 2}}{\text{R} \times \text{P} \, (c)}$

29. $\dfrac{\text{B} - \text{Kt 5 ch.}}{\text{Kt} \times \text{B}}$

30. $\dfrac{\text{P} \times \text{Kt ch.}}{\text{K} \times \text{P}}$

31. $\dfrac{\text{R} - \text{K 5 ch.}}{\text{K} - \text{B 3}}$

32. $\dfrac{\text{R} \times \text{B}}{\text{Resigns.}}$

Chapter VIII.

THE KING'S ROOK'S PAWN'S GAMBIT— ANALYSIS.

	(1)	(2)	(3)
1.	$\dfrac{\text{P} - \text{K 4}}{\text{P} - \text{K 4}}$	—	—
2.	$\dfrac{\text{P} - \text{K B 4}}{\text{P} \times \text{P}}$	—	—
3.	$\dfrac{\text{P} - \text{K R 4}}{\text{B} - \text{K 2} \,!}$	—	$\dfrac{}{\text{P} - \text{Q 4}}$
4.	$\dfrac{\text{Q} - \text{Kt 4}}{\text{P} - \text{Q 4} \,!}$	$\dfrac{\text{Kt} - \text{K B 3}}{\text{Kt} - \text{K B 3}}$	$\dfrac{\text{P} \times \text{P}}{\text{Q} \times \text{P}}$
5.	$\dfrac{\text{Q} \times \text{P (B 5)}}{\text{P} \times \text{P}}$	$\dfrac{\text{P} - \text{Q 3}}{\text{P} - \text{Q 4}}$	$\dfrac{\text{Q} - \text{K 2 ch.}}{\text{B} - \text{K 3}}$
6.	$\dfrac{\text{Q} \times \text{P (K 5)}}{\text{Kt} - \text{K B 3}}$	$\dfrac{\text{P} \times \text{P}}{\text{Kt} \times \text{P}}$	$\dfrac{\text{Kt} - \text{Q B 3}}{\text{Q} - \text{Q 2}}$
7.	$\dfrac{\text{Q} - \text{B 3}}{\text{0} - \text{0}}$	$\dfrac{\text{P} - \text{B 4}}{\text{Kt} - \text{K 6}}$	$\dfrac{\text{P} - \text{Q 3}}{\text{B} - \text{Q 3}}$

(a) Was this Pawn worth the loss of time incurred in seizing it ?

(b) This is probably his best move.

(c) He seems to have thoroughly convinced himself that nothing is to be done.

	(1)	(2)	(3)
8.	$\dfrac{\text{B}-\text{B }4}{\text{B}-\text{K Kt }5}$	$\dfrac{\text{B}\times\text{Kt}}{\text{P}\times\text{B}}$	$\dfrac{\text{Kt}-\text{R }3}{\text{Kt}-\text{Q B }3}$
9.	$\dfrac{\text{Q}\times\text{Kt P}}{\text{Q}-\text{Q }3}$	$\dfrac{\text{P}-\text{Q }4}{\text{B}-\text{K Kt }5}+$	$\dfrac{\text{Kt}-\text{Q Kt }5}{0-0-0}$
10.	$\dfrac{\text{Q}-\text{Kt }3\ (a)}{\text{Kt}-\text{B }3}$		$\dfrac{\text{Kt}\times\text{B ch.}}{\text{P}\times\text{Kt}}$
11.	$\dfrac{\text{Q}-\text{Q }3}{\text{Kt}-\text{Q }5}$		$\dfrac{\text{Kt}\times\text{P}}{\text{B}-\text{K Kt }5}$
12.	$\dfrac{\text{P}-\text{B }3}{\text{Q}-\text{K }4}\text{ ch.}$		$\dfrac{\text{Q}-\text{Q }2}{\text{R}-\text{K }1\text{ ch.}+}$
13.	$\dfrac{\text{K}-\text{B }1}{\text{Kt}-\text{B }4}$ and wins.		

CHAPTER IX.

THE BISHOP'S GAMBIT—ANALYSIS.

	(1)	(2)	(3)
1.	$\dfrac{\text{P}-\text{K }4}{\text{P}-\text{K }4}$	—	—
2.	$\dfrac{\text{P}-\text{K B }4}{\text{P}\times\text{P}}$	—	—
3.	$\dfrac{\text{B}-\text{B }4}{\text{Q}-\text{R }5\text{ ch.}}$	—	—
4.	$\dfrac{\text{K}-\text{B }1}{\text{P}-\text{K Kt }4}$	—	—
5.	$\dfrac{\text{Kt}-\text{Q B }3}{\text{B}-\text{Kt }2}$	—	—
6.	$\dfrac{\text{Kt}-\text{B }3}{\text{Q}-\text{R }4}$	$\dfrac{\text{P}-\text{Q }4}{\text{P}-\text{Q }3}$	—
7.	$\dfrac{\text{P}-\text{K R }4}{\text{P}-\text{K R }3}$	$\dfrac{\text{P}-\text{K }5}{\text{P}\times\text{P}}$	—
8.	$\dfrac{\text{P}-\text{Q }4}{\text{P}-\text{Q }3}$	$\dfrac{\text{Kt}-\text{Q }5}{\text{K}-\text{Q }1}$	—

(a) If 10. $\dfrac{\text{Q}\times\text{R}}{\text{Kt}-\text{B }3}$; 11. $\dfrac{\text{Q}-\text{Kt }7}{\text{Q}-\text{Kt }6}\text{ ch.}$; 12. $\dfrac{\text{K}-\text{B }1}{\text{Kt}-\text{K }5}$ and wins.

	(1)	(2)	(3)
9.	$\dfrac{\text{P–K 5}}{\text{P} \times \text{P}}$	$\dfrac{\text{P} \times \text{P}}{\text{B–Q 2}}$	—
10.	$\dfrac{\text{Kt–Q 5}}{\text{K–Q 1}}$	$\dfrac{\text{Kt–K B 3}}{\text{Q–R 4}}$	—
11.	$\dfrac{\text{P} \times \text{P}}{\text{B–Q 2}}$	$\dfrac{\text{B–Q 2}}{\text{Kt–K 2}}$	$\dfrac{\text{P–K R 4}}{\text{P–K R 3}}$
12.	$\dfrac{\text{K–Kt 1}}{\text{Q–Kt 3}}$	$\dfrac{\text{B–B 3}}{\text{R–K 1}}$	$\dfrac{\text{K–Kt 1}}{\text{Q–Kt 3}}$

Nos. 1 to 21.   Position after Black's 5th move.

BLACK.

WHITE.

	(1)	(2)	(3)
13.	$\dfrac{\text{P} \times \text{P}}{\text{P} \times \text{P}}$	$\dfrac{\text{Kt} \times \text{Kt}}{\text{R} \times \text{Kt}}$	$\dfrac{\text{P} \times \text{P}}{\text{P} \times \text{P}}$
14.	$\dfrac{\text{R} \times \text{R}}{\text{B} \times \text{R}}$	$\text{Q–Q 5} =$	$\dfrac{\text{R} \times \text{R}}{\text{B} \times \text{R}}$
15.	$\dfrac{\text{K Kt} \times \text{P}}{\text{Q} \times \text{Kt}}$		$\dfrac{\text{Kt} \times \text{Kt P !} (a)}{\text{Q} \times \text{Kt}}$
16.	$\dfrac{\text{B} \times \text{P}}{\text{Q–K Kt 3 !}}$		$\dfrac{\text{B} \times \text{P}}{\text{Q–B 4}}$
17.	$\dfrac{\text{P–K 6}}{\text{P} \times \text{P}}$		$\dfrac{\text{P–K 6}}{\text{P} \times \text{P}}$

(a) Petroff's attack.

	(1)	(2)	(3)
18.	$\dfrac{\text{Kt}\times\text{P}}{\text{P}-\text{K }4}$		$\dfrac{\text{Kt}\times\text{P}}{\text{Q}-\text{B }4\text{ ch. !}}$
19.	$\dfrac{\text{Kt}\times\text{R}}{\text{P}\times\text{B}}$		$\dfrac{\text{K}-\text{R }1}{\text{Q}\times\text{B}}$
20.	$\dfrac{\text{B}\times\text{Kt}}{\text{Q}\times\text{B}}$		$\dfrac{\text{Q}-\text{Q }6}{\text{P}-\text{K }4\text{ !}}$
21.	$\dfrac{\text{Q}-\text{Q }6}{\text{Kt}-\text{Q R }3}$		$\dfrac{\text{R}-\text{Q }1\text{ !}}{\text{P}\times\text{B}}$

Nos. 3, 4, 5, and 6.   Position after White's 16th move.

BLACK.

WHITE.

22.	$\dfrac{\text{R}-\text{Q }1}{\text{Q}-\text{B }2}$	$\dfrac{\text{Kt}\times\text{R}}{\text{Kt}-\text{K }2\text{ !}}$
23.	$\dfrac{\text{P}-\text{Q Kt }4}{\text{Q}-\text{K }2}$	$\overline{\text{Q}\times\text{Kt ch.}}$
24.	$\dfrac{\text{Q}\times\text{B P}}{\text{Q}\times\text{Q Kt P}}$	
25.	$\dfrac{\text{Q}-\text{B }7}{\text{Q}-\text{K }2}$	
26.	$\dfrac{\text{Q}-\text{Kt }8\text{ ch.}}{\text{Q}-\text{K }1}$	
27.	$\dfrac{\text{Q}-\text{Kt }5\text{ ch.}}{\text{K}-\text{B }1}$	

	(4)	(5)	(6)
1.	—	—	—
2.	--	—	—
3.	—	—	—
4.	—	—	—
5.	—	—	—
6.	—	--	—
7.	—	—	—
8.	—	--	—
9.	—	—	—
10.	—	—	—
11.	—	—	—
12.	—	—	—
13.	—	—	—
14.	—	—	—
15.	—	—	—
16.	$\dfrac{}{\text{Q—Kt 3}}$	—	—
17.	$\dfrac{\text{P—K 6}}{\text{P×P}}$	—	—
18.	$\dfrac{\text{Kt×P}}{\text{P—K 4}}$	—	—
19.	$\dfrac{\text{Kt—K 6 ch.}}{\text{K—K 1}}$	$\dfrac{}{\text{K—B 1}}$	$\dfrac{}{\text{K—K 2}}$
20.	$\dfrac{\text{Q—Q 6}}{\text{B×Kt}}$	$\dfrac{\text{Q—Q 6}}{\text{Kt—Q R 3}}$	$\dfrac{\text{B—Kt 5 ch.}}{\text{B—B 3}}$
21.	$\dfrac{\text{B×B}}{\text{Kt—Q B 3}}$	$\dfrac{\text{B—K Kt 5}}{\text{B—B 3 !}}$	$\dfrac{\text{Q—Q 5}}{\text{B×Kt 1}}$

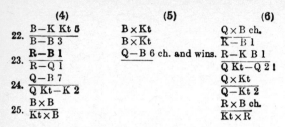

	(4)	(5)	(6)
22.	$\dfrac{\text{B—K Kt 5}}{\text{B—B 3}}$	$\dfrac{\text{B} \times \text{Kt}}{\text{B} \times \text{Kt}}$	$\dfrac{\text{Q} \times \text{B ch.}}{\text{K—B 1}}$
23.	$\dfrac{\textbf{R—B 1}}{\text{R—Q 1}}$	Q—B 6 ch. and wins.	$\dfrac{\text{R—K B 1}}{\text{Q Kt—Q 2 !}}$
24.	$\dfrac{\text{Q—B 7}}{\text{Q Kt—K 2}}$		$\dfrac{\text{Q} \times \text{Kt}}{\text{Q—Kt 2}}$
25.	$\dfrac{\text{B} \times \text{B}}{\text{Kt} \times \text{B}}$		$\dfrac{\text{R} \times \text{B ch.}}{\text{Kt} \times \text{R}}$

Nos. 4, 5, and 6.   Position after White's 19th move.

BLACK.

WHITE.

26.	$\dfrac{\text{Q} \times \text{K P}}{\text{R—Q 7}}$	$\dfrac{\text{Q—Q 6 ch.}}{\text{Q—K 2}}$
27.	$\dfrac{\text{Q—Kt 8 ch.}}{\text{R—Q 1}}$	Q × Kt ch. and wins.
28.	$\dfrac{\text{Q—B 4}}{\text{Kt—Q 4 !}}$	
29.	$\dfrac{\text{Q—K 5}}{\text{Q—K 5}}$	
30.	$\dfrac{\text{B—B 7 db. ch.}}{\text{K—Q 2}}$	
31.	$\dfrac{\text{Q} \times \text{Q}}{\text{Kt} \times \text{Q}}$	
32.	B × Kt and wins.	

	(7)	(8)	(9)
1.	--	—	—
2.	—	—	—
3.	—	—	—
4.	—	—	—
5	—	—	—

Nos. 7 and 8.   Position after White's 13th move.

BLACK.

WHITE.

6.	—	—	—
7.	—	—	—
8.	—	—	$\dfrac{\text{Kt}-\text{K B 3}}{\text{Q}-\text{R 4}}$
9.	$\dfrac{\text{Kt}-\text{K B 3}}{\text{Q}-\text{R 4}}$	—	$\dfrac{\text{P}-\text{K R 4}}{\text{Kt}-\text{K 2}}$
10.	$\dfrac{\text{P}-\text{K R 4}}{\text{P}-\text{K R 3}}$	—	$\dfrac{\text{Kt}\times\text{Kt P}}{\text{Q}\times\text{Q ch.}}$

	(7)	(8)	(9)
11.	$\dfrac{\text{K}-\text{Kt}\,1}{\text{Q}-\text{Kt}\,3}$	—	$\dfrac{\text{Kt}\times\text{Q}}{\text{P}-\text{K B}\,3}$
12.	$\dfrac{\text{Kt}\times\text{K P}}{\text{Q}-\text{B}\,4}$	—	$\dfrac{\text{Kt}-\text{K}\,6\,!}{\text{B}\times\text{Kt}}$
13.	$\dfrac{\text{Q}-\text{R}\,5}{\text{B}\times\text{Kt}}$	$\dfrac{}{\text{B}-\text{K}\,3}$	$\dfrac{\text{B}\times\text{B}}{\text{P}\times\text{P}\,!}$
14.	$\dfrac{\text{P}\times\text{B}}{\text{P}-\text{Q B}\,3}$	$\dfrac{\text{P}\times\text{P}}{\text{P}\times\text{P}}$	$\dfrac{\text{B}\times\text{P}}{\text{Kt}-\text{R}\,3}$
15.	$\dfrac{\text{B}-\text{Q}\,2}{\text{P}\times\text{Kt}}$	$\dfrac{\text{Q}\times\text{R}}{\text{B}\times\text{Q}}$	$\dfrac{\text{Kt}-\text{B}\,2}{\text{Kt}-\text{B}\,4}$
16.	$\dfrac{\text{B}\times\text{P}\ (\text{Q}\,5)}{\text{Kt}-\text{Q B}\,3}$	$\dfrac{\text{R}\times\text{B}}{\text{P}-\text{K B}\,3}$	$\dfrac{\text{B}-\text{R}\,3}{\text{Kt}-\text{Q}\,4}$
17.	$\dfrac{\text{P}\times\text{P}}{\text{B}-\text{K}\,3}$	$\dfrac{\text{B}-\text{Q}\,3}{\text{Q}\times\text{B}}$	$\dfrac{\text{B}-\text{Kt}\,3}{\text{C}-\text{O}\,+}$
18.	$\dfrac{\text{B}\times\text{B}}{\text{P}\times\text{B}}$	$\dfrac{\text{Kt}\times\text{Q}}{\text{B}\times\text{Kt}}$	
19.	$\dfrac{\text{R}-\text{K B}\,1}{\text{Q}\times\text{Q B P}}$	$\dfrac{\text{B}\times\text{P}}{\text{P}\times\text{B}}$	
20.	$\dfrac{\text{B}\times\text{P}}{\text{Q}-\text{B}\,4\ \text{ch.}}$	$\dfrac{\text{Kt}\times\text{P}}{\text{B}-\text{B}\,2}$	
21.	$\dfrac{\text{K}-\text{R}\,2}{\text{Kt}\times\text{P}}$	R—K 1 and wins.	
22.	P—Kt 6 and wins.		

	(10)	(11)	(12)
1.	—	—	—
2.	—	—	—
3.	-	—	—
4.	—	—	—
5.	—	—	—
6.	—	—	—
7.	—	—	—

	(10)	(11)	(12)
8.	$\dfrac{\text{Kt}-\text{Q 5}}{\text{B}-\text{Kt 5}}$	—	—
9.	$\dfrac{\text{Kt}-\text{K B 3}}{\text{Q}-\text{R 4 }(a)}$	$\dfrac{}{\text{K}-\text{Q 1}}$	$\dfrac{}{\text{Q}-\text{R 3}}$
10.	$\dfrac{\text{Kt}\times\text{P ch.}}{\text{K}-\text{Q 1}}$	$\dfrac{\text{Kt}\times\text{Q !}}{\text{B}\times\text{Q}}$	$\dfrac{\text{Kt}\times\text{P ch.}}{\text{K}-\text{Q 1}}$
11.	$\dfrac{\text{Kt}\times\text{R}}{\text{P}-\text{K 5}}$	$\dfrac{\text{Kt}-\text{B 5}}{\text{B}-\text{B 1 !}}$	$\dfrac{\text{Kt}\times\text{R}}{\text{P}-\text{K 5}}$

Nos. 10, 11, and 12.   Position after White's 9th move.

BLACK.

WHITE.

	(10)	(11)	(12)
12.	$\dfrac{\text{B}-\text{K 2}}{\text{P}\times\text{Kt}}$	$\dfrac{\text{B}\times\text{P}}{\text{K P}\times\text{B !}}$	$\dfrac{\text{Kt}\times\text{Kt P}}{\text{Q}\times\text{Kt}}$
13.	$\dfrac{\text{B}\times\text{P}}{\text{B}\times\text{B}}$	$\dfrac{\text{R}\times\text{B}}{\text{Kt}-\text{Q B 3}}$	$\dfrac{\text{B}-\text{K 2}}{\text{B}\times\text{B ch.}}$
14.	$\dfrac{\text{Q}\times\text{B}}{\text{Q}\times\text{Q ch.}}$	$\dfrac{\text{P}-\text{K R 4}}{\text{P}-\text{K B 3}}$	$\dfrac{\text{Q}\times\text{B}}{\text{P}-\text{K 6}}$
15.	$\dfrac{\text{P}\times\text{Q}}{\text{B}\times\text{P}}$	$\dfrac{\text{Kt}-\text{Q B 3 !}}{\text{K Kt}-\text{K 2}}$	$\dfrac{\text{Q}-\text{B 4}}{\text{Q}-\text{K 2}}$

(a) If 9. $\dfrac{}{\text{B}\times\text{Kt}}$; 10. $\dfrac{\text{Q}\times\text{B}}{\text{K}-\text{Q 1}}$; 11. $\dfrac{\text{Kt}\times\text{K B P}}{\text{Kt}-\text{Q 2 !}}$; 12. $\dfrac{\text{Kt}-\text{K 2}+}{}$

	(10)	(11)	(12)
			$\dfrac{\text{Q}-\text{Q 5 ch.}}{\text{K}-\text{K 1}}$
16.	$\dfrac{\text{B}\times\text{P !}}{\text{P}\times\text{B}}$	$\dfrac{\text{Kt}\times\text{Kt}}{\text{B}\times\text{Kt}}$	$\overline{\text{Q}-\text{B 5}}$
17.	$\dfrac{\text{Q R}-\text{Q 1}}{\text{Kt}-\text{Q B 3}}$	$\dfrac{\text{R P}\times\text{P}}{\text{B P}\times\text{P}}$	
18.	$\dfrac{\text{P}-\text{Q B 3}}{\text{K}-\text{B 1}}$	$\dfrac{\text{R}-\text{R 6}}{\text{B}-\text{B 1}}$	
19.	$\dfrac{\text{P}\times\text{B}}{\text{K}-\text{Kt 1}}$	$\dfrac{\text{R}-\text{K 6}}{\text{K}-\text{Q 2}}$	
20.	$\dfrac{\text{P}-\text{Q 5}}{\text{Kt}-\text{Q 1}}$	$\dfrac{\text{Kt}-\text{K 4}}{\text{B}-\text{K 2 !}}$	
21.	$\overline{\text{R}-\text{Q B 1}} +$	$\dfrac{\text{Kt}-\text{B 5 ch.}}{\text{K}-\text{B 1}}$	
22.		$\dfrac{\text{Kt}\times\text{P}}{\text{K}\times\text{Kt}}$	
23.		$\overline{\text{B}-\text{Q 5}} +$	

	(13)	(14)	(15)
1.	—	—	—
2.	—	—	—
3.	—	—	—
4.	—	—	—
5.	—	—	—
6.	—	—	—
7.	$\dfrac{\text{Kt}-\text{B 3}}{\text{Q}-\text{R 4}}$	—	$\dfrac{\text{B}-\text{K 2}}{\text{Kt}-\text{K 2 !}}$
8.	$\dfrac{\text{P}-\text{K R 4}}{\text{P}-\text{K R 3}}$	—	$\dfrac{\text{Kt}-\text{B 3}}{\text{Q}-\text{R 3}}$
9.	$\dfrac{\text{P}-\text{K 5}}{\text{P}\times\text{P}}$	$\overline{\text{Q}-\text{Kt 3}}$	$\dfrac{\text{P}-\text{K R 4}}{\text{P}-\text{Kt 5}}$
10.	$\dfrac{\text{Kt}\times\text{K P}}{\text{Q}\times\text{Q ch.}}$	$\dfrac{\text{Q}-\text{K 2}}{\text{K}-\text{Q 1 !}}$	$\dfrac{\text{Kt}-\text{K 1}}{\text{P}-\text{K B 4 !}}$
11.	$\dfrac{\text{Kt}\times\text{Q}}{\text{B}-\text{K 3}}$	$\dfrac{\text{B}-\text{Q 3}}{\text{B}-\text{B 4 !}}$	$\dfrac{\text{P}\times\text{P}}{\text{Kt}\times\text{P}}$

	(13)	(14)	(15)
12.	$\dfrac{B \times B}{P \times B}$	$\dfrac{B \times B}{Q \times B}$	$\dfrac{B \times Kt\ P}{Kt - Kt\ 6\ ch.}$
13.	$\dfrac{Kt - Kt\ 6}{R - R\ 2}$	$\dfrac{K\ P \times P}{B\ P \times P}$	$\dfrac{K - Kt\ 1}{B \times B}$
14.	$\dfrac{P \times P}{B \times P}$	$\dfrac{P \times P}{P \times P}$	$\dfrac{Q \times B}{B \times P\ ch.}$
15.	$\dfrac{P \times P\ +}{-}$	$\dfrac{R \times R}{B \times R}$	$\dfrac{K - R\ 2}{Kt \times R\ !}$

Nos. 13 and 14.   Position after White's 9th move.

BLACK.

WHITE.

	(14)	(15)
16.	$\dfrac{Kt - K\ 4}{K - Q\ 2}$	$\dfrac{K \times Kt\ !}{Kt - B\ 3}$
17.	$\dfrac{Kt \times P}{B \times P}$	$\dfrac{B \times P}{Q - Kt\ 3}$
18.	$\dfrac{Kt \times B}{Q \times Kt}$	$\dfrac{Q - K\ 2\ ch.}{K - Q\ 2\ +}$
19.	$Q - K\ 4\ +$	

	(16)	(17)	(18)
1.	—	—	—
2.	—	—	—

	16)	(17)	(18)
3.	—	—	—
4.	—	—	—
5.	—	—	—
6.	—	—	—

Nos. 15, 16, and 17.   Position after Black's 10th move.

BLACK.

WHITE.

7.			$\dfrac{\text{Q}-\text{R 3}}{\text{P}-\text{K R 4}}$
8.	—	—	$\dfrac{\text{P}-\text{K R 4}}{\text{P}-\text{K B 3}}$
9.	—	—	$\dfrac{\text{Kt}-\text{B 3}}{\text{B}-\text{Kt 5}}$
10.	—	—	$\dfrac{\text{P}-\text{K 5 !}}{\text{Q P}\times\text{P}}$
11.	$\dfrac{\text{P}-\text{K Kt 3}}{\text{Q}-\text{K 3 !}}$	$\dfrac{\text{Kt}-\text{Q 3}}{\text{B}\times\text{P !}}$	$\dfrac{\text{P}\times\text{P}}{\text{P}\times\text{P}}$
12.	$\dfrac{\text{P}-\text{Q 5}}{\text{Q}-\text{B 2}}$	$\dfrac{\text{Kt}\times\text{P}}{\text{B}\times\text{Kt !}}$	$\dfrac{\text{Kt}\times\text{P}}{\text{B}\times\text{B ch.}}$

	(16)	(17)	(18)
13.	$\dfrac{\text{Kt}-\text{Kt 5}}{\text{Kt}-\text{R 3}}$	$\dfrac{\text{Kt}-\text{Q 5}}{\text{Q}-\text{Kt 2 !}}$	$\dfrac{\text{Q}\times\text{B}}{\text{Kt}-\text{K 2}}$
14.	$\dfrac{\text{P}\times\text{P !}}{\text{P}\times\text{P}}$	$\dfrac{\text{Kt}\times\text{P ch.}}{\text{K}-\text{Q 2}}$	$\dfrac{\text{Q}-\text{B 4}}{\text{Q}-\text{Q R 3}}$
15.	$\dfrac{\text{K B}\times\text{P}}{\text{B}\times\text{B}}$	$\dfrac{\text{Kt}\times\text{R}}{\text{B}\times\text{Kt P}}$	$\underline{\text{Kt}-\text{Kt 5}}$ and wins.
16.	$\dfrac{\text{Q}\times\text{B}}{\text{Kt}\times\text{P}}$	$\dfrac{\text{B}\times\text{B}}{\text{Q}\times\text{B}}$	
17.		$\dfrac{\text{P}\times\text{P !}}{\text{P}-\text{K R 4}}$	
18.		$\dfrac{\text{R}-\text{Q Kt 1}}{\text{Q}-\text{B 3 !}}$	

Nos. 15 to 19.   Position after White's 7th move.

BLACK.

WHITE.

	(19)	(20)	(21)
1.	—	—	—
2.	—	—	—
3.	—	—	—

	(19)	(20)	(21)
4.	—	—	—
5.	—	—	—
6.	—	$\overline{\text{Kt—K 2}}$	—
7.	$\overline{\text{Kt—Q B 3}}$	$\dfrac{\text{Kt—B 3 !}}{\text{Q—R 4 !}}$	$\dfrac{\text{P—K 5}}{\overline{\text{Kt—B 4}}}$
8.	$\dfrac{\text{Kt—Kt 5}}{\text{K—Q 1}}$	$\dfrac{\text{P—K R 4}}{\overline{\text{P—K R 3}}}$	$\dfrac{\text{Kt—B 3}}{\overline{\text{Q—R 4}}}$
9.	$\dfrac{\text{P—K 5}}{\overline{\text{P—Q R 3}} \text{ !}}$	$\dfrac{\text{P—K 5 !}}{\overline{\text{P—K B 3}} \text{ ! } (a)}$	$\dfrac{\text{K—Kt !}}{\overline{\text{Kt—B 3}}}$
10.	$\dfrac{\text{Kt—Q B 3}}{\overline{\text{B—B 4}} \text{ !}}$	$\dfrac{\text{B—K 2}}{\overline{\text{Q—Kt 3}}}$	$\dfrac{\text{Kt—Kt 5}}{\overline{\text{K—Q 1}}}$
11.	$\dfrac{\text{Kt—B 3}}{\overline{\text{Q—R 3}}}$	$\dfrac{\text{B—Q 3}}{\overline{\text{P—K B 4}}}$	$\dfrac{\text{P—K R 4}}{\overline{\text{Kt×R P}}}$
12.	$\dfrac{\text{P—K R 4}}{\overline{\text{P—K B 3}}}$	$\dfrac{\text{P×P}}{\overline{\text{P×P}}}$	$\dfrac{\text{K—B 2}}{\overline{\text{P—Q R 3}}}$
13.	$\dfrac{\text{Kt—Q 5 !}}{\overline{\text{B—K 5}} \text{ !}}$	$\dfrac{\text{R×R}}{\overline{\text{B×R}}}$	$\dfrac{\text{Kt—B 3}}{\overline{\text{Q—Kt 5}}}$
14.	$\dfrac{\text{Kt×K B P !}}{\overline{\text{B×K Kt !}}}$	$\dfrac{\text{P—K Kt 3}}{\overline{\text{Q—R 4}}}$	$\dfrac{\text{Kt×Kt}}{\overline{\text{Q×Q}}}$
15.	$\dfrac{\text{B×B}}{\overline{\text{Kt×Kt}}}$	$\dfrac{\text{P×P}}{\overline{\text{Q—R 6}} \text{ ch.}}$	$\dfrac{\text{Kt×Q}}{\overline{\text{P×Kt}}}$
16.	$\dfrac{\text{P×Kt}}{\overline{\text{Q×B P}}}$	$\dfrac{\text{K—B 2}}{\overline{\text{P—Kt 5}}}$	$\dfrac{\text{P—B 3}}{\overline{\text{P—B 3}}}$
17.	$\dfrac{\text{R P×P}}{\overline{\text{Q×Kt P}}}$	$\dfrac{\text{Kt—K Kt 1}}{\overline{\text{Q—R 7}} \text{ ch.}}$	$\dfrac{\text{B×P}}{\overline{\text{P×P}}}$
18.		$\dfrac{\text{K—B 1}}{\overline{\text{P—Kt 6}}}$	$\dfrac{\text{P×P}}{\overline{\text{B×P}}}$
19.		$\dfrac{\text{B—K 3}}{} =$	$\dfrac{\text{R×P}}{\overline{\text{R—B 1}}}$
20.			$\dfrac{\text{K—K 3}}{} =$

(a) I 19. $\dfrac{}{\text{Kt—B 4}}$; 10. $\dfrac{\text{K—Kt 1}}{}$.

	(22)	(23)	(24)
1.	—	—	—
2.	—	—	—
3.	—	—	—
4.	—	—	—
5.	$\dfrac{\text{Kt} - \text{K B 3}}{\text{Q} - \text{R 4}}$	—	—

Nos. 22 to 25. Position after Black's 6th move.

BLACK.

WHITE.

	(22)	(23)	(24)
6.	$\dfrac{\text{P} - \text{K R 4}}{\text{B} - \text{Kt 2}}$	—	—
7.	$\dfrac{\text{P} - \text{Q 4}}{\text{P} - \text{K R 3}}$	$\dfrac{\text{K} - \text{Kt 1}}{\text{B} - \text{Q 5}}$	$\dfrac{\text{R} - \text{R 2}}{\text{P} - \text{Kt 5}}$
8.	$\dfrac{\text{P} - \text{K 5}}{\text{Kt} - \text{K 2}}$	$\dfrac{\text{K} - \text{R 2}}{\text{P} - \text{Kt 5}}$	$\dfrac{\text{Kt} - \text{Kt 5}}{\text{Kt} - \text{K R 3}}$
9.	$\dfrac{\text{Kt} - \text{B 3}}{\text{Kt} - \text{B 4}}$	$\dfrac{\text{Kt} \times \text{B}}{\text{P} - \text{Kt 6 ch.}}$	$\dfrac{\text{P} - \text{Q 4}}{\text{P} - \text{Q 4}}$
10.	$\dfrac{\text{Kt} - \text{K 4}}{\text{P} - \text{Q 3}}$	$\dfrac{\text{K} - \text{R 3}}{\text{P} - \text{Q 4 d. ch.}}$	$\dfrac{\text{B} \times \text{P !}}{\text{P} - \text{Kt 6}}$

	(22)	(23)	(24)
11.	$\dfrac{\text{K P} \times \text{P}}{\text{B P} \times \text{P}}$	$\dfrac{\text{Kt} - \text{B 5}}{\text{Q} \times \text{Q}}$	$\dfrac{\text{B} \times \text{P ch.}}{\text{Q} \times \text{B}}$
12.	$\dfrac{\text{Q} - \text{K 2}}{\text{Kt} - \text{Q 1}}$	$\dfrac{\text{R} \times \text{Q}}{\text{Kt} - \text{K R 3}}$	$\dfrac{\text{Kt} \times \text{Q}}{\text{B} - \text{Kt 5}}$
13.	$\dfrac{\text{P} - \text{B 3}}{\text{R} - \text{K 1}}$	$\dfrac{\text{P} - \text{R 5}}{\text{P} \times \text{K P}}$	$\dfrac{\text{Q} - \text{K 1}}{\text{P} \times \text{R}}$
14.	$\dfrac{\text{K} - \text{Kt 1}}{\text{P} - \text{Kt 5}}$	$\dfrac{\text{K} - \text{R 4}}{\text{Kt} \times \text{Kt ch.}}$	$\dfrac{\text{K} - \text{B 2}}{\text{B} \times \text{P ch. and wins.}}$
15	$\dfrac{\text{Kt} - \text{Q 2}}{\text{P} - \text{B 6}}$	$\dfrac{\text{K} - \text{Kt 5}}{\text{P} - \text{B 6}}$	
16.	$\dfrac{\text{Q} - \text{Q 3}}{\text{P} \times \text{P}}$	$\dfrac{\text{K} - \text{B 4}}{\text{P} - \text{B 7 and wins.}}$	
17.	$\dfrac{\text{K} \times \text{P}}{\text{P} - \text{Q 4}}$		
18.	$\dfrac{\text{B} \times \text{P}}{\text{Kt} \times \text{R P ch. +}}$		

	(25)	(26)	(27)
1.	—	—	—
2.	—	—	—
3.	—	—	—
4.	—	$\dfrac{}{\text{Kt} - \text{Q B 3}}$	$\dfrac{}{\text{P} - \text{K Kt 4}}$
5.	—	$\dfrac{\text{Kt} - \text{K B 3}}{\text{Q} - \text{R 4}}$	$\dfrac{\text{Q} - \text{B 3}}{\text{Kt} - \text{Q B 3}}$
6.	—	$\dfrac{\text{P} - \text{Q 4}}{\text{P} - \text{K Kt 4}}$	$\dfrac{\text{P} - \text{K Kt 3}}{\text{Q} - \text{R 3}}$
7.	$\dfrac{\text{B} - \text{K 2}}{\text{P} - \text{Kt 5}}$	$\dfrac{\text{P} - \text{K R 4}}{\text{B} - \text{Kt 2}}$	$\dfrac{\text{P} \times \text{P}}{\text{P} \times \text{P}}$
8.	$\dfrac{\text{Kt} - \text{K 1}}{\text{Kt} - \text{K B 3}}$	$\dfrac{\text{Kt} - \text{B 3}}{\text{Kt} \times \text{P}}$	$\dfrac{\text{P} - \text{Q 3}}{\text{Kt} - \text{Q 5}}$
9.	$\dfrac{\text{Kt} - \text{B 3}}{\text{Q} - \text{Kt 3}}$	$\dfrac{\text{Kt} \times \text{Kt}}{\text{Q} \times \text{Q}}$	$\dfrac{\text{Q} - \text{B 2}}{\text{B} - \text{B 4}}$
10.	$\dfrac{\text{P} - \text{Q 3}}{\text{Kt} - \text{R 4}}$	$\dfrac{\text{Kt} \times \text{Q}}{\text{B} \times \text{Kt}}$	$\dfrac{\text{Q B} \times \text{P}}{\text{Kt} \times \text{P}}$

	(25)	(26)	(27)
11.	Kt--Q 5 / Kt—Kt 6 ch.	P×P / B—K 4	B×Q / B×Q
12.	K—Kt 1 / B—Q 5 ch.	R—R 4 / Kt—K 2	B—Kt 7 / B—Q 5
13.	K—R 2 / Kt×B +	Q B×P / Kt—Kt 3	
		B×B	
		Kt×B	

	(28)	(29)	(30)
1.	—	—	—
2.	—	—	—
3.	—	—	P—K Kt 4
4.	—	—	P—K R 4 / B—Kt 2
5.	—	P—Q 3	P—Q 4 / P—K R 3
6.	—	P—K Kt 3 / Q—Kt 5	P×P / P×P
7.	—	P—Q 4 / Q×Q	R×R / B×R
8.	B—Q 3	Kt×Q / B—R 3	Q—R 5 / Q—B 3
9.	Kt—B 3 ! / Kt—K 2	P×P / P×P	P—K 5 / Q—Kt 2
10.	Kt—Q 5 / P—B 4	Kt—B 3 / B—R 6 ch.	Kt—K R 3 +
11.	K Kt—K 2 / R—K B 1	K—B 2 / Kt—K 2	
12.	B×P / B×B	Kt—K 2 / Kt—Kt 3	
13.	Kt×B / Kt—K 4	Kt—K 1 +	
14.	Q—R 5 ch. / Q×Q		
15.	Kt×Q / P×P d. ch. and wins.		

	(31)	(32)	(33)
1.	—	—	—
2.	—	—	—
3.	$\overline{\text{P}-\text{K B 4}}$	—	—
4.	$\frac{\text{Q}-\text{K 2}}{\text{Q}-\text{R 5 ch.}}$	$\frac{\text{Kt}-\text{Q B 3}}{\text{Q}-\text{R 5 ch.}}$	—
5.	$\frac{\text{K}-\text{Q 1 !}}{\text{P}\times\text{P}}$	$\frac{\text{K}-\text{B 1}}{\text{Kt}-\text{K B 3}}$	$\overline{\text{P}\times\text{P}}$
6.	$\frac{\text{Q}\times\text{P ch.}}{\text{B}-\text{K 2}}$	$\frac{\text{Kt}-\text{B 3}}{\text{Q}-\text{R 4}}$	$\frac{\text{Kt}\times\text{P}}{\text{P}-\text{Q B 3}}$
7.	$\frac{\text{P}-\text{Q 4}}{\text{Kt}-\text{K B 3}}$	$\frac{\text{P}-\text{K 5}}{\text{Kt}-\text{K 5}}$	$\frac{\text{Q}-\text{K 2}}{\text{K}-\text{Q 1}}$
8.	$\frac{\text{Q}\times\text{B P}}{\text{Q}\times\text{Q}}$	$\frac{\text{Kt}-\text{Q 5}}{\text{Kt}-\text{Kt 6 ch.}}$	$\frac{\text{Kt}-\text{K B 3}}{\text{Q}-\text{K 2}}$
9.	$\frac{\text{B}\times\text{Q}}{}$ $=$	$\frac{\text{K}-\text{Kt 1}}{\text{Kt}\times\text{R}}$	$\frac{\text{Q Kt}-\text{K K 5}}{\text{Q}\times\text{Q ch.}}$
10.		$\frac{\text{Kt}\times\text{P ch.}}{\text{K}-\text{Q 1}}$	$\frac{\text{B}\times\text{Q}}{\text{K}-\text{K 1}}$
11.		$\frac{\text{Kt}\times\text{R}}{\text{Kt}-\text{Kt 6}}$	$\frac{\text{Kt}-\text{K 5}}{\text{B}-\text{K 2}}$
12.		$\frac{\text{P}\times\text{Kt}}{\text{P}\times\text{P}}$	$\frac{\text{Kt}-\text{B 7}}{\text{B}\times\text{Kt}}$
13.		$\frac{\text{P}-\text{Q 4}}{\text{B}-\text{K 2}}$	$\frac{\text{Kt}\times\text{B}}{\text{P}-\text{K R 3}}$
14.		$\frac{\text{B}-\text{B 4}}{\text{Q}-\text{Kt 5}}$	$\frac{\text{B}-\text{R 5 ch.}}{\text{K}-\text{K 2}}$
15.		$\frac{\text{Kt}-\text{Kt 5}}{\text{Q}\times\text{B}}$	$\frac{\text{Kt}-\text{B 7}}{\text{Kt}-\text{K B 3}}$
16.		$\frac{\text{Kt}-\text{B 7 ch.}}{\text{K}-\text{K 1}}$	$\frac{\text{Kt}\times\text{R}}{\text{Kt}\times\text{B}}$
17.		$\frac{\text{Q}-\text{Q 3}}{\text{B}-\text{Q 1}}$	$\frac{\text{Kt}-\text{Kt 6 ch.}}{\text{K}-\text{B 3}}$
18.		$\frac{\text{Kt}-\text{Q 6 ch.}}{\text{K}-\text{B 1}}$	$\frac{\text{Kt}-\text{R 4}}{\text{P}-\text{K Kt 4}}$
19.		$\overline{\text{R}-\text{K B 1}}$ and wins.	$\overline{\text{Kt}-\text{K B 3}}$ +

	(34)	(35)	(36)
1.	—	—	—
2.	—	—	—
3.	$\overline{P-Q\,4}$	—	$\overline{P-Q\,B\,3}$
4.	$\dfrac{B\times P}{Kt-K\,B\,3}$	—	$\dfrac{P-Q\,4}{P-Q\,4}$
5.	$\dfrac{Q-K\,2}{Kt\times B}$	$\dfrac{Kt-Q\,B\,3}{B-Q\,Kt\,5}$	$\dfrac{P\times P}{P\times P}$
6.	$\dfrac{P\times Kt\ d.\ ch.}{B-K\,2}$	$\dfrac{K\,Kt-K\,2}{B\times Kt}$	$\dfrac{B-Kt\,5\ ch.}{Kt-B\,3}$
7.	$\dfrac{Q-B\,3}{B-R\,5\ ch.}$	$\dfrac{Q\,P\times B}{P-B\,3}$	$\dfrac{Q\,B\times P}{Q-Kt\,3}$
8.	$\dfrac{P-K\,Kt\,3}{P\times P}$	$\dfrac{B-B\,4}{Q\times Q\ ch.}$	$\dfrac{Q-K\,2\ ch.}{B-K\,3}$
9.	$\dfrac{P\times P}{B-Kt\,4}$	$\dfrac{K\times Q}{Kt\times P}$	$\dfrac{P-B\,3}{0-0-0}$
10.	$\overline{Kt-B\,3}$ =	$\overline{K-K\,1}$ =	$\overline{Kt-B\,3}$ =

	(37)	(38)	(39)
1.		—	—
2			—
3.	$\overline{Q-R\,5}\ ch.$	—	—
4.	$\dfrac{K-B\,1}{B-B\,4}$	$\overline{Kt-K\,B\,3}$	$Q\overline{-B\,3}$
5	$\dfrac{P-Q\,4}{B-Kt\,3}$	$\dfrac{Kt-K\,B\,3}{Q-R\,4}$	$\dfrac{Kt-Q\,B\,3}{P-B\,3}$
6.	$\dfrac{Kt-K\,B\,3}{Q-K\,2}$	$\dfrac{P-K\,R\,4}{P-K\,Kt\,4}$	$\dfrac{P-Q\,4}{P-Q\,3}$
7.	$\dfrac{Q\,B\times P}{Q\times K\,P}$	$\dfrac{Kt-B\,3}{P-K\,R\,3}$	$\dfrac{Kt-B\,3}{P-K\,Kt\,4}$
8.	$\dfrac{B\times P\ ch.}{K-B\,1}$	$\dfrac{P-K\,5}{Kt-Kt\,1}$	$\dfrac{P-K\,R\,4}{P-K\,R\,3}$
9.	$\dfrac{B-Kt\,3}{Kt-K\,R\,3}$	$\dfrac{B-K\,2}{P-Kt\,5}$	$\dfrac{P-K\,5}{P\times K\,P}$

	(37)	(38)	(39
10.	$\dfrac{\text{Kt}-\text{B }3}{\text{Q}-\text{K }2}$	$\dfrac{\text{Kt}-\text{R }2}{\text{Q}\times\text{K P}}$	$\dfrac{\text{P}\times\text{P}}{\text{Q}-\text{Kt }2}$
11.	$\dfrac{\text{B}-\text{Kt }3}{\text{P}-\text{B }3}$	$\dfrac{\text{P}-\text{Q }4+}{}$	$\dfrac{\text{Q}-\text{Q }4}{\text{B}-\text{K Kt }5}$
12.	$\dfrac{\text{Q}-\text{Q }2}{\text{P}-\text{Q }4}$		$\dfrac{\text{P}\times\text{P}}{\text{P}\times\text{P}}$
13.	$\dfrac{\text{R}-\text{K }1+}{}$		$\dfrac{\text{R}\times\text{R}}{\text{Q}\times\text{R}}$
14.			$\dfrac{\text{Kt}\times\text{P}}{\text{Q}-\text{R }8\text{ ch.}}$
15.			$\dfrac{\text{Q}-\text{Kt }1}{\text{Q}\times\text{Q ch.}}$
16.			$\text{K}\times\text{Q}+$

	(40)	(41)	(42)
1.	—	—	—
2.	—	—	—
3.	—	—	—
4.	—	$\dfrac{\text{P}-\text{Q }3}{}$	—
		$\dfrac{\text{Q}-\text{B }3}{\text{P}-\text{K Kt }4}$	
5.	$\dfrac{\text{Kt}-\text{K }2}{}$	$\dfrac{\text{Q}-\text{B }3}{\text{P}-\text{K Kt }4}$	$\dfrac{\text{P}-\text{Q }4}{\text{B}-\text{K }3}$
6.	$\dfrac{\text{P}-\text{Q }4}{\text{P}-\text{Q }3}$	$\dfrac{\text{P}-\text{K Kt }3}{\text{Q}-\text{Kt }5}$	$\dfrac{\text{Q}-\text{Q }3}{\text{B}\times\text{B}}$
7.	$\dfrac{\text{Kt}-\text{B }3}{\text{P}-\text{K Kt }4}$	$\dfrac{\text{P}-\text{Q }3}{\text{B}-\text{R }3}$	$\dfrac{\text{Q}\times\text{B}}{\text{P}-\text{Q B }3}$
8.	$\dfrac{\text{P}-\text{K R }4}{\text{P}-\text{K R }3}$	$\dfrac{\text{Q}\times\text{Q}}{\text{B}\times\text{Q}}$	$\dfrac{\text{Q}-\text{Kt }3}{\text{P}-\text{Q Kt }3}$
9.	$\dfrac{\text{P}-\text{K }5}{\text{Q}-\text{Kt }2}$	$\dfrac{\text{P}-\text{K R }4}{\text{P}\times\text{R P}}$	$\dfrac{\text{Q}-\text{K R }3}{\text{Q}\times\text{Q}}$
10.	$\dfrac{\text{R P}\times\text{P}}{\text{R P}\times\text{P}}$	$\dfrac{\text{B}\times\text{B}=}{}$	$\dfrac{\text{Kt}\times\text{Q}}{\text{Kt}-\text{B }3}$
11.	$\dfrac{\text{R}\times\text{R}}{\text{Q}\times\text{R}}$		$\dfrac{\text{Kt}-\text{B }3}{\text{Q Kt}-\text{Q }2=}$
12.	$\dfrac{\text{Kt}-\text{K }4}{\text{P}\times\text{P}}$		

(40) *(contd.)*

13. $\dfrac{P \times P}{Q - R\,8 \text{ ch.}}$

14. $\dfrac{Kt - Kt\,1}{Kt - Q\,2}$

15. $\dfrac{Kt \times P}{Kt \times P}$

16. $\dfrac{}{Q - K\,2\,+}$

THE BISHOP'S GAMBIT—GAMES.

	(1) McDonnell / La Bourdonnais	(2) McDonnell / La Bourdonnais	(3) McDonnell / La Bourdonnais
1.	$\dfrac{P-K\,4}{P-K\,4}$	$\dfrac{P-K\,4}{P-K\,4}$	$\dfrac{P-K\,4}{P-K\,4}$
2.	$\dfrac{P-K\,B\,4}{P\times P}$	$\dfrac{P-K\,B\,4}{P\times P}$	$\dfrac{P-K\,B\,4}{P\times P}$
3.	$\dfrac{B-B\,4\,(a)}{Q-R\,5 \text{ ch.}}$	$\dfrac{B-B\,4}{Q-R\,5 \text{ ch.}}$	$\dfrac{B-B\,4}{Q-R\,5 \text{ ch.}}$
4.	$\dfrac{K-B\,1}{P-K\,Kt\,4}$	$\dfrac{K-B\,1}{P-K\,Kt\,4}$	$\dfrac{K-B\,1}{P-Q\,3}$
5.	$\dfrac{Kt-Q\,B\,3}{B-Kt\,2}$	$\dfrac{Kt-Q\,B\,3}{B-Kt\,2}$	$\dfrac{P-Q\,4}{B-Kt\,5}$
6.	$\dfrac{P-Q\,4}{P-Q\,3}$	$\dfrac{P-Q\,4}{Kt-Q\,B\,3}$	$\dfrac{Q-Q\,3}{Kt-Q\,B\,3}$
7.	$\dfrac{B-K\,2}{Q\,Kt-B\,3}$	$\dfrac{P-K\,5}{K\,Kt-K\,2}$	$\dfrac{B\times P \text{ ch. }(b)}{K\times B}$
8.	$\dfrac{P-K\,5}{K\,Kt-K\,2}$	$\dfrac{Kt-B\,3}{Q-R\,4}$	$\dfrac{Q-Kt\,3 \text{ ch.}}{K-Kt\,3}$
9.	$\dfrac{Kt-Kt\,5}{0-0}$	$\dfrac{Kt-K\,4}{P-K\,R\,3}$	$\dfrac{Q\times P}{Kt\times P}$
10.	$\dfrac{Kt\times B\,P}{R-Kt\,1}$	$\dfrac{Kt-B\,6 \text{ ch.}}{B\times Kt}$	$\dfrac{Q\times R}{Kt-K\,B\,3\,(c)}$
11.	$\dfrac{Kt-B\,3}{Q-R\,3}$	$\dfrac{P\times B}{P-Q\,4}$	$\dfrac{Kt-Q\,R\,3}{P-B\,6\,(d)}$

(a) This was a favourite opening of McDonnell's; he bestowed much time and labour on its analysis, and discovered many skilful methods of diversifying the attack.

(b) This is not good play, because to recover the Piece, White is obliged to take his Queen too far from the point of action.

(c) Indispensable, to prevent the Queen checking at K 8.

(d) The winning move.

	(1)	(2)	(3)
12.	$\dfrac{\text{P} \times \text{P}}{\text{Kt—B 4}}$	$\dfrac{\text{B—Q 3}}{\text{Kt—B 4}}$	$\dfrac{\text{P—K Kt 3}}{\text{B—R 6 ch.}}$
13.	$\dfrac{\text{P—B 3}}{\text{Kt—Kt 6 ch.}}$	$\dfrac{\text{Q—K 1 ch.}}{\text{K—Q 1}}$	$\dfrac{\text{K—K 1}}{\text{Q—Kt 5}}$
14.	$\dfrac{\text{P} \times \text{Kt}}{\text{Q} \times \text{R ch.}}$	$\dfrac{\text{Kt—K 5}}{\text{Kt (B 4)} \times \text{P } (b)}$	$\dfrac{\text{B—K 3}}{\text{P—Q 4 } (f)}$
15.	$\dfrac{\text{K—B 2}}{\text{P} \times \text{P ch.}}$	$\dfrac{\text{P—B 3}}{\text{Kt} \times \text{Kt}}$	$\dfrac{\text{Q} \times \text{R P}}{\text{Kt—B 3}}$
16.	$\dfrac{\text{K} \times \text{P}}{\text{Q} \times \text{Q}}$	$\dfrac{\text{Q} \times \text{Kt}}{\text{Kt—B 3}}$	$\dfrac{\text{Q} \times \text{P}}{\text{P—Q 5}}$
17.	$\dfrac{\text{B} \times \text{Q}}{\text{P—K R 3}}$	$\dfrac{\text{Q} \times \text{Q P ch.}}{\text{K—K 1}}$	$\dfrac{\text{B—Q 2}}{\text{Q} \times \text{K P ch.}}$
18.	$\dfrac{\text{P—Kt 3}}{\text{P—Kt 4}}$	$\dfrac{\text{B—Kt 5 } (c)}{\text{B—K 3}}$	$\dfrac{\text{K—Q 1}}{\text{P—B 7}}$
19.	$\dfrac{\text{B—K 3}}{\text{P—B 4}}$	$\dfrac{\text{B} \times \text{Kt ch.}}{\text{K—B 1}}$	$\dfrac{\text{Kt} \times \text{B}}{\text{Q—B 6 ch.}}$
20.	$\dfrac{\text{P—Q 5}}{\text{P—B 5 ch.}}$	$\dfrac{\text{Q—B 5 ch.}}{\text{K—Kt 1}}$	$\dfrac{\text{K—B 1}}{\text{Q} \times \text{R ch. and wins}}$
21.	$\dfrac{\text{K—R 2}}{\text{P} \times \text{B}}$	$\dfrac{\text{B—B 3}}{\text{Q—Kt 3}}$	—
22.	$\dfrac{\text{P} \times \text{Kt}}{\text{P—K Kt 5}}$	$\dfrac{\text{Q—Q 4}}{\text{P—B 4}}$	—
23.	$\dfrac{\text{Kt—Q 4}}{\text{B—K 4 ch.}}$	$\dfrac{\text{Q—K 5}}{\text{R—K 1}}$	—
24.	$\dfrac{\text{K—Kt 1}}{\text{B} \times \text{P}}$	$\dfrac{\text{B—K 2 } (d)}{\text{P—B 6}}$	—
25.	$\dfrac{\text{Kt (B 7)} \times \text{P}}{\text{B—Q B 4}}$	$\dfrac{\text{K—B 2 } (e)}{\text{P} \times \text{B}}$	—
26.	$\dfrac{\text{P—Kt 4 } (a)}{\text{B—Kt 3}}$	$\dfrac{\text{B—K 3}}{\text{P—Kt 3}}$	—
27.	$\dfrac{\text{Kt—Q 6}}{\text{B} \times \text{Kt}}$	$\dfrac{\text{P—K R 4}}{\text{B—Q 2}}$	—

(a) B—K 2 would have been better play we believe.

(b) Had Black checked with his Knight and taken the Rook, he would have been mated in five moves.

(c) This portion of the game is played by Mr. McDonnell with great judgment.

(d) It would have been better to take the Q B P with Q.

(e) It is obvious he would have lost his Queen by taking the Pawn.

(f) An excellent move to exclude the Queen.

(g) This is not advisable play.

	(1)	(2)	(1) (*contd.*)
28.	$\dfrac{\text{P}\times\text{B}}{\text{R}\times\text{P}}$	$\dfrac{\text{Q}-\text{Q}5}{\text{Q}\times\text{P ch.}}$	36. $\dfrac{\text{R}\times\text{P}}{\text{R}\times\text{R ch.}}$
29.	$\dfrac{\text{Kt}\times\text{B}}{\text{R}\times\text{Kt}}$	$\dfrac{\text{K}\times\text{P}}{\text{B}-\text{Kt}5\text{ ch.}}$	37. $\dfrac{\text{K}\times\text{R}}{\text{P}-\text{K R}4}$
30.	$\dfrac{\text{P}-\text{Q}5}{\text{K}-\text{B}2}$	$\dfrac{\text{K}-\text{Q}2}{\text{R}-\text{Q}1}$	38. $\dfrac{\text{K}-\text{K}4}{\text{P}-\text{R}5}$
31.	$\dfrac{\text{B}-\text{Kt}3}{\text{K}-\text{K}2}$	Resigns	39. $\dfrac{\text{B}-\text{Q}1}{\text{P}-\text{R}6}$
32.	$\dfrac{\text{K}-\text{B}1}{\text{R}-\text{K}5}$	—	40. $\dfrac{\text{P}\times\text{P}}{\text{P}\times\text{P}}$
33.	$\dfrac{\text{K}-\text{K}2}{\text{R}-\text{K B}1}$	—	41. $\dfrac{\text{B}-\text{B}3}{\text{P}-\text{R}7}$
34.	$\dfrac{\text{K}-\text{Q}3}{\text{R}-\text{K}4}$	—	42. $\dfrac{\text{B}-\text{Kt}2}{\text{R}-\text{K B}8}$
35.	$\dfrac{\text{R}-\text{K}1}{\text{K}-\text{Q}3}$ (*a*)	—	43. Resigns

	(4)	(5)	(6)
	$\dfrac{\text{Mr. ——}}{\text{Staunton}}$	$\dfrac{\text{Devinck}}{\text{Kieseritsky}}$	$\dfrac{\text{Max Lange}}{\text{Anderssen}}$
1.	$\dfrac{\text{P}-\text{K}4}{\text{P}-\text{K}4}$	$\dfrac{\text{P}-\text{K}4}{\text{P}-\text{K}4}$	$\dfrac{\text{P}-\text{K}4}{\text{P}-\text{K}4}$
2.	$\dfrac{\text{P}-\text{K B}4}{\text{P}\times\text{P}}$	$\dfrac{\text{P}-\text{K B}4}{\text{P}\times\text{P}}$	$\dfrac{\text{P}-\text{K B}4}{\text{P}\times\text{P}}$
3.	$\dfrac{\text{B}-\text{B}4}{\text{P}-\text{Q}4}$	$\dfrac{\text{B}-\text{B}4}{\text{P}-\text{Q Kt}4}$	$\dfrac{\text{B}-\text{B}4}{\text{Q}-\text{R}5\text{ ch.}}$
4.	$\dfrac{\text{P}\times\text{P}\ (b)}{\text{Kt}-\text{K B}3}$	$\dfrac{\text{B}\times\text{Kt P}}{\text{Q}-\text{R}5\text{ ch.}}$	$\dfrac{\text{K}-\text{B}1}{\text{P}-\text{K Kt}4}$
5.	$\dfrac{\text{Q}-\text{B}3}{\text{B}-\text{Q}3}$	$\dfrac{\text{K}-\text{B}1}{\text{B}-\text{Kt}2}$	$\dfrac{\text{Kt}-\text{Q B}3}{\text{B}-\text{Kt}2}$
6.	$\dfrac{\text{P}-\text{K R}3}{0-0}$	$\dfrac{\text{Kt}-\text{Q B}3}{\text{B}-\text{Kt}5}$	$\dfrac{\text{P}-\text{Q}4}{\text{Kt}-\text{K}2}$
7.	$\dfrac{\text{P}-\text{B}3}{\text{P}-\text{B}3}$	$\dfrac{\text{Q}-\text{B}3}{\text{P}-\text{K B}4}$	$\dfrac{\text{P}-\text{K Kt}3}{\text{P}\times\text{P}}$
8.	$\dfrac{\text{P}\times\text{P}}{\text{Kt}\times\text{P}}$	$\dfrac{\text{P}-\text{Q}3}{\text{B}\times\text{Kt}}$	$\dfrac{\text{K}-\text{Kt}2}{\text{Q}-\text{R}3}$
9.	$\dfrac{\text{P}-\text{Q}4}{\text{Kt}-\text{K}5}$	$\dfrac{\text{P}\times\text{B}}{\text{P}\times\text{P}}$	$\dfrac{\text{P}\times\text{P}}{\text{Q}-\text{K Kt}3}$

(*a*) This game is very cleverly played by La Bourdonnais.
(*b*) It is better to take the Pawn with the Bishop.

	(4)	(5)	(6)
10.	$\dfrac{\text{Q B}\times\text{P}}{\text{Q}-\text{R 5 ch.}}$	$\dfrac{\text{P}\times\text{P}}{\text{Kt}-\text{K B 3}}$	$\dfrac{\text{Kt}-\text{B 3}}{\text{P}-\text{K R 3}}$
11.	$\dfrac{\text{P}-\text{K Kt 3}}{\text{Kt}\times\text{Kt P}}$	$\dfrac{\text{B}-\text{Q 3}}{0-0}$	$\dfrac{\text{R}-\text{B 1}}{0-0\ (a)}$
12.	$\dfrac{\text{B}\times\text{B}}{\text{Kt}\times\text{R d. c}\text{ł.}}$	$\dfrac{\text{B}-\text{R 3}}{\text{P}-\text{Q 3}}$	$\dfrac{\text{Kt}-\text{K 5}}{\text{B}\times\text{Kt}}$
13.	$\dfrac{\text{K}-\text{B 1}}{\text{B}-\text{K 3}}$	$\dfrac{\text{B}-\text{B 4 ch.}}{\text{K}-\text{R 1}}$	$\dfrac{\text{P}\times\text{B}}{\text{Kt}-\text{Q B 3}}$
14.	$\dfrac{\text{B}-\text{Q 3}}{\text{Q R}-\text{Q 1}}$	$\dfrac{\text{B}-\text{Q 5}}{\text{Kt}\times\text{B}}$	$\dfrac{\text{R}-\text{B 6}}{\text{Q}-\text{Kt 2}}$
15.	$\dfrac{\text{B}-\text{R 2}}{\text{B}-\text{Q 4}}$	$\dfrac{\text{P}\times\text{Kt}}{\text{Kt}-\text{Q 2}}$	$\dfrac{\text{Q}-\text{R 5}}{\text{Kt}\times\text{P}\,(b)}$
16.	$\dfrac{\text{Q}-\text{B 4}}{\text{Q}-\text{R 4}}$	$\dfrac{\text{P}-\text{B 4}}{\text{Kt}-\text{K 4}}$	$\dfrac{\text{R}\times\text{R P}}{\text{Kt}\times\text{B}}$
17	$\dfrac{\text{Kt}-\text{Q 2}}{\text{Kt}-\text{K 2}}$	$\dfrac{\text{Q}-\text{B 3}}{\text{P}-\text{B 6}}$	$\dfrac{\text{B}\times\text{P}}{\text{Kt}-\text{K Kt 3}}$
18.	$\dfrac{\text{P}-\text{B 4}}{\text{Kt}-\text{Kt 3}}$	$\dfrac{\text{P}-\text{K Kt 3}}{\text{Q}\times\text{B P ch.}}$	$\dfrac{\text{Kt}-\text{Q 5}}{\text{Kt}-\text{K 6 ch.}}$
19.	$\dfrac{\text{Q}-\text{Kt 4}}{\text{Q}-\text{R 3}}$	$\dfrac{\text{Q}\times\text{Q}}{\text{Kt}\times\text{Q}}$	$\dfrac{\text{B}\times\text{Kt}}{\text{P}-\text{Q 3}}$
20.	$\dfrac{\text{R}-\text{Q 1}}{\text{Q}-\text{K 6}}$	$\dfrac{\text{B}-\text{Kt 4}}{\text{P}-\text{B 7}}$	$\dfrac{\text{R}-\text{R 1}}{\text{R}-\text{K 1}}$
21.	$\dfrac{\text{Q}-\text{B 5}}{\text{B}-\text{Kt 7 ch.}}$	$\dfrac{\text{Kt}-\text{R 3}}{\text{B}\times\text{Q P and wins.}}$	$\dfrac{\text{B}-\text{Q 4 }(c)}{\text{Resigns}}$
22.	$\dfrac{\text{K}\times\text{B}}{\text{Kt}-\text{R 5 ch. \& wins.}}$		

Notes by Mr. Max Lange.

(a) 11. $\overline{\text{R}-\text{B 1}}$ seems better, which may be followed by—

12. $\dfrac{\text{P}-\text{Kt 3}}{\text{P}-\text{R 3}}$, or 12. $\overline{\text{P}-\text{Q 3}}$.

(b) 15. $\overline{\text{K}-\text{R 2}}$ would perhaps be more prudent, though White would still have a chance of an equally powerful attack by playing B—K 3, followed by Q R—K B 1.

(c) Notwithstanding the equality of forces, Black cannot save the game. If 21. $\overline{\text{Q}\times\text{B}}$, then 22. $\dfrac{\text{R}\times\text{Kt ch.}}{\text{R}-\text{K 4}}$, and wins. If 21. $\overline{\text{R}-\text{K 4}}$;

22. $\dfrac{\text{B}\times\text{R}}{\text{P}\times\text{B}}$; 23. $\dfrac{\text{Kt}-\text{K 7 ch.}}{\quad}$, and 24. $\dfrac{\text{Kt}\times\text{Kt}}{\quad}$, and White must win.

	(7)	(8)	(9)
	Max Lange	Max Lange	Schumoff
	Anderssen	Anderssen	Jaenisch
1.	P—K 4 / P—K 4	P—K 4 / P—K 4	P—K 4 / P—K 4
2.	P—K B 4 / P×P	P—K B 4 / P×P	P—K B 4 / P×P
3.	B—B 4 / Q—R 5 ch.	B—B 4 / Q—R 5 ch.	B—B 4 / Q—R 5 ch.
4.	K—B 1 / P—K Kt 4	K—B 1 / P—K Kt 4	K—B 1 / P—K Kt 4
5.	Kt—Q B 3 / B—Kt 2	Kt—Q B 3 / B—Kt 2	Kt—Q B 3 / B—Kt 2
6.	P—K Kt 3 / P×P	P—Q 4 / Kt—K 2	P—Q 4 / P—Q 3
7.	K—Kt 2 / Q—R 3	P—K Kt 3 / P×P	Kt—Q 5 / K—Q 1
8.	P×P / Q—K Kt 3	K—Kt 2 / Q—R 3	P—K 5 / Kt—Q B 3 (a)
9.	P—Q 4 / P—Q 3	P×P / Q—K Kt 3	Kt—K B 3 / Q—R 4
10.	Kt—B 3 / P—K R 3	Kt—K B 3 / P—K R 3	P—K R 4 / P—K R 3
11.	R—B 1 / B—K 3	R—B 1 / R—B 1	P—Q Kt 4 (b) / K Kt—K 2
12.	Q—Q 3 / Kt—Q 2	P—Kt 3 / P—Q 3	Kt×B P / K×Kt
13.	Kt—Q Kt 5 / K—Q 1	P—K 5 / B—Kt 5	P×P ch. / K×P
14.	B×B / Q×B	Kt—Kt 5 / Kt—R 3	P—Kt 5 / Kt—R 4

Notes by Jaenisch.

(a) This, in our opinion, is the best defence in the present variation of the Bishop's Gambit. The natural move, 8. $\dfrac{}{\text{P—Q B 3}}$ is inferior, for it would be followed by 9. $\dfrac{\text{Kt—Q B 3}}{\text{P—Q 4}}$; 10. $\dfrac{\text{B—K 2}}{}$; and the defence of the Gambit Pawn would become extremely difficult in the end.

(b) An ingenious and subtle preparation for the sacrifice of the Knight on the 12th move.

	(7)	(8)	(9)
15.	$\dfrac{\text{B}\times\text{P ch.}}{\text{B}-\text{B 3}}$	$\dfrac{\text{P}\times\text{P}}{\text{P}\times\text{P}}$	$\dfrac{\text{B}-\text{R 3 ch.}}{\text{K}-\text{Q 2 } (a)}$
16.	$\dfrac{\text{B}-\text{B 4}}{\text{P}-\text{R 3}}$	$\dfrac{\text{B}-\text{R 3}}{0-0-0}$	$\dfrac{\text{Kt}-\text{K 5 ch.}}{\text{B}\times\text{Kt}}$
17.	$\dfrac{\text{Q}-\text{R 3}}{\text{B}-\text{K 2}}$	$\dfrac{\text{Kt}\times\text{R P ch}}{\text{K}-\text{Kt}}$	$\dfrac{\text{Q}\times\text{Q}}{\text{Kt}\times\text{B}}$
18.	$\dfrac{\text{P}-\text{Q 5}}{\text{Q}\times\text{K P}}$	$\dfrac{\text{Kt}-\text{Kt 5}}{\text{Kt}-\text{K B 4}}$	$\dfrac{\text{B}\times\text{Kt } (b)}{\text{Kt}-\text{K 6 ch.}}$
19.	$\dfrac{\text{Q}-\text{B 3}}{\text{P}\times\text{Kt}}$	$\dfrac{\text{Q}-\text{Q 3}}{\text{K R}-\text{K 1}}$	$\dfrac{\text{K}-\text{B 2}}{\text{K}\times\text{B}}$
20.	$\dfrac{\text{Q}\times\text{R}}{\text{Kt}-\text{Q B 3}}$	$\dfrac{\text{Q R}-\text{K 1}}{\text{R}\times\text{R}}$	$\dfrac{\text{P}\times\text{P}}{\text{B}-\text{Kt 5}}$
21.	$\dfrac{\text{B}\times\text{P}}{\text{K}-\text{Q 2}}$	$\dfrac{\text{R}\times\text{R}}{\text{Q}-\text{R 4}}$	$\dfrac{\text{Q}-\text{R 4}}{\text{B}\times\text{P}}$
22.	$\dfrac{\text{Q R}-\text{K 1}}{\text{Q}\times\text{Q P}}$	$\dfrac{\text{Kt}-\text{Kt 1}}{\text{Kt}-\text{B 2}}$	$\dfrac{\text{P}\times\text{P d. ch}}{\text{K}-\text{B 1}}$
23.	$\dfrac{\text{R}\times\text{B ch.}}{\text{K}\times\text{R}}$	$\dfrac{\text{Kt}\times\text{Kt}}{\text{B}\times\text{P}}$	$\dfrac{\text{Q}-\text{Kt 5}}{\text{Kt}-\text{B 4 d. ch.}}$
24.	$\dfrac{\text{B}-\text{Kt 5}}{\text{Resigns}}$	$\dfrac{\text{Kt}-\text{R 6 ch.}}{\text{K}-\text{R 2}}$	$\dfrac{\text{K}-\text{K 1 } (c)}{\text{R}-\text{K 1 ch.}}$
25.		$\dfrac{\text{B}-\text{B 1}}{\text{P}-\text{Q 4}}$	$\dfrac{\text{K}-\text{Q 2}}{\text{R}-\text{K Kt 1}}$

(a) An incredible error, which, however, we were afterwards enabled to redeem in a manner sufficiently striking. It will be seen, however, that playing the K—B 2 would have been attended by consequences anything but favourable to Black, for suppose 15. $\overline{\text{K}-\text{B 2}}$; 16. $\dfrac{\text{Q}-\text{K 1}}{}$, &c. We believe the best resource consists in playing at move 14. $\overline{\text{Kt}-\text{B 4}}$; instead of $\overline{\text{Kt}-\text{R 4}}$. It is, however, difficult to judge correctly in our own cause.

(b) 18. $\dfrac{\text{Q}\times\text{B P}}{}$ or $\dfrac{\text{P}\times\text{B}}{}$ would have given White the victory. The fault, 18. $\dfrac{\text{B}\times\text{Kt}}{}$ led immediately to the loss of the game.

(c) 24. $\dfrac{\text{K}-\text{B 1}}{}$ would have been followed by 24. $\overline{\text{Kt}-\text{Kt 6 ch.}}$; 25 $\dfrac{\text{K}-\text{K 1}}{\text{B}-\text{B 6 ch}}$; 26. $\dfrac{\text{K}-\text{B 2}}{\text{Kt}-\text{K 5 ch.}}$, &c.

	(7)	(8)	(9)
26.		$\dfrac{\text{Kt}-\text{B 7}}{\text{P}\times\text{B}}$	$\dfrac{\text{Q}\times\text{Kt }(a)}{\text{B}-\text{K 6 ch. and wins.}}$
27.		$\dfrac{\text{P}\times\text{P}}{\text{B}\times\text{Kt}}$	

(8) (contd.)

28. $\dfrac{\text{Kt}-\text{Kt 5 ch.}}{\text{K}-\text{Kt 3}}$	33. $\dfrac{\text{Q}-\text{R 8 ch.}}{\text{K}-\text{Kt 3}}$	38. $\dfrac{\text{R}-\text{Kt 4 ch.}}{\text{K}-\text{B 6}}$
29. $\dfrac{\text{Q}\times\text{R ch.}}{\text{K}-\text{R 3}}$	34. $\dfrac{\text{Kt}-\text{Q 5 ch.}}{\text{B}\times\text{Kt}}$	39. $\dfrac{\text{Q}-\text{B 5 ch.}}{\text{K}-\text{Q 7}}$
30. $\dfrac{\text{Kt}-\text{B 7 ch.}}{\text{K}-\text{R 2}}$	35. $\dfrac{\text{R}-\text{Kt 1 ch.}}{\text{K}-\text{B 4}}$	40. $\dfrac{\text{Q}-\text{Q 4 ch.}}{\text{K}-\text{B 8}}$
31. $\dfrac{\text{K}\times\text{B}}{\text{B}-\text{B 6}}$	36. $\dfrac{\text{Q}-\text{K B 8 ch.}}{\text{K}-\text{Q 5}}$	41. $\dfrac{\text{Q}-\text{Kt 2 ch. and}}{\text{White won ultimately.}}$
32. $\dfrac{\text{B}-\text{K 3 ch.}}{\text{Kt}\times\text{B}}$	37. $\dfrac{\text{P}\times\text{B}}{\text{Q}-\text{K 7}}$	

	(10)	(11)	(12)
	$\dfrac{\text{Delta}}{\text{Gamma}}$	$\dfrac{\text{Gamma}}{\text{Lowenthal}}$	$\dfrac{\text{Mucklow }(b)}{\text{Ranken}}$
1.	$\dfrac{\text{P}-\text{K 4}}{\text{P}-\text{K 4}}$	$\dfrac{\text{P}-\text{K 4}}{\text{P}-\text{K 4}}$	$\dfrac{\text{P}-\text{K 4}}{\text{P}-\text{K 4}}$
2.	$\dfrac{\text{P}-\text{K B 4}}{\text{P}\times\text{P}}$	$\dfrac{\text{P}-\text{K B 4}}{\text{P}\times\text{P}}$	$\dfrac{\text{P}-\text{K B 4}}{\text{P}\times\text{P}}$
3.	$\dfrac{\text{B}-\text{B 4}}{\text{Q}-\text{R 5 ch.}}$	$\dfrac{\text{B}-\text{B 4}}{\text{Q}-\text{R 5 ch.}}$	$\dfrac{\text{B}-\text{B 4}}{\text{Q}-\text{R 5 ch.}}$
4.	$\dfrac{\text{K}-\text{B 1}}{\text{P}-\text{K Kt 4}}$	$\dfrac{\text{K}-\text{B 1}}{\text{Kt}-\text{Q B 3}}$	$\dfrac{\text{K}-\text{B 1}}{\text{P}-\text{K Kt 4}}$
5.	$\dfrac{\text{Kt}-\text{Q B 3}}{\text{B}-\text{Kt 2}}$	$\dfrac{\text{P}-\text{Q 4}}{\text{P}-\text{K Kt 4}}$	$\dfrac{\text{Kt}-\text{Q B 3}}{\text{B}-\text{Kt 2}}$

(a) 26. $\dfrac{\text{P}-\text{R 7}}{}$ would have been of no avail, on account of 26. $\dfrac{}{\text{R}\times\text{Q}}$; 27. $\dfrac{\text{P}-\text{R 8 (Q)}}{\text{B}\times\text{Q}}$, &c.

(b) This is not the amateur who took part in the Chess Tournament of 1851.

	(10)	(11)	(12)
6.	P—K Kt 3 / P×P	Kt—Q B 3 / B—Kt 2	P—K 5 / Kt—Q B 3 (g)
7.	K—Kt 2 / Q—R 3	P—K 5 / P—Q R 3 (b)	Kt—B 3 / Q—R 4
8.	P×P / Q—K Kt 3	Kt—Q 5 / K—Q 1	P—Q 4 / K Kt—K 2
9.	P—Q 4 / P—K R 3	P—B 3 / Kt—K 2	Kt—K 4 / P—K R 3
10.	Kt—B 3 / Kt—K 2	Kt—K B 3 / Q—R 4	Kt—B 6 ch. / B×Kt
11.	Q—Q 3 / P—Q 3	K—Kt 1 / Kt—B 4 (c)	P×B / Kt—B 4
12.	B—K 3 / 0—0	P—K R 4 / Kt×R P	P—Q 5 / Kt—K 4
13.	Q R—K B 1 / P—Q B 3	R×Kt (d) / P×R	Q—K 1 / Kt—K 6 ch.
14.	Q—Q 2 / B—Kt 5	Kt×K B P / Q—Kt 5	B×Kt / Kt×Kt
15.	Kt×P (a) / P×Kt	B×P / B—B 1 (e)	P×Kt / P×B
16.	Q B×P / Kt—B 1	B—R 5 / Q—Kt 6	White mates in 5
17.	R—R 4 / B—K 3	Kt—Kt 5 / Kt×K P (f)	
18.	P—Q 5 / P×P	P×Kt / B—B 4 ch.	
19.	P×P / B—B 4	K—R 1 / K—K 2	

(a) Cleverly conceived. White gains two Pawns for his Piece, and puts the adversary's two Knights and the Q R completely *hors de combat*.

(b) Black gives his opponent too much time by this move. In the Gambits a lost move, whether in attack or defence, is seldom retrievable.

(c) Better to have taken off the Q Kt.

(d) The K R P was thrown forward by White with the intention of risking this sacrifice, which seems quite sound.

(e) Black seems to have no good move at this point.

(f) It is quite immaterial what he plays.

(g) I find a note appended to this move by one of the players:—
" P—B 6 is the proper move."

	(10)	(11)	(12)
20.	R×B (a) / Q×R	Kt—Q 5 ch. / K—B 1	
21.	B—Q 3 / B×Kt	Kt—K 6 ch / P×Kt	
22.	Q×B (b) and wins.	B—R 6 ch. / Resigns	

	(13)	(14)	(15)
	Schulten / Morphy	Goltz / Heydebrand	Morphy, Walker, Greenaway / Lowenthal, Mongredien, Medley
1.	P—K 4 / P—K 4	P—K 4 / P—K 4	P—K 4 / P—K 4
2.	P—K B 4 / P×P	P—K B 4 / P×P	P—K B 4 / P×P
3.	B—B 4 / P—Q 4	B—B 4 / P—Q 4	B—B 4 / P—Q 4
4.	P×P (c) / B—Q 3	P×P / B—Q 3	B×P / Kt—K B 3
5.	Kt—Q B 3 / Kt—K B 3	Kt—K B 3 / Kt—Q 2	Kt—K B 3 / Kt×B
6.	P—Q 4 / 0—0	P—Q 4 / Kt—Kt 3	P×Kt / Q×P
7.	K Kt—K 2 / P—B 6 (d)	Q—K 2 o / Kt—K 2	Kt—B 3 / Q—K R 4

(a) Very well played. Th game is virtually won from this point.

(b) Instead of this move he might have played thus :—

22. R—R 8 ch. / K×R (If 22. Q×R / B×R ; 23. B×Q / B—Kt 2 ; 24. Q—K 2, and wins);

23. Q×B ch. / Q—K 4 ; 24. B—B 6 ch. and White wins.

(c) Not so strong as 4. B×P, and if 4. Kt—K B 3 ; 5. Kt—Q B 3 ; or 5. Q—B 3

(d) A sacrifice quite characteristic of Morphy's style.

	(13)	(14)	(15)
8.	$\dfrac{P \times P}{Kt - R\,4}$	$\dfrac{0 - 0}{0 - 0}$	$\dfrac{P - Q\,4}{B - Q\,3}$
9.	$\dfrac{P - K\,R\,4}{R - K\,1}$.	$\dfrac{Kt - B\,3}{B - K\,Kt\,5}$	$\dfrac{Q - K\,2\ ch.}{K - Q\,1}$
10.	$\dfrac{Kt - K\,4}{B - Kt\,6\ ch.}$	$\dfrac{B - Kt\,3}{P - Q\,R\,4}$	$\dfrac{0 - 0}{P - K\,Kt\,4}$
11.	$\dfrac{K - Q\,2\ (a)}{B - Q\,3}$	$\dfrac{P - Q\,R\,3}{P - R\,5}$	$\dfrac{Q - Kt\,5}{P - K\,B\,4}$
12.	$\dfrac{K - B\,3}{P - Q\,Kt\,4\ (b)}$	$\dfrac{B - R\,2}{P - Kt\,4}$	$\dfrac{Q - Q\,5}{Kt - B\,3}$
13.	$\dfrac{B \times P}{P - Q\,B\,3}$	$\dfrac{K - R\,1}{P - K\,B\,3}$	$\dfrac{Kt - K\,5}{R - B\,1}$
14.	$\dfrac{Kt \times B}{Q \times Kt}$	$\dfrac{Q - B\,2}{Kt - B\,4}$	$\dfrac{B - Q\,2}{Kt - K\,2}$
15.	$\dfrac{B - R\,4}{B - R\,3}$	$\dfrac{Kt - Kt\,5}{R - R\,4}$	$\dfrac{Q - B\,4}{R - B\,3}$
16.	$\dfrac{R - K\,1}{Kt - Q\,2}$	$\dfrac{P - B\,4}{R \times Kt\ (d)}$	$\dfrac{Q\,R - K\,1}{P - B\,3}$
17.	$\dfrac{P - Kt\,3}{Kt - Kt\,3}$	$\dfrac{P \times R}{Q - K\,1}$	$\dfrac{Kt - R\,4}{B - Q\,2}$
18.	$\dfrac{B \times P}{Q\,R - Q\,B\,1}$	$\dfrac{B - Q\,2}{Kt - Kt\,6\ ch.}$	$\dfrac{Kt - B\,5}{B - B\,1}$
19.	$\dfrac{K - Q\,2\ (c)}{R \times B}$	$\dfrac{P \times Kt}{P \times P}$	$\dfrac{R - B\,3}{P - Kt\,5}$
20.	$\dfrac{P \times R}{B \times Kt}$	$\dfrac{Q - Kt\,1}{Q - R\,4\ ch.}$	$\dfrac{R - Q\,Kt\,3}{P - Q\,Kt\,3}$
21.	$\dfrac{R \times B}{Q \times P\ ch.}$	$\dfrac{Kt - R\,2}{B - K\,7}$	Drawn.
22.	$\dfrac{K - K\,1}{Q - Kt\,8\ ch.}$	$\dfrac{K\,R - K\,1}{R - K\,1}$	
23.	$\dfrac{K - Q\,2}{R - Q\,1\ ch.}$	$\dfrac{B - Kt\,4}{R - K\,5}$	

(a) If 11. $\dfrac{K - B\,1}{}$, Black could play 11. $\dfrac{}{R \times Kt}$ with advantage.

(b) The usual sacrifice again.

(c) If 19. $\dfrac{K - Kt\,2}{}$, then 19 $\dfrac{}{R \times B}$; 20. $\dfrac{P \times R}{B \times Kt}$; 21. $\dfrac{R \times B}{Kt - R\,5\ ch.}$

(d) Preparatory to a manœuvre on the King's side by which Black gains an irresistible attack, and finally wins the game.

	(13)	(14)	(15)
24.	K−B 3 Q−B 4 ch.	B×B P×B	
25.	K−Kt 2 Kt−R 5 ch.	R×B R−R 5 (a)	
26.	Resigns ————	R−K 8 ch. K−Kt 2	
27.	—	R−K 7 ch. K−R 3	
28.	—	R×P ch. K×R	
29.	—	Q−Kt 1 ch. K−Kt 2	
30.	—	K−Kt 1 R×Kt	
31.	—	K−B 1 R−R 8 mate	

	(16)	(17)	(18)
	Anderssen Kieseritsky	Charousek Lasker	Charousek Tchigorin
1.	P−K 4 P−K 4	P−K 4 P−K 4	P−K 4 P−K 4
2.	P−K B 4 P×P	P−K B 4 P×P	P−K B 4 P×P
3.	B−B 4 P−Q Kt 4	B−B 4 P−Q 4	B−B 4 Kt−Q B 3
4.	B×Kt P Q−R 5 ch.	B×P Q−R 5 ch.	P−Q 4 Kt−B 3
5.	K−B 1 Kt−K B 3	K−B 1 P−K Kt 4	P−K 5 P−Q 4
6.	Kt−K B 3 Q−R 3	Kt−K B 3 Q−R 4	B−Kt 3 B−K Kt 5
7.	P−Q 3 Kt−R 4	P−K R 4 B−Kt 2	Q−Q 3 Kt−K R 4
8.	Kt−R 4 P−Q B 3	Kt−B 3 P−Q B 3	Kt−K R 3 Kt−Kt 5

(a) All this is in the best style.

	(16)	(17)	(18)
9.	Kt—B 5 / Q—Kt 4	B—B 4 / B—Kt 5	Q—Q B 3 / Kt—R 3
10.	P—K Kt 4 / Kt—K B 3	P—Q 4 / Kt—Q 2	0—0 / B—K 7 (b)
11.	R—Kt 1 / P×B	K—B 2 / B×Kt	B—R 4 ch. / P—B 3
12.	P—K R 4 / Q—Kt 3	P×B / 0—0—0	B×P ch. / P×B
13.	P—R 5 / Q—Kt 4	P×P / Q×P	Q×P ch. / K—R 2
14.	Q—B 3 / Kt—Kt 1	Kt—K 2 / Q—K 2	Kt×P / Kt×Kt
15.	B×P / Q—B 3	P—B 3 / Kt—K 4	B×Kt / P—K R 3 (c)
16.	Kt—Q B 3 / B—Q B 4	Q—R 4 / Kt×B	Kt—B 3 / B—B 5
17.	Kt—Q 5 / Q×Q Kt P	Q×Kt / Kt—B 3	P—K 6 ! / R—Q B 1
18.	B—Q 6 / B×R	B×P / Kt—Q 2	B—B 7 ! / P×P
19.	P—K 5 / Q×R ch.	Q—R 4 / P—Q R 3	B×Q ch. / R×B
20.	K—K 2 / Kt—Q R 3	Q—R 5 / Kt—B 1	Q—Kt 7 ch. / R—Q 2
21.	Kt×Kt P ch. / K—Q 1	Kt—Kt 3 / Kt—K 3	R—B 7 ch. / K×R
22.	Q—B 6 ch. / Kt×Q	Kt—B 5 / Q—B 1	Q×R ch. / B—K 2
23.	B—K 7 mate (a)	B—Kt 3 / R—Q 2	R—K 1 / R—K 1
24.		Kt×B / Q×Kt	P—Q Kt 3 / K—B 1
25.		Q—K 5 / Q×Q	P×B / Resigns (d)

(a) Known as the " Immortal Game "—one of the finest on record.
(b) He should have played 10. P—K Kt 4.
(c) If 15.   B×R
      16. K×B   Kt—B 2
      17. B—Kt 5 ch.   P—B 3
      18. P×P ch., &c.
(d) A very fine game of Charousek's—a real chess genius.

(17) *(contd.)*

26. $\dfrac{\text{B}\times\text{Q}}{\text{P—B 3}}$

27. $\dfrac{\text{B}\times\text{P}}{\text{R—B 1}}$

28. $\dfrac{\text{R—B 6}}{\text{Kt—B 5}}$

29. $\dfrac{\text{K—K 3}}{\text{Kt—Kt 7 ch.}}$

30. $\dfrac{\text{K—Q 2}}{\text{R (Q 2)—K B 2}}$

31. $\dfrac{\text{P—K 5}}{\text{Kt—B 5}}$

32. $\dfrac{\text{Q R—R 1}}{\text{R—Kt 1}}$

33. $\dfrac{\text{P—B 4}}{\text{Kt—K 3}}$

34. $\dfrac{\text{K—K 3}}{\text{Kt—B 1}}$

35. $\dfrac{\text{P—Q 5}}{\text{R—Q 2}}$

36. $\dfrac{\text{P—K 6}}{\text{Resigns}}$

CHAPTER X.

THE KING'S GAMBIT DECLINED—ANALYSIS.

	(1)	(2)	(3)
1.	$\dfrac{\text{P—K 4}}{\text{P—K 4}}$	—	—
2.	$\dfrac{\text{P—K B 4}}{\text{B—B 4}}$	—	P—Q 3 ?
3.	$\dfrac{\text{Kt—K B 3}}{\text{P—Q 3}}$	—	$\dfrac{\text{Kt—K B 3}}{\text{B—Kt 5}}$
4.	$\dfrac{\text{P—B 3}}{\text{B—K Kt 5}}$	—	$\dfrac{\text{B—B 4}}{\text{Kt—Q B 3}}$
5.	$\dfrac{\text{B—K 2 !}}{\text{B}\times\text{Kt}}$	$\dfrac{\text{P—Q 4}}{\text{P}\times\text{P}}$	$\dfrac{\text{P—B 3}}{\text{B}\times\text{Kt}}$
6.	$\dfrac{\text{B}\times\text{B}}{\text{Kt—Q B 3}}$	$\dfrac{\text{P}\times\text{P}}{\text{B}\times\text{Kt}}$	$\dfrac{\text{Q}\times\text{B}}{\text{Kt—B 3}}$
7.	$\dfrac{\text{P—Q Kt 4}}{\text{B—Kt 3}}$	$\dfrac{\text{P}\times\text{B}}{\text{Q—R 5 ch.}}$	
8.	$\dfrac{\text{P—Kt 5}}{\text{Q Kt—K 2}}$	$\dfrac{\text{K—K 2}}{\text{B—Kt 3}}$	
9.	P—Q 4	$\dfrac{\text{B—K 3}}{\text{Kt—K B 3}}$	
10.		$\dfrac{\text{Kt—B 3}}{\text{Kt—B 3}}$ =	

2

	(4)	(5)	(6)
1.	—	—	—
2.	—	P—Q 4 (a)	—
3.	B—B 4 / P×P	P×Q P / Q×P	—
4.	Kt—K B 3 / B—K 3	Kt—Q B 3 / Q—K 3	—
5.	B×B / P×B	Kt—B 3 / P×P d. ch.	—
6.	P—Q 4 / P—K Kt 4	K—B 2 / P—Q B 3	Q—Kt 3 ch. / P—Q 4
7.	P—K R 4 / P—Kt 5	P—Q 4 / B—Q 3	Kt—K B 3 / B—Kt 5 ch.
8.	Kt—Kt 5 / Q—B 3	B—Q 3 / Kt—K 2	P—B 3 / R—K 1 ch.
9.	Q×P +	R—K 1 +	B—K 2
10.			B—B 4 / B—Kt 5
11.			B×P ch. / K×B
12.			Kt—K 5 ch. / K—K 1
13.			Kt×B / Kt×Kt
14.			Q×Kt / Q×P ch.
15.			K—B 3 / Kt—Q 2

	(7)	(8)	(9)
1.	—	—	—
2.	—	—	B—B 4 / Kt—Kt B 3
3.	P—K 5	P×P	P—Q 3

(a) The Falkbeer Counter Gambit.

	(7)	**(8)**	**(9)**
4.	B—Kt 5 ch. / P—B 3	B—Kt 5 ch. / B—Q 2	P—B 3 / B—K Kt 5
5.	P×P / P×P	Q—K 2 ch. / Q—K 2	B—B 4 / Kt—Q B 3
6.	B—B 4 / Kt—K B 3	Kt—Q B 3 / Kt—K B 3	P—Q Kt 4 / B—Kt 3
7.	P—Q 4 / Kt—Q 2 !	B×B ch. / Kt×B	P—Q R 4 / P—Q R 3
8.	Kt—K 2 / Kt—Kt 3	P—Q 4 / 0—0—0	P—Q 3 / Kt—B 3
9.	B—Kt 3 / B—R 3	Q×Q / B×Q	P—R 3 / B×Kt
10.	Kt—Q B 3 / B—Kt 5	B×P / Kt—Kt 3 =	Q×B
11.	0—0 / B (Kt 5)×Kt		
12.	P×B / K Kt—Q 4		
13.	R—K 1 / P—K B 4 (or 0—0)		
14.	P—Kt 4		

	(10)	**(11)**	**(12)**
1.	—	--	—
2.	—	—	—
3.	—	--	--
4.	Kt—K B 3	B—B 4 / Kt—K B 3	Kt—Q B 3
5.	P—Q 3 / 0—0	P—Q 3 / B—K Kt 5	P—B 3 / Kt—B 3
6.	Kt—B 3 / P—Q R 3	Kt—B 3 / Kt—B 3	P—Q 4 / P×Q P
7.	P—B 5 / P—Q Kt 4	P—K R 3 / B×Kt	P×P / B—Kt 3

	(10)	(11)	(12)
8.	$\dfrac{\text{B}-\text{Kt } 3}{\text{B}-\text{Kt } 2}$	$\dfrac{\text{Q} \times \text{B}}{\text{Kt}-\text{Q } 5}$	$\dfrac{0-0}{0-0}$
9.	$\dfrac{\text{B}-\text{Kt } 5}{\quad}$	$\dfrac{\text{Q}-\text{Kt } 3}{\text{Kt} \times \text{P ch.}}$	
10.		$\dfrac{\text{K}-\text{Q } 1}{\text{Kt} \times \text{Q R}}$	
11.		$\dfrac{\text{Q} \times \text{P}}{\text{R}-\text{K B 1}}$	
12.		$\dfrac{\text{P} \times \text{P}}{\text{P} \times \text{P}}$	

Nos. **9** to **12.**   Position after Black's 3rd move.

BLACK.

WHITE.

	(13)	(14)	(15)
1.	—	—	—
2.	$\overline{\text{Kt}-\text{B } 3}$	$\overline{\text{P}-\text{Q } 4}$	—
3.	$\dfrac{\text{P} \times \text{P}}{\text{Kt} \times \text{P}}$	$\dfrac{\text{P} \times \text{Q P}}{\text{P} \times \text{P}}$	$\overline{\text{P}-\text{K } 5}$
4.	$\dfrac{\text{Kt}-\text{K B } 3}{\text{Kt}-\text{Kt } 4}$	$\dfrac{\text{B}-\text{Kt } 5 \text{ ch.}}{\text{P}-\text{B } 3}$	$\dfrac{\text{B}-\text{Kt } 5 \text{ ch.}}{\text{P}-\text{B } 3}$

	(13)	(14)	(15)
5.	P—Q 4 / Kt×Kt ch.	Q—K 2 ch. / B—K 2	P×P / Kt×P
6.	Q×Kt / Q—R 5 ch.	P×P / P×P	P—Q 4 / Q—R 4 ch.
7.	Q—B 2 / Q×Q	B—B 4 / Kt—B 3	Kt—B 3 / B—Q Kt 5
8.	K×Q / Kt—B 3	K Kt—B 3 / B—K Kt 5	B—Q 2 / Kt—B 3
9.	P—B 3 / P—Q 3	P—Q 3 / 0—0	B×Kt ch. / P×B
10.		0—0 / B—B 4 ch.	P—Q R 3 / B×Kt
11.		K—R 1 / R—K 1	B×B / Q—Q 4

THE KING'S GAMBIT DECLINED—GAMES.

	(1) Devinck / Kieseritsky	(2) Max Lange / Dr. Rinne	(3) Max Lange / Amateur
1.	P—K 4 / P—K 4	P—K 4 / P—K 4	P—K 4 / P—K 4
2.	P—K B 4 / P—Q 3	P—K B 4 / P—Q 4	P—K B 4 / P—Q 4
3.	Kt—K B 3 / Kt—Q B 3	Kt—K B 3 / Q P×P	P×Q P / P—K 5
4.	B—B 4 / B—K 3	Kt×P / B—K 3	B—Kt 5 ch. (a) / P—B 3
5.	B×B / P×B	Kt—Q B 3 / Kt—K B 3	P×P / P×P
6.	P×P / Kt×P	Q—K 2 / B—K B 4	B—B 4 / Kt—K B 3

Notes by Max Lange.

(a) This is perhaps White's best move, as it at all events in some measure frees his game, which Black's K P threatens to cramp.

	(1)	(2)	(3)
7.	P—Q 4 / Kt×Kt ch.	Q—Kt 5 ch. / Q Kt—Q 2	P—Q 4 / Q Kt—Q 2 (a)
8.	Q×Kt / Q—B 3	B—B 4 / B—K 3	B—K 3 / Kt—Kt 3
9.	0—0 / Q×Q	Kt×Kt / B×Kt	Kt—Q 2 / Kt×B
10.	R×Q / B—K 2	Q×P / P—B 3	Kt×Kt / Kt—Kt 5
11.	B—K 3 / B—B 3	Q—Kt 3 / Q—K 2	Q—K 2 / B—R 3
12.	Kt—Q 2 / Kt—K 2	0—0 / B—K 3	0—0—0 (b) / Kt×B
13.	Q R—K B 1 / Kt—Kt 3	B×B / Q×B	Q×Kt / B×Q
14.	P—K Kt 3 / P—K 4	Q×Q / P×Q	Q×P ch. / K—Q 2
15.	P—B 3 / R—K B 1	R—K 1 / B—B 4 ch.	P—Q 5 / B×Q P
16.	Kt—B 4 / K—K 2	K—R 1 / 0—0	R×B ch. / P×R
17.	P—K R 4 / P—Q Kt 4	Kt×P / Kt×Kt	Q×P ch. / K—B 2
18.	P×P / Kt×P (K 5)	R×Kt / Q R—K 1	Q—B 4 ch. / K—Kt 2
19.	Kt×Kt / B×Kt	P—Q 4 / B—Q 3	Kt—B 3 / B—Q 3
20.	R×R / R×R	B—Q 2 and won ultimately.	R—Q 1 / Q—Kt 3
21.	R×R / K×R		Q—Q 5 ch. / K—B 2

(a) This move, recommended by Mr. Staunton, is considered by Jaenisch to give Black the better game, but the investigation given in the "Schachzeitung" (1855), is more elegant than correct.

(b) Perhaps 12. $\dfrac{Q \times Kt}{}$ is simpler, though Castling gives rise to a strong attack. The following is bad for Black :—12. $\dfrac{0—0}{B \times Kt}$; 13. $\dfrac{Q \times B}{Kt \times B}$; 14. $\dfrac{Q \times P \text{ ch.}}{K—K 2}$; 15. $\dfrac{Q \times P \text{ ch.}}{}$ &c.

	(1)	(2)	(3)
22.	$\dfrac{K-B\,2}{P-Q\,R\,4}$		$\dfrac{Q\times P \text{ ch.}}{K-B\,3}$
23.	$\dfrac{B-Q\,4}{P-B\,4}$		$\dfrac{Kt-K\,5 \text{ ch.}}{K-Kt\,4}$
24.	$\dfrac{B\times B}{P\times B}$		$\dfrac{Q-B\,4 \text{ ch.}}{K-R\,4}$
25.	$\dfrac{K-B\,3}{P-R\,4}$		$\dfrac{Q-Q\,5 \text{ ch. and wins.}}{}$
26.	$\dfrac{P-K\,Kt\,4}{P-Kt\,3}$	(1) *(contd.)*	
27.	$\dfrac{P\times P}{P\times P}$	31. $\dfrac{K-B\,2}{K-B\,4}$	
28.	$\dfrac{K-K\,3}{P-B\,5}$	32. $\dfrac{P-Kt\,4 \text{ ch.}}{P\times P}$	
29.	$\dfrac{P-R\,3}{K-K\,2}$	33. $\dfrac{R\,P\times P \text{ ch.}}{K-B\,3}$	
30.	$\dfrac{K-Q\,2}{K-Q\,3}$	Drawn.	

	(4)	(5)	6
	Cook	Tchigorin	Schlechter
	Locock	Marco	Jorowski
1.	$\dfrac{P-K\,4}{P-K\,4}$	$\dfrac{P-K\,4}{P-K\,4}$	$\dfrac{P-K\,4}{P-K\,4}$
2.	$\dfrac{P-K\,B\,4}{P-Q\,4\ (a)}$	$\dfrac{P-K\,B\,4}{B-B\,4}$	$\dfrac{P-K\,B\,4}{B-B\,4}$
3.	$\dfrac{Kt-K\,B\,3}{Q\,P\times P}$	$\dfrac{Kt-K\,B\,3}{P-Q\,3}$	$\dfrac{Kt-K\,B\,3}{P-Q\,3}$
4.	$\dfrac{Kt\times P}{B-K\,3}$	$\dfrac{P-B\,3}{B-K\,Kt\,5}$	$\dfrac{Kt-B\,3}{Kt-K\,B\,3}$
5.	$\dfrac{P-Q\,4}{Kt-K\,B\,3}$	$\dfrac{B-K\,2\,!}{B\times Kt}$	$\dfrac{B-B\,4}{Kt-B\,3}$
6.	$\dfrac{Kt-Q\,B\,3}{B-Q\,Kt\,5}$	$\dfrac{B\times B}{P\times P}$	$\dfrac{P-Q\,3}{P-Q\,R\,3}$
7.	$\dfrac{B-K\,2}{Kt-Q\,4}$	$\dfrac{P-Q\,4}{Q-R\,5 \text{ ch.}}$	$\dfrac{P-B\,5}{Kt-Q\,R\,4}$

(*a*) The Falkbeer Counter Gambit—declining one Gambit by offering another. Theoretically unsound, it leads to an interesting game.

	(4)	(5)	(6)
8.	0-0 / Kt×Kt	P-Kt 3 / P×P	P-Q R 3 / Kt×B
9.	P×Kt / B×B P	P×P / Q×Kt P ch.	P×Kt / P-B 3
10.	B-K 3 / B×R	K-K 2 / B-Kt 3	B-Kt 5 / P-Kt 4
11.	P-B 5 / B-B 1	R-Kt 1 / Q-R 7 ch.	Q-Q 3 / P×P
12.	B-Kt 5 ch. / P-B 3	R-Kt 2 / Q-R 6	Q×B P / P-Q R 4
13.	Kt×K B P ! / K×Kt	R×P / Kt-Q 2	B×Kt / P×B
14.	Q-R 5 ch. / K-B 1	Q-Kt 1 / K Kt-B 3	Kt-Q R 4 / B-R 3
15.	P-B 6 / P×P	B-K 3 / 0-0-0	Q-B 3 / B-R 2
16.	B-Q B 4 / Q-Q 2	Kt-Q 2 / K R-Kt 1	Q×B P ch. / K-K 2
17.	R×P ch. / K-K 2	P-R 4 / P-Q R 3	0-0-0 / Q-Q Kt 1
18.	R-B 7 ch. / K-Q 1	P-Kt 4 / P-K R 4	Kt-B 3 / R-Q B 1
19.	Q-Kt 5 ch. / K-B 2	P-R 5 / B-R 2	Kt-Q 5 ch. / K-Q 1
20.	B-B 4 ch. / K-Kt 3	Q-Kt 5 / K-Kt 1	Kt-Kt 4 / B-K 6 ch.
21.	Q-B 5 mate	P-Kt 5 / R×R	K-Kt 1 / B-B 4
22.		Q×R / P×P	Kt×B / R×Q
23.		Q×P / R-K B 1	Kt×Q / R×Kt
24.		Q-Kt 3 / Q-R 7 ch.	K-R 2 and wins.
25.		K-Q 3 / Kt-K 4 ch. (a)	
26.		P×Kt / B×B	

(a) Quite sound.

(5) (*contd.*)

27. $\dfrac{\text{Kt}-\text{B 1}\ (a)}{\text{Q}\times\text{P}}$ 29. $\dfrac{\text{K}-\text{K 2}}{\text{Q}-\text{R 7 ch.}}$ 31. $\dfrac{\text{R}-\text{K B 1}}{\text{R}\times\text{R}}$

28. $\dfrac{\text{Kt}\times\text{B}}{\text{Kt}-\text{Q 2}}$ 30. $\dfrac{\text{B}-\text{Kt 2}}{\text{Kt}-\text{K 4}}$ 32. $\dfrac{}{\text{K}\times\text{R and wins.}}$

(a) If 27. K×B   Kt—Kt 5 ch.
    28. B×Kt   P×B and R—B 7

BOOK V.

Chapter I.

THE QUEEN'S GAMBIT—ANALYSIS

	(1)	(2)	(3)
1.	P–Q 4 / P–Q 4	—	—
2.	P–Q B 4 / P×P	—	—
3.	P–K 3 / P–K 4 (P–Q Kt 4?)	P–Q B 4	P–K 4 / P–K 4
4.	B×P / P×P	B×P / P×P	P–Q 5 / P–K B 4
5.	P×P / Kt–K B 3	P×P / Kt–Q B 3	B×P / Kt–K B 3
6.	Kt–Q B 3 / B–Q 3	Kt–K 2 / P–K 4	Kt–K B 3 / B–Q 3
7.	Kt–B 3 / Kt–B 3	B–K 3 / P×P	P×P / B×P
8.	0–0 / 0–0	Kt×P / Kt×Kt	0–0 / 0–0
9.	P–K R 3 / P–K R 3 =	B×Kt / Q–K 2 ch.	Kt–B 3 / Q Kt–Q 2
10.		B–K 2 / Q–Kt 5 ch.	
11.		Q–Q 2 / Q×Q ch.	
12.		Kt×Q + / Kt–K 2	

	(4)	(5)	(6)
1.	—	—	—
2.	—	—	—
3.	$\dfrac{\text{Kt}-\text{Q B 3}}{\text{Kt}-\text{K B 3}}$	$\overline{\text{P}-\text{Q B 4}}$	$\dfrac{\text{P}-\text{K 4}}{\text{P}-\text{K B 4}}$
4.	$\dfrac{\text{P}-\text{K 3}}{\text{P}-\text{K 4}}$	$\dfrac{\text{P}-\text{Q 5}}{\text{P}-\text{K 3}}$	$\dfrac{\text{P}-\text{K 5}}{\text{B}-\text{K 3}}$
5.	$\dfrac{\text{B}\times\text{P}}{\text{P}\times\text{P}}$	$\dfrac{\text{P}-\text{K 4}}{\text{P}\times\text{P}}$	$\dfrac{\text{Kt}-\text{Q R 3}}{\text{Kt}-\text{Q B 3}}$
6.	$\dfrac{\text{P}\times\text{P}}{\text{B}-\text{Q 3}}=$	$\dfrac{\text{P}\times\text{P}}{\text{B}-\text{Q 3}}$	$\dfrac{\text{B}-\text{K 3}}{\text{Kt}-\text{R 4}}$
7.		$\dfrac{\text{B}\times\text{P}}{\text{Kt}-\text{K 2}}=$	$\dfrac{\text{Q}-\text{R 4 ch.}}{\text{P}-\text{B 3}}$
8.			$\dfrac{\text{B}-\text{Q 2}}{\text{Q}\times\text{P}}$
9.			$\dfrac{\text{Q}\times\text{Kt}}{\text{Q}\times\text{Kt P}}$
10.			$\dfrac{\text{B}-\text{B 3}}{\text{Q}-\text{Kt 3}}$
11.			$\dfrac{\text{Q}\times\text{Q}}{\text{P}\times\text{Q}}$
12.			$\dfrac{\text{Kt}\times\text{P}}{\text{P}-\text{Q Kt 4}}$
13.			$\dfrac{\text{Kt}-\text{K 3}}{\text{P}-\text{B 5}}$
14.			$\dfrac{\text{Kt}-\text{B 2}}{\text{R}\times\text{P}}$
15.			$\dfrac{\text{B}-\text{Q 3}}{\text{R}\times\text{R ch.}}$
16.			$\dfrac{\text{B}\times\text{R}}{} +$

THE QUEEN'S GAMBIT—GAMES.

	(1)	(2)
	$\dfrac{\text{La Bourdonnais}}{\text{McDonnell}}$	$\dfrac{\text{Harrwitz, Sazias, Another}}{\text{Kieseritsky, Henderson, Kling}}$
1	$\dfrac{\text{P}-\text{Q 4}}{\text{P}-\text{Q 4}}$	$\dfrac{\text{P}-\text{Q 4}}{\text{P}-\text{Q 4}}$
2.	$\dfrac{\text{P}-\text{Q B 4}}{\text{P}\times\text{P}}$	$\dfrac{\text{P}-\text{Q B 4}}{\text{P}\times\text{P}}$

	(1)	(2)
3.	$\dfrac{\text{P−K 3}}{\text{P−K 4}}$	$\dfrac{\text{P−K 4}}{\text{P−K B 4 } (e)}$
4.	$\dfrac{\text{B×P}}{\text{P×P}}$	$\dfrac{\text{P×P } (f)}{\text{Q B×P}}$
5.	$\dfrac{\text{P×P}}{\text{Kt−K B 3}}$	$\dfrac{\text{K B×P}}{\text{Kt−K B 3}}$
6.	$\dfrac{\text{Kt−Q B 3}}{\text{B−K 2 } (a)}$	$\dfrac{\text{Kt−K 2}}{\text{B−K 5}}$
7.	$\dfrac{\text{Kt−B 3}}{\text{0−0}}$	$\dfrac{\text{0−0}}{\text{Kt−B 3}}$
8.	$\dfrac{\text{P−K R 3 } (b)}{\text{Q Kt−Q 2}}$	$\dfrac{\text{Q−Kt 3}}{\text{B−Q 4}}$
9.	$\dfrac{\text{B−K 3}}{\text{Kt−Kt 3}}$	$\dfrac{\text{B×B}}{\text{Q×B}}$
10.	$\dfrac{\text{B−Kt 3}}{\text{P−B 3}}$	$\dfrac{\text{Q×Q Kt P}}{\text{Kt×Q P } (g)}$
11.	$\dfrac{\text{0−0}}{\text{Kt (B 3)−Q 4}}$	$\dfrac{\text{Q−R 6}}{\text{P−K 4}}$
12.	$\dfrac{\text{Q−K 2}}{\text{P−K B 4}}$	$\dfrac{\text{Q Kt−B 3}}{\text{Q−B 3}}$
13.	$\dfrac{\text{Kt−K 5}}{\text{P−B 5}}$	$\dfrac{\text{Q×Q}}{\text{Kt×Q}}$
14.	$\dfrac{\text{B−Q 2}}{\text{P−Kt 4 } (c)}$	$\dfrac{\text{P−B 4}}{\text{B−B 4 ch.}}$
15.	$\dfrac{\text{Q R−K 1}}{\text{K−Kt 2}}$	$\dfrac{\text{K−R 1}}{\text{0−0}}$
16.	$\dfrac{\text{Kt×Kt}}{\text{Kt×Kt}}$	$\dfrac{\text{P−K R 3}}{\text{Q R−K 1}}$
17.	$\dfrac{\text{Kt×P } (d)}{\text{P×Kt}}$	$\dfrac{\text{P×P}}{\text{Kt×P}}$

(a) This is a fault. The Bishop should always be played to Q 3 at the present stage.

(b) An indispensable move in this opening.

(c) The advance of these Pawns should rarely be ventured by any but the experienced player.

(d) Capitally played.

(e) This leads to the objectionable defence of Mr. Schwartz, which has been previously examined.

(f) Bishop takes Pawn would be likewise good play.

(g) Very neatly played.

	(1)	(2)
18.	$\dfrac{\text{B} \times \text{Kt}}{\text{Q} \times \text{B}}$	$\dfrac{\text{B—Kt 5}}{\text{R—K 3}}$
19.	$\dfrac{\text{Q} \times \text{B ch.}}{\text{R—B 2}}$	$\dfrac{\text{Q R—Q 1}}{\text{Kt—B 5}}$
20.	$\dfrac{\text{Q—Kt 4}}{\text{B—B 4}}$	$\dfrac{\text{P—Q Kt 3}}{\text{Kt—K 6}}$
21.	$\dfrac{\text{R—K 5}}{\text{Q—Q 2}}$	$\dfrac{\text{B} \times \text{Kt}}{\text{R} \times \text{B}}$
22.	$\dfrac{\text{P—Q 5 } (a)}{\text{P} \times \text{P}}$	$\dfrac{\text{R—B 3}}{\text{R—K 1}}$
23.	$\dfrac{\text{Q—Q 4}}{\text{K—R 3}}$	$\dfrac{\text{Kt—B 4}}{\text{Kt—K 5}}$
24.	$\dfrac{\text{P—K R 4}}{\text{B—K 3}}$	$\dfrac{\text{Kt} \times \text{Kt}}{\text{R} \times \text{Kt } (c)}$
25.	$\dfrac{\text{K R—K 1}}{\text{R—K 1}}$	$\dfrac{\text{R} \times \text{R}}{\text{B} \times \text{R}}$
26.	$\dfrac{\text{R} \times \text{Kt P } (b)}{\text{Q R—K B 1}}$	$\dfrac{\text{R—Q 8 ch.}}{\text{K—B 2}}$
27.	$\dfrac{\text{Q—K 5}}{\text{B—Kt 5}}$	$\dfrac{\text{Kt—Q 5}}{\text{R—Q 5}}$
28.	$\dfrac{\text{R—R 5 ch.}}{\text{B} \times \text{R}}$	$\dfrac{\text{R—Q 7 ch.}}{\text{K—K 3}}$
29.	$\dfrac{\text{Q—Kt 5 mate.}}{}$	$\dfrac{\text{R—K 7 ch.}}{\text{K} \times \text{Kt}}$

(2) (contd.)			
30.	$\dfrac{\text{R} \times \text{B}}{\text{R—K 5}}$	35.	$\dfrac{\text{K—R 3}}{\text{K—Kt 4}}$
31.	$\dfrac{\text{R—Q 3 ch.}}{\text{K—B 3}}$	36.	$\dfrac{\text{P—K Kt 4}}{\text{P—B 4}}$
32.	$\dfrac{\text{K—R 2}}{\text{R—K 7}}$	37.	$\dfrac{\text{K—Kt 3}}{\text{P—R 5}}$
33.	$\dfrac{\text{P—R 3}}{\text{P—Q R 4}}$	38.	$\dfrac{\text{P} \times \text{P ch.}}{\text{K} \times \text{P}}$
34.	$\dfrac{\text{P—K R 4}}{\text{R—K 5}}$	39.	$\dfrac{\text{R—Q 7}}{\text{P—B 5}}$
		40.	$\dfrac{\text{R} \times \text{Kt P}}{\text{P—B 6 and wins.}}$

(a) An excellent move.

(b) The best mode of taking the Pawn.

(c) It would have been better perhaps to have taken this Knight with the Q R.

Chapter II.

THE QUEEN'S GAMBIT DECLINED—ANALYSIS

	(1)	(2)	(3)
1.	$\dfrac{\text{P—Q 4}}{\text{P—Q 4}}$	—	—
2.	$\dfrac{\text{P—Q B 4}}{\text{P—K 3}}$	$\overline{\text{P—Q B 4}}$	—
3.	$\dfrac{\text{Kt—Q B 3}}{\text{Kt—K B 3}}$	$\dfrac{\text{P}\times\text{B P}}{\overline{\text{P—Q 5 !}}}$	—
4.	$\dfrac{\text{P—K 3}}{\overline{\text{P—Q B 4}}}$	$\dfrac{\text{P—Q Kt 4}}{\overline{\text{P—Q R 4}}}$	$\overline{\text{P—K 4}}$
5.	$\dfrac{\text{Kt—B 3}}{\overline{\text{Kt—Q B 3}}}$	$\dfrac{\text{P—Kt 5}}{\overline{\text{P—K 4}}}$	$\dfrac{\text{Kt—K B 3}}{\overline{\text{P—B 3}}}$
6.	$\dfrac{\text{P—Q R 3}}{\overline{\text{P—Q R 3}}}$	$\dfrac{\text{Kt—K B 3}}{\overline{\text{P—B 3}}}$	$\dfrac{\text{P—K 3}}{\overline{\text{P}\times\text{P}}}$
7.		$\dfrac{\text{P—K 3}}{\overline{\text{B}\times\text{P}}}$	$\dfrac{\text{Q}\times\text{Q ch.}}{\overline{\text{K}\times\text{Q}}}$
8.		$\dfrac{\text{P}\times\text{P}}{\overline{\text{P}\times\text{P}}}$	$\dfrac{\text{B}\times\text{P}}{\overline{\text{P—Q R 4}}}$
9.		$\underline{\text{B—Kt 2 +}}$	$\dfrac{\text{P—Kt 5}}{\overline{\text{Kt—Q 2}}}$
10.			$\dfrac{\text{P—B 6}}{\overline{\text{P}\times\text{P}}}$
11.			$\dfrac{\text{P—Q R 4}}{\overline{\text{P—Q B 4}}}$
12.			Q Kt—Q 2 +

	(4)	(5)	(6)
1.	—	$\dfrac{\text{P—Q 4}}{\overline{\text{P—Q 4}}}$	—
2.	$\overline{\text{P—Q B 3}}$	$\dfrac{\text{P—Q B 4}}{\overline{\text{P—K 3}}}$	—
3.	$\dfrac{\text{P—B 3}}{\overline{\text{Kt—B 3}}}$	$\dfrac{\text{Kt—Q B 3}}{\overline{\text{Kt—K B 3}}}$	$\overline{\text{P—Q B 3}}$

	(4)	(5)	(6)
4.	Kt—Q B 3 / B—B 4	B—B 4 / P—Q B 4	P—K 3 / Kt—B 3
5.	P—K 3 / P—K 3	P—K 3 / Kt—B 3	P—B 3 / B—Kt 5
6.	B—Q 3 / B×B	Kt—B 3 / P×Q P	Kt—R 3 / Q Kt—Q 2
7.	Q×B / B—Kt 5	K P×P / P×P	Kt—B 4 / 0—0
8.	P—K 4 / B×Kt ch.	B×P / B—K 2	B—Q 2
9.	P×B / Q Kt—Q 2	0—0 / 0—0	
10.	B P×P / B P×P	R—B 1 / B—Q 2	
11.	P—K 5 / Kt—K R 4	Q—K 2 / Q—R 4	
12.	Kt—K 2 +		

	(7)	(8)	(9)
1.	—	—	—
2.	P—Q B 3	P—K 3	—
3.	P—K 3 / B—B 4	P—K 3 / Kt—K B 3	Kt—Q B 3 / Kt—K B 3
4.	P—Q R 3 / P—K 3	Kt—Q B 3 / P—B 4	B—Kt 5 / B—K 2
5.	P—B 5 / P—Q R 4	Kt—B 3 / Kt—B 3	Kt—B 3 / Q Kt—Q 2
6.	Q—Kt 3 / Q—B 2	P—Q R 3 / B—K 2	P—K 3 / 0—0
7.	Kt—Q B 3 / Kt—Q 2	B—Q 3 / 0—0	P—B 5 / Kt—K 5
8.	Kt—R 4 / K Kt—B 3	0—0 / P—Q Kt 3	Kt×Kt / P×Kt
9.	Kt—K 2 / B—K 2	P—Q Kt 3 / B—Kt 2	B×B / Q×B
10.	K Kt—Q B 3	B P×P / K P×P	Kt—Q 2 / Kt—B 3

	(7)	(8)	(9)
11.	—	$\frac{B-Kt\,2}{P\times P}$	$\frac{Kt-B\,4}{P-Q\,Kt\,3}$
12.	—	$\frac{P\times P}{R-B\,1}$	$\frac{P-Q\,Kt\,4}{Kt-Q\,4}$

	(10)	(10a)	(11)
1.	—	—	—
2.	—	—	—

Nos. 9 to 14.   Position after White's 4th move.

BLACK.

WHITE.

	(10)	(10a)	(11)
3.	—	—	—
4.	—	$\overline{P-B\,3}$	$\overline{B-K\,2}$
5.	$\frac{P-K\,3}{0-0}$	$\frac{P-K\,3}{Q\,Kt-Q\,2}$	$\frac{P-K\,3}{0-0}$
6.	$\frac{Kt-B\,3}{P-Q\,Kt\,3}$	$\frac{Kt-B\,3}{Q-R\,4}$	$\frac{Kt-B\,3}{Q\,Kt-Q\,2}$
7.	$\frac{B-Q\,3}{B-Kt\,2}$	$\frac{Kt-Q\,2}{Kt-K\,5}$	$\frac{B-Q\,3}{P\times P}$

	(10)	**(10a)**	**(11)**
8.	$\dfrac{P \times P}{P \times P}$	$\dfrac{P \times P}{Kt \times K\ Kt}$	$\dfrac{B \times B\ P}{P - B\ 4}$
9.	$\dfrac{Kt - K\ 5}{Q\ Kt - Q\ 2}$	$\dfrac{Q \times Kt}{K\ P \times P}$	$\dfrac{B - Q\ 3}{P - Q\ R\ 3}$
10.	$\dfrac{P - B\ 4}{Kt - K\ 5}$	$\dfrac{B - Q\ 3}{B - Kt\ 5}$	$\dfrac{0 - 0}{P - Kt\ 4}$
11.	$\dfrac{0 - 0}{}$	$\dfrac{0 - 0}{0 - 0}$	

	(12)	**(13)**	**(14)**
1.	—	—	—
2.	—	—	—
3.	—	—	—
4.	—	—	—
5.	—	—	—
6.	—	—	—
7.	—	$\dfrac{R - B\ 1}{P - B\ 3}$	$\dfrac{P - Q\ Kt\ 3}{}$
8.	—	$\dfrac{B - Q\ 3}{P \times P}$	$\dfrac{P \times P}{P \times P}$
9.	$\dfrac{0 - 0}{P - Q\ R\ 3}$	$\dfrac{B \times P}{Kt - Q\ 4}$	$\dfrac{B - Q\ 3}{B - Kt\ 2}$
10.	$\dfrac{Kt - K\ 5}{Kt \times Kt}$	$\dfrac{B \times B}{Q \times B}$	$\dfrac{0 - 0}{P - B\ 4}$
11.	$\dfrac{P \times Kt}{Kt - Q\ 2}$		
12.	$\dfrac{B \times B}{Q \times B}$		
13.	$\dfrac{P - B\ 4}{P - Q\ Kt\ 4}$		
14.	$\dfrac{B - Q\ 3}{P - B\ 4}$		

	(15)	(16)	(17)
1.	—	—	—
2.	—	—	—
3.	—	$\dfrac{\text{P}-\text{K }3}{\text{Kt}-\text{K B }3}$	$\dfrac{\text{Kt}-\text{Q B }3}{\text{P}-\text{Q B }4}$
4.	$\dfrac{\text{Kt}-\text{B }3}{\text{B}-\text{K }2}$	$\dfrac{\text{Kt}-\text{Q B }3}{\text{P}-\text{B }4}$	$\dfrac{\text{P}-\text{K }3}{\text{Kt}-\text{Q B }3}$
5.	$\dfrac{\text{P}-\text{K }3}{0-0}$	$\dfrac{\text{Kt}-\text{B }3}{\text{Kt}-\text{B }3}$	$\dfrac{\text{Kt}-\text{B }3}{\text{Kt}-\text{B }3}$
6.	$\dfrac{\text{B}-\text{Q }3}{\text{P}-\text{Q B }4}$	$\dfrac{\text{P}-\text{Q R }3}{\text{B}-\text{K }2}$	$\dfrac{\text{B}-\text{Q }3}{\text{B}-\text{K }2}$
7.	$\dfrac{0-0}{\text{P}\times\text{Q P}}$	$\dfrac{\text{Q P}\times\text{P}}{\text{P}\times\text{P}}$	$\dfrac{0-0}{0-0}$
8.	$\dfrac{\text{K P}\times\text{P}}{\text{P}\times\text{P}}$	$\dfrac{\text{Q}\times\text{Q ch.}}{\text{K}\times\text{Q}}$	$\dfrac{\text{P}-\text{Q Kt }3}{\text{P}-\text{Q Kt }3}$
9.	$\dfrac{\text{B}\times\text{P}}{\text{Q Kt}-\text{Q }2}$	$\dfrac{\text{B}\times\text{P}}{\text{B}\times\text{P}}$	$\dfrac{\text{B}-\text{Kt }2}{\text{B}-\text{Kt }2}$
10.	$\dfrac{\text{B}-\text{Kt }3}{\text{Kt}-\text{Kt }3}$	$\dfrac{\text{P}-\text{Q Kt }4}{\text{B}-\text{Kt }3}$	$\dfrac{\text{R}-\text{B }1}{\text{R}-\text{B }1}$
11.	$\dfrac{\text{B}-\text{Kt }5}{\text{B}-\text{Q }2}$	$\dfrac{\text{B}-\text{Kt }2}{\text{K}-\text{K }2}$	
12.	$\dfrac{\text{Q}-\text{Q }3}{\text{R}-\text{B }1}$	$\dfrac{\text{K}-\text{K }2}{\text{B}-\text{Q }2}$	

THE QUEEN'S GAMBIT DECLINED—GAMES.

	(1) St. Amant / Staunton	(2) Blackburne / Lipschütz	(3) Englisch / Schiffers
1.	$\dfrac{\text{P}-\text{Q }4}{\text{P}-\text{Q }4}$	$\dfrac{\text{P}-\text{Q }4}{\text{P}-\text{Q }4}$	$\dfrac{\text{P}-\text{Q }4}{\text{P}-\text{Q }4}$
2.	$\dfrac{\text{P}-\text{Q B }4}{\text{P}-\text{K }3}$	$\dfrac{\text{P}-\text{Q B }4}{\text{P}-\text{K }3}$	$\dfrac{\text{P}-\text{Q B }4}{\text{P}-\text{K }3}$
3.	$\dfrac{\text{Kt}-\text{Q B }3}{\text{Kt}-\text{K B }3}$	$\dfrac{\text{Kt}-\text{Q B }3}{\text{Kt}-\text{K B }3}$	$\dfrac{\text{Kt}-\text{Q B }3}{\text{Kt}-\text{K B }3}$
4.	$\dfrac{\text{Kt}-\text{B }3}{\text{P}-\text{Q R }3}$	$\dfrac{\text{Kt}-\text{B }3}{\text{P}-\text{Q Kt }3}$	$\dfrac{\text{B}-\text{Kt }5}{\text{B}-\text{K }2}$
5.	$\dfrac{\text{P}-\text{B }5}{\text{B}-\text{K }2}$	$\dfrac{\text{B}-\text{Kt }5}{\text{B}-\text{K }2}$	$\dfrac{\text{P}-\text{K }3}{0-0}$

	(1)	(2)	(3)
6.	B—Kt 5 (a) / 0—0	P—K 3 / B—Kt 2	Kt—B 3 / R—K 1
7.	P—K 3 / P—Q Kt 3 (b)	R—Q B 1 / Q Kt—Q 2	B—K 2 / Q Kt—Q 2
8.	P—Q Kt 4 / B—Kt 2	P×P / P×P	0—0 / P—B 3
9.	B×Kt / B×B	B—Q 3 / 0—0	R—B 1 / Kt—B 1
10.	B—Q 3 / P—Q R 4	0—0 / Kt—K 5	Q—Kt 3 / Kt—Kt 3
11.	P—Q R 3 / Kt—Q 2 (c)	B—K B 4 / P—Q B 4	K R—Q 1 / P—K R 3
12.	B P×P / B P×P	Q—K 2 / P—B 4	B×Kt / B×B
13.	0—0 / Q—K 2 (d)	K R—Q 1 / P—Q B 5	B—Q 3 / Kt—R 5
14.	Q—Kt 3 (e) / P×P	B×Kt / B P×B	Kt×Kt / B×Kt
15.	P×P / K R—B 1	Kt—K 5 / Kt—B 3	P—K 4 / P×K P
16.	B—Kt 5 (f) / Kt—B 1	P—K Kt 4 / Q—K 1	B×P / B—B 3
17.	K R—B 1 / Kt—Kt 3	Q—B 1 / B—Q 3	Kt—K 2 / Q—B 2
18.	B—K 2 / Q—Q 1	P—K R 3 / Q R—Q 1	Q—K B 3 / B—Q 2

(a) It has been previously remarked that the Q B in these games can seldom be advantageously played to the King's side.

(b) This appears the only safe and effectual way of bringing the Q B into play.

(c) Threatening to gain a Pawn.

(d) A much better move than advancing the **K P** one step, which would have cost Black at least a Pawn (e.g.)

11.	P—K 4
12. P×P	Kt×P
13. Kt×Kt	B×Kt
14. B×P ch.	K×B
15. Q—R 5 ch.	K—Kt 1
16. Q×B, &c.	

(e) Well played.

(f) A lost move.

	(1)	(2)	(3)
19.	Kt—Kt 5 / B—K 2	Q—Kt 2 / P—Q Kt 4	P—Q Kt 3 / Q R—Q 1
20.	Kt—K 1 / B—R 3 (a)	Kt—K 2 / P—Kt 5	B—B 2 / B—Kt 4
21.	P—B 4 / Kt—R 5	Kt—Kt 3 / Kt—Q 2	R—Kt 1 / P—K B 4
22.	K—B 2 / Kt—B 4	Kt×Kt / R×Kt	Kt—Kt 3 / B—B 1
23.	K Kt—B 3 / B×Kt	Kt—K 2 / B×B	Kt—K 2 / P—K 4
24.	R×R / R×R	Kt×B / Q R—K B 2	P×K P / Q×P
25.	B×B / Kt—Q 3	P—Kt 5 / R—B 4	Kt—Kt 3 / P—K Kt 3
26.	B—Q 3 / P—Q Kt 4	K—R 1 / P—Q R 4	Kt—K 1 / Q—K 7
27.	Kt—K 5 / Kt—B 5	R—K Kt 1 / B—Q B 1	R×R / B×R
28.	Kt—B 6 / Q—Q 3	Q—Kt 3 / Q—R 5	Q—B 3 / Q—K 4
29.	Kt×B ch. / Q×Kt	P—Q Kt 3 / P×P	Q—B 3 / B—Kt 3
30.	B×Kt / Q P×B (b)	P×P / Q×P	B—Q 3 / P—K R 4 ! (c)
31.	Q—Kt 2 / R—R 5	R—B 7 / P—R 5	P—Q Kt 4 / P—Q 5
32.	R—Q Kt 1 / Q—R 2	P—Kt 6 / P—K R 3	Q—Q 1 / B×P ch
33.	Q—B 2 / P—Kt 3	R×P ch. / K×R	K×B / Q—Q 5 ch.
34.	P—R 4 / Q—K 2	Kt—R 5 ch. / R×Kt	K—B 3 / P—B 5 (d)
35.	R—K R 1 / Q×Kt P	Q—B 7 ch. / K—B 3	Resigns.

(a) From this point the game is in Black's favour.

(b) Black properly takes with the Q P, foreseeing, in the event of the capital Pieces being changed off, that a White passed P on the Q Kt file would be out of reach of his King.

(c) The key move of a very fine ending.

(d) Crushing.

	(1)	(2)	(3)
36.	Q—K 4 / Q—Kt 7 ch.	Q—Q 6 ch. and mates in 3 moves (c)	
37.	K—Kt 3 / R—R 7		
38.	R—K B 1 / P—Kt 5		
39.	Q—Kt 7 / P—R 4		(1) (contd.)
40.	K—R 3 / P—B 6		

	(1)		(3)
40.		46. R×R / Q×R	52. Q—Q B 1 / Q—B 4 ch.
41.	R—K Kt 1 / Q—K B 7	47. Q×Kt P / Q—Kt 8	53. K—R 2 / Q—Q 6
42.	Q—Kt 8 ch. / K—R 2	48. Q—Kt 7 / K—Kt 2	54. P—B 5 / Q—K 7 ch.
43.	Q—K B 8 / Q×K P ch.	49. Q—K 4 / Q—B 4	55. K—R 3 / Q—Q 8
44.	P—Kt 3 / R—R 2	50. Q—K 1 / P—B 7	56. P×P ch. / P×P
45.	R—Q R 1 (a) / Q×Q P (b)	51. Q—R 1 ch. / K—R 2	57. Resigns

	(4) Tinsley / Alapin	(5) Steinitz / Lasker	(6) Steinitz / Lasker
1.	P—Q 4 / P—Q 4	P—Q 4 / P—Q 4	P—Q 4 / P—Q 4
2.	P—Q B 4 / P—K 3	P—Q B 4 / P—K 3	P—Q B 4 / P—K 3
3.	P—K 3 / Kt—K B 3	Kt—Q B 3 / P—Q B 3	Kt—Q B 3 / Kt—K B 3
4.	Kt—Q B 3 / P—Q Kt 3	P—K 3 / Kt—B 3	B—B 4 / B—K 2
5.	Kt—B 3 / B—Kt 2	Kt—B 3 / B—Q 3	P—K 3 / O—O
6.	B—Q 3 / P×P	B—Q 3 / Q Kt—Q 2	P—B 5 / Kt—K 5

(a) High praise is due to White for the pertinacious ingenuity with which he struggled to draw the game.

(b) Had he taken the Rook, White would have drawn the game.

(c) "A magnificent finish in Blackburne's happiest style."

	(4)	(5)	(6)
7.	$\dfrac{B \times P}{B - K\,2}$	$\dfrac{0 - 0}{0 - 0}$	$\dfrac{Kt \times Kt}{P \times Kt}$
8.	$\dfrac{0 - 0}{0 - 0}$	$\dfrac{P - K\,4\,!}{P \times K\,P}$	$\dfrac{Q - B\,2\,!}{P - B\,4}$
9.	$\dfrac{B - Q\,3}{P - B\,4}$	$\dfrac{Kt \times P}{Kt \times Kt}$	$\dfrac{B - B\,4}{Kt - B\,3}$
10.	$\dfrac{P - Q\,Kt\,3}{P \times P}$	$\dfrac{B \times Kt}{P - K\,R\,3}\,(a)$	$\dfrac{P - Q\,R\,3}{B - B\,3}\,(b)$
11.	$\dfrac{Kt \times P}{Q\,Kt - Q\,2}$	$\dfrac{B - B\,2}{P - K\,B\,4}$	$\dfrac{0 - 0 - 0}{K - R\,1}$
12.	$\dfrac{B - Kt\,2}{Kt - B\,4}$	$\dfrac{R - K\,1}{Kt - B\,3}$	$\dfrac{P - B\,3}{Q - K\,2\,!}$
13.	$\dfrac{P - B\,4}{Kt \times B}$	$\dfrac{B - Q\,2}{B - Q\,2}$	$\dfrac{B - K\,Kt\,3\,!}{P - B\,5}$
14.	$\dfrac{Q \times Kt}{P - K\,4}$	$\dfrac{B - B\,3}{Q - B\,2}$	$\dfrac{Q \times P\,!\,(c)}{P \times B}$
15.	$\dfrac{P \times P}{Kt - Kt\,5}$	$\dfrac{Kt - K\,5\,!}{B - K\,1}$	$\dfrac{P \times P}{P - K\,Kt\,3}\,(d)$
16.	$\dfrac{P - K\,6}{Q - Q\,3}$	$\dfrac{Q - Q\,3}{P - K\,Kt\,4\,?}$	$\dfrac{Q \times Kt\,P}{B - Q\,2}$
17.	$\dfrac{P \times P\ ch.}{R \times P}$	$\dfrac{Q - R\,3}{Q - Kt\,2}$	$\dfrac{P - B\,4}{R - B\,2}$
18.	$\dfrac{P - Kt\,3}{Kt \times R\,P}$	$\dfrac{Q\,R - Q\,1\,!}{P - Kt\,5}$	$\dfrac{P - K\,Kt\,4\,!}{R - Kt\,2}$
19.	$\dfrac{P - Kt\,4}{Kt \times R}$	$\dfrac{Q - K\,3}{B - R\,4}$	$\dfrac{Q - R\,6}{R \times P}$
20.	$\dfrac{R \times Kt}{B - R\,3}$	$\dfrac{Kt \times B\,P\,!}{B \times P\ ch.}$	$\dfrac{B - Q\,3}{R - Kt\,2}$

(a) Better is Kt—B 3.
(b) If 10.   P—K Kt 4 ?
   11. B—K Kt 3   P—B 5
   12. Q×P   P×B
   13. R P×P, &c.
(c) Quite sound.
(d) If 15.   P—K Kt 4
   16. B—K 2   R—B 2
   17. P—B 4   P—Kt 5
   18. Kt—K 2

	(4)	(5)	(6)
21.	Q×B (a) / Q×P ch.	K×B / P—Kt 6 ch.	Kt—B 3 / Q—B 2
22.	K—R 1 / B—Q 3	Q×P / Q×Q ch.	P—K Kt 4 / Q R—K Kt 1
23.	P—K 5 / B×P	P×Q / B×R	P—Kt 5 / B—Q 1
24.	Kt—B 3 / R×Kt	B×B / P×Kt	R—R 2 / R—Kt 3
25.	Q—B 4 ch. / K—R 1 (b)	R×P (c) / Kt—K 5	Q—R 5 / R (Kt 3)—Kt 2
26.	Resigns	R×B P / Kt×B	Q R—R 1 / Q×Q
27.		P×Kt / K—Kt 2	R×Q / R—B 1
28.		R—R 6 and wins.	R×P ch. / R×R
29.			R×R ch. / K—Kt 1
30.			R×B / R—B 2
31.			B—B 4 ! / Resigns

	(7)	(8)	(9)
	Steinitz / Lasker	Pillsbury / Lasker	Schlechter / Marco
1.	P—Q 4 / P—Q 4	P—Q 4 / P—Q 4	P—Q 4 / P—Q 4
2.	P—Q B 4 / P—K 3	P—Q B 4 / P—K 3	P—Q B 4 / P—K 3
3.	Kt—Q B 3 / Kt—K B 3	Kt—Q B 3 / Kt—K B 3	Kt—Q B 3 / Kt—K B 3

(a) If 21. R×R / B×Q
    22. R×P ch. / K×R
    23. Kt—B 5 ch. / K—B 2
    24. Kt×Q / B×Kt, &c.
(b) A beautiful finish.
(c) If 25. / R—Q B 1
    26. B—B 3 / P—B 4
    27. P—Q 5

	(7)	(8)	(9)
4.	$\dfrac{\text{B—B 4}}{\text{B—K 2}}$	$\dfrac{\text{Kt—B 3}}{\text{P—B 4}}$	$\dfrac{\text{B—Kt 5}}{\text{B—K 2}}$
5.	$\dfrac{\text{P—K 3}}{\text{0—0}}$	$\dfrac{\text{B—Kt 5}}{\text{P}\times\text{Q P !}}$	$\dfrac{\text{P—K 3}}{\text{0—0}}$
6.	$\dfrac{\text{R—Q B 1}}{\text{P—B 4 !}}$	$\dfrac{\text{Q}\times\text{P}}{\text{Kt—B 3}}$	$\dfrac{\text{Kt—B 3}}{\text{Q Kt—Q 2}}$
7.	$\dfrac{\text{Q P}\times\text{P}}{\text{B}\times\text{P}}$	$\dfrac{\text{Q—R 4}}{\text{B—K 2}}$	$\dfrac{\text{R—B 1 !}}{\text{P—Q R 3}}$
8.	$\dfrac{\text{P}\times\text{P}}{\text{P}\times\text{P}}$	$\dfrac{\text{0—0—0}}{\text{Q—R 4}}$	$\dfrac{\text{P—B 5}}{\text{P—Kt 4}}$
9.	$\dfrac{\text{Kt—B 3}}{\text{Kt—B 3}}$	$\dfrac{\text{P—K 3}}{\text{B—Q 2}}$	$\dfrac{\text{P—Q Kt 4}}{\text{P—B 3}}$
10.	$\dfrac{\text{B—Q 3}}{\text{P—Q 5 !}}$	$\dfrac{\text{K—Kt 1 !}}{\text{P—K R 3}}$	$\dfrac{\text{B—Q 3}}{\text{P—Q R 4}}$
11.	$\dfrac{\text{P}\times\text{P}}{\text{Kt}\times\text{P}}$	$\dfrac{\text{P}\times\text{P}}{\text{P}\times\text{P}}$	$\dfrac{\text{P—Q R 3}}{\text{R—K 1}}$
12.	$\dfrac{\text{0—0}}{\text{B—K Kt 5}}$	$\dfrac{\text{Kt—Q 4 (a)}}{\text{0—0}}$	$\dfrac{\text{0—0}}{\text{Kt—R 4}}$
13.	$\dfrac{\text{Kt—Q Kt 5}}{\text{B}\times\text{Kt}}$	$\dfrac{\text{B}\times\text{Kt}}{\text{B}\times\text{B}}$	$\dfrac{\text{B}\times\text{B}}{\text{Q}\times\text{B}}$
14.	$\dfrac{\text{P}\times\text{B}}{\text{Kt—K 3}}$	$\dfrac{\text{Q—R 5 ?}}{\text{Kt}\times\text{Kt}}$	$\dfrac{\text{Kt—K 5}}{\text{Kt}\times\text{Kt}}$
15.	$\dfrac{\text{B—K 5 ?}}{\text{Kt—R 4 !}}$	$\dfrac{\text{P}\times\text{Kt}}{\text{B—K 3}}$	$\dfrac{\text{B}\times\text{P ch.}}{\text{K—B 1}}$
16.	$\dfrac{\text{K—R 1}}{\text{Q—Kt 4}}$	$\dfrac{\text{P—B 4}}{\text{Q R—B 1}}$	$\dfrac{\text{Q}\times\text{Kt}}{\text{Kt—B 5}}$
17.	$\dfrac{\text{B—Kt 3}}{\text{Q R—Q 1}}$	$\dfrac{\text{P—B 5 ?}}{\text{R}\times\text{Kt}}$	$\dfrac{\text{B—Q 3}}{\text{Q—B 3}}$
18.	$\dfrac{\text{Q—B 2}}{\text{Q—R 3 !}}$	$\dfrac{\text{P}\times\text{B}}{\text{R—Q R 6 !}}$	$\dfrac{\text{B}\times\text{Kt}}{\text{Kt P}\times\text{B}}$
19.	$\dfrac{\text{Q R—Q 1}}{\text{R—B 1}}$	$\dfrac{\text{P}\times\text{P ch. (b)}}{\text{R}\times\text{P}}$	$\dfrac{\text{P—Kt 5}}{\text{B—Q 2}}$

(a) If 12. B×Kt   B×B
     13. R×P   Q×R
     14. Kt×Q   B×Q
     15. Kt—B 7 ch.   K—Q 1
     16. Kt×R   B×P !

(b) If 19. P—K 7   R—K 1
     20. P×R   Q—Kt 3 ch.
     21. K—B 2   R—B 1 ch., &c.

	(7)	**(8)**	**(9)**
20.	$\dfrac{\text{Q}-\text{Kt 3}}{\text{P}-\text{Q R 3}}$	$\dfrac{\text{P}\times\text{R}}{\text{Q}-\text{Kt 3 ch.}}$	$\dfrac{\text{P}\times\text{P}}{\text{B}\times\text{P}}$
21.	$\dfrac{\text{Kt}-\text{B 3}}{\text{Kt}-\text{Q 5 !}}$	$\dfrac{\text{B}-\text{Kt 5}}{\text{Q}\times\text{B ch.}}$	$\dfrac{\text{R}-\text{Kt 1}}{\text{P}-\text{Kt 3}}$
22.	$\dfrac{\text{Q}\times\text{Kt P}}{\text{Kt}\times\text{B ch.}}$	$\dfrac{\text{K}-\text{R 1}}{\text{R}-\text{B 2}}$	$\dfrac{\text{Q}-\text{R 6 ch.}}{\text{K}-\text{K 2}}$
23.	$\dfrac{\text{P}\times\text{Kt}}{\text{K}-\text{Kt 1}}$	$\dfrac{\text{R}-\text{Q 2}}{\text{R}-\text{B 5}}$	$\dfrac{\text{R}-\text{Kt 6}}{\text{K}-\text{Q 2}}$
24.	$\dfrac{\text{Q}\times\text{R P}}{\text{R}-\text{Kt 3}}$	$\dfrac{\text{K R}-\text{Q 1}}{\text{R}-\text{B 6 !}}$	$\dfrac{\text{Q}-\text{R 3}}{\text{Q}-\text{Kt 4}}$
25.	$\dfrac{\text{Q}-\text{B 4}}{\text{R}\times\text{P}}$	$\dfrac{\text{Q}-\text{B 5}}{\text{Q}-\text{B 5}}$	$\dfrac{\text{K R}-\text{Kt 1}}{\text{R}-\text{R 1}}$
26.	$\dfrac{\text{P}-\text{K R 4}}{\text{B}-\text{R 2}}$	$\dfrac{\text{K}-\text{Kt 2}}{\text{R}\times\text{P !}}$	$\dfrac{\text{Q}-\text{B 3}}{\text{P}-\text{B 4}}$
27.	$\dfrac{\text{B}-\text{K 4}}{\text{Q}-\text{Q 3 !}}$	$\dfrac{\text{Q}-\text{K 6 ch.}}{\text{K}-\text{R 2}}$	$\dfrac{\text{R}\times\text{B !}}{\text{K}\times\text{R}}$
28.	$\dfrac{\text{P}-\text{B 4 ?}}{\text{Q}-\text{Q 2 !}}$	$\dfrac{\text{K}\times\text{R}}{\text{B mates in } \mathbf{5}}$	$\dfrac{\text{Kt}\times\text{P}}{\text{Q R}-\text{Q Kt 1}}$
29.	$\dfrac{\text{B}-\text{Kt 2}}{\text{Q}-\text{Kt 5}}$		$\dfrac{\text{Kt}-\text{B 4 ch.}}{\text{K}-\text{Q 2}}$
30.	$\dfrac{\text{Q}-\text{Q 3}}{\text{Kt}-\text{B 4}}$		$\dfrac{\text{R}-\text{Kt 7 ch.}}{\text{R}\times\text{R}}$
31.	$\dfrac{\text{Kt}-\text{K 4}}{\text{B}-\text{K 6 (!)}}$		$\dfrac{\text{Q}\times\text{R ch.}}{\text{K}-\text{K 1}}$
32.	$\dfrac{\text{R}-\text{B 3}}{\text{R}\times\text{B}}$		$\dfrac{\text{P}-\text{B 6}}{\text{Resigns.}}$
33.	$\dfrac{\text{K}\times\text{R}}{\text{Kt}\times\text{P ch.}}$		
34.	$\dfrac{\text{K}-\text{R 2}}{\text{Kt}\times\text{R ch.}}$		
35.	$\dfrac{\text{K}-\text{Kt 2}}{\text{Kt}-\text{R 5 ch.}}$		
36.	$\dfrac{\text{K}-\text{R 2}}{\text{Kt}-\text{B 4}}$		

(7) (*contd.*)

37.	$\dfrac{\text{R}-\text{Q Kt 1}}{\text{P}-\text{R 4}}$	39.	$\dfrac{\text{P}-\text{R 3}}{\text{R}\times\text{P}}$
38.	$\dfrac{\text{R}-\text{Kt 5}}{\text{R}-\text{R 1}}$	40.	$\dfrac{\text{Resigns }(a)}{}$

(a) For if 40. Q × R   Q − K 7 ch. !

Chapter III.

THE SICILIAN DEFENCE—ANALYSIS.

	(1)	(2)	(3)
1.	$\dfrac{\text{P—K 4}}{\text{P—Q B 4}}$	—	—
2.	$\dfrac{\text{Kt—K B 3}}{\text{P—K 3}}$	—	—
3.	$\dfrac{\text{P—Q 4}\ (a)}{\text{P—Q 4}}$	—	$\dfrac{\text{P}\times\text{P}}{}$
4.	$\dfrac{\text{P}\times\text{Q P}}{\text{K P}\times\text{P}}$	—	$\dfrac{\text{Kt}\times\text{P}}{\text{B—B 4}}$
5.	$\dfrac{\text{P—B 4}}{\text{P}\times\text{Q P}}$	$\dfrac{\text{B—Kt 5 ch.}}{\text{Kt—B 3}}$	$\dfrac{\text{Kt—Q B 3}}{\text{Q—Kt 3}}$
6.	$\dfrac{\text{P}\times\text{P}}{\text{Q}\times\text{P}}$	$\dfrac{\text{B—K 3}}{\text{P}\times\text{P}}$	$\dfrac{\text{Kt—R 4}}{\text{Q—R 4 ch.}}$
7.	$\dfrac{\text{Q}\times\text{P}}{\text{Q}\times\text{Q}}$	$\dfrac{\text{Kt}\times\text{P}}{\text{B—Q 2}}$	$\dfrac{\text{P—B 3}}{}=$
8.	$\dfrac{\text{Kt}\times\text{Q}}{\text{B—Q B 4}}$	$\dfrac{\text{P—Q B 4}}{\text{P}\times\text{P}}$	
9.	$\dfrac{\text{Kt—Kt 3}}{\text{B—Kt 3}}$	$\dfrac{\text{B}\times\text{P}}{\text{B—Kt 5 ch.}}$	
10.	$\dfrac{\text{B—Q B 4}}{\text{Kt—K B 3}}$	$\dfrac{\text{Kt—Q B 3}}{\text{K Kt—K 2}}$	
11.	$\dfrac{\text{0—0}}{\text{0—0}}=$	$\dfrac{\text{0—0}}{\text{B}\times\text{Kt}}$	
12.		$\dfrac{\text{P}\times\text{B}}{\text{0—0}}=$	

(a) If 3. $\dfrac{\text{Kt—B 3}}{\text{Kt—Q B 3}}$; 4. $\dfrac{\text{B—Kt 5}}{\text{P—Q R 3}}$

	(4)	(5)	(6)
1.	—	—	—
2.	$\dfrac{\text{P--Q 4}}{\text{P} \times \text{P}}$	—	—
3.	$\dfrac{\text{Q} \times \text{P}}{\text{Kt--Q B 3}}$	—	$\dfrac{\text{Kt--K B 3}}{\text{P--K 4}}$
4.	$\dfrac{\text{Q--Q 1}}{\text{Kt--B 3}}$	$\dfrac{\text{P--B 4}}{\text{P} \times \text{P}}$	$\dfrac{\text{B--Q B 4}}{\text{Kt--K B 3(or B--K 2)}}$
5.	$\dfrac{\text{Kt--Q B 3}}{\text{P--K 3}}$	$\dfrac{\text{P} \times \text{P}}{\text{Kt--B 3}}$	$\dfrac{\text{Kt--Kt 5}}{\text{P--Q 4}}$
6.	$\dfrac{\text{B--K Kt 5}}{\text{B--K 2}} =$	$\dfrac{\text{P--K Kt 4}}{\text{Q--R 5 ch.}}$	$\dfrac{\text{P} \times \text{P}}{\text{P--K R 3}}$
7.		$\dfrac{\text{Kt--B 3}}{\text{P--K R 4}}$	$\dfrac{\text{Kt--K B 3}}{\text{B--K Kt 5}}$
8.		$\dfrac{\text{P--Kt 5}}{\text{Kt--K 5}}$	$\dfrac{\text{P--K R 3}}{\text{Q--B 2}}$
9.		$\dfrac{\text{Q--Q 3}}{\text{Kt} \times \text{Kt}}$	$\dfrac{\text{P} \times \text{B}}{\text{Q} \times \text{B}}$
10.		$\dfrac{\text{P} \times \text{Kt}}{\text{P--Q 3}}$	$\dfrac{\text{Kt} \times \text{K P}}{\text{Q} \times \text{Q P}}$
11.		$\dfrac{\text{B--K R 3}}{\text{Kt--K 4}}$	$\dfrac{\text{0--0}}{\text{B--Q 3}}$
12.		$\dfrac{\text{Q--Q 2}}{\text{B--Q 2} +}$	$\dfrac{\text{B--B 4}}{\text{0--0}}$
13.			$\dfrac{\text{P--B 4}}{\text{Q--K 5}}$
14.			$\dfrac{\text{Q--B 3}}{\text{Q} \times \text{Q}}$
15.			$\dfrac{\text{P} \times \text{Q}}{\text{Kt--B 3}}$
16.			$\dfrac{\text{Kt} \times \text{Kt}}{\text{B} \times \text{B}} =$

	(7)	(8)	(9)
1.	—	—	—
2.	—	$\dfrac{\text{P--K B 4}}{\text{P--K 3}}$	$\dfrac{\text{Kt--Q B 3}}{\text{Kt--K B 3}}$
3.	$\dfrac{}{\text{Kt--Q B 3}}$	$\dfrac{\text{Kt--K B 3}}{\text{P--Q 4}}$	$\dfrac{\text{Kt--K B 3}}{\text{P--K 3}}$

	(7)	(8)	(9)
4.	$\dfrac{\text{Kt}\times\text{P}}{\text{P}-\text{K 3}\,(x)}$	$\dfrac{\text{P}-\text{K 5}}{\text{Kt}-\text{Q B 3}}$	$\dfrac{\text{B}-\text{K 2}}{\text{P}-\text{Q 4}}$
5.	$\dfrac{\text{Kt}-\text{Kt 5}}{\text{P}-\text{Q R 3}}$	$\dfrac{\text{P}-\text{B 3}}{\text{P}-\text{B 3}}$	$\dfrac{\text{P}-\text{Q 3}}{\text{P}\times\text{P}}$
6.	$\dfrac{\text{Kt}-\text{Q 6 ch.}}{\text{B}\times\text{Kt}}$	$\dfrac{\text{B}-\text{Q 3}}{\text{Kt}-\text{R 3}}$	$\dfrac{\text{P}\times\text{P}}{\text{Q}\times\text{Q ch.}}$
7.	$\dfrac{\text{Q}\times\text{B}}{\text{Q}-\text{K 2}}$	$\dfrac{\text{B}-\text{B 2}}{\text{Q}-\text{Kt 3}+}$	$\dfrac{\text{B}\times\text{Q}}{\text{Kt}-\text{B 3}}$
8.	$\dfrac{\text{Q}-\text{Kt 3}+}{}$		$\dfrac{\text{Kt}-\text{B 3}}{\text{B}-\text{Q 2}}$
9.			$\dfrac{\text{B}-\text{K 3}}{0-0}=$

	(10)	(11)	(12)
1.	—	—	—
2.	$\dfrac{\text{P}-\text{Q B 4}}{\text{P}-\text{K 3}}$	$\dfrac{\text{P}-\text{Q Kt 4}}{\text{P}\times\text{P}}$	—
3.	$\dfrac{\text{Kt}-\text{K B 3}}{\text{Kt}-\text{Q B 3}}$	$\dfrac{\text{P}-\text{Q 4}}{\text{P}-\text{Q 4}}$	$\dfrac{\text{P}-\text{K 3}}{}$
4.	$\dfrac{\text{Kt}-\text{B 3}}{\text{P}-\text{K Kt 3}}$	$\dfrac{\text{P}-\text{K 5}}{\text{B}-\text{B 4}}$	$\dfrac{\text{P}-\text{Q R 3}}{\text{P}\times\text{P}}$
5.	$\dfrac{\text{P}-\text{Q 3}}{\text{B}-\text{Kt 2}}$	$\dfrac{\text{P}-\text{Q R 3}}{\text{P}\times\text{P}}$	$\dfrac{\text{B}\times\text{P}}{\text{B}\times\text{B}}$
6.	$\dfrac{\text{B}-\text{K 2}}{\text{K Kt}-\text{K 2}+}$	$\dfrac{\text{B}\times\text{P}}{\text{Q Kt}-\text{B 3}+}$	$\dfrac{\text{R}\times\text{B}}{\text{Q Kt}-\text{B 3}}$
7.			$\dfrac{\text{P}-\text{K B 4}}{\text{P}-\text{Q 4}}$
8.			$\dfrac{\text{P}-\text{K 5}}{\text{Kt}-\text{R 3}}$
9.			$\dfrac{\text{Kt}-\text{K B 3}}{0-0+}$

(a) If 4. $\dfrac{}{\text{P}-\text{K 4}}$;   5. $\dfrac{\text{Kt}-\text{Kt 5}}{\text{P}-\text{Q 3}}$;   6. $\dfrac{\text{B}-\text{K 3}}{}$

	(13)	(14)	(15)
1.	—	P—K 4 / P—Q B 4	—
2.	B—B 4 / P—K 3	Kt—Q B 3 / Kt—Q B 3	—
3.	Kt—Q B 3 / P—Q R 3	Kt—B 3 / P—K Kt 3	—
4.	P—Q R 4 / Kt—K 2	P—Q 4 / P×P	—
5.	P—Q 4 / P—Q 4	Kt×P / B—Kt 2	—
6.	K×P / K P×P	B—K 3 / Kt—B 3	P—Q 3
7.	B—K 2 / P×P	B—K 2 / 0—0	B—K 2 / Kt—B 3
8.	Q×P / Kt—B 3	Q—Q 2 / P—Q 3	0—0 / 0—0
9.		P—K R 3 / B—Q 2	P—K R 3 / B—Q 2
10.		0—0 / R—B 1	
11.		Q R—Q 1 / Q—R 4	

	(16)	(17)	(18)
1.	—	—	—
2.	—	—	—
3.	Kt—B 3	—	P—K 3
4.	P—Q 4 / P×P	—	P—Q 4 / P×P
5.	Kt×P / P—Q 3	—	Kt×P / Kt—B 3
6.	B—Q Kt 5 / B—Q 2	B—K 2 / P—K 3	K Kt—Kt 5 / B—Kt 5
7.	0—0 / P—K Kt 3	B—K 3 / P—Q R 3	Kt—Q 6 ch. / K—K 2
8.	K Kt—K 2	0—0 / B—K 2	B—K B 4 / P—K 4

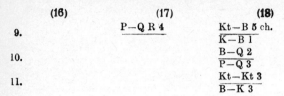

	(16)	(17)	(18)
9.		P—Q R 4	Kt—B 5 ch.
			K—B 1
10.			B—Q 2
			P—Q 3
11.			Kt—Kt 3
			B—K 3

Nos. 14 to 20. Position after White's 3rd move.

BLACK.

WHITE.

	(19)	(20)
1.	—	—
2.	—	—
3.	—	—
4.	—	—
5.	—	P—Q R 3
6.	Kt×Kt	B—K 2
	Kt P×Kt	Kt—B 3

	(19)	(20)
7.	$\dfrac{\text{P—Kt 5}}{\text{Kt—Q 4}}$	$\dfrac{\text{Kt}\times\text{Kt}}{\text{Kt P}\times\text{Kt}}$
8.	$\dfrac{\text{Kt—K 4}}{\text{P—K B 4}}$	$\dfrac{\text{P—K 5}}{\text{Kt—Q 4}}$
9.	$\dfrac{\text{Kt—Q 6 ch.}}{\text{B}\times\text{Kt}}$	$\dfrac{\text{Kt—K 4}}{\text{P}\times\text{B 4}}$
10.	$\dfrac{\text{P}\times\text{B}}{\text{0—0}}$	
11.	$\dfrac{\text{B—K 2}}{\text{P—K 4}}$	
12.	$\dfrac{\text{0—0}}{}$	

THE SICILIAN DEFENCE—GAMES.

	(1) McDonnell / La Bourdonnais	(2) Cochrane / Staunton	(3) Cochrane / Staunton	(4) Horwitz / Staunton
1.	$\dfrac{\text{P—K 4}}{\text{P—Q B 4}}$	$\dfrac{\text{P—K 4}}{\text{P—Q B 4}}$	$\dfrac{\text{P—K 4}}{\text{P—Q B 4}}$	$\dfrac{\text{P—K 4}}{\text{P—Q B 4}}$
2.	$\dfrac{\text{Kt—K B 3}}{\text{Kt—Q B 3}}$	$\dfrac{\text{P—Q 4}}{\text{P}\times\text{P}}$	$\dfrac{\text{P—Q 4}}{\text{P}\times\text{P}}$	$\dfrac{\text{B—B 4}}{\text{P—K 3}}$
3.	$\dfrac{\text{P—Q 4}}{\text{P}\times\text{P}}$	$\dfrac{\text{Q}\times\text{P}}{\text{Kt—Q B 3}}$	$\dfrac{\text{Kt—K B 3}}{\text{P—K 4}}$	$\dfrac{\text{Kt—Q B 3}}{\text{Kt—Q B 3}}$
4.	$\dfrac{\text{Kt}\times\text{P}}{\text{Kt}\times\text{Kt}\ (a)}$	$\dfrac{\text{Q—Q 1}}{\text{P—K 4}}$	$\dfrac{\text{B—Q B 4}}{\text{Kt—K B 3}}$	$\dfrac{\text{P—B 4}}{\text{P—Q R 3}}$
5	$\dfrac{\text{Q}\times\text{Kt}}{\text{P—K 3}}$	$\dfrac{\text{B—Q B 4}}{\text{Kt—B 3}}$	$\dfrac{\text{Kt—Kt 5}}{\text{P—Q 4}}$	$\dfrac{\text{P—Q R 4}}{\text{P—K Kt 3}}$
6.	$\dfrac{\text{B—Q B 4}}{\text{Kt—K 2}}$	$\dfrac{\text{Kt—K B 3}}{\text{B—B 4}\ (b)}$	$\dfrac{\text{P}\times\text{P}}{\text{P—K R 3}}$	$\dfrac{\text{Kt—B 3}}{\text{B—Kt 2}}$
7.	$\dfrac{\text{Kt—B 3}}{\text{Kt—B 3}}$	$\dfrac{\text{0—0}}{\text{0—0}}$	$\dfrac{\text{Kt—K B 3}}{\text{B—K Kt 5}}$	$\dfrac{\text{0—0}}{\text{Kt—R 3}}$
8.	$\dfrac{\text{Q—Q 1}}{\text{B—B 4}}$	$\dfrac{\text{Kt—B 3}}{\text{P—K R 3}}$	$\dfrac{\text{P—K R 3}}{\text{Q—B 2}}$	$\dfrac{\text{P—Q 3}}{\text{P—B 4}}$

(a) This is not so good as P—K 4.
(b) Had he taken the K P, White would have played B×P ch.,
and then Q—Q 5.

	(1)	(2)	(3)	(4)
9.	0-0 / 0-0	P-Q R 3 (b) / P-Q R 3	P×B / Q×B	Q-K 1 / 0-0 (e)
10.	K-R 1 / P-B 4	B-Q 5 / P-Q 3	Kt×K P / Q×Q P	B-K 3 / P-Kt 3
11.	P×P / R×P	B×Kt / P×B	0-0 / B-Q 3	P-R 3 / Kt-K 2 (f)
12.	B-Q 3 / R-B 1	Kt-K1 / Kt-Kt 5	B-B 4 / 0-0	P-K 5 / B-Kt 2
13.	Q-R 5 / R-B 4 (a)	P-R 3 / Kt-B 3	R-K 1 (d) / R-K 1	P-Q 4 / P×P
14.	B×R / P×B	K-R 1 / Kt-R 2	P-B 4 / Q-R 4	Kt×P / Q-B 2
15.	Q×B P / P-Q 3	Kt-Q 3 / B-R 2	B-Q 2 / Q-B 2	P-Q Kt 3 / Kt-B 3
16.	Q-Q 5 ch. / K-R 1	P-B 4 / Q-R 5	Kt-Q 3 / R×R ch.	Q-B 2 / Q R-Q Kt 1 (g)
17.	B-Kt 5 / Q-B 1	Q-B 3 / P-K B 4	B×R / Q×P	Q R-Q 1 (h) / Kt×Kt
18.	Kt-K 4 / Kt-Kt 5	P×B P / B×B	Q-B 3 / Kt-B 3	B×Kt / B-B 1 (i)
19.	Q-Kt 3 / B-B 4	P-K Kt 4 / Kt-Kt 4	B-Q 2 / R-K 1	Q-K 2 / Q-Kt 2 (j)
20.	Q R-K 1 / B-Q 2	Q-Kt 2 (c) / Kt×P	P-Kt 5 / P×P	B-B 2 (k) / Kt-B 2

(a) He appears to have no better move.

(b) With the intention of advancing the Q Kt P and removing the adverse Knight from the support of the K P.

(c) If White had ventured to take the Knight, Black would have played the B—K 5, winning the Queen.

(d) P—Q B 4 would, perhaps, have been better play.

(e) This game is opened with remarkable care and prudence on both sides.

(f) Threatening to win a Piece shortly, by P—Q 4.

(g) Imperative, for preserving the Kt P.

(h) He might have gained three Pawns for a Piece by Kt×K P.

(i) The only move to save the Pawn, for Q—B 3 would have been unavailing.

(j) Black is driven to this abject defence for a time to preserve his Pawns.

(k) Well played. To understand the merit of this move, the student should observe that during the whole of the attack and defence on the Queen's side, Black has been looking for that moment

	(1)	(2)	(3)	(4)
21.	P—Q R 4 and wins.	Q—R 2 / Q×P	B×P / Kt—Q Kt 5 (a)	K—Q 3 / K R—K 1
22.		Q—Kt 2 / Q—R 5	B—B 4 / B×B	K R—Q 1 / B—R 3 (b)
23.		Q—R 2 / P—K 5	Kt×B / Q—Q B 8 ch.	P—K Kt 3 / B—K B 1
24.		Kt—K 1 / B—Kt 8	K—R 2 / Q×P	K—R 2 / Q—B 3 (c)
25.		R×B / Kt—B 7 ch	Resigns	R (Q 3)—Q 2 / B—Kt 5
26.		K—Kt 2 / B—R 6 ch.		B—Q 4 / B×Kt
27.		Resigns.		B×B / P—Q Kt 4
28.				R—Q 6 (d) / Kt×R

to throw forward his Q P, when White, by taking it *en passant*, would expose an unprotected Piece to the range of the Black K B. Hitherto White has very cleverly thwarted him, and effectually prevented his advancing the Pawn beneficially ; but now, having his Q R bearing on the file, he changes his tactics, and seemingly affords his adversary the very opportunity desired ; since if Black at this point plays on his Q P, White cannot take it in passing without losing his Knight. Upon looking into the position, however, it will be seen that if Black throws forward his Q P, White, instead of taking it *en passant*, would simply take it with his Knight ; and if the Knight were taken, would win the adverse Queen by the check of the Bishop.

(*a*) Black might also have secured the game thus :—

21.		Q×Kt
22.	Q×Q	R—K 8 ch.
23.	Q—B 1	B—R 7 ch.
24.	K×B	R×Q

Locking up White's remaining Pieces, and winning easily.

(*b*) An important move, far better than playing the Bishop to his square at once, because it compels his adversary to make a move in some degree prejudicial to his game.

(*c*) Black has now an irresistible position. He threatens to gain a Piece by pushing on the Q Kt P.

(*d*) The ingenuity of desperation ; he sacrifices the exchange, for the purpose, if possible, of playing Q—K 5.

(4) (contd.)

29. $\dfrac{\text{P} \times \text{Kt}}{\text{B} - \text{Kt } 2}$ (a)

30. $\dfrac{\text{P} \times \text{P}}{\text{P} \times \text{P}}$

31. $\dfrac{\text{B} \times \text{P}}{\text{Q} \times \text{B}}$

32. $\dfrac{\text{B} \times \text{P}}{\text{B} - \text{B } 6}$

33. $\dfrac{\text{R} - \text{Q } 3}{\text{B} \times \text{Q}}$

34. $\dfrac{\text{R} \times \text{Q}}{\text{K R} - \text{Q } 1}$

35. $\dfrac{\text{B} \times \text{P ch.}}{\text{K} - \text{B } 1}$

36. $\dfrac{\text{P} - \text{Q } 7}{\text{B} - \text{Kt } 4}$

37. $\dfrac{\text{P} - \text{K R4}}{\text{B} \times \text{P}}$

38. $\dfrac{\text{B} - \text{B } 4}{\text{B} - \text{Kt } 4}$

39. $\dfrac{\text{B} \times \text{B}}{\text{R} \times \text{B}}$

40. $\dfrac{\text{K} - \text{R } 3}{\text{P} - \text{K R } 4}$

41. $\dfrac{\text{R} - \text{B } 6}{\text{K} - \text{Kt } 2}$

42. $\dfrac{\text{R} - \text{B } 7 \text{ ch.}}{\text{K} - \text{R } 3}$

43. $\dfrac{\text{R} - \text{B } 4}{\text{R} - \text{Q } 8}$

44. $\dfrac{\text{P} - \text{Q Kt } 4}{\text{Q R} - \text{Q } 4}$

45. $\dfrac{\text{K} - \text{Kt } 2}{\text{R} - \text{Q } 7 \text{ ch.}}$

46. $\dfrac{\text{K} - \text{B } 3}{\text{R} - \text{Q } 5}$

47. $\dfrac{\text{R} - \text{B } 8}{\text{R} \times \text{P}}$

48. $\dfrac{\text{K} - \text{K } 3}{\text{R (Q 8)} - \text{Q } 5}$ and wins.

	(5)	**(6)**	**(7)**	**(8)**
	Horwitz	Morphy	Berger	Janowski
	Staunton	Lowenthal	—	Marshall
1.	$\dfrac{\text{P} - \text{K } 4}{\text{P} - \text{Q B } 4}$	$\dfrac{\text{P} - \text{K } 4}{\text{P} - \text{Q B } 4}$	$\dfrac{\text{P} - \text{K } 4}{\text{P} - \text{Q B } 4}$	$\dfrac{\text{P} - \text{K } 4}{\text{P} - \text{Q B } 4}$
2.	$\dfrac{\text{P} - \text{K B } 4}{\text{P} - \text{K } 3}$	$\dfrac{\text{P} - \text{K B } 4}{\text{P} - \text{K } 3}$	$\dfrac{\text{Kt} - \text{Q B } 3}{\text{Kt} - \text{Q B } 3}$	$\dfrac{\text{Kt} - \text{K B } 3}{\text{P} - \text{K } 3}$
3.	$\dfrac{\text{Kt} - \text{K B } 3}{\text{Kt} - \text{Q B } 3}$	$\dfrac{\text{Kt} - \text{K B } 3}{\text{P} - \text{Q } 4}$	$\dfrac{\text{Kt} - \text{B } 3}{\text{Kt} - \text{B } 3}$	$\dfrac{\text{Kt} - \text{B } 3}{\text{P} - \text{Q } 4}$
4.	$\dfrac{\text{P} - \text{B } 4}{\text{P} - \text{Q } 3}$	$\dfrac{\text{P} \times \text{P}}{\text{P} \times \text{P}}$	$\dfrac{\text{P} - \text{Q } 4}{\text{P} \times \text{P}}$	$\dfrac{\text{P} \times \text{P}}{\text{P} \times \text{P}}$
5.	$\dfrac{\text{B} - \text{K } 2}{\text{Kt} - \text{K } 2}$	$\dfrac{\text{P} - \text{Q } 4}{\text{B} - \text{K Kt } 5}$ (b)	$\dfrac{\text{Kt} \times \text{P}}{\text{P} - \text{Q } 3}$	$\dfrac{\text{P} - \text{Q } 4}{\text{Kt} - \text{Q B } 3}$
6.	$\dfrac{0 - 0}{\text{Kt} - \text{Kt } 3}$	$\dfrac{\text{B} - \text{K } 2}{\text{B} \times \text{Kt}}$	$\dfrac{\text{B} - \text{K } 2}{\text{P} - \text{K Kt } 3}$	$\dfrac{\text{P} \times \text{P}}{\text{Kt} - \text{B } 3}$

(a) He would evidently have lost the game by taking the Bishop. The present move not only gives White no time to plant his Queen at K 5, but prevents another very dangerous move, viz. R—Q 5.

(b) Injudicious ; since by taking the Knight, he only assists White to post his K B in a most threatening attitude.

	(5)	(6)	(7)	(8)
7.	P—Q 3 / B—K 2	B×B / Kt—K B 3	B—K 3 / B—Kt 2	B—K 3 / B—K 2
8.	Kt—B 3 / B—B 3	0—0 / B—K 2 (c)	P—K R 3 / P—Q R 3	B—Q Kt 5 / 0—0
9.	Q—K 1 / P—Q R 3	B—K 3 / P×P	Q—Q 2 / 0—0	0—0 (d) / B—Kt 5
10.	K—R 1 / 0—0	Q B×P / 0—0	R—Q 1 / B—Q 2	B×Kt / P×P
11.	B—K 3 / R—Kt 1	Kt—B 3 / Kt—B 3	0—0 / Kt×Kt	B—Q 4 / Kt—K 5
12.	P—Q R 4 / Kt—Q 5	B×Kt / B×B	B×Kt / B—B 3	Kt—Q R 4 (?) / Kt—Kt 4 ! (e)
13.	B—Q 1 / B—Q 2 (a)	Kt×P / B×P	Q—K 3 / Kt—Q 2	B—K 3 / B×Kt (!)
14.	B×Kt / P×B	R—Kt 1 / B—Q 5 ch.	B×B / K×B	P×B / P—Q 5
15.	Kt—K 2 / P—Kt 4	K—R 1 / R—Kt 1	Q—Kt 3 / P—B 3	B×Kt / B×B
16.	B P×P / P×P	P—B 3 / B—B 4	B—Kt 4 / Kt—B 4	P—K B 4 / B×P
17.	P—R 5 / P—K 4 (b)	P—B 5 / Q—R 5	K R—K 1 / P—Q R 4	Q—Kt 4 / Q—B 3
18.	P—B 5 / Kt—K 2	P—Kt 3 / Q—Kt 4	P—K 5 / B P×P	K R—K 1 / Q R—K 1
19.	P—K Kt 4 / Kt—B 3	P—B 6 / Kt—K 4	K R×P / Kt—Q 2	Q—Kt 2 / R—K 3
20.	R—K Kt 1 / B—Kt 4	P×P / K R—Q 1	B×Kt / Q×B	Q R—Q 1 / R (B 1)—K 1

(a) It would, perhaps, have been prudent to return the Knight to B 3.

(b) Black's necessity to sustain the doubled Pawn gave White an opportunity of opening a powerful attack on the King's side.

(c) 8. P×P, and then 9. Kt—Q B 3, would have been far preferable.

(d) He should have played 9. P—K R 3.

(e) Threatening—

13.		Kt×Kt ch.
14.	P×Kt	B—R 6
15.	R—K 1	B×P !

	(5)	(6)	(7)	(8)
21.	B—Kt 3 (a) / B—K 6	B—K 4 / Q×P (Kt 7)	Q—K 3 / R—B 2	R×R / R×R
22.	R—Kt 2 / R—R 1	Q—R 5 / R—Q 3	R—K 6 / P—Q Kt 4	K—B 1 / Q—K 4
23.	P—R 6 / Kt—Kt 1	B×P ch. / K—B 1	R—K 1 / R—R 2	Q—B 3 / R—B 3
24.	P—Kt 5 / K—R 1 (b)	B—K 4 / R—R 3	Kt—K 2 / K—B 1	K—Kt 2 / B×P
25.	Q—R 4 / R×P	Q—B 5 / Q×P (h)	Kt—B 4 / K—K 1	Q—K R 3 / P—K R 3
26.	R—K B 1 (c) / Kt—B 3	R—Kt 2 / R—K 1	Q—Q 4 / K—Q 1	P—Q B 3 / Q—K 7
27.	R—Kt 3 / Kt—Kt 5	Kt—B 6 / R—K 3	Q—R 8 ch. / Q—K 1	R—K B 1 / B—K 4
28.	B×P (d) / R×B	R—Kt 2 / Q×R ch. (i)	R×Q P ch. / K—B 2	K—Kt 1 / P—Q 6
29.	Q—R 5 / Q—K Kt 1(e)	B×Q / R (R 3)×Kt	Kt—K 6 ch. / K—Kt 2	P—K B 4 / P—Q 7 & wins.
30.	Kt—R 4 / P—Q 4 (f)	Q×K R / R×Q	Kt—Q 8 ch. / K—R 1	—
31.	R—R 3 / P—Kt 3 (g)	R×R / Kt—Kt 5	R×B / Resigns.	—

(a) Very well played.

(b) A little examination will show that this was indispensable.

(c) White plays here with becoming care and foresight. He knew well the importance of getting his K R—K 3, with the object of afterwards placing it behind the Queen on the Rook's file, and he saw the difficulty of accomplishing it while Black's Bishop could be played to K B 7, a move effectually barred by the Q R being stationed at K B sq.

(d) This is an error. White forgot that on pushing forward his Kt P, as he meditated, Black could exchange Queens. His best move, we believe, was P—K B 6, from which many beautiful variations spring. He might also have played K R to his 3rd, and in either case would have had an irresistible attack.

(e) Played with the conviction that White, overlooking the Q R in reserve, would dash at a mate with his Knight.

(f) This may be called "The game move." By bringing the banished Rook into operation at the proper moment, Black completely paralyses his opponent's attack.

(g) Leaving White nothing but to retreat.

(h) Tempting, but very dangerous.

(i) He has nothing better.

	(5)	(6)		(6) (*contd.*)
32.	$\dfrac{\text{Q—Kt 4}}{\text{Kt×P}}$	$\dfrac{\text{R—B 5}}{\text{P—Kt 3}}$	44.	$\dfrac{\text{R—B 6}}{\text{P—B 5 ch.}}$
33.	$\dfrac{\text{Q—Kt 2}}{\text{Q P×P}}$	$\dfrac{\text{B—Q 5}}{\text{Kt—R 3}}$	45.	$\dfrac{\text{K×P}}{\text{B—B 7}}$
34.	$\dfrac{\text{Kt×P ch.}(a)}{\text{R×Kt}}$	$\dfrac{\text{R—B 6}}{\text{K—Kt 2}}$	46.	$\dfrac{\text{K—K 4}}{\text{B—B 4}}$
35.	$\dfrac{\text{P×R}}{\text{R×R ch.}}$	$\dfrac{\text{R—B 6}}{\text{P—R 4}}$	47.	$\dfrac{\text{R—B 5 ch.}}{\text{K×P}}$
36.	$\dfrac{\text{Q×R}}{\text{Kt—B 7 ch.}(b)}$	$\dfrac{\text{R—B 7}}{\text{K—Kt 3}}$	48.	$\dfrac{\text{R×B}}{\text{P×R}}$
37.	$\dfrac{\text{Q×Kt}}{\text{B×Q}}$	$\dfrac{\text{K—Kt 2}}{\text{P—B 3}}$	49.	K—Q5 and wins.
38.	$\dfrac{\text{R×P ch.}}{\text{Q×R}}$	$\dfrac{\text{K—B 3}}{\text{Kt—B 4}}$		
39.	$\dfrac{\text{P×Q}}{\text{K×P}}$	$\dfrac{\text{B—K 4}}{\text{K—Kt 4}}$		
40.	$\dfrac{\text{K—Kt 2}}{\text{P—K 6}}$	$\dfrac{\text{B×Kt}}{\text{K×B}}$		
41.	$\dfrac{\text{K—B 3}}{\text{B—B 3 ch.}}$	$\dfrac{\text{P—K R 4}}{\text{K—Kt 3}}$		
42.	$\dfrac{\text{K—Kt 4}}{\text{P—Q 6}}$	$\dfrac{\text{R—B 6}}{\text{K—R 4}}$		
43.	Resigns.	$\dfrac{\text{K—Kt 3}}{\text{P—B 4}}$		

(*a*) He would obviously have lost his Queen had he taken the doubled Pawn with her.

(*b*) We have here one of those positions where the young player, flushed with success, is too apt to suffer a victory within his reach to elude him. Nine out of ten inexperienced amateurs would now snatch at the Rook, conceiving the check with the Knight sheer loss of time; and would be astounded to learn that they had lost the game by their impetuosity. Let us suppose Black to have played in this manner :—

36.		B×R
37.	Q—B 6 ch.	Q—Kt 2
38.	Q—Q 8 ch.	Q—Kt 1
39.	P—Kt 7 ch.	K×P
40.	Q—B 6 mate ! !	

CHAPTER IV.

THE FRENCH DEFENCE—ANALYSIS.

	(1)	(2)	(3)
1.	$\dfrac{\text{P—K 4}}{\text{P—K 3}}$	—	—
2.	$\dfrac{\text{P—Q 4}}{\text{P—Q 4}}$	—	—
3.	$\dfrac{\text{P} \times \text{P}}{\text{P} \times \text{P}}$	—	$\dfrac{\text{P—K 5}}{\text{P—Q B 4}}$
4.	$\dfrac{\text{P—Q B 4 ?}}{\text{B—Kt 5 ch.}}$	$\dfrac{\text{Kt—K B 3}}{\text{Kt—K B 3}}$	$\dfrac{\text{B—Kt 5 ch}}{\text{Kt—B 3}}$
5.	$\dfrac{\text{B—Q 2}}{\text{Q—K 2 ch.}}$	$\dfrac{\text{B—K 3}}{\text{B—K 3}}$	$\dfrac{\text{B} \times \text{Kt}}{\text{P} \times \text{B}}$
6.	$\dfrac{\text{Q—K 2}}{\text{B—K 3}}$	$\dfrac{\text{B—Q 3}}{\text{B—Q 3}}$	$\dfrac{\text{P—Q B 3}}{\text{Q—Kt 3}}$
7.	$\dfrac{\text{P} \times \text{P}}{\text{B} \times \text{B ch.}}$	$\dfrac{\text{0—0}}{\text{0—0}} =$	$\dfrac{\text{Kt—B 3}}{\text{B—Q R 3}}$
8.	$\dfrac{\text{Kt} \times \text{B}}{\text{B} \times \text{P}}$		$\dfrac{\text{Q Kt—Q 2}}{\text{P} \times \text{P}}$
9.	$\dfrac{\text{K Kt—B 3 (or Q} \times \text{Q)}}{\text{Kt—Q B 3}}$		$\dfrac{\text{P} \times \text{P}}{\text{P—Q B 4}}$
10.	$\dfrac{\text{Q—K 3}}{\text{B} \times \text{Kt}}$		$\dfrac{\text{Kt—Kt 3}}{\text{P} \times \text{P}}$
11.	$\dfrac{\text{Kt} \times \text{B}}{\text{0—0—0}}$		$\dfrac{\text{K Kt} \times \text{P}}{\text{B—Kt 5 ch.}}$
12.	$\dfrac{\text{Q R—Q 1}}{\text{Q—Kt 5 ch.}}$		$\dfrac{\text{B—Q 2}}{\text{Kt—K 2}}$
13.	$\dfrac{\text{Q—Q 2}}{\text{Kt} \times \text{P} +}$		$\dfrac{\text{K Kt—K 2}}{\text{Kt—B 3}}$
14.			$\dfrac{\text{P—B 4}}{\text{Q—K 6}}$
15.			$\dfrac{\text{Q Kt—B 1}}{\text{0—0 +}}$

	(4)	(5)	(6)
1.	—	—	$\dfrac{\text{P—K 4}}{\text{P—K 3}}$
2.	$\dfrac{\text{P—K B 4}}{\text{P—Q 4}}$	—	$\dfrac{\text{P—Q 4}}{\text{P—Q 4}}$
3.	$\dfrac{\text{P}\times\text{P}}{\text{P}\times\text{P}}$	$\dfrac{\text{P—K 5}}{\text{P—Q B 4}}$	$\dfrac{\text{Kt—Q B 3}}{\text{Kt—K B 3}}$
4.	$\dfrac{\text{Kt—K B 3}}{\text{P—Q B 4}}$	$\dfrac{\text{Kt—K B 3}}{\text{Kt—Q B 3}}$	$\dfrac{\text{B—Kt 5}}{\text{B—K 2}}$
5.	$\dfrac{\text{P—Q 4}}{\text{Kt—Q B 3}}$	$\dfrac{\text{P—B 3}}{\text{P—B 3}}$	$\dfrac{\text{B}\times\text{Kt}}{\text{B}\times\text{B}}$
6.	$\dfrac{\text{P—B 3}}{\text{Kt—B 3}}$	$\dfrac{\text{Kt—R 3}}{\text{Kt—R 3}}$	$\dfrac{\text{P—K 5}}{\text{B—K 2}}$
7.	$\dfrac{\text{B—K 3}}{\text{Q—Kt 3}}$	$\dfrac{\text{Kt—B 2}}{\text{B—K 2}}$	$\dfrac{\text{Kt—B 3}}{\text{0—0}}$
8.	$\dfrac{\text{Q—Kt 3}}{\text{Kt—R 4}}$	$\dfrac{\text{P—Q 4}}{\text{0—0}}$	$\dfrac{\text{B—Q 3}}{\text{Kt—Q 2}}$
9.	$\dfrac{\text{Q}\times\text{Q}}{\text{P}\times\text{Q}}$		$\dfrac{\text{P—K B 4}}{\text{P—K B 3}}$
10.	$\dfrac{\text{B—Kt 5 ch.}}{\text{B—Q 2}}$		$\dfrac{\text{Kt—K Kt 5}}{\text{P}\times\text{Kt}}$
11.	$\dfrac{\text{B}\times\text{B ch.}}{\text{Kt}\times\text{B}}$		$\dfrac{\text{B}\times\text{P ch.}}{\text{K}\times\text{B}}$
12.			$\dfrac{\text{P}\times\text{P ch.}}{\text{K—Kt 1}}$
13.			$\dfrac{\text{R—R 8 ch.}}{\text{K}\times\text{R}}$
14.			$\dfrac{\text{Q—R 5 ch.}}{\text{K—Kt 1}}$
15.			P—Kt 6 and wins.

	(7)	(8)	(9)
1.	—	—	—
2.	—	—	—
3.	—	—	—
4.	$\dfrac{}{\text{B—Kt 5}}$	$\dfrac{\text{P—K 5}}{\text{K Kt—Q 2}}$	$\dfrac{\text{P}\times\text{P}}{\text{P}\times\text{P}}$

	(7)	(8)	(9)
5.	$\dfrac{\text{B}-\text{Q}\,3}{\text{P}-\text{K R}\,3}$	$\dfrac{\text{P}-\text{K B}\,4}{\text{P}-\text{Q B}\,4}$	$\dfrac{\text{Kt}-\text{B}\,3}{\text{B}-\text{Q}\,3}$
6.	$\dfrac{\text{B}\times\text{Kt}}{\text{Q}\times\text{B}}$	$\dfrac{\text{P}\times\text{P}}{\text{B}\times\text{P}}$	$\dfrac{\text{B}-\text{Q}\,3}{0-0}$
7.	$\dfrac{\text{Kt}-\text{B}\,3}{\qquad}$	$\dfrac{\text{Q}-\text{Kt}\,4}{\text{P}-\text{K Kt}\,3}$	$\dfrac{0-0}{\text{B}-\text{K Kt}\,5}$

Nos. 6 to 9.   Position after Black's 3rd move.

BLACK.

WHITE.

	(8)	(9)
8.	$\dfrac{\text{P}-\text{K R}\,4}{\text{P}-\text{K R}\,4}$	$\dfrac{\text{B}-\text{K Kt}\,5}{\text{P}-\text{B}\,3}$
9.	$\dfrac{\text{Q}-\text{R}\,3}{\text{Q}-\text{Kt}\,3}$	$\dfrac{\text{Kt}-\text{K}\,2}{\text{Q Kt}-\text{Q}\,2}$
10.	$\dfrac{\text{Kt}-\text{B}\,3}{\text{Q Kt}-\text{B}\,3}$	$\dfrac{\text{Kt}-\text{Kt}\,3}{\text{Q}-\text{B}\,2}$
11.	$\dfrac{\text{B}-\text{Q}\,3}{\text{Kt}-\text{Kt}\,5}$	$\dfrac{\text{Q}-\text{Q}\,2}{\text{Kt}-\text{R}\,4}$
12.		$\dfrac{\text{Kt}\times\text{Kt}}{\text{B}\times\text{Kt}}$

	(10)	(11)	(12)
1.	—	—	—
2.	—	—	—
3.	B—Kt 5	P×P / P×P	—
4.	P×P / P×P	Kt—K B 3 / Kt—K B 3	B—K 3 / Kt—K B 3
5.	Kt—B 3 / B—Kt 5	B—Q 3 / B—Q 3	B—Q 3 / B—Q 3
6.	B—Q 3 / Kt—K B 3	0—0 / 0—0	Kt—Q B 3 / P—B 3
7.	0—0 / 0—0	B—K Kt 5 / B—K Kt 5	K Kt—K 2 / B—K Kt 5
8.	—	Q Kt—Q 2 / P—B 3	Q—Q 2 / Q Kt—Q 2
9.	—	R—K 1 / Q Kt—Q 2	P—K R 3 / B—R 4
10.	—	P—K R 3 / B—R 4	P—B 4 / B×Kt
11.	—	P—K Kt 4 / B—Kt 3	Kt×B / Kt—K 5
12.	—	B×B / P×B	B×Kt / P×B

THE FRENCH DEFENCE—GAMES.

	(1) Szen / Boncourt	(2) Kieseritsky / St. Amant	(3) Harrwitz / Horwitz
1.	P—K 4 / P—K 3	P—K 4 / P—K 3	P—K 4 / P—K 3
2.	P—Q 4 / P—Q 4	P—K B 4 (a) / P—Q 4	P—Q 4 / P—Q 4
3.	P×P / P×P	P×P / P×P	P×P / P×P

(a) This is not so good a reply as P—Q 4.

	(1)	(2)	(3)
4.	P – Q B 4 / Kt – K B 3	P – Q 4 / P – Q B 4	P – Q B 4 / Kt – K B 3
5.	Kt – Q B 3 / B – Q Kt 5	P × P (a) / B × P	Kt – Q B 3 / B – K 2
6.	P – Q R 3 / B × Kt ch.	B – Kt 5 ch. / Kt – B 3	P × P / Kt × P
7.	P × B / Kt – K 5	Q – K 2 ch. / K Kt – K 2	B – Q B 4 / B – K 3
8.	Q – Kt 3 / P – Q B 3	Kt – K B 3 / B – K Kt 5	Q – Kt 3 / B – Q Kt 5
9.	B – Q 3 / 0 – 0	B – K 3 / Q – Kt 3	Kt – B 3 / Kt – Q B 3
10.	Kt – K 2 / P × P	B × B / Q × B (B 5)	0 – 0 / B × Kt
11.	B × P / P – Q Kt 4	Kt – B 3 / 0 – 0	P × B / 0 – 0
12.	B – Q 3 / B – B 4	0 – 0 – 0 / Q R – Q 1	Kt – Kt 5 (c) / Kt – R 4
13.	Q – B 2 / R – K 1	B – Q 3 (b) / K – R 1	Q – B 2 (d) / P – K Kt 3
14.	0 – 0 / B – Kt 3	P – K R 3 / B – B 4	Kt × B / P × Kt
15.	Kt – B 4 / Kt – Q 3	P – K Kt 4 / B × B	B – Q 3 / Kt – Q B 3
16.	Kt × B / R P × Kt	Q × B / Kt – Kt 5	B – K R 6 / R – B 2 (e)
17.	B – K B 4 / Kt – R 3	Q – Q 4 / Q – R 4	B × P / R – Q 2

(a) P – Q B 4, or Kt – K B 3, is better, because the present move brings the adverse Bishop into powerful play.

(b) Threatening $\dfrac{\text{B} \times \text{P ch.}}{}$, and if $\dfrac{}{\text{K} \times \text{B}}$, then $\dfrac{\text{Kt} - \text{Kt } 5 \text{ ch.}}{}$, &c.

(c) An excellent move, relieving himself at once from the threatened danger to his Queen, and opening a most formidable attack upon the adverse King.

(d) Threatening mate, and thus escaping the loss of exchange.

(e) We should have preferred an attempt to carry the war into the enemy's territory, by playing Q – R 5, and Kt – B 5 afterwards.

	(1)	(2)	(3)
18.	K R—K 1 / Q—Q 2	P—R 3 / Kt (Kt 5)—B 3	B—K 4 / Q—R 5 (c)
19.	P—Q R 4 / Kt—B 2	Q—Q 3 / P—Q R 3	B×Kt / R×B
20.	B×Kt / Q×B	K R—K 1 / P—Q Kt 4	B—K B 3 (d) / R—R 4
21.	R×R ch. / R×R	Kt—Q 4 / P—Kt 5	P—K R 3 / K—R 1
22.	P×P / P×P	Kt—Kt 3 / Q—B 2	Q—Kt 3 (e) / R—K Kt 1 (f)
23.	R×P / R—K 8 ch	Kt—K 2 / P×P	Q×K P / R—Kt 3 (g)
24.	B—B 1 / Q—Q B 3	P×P / Kt—R 4	Q—B 8 ch. / R—Kt 1
25.	Q—Q 2 / R—Kt 8	Q—B 3 / Kt—B 5	Q—K 6 / R—Kt 3
26.	Q—Q 3 / R—B 8	Q—Kt 4 (a) / R—Q Kt 1	Q—Q 7 / R—Kt 2
27.	R—R 3 / Kt—Q 4	Q—R 4 / K R—Q B 1	Q—B 8 ch. / R—Kt 1
28.	Q—B 3 / P—B 3	P—B 5 / Q—K 4 (b) and Black won ultimately.	Q—K 6 / Kt—Q 1
29.	Q—Q 3 / Kt—B 5		Q—Q 7 / Q—K 5

(a) Badly played, as it enables Black to strengthen his attack without losing time.

(b) Overlooking the obvious move of Kt—Kt 3, which wins at once.

(c) Black now turns the assault upon his opponent, and the attack and counter-attack are admirably sustained.

(d) B—Q 2 would, perhaps, have been better.

(e) This is ingeniously imagined, but it gives Black too much time.

(f) Losing moves. He should have played Q—K 5, when the following variation was probable :—

22.		Q—K 5
23.	K—R 2	R—K Kt 1
24.	P—Kt 3	Q—Kt 5
25.	P—K R 4	Q or R×P ch.

And wins.

(g) Again Black loses time. Why not play Kt—Q 1 directly ?

	(1)	(2)	(3)
30.	$\dfrac{P-Q\,5}{Q\times Q\,P}$		$\dfrac{P-Kt\,3}{Kt-K\,3}$
31.	$\dfrac{Q\times Q\text{ ch.}}{Kt\times Q}$		$\dfrac{K\,R-Q\,1\,(a)}{R\times R\,P}$
32.	$\dfrac{P-Kt\,3}{Kt\times P}$ and wins.		$\dfrac{K-B\,1}{R\,(R\,6)\times P}$

(3) (*contd.*)

33.	$\dfrac{P\times R}{Q\times B}$		
34.		$\dfrac{Q-Q\,5}{R-B\,1\text{ ch.}}$	36. $\dfrac{K-R\,3}{Kt-B\,5\text{ ch. and}}$ wins.
35.		$\dfrac{K-Kt\,2}{R-B\,7\text{ ch.}}$	

	(4) Bird / Brien	(5) Falkbeer / St. Amant	(6) Mackenzie / Mason
1.	$\dfrac{P-K\,4}{P-K\,3}$	$\dfrac{P-K\,4}{P-K\,3}$	$\dfrac{P-K\,4}{P-K\,3}$
2.	$\dfrac{P-Q\,4}{P-Q\,4}$	$\dfrac{P-Q\,4}{P-Q\,4}$	$\dfrac{P-Q\,4}{P-Q\,4}$
3.	$\dfrac{P\times P}{P\times P}$	$\dfrac{P\times P}{P\times P}$	$\dfrac{Kt-Q\,B\,3}{Kt-K\,B\,3}$
4.	$\dfrac{B-Q\,3}{Kt-K\,B\,3}$	$\dfrac{B-K\,3}{Kt-K\,B\,3}$	$\dfrac{P\times P}{P\times P}$
5.	$\dfrac{Kt-K\,B\,3}{B-Q\,3}$	$\dfrac{P-Q\,B\,4}{B-K\,2}$	$\dfrac{Kt-B\,3}{B-Q\,3}$
6.	$\dfrac{0-0}{0-0}$	$\dfrac{Kt-Q\,B\,3}{0-0}$	$\dfrac{B-Q\,3}{0-0}$
7.	$\dfrac{B-K\,3}{P-K\,R\,3}$	$\dfrac{Q-Kt\,3}{P-B\,3}$	$\dfrac{0-0}{Kt-B\,3}$
8.	$\dfrac{Kt-K\,5}{R-K\,1}$	$\dfrac{B-Q\,3}{P-Q\,Kt\,3}$	$\dfrac{B-K\,Kt\,5}{Kt-K\,2}$
9.	$\dfrac{P-K\,B\,4}{P-R\,3}$	$\dfrac{K\,Kt-K\,2}{B-K\,3}$	$\dfrac{B\times Kt}{P\times P}$
10.	$\dfrac{Kt-Q\,2}{Kt-B\,3}$	$\dfrac{P-K\,R\,3}{P-B\,4}$	$\dfrac{Kt-K\,R\,4}{K-Kt\,2}$

(a) P—Q 5 seems much more effective, and leads to many striking variations

	(4)	(5)	(6)
11.	P—B 3 / Kt—K 2	P—Kt 4 / Kt—B 3	Q—R 5 / R—R 1
12.	Q Kt—B 3 / Kt—B 4	B P×P / K Kt×P	P—K B 4 / P—Q B 3
13.	B—K B 2 / Kt—K 5	Q—B 2 / P×P	R—B 3 / Kt—Kt 3
14.	Q—B 2 / P—K B 3	B×P / Kt—Kt 5	Q R—K B 1 / Q—B 2
15.	P—K Kt 4 / P×Kt	Q—Q 2 / Kt (B 3)×B	Kt—K 2 / B—Q 2
16.	B P×P / B—B 1	Kt×Kt / Q×Kt	Kt—Kt 3 / Q R—K Kt 1
17.	P×Kt / B×P	B×P ch. / K×B	Q—R 6 ch. / K×Q
18.	B—Kt 3 / B—K R 6	Q×Q / Kt—B 7 ch.	Kt (R 4)—B 5 ch. / B×Kt
19.	K R—K 1 / Kt×B	K—Q 2 / Kt×Q	Kt×B ch. / K—R 4
20.	P×Kt / P—K Kt 4	P—B 4 / Q R—Q 1	P—Kt 4 ch. / K×P
21.	R—K 2 / B—K Kt 5	Q R—K B 1 / B—B 5	R—Kt 3 ch. / K—R 4
22.	R—B 2 / B×Kt	R—B 2 / B—B 4	B mates

and Black won.

23.	R×B / R—K 2
24.	Q R—K B 1 / Q—Q 2
25.	Q—B 2 / B—Kt 2
26.	B—Kt 1 / Q—K 3
27.	Q—B 2 / B—B 1
28.	R—B 6 / Q—R 6
29.	Q—B 2 / B—Kt 2

(4)	(contd.)
30.	B—B 5 / Q—R 4
31.	B—Kt 6 / Q—R 6
32.	R—B 7 / R×R
33.	B×R ch. / K—R 1
34.	P—K 6 / B—B 1

35.	Q—K 3 / B—K 2
36.	Q—K 5 ch. / K—R 2
37.	B—R 4 / R—K B 1
38.	R×R / B×R
39.	P—K 7 / B—Kt 2
40.	B—Kt 6 ch. and wins.

	7)	(8)	(9)
	Pollock	Blackburne	Blackburne
	Lee	Bird	Schwarz
1.	P–K 4 / P–K 3	P–K 4 / P–K 3	P–K 4 / P–K 3
2.	Kt–Q B 3 / P–Q 4	P–Q 4 / P–Q Kt 3	P–Q 4 / P–Q 4
3.	Kt–B 3 / Kt–K B 3	B–Q 3 / B–Kt 2	Kt–Q B 3 / Kt–K B 3
4.	P–K 5 / K Kt–Q 2	Kt–K R 3 / Kt–K B 3	P×P / P×P
5.	P–Q Kt 3 / B–K 2	P–K B 3 / P–B 4	Kt–B 3 / B–Q 3
6.	B–Kt 2 / P–Q R 3	P–B 3 / P×P	B–Q 3 / P–B 3
7.	B–Q 3 / P–Q B 4	P×P / Kt–B 3	0–0 / 0–0
8.	0–0 / Kt–Q B 3	B–K 3 / B–Kt 5 ch.	Kt–K 2 / B–K Kt 5
9.	Q–K 2 / Kt–Kt 5	Kt–Q 2 / P–Q 4	Kt–Kt 3 / Q–B 2
10.	Q R–K 1 / 0–0	P–K 5 / Kt–Q 2	B–K 3 / Q Kt–Q 2
11.	P–Q R 3 / Kt×B	0–0 / B–K 2	Q–Q 2 / K R–K 1
12.	Q×Kt / P–Q Kt 4	R–B 1 / P–B 4	Q R–K 1 / Kt–K 5
13.	Kt–K 2 / Kt–Kt 3	P–B 4 / Kt–Kt 5	Q–B 1 / B×K Kt
14.	Kt–Kt 3 / B–Q 2	B–Kt 1 / B–R 3	P×B / Kt×Kt
15.	K–R 1 / P–Q R 4	R–K B 2 / R–Q B 1	R P×Kt / B×P
16.	Kt–Kt 1 / P–R 5	Kt–B 3 / P–R 3	K–Kt 2 / B–Q 3
17.	P–K B 4 / P–Kt 3	P–K Kt 4 / R×R	R–R 1 / Kt–B 1
18.	Kt–R 3 / P×P	B×R / P×P	R–R 3 / P–K Kt 3
19.	P×P / P–B 5	B–Kt 6 ch. / K–B 1	Q R–R 1 / Q R –Q 1

	(7)	(8)	(9)
20.	$\dfrac{\text{Q}-\text{K 3}}{\text{P}\times\text{P}}$	$\dfrac{\text{Kt (B 3)}-\text{Kt 5}}{\text{P}\times\text{Kt}}$	$\dfrac{\text{B}-\text{K Kt 5}}{\text{R}-\text{Q 2}}$
21.	$\dfrac{\text{P}-\text{B 5 !}}{\text{K P}\times\text{P}}$	$\dfrac{\text{Q}\times\text{P}}{\text{B}-\text{Q 6}}$	$\dfrac{\text{P}-\text{Q B 4}}{\text{P}\times\text{P}}$
22.	$\dfrac{\text{Q}-\text{R 6}}{\text{B}-\text{K 3}}$	$\dfrac{\text{P}\times\text{P d. ch.}}{\text{Kt}-\text{B 3}}$	$\dfrac{\text{B}\times\text{B P}}{\text{P}-\text{K R 4}}$
23.	$\dfrac{\text{R}\times\text{P}}{\text{B}\times\text{R}}$	$\dfrac{\text{Kt P}\times\text{Kt}}{\text{P}\times\text{P}}$	$\dfrac{\text{R}-\text{R 4 }(a)}{\text{P}-\text{Kt 4}}$
24.	$\dfrac{\text{Kt}\times\text{B}}{\text{P}\times\text{Kt}}$	$\dfrac{\text{P}\times\text{P}}{\text{B}-\text{Q 3}}$	$\dfrac{\text{B}-\text{Kt 3}}{\text{Kt}-\text{K 3}}$
25.	$\dfrac{\text{R}-\text{K 3}}{\text{R}-\text{R 5}}$	$\dfrac{\text{B}-\text{B 7}}{\text{K}\times\text{B}}$	$\dfrac{\text{B}-\text{B 6}}{\text{Kt}-\text{B 5 ch.}}$
26.	$\dfrac{\text{P}-\text{K 6}}{\text{R}-\text{K Kt 5}}$	$\dfrac{\text{Q}-\text{Kt 7 ch.}}{\text{K}-\text{K 1}}$	$\dfrac{\text{Q}\times\text{Kt}}{\text{B}\times\text{Q}}$
27.	$\dfrac{\text{Kt}-\text{Kt 5 !!}}{\text{R}\times\text{Kt}}$	$\dfrac{\text{P}-\text{B 7 ch.}}{\text{Resigns.}}$	$\dfrac{\text{R}\times\text{P}}{\text{P}\times\text{R}}$
28.	$\dfrac{\text{R}-\text{R 3}}{\text{Resigns.}}$		$\dfrac{\text{R}\times\text{P}}{\text{Resigns.}}$

Chapter V

THE CENTRE COUNTER—ANALYSIS.

	(1)	(2)	(3)
1.	$\dfrac{\text{P}-\text{K 4}}{\text{P}-\text{Q 4}}$	—	—
2.	$\dfrac{\text{P}\times\text{P !}}{\text{Q}\times\text{P}}$	—	—
3.	$\dfrac{\text{Kt}-\text{Q B 3}}{\text{Q}-\text{Q 1 !}}$	$\overline{\text{Q}-\text{K 4 ch.}}$	—
4.	$\dfrac{\text{P}-\text{Q 4}}{\text{B}-\text{B 4}}$	$\dfrac{\text{B}-\text{K 2}}{\text{B}-\text{Kt 5}}$	$\overline{\text{Kt}-\text{Q B 3}}$

(a) " The initiation of a most beautiful final combination. The latter part of this game is one of the most brilliant combinations ever made in actual play."—Hoffer.

	(1)	(2)	(3)
5.	$\dfrac{\text{Kt}-\text{B }3}{\text{P}-\text{K }3}$	$\dfrac{\text{P}-\text{Q }4}{\text{Q}-\text{K }3}$	$\dfrac{\text{Kt}-\text{B }3}{\text{Q}-\text{B }3}$
6.	$\dfrac{\text{B}-\text{Q B }4+}{}$	$\dfrac{\text{P}-\text{Q }5}{\text{Q}-\text{K }4}$	$\dfrac{\text{Kt}-\text{Q Kt }5\,!}{\text{K}-\text{Q }1}$
7.	—	$\dfrac{\text{P}-\text{K B }4}{\text{B}\times\text{B}}$	$\dfrac{0-0}{\text{B}-\text{Kt }5}$
8.	—	$\dfrac{\text{K Kt}\times\text{B}}{\text{Q}-\text{Q }3}$	$\dfrac{\text{P}-\text{Q }4}{\text{P}-\text{Q R }3}$
9.	—	$\dfrac{\text{Kt}-\text{K }4}{\text{Q}-\text{Kt }5\text{ ch.}}$	$\dfrac{\text{P}-\text{Q }5}{\text{Kt}-\text{Kt }5}$
10.	—	$\dfrac{\text{Kt}-\text{B }3}{\text{P}-\text{K }3}$	$\dfrac{\text{Kt}-\text{B }3}{\text{B}-\text{B }4}$
11.	—	$\dfrac{0-0+}{}$	$\dfrac{\text{Kt}-\text{Q }4}{\text{Q}-\text{Kt }3}$
12.	—	—	$\dfrac{\text{P}-\text{Q R }3}{\text{B}\times\text{P}}$
13.	—	—	$\dfrac{\text{Kt}\times\text{B}}{\text{Kt}\times\text{Kt}}$
14.	—	—	$\dfrac{\text{B}-\text{Q }3 \text{ and wins.}}{}$

	(4)	(5)	(6)
1.	—	—	—
2.	—	—	$\dfrac{\text{Kt}-\text{K B }3}{}$
3.	—	$\dfrac{\text{P}-\text{Q }4}{\text{Q}-\text{K }5\text{ ch.}}$	$\dfrac{\text{B}-\text{Kt }5\text{ ch.}}{\text{B}-\text{Q }2}$
4.	—	$\dfrac{\text{B}-\text{K }3}{\text{B}-\text{B }4}$	$\dfrac{\text{B}-\text{B }4}{\text{P}-\text{Q Kt }4}$
5.	—	$\dfrac{\text{Kt}-\text{Q B }3}{\text{Q}\times\text{B P}}$	$\dfrac{\text{B}-\text{Kt }3}{\text{B}-\text{Kt }5}$
6.	$\dfrac{\text{P}-\text{Q }4}{\text{B}-\text{Kt }5}$	$\dfrac{\text{Q}\times\text{Q}}{\text{B}\times\text{Q}}$	$\dfrac{\text{P}-\text{K B }3}{\text{B}-\text{B }1}$
7.	$\dfrac{\text{Kt}-\text{Q }5}{\text{Q}-\text{Q }3}$	$\dfrac{\text{R}-\text{B }1}{\text{B}-\text{B }4}$	$\dfrac{\text{Q}-\text{K }2}{\text{P}-\text{Q R }3}$
8.	$\dfrac{\text{P}-\text{B }4}{\text{B}\times\text{Kt}}$	$\dfrac{\text{Kt}-\text{Q }5+}{}$	$\dfrac{\text{P}-\text{Q B }4}{\text{P}-\text{B }3}$
9.	$\dfrac{\text{B}-\text{K B }4}{\text{B}\times\text{B}}$	—	$\dfrac{\text{Q P}\times\text{P}}{\text{Kt}\times\text{P}}$

	(4)	(5)	(6)
10.	Q×B / Kt×P	—	P×P / Kt—Q 5
11.	Q—K 4 / Kt—K B 3	—	Q—K 3 / P×P
12.	Q×Q Kt / Q—K 3 ch.	—	Kt—K 2 / Kt×Kt
13.	Kt—K 3 +	—	K×Kt / B—R 3
14.	—	—	R—Q 1 / P—Kt 5 d. ch.
15.	—	—	P—Q 3 / P—K 3
16.	—	—	P—Q R 3 +

	(7)	(8)	(9)
1.	—	—	—
2.	—	—	P—K 5 / P—Q 5
3.	—	—	P—K B 4 / P—Q B 4
4.	—	—	Kt—K B 3 / Kt—Q B 3
5.	—	P—Q R 4	P—Q 3 / P—K 3
6.	Kt—K B 3 / Kt×P	P—Q R 3 / B—Kt 5	B—K 2 / P—B 3 ⇒
7.	Kt—B 3 / Kt×Kt	P—K B 3 / B—B 1	
8.	Kt—K 5 / Q—Q 5	Kt—B 3 / B—R 3	
9.	Q×B / Q×Kt ch.	P—Q 3 / P—Kt 5	
10.	K—B 1 / P—K B 4	P×P / P×P	
11.	Q—B 3 / Kt—K 5	Kt—R 4 / B—Kt 2	
12.	P—Q 3 +	B—Q 2 +	

THE CENTRE COUNTER-GAMES.

	(1) Mr. H. —— V. H. der Laza	(2) Lowenthal Staunton	(3) Lasker Allchin
1.	P—K 4 / P—Q 4	P—K 4 / P—Q 4	P—K 4 / P—Q 4
2.	P×P / Kt—K B 3	P×P / Kt—K B 3	P×P / Kt—K B 3
3.	B—Kt 5 ch. / B—Q 2	B—B 4 / Kt×P	P—Q 4 (c) / Kt×P
4.	B—B 4 / P—Q Kt 4	P—Q 4 / P—K 3	Kt—K B 3 / B—Kt 5
5.	B—Kt 3 / B—Kt 5	Kt—K B 3 / B—Q 3	P—B 4 / Kt—Kt 3
6.	P—K B 3 / B—B 1	0—0 / 0—0	Kt—B 3 / P—K 4
7.	Kt—B 3 (a) / P—Kt 5	B—Q 3 / B—B 5	P—B 5 / P×P
8.	Kt—K 4 / Kt×P	Q Kt—Q 2 / Kt—Q B 3	Kt—K 4 / Kt (Kt 3)—Q 2
9.	B×Kt / Q×B	P—Q R 3 / Kt—B 3	Q×P / Q—K 2
10.	Kt—K 2 / P—K B 4	Kt—K 4 / B×B	B—Q Kt 5 / Kt—Q B 3
11.	Kt—B 4 / Q—Kt 4	R×B / Q—K 2	B×Kt / P×B
12.	Kt—Kt 3 / P—K 4	R—K 1 / P—Q Kt 3	0—0 / B×Kt
13.	Kt (B 4)—K 2 / B—B 4 (b)	Kt×Kt ch. / P×Kt	P×B / 0—0
14.	P—Q 4 / P×P	P—Q 5 / Kt—K 4	Q—R 4 / Kt—K 4
15.	Kt×Q P / B×Kt	Kt×Kt / P×Kt	K—Kt 2 / Q—K 3

(a) Instead of this move, he ought to have played Q—K 2.
(b) By this move, White is deprived of the power of castling.
(c) Hardly so good as 3 B—Kt 5 ch.

	(1)	(2)	(3)
16.	$\dfrac{Q \times B}{0-0}$	$\dfrac{B \times P \text{ ch.}}{K \times B}$	$\dfrac{Q \times R\ P}{Q-B\ 4}$
17.	$\dfrac{B-B\ 4\ (a)}{Kt-Q\ B\ 3}$	$\dfrac{Q-R\ 5\ \text{ch.}}{K-Kt\ 2}$	$\dfrac{Q-R\ 8\ \text{ch.}}{K-Q\ 2}$
18.	$\dfrac{Q-Q\ 3}{R-K\ 1\ \text{ch.}}$	$\dfrac{R-K\ 3}{R-K\ Kt\ 1}$	$\dfrac{R-Q\ 1\ \text{ch.}\ (c)}{K-K\ 3}$
19.	$\dfrac{K-B\ 2}{Q-Kt\ 3\ \text{ch.}}$	$\dfrac{R-Kt\ 3\ \text{ch.}}{K-B\ 1}$	$\dfrac{Q \times R}{Q \times P\ \text{ch.}}$
20.	$\dfrac{B-K\ 3\ (b)}{R \times B}$	$\dfrac{Q-R\ 6\ \text{ch.}}{K-K\ 1}$	$\dfrac{K-Kt\ 1}{B-K\ 2}$
21.	$\dfrac{Q \times R}{P-B\ 5}$	$\dfrac{R \times R\ \text{ch.}}{K-Q\ 2}$	$\dfrac{Q-Q\ 4}{Q-Kt\ 5\ \text{ch.}}$
22.	$\dfrac{Q \times Q}{P \times Kt\ \text{ch.}}$	$\dfrac{P \times P\ \text{ch.}}{Q \times P}$	$\dfrac{K-R\ 1}{Q-B\ 6\ \text{ch.}}$
23.	$\dfrac{P \times P}{R\ P \times Q}$	$\dfrac{R-Q\ 1\ \text{ch.}}{K-B\ 3}$	$\dfrac{K-Kt\ 1}{Q-Kt\ 5\ \text{ch.}}$
24.	$\dfrac{K\ R-Q\ 1}{B-B\ 4}$	$\dfrac{Q \times Q\ \text{ch.}}{P \times Q}$	$\dfrac{K-R\ 1}{Q-B\ 6\ \text{ch.}}$
25.	$\dfrac{R-Q\ 2}{K-B\ 2}$	$\dfrac{Q\ R-Q\ 8}{\text{Resigns.}}$	$\dfrac{K-Kt\ 1}{\text{Drawn.}}$
26.	$\dfrac{P-Kt\ 4}{B-K\ 3}$		

(1) (contd.)

	(1)			
27.	$\dfrac{P-R\ 3}{P \times P}$	30.	$\dfrac{K-R\ 4}{R-R\ 5}$	33. $\dfrac{K-R\ 5}{R-Kt\ 4}\ \text{ch.}$
28.	$\dfrac{P \times P}{Kt-K\ 4}$	31.	$\dfrac{R-K\ 2}{Kt \times Kt\ P}$	34. $\dfrac{K-R\ 4}{R-Kt\ 5}\ (d)$
29.	$\dfrac{K-Kt\ 3}{P-R\ 3}$	32.	$\dfrac{P \times Kt}{R \times P\ \text{ch.}}$	

(a) He has perhaps no better move in his present bad position.

(b) To avoid the shutting up of his K R, he is obliged to sacrifice two minor Pieces for a Rook and Pawn.

(c) An ill-considered move, which robs him of victory. 18. Q—R 3 would have assured him a win. Played in the Petrograd Tournament, 1914.

(d) Here Black proffered to make the game drawn, remarking that he might perhaps win by venturing R—B 5.

Chapter VI.

THE VIENNA GAME—ANALYSIS.

	(1)	(2)	(3)
1.	P—K 4 / P—K 4	—	—
2.	Kt—Q B 3 / Kt—K B 3	—	—
3.	P—B 4 / P—Q 4	—	—
4.	P—Q 3 / Q P×P	—	P×Q P / Kt×P
5.	B P×P / Kt—Kt 5	—	Kt×Kt / Q×Kt
6.	P—Q 4 / P—K 6	—	P×P / Kt—B 3
7.	Kt—R 3 / P—K B 3	Kt—Q B 3	Kt—B 3 / B—K Kt 5
8.	B—B 4 / P×P	B—Kt 5 / Q—R 5 ch.	B—K 2 / Kt×P =
9.	0—0 / P×P	K—B 1 / Kt—B 7	
10.	B—B 7 ch. / K—K 2	Q—K 1 / Q×P	
11.	Kt—Q 5 ch. and wins.	B×P / Q×P	
12.		B×Kt / Q×Q ch.	
13.		R×Q ch. / K—Q 1	
14.		B×Kt / P×B	
15.		Kt—K Kt 5+	

	(4)	(5)	(6)
1.	—	—	—
2.	—	$\dfrac{\text{B—B 4}}{\text{P—B 4}}$	$\dfrac{\text{B—Kt 5}}{\text{Kt—B 3}}$
3.	—	$\dfrac{\text{P—Q 3}}{}$	$\dfrac{\text{B×Kt}}{\text{P×B}}$
4.	$\dfrac{\text{B P×P}}{\text{Kt×P}}$	$\dfrac{\text{Kt—B 3}}{\text{Kt—Q B 3}}$	$\dfrac{\text{P×B}}{\text{P—Q 3}} =$
5.	$\dfrac{\text{Kt—B 3}}{\text{B—K Kt 5}}$	$\dfrac{\text{Kt—K Kt 5}}{}$ (a)	
6.	$\dfrac{\text{P—Q 3}}{\text{Kt×Kt}}$		
7.	$\dfrac{\text{P×Kt}}{\text{Kt—B 3}}$		
8.	$\dfrac{\text{P—Q 4}}{\text{P—B 3}} =$		

	(7)	(8)	(9)
1.	$\dfrac{\text{P—K 4}}{\text{P—K 4}}$	—	—
2.	$\dfrac{\text{Kt—Q B 3}}{\text{Kt—K B 3}}$	—	—
3.	$\dfrac{\text{P—B 4}}{\text{P—Q 4}}$	—	—
4.	$\dfrac{\text{B P×P}}{\text{Kt×P}}$	—	$\dfrac{\text{P×Q P}}{\text{Kt×P}}$
5.	$\dfrac{\text{Q—B 3}}{\text{P—K B 4}}$	$\dfrac{\text{Kt—B 3}}{\text{B—Q Kt 5}}$	$\dfrac{\text{Kt×Kt}}{\text{Q×Kt}}$
6.	$\dfrac{\text{P—Q 3}}{\text{Kt×Kt}}$	$\dfrac{\text{Q—K 2}}{\text{B×Kt}}$	$\dfrac{\text{P×P}}{\text{Kt—B 3}}$
7.	$\dfrac{\text{P×Kt}}{\text{P—Q 5}}$	$\dfrac{\text{Kt P×B}}{\text{0—0}}$	$\dfrac{\text{Kt—B 3}}{\text{B—K Kt 5}}$
8.	$\dfrac{\text{B—Kt 2}}{\text{B—B 4}}$	B—Kt 2	$\dfrac{\text{B—K 2}}{\text{Kt×P}}$
9.	$\dfrac{\text{0—0—0}}{\text{Kt—B 3}}$		$\dfrac{\text{0—0}}{\text{B—B 4 ch.}}$

(a) And we reproduce a well-known position in the King's Gambit Declined.

	(7)	(8)	(9)
10.	$\dfrac{\text{Q—Kt 3}}{\text{0—0}}$		$\dfrac{\text{K—R 1}}{\text{Kt—Kt 3}}$
11.	$\dfrac{\text{Kt—B 3}}{\text{P—B 5}}$		$\dfrac{\text{P—Q 4}}{\text{B—K 2}}$
12.	$\dfrac{\text{Q—B 2}}{\text{B—K Kt 5}}$		$\dfrac{\text{P—B 4}}{\text{Q—K R 4}}$
13.	$\dfrac{\text{P×P}}{\text{B×Kt}}$		

Nos. 7 to 10.   Position after Black's 3rd move.

BLACK.

WHITE.

	(10)	(11)
1.	—	—
2.	—	—
3.	—	$\dfrac{\text{P—K Kt 3}}{\text{B—Q B 4}}$
4.	$\dfrac{\text{P—Q 3}}{\text{Kt—B 3}}$	$\dfrac{\text{B—Kt 2}}{\text{0—0}}$
5.	$\dfrac{\text{P×KP}}{\text{Q Kt×P}}$	$\dfrac{\text{K Kt—K 2}}{\text{P—Q 3}}$

	(10)	(11)
6.	P—Q 4 / Kt—Kt 5	0—0 / Kt—B 3
7.	P—K 5 / Kt—K 5	P—Q 3 / Kt—K 2
8.	Kt—K B 3 / B—Q Kt 5	P—Q 4 / P×P
9.	B—Q 2 : / B—Kt 5	Kt×P

THE VIENNA GAME—GAMES.

	(1) Max Lange / Alvensleben	(2) Max Lange / Guretzki-Comitz	(3) Hampe / Lowenthal
1.	P—K 4 / P—K 4	P—K 4 / P—K 4	P—K 4 / P—K 4
2.	Kt—Q B 3 / Kt—K B 2	Kt—Q B 3 / B—B 4	Kt—Q B 3 (a) / Kt—K B 3
3.	P—B 4 / P—Q 4	P—B 4 / B×Kt	B—B 4 / P—Q Kt 4
4.	P—Q 3 / Q P×P	R×B / P×P	B×Kt P / P—B 3
5.	B P×P / Kt—Kt 5	P—Q 4 / Q—R 5 ch.	B—R 4 / B—B 4 (b)
6.	P—Q 4 / P—K 6	P—Kt 3 / P×P	Kt—B 3 / 0—0
7.	Kt—R 3 / P—K B 3	R×P / Q×R P	0—0 / P—Q 4
8.	B—B 4 / P×P	Q—B 3 / P—K Kt 3	Kt×K P / P×P
9.	0—0 / P×P	B—Q B 4 / P—K B 3	Kt×B P / Q—B 2
10.	B—B 7 ch. / K—K 2	Kt—Q 5 / K—Q 1	Kt×Kt / Kt—Kt 5 (c)

(a) A favourite mode of opening with Mr. Hampe.
(b) This may be termed Evans' Gambit *au second*.
(c) The game now becomes of singular interest, and the after play of Black will be found to deserve the highest praise

	(1)	(2)	(3)
11.	$\dfrac{\text{Kt}-\text{Q 5 ch.}}{\text{K}-\text{Q 3}}$	$\dfrac{\text{B}-\text{K Kt 5}}{\text{P}-\text{B 3}}$	$\dfrac{\text{P}-\text{K Kt 3}}{\text{Kt}-\text{K 4}}$
12.	$\dfrac{\text{Kt}\times\text{K P}}{\text{Kt}\times\text{Kt}}$	$\dfrac{\text{B}\times\text{P ch.}}{\text{K}-\text{K 1}}$	$\dfrac{\text{Kt}-\text{Q 7}}{\text{Kt}-\text{B 6 ch.}}$
13.	$\dfrac{\text{Q}\times\text{P ch.}}{\text{K}-\text{B 3}}$	$\dfrac{\text{Kt}-\text{B 7 ch.}}{\text{K}-\text{B 1}}$	$\dfrac{\text{K}-\text{R 1}}{\text{B}-\text{Kt 2 }(a)}$
14.	$\dfrac{\text{Q}-\text{B 3 ch.}}{\text{K}-\text{Kt 3}}$	$\dfrac{\text{Q}-\text{R 3 ch.}}{\text{P}-\text{B 4}}$	$\dfrac{\text{Kt}\times\text{B}}{\text{Q}\times\text{Kt}}$
15.	$\dfrac{\text{B}\times\text{Kt ch.}}{\text{P}-\text{B 4}}$	$\dfrac{\text{Q}\times\text{P ch.}}{\text{P}-\text{Q 3}}$	$\dfrac{\text{K}-\text{Kt 2}}{\text{Q}-\text{K R 4}}$
16.	$\dfrac{\text{P}-\text{Q Kt 4}}{\text{K}-\text{B 2}}$	$\dfrac{\text{Q}\times\text{P ch.}}{\text{Kt}-\text{K 2}}$	$\dfrac{\text{P}-\text{K R 3}}{\text{P}-\text{K 6}}$
17.	$\dfrac{\text{P}\times\text{P}}{\text{B}\times\text{Kt}}$	$\dfrac{\text{Q}-\text{Q 8 mate.}}{}$	$\dfrac{\text{Q P}\times\text{P}}{\text{Kt}-\text{K 8 db. ch.}}$
18.	$\dfrac{\text{P}\times\text{B}}{\text{Kt}-\text{Q 2}}$		$\dfrac{\text{K}-\text{R 2}}{\text{Kt}-\text{B 6 ch.}}$
19.	$\dfrac{\text{B}-\text{B 4 ch.}}{\text{K}-\text{B 1}}$		$\dfrac{\text{K}-\text{Kt 2}}{\text{Q R}-\text{Q 1}}$
20.	$\dfrac{\text{B}-\text{K 6}}{\text{Q}-\text{K 2}}$		Resigns. (b)
21.	$\dfrac{\text{P}-\text{B 6}}{\text{Q}-\text{B 4 ch.}}$		
22.	$\dfrac{\text{Q}\times\text{Q}}{\text{B}\times\text{Q ch.}}$		
23.	$\dfrac{\text{K}-\text{Kt 2}}{\text{P}\times\text{P}}$		

(1) (contd.)

24.	$\dfrac{\text{Q R}-\text{Q 1}}{\text{R}-\text{Q 1}}$	26.	$\dfrac{\text{R}-\text{Q 1}}{\text{Resigns.}}$
25.	$\dfrac{\text{R}\times\text{Kt}}{\text{R}\times\text{R}}$		

	(4)	(5)	(6)
	$\dfrac{\text{Hampe}}{\text{Lowenthal}}$	$\dfrac{\text{Hampe}}{\text{Falkbeer}}$	$\dfrac{\text{Lowenthal and "Alter"}}{\text{Staunton and Barnes}}$
1.	$\dfrac{\text{P}-\text{K 4}}{\text{P}-\text{K 4}}$	$\dfrac{\text{P}-\text{K 4}}{\text{P}-\text{K 4}}$	$\dfrac{\text{P}-\text{K 4}}{\text{P}-\text{K 4}}$

(a) Very well played.
(b) Because he must now move his Queen to a square where she can be won by the Knight, giving discovered check.

	(4)	(5)	(6)
2.	$\dfrac{\text{Kt—Q B 3}}{\text{Kt—K B 3 (a)}}$	$\dfrac{\text{Kt—Q B 3 (c)}}{\text{Kt—K B 3}}$	$\dfrac{\text{Kt—Q B 3}}{\text{Kt—K B 3}}$
3.	$\dfrac{\text{B—B 4}}{\text{B—B 4}}$	$\dfrac{\text{B—B 4 (d)}}{\text{P—Q Kt 4}}$	$\dfrac{\text{P—B 4}}{\text{P—Q 4}}$
4.	$\dfrac{\text{P—Q 3}}{\text{P—Q 3}}$	$\dfrac{\text{B×Kt P}}{\text{P—B 3}}$	$\dfrac{\text{P×K P}}{\text{Kt×P}}$
5.	$\dfrac{\text{B—K Kt 5}}{\text{B—K 3}}$	$\dfrac{\text{B—B 4}}{\text{B—B 4}}$	$\dfrac{\text{Kt—B 3}}{\text{B—K Kt 5}}$
6.	$\dfrac{\text{Kt—Q 5}}{\text{B×Kt}}$	$\dfrac{\text{P—Q 3}}{\text{P—Q 4}}$	$\dfrac{\text{B—K 2}}{\text{Kt—Q B 3}}$
7.	$\dfrac{\text{B×B}}{\text{P—B 3}}$	$\dfrac{\text{P×P}}{\text{P×P}}$	$\dfrac{\text{B—Kt 5}}{\text{B—Kt 5}}$
8.	$\dfrac{\text{B—Kt 3}}{\text{Q Kt—Q 2}}$	$\dfrac{\text{B—Kt 5 ch.}}{\text{B—Q 2}}$	$\dfrac{\text{Q—K 2}}{\text{Kt—Kt 4}}$
9.	$\dfrac{\text{Kt—B 3}}{\text{0—0}}$	$\dfrac{\text{B×B ch.}}{\text{Q Kt×B}}$	$\dfrac{\text{Q—B 2}}{\text{Q B×Kt}}$
10.	$\dfrac{\text{0—0}}{\text{P—K R 3}}$	$\dfrac{\text{P—K R 3 (e)}}{\text{Q—Kt 3}}$	$\dfrac{\text{P×B}}{\text{0—0}}$
11.	$\dfrac{\text{B—K R 4}}{\text{P—K Kt 4 (b)}}$	$\dfrac{\text{Q—K 2}}{\text{0—0}}$	$\dfrac{\text{B×Kt}}{\text{P×B}}$
12.	$\dfrac{\text{B—Kt 3}}{\text{Q—K 2}}$	$\dfrac{\text{Kt—Q 1}}{\text{P—K 5 (f)}}$	$\dfrac{\text{Kt—K 2}}{\text{P—B 3}}$

(a) This is considered the best reply, but the second player may safely move B—B 4; or, if he wish a lively game, can adopt the counter gambit 2. P—K B 4.

(b) We rarely like the advance of this Pawn so early in the game.

(c) To this opening Mr. Hampe is extremely partial, and in the use of it he certainly exhibits great originality and resource.

(d) P—K B 4, as was before remarked, leads to many striking situations, and is perhaps the most lively form this game can take.

(e) This was an error, seemingly irreparable, for White never afterwards appears to have had time to liberate his men. We believe he should have played Kt—R 3.

(f) Mr. Falkbeer has now a powerful attack, and he maintains it capitally.

	(4)	(5)	(6)
13.	$\dfrac{\text{K}-\text{R 1}}{\text{K}-\text{R 1}}$	$\dfrac{\text{P}-\text{Q B 3 } (c)}{\text{P}\times\text{P}}$	$\dfrac{\text{P}-\text{K R 4}}{\text{Kt}-\text{K 3}}$
14.	$\dfrac{\text{P}-\text{K R 4}}{\text{Kt}-\text{R 4}}$	$\dfrac{\text{Q}\times\text{P}}{\text{Kt}-\text{K 4}}$	$\dfrac{\text{P}-\text{B 3}}{\text{B}-\text{R 4}}$
15.	$\dfrac{\text{Q}-\text{Q 2 } (a)}{\text{R}-\text{K Kt 1}}$	$\dfrac{\text{Q}-\text{B 2}}{\text{Q}-\text{R 3 } (d)}$	$\dfrac{\text{P}-\text{Q}}{\text{P}\times\text{P}}$
16.	$\dfrac{\text{P}\times\text{P}}{\text{Kt}\times\text{B ch.}}$	$\dfrac{\text{Kt}-\text{K 2}}{\text{Kt}-\text{Q 6 ch.}}$	$\dfrac{\text{P}\times\text{P}}{\text{P}-\text{Q 5}}$
17.	$\dfrac{\text{P}\times\text{Kt}}{\text{P}\times\text{P}}$	$\dfrac{\text{K}-\text{B 1}}{\text{Kt}-\text{K 5}}$	$\dfrac{\text{B}-\text{Q 2}}{\text{Q}-\text{Q 4}}$
18.	$\dfrac{\text{P}-\text{B 3}}{\text{R}-\text{Kt 2}}$	$\dfrac{\text{B}-\text{K 3}}{\text{B}\times\text{B}}$	$\dfrac{\text{K R}-\text{B 1}}{\text{B}-\text{Kt 3}}$
19.	$\dfrac{\text{P}-\text{Q 4}}{\text{B}-\text{Kt 3}}$	$\dfrac{\text{P}\times\text{B}}{\text{P}-\text{B 4}}$	$\dfrac{\text{Q}-\text{Kt 3}}{\text{P}-\text{Q 6}}$
20.	$\dfrac{\text{P}-\text{R 4}}{\text{P}-\text{R 4}}$	$\dfrac{\text{P}-\text{K Kt 3}}{\text{Kt}\times\text{P ch. } (e)}$	$\dfrac{\text{Kt}-\text{B 1}}{\text{Q R}-\text{Q 1}}$
21.	$\dfrac{\text{K}-\text{R 2 } (b)}{\text{Kt}-\text{B 3}}$	$\dfrac{\text{Kt}\times\text{Kt}}{\text{P}-\text{B 5}}$	$\dfrac{\text{Kt}-\text{Kt 3}}{\text{P}-\text{Q R 4}}$

(a) At first sight it appears as if White could now sacrifice his Knight, and get a winning attack; but on carefully looking through the variation, the student will find Black can escape. For suppose 15. $\dfrac{\text{Kt}\times\text{Kt P}}{\text{Kt}\times\text{B ch.}}$; 16. $\dfrac{\text{P}\times\text{Kt}}{\text{P}\times\text{Kt}}$; 17. $\dfrac{\text{Q}-\text{R 5 ch.}}{\text{K}-\text{Kt 2}}$, and we cannot see how White, owing to the peculiar situation of his King, can ever maintain the attack.

(b) This appears to be utterly useless, and worse.

(c) White's case is too perilous for timid measures. His Pieces are locked up, and it is obvious that, if exposed to the combined action of the enemy's Rooks and Knights, the position of his King cannot long be tenable. For these reasons, in Mr. Hampe's predicament, we should at once have sacrificed the Queen's Pawn. By throwing that Pawn forward on the adverse Bishop, and then playing B—K 3, he must have prevented the opening of the King's file, and might have gained time to bring his forces into the field.

(d) A fine move admirably followed up.

(e) We are gone retrograde we fear in chess, as in other things during the last few years; for a succession of ingenious combinations occurring in a single *partie* is quite a rarity, and has upon us all the freshening influence of some unexpected novelty. When will our amateurs shake off their apathy, and give us something as smart in style and sound in calculation as this sparkling little game?

	(4)	(5)	(6)
22.	R — R 1 / R — R 2 ch.	P × P / R × P ch.	P — Q B 4 / Q × Q B P
23.	K — Kt 1 / R × R ch.	K — Kt 2 / Q — K Kt 3	B — B 3 / B — Q 5
24.	K × R / Kt × P	Q — Q 2 / Q R — K B 1	Kt × B / Kt × Kt
25.	Q — K 1 / P — K B 4	R — K Kt 1 / R — B 6	K — Q 2 / Kt — K 3
26.	P — Kt 4 / Q — R 2 ch.	K — R 2 / Q — K 3	P — B 4 / Kt — B 4
27.	K — Kt 1 / P × Q P	R — Kt 2 / Kt — B 5	Q R — K 1 / Kt — K 5 ch.
28.	Kt × Q P / P — B 4	Kt — B 2 / Kt × R	R × Kt / Q × R
29.	P × P / P × Kt	Kt — Kt 4 / Kt — K 6	R — B 2 / R — B 2
30.	Q × Kt / P — Q 6 d. ch. and mates next move.	R — K 1 / Kt × Kt ch.	Q — K 3 / Q — B 4 and won ultimately
31.		P × Kt / Q — Q 3	
32		Resigns.	

	(7) Falkbeer / Anderssen	(8) Berger / Froelick	(9) Mieses / Blackburne
1.	P — K 4 / P — K 4	P — K 4 / P — K 4	P — K 4 / P — K 4
2.	Kt — Q B 3 / P — K B 4	Kt — Q B 3 / Kt — Q B 3	Kt — Q B 3 / Kt — K B 3
3.	P × P / Kt — K B 3	Kt — B 3 / P — Q 3	P — K Kt 3 / Kt — B 3
4.	P — K Kt 4 / B — Q B 4	B — Kt 5 / B — Kt 5	B — Kt 2 / P — Q 3
5.	P — Kt 5 / 0 — 0	Kt — Q 5 / K Kt — K 2	P — Q 3 / B — K 2
6.	P × Kt / Q × P	P — B 3 / P — Q R 3	K Kt — K 2 / 0 — 0

(7)	(8)	(9)
7. $\dfrac{\text{Q}-\text{B }3}{\text{B}-\text{Kt }3}$	$\dfrac{\text{B}--\text{R }4}{\text{P}-\text{Q Kt }4}$	$\dfrac{\text{P}-\text{K R }3}{\text{Kt}-\text{K }1\,!}$
8. $\dfrac{\text{P}-\text{Q }3}{\text{P}-\text{Q B }3}$	$\dfrac{\text{B}-\text{Kt }3}{\text{Kt}-\text{R }4}$	$\dfrac{\text{P}-\text{K Kt }4}{\text{P}-\text{K Kt }3\,?}$
9. $\dfrac{\text{Kt}-\text{K }4}{\text{Q}-\text{K }2}$	$\dfrac{\text{Kt}\times\text{K P}}{\text{B}\times\text{Q}}$	$\dfrac{\text{B}-\text{R }6}{\text{Kt}-\text{Kt }2}$
10. $\dfrac{\text{B}-\text{Q }2}{\text{P}-\text{Q }4}$	$\dfrac{\text{Kt}-\text{K B }6\text{ ch.}}{\text{P}\times\text{Kt}}$	$\dfrac{\text{Q}-\text{Q }2}{\text{B}-\text{K }3}$
11. $\dfrac{\text{P}-\text{B }6}{\text{Q}-\text{Q B }2}$	$\dfrac{\text{B}\times\text{P mate.}}{}$	$\dfrac{0-0-0}{\text{Kt}-\text{Q }5}$
12. $\dfrac{0-0-0}{\text{P}\times\text{Kt}}$		$\dfrac{\text{Kt}\times\text{Kt}}{\text{P}\times\text{Kt}}$
13. $\dfrac{\text{Q P}\times\text{P}}{\text{R}\times\text{P}}$		$\dfrac{\text{Kt}-\text{K }2}{\text{P}-\text{Q B }4}$
14. $\dfrac{\text{B}-\text{B }4\text{ ch.}}{\text{K}-\text{R }1}$		$\dfrac{\text{P}-\text{K B }4\ (a)}{\text{P}-\text{B }3}$
15. $\dfrac{\text{Q}-\text{R }5}{\text{Q Kt}-\text{Q }2}$		$\dfrac{\text{P}-\text{B }5}{\text{B}-\text{B }2}$
16. $\dfrac{\text{P}-\text{K B }4}{\text{R}-\text{K B }1}$		$\dfrac{\text{P}-\text{K R }4}{\text{P}-\text{Q R }4}$
17. $\dfrac{\text{Kt}-\text{K B }3}{\text{Kt}-\text{K B }3}$		$\dfrac{\text{Kt}-\text{Kt }3\ (b)}{\text{B}\times\text{P}}$
18. $\dfrac{\text{Q}-\text{R }4}{\text{B}-\text{K Kt }5}$		$\dfrac{\text{P}\times\text{P }?}{\text{P}\times\text{P}}$
19. $\dfrac{\text{Kt}\times\text{K P}}{\text{B}-\text{K R }4}$		$\dfrac{\text{P}-\text{R }5}{\text{P}-\text{K Kt }4}$
20. $\dfrac{\text{B}-\text{B }3}{\text{B}-\text{K }6\text{ ch.}}$		$\dfrac{\text{Kt}-\text{B }5}{\text{Kt}\times\text{Kt }!}$
21. $\dfrac{\text{K}-\text{Kt }1}{\text{B}\times\text{K B P}}$		$\dfrac{\text{B}\times\text{R}}{\text{Kt}-\text{K }6}$
22. $\dfrac{\text{Q}\times\text{B}}{\text{Kt}-\text{Q }4}$		$\dfrac{\text{B}\times\text{B}}{\text{Q}\times\text{B}}$

(a) Threatening—

15. P—B 5	P×P
16. K P×P	B—Q 2
17. K R—B 1	Kt—K 1
18. B×R	

(b) He should have played it to Kt 1.

	(7)	(8)	(9)
23.	R×Kt / R×Q		Q R—Kt 1 / P—R 5
24.	R—Q 7 / Q—B 1		Q—K 2 / B—K 3
25.	Kt—Kt 6 / R P×Kt		K—Q 2 / Q—Q 1
26.	R×K Kt P / R—K B 6		R—R 1 / P—R 6 !
27.	B—K 5 / Q—K B 1		K R—Q Kt 1 / P—R 7
28.	R—K B 7 d. ch. / K—Kt 1		R—Kt 1 / Q—Kt 3 !
29.	R×R d. ch. / K—R 2		K—B 1 / P—B 5
30.	R×Q and wins.		P×P / Kt×P (B 4)
31.			P—Kt 3 / P—Q 6 and wins.

CHAPTER VII.

MISCELLANEOUS OPENINGS—ANALYSIS.

FIANCHETTO.

	(1)	(2)	(3)
1.	P—K 4 / P—Q Kt 3	—	—
2.	P—Q 4 / B—Kt 2	—	—
3.	B—Q 3 / P—K 3	P—K B 4	P—Kt 3
4.	P—K B 4 / P—Q 4	P×P / B×P	P—K B 4 / B—Kt 2
5.	P—K 5 / P—Q B 4	Q—R 5 ch. / P—Kt 3	Kt—K B 3 / P—Q 3

	(1)	(2)	(3)
6.	$\dfrac{\text{P—B 3}}{\text{Kt—K.B 3}}=$	$\dfrac{\text{P} \times \text{P}}{\text{B—K Kt 2}}$	$\dfrac{\text{B—K 3}}{\text{Kt—Q 2}}$
7.		$\dfrac{\text{P} \times \text{P d. ch.}}{\text{K—B 1}}$	$\dfrac{\text{P—B 4}}{\text{P—K 3}}$
8.		$\dfrac{\text{P} \times \text{Kt (Q) ch.}}{\text{K} \times \text{Q}}$	$\dfrac{\text{Kt—B 3}}{\text{Kt—K 2}}$
9.		$\dfrac{\text{Q—Kt 4}}{\text{B} \times \text{R}}$	$\dfrac{\text{Q—K 2}}{\text{0—0}}$
10.		$\dfrac{\text{P—K R 4}}{\text{P—K 3}}$	$\dfrac{\text{0—0—0}}{\text{P—K B 4}}$
11.		$\dfrac{\text{P—R 5}}{\quad}+$	$\dfrac{\text{Kt—K Kt 5}}{\text{P} \times \text{P}}$
12.			$\dfrac{\text{B} \times \text{P}}{\text{B} \times \text{B}}$
13.			$\dfrac{\text{Q Kt} \times \text{B}}{\quad}+$

QUEEN'S PAWN—DUTCH DEFENCE.

	(1)	(2)	(3)
1.	$\dfrac{\text{P—Q 4}}{\text{P—K B 4}}$	—	—
2.	$\dfrac{\text{P—Q B 4}}{\text{Kt—K B 3}}$	$\dfrac{\text{P—K 4}}{\text{P} \times \text{P}}$	$\dfrac{\text{P—K R 3}}{\text{Kt—K B 3}}$
3.	$\dfrac{\text{Kt—Q B 3}}{\text{P—Q 3}}$	$\dfrac{\text{Kt—Q B 3}}{\text{Kt—K B 3}}$	$\dfrac{\text{P—K Kt 4}}{\text{P—Q 4 !}}$
4.	$\dfrac{\text{B—B 4}}{\text{P—B 3}}$	$\dfrac{\text{B—K Kt 5}}{\text{P—B 3}}$	$\dfrac{\text{P—Kt 5}}{\text{Kt—K 5}}$
5.	$\dfrac{\text{P—K 3}}{\text{Q—B 2}}$	$\dfrac{\text{B} \times \text{Kt}}{\text{K P} \times \text{B}}$	$\dfrac{\text{P—K R 4}}{\text{P—B 4}}$
6.	$\dfrac{\text{Kt—B 3}}{\text{Kt—R 4}}$	$\dfrac{\text{Kt} \times \text{P}}{\text{P—Q 4}}$	$\dfrac{\text{P—Q B 3}}{\text{P—K 3}}$
7.	$\dfrac{\text{B—Kt 5}}{\text{P—K R 3}}$	$\dfrac{\text{Kt—Kt 3}}{\text{B—Q 3}}$	$\dfrac{\text{Kt—B 3}}{\text{Kt—Q B 3}}$
8.	$\dfrac{\text{B—R 4}}{\text{P—K Kt 4}}$	$\dfrac{\text{B—Q 3}+}{\text{0—0}}$	$\dfrac{\text{B—B 4}}{\text{B—Q 3}}$
9.	$\dfrac{\text{Kt—Q 2}}{\text{Kt—B 3}}$		$\dfrac{\text{B} \times \text{B}}{\text{Q} \times \text{B}}=$
10.	$\dfrac{\text{B—Kt 3}}{\text{P—K 4}}\Rightarrow$		

QUEEN'S PAWN.

	(1)	(2)
1	$\dfrac{\text{P—Q 4}}{\text{P—Q B 4}}$	—
2.	$\dfrac{\text{P—Q 5}}{\text{P—K 4}}$	$\dfrac{}{\text{P—B 4}}$
3.	$\dfrac{\text{P—Q B 4}}{\text{P—B 4}}$	$\dfrac{\text{Kt—Q B 3}}{\text{P—Q 3}}$
4.	$\dfrac{\text{Kt—Q B 3+}}{\text{P—Q 3}}$	$\dfrac{\text{P—K 4}}{\text{P×P}}$
5.		$\dfrac{\text{Kt×P}}{\text{P—K 4}}$
6.		$\dfrac{\text{B—K Kt 5}}{\text{Q—R 4 ch.}}$
7.		$\dfrac{\text{P—B 3}}{\text{B—B 4}}$
8.		$\dfrac{\text{Kt—Kt 3}}{\text{B—Kt 3}}$
9.		$\dfrac{\text{B—Q 3}}{\text{B×B}}$
10.		$\dfrac{\text{Q×B+}}{}$

BIRD 8.

	(1)	(2)
1.	$\dfrac{\text{P—K B 4}}{\text{P—Q 4}}$	—
2.	$\dfrac{\text{Kt—K B 3}}{\text{B—Kt 5}}$	$\dfrac{}{\text{P—Q B 4}}$
3.	$\dfrac{\text{Kt—K 5}}{\text{B—B 4}}$	$\dfrac{\text{P—K 3}}{\text{Kt—Q B 3}}$
4.	$\dfrac{\text{P—K Kt 4 ?}}{\text{P—K 3}}$	$\dfrac{\text{B—Kt 5}}{\text{P—Q R 3}}$
5.	$\dfrac{\text{P—Kt 5}}{\text{P—K B 3}}$	$\dfrac{\text{B×Kt ch.}}{\text{P×B}}$
6.	$\dfrac{\text{Kt—K B 3}}{\text{P×P}}$	$\dfrac{\text{0—0}}{\text{P—K 3}}$
7.	$\dfrac{\text{Kt×P}}{\text{B—K 2}}$	$\dfrac{\text{P—B 4}}{\text{Kt—R 3}}$

	(1)	(2)
8.	P-K R 4 / P--K R 3	Q-K 2 / B-Q 3
9.	Kt-K B 3 / B-K Kt 5 +	Kt-B 3 / Q-K 2
10.		P-Q Kt 3 / P-B 3
11.		P-Q 3 / 0-0
12.		P-K 4 / P×K P
13.		P×P / P-K 4
14.		P-B 5 +

ENGLISH.

	(1)	(2)	(3)
1.	P-Q B 4 / P-Q B 4	P-K 4	—
2.	P-B 4 / P-B 4	Kt-Q B 3 / P-K B 4	—
3.	P-Q 3 / Kt-K B 3	P-K 3 / Kt-K B 3	P-Q 4 / P-K 5
4.	Kt-Q B 3 / P-Q 3	P-Q 4 / P-K 5	P-Q 5 / P-B 3
5.	P-K 4 / Kt-B 3	Kt-R 3 +	P-Q 6 / Q-B 3
6.	Kt-B 3 / P-K 4		P-B 5 / P-Q Kt 3
7.	B-Q 2 / Q-K 2		P×P / P×P
8.	P-Q R 3 / P-K Kt 3		Kt-R 4 / B×P
9.	P-K Kt 3 / B-Kt 2		Kt×P / B-Kt 5 ch.
10.	Kt-Q 5 / Kt×Kt		B-Q 2 / Q×P
11.	B P×Kt / Kt-Q 5		Kt×R / B×B ch.

	(1)	(2)	(3)
12.	$\dfrac{\text{Kt} \times \text{Kt}}{\text{B P} \times \text{Kt}}$		$\dfrac{\text{Q} \times \text{B}}{\text{Q} \times \text{R ch.}}$
13.			$\dfrac{\text{Q}-\text{Q 1}}{\text{Q} \times \text{P}+}$

MISCELLANEOUS OPENINGS—GAMES.

	(1)	(2)
	QUEEN'S COUNTER GAMBIT.	DUTCH OPENING
	$\dfrac{\text{Lasker}}{\text{Alechin}}$	$\dfrac{\text{Blackburne}}{\text{Niemzowitcb}}$
1.	$\dfrac{\text{P}-\text{Q 4}}{\text{P}-\text{Q 4}}$	$\dfrac{\text{P}-\text{K 3}}{\text{P}-\text{Q 3}}$
2.	$\dfrac{\text{P}-\text{Q B 4}}{\text{P}-\text{K 4}}$	$\dfrac{\text{P}-\text{K B 4}}{\text{P}-\text{K 4}}$
3.	$\dfrac{\text{Q P} \times \text{P}}{\text{P}-\text{Q 5}}$	$\dfrac{\text{P} \times \text{P}}{\text{P} \times \text{P}}$
4.	$\dfrac{\text{Kt}-\text{K B 3}}{\text{Kt}-\text{Q B 3}}$	$\dfrac{\text{Kt}-\text{Q B 3}}{\text{B}-\text{Q 3}}$
5.	$\dfrac{\text{P}-\text{Q R 3}}{\text{B}-\text{K Kt 5}}$	$\dfrac{\text{P}-\text{K 4}}{\text{B}-\text{K 3}}$
6.	$\dfrac{\text{Q Kt}-\text{Q 2}}{\text{Q}-\text{K 2}}$	$\dfrac{\text{Kt}-\text{B 3}}{\text{P}-\text{K B 3}}$
7.	$\dfrac{\text{P}-\text{R 3}}{\text{B} \times \text{Kt}}$	$\dfrac{\text{P}-\text{Q 3}}{\text{Kt}-\text{K 2}}$
8.	$\dfrac{\text{Kt} \times \text{B}}{\text{0}-\text{0}}$	$\dfrac{\text{B}-\text{K 3}}{\text{P}-\text{Q B 4}}$
9.	$\dfrac{\text{Q}-\text{Q 3}}{\text{P}-\text{K R 3}} (a)$	$\dfrac{\text{Q}-\text{Q 2}}{\text{Q Kt}-\text{B 3}}$
10.	$\dfrac{\text{P}-\text{K Kt 3}}{\text{P}-\text{K Kt 3}}$	$\dfrac{\text{B}-\text{K 2}}{\text{Kt}-\text{Q 5}}$
11.	$\dfrac{\text{B}-\text{Kt 2}}{\text{B}-\text{Kt 2}}$	$\dfrac{\text{0}-\text{0}}{\text{0}-\text{0}}$
12.	$\dfrac{\text{0}-\text{0}}{\text{Kt} \times \text{P}}$	$\dfrac{\text{Kt}-\text{Q 1}}{\text{K Kt}-\text{B 3}}$
13.	$\dfrac{\text{Kt} \times \text{Kt}}{\text{B} \times \text{Kt}}$	$\dfrac{\text{P}-\text{B 3}}{\text{Kt} \times \text{B ch.}}$

(a) If 9.   Kt × P
      10. Q—B 5 ch.   Kt—Q 2
      11. Kt × P   Kt—R 3
      12. Q—Q R 5, &c.

	(1)	(2)
14.	$\dfrac{\text{P—Q Kt 4}}{\text{P—K B 4}}$	$\dfrac{\text{Q} \times \text{Kt}}{\text{R—K 1}}$
15.	$\dfrac{\text{P—B 5}}{\text{Q—K 3}}$	$\dfrac{\text{Kt—R 4}}{\text{B—B 1}}$
16.	$\dfrac{\text{P—B 6}}{\text{Kt—K 2}}$	$\dfrac{\text{Kt—B 5}}{\text{K—R 1}}$
17.	$\dfrac{\text{P} \times \text{P ch.}}{\text{K—Kt 1}}$	$\dfrac{\text{P—K Kt 4}}{\text{Q—Q 2}}$
18.	$\dfrac{\text{B—Kt 2}}{\text{R—Q 3}}$	$\dfrac{\text{Kt—B 2}}{\text{P—Q R 4}}$
19.	$\dfrac{\text{Q R—B 1}}{\text{K R—Q 1}}$	$\dfrac{\text{P—Q R 3}}{\text{P—Q Kt 4}}$
20.	$\dfrac{\text{R—B 2}}{\text{P—B 5}}$	$\dfrac{\text{R—Q 1}}{\text{R—Kt 1}}$
21.	$\dfrac{\text{P} \times \text{P}}{\text{B} \times \text{P}}$	$\dfrac{\text{R—Q 2}}{\text{P—Kt 5}}$
22.	$\dfrac{\text{R—Q 1}}{\text{Kt—B 4}}$	$\dfrac{\text{R P} \times \text{P}}{\text{R P} \times \text{P}}$
23.	$\dfrac{\text{B—B 1}}{\text{Kt—K 6}}$ (a)	$\dfrac{\text{P—B 4}}{\text{R—R 1}}$

(a) Very lively play that requires exceeding careful defence. If
24. P×Kt. P×P wins easily (see Diagram).

Position after Black's 23rd move.

BLACK—ALECHIN.

WHITE—LASKER.

	(1)	(2)
24.	$\dfrac{\text{R}-\text{B 5}}{\text{Q}-\text{B 3 } (a)}$	$\dfrac{\text{Q}-\text{B 3}}{\text{R}-\text{R 7}}$
25.	$\dfrac{\text{Q}-\text{K 4}}{\text{Kt}\times\text{R}}$	$\dfrac{\text{P}-\text{Kt 5}}{\text{P}-\text{Kt 3}}$
26.	$\dfrac{\text{B}\times\text{B}}{\text{Kt}-\text{B 6}}$	$\dfrac{\text{Kt}-\text{Kt 4}}{\text{P}\times\text{Kt}}$
27.	$\dfrac{\text{B}\times\text{R}}{\text{Q}\times\text{B}}$	$\dfrac{\text{Kt}\times\text{B P}}{\text{Kt}-\text{Q 5}}$
28.	$\dfrac{\text{Q}-\text{K 5}}{\text{Q}-\text{Kt 3}}$	$\dfrac{\text{Q}-\text{B 2}}{\text{Q}-\text{B 3}}$
29.	$\dfrac{\text{Q}-\text{K 7}}{\text{Q}-\text{Q 3}}$	$\dfrac{\text{Kt}\times\text{R}}{\text{Q}\times\text{Kt}}$
30.	$\dfrac{\text{R}-\text{K 5}}{\text{P}-\text{Q 6}}$	$\dfrac{\text{B}\times\text{Kt}}{\text{K P}\times\text{B}}$
31.	$\dfrac{\text{P}\times\text{P}}{\text{Q}\times\text{P}}$	$\dfrac{\text{P}\times\text{P}}{\text{B}-\text{K 2}}$
32.	$\dfrac{\text{R}-\text{K 3}}{\text{Q}-\text{Q 8 ch.}}$	$\dfrac{\text{R}-\text{K 1}}{\text{Q}-\text{B 2}}$
33.	$\dfrac{\text{K}-\text{R 2}}{\text{Kt}-\text{Kt 4}}$	$\dfrac{\text{Q}-\text{R 4}}{\text{R}-\text{R 1}}$
34.	$\dfrac{\text{R}-\text{K 6}}{\text{Kt}\times\text{P}}$	$\dfrac{\text{R}-\text{K B 2}}{\text{B}-\text{B 3}}$
35.	$\dfrac{\text{R}-\text{K B 6 }(b)}{\text{Resigns}}$	$\dfrac{\text{Q}-\text{Kt 4}}{\text{R}-\text{K 1}}$

(2) *(contd.)*

36.	$\dfrac{\text{R}\times\text{R}}{\text{Q}\times\text{R}}$	39.	$\dfrac{\text{P}-\text{Kt 6}}{\text{P}\times\text{P}}$
37.	$\dfrac{\text{R}-\text{K 2}}{\text{Q}-\text{Q 2}}$	40.	$\dfrac{\text{R}\times\text{P}}{\text{Q}-\text{K R 2}}$
38.	$\dfrac{\text{R}-\text{K 6}}{\text{B}-\text{R 1}}$	41.	$\dfrac{\text{Q}-\text{Kt 3}}{\text{Q}-\text{R 4}}$
		42.	$\dfrac{\text{R}-\text{Kt 4}}{\text{Resigns }(c)}$

(a) If 24.   Kt×R

    25. B×B   Kt×P

    26. K×Kt   R−K B 1

    27. Q−K B 3 and wins.

(b) Followed by R−B 8.   A fine game on both sides.   Played in the Petrograd Tournament, 1914.

(c) Played in the Petrograd Tournament, 1914.   A finely played game by the *doyen* of English chess.

(3)	(4)	(5)
QUEEN'S PAWN.	QUEEN'S PAWN.	
Lasker / Tarrasch	Capablanca / Bernstein	Zukertort / Blackburne

	(3)	(4)	(5)
1.	P—Q 4 / P—Q 4	P—Q 4 / P—Q 4	P—Q B 4 / P—K 3
2.	Kt—K B 3 / P—Q B 4	Kt—K B 3 / Kt—K B 3	P—K 3 / Kt—K B 3
3.	P—Q B 4 / P—K 3	P—B 4 / P—K 3	Kt—K B 3 / P—Q Kt 3
4.	P×Q P / K P×P	Kt—B 3 / Q Kt—Q 2	B—K 2 / B—Kt 2
5.	P—K Kt 3 / Kt—Q B 3	B—Kt 5 / B—K 2	0—0 / P—Q 4
6.	B—Kt 2 / Kt—B 3	P—K 3 / P—B 3	P—Q 4 / B—Q 3
7.	0—0 / B—K 2	B—Q 3 / P×P	Kt—B 3 / 0—0
8.	P×P / B×P	B×B P / P—Kt 4	P—Q Kt 3 / Q Kt—Q 2
9.	Q Kt—Q 2 (a) / P—Q 5	B—Q 3 / P—Q R 3	B—Kt 2 / Q—K 2
10.	Kt—Kt 3 / B—Kt 3	P—K 4 / P—K 4	Kt—Q Kt 5 / Kt—K 5
11.	Q—Q 3 / B—K 3	P×P / Kt—Kt 5	Kt×B / P×Kt
12.	R—Q 1 / B×Kt	B—K B 4 / B—B 4	Kt—Q 2 / Q Kt—B 3
13.	Q×B / Q—K 2	0—0 / Q—B 2	P—B 3 / Kt×Kt
14.	B—Q 2 / 0—0	R—B 1 / P—B 3	Q×Kt / P×P
15.	P—Q R 4 / Kt—K 5	B—Kt 3 / P×P	B×P / P—Q 4
16.	B—K 1 / Q R—Q 1	P—Q Kt 4 ! (b) / B—R 2	B—Q 3 / K R—B 1

(a) Or 9. Kt—Q B 3.

(b) The first move of an exceptionally deep combination.

	(3)	**(4)**	**(5)**
17.	$\dfrac{\text{P}-\text{R 5}}{\text{B}-\text{B 4}}$	$\dfrac{\text{B}\times\text{Kt P !}}{\text{R P}\times\text{B}}$	$\dfrac{\text{Q R}-\text{K 1}}{\text{R}-\text{B 2}}$
18.	$\dfrac{\text{P}-\text{R 6}}{\text{P}\times\text{P}}$	$\dfrac{\text{Kt}\times\text{Kt P}}{\text{Q}-\text{Q 1}}$	$\dfrac{\text{P}-\text{K 4}}{\text{Q R}-\text{Q B 1}}$
19.	$\dfrac{\text{Q R}-\text{B 1}}{\text{R}-\text{B 1}}$	$\dfrac{\text{Kt}-\text{Q 6 ch.}}{\text{K}-\text{B 1}}$	$\dfrac{\text{P}-\text{K 5}}{\text{Kt}-\text{K 1}}$
20.	$\dfrac{\text{Kt}-\text{R 4}}{\text{B}-\text{Kt 3}}$	$\dfrac{\text{R}\times\text{P}}{\text{Kt}-\text{Kt 3}}$	$\dfrac{\text{P}-\text{B 4}}{\text{P}-\text{Kt 3}}$
21.	$\dfrac{\text{Kt}-\text{B 5 }(a)}{\text{Q}-\text{K 4}}$	$\dfrac{\text{B}-\text{R 4}}{\text{Q}-\text{Q 2}}$	$\dfrac{\text{R}-\text{K 3 }(c)}{\text{P}-\text{B 4}}$
22.	$\dfrac{\text{B}\times\text{Kt}}{\text{Q}\times\text{B}}$	$\dfrac{\text{Kt}\times\text{B }(b)}{\text{Q}\times\text{R}}$	$\dfrac{\text{P}\times\text{P } e.p.}{\text{Kt}\times\text{P}}$
23.	$\dfrac{\text{Kt}-\text{Q 6}}{\text{Q}\times\text{P}}$	$\dfrac{\text{Q}-\text{Q 8 ch.}}{\text{Q}-\text{K 1}}$	$\dfrac{\text{P}-\text{B 5}}{\text{Kt}-\text{K 5}}$
24.	$\dfrac{\text{Kt}\times\text{R}}{\text{R}\times\text{Kt}}$	$\dfrac{\text{B}-\text{K 7 ch.}}{\text{K}-\text{B 2}}$	$\dfrac{\text{B}\times\text{Kt}}{\text{P}\times\text{B}}$
25.	$\dfrac{\text{Q}-\text{Q 5}}{\text{Q}-\text{K 3}}$	$\dfrac{\text{Kt}-\text{Q 6 ch.}}{\text{K}-\text{Kt 3}}$	$\dfrac{\text{P}\times\text{Kt P}}{\text{R}-\text{B 7 }(d)}$
26.	$\dfrac{\text{Q}-\text{B 3}}{\text{P}-\text{R 3}}$	$\dfrac{\text{Kt}-\text{R 4 ch.}}{\text{K}-\text{R 4}}$	$\dfrac{\text{P}\times\text{P ch.}}{\text{K}-\text{R 1}}$
27.	$\dfrac{\text{B}-\text{Q 2}}{\text{Kt}-\text{K 4}}$	$\dfrac{\text{Kt}\times\text{Q}}{\text{R}\times\text{Q}}$	$\dfrac{\text{P}-\text{Q 5 ch.}}{\text{P}-\text{K 4}}$

(a) A good move, winning the exchange.

(b) Sacrificing further material to feed the attack. If—

22.	Q × Q
23. R × Q	R × Kt
24. R × R	Kt × R
25. R — Q 8 ch., &c.	

(c) The beginning of one of the deepest combinations on record.

(d) He has nothing better, for if—

25.	P × P
26. R — Kt 3	Q — Kt 2 *
27. P — Q 5	P — K 4
28. Q — Kt 5	R — K 1
29. R — B 6	

* If

26.	Q — R 2
27. R — B 6	R — Kt 2
28. R — R 3 wins.	

	(3)	(4)	(5)
28.	R×R ch. / Q×R	Kt×P ch. / K—R 3	Q—Kt 4 ! (d) / Q R—B 4 (e)
29.	Q—K 4 / Kt—Q 2	Kt (Kt 7)—B 5 ch. / K—R 4	R—B 8 ch. / K×P (f)
30.	R—Q B 1 / Q—B 1	P—K R 3 (b) / Kt—B 1	Q×P ch. / K—Kt 2
31.	B×P (a) / Kt—B 4	P×Kt ch. / K×P	B×P ch. / K×R
32.	Q—Kt 4 / P—B 4	B×R / R×B	B—Kt 7 ch. / K—Kt 1
33.	Q—Kt 6 / Q—B 2	P—Kt 3 / R—Q 7	Q×Q / Resigns (g).
34.	Q×Q ch. / K×Q	K—Kt 2 / R—K 7 (c)	
35.	B—Kt 5 / Kt—Q 6	P—R 4 / Kt—Kt 3	
36.	R—Q Kt 1 / K—K 3	Kt—K 3 ch. / K—R 4	
37.	P—Kt 3 / K—Q 4	P—R 5 / Kt—Q 2	
38.	P—B 3 / P—R 4	Kt (R 4)—B 5 / Kt—B 3	

(a) If 31. $\overline{\text{P×B}}$;   32. $\dfrac{\text{Q—Kt 4}}{}$ wins the Knight.

(b) If 30.   Kt—R 3
    31. Kt—Kt 7 mate.

(c) If 34.   R×R P
    35. Kt—B 3

(d) Crushing.

(e) If 28. Q×Q, White mates in 7 moves, thus:—

    29. B×P ch.   K×P
    30. R—R 3 ch.   K—Kt 3
    31. R—Kt 3 ch.   K—R 3
    32. R—B 6 ch.   K—R 4
    33. R (B 6)—B 5 ch.   K—R 3
    34. B—B 4 ch.   K moves
    35. R mates.

(f) If 29.   Q×R
    30. B×P ch.   K×P
    31. Q×P ch., and mate in 4.

(g) One of the very greatest games on record.

	(3)	(4)	(5)
39.	$\dfrac{\text{P—R 4}}{\text{Kt—B 4}}$	$\dfrac{\text{P—Kt 5}}{\text{B—Q 5}}$	
40.	$\dfrac{\text{P—R 5}}{\text{P—Q 6}}$	$\dfrac{\text{K—B 3}}{\text{R—R 7}}$	
41.	$\dfrac{\text{K—B 1}}{\text{P—R 5}}$	$\dfrac{\text{P—R 6}}{\text{B—R 2}}$	
42.	$\dfrac{\text{P}\times\text{P}}{\text{Kt}\times\text{P}}$	$\dfrac{\text{R—B 1}}{\text{R—Kt 7}}$	
43.	$\dfrac{\text{B—B 6 }(a)}{\text{K—K 3}}$	$\dfrac{\text{P—Kt 4 ch.}}{\text{K—Kt 4}}$	
44.	$\dfrac{\text{B}\times\text{P}}{\text{K—B 2}}$	$\dfrac{\text{R—B 7}}{\text{Resigns }(b)\text{.}}$	
45.	$\dfrac{\text{B—K 5}}{\text{Kt—B 4}}$		
46.	$\dfrac{\text{R—Q 1}}{\text{Resigns.}}$		

(*a*) A pretty move, to which there is no answer.   Played in the Petrograd Tournament, 1914.

(*b*) The whole game has been magnificently played by White. Rarely has the depth and subtlety of Capablanca's combination beginning at his sixteenth move been equalled in actual play.   This game was unanimously awarded the first Brilliancy Prize at the Petrograd Tournament, 1914.

SYNOPSIS OF BOOK VI.

THE END GAME.

CHAPTER I.

King and Queen against King.
King and Rook against King.
King and two Bishops against King.
King, Bishop, and Knight against King.
King and two Knights against King.
King and Pawn—King, Bishop, and Pawn—and King, Knight, and Pawn, against King.

CHAPTER II.

Queen against a Knight or Bishop.
Queen against Rook.
Queen against Rook and Pawn.
Queen against two Bishops.
Queen against two Knights.
Queen against Knight and Bishop.
Queen against Queen and Pawn.
Queen against Pawn.

CHAPTER III.

Rook against Bishop.
Rook against Knight.
Rook and Pawn against Bishop.
Rook against three minor Pieces.
Rook and Pawn against Rook.
Rook against one or more Pawns.
Rook against two Rooks.
Rook against Rook and Bishop.
Rook against Rook and Knight.

CHAPTER IV.

Endings with Kings and Pawns only.
King and Pawn against King and Pawn.
King and two Pawns against King and Pawn.
King and two Pawns against King and two Pawns.
King and two Pawns against King and three Pawns.
King and Pawns against King and three Pawns.

BOOK VI.

THE END GAME.

To play the end game with correctness and skill is an important and a very rare accomplishment, except among the magnates of the game. To the inexperienced player, a want of knowledge of the principles which should govern the action of his forces when the field is comparatively vacant, is a constant source of embarrassment and mortification. How often, while he is exulting in a fancied victory, when in fact it seems within his grasp, and he is dismissing the last uncertainty of its result, do we see it snatched from him in a moment! The well-timed advance of some unheeded Pawn—the perpetual and unavoidable check by the sole remaining Piece of his opponent— or the still more tantalizing dilemma of a forced stalemate—will often reverse the fortunes of the day or make the contest null. You should, therefore, make it an especial point of study, to comprehend the various classes of positions which most frequently occur towards the terminating stages of the conflict. To enable you to do so, we will now begin with the simpler class of checkmates, consisting of the King alone against an adverse force of different degrees, proceeding onward to the more difficult and complex situations which arise, when both parties are left with nearly equal forces at the end.

CHAPTER I.

KING AND QUEEN AGAINST KING.

THIS is one of the simplest of all checkmates. It is only necessary to force the single King to the nearest side of the chess-board, and then bringing up your own King, you mate in a very few moves. There is, however, one danger to be guarded against, viz., that of *stalemating* your adversary. The power of the Queen being so great, renders you very liable to this error. Place the Pieces as in Diagram 1, and find how to effect mate in two moves—observing the probability there is of giving stalemate.

KING AND ROOK AGAINST KING.

THIS is also a very easy checkmate, though less so than the preceding one. A little practice, however, will enable you readily to master it. In fact, in the most favourable position for Black, he cannot protract

mate beyond eighteen or nineteen moves. As before, he must be
driven to the side of the board, and then your King being placed in
front of him, with one square between, mate is given by a check
from the Rook on the same side line upon which the King stands.
An example (see Diagram 2) will make this quite plain.

WHITE.	BLACK.
1. R—R 7	K—B 1
2. K—K 2	K—Kt 1
3. R—R 7	K—B 1
4. K—K 3	K—K 1
5. K—K 4	K—Q 1
6. K—Q 5	K—B 1
7. K—Q 6	K—Kt 1
8. R—R 7	

(8. R—Q B 7 is still better, but the present move exhibits the
           principle more clearly.)

8.	K—B 1
9. R—K Kt 7	K—Kt 1
10. K—B 6	K—R 1
11. K—Kt 6	K—Kt 1
12. R—Kt 8 (checkmate).	

Diagram 1.   Diagram 2.

BLACK.   BLACK.

WHITE.   WHITE.

In the following situation (see Diagram 3), examine how to give
mate in three moves.

KING AND TWO BISHOPS AGAINST KING.

The two Bishops also win, without much difficulty, against the King alone; but in this case the King must be forced, not only to a side of the board, but into one of the corners, or, at any rate, into a square adjoining a corner one. The following example (see Diagram 4) will be a sufficient illustration :—

	WHITE.	BLACK.
1.	B—K R 3	K—Q 1
2.	B—B 4	K—K 2
3.	K—K 2	K—B 3
4.	K—B 3	K—K 2
5.	B—B 5	K—B 3
6.	K—Kt 4	K—K 2
7.	K—Kt 5	K—Q 1
8.	K—B 6	K—K 1
9.	B—B 7	K—B 1
10.	B—Q 7	K—Kt 1
11.	K—Kt 6	K—B 1
12.	B—Q 6 ch.	K—Kt 1
13.	B—K 6 ch.	K—R 1
14.	B—K 5 mate	

Diagram 3.

Diagram 4.

BLACK.

BLACK.

WHITE.

WHITE.

KING, BISHOP, AND KNIGHT AGAINST KING.

THIS is a much more difficult checkmate than any of the preceding ones, and should you be left with such a force at the termination of a game, you would probably find it quite impossible to win within the stipulated number of moves. This position merits a close examination, and you will then see that in this case, the King must not only be driven into a corner of the board, but into one of them which is commanded by your Bishop.

You will observe in this position (see Diagram 5), that the Black King is in the most unfavourable situation for White, since he occupies a corner square which is not commanded by the Bishop.

	WHITE.	BLACK.
1.	Kt—B 7 ch.	K—Kt 1
2.	B—K 4	K—B 1
3.	B—R 7	K—K 1
4.	Kt—K 5	K—B 1 or (A)
5.	Kt—Q 7 ch.	K—K 1
6.	K—K 6	K—Q 1
7.	K—Q 6.	K—K 1 !
8.	B—Kt 6 ch.	K—Q 1
9.	Kt—B 5	K—B 1
10.	B—B 7	K—Q 1
11.	Kt—Q 7 ch.	K—B 1
12.	K—B 6	K—Kt 1
13.	K—Kt 6	K—B 1
14.	B—K 6 ch.	K—Kt 1
15.	Kt—B 5	K—R 1
16.	B—Q 7	K—Kt 1
17.	Kt—R 6 ch.	K—R 1
18.	B—B 6 mate.	

(A.)

4.		K—Q 1
5.	K—K 6	K—B 2
6.	Kt—Q 7	K—B 3

(This is his best move, to avoid the corner square ; if, instead of this, Black play K—Kt 2, White's best move is the B—Q 3, and if Black then play K—B 3, White can move B—B 4, and B—Kt. 5.)

7.	B—Q 3	K—B 2 !
8.	B—Kt 5	K—Q 1
9.	Kt—K 5	K—B 2
10.	Kt—B 4	K—Q 1
11.	K—Q 6	K—B 1

12. Kt—R 5	K—Q 1
13. Kt—Kt 7 ch.	K—B 1
14. K—B 6	K—Kt 1
15. Kt—Q 6	K—R 2
16. K—B 7	K—R 1
17. B—B 4	K—R 2
18. Kt—B 8 ch.	K—R 1
19. B—Q 5 mate.	

It not unfrequently happens, however, that when Black has a Pawn besides the King, mate can be given without the necessity of driving him to the corner commanded by your Bishop, because you do not then incur the risk of stalemating him. The following position illustrates this. (See Diagram 6.)

Diagram 5.

BLACK.

Diagram 6.

BLACK.

WHITE.

WHITE.

White to move and mate in six.

WHITE.	BLACK.
1. B—Kt 4	K—R 2
2. B—B 5 ch.	K—R 1 !
3. K—Kt 6	P—Kt 5
4. K—R 6	P—Kt 6
5. B—Q 6	P—Kt 7
6. Kt—Kt 6 mate.	

KING AND TWO KNIGHTS AGAINST KING.

THE two Knights, with the assistance of the King, cannot force checkmate; unless, indeed, the adversary has a Pawn, which may sometimes be made the means of effecting it with only a single

Knight, as will be seen hereafter. Many singular positions occur with the Knights, where the adverse Pawns, or even Pieces, may be made to assist in crowding, and finally in checkmating, their own monarch. The following is an example :—

Diagram 7.

BLACK.

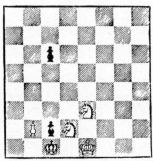

WHITE.

White mates in six moves, thus :—

WHITE.	BLACK.
1. Kt (K 3)—B 4	P—B 4
2. P—Kt 4	P×P
3. K—K 2	P—Kt 6
4. K—K 1	P—Kt 7
5. Kt.—K 5	P—Kt 8 (Queen)
6. Kt—Q 3 mate.	

KING AND PAWN,—KING, BISHOP, AND PAWN,—AND KING, KNIGHT, AND PAWN,—AGAINST KING.

WHEN one Pawn only is left on the board, supported by its King, and the adverse King is either in front of the Pawn, or within such distance as to be able to intercept it, it becomes a point of great nicety in some cases, to calculate whether or not you have the power of Queening the Pawn, and therefore of winning the game. This frequently depends upon your gaining the opposition, which you cannot always do.

In the annexed position (see Diagram 8) you have the opposition, and if Black have to play you will win.   Thus :—

1.	K — K 1
2. P—K 7	K — Q 2
3. K—B 7 and	
4. P—K 8 (Queen)	

But if White move first, the game is drawn ; for if 1. P—K 7 ch., Black moves King to his square, and you must either abandon the Pawn or give stalemate.   You will find, on trial, that any other mode of play on your part will produce the same result,—from which is deduced this important general rule : That if you can advance the Pawn to its 7th sq., *not giving check*, you will win ; but that if the Pawn checks at this point, you will only draw.

Diagram 8.   Diagram 9.

BLACK.   BLACK.

WHITE.   WHITE.

In this position (see Diagram 9) White will win either with or without the move ; for if Black have to play, he is forced to allow the White King to be moved either to B 7 or Q 7 ; and if White moves he gains the opposition, by K—B 6 or Q 6, and then P—K 6. It is evident that this would equally hold good if the White Pawn were any number of squares less advanced ; so that you invariably win, if you can succeed in placing your King on the sixth square of the file occupied by your Pawn, and in front of it ; providing, of course, that the Black King cannot attack the Pawn, so as to compel you to retreat in order to support it.   It is perhaps scarcely necessary to observe, that if the Pawn be upon either of the Rooks' files, these remarks will not apply—this contingency will be considered hereafter.

Recurring to the last position (Diagram 9), place your King and Pawn each one square further back, that is, K at K 5, and P at K 4.

If White has the move he wins by K—K 6 as before ; but if Black play first he will draw the game (*e.g.*).

WHITE.	BLACK.
	K—K 2
1.	
2. K—B 5	K—B 2
3. P—K 5	K—K 2
4. P—K 6	K—K 1

It is obvious, that if instead Black had moved K—Q 1 or B 1, White would have won, as in the first example.

5. K—B 6	K—B 1

And draws as before.

The student is recommended to devote a little time to the careful examination of the preceding positions and variations, with such others arising out of them, as will readily suggest themselves ; after which, he will not find much difficulty in understanding the following one. (See Diagram 10.)

This position was first given by Lolli, and has been subsequently quoted by most of the later authors. An analysis of it will exhaust the principal varieties of this branch of the subject. The winning of it for White, depends altogether upon his having the move or the contrary. In the first place, suppose White plays first :—

WHITE.	BLACK.
1. K—Q 2	K—K 2
2. K—K 3	K—K 3
3. K—K 4	K—B 3
4. K—Q 5	K—K 2
5. K—K 5	K—B 2
6. K—Q 6	

If Black plays K—B 3, White plays P—K 4, then P—K 5, and on Black afterwards moving K—K 1, White gains the opposition, as shown before.

6.	K—K 1 or B 1
7. K—K 6	

And then advances Pawn, winning.

Next suppose Black has the move, and he will draw :—

WHITE.	BLACK.
1.	K—K 2
2. K—Q 2	K—K 3
3. K—K 3	K—K 4
4. K—Q 3	K—Q 4
5. P—K 3 or K 4 ch.	K—K 4

And it is clear that, play as you may, White can only draw the game.

The only exception in all the foregoing cases is to be found, as has already been remarked, when the Pawn is upon either of the Rooks' files. In these instances, Black will invariably draw the game when his King can be placed on any part of the file in front of the Pawn, it being quite immaterial at what distance the adverse King and Pawn may be. Even, as in the next example, which is to be found in Ponziani, Black will draw the game, if he have not the move, against two Pawns in a somewhat similar position. For White being to move, he can only play K—R 8, to which Black must reply by K—B 1; and if White then advance B P, it will be taken; or if he play R P, Black returns to B 2, and his adversary is stalemated. (See Diagram 11.)

Diagram 10.   Diagram 11.

BLACK.   BLACK.

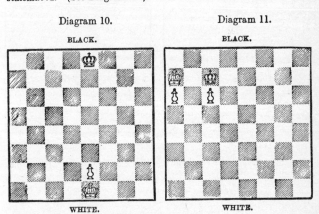

WHITE.   WHITE.

Two *united* Pawns, with their King, always win against King alone. Another advantage in having two Pawns thus situated is, that they can always maintain themselves until the arrival of the King to their support, for should one be taken, the other will Queen. In the next position (see Diagram 12), White wins by K—Kt 5, then Queening R P, and upon that being taken, playing K—R 6 or B 6, having the opposition. It is curious, however, that if White had a Bishop in place of a Pawn, at R 7, he could only draw the game, for he could not drive the adverse King from the corner; and should he sacrifice the Bishop at Kt 8, he could not afterwards gain the opposition.

Of course, in all ordinary cases, a Pawn, with the support of one of the minor Pieces in addition to the King, must win with ease. Besides the case just mentioned, however, there are one or two important exceptions to this rule,—an acquaintance with which will sometimes enable you to save an otherwise desperate game.

Of these, the one of most consequence has reference to the Bishop, and may be thus expressed : That if you are left with a Pawn on a Rook's file, and a Bishop which does not command the 8th square of that file, or, in other words, the square on which your Pawn should go to Queen, you will not be able to win, unless the adverse King can be prevented from getting before the Pawn.

Diagram 12.   Diagram 13.

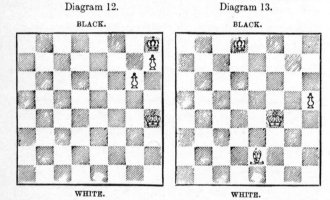

BLACK.   BLACK.

WHITE.   WHITE.

In this position (see Diagram 13), Black having to play, the game, you will find, can only be drawn. Thus :—

WHITE.	BLACK.
1.	K—K 2

(If he play the K—K 1, you can win.)

| 2. B—B 4 or (A) | K—B 3 |

And play as you may, the game is drawn.

(A.)

| 1. | K—K 2 |
| 2. P—R 6 | K—B 2 |

And draws the game.

The peculiarity of this latter variation is, that if Black, after the Pawn is moved, play K—B 3, you win by B—R 5.

We may conclude this Chapter with two ingenious positions from the excellent German Treatise so often referred to already, in which a single King draws the game against Knight and Pawn.

The first of these positions (Diagram 14) strikingly exemplifies an important peculiarity of the Knight, viz., that he can never gain a move. White would now win if Black had to move; but having himself to play, the case is different; for in order to force away the

Black King, the Knight, must be able to occupy one of the squares commanding Q B 8 or Q B 7 not giving check, which (since the moves required by a Knight to reach a given point cannot be altered from an even to an odd number) you will find he can never do. Suppose,—

WHITE.	BLACK.
1. Kt—K 3	K—B 2
2. Kt—Q 5 ch.	K—B 1
3. Kt—K 7 ch.	K—B 2

&c., &c.

Diagram 14.

BLACK.

WHITE.

Diagram 15.

BLACK.

WHITE.

Diagram 15. Here also it is clear that White cannot win, for the Knight cannot command the R 8 square without leaving the Pawn to be taken, and should the King attempt to support it, you inevitably give stalemate.

CHAPTER II.

ENDINGS in which there are Pieces or Pawns on both sides, are of course much more difficult and complicated in their nature than such as have yet been examined. In many cases, indeed, the variations are too numerous to admit of complete demonstration, whilst in others, the result continually changes according to the different parts of the board which the same Pieces may occupy. All that we can attempt here, therefore, is to mention the principal instances, in which the issue is determinate and fixed; and to give as accurate an approximation as possible in those that remain. We need only premise further, that the reader will find a careful study of these peculiar endings of the greatest advantage, not only as regards his acquaintance with the positions actually given, many of which in play may never occur, but still more particularly as to his general knowledge of the powers and range of the various Pieces, and of the methods of most effectually combining and playing them.

QUEEN AGAINST A KNIGHT OR BISHOP.

(In all cases, each party is of course understood to have a King in addition to the Pieces named.)

The Queen wins easily against one of the minor Pieces, except when in such a position that the weaker party, by the sacrifice of the Piece, may force a stalemate. As an example, see Diagram 16.

Diagram 16.   Diagram 17.

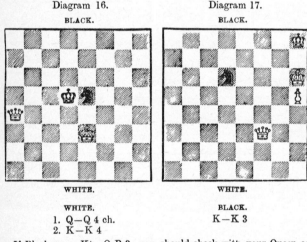

WHITE.	BLACK.
1. Q—Q 4 ch.	K—K 3
2. K—K 4	

If Black move Kt—Q B 3, you should check with your Queen at Q 5, and then take the Knight; but if he play—

2.	Kt—Kt 3
3. Q.—Kt 6 ch.	K—B 2
4. K—B 5	Kt—K 2 ch.
5. K—Kt 5	Kt—Q 4
6. Q—Q 6	Kt—K 2
7. Q—B 6 ch.	K—K 1
8. Q—K 6	K—Q 1
9. K—B 6	Kt—B 1
10. Q—Q B 6	

And White wins the Knight.

Whenever the Knight is at a distance from the King, White may generally win it in a few moves by a divergent check, or by attacking and confining the Knight; but you must always be careful to prevent your King and Queen being attacked at the same time by the adverse Knight; and to avoid positions in which Black may draw by giving up his Knight, as in the following (see Diagram 17), where Black having to move, can make a drawn game.

In the same manner, the Queen easily wins against a Bishop.

QUEEN AGAINST ROOK.

HERE also, as in the last case, the Queen wins in all general positions the exceptions being of the same nature as before, viz., being founded on the possibility of making a stalemate.

Diagram 18.   Diagram 19.

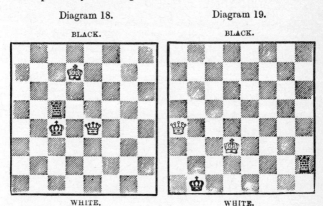

Philidor gives this position (see Diagram 18), and the method of playing it. Black being already in check, he plays:—

WHITE.	BLACK.
1.	K—Kt 6
2. K—Q 6	R—B 7

(Should Black play 2. R—B 5, White's reply is 3. Q—K 1, and then to advance his King.)

3. K—Q 5

(To check would be a loss of time.)

| 3. | K—Kt 7 |
| 4. K—Q 4 | K—R 8 |

(Inviting White to take the Rook, and thus give stalemate.'

5. K—Q 3	R—Kt 7
6. Q—R 4 ch.	K—Kt 8 or (A.)
7. K—B 3	R—K R 7
8. Q—Kt 5 ch.	K—R 8
9. Q—R 6 ch.	K—Kt 8
10. Q—Kt 6 ch.	K—R 7
11. Q—R 7 ch.	K—Kt 8
12. Q—Kt 8 ch.	

Then takes Rook, and wins.

(A.)

6.	R—Q R 7
7. Q—Q 1 ch.	K—Kt 7
8. Q—B 2 ch.	K—R 6
9. Q—B 3 ch.	K—R 5
10. K—B 4	

And wins.

With the exceptions already referred to, White can always force the single King to a side of the board, and afterwards win the Rook, either by a divergent check, or as in the last variation. We give one other example of the same kind (see Diagram 19), with the method of playing it.

WHITE.	BLACK.
1. Q—K Kt 4	

If Black plays R—R 2, White moves Q—B 5, and if ;

1.	R—B 7
2. Q—Q 1 ch.	R—B 8
3. Q—Kt 3 ch.	K—R 8
4. Q—R 4 ch.	

If instead White plays K—K 2, Black moves R—B 7 ch., and will draw the game.

4.	K—Kt 7
5. K—Q 2	R—Q Kt 8
6. Q—Kt 5 ch.	K—R 7
7. Q—R 6 ch.	K—Kt 6
8. Q—R 5	R—Kt 7 ch.
9. K—Q 3	R—Kt 8
10. Q—Kt 5 ch.	K—R 7
11. Q—R 4 ch.	K—Kt 7
12. K—Q 2	

And wins.

In this position (see Diagram 20), which is given by Ponziani, Black having the move, will draw the game ; thus,—

1.	R—R 2 ch.
2. K—Kt 2	R—Kt 2 ch.
3. K—B 3	R—B 2 ch.

4.	K—Kt 4	R—Kt 2 ch.
5.	K—B 5	R—B 2 ch.
6.	K—Kt 6	R—Kt 2 ch.
7.	K—R 6	R—R 2 ch.

&c., for if White should take the Rook, his adversary is stalemated.

Diagram 20.

BLACK.

WHITE.

QUEEN AGAINST ROOK AND PAWN.

WITH few exceptions, arising from peculiar situations, the Queen wins also against a Rook and Pawn, though with greater difficulty than before. The two following positions, illustrating both a won and a drawn game, are from Philidor.

Here White having to play, will win. The following is Philidor's analysis, and seems satisfactorily to prove this :—

WHITE.		BLACK.
1.	Q—R 7 ch.	K—K 3 !
2.	Q—Q B 7	R—Q B 4
3.	Q—Q 8 (a)	R—K 4
4.	Q—K 8 ch.	K—Q 4
5.	Q—Q B 8	R—K 5 ch.

(Had the Rook instead been played to R 4, White would have checked with Queen at R 8, and in two or three more moves would win the Pawn at least.)

6.	K—B 5	R—K 4 ch.
7.	K—B 6	R—K 5

(a) This is the position which White must endeavour to gain, in order to force the King to Q 4, in front of the Pawn.

If instead he had played K—Q 5, the Queen would advance to B 6.)

8.	Q—K B 5 ch.	R—K 4
9.	Q—Q 3 ch.	K—B 4
10.	Q—Q 2	K—B 3
11.	Q—Q 4	K—Q 2

(He might also have played to B 2. See Variation.)

12.	Q—Q B 4	R—Q B 4
13.	Q—K B 7 ch.	K—B 3
14.	K—K 7	

This is the important point, to be able to play the King behind the Pawn.)

14.		R—K 4 ch.
15.	K—Q 8	R—Q B 4
16.	Q—Q 7 ch.	K—Q 4
17.	K—K 7	R—B 3
18.	Q—K B 5 ch.	K—B 5
19.	K—Q 7	R—B 4
20.	Q—K 4 ch.	K—Kt 6
21.	K × P	

And wins.

Diagram 21.

BLACK.

WHITE.

VARIATION.

On Black's 11th move.

	WHITE.	BLACK.
11.		K—B 2
12.	Q—Q R 4	R—Q B 4
13.	Q—R 7 ch.	K—B 3
14.	K—K 7	

And wins, as above.

In the next position (see Diagram 22) Black may draw the game either

with the move or without it, for his King cannot be forced in front
of the Pawn as in the last example.   Suppose,—

WHITE.	BLACK.
1. Q—Kt 8 ch.	K—K 2
2. Q—Kt 8	R—Q B 3
3. K—K 5	R—K 3 ch.
4. K—Q 5	

And the game is drawn.

The Rook, with the aid of two united Pawns, will frequently draw
against the Queen, and still more easily with one or both of the minor
Pieces.   In the latter case they may sometimes win, as in the following
situation (see Diagram 23) from Ponziani.

WHITE.	BLACK.
1.	B—R 5 ch.
2. K—B 1	R—K 1
3. Q—Kt 4 (a)	B—B 7
4. P—B 7	R—Q R 1
5. Q×Kt ch.	K×Q
6. K×B	K—Q 4
7. P—Kt 6	K—K 3
8. P—R 5	K—B 3

And wins.

(A.)

3. P—Kt 6	R×Q
4. P×R	Kt--Q 3
5. P—Kt 7	B—Kt 6

And wins.

Diagram 22.   Diagram 23.

BLACK.   BLACK.

WHITE.   WHITE.

(a) (Or P—Kt 6. See A.)

QUEEN AGAINST TWO BISHOPS.

THE Queen usually wins against two of the minor Pieces, at least, if they are on different parts of the board, or at a distance from their King. There are, however, many instances in which, by skilful play, the weaker force may draw the game, nor are the principal writers by any means yet agreed as to the number and description of such cases.

The two Bishops will be able to draw when they can assume a position similar to the following (see Diagram 24), or in other words, such a position in front of their King, that the adverse King cannot approach.

Diagram 24.

BLACK.

WHITE.

This situation is from Lolli, who gives the following moves to prove that White cannot win; and, indeed, it is pretty evident that the White King can never cross the line formed by the two Bishops.

White moves first.

WHITE.	BLACK.
1. Q — Q 7 ch.	K — Kt 1 !
2. Q — K 6	K — Kt 2
3. K — B 4	B — R 2
4. Q — Q 7 ch.	K — Kt 3
5. Q — K 8 ch.	K — Kt 2
6. K — Kt 4	B — Kt 3
7. Q — K 6	B — R 2
8. Q — Q 7 ch.	K — Kt 3
9. Q — K 8 ch.	K — Kt 2
10. K — R 5	B — B 4

The game is drawn.

Should Black on his first move play a Bishop in place of the King, he would lose. The reason is, that your King could then be played to B 5; for instance,—

WHITE.	BLACK.
1. Q—Q 7 ch.	B—B 2
2. K—B 5	B—B 6
3. Q—B 7	B—R 8
4. Q—R 7	B—Kt 7
5. Q—Kt. 6	B—R 6
6. Q—Q 4 ch.	K—Kt 1
7. K—B 6	K—B 1
8. Q—Q 8 ch.	B—K 1
9. K—K 6	B—Kt 5
10. Q—B 6 ch.	K—Kt. 1
11. Q—Kt 5 ch.	K—B 1
12. Q—B 4 ch.	

And wins a Bishop.

And although Black may vary his defence in many parts, you will find that in a similar manner you can always, after this first error of B—B 2, force him to assume a position of the same kind, and win one of the Bishops.

QUEEN AGAINST TWO KNIGHTS.

THE power of the Queen against the two Knights has been a subject of considerable discussion. It has been laid down by Lolli and other old authors that, with one or two exceptions only, the Queen could always win in these cases, and this opinion was entertained for a long time. MM. V. H. d. Laza and Bilguer, however, considered this decision to rest on no sufficient grounds, and with the spirit of patient research which distinguished the whole of their treatise, succeeded, if not in demonstrating, yet in showing a very high degree of probability in support of their opinion that Black can frequently obtain a draw.

The kind of exception already referred to as having been so long supposed the only one in which the Knights could draw is the following (see Diagram 25, p. 444).

Here it is obvious that the White King can never move from the corner, and you will find that so long as Black keeps his King near the Knights and does not play him on to the Rook's file (in which case White might, by occupying the Knight's file with his Queen, break up the position) the game is drawn. Should Black move his King away from the Knights, the latter would speedily be forced into one of the Rook's squares, and prevented from moving, and then being compelled to move a Knight, Black would lose at once.

Another position, strictly analogous to the above, and which, therefore, does not invalidate the general principle, has been made public by Mr. Walker.

Leaving those few instances in which the White King can be prevented from moving out of the corner and coming into play, it was always considered that the strongest situation in which the Black force could be placed, was one where the two Knights should mutually defend each other, and be within reach of their King. The opinion, however, or we may rather say the discovery, of Von H. d. Laza, is that, to use his own words, " it is even more easy to draw the game against the Queen with two Knights than with two Bishops, and the whole secret consists in placing the Knights before their King in the same position as the Bishops, that is to say, side by side, and not so that they may defend each other."

Diagram 25.   Diagram 26.

BLACK.   BLACK.

WHITE.   WHITE.

He then proceeds to support his assertion thus :—" In the well-known position examined by Lolli, and pronounced by subsequent writers as one in which the Queen must win, I think the game ought to be drawn." The position alluded to is given above (see Diagram 26) :—

WHITE.	BLACK.
" 1. K—Kt 3	K—Q 6

(It would be equally good to play Kt—Q 6.)

2. Q—Q 5 ch.	K—B 6
3. K—B 4	Kt—Q 6 ch.
4. K—B 3	

" Lolli now makes Black play Kt—K 4 ch., a move which speedily loses the game. Suppose him, however, to play—

4.	Kt—Kt 5
5. Q—Q 1	Kt—Q 7 ch.

6. K—K 2	Kt—Kt 6
7. Q—K 1 ch.	K—B 5
8. Q—R 4 ch.	K—B 6
9. Q—B 6 ch.	Kt—Q 5 ch.
10. K—B 2	Kt—Q 4

And I cannot discover how White will win the game.

Diagram 27.   Diagram 28.

BLACK.   BLACK.

WHITE.   WHITE.

"The two following positions (see Diagrams 27 and 28) are certainly very favourable for the Queen and King, and yet it is, if not quite impossible, at least extremely difficult, to bring the King into action and win the game.

Diagram 27.

WHITE.	BLACK.
1. Q—K 6	K—Kt 2
2. K—B 3	Kt—R 2

This appears to be a better move than Kt—R 5 ch.

3. K—Kt 4	Kt (R 2)—B 1
4. Q—Q 6	K—B 2
5. R—Q 5 ch.	K—Kt 2
6. K—Kt 5 ?	Kt—R 2 ch.

Winning the Queen next move."

In Diagram 28 the best mode of defence is the following:—

WHITE.	BLACK.
1.	Kt—B 1 ch.
2. K—B 6	Kt—K 2 ch.
3. K—Kt 5	Kt—Q 3 ch.

And I know not how White can win.

In this ending White should endeavour, therefore, where Black's Knights support each other, to drive the Black King into a position where he cannot move, thus forcing a Knight to move, when he can win one of them with a divergent check.

Black should try and keep his Knights together (but not supporting each other), in the centre of the board, with his King near them.

QUEEN AGAINST KNIGHT AND BISHOP.

THIS kind of ending is analogous in character to the last, and the discovery of MM. V. H. d. Laza and Bilguer equally applies to it. Except in some few positions. such as the following (see Diagram 29), where, as with the two Knights, the White King can be imprisoned in the corner, and that of the adversary is in the neighbourhood of his two Pieces, it has always been laid down that the Queen wins. Again, however, we incline to agree with V. H. d. Laza, that, though with greater difficulty, "a King with Bishop and Knight can in many cases draw the game against a King and Queen." "The system of defence which I am about to lay down," he says, "is the invention of my late friend, Von Bilguer, and has hitherto been known only to himself and me."

Diagram 29.

BLACK.

WHITE.

Diagram 30.

BLACK.

WHITE.

"Let us suppose the Black King to stand on K R 8, then if we place his Knight on K R 7, the latter attacks three squares, viz., Kt 5, B 6, and B 8, and it is evident that the adverse party can only win by bringing his King near the other, which is to be effected by passing over his R 4, B 4, or B 2 ; but if we now place Black's Bishop at K Kt 6, all the squares around are for the moment defended, and before mate could be given, Black must be compelled to quit his entrenchments, and then it remains to be shown that it is impossible for him to take up a similar position."

Diagram 30.

WHITE.	BLACK.
1. Q—Q 5	K—Kt 3
2. Q—Kt 2 ch.	K—B 2

(If instead of this move White plays Q—Kt 8, Black must move B—Kt 4 or R 5, and then again back to B 3, as circumstances may require.)

3. Q—Kt 4	B—K 4

(Since it is of great importance to defend the K Kt 3 against the Q, Black can only move his B, which he must play to K 2 or K 4.)

4. Q—B 4 ch.	K—Kt 3
5. Q—K 4 ch.	K—B 3

It must now be examined whether White can force the game, or if Black cannot again take up a safe position.

6. K—B 6	Kt—B 4

(In order to cut off afterwards the White squares from the adverse King.)

7. Q—B 3	K—K 3
8. Q—K 4	K—B 3

(Should White play K—B 5, Black, by answering with B—Q 3 ch., would gain a position similar to the primitive situation of the Pieces, and if he plays Q—Q 5 ch., the Black King must be moved to B 3, the result of which shall be analysed in the accompanying variation.)

9. K—Q 5	Kt—K 2 ch.
10. K—B 4	Kt—B 4
11. K—Q 3	Kt—Q 3
12. Q—Q 5	K—B 4
13. K—K 3	K—B 3
14. K—B 3	Kt—B 4
15. Q—B 6 ch.	Kt—Q 3
16. K—Kt 4	K—K 3

Drawn.

VARIATION.

Beginning at White's 8th move.

WHITE.	BLACK.
8. Q—Q 5 ch.	K—B 3
9. K—Q 7	Kt—Kt 2
10. K—Q 8	Kt—K 3 ch.
11. K—B 8	K—B 4
12. K—Q 7	Kt—B 5

And White has gained nothing.

In this position (see Diagram 31) White wins by 1. Q—K R **3**.

If Black has the move and plays—

WHITE.	BLACK.
	1.
2. Q—Q 4	B—R 5
3. Q—K 5 ch., and wins.	B—Kt 4

Or if—

	1. B—Kt 3
2. Q—K Kt 3 ch.	K—Q 8
3. Q—Kt 4 ch.	K—B 8
4. Q—Kt 4	B—Q 1
5. Q—Q 6	B—R 5
6. Q—R 3 ch.	K—Q **8**
7. Q—R 4 ch., and wins.	

Diagram 31.

BLACK.

WHITE.

On the whole, as regards this part of the subject, it may be safely assumed, that when you are left, at the end of a game, with the Queen against any two of the minor Pieces, the probability is very great in favour of your easily gaining it, and that this probability is converted almost into certainty, when the two Pieces are far removed from each other or from their King, or when they cannot prevent your King from entering into their game. At the same time there appear to be many positions that the weaker force may occasionally take up, in which by a very careful and accurate system of defence, they may succeed in maintaining their entrenchments, and thus produce a drawn game. The innumerable variations, however, are very far from being exhausted, and leave ample scope for the researches of future analysts.

QUEEN AGAINST QUEEN AND PAWN.

In cases of this kind the game is usually drawn without difficulty, and most generally so by means of a perpetual check, though the same object may sometimes be attained by an exchange of Queens, when your King is able to stop the Pawn. When, however, the Pawn is advanced to its 7th square, and more particularly if defended by its King, the task is one of more difficulty, and many instructive situations occur where the Pawn may be Queened and the game therefore won. We subjoin an example or two of each kind, by way of illustration.

Diagram 32.   Diagram 33.

BLACK.   BLACK.

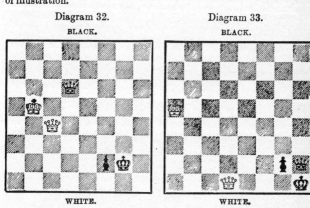

WHITE.   WHITE.

Here (see Diagram 32), with the move, White will draw the game: for suppose,—

WHITE.	BLACK.
1. Q—Kt 4 ch.	Q—Kt 6
2. Q—Q 4 ch.	K—Kt 8
3. Q—Q 4.	K—R 7
4. Q—R 8 ch.	Q—R 6
5. Q—K 5 ch.	K—Kt 8
6. Q—Kt 5 ch.	Q—Kt 7
7. Q—K 3	

And he will always be able to make a drawn game.

In the next case (see Diagram 33), you would be ready to suppose that, as Black must Queen the Pawn, he will win; it will be seen on examination, however, that the game is really drawn. Black being in check plays—

1.		P—Kt 8 (Q)
2.	Q—B 3 ch.	Q (R 7)—Kt 7
3.	Q—R 5 ch.	Q (Kt 8)—R 7
4.	Q—K 1 ch.	Either Q interposes.

Perpetual check.

The ingenious position Diagram 34 is given by Mr. Lewis; Black, with the move, ought to win. You are recommended to endeavour to discover the method of doing so before looking at the solution.

	WHITE.	BLACK.
1.		Q—Kt 4
2.	K moves	

(For it is clear that the Queen cannot move without allowing the Pawn to advance.)

2.		K—Q 8
3.	Q—R 1 ch.	P—B 8 (Q)

And wins.

Diagram 34.

BLACK.

WHITE.

Diagram 35.

BLACK.

WHITE.

White to move, wins. (See Diagram 35.)

	WHITE.	BLACK.
1.	P—R 8 (Q) ch.	K—B 5

(If instead 1. . . . K—B 4, 2. Q—Q 5 ch., and then forces the exchange of Queens.)

2.	Q—K B 8 ch.	K—K 5
3.	Q—K 7 ch.	K—B 6

(If to B 5, the Queen checks at B 7.)

4.	Q—K B 6 ch.	K—K 5
5.	Q—K 6 ch.	K—B 6
6.	Q—K B 5 ch.	K—K 7
7.	Q—Q 3 ch.	

Then forces an exchange of Queens, and wins with his remaining Pawn.

QUEEN AGAINST PAWN.

In all ordinary situations, the Queen of course easily stops a single Pawn and wins against it; if, however, the latter has reached its 7th square, and has the support of its King, there are instances in which the game may be drawn. The first position (see Diagram 36) will show the method of winning, and we shall afterwards point out the exceptions.

Diagram 36.

BLACK.

WHITE.

WHITE.	BLACK.
1. Q—B 5 ch.	K—Kt 7
2. Q—K 4 ch.	K—B 7
3. Q—B 4 ch.	K—Kt 7
4. Q—K 3	K—B 8
5. Q—B 3 ch.	K—K 8
6. K—Q 4	K—Q 8
7. Q—Q 3 ch.	K—K 8
8. K—K 3	K—B 8
9. Q×P ch., and wins.	

The same mode of procedure can always be adopted, unless the single Pawn should be either on the Bishop's or Rook's file, in which case Black may usually make a drawn game, owing to the power which he then has of making a stalemate. His having this alternative, however, altogether depends upon the distance which the adverse King may chance to be from the scene of action. In the next position (Diagram 37) the game is drawn.

WHITE.	BLACK.
1. Q—Kt 4 ch.	K—R 8
2. Q—B 3 ch.	K—Kt 8
3. Q—Kt 3 ch.	K—R 8

And it is evident, that if White takes the Pawn, his adversary is stalemated.

The result is the same when the Pawn is on the Rook's file, as you will at once see by making the experiment.

The following position (see Diagram 38), from Lolli, is a very ingenious exception to this rule, and will well repay your attention.

WHITE.	BLACK.
1. K — B 3 d. ch.	K — B 7
2. Q — K Kt 2 ch.	K — Kt 6
3. Q — B 1	K — Kt 7
4. Q — K 2 ch.	K — Kt 6
5. Q — Q 1 ch.	K — Kt 7
6. Q — Q 2 ch.	K — Kt 8
7. K — Kt 4	P — R 8 (Q)
8. K — Kt 3	

And wins.

Diagram 37.   Diagram 38.

BLACK.   BLACK.

WHITE.   WHITE

CHAPTER III.

ROOK AGAINST BISHOP.

It is not very difficult to draw the game with a Bishop against a Rook. As it is necessary that the two Kings should be opposite each other (except in the corners of the board), before checkmate can be given with the Rook, it follows, that if you can so play your Bishop as to prevent his King facing yours, the game will be drawn. It is seldom good play to interpose the Bishop when the King is checked, and your Bishop should generally be at a distance from your King. (See Diagram No. 39.)

WHITE.	BLACK.
1. B—Kt 7	R—Q Kt 3
2. B—Q 5	R—Kt 7
3. B—B 6	R—B 7 ch.
4. K—Kt 1	

If instead White had played K—K 1, he would have lost the game. See (A.)

4.	K—K 7
5. B—Q 5	K—K 8
6. B—B 6	R—B 3
7. B—Kt 7	R—Kt 3 ch.
8. K—R 2	

Not to R 1, because Black would play K—B 7, and win.

8.	K—B 7
9. K—R 3, &c.	

And the game is drawn.

(A.)

WHITE.	BLACK.
4. K—K 1	R—Q B 7
5. B—R 4	R—B 8 ch.
6. B—Q 1	R—Kt 8

And wins.

Diagram 39. Diagram 40.

BLACK. BLACK.

WHITE. WHITE.

The most secure position, though not, as Philidor asserts, the only safe one, for the weaker force, is that where the King can be played to a corner square of a different colour to that on which the Bishop runs, as in this situation you have only to move your King or Bishop to K 1, or R 2, and cannot be compelled to leave the corner.

Diagram 40.

White to move and mate in seven.

WHITE.	BLACK.
1. R—Q B 2	B—Kt 6 (a)
2. R—B 8 ch.	B—Kt 1
3. K—Q 6	P—Kt 6
4. R—B 7	B—Q 4 !
5. K × B	K—Kt 1
6. K—K 6	K moves.
7. R mates.	

ROOK AGAINST KNIGHT.

In ordinary positions, and where the Knight is near to, or cannot be prevented approaching, his King, the weaker party will be able to draw the game. The method of doing so, however, is not very easy, and there are many positions (of which we shall give some examples) where the Rook can win.

Diagram 41.

White to play.

WHITE.	BLACK.
1. R—R 8	K—Q 1
2. R—Kt 8	K—B 2
3. R—Kt 4	K—Q 1
4. R—Kt 7	K—K 1
5. R—Q 7	Kt—Kt 3
6. R—Q Kt 7 (or A.)	Kt—B 1
7. R—K B 7	K—Q 1
8. R—K R 7	Kt—Kt 3
9. K—Q 6	Kt—B 1 ch.
10. K—B 6	Kt—K 2 ch.
11. K—Kt 7	K—K 1
12. K—B 7	K—B 1
13. K—Q 7	Kt—Kt 1
14. K—Q 8	Kt—B 3
15. R—R 8 ch.	Kt—Kt 1
16. R—R 4	K—Kt 2
17. K—K 8	Kt—B 3 ch.
18. K—K 7	Kt—Kt 1 ch.
19. R—K 6	K—B 1
20. R—K B 4 ch.	K—K 1

(a) If the Pawn is moved instead, the result is the same.

21. R—B 7	Kt—R 3
22. R—K Kt 7	K—B 1
23. R—K R 7	Kt—Kt 1
24. R—K B 7 ch.	K—K 1
25. R—Q Kt 7	K—B 1

And Black will draw the game.

(A.)

| 6. R—Q B 7 | K—Q 1 |
| 7. K—Q 6 | Kt—B 1 ch. |

(If Black plays 7. Kt—R 1, he would lose the game.)

| 8. K—B 6 | Kt—K 2 |

Checking, &c., as before.

By carefully pursuing this system, he will always be able to draw the game.

Diagram 41.   Diagram 42.

BLACK.   BLACK.

WHITE.   WHITE.

Diagram 42.

This position, Black having the move, was considered for some time a drawn game. It has been shown, however, that White can win.

| WHITE. | BLACK. |
| 1. | K—K 1 ! |

For if Black plays 1. Kt—B 3, White checks with R, followed by K—K 6; and if instead Black plays K—B 1, White plays R—R 4, and in a few moves will equally win the Knight.)

| 2. K—K 6 | K—B 1 |
| 3. R—R 4 | Kt—K 6 |

(Any other move loses the Knight at once.)

4. R—K 4	Kt—B 7

(If to Kt 7, White moves K—B 6.)

5. K—Q 5	K moves
6. K—B 4	K moves
7. R—K 2	Kt—R 6 ch.
8. K—Kt 4	Kt—Kt 8
9. R—Q Kt 2	

And wins.

In the following position (see Diagram 43) White will win either with or without the move.

Diagram 43.

BLACK.

WHITE.

WHITE.	BLACK.
1.	Kt—R 2 ch.
2. K—B 7	Kt—Kt 4 ch.

If 2. Kt—B 1, White should play R—R 8, for if K × Kt at once, Black is stalemated.

3. K—Kt 6

And wins.

The two last examples forcibly illustrate the importance of keeping the Knight near his King, and of not playing either the King or Knight to a corner square, or even to a Knight's square, if it can be avoided. In all cases the danger increases to the weaker force, as he is compelled to recede from the centre squares to any of the side lines. The principle to be observed is, therefore, precisely opposite to the one recommended in the case of Bishop against Rook, where the corner squares are the most secure of any.

ROOK AND PAWN AGAINST BISHOP.

NOTWITHSTANDING that the Rook is much more powerful than the Bishop, and more particularly so towards the end of a game, it is singular that there are many positions in which the former cannot do more than draw the game. We give some examples of both results.

Diagram 44.

This situation is given by Philidor, and may either be won by White or only drawn, according as he plays correctly or otherwise. In the first place, suppose—

WHITE.	BLACK.
1. R—Q R 1	B—Kt 1 !
2. R—R 6 ch.	B—Q 3

(The object of White is to be able to play his King in front of the Pawn, which, as you will see, speedily gives him the victory.)

3. R—Q Kt 6	K—Q 2
4. K—Q 5	B—Kt 6
5. R—Kt 7 ch.	B—B 2
6. R—R 7	K—B 1 or Q 1
7. K—B 6	

And then advances the Pawn, winning easily.

But if White had first played P—Q 5 ch. Black might have drawn the game as follows :—

WHITE.	BLACK.
1. P—Q 5 ch.	K—Q 2
2. K—Q 4	B—Kt 6
3. R—Q R 1	B—B 5
4. R—R 7 ch.	K—Q 3
5. K—K 4	B—Kt 6

(Black must exercise great care here; had he played 5. B—R 7 White would have moved 6. R—K Kt 7, and won the game.)

6. R—K Kt 7	B—K 8
7. R—Kt 6 ch.	K—Q 2
8. P—Q 6	

(Were White to attempt first to support the Pawn by playing K—K 5, the check from the Bishop would force him to retire.)

8.	K—B 3
9. K—K 5	B—Kt 5

And it is obvious that White can never advance the Pawn without immediately losing it.

Diagram 45.

In this situation, Black draws the game, either with or without the move. Suppose White begins,—

WHITE.	BLACK.
1. R—Q Kt 7	B—B 5
2. R—Q B 7	B—R 7

This is the proper square for Black to play his Bishop to ; if he moves it to Kt 4 or Kt 6, White can win tne game. Suppose, in the first case :—

2.	B—Kt 4
3. K—B 5	B—K 7 !
4. P—B 7	K—Kt 2 !
5. K—K 6	B—R 4 !
6. R—Kt 7	B—Kt 3.
7. P—B 8 (Q) ch.	K × Q
8. K—B 6	

And wins.

Diagram 44.　　　　　　　　Diagram 45.

BLACK.　　　　　　　　　BLACK.

WHITE.　　　　　　　　　WHITE.

In the second place,—

2.	B—K 7
3. P—B 7	K—Kt 2 !
4. K—B 5	B—R 4 or Q 6 ch.
5. K—K 6	B—Kt 3 !
6. P—B 8 (Q) ch.	K × Q
7. K—B 6	

And wins.

If, in the third place, Black plays—

2.	B—Kt 6

White wins by K—Kt 6, and afterwards checking with the Rook.

When, however, the Pawn is on the Knight's file, the Rook, in a similar position, will win. (See Diagram 46.)

WHITE.	BLACK.
1. P—Kt 7 ch.	

(If 1. . . . B×P White wins by K—Kt 6), therefore,—

| 1. | K—R 2 |
| 2. R—Kt 1 | |

(If 2. . . . B×P, 3. R—R 1 ch. and K—Kt 6 as before), therefore,—

2.	B—Q 5
3. R—Kt 4	B—B 7
4. R—Kt 4	K—Kt 1
5. K—Kt 6	B—Q 4
6. R—K B 4	B×P
7. R—Q B 4, &c.	

Winning.

Diagram 46.   Diagram 47.

BLACK.   BLACK.

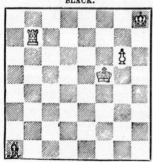 

WHITE.   WHITE.

Diagram 47.

(White to play and mate in 10.)

WHITE.	BLACK.
1. P—Kt 7 ch.	K—Kt 1
2. B—B 4 ch.	R—B 2
3. K—Kt 6	P—R 4
4. B—K 5	P—R 5
5. K—R 7	P—Kt 4 (d. ch.) !
6. K—Kt 8	P—R 6
7. K—B 8	P—R 7
8. B×P	P—Kt 5
9. B—K 5	P—Kt 6
10. K—K 8	P—Kt 7
11. K—Q 8	P—Kt 8 (Q)
12. B×R mate.	

ROOK AGAINST THREE MINOR PIECES.

THREE minor Pieces are much stronger than a Rook, and in cases where two of them are Bishops will usually win without much difficulty, because the player of the Rook is certain soon to be compelled to lose it for one of his adversary's Pieces. If, however, there are two Knights and one Bishop opposed to a Rook, the latter may generally be exchanged for the Bishop, and as two Knights are insufficient in themselves to mate, the game will be drawn.

Diagram 48.   Diagram 49.

BLACK.   BLACK.

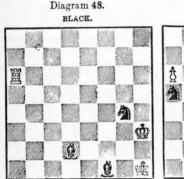

WHITE.   WHITE.

Diagram 48.

Black wins. For suppose,—

	WHITE.	BLACK.
1.	R—R 3 ch.	B—K 6
2.	R—R 2	K—Kt 6
3.	R—R 2	B—K B 5
4.	R—R 2	B—R 6
5.	R—R 3 ch.	B—K 6
6.	R—R 2	Kt—B 7 ch.
7.	K—Kt 1	B—Kt 7
8.	R—K 2	Kt—R 6 mate.

Diagram 49.

In this position also Black, with the move, will win, as his adversary will not be able to exchange his Rook for the Bishop.

	WHITE.	BLACK.
1.		K—B 7
2.	R—Q 1	Kt—Kt 6 ch.
3.	K—Kt 2	

(If 3. K—B 2   B × R ch.
4. K × B   Kt—K 6 mate.)

3.		B × R
4.	P—R 7	B—B 6
5.	K × Kt	K—Kt 8
6.	P—R 4	Kt × P
7.	K—B 4	Kt—Kt 3
8.	K—B 5	Kt—B 5
9.	K—Q 6	Kt—Q 6
10.	K—B 7	Kt—Kt 5
11.	K—Kt 8	Kt—R 6 ch

And wins.

ROOK AND PAWN AGAINST ROOK.

THIS is a more important ending, as being one of more probable occurrence in actual play than many of those we have been examining. The single Rook will frequently draw against Rook and Pawn when his King is in front of the Pawn.

Diagram 50.   Diagram 51.

BLACK.   BLACK.

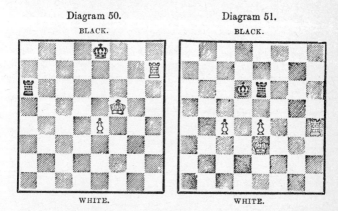

WHITE.   WHITE.

The first position (see Diagram 50) is given by Philidor, and is intended to show the method by which Black may draw the game, and also the mode of play which White must adopt should his adversary not play the correct defence. White, having to play, moves—

| WHITE. | BLACK. |
| 1. P—K 5 | R—Q Kt 3 |

(If he plays R—R 8, Philidor thinks he ought to lose the game. See Variation.)

2. R—R 7	R—Q B 3
3. P—K 6	R—B 8
4. K—B 6	R—B 8 ch

And will draw.

VARIATION.

WHITE.	BLACK.
1. P—K 5	R—R 8 ;
2. K—B 6	R—B 8 ch
3. K—K 6	K—B 1
4. R—R 8 ch.	K—Kt 2
5. R—K 8	R—K 8
6. K—Q 7	K—B 2 (a)
7. P—K 6 ch.	K—Kt 2
8. K—K 7	R—K 7
9. R—Q 8	R—K 8
10. R—Q 2	R—K 6
11. R—Kt 2 ch.	K—R 2
12. K—B 7	R—B 6 ch.
13. K—K 8	R—K 6 ;
14. P—K 7	R—Q 6
15. R—Q B 2	K—Kt 2
16. R—B 7	R—Q 7
17. R—Q 7	R—Q Kt 7
18. R—Q 1	R—Kt 1
19. K—Q 7	R—Kt 2 ch.
20. K—K 6	R—Kt 3 ch.
21. R—Q 6	R—Kt 1
22. R—Q 8 and wins.	

Diagram 51.

White wins.

WHITE.	BLACK.
1.	K—B 4
2. R—R 8	K×P
3. R—B 8 ch.	K—Kt 4
4. K—Q 4	

Diagram 52.

Black, with the move, draws.

WHITE.	BLACK.
1.	R—R 7 ch.
2. K—Kt 6	R—Q 7

And White dare not take on account of the stalemate.

(a) If 6. . . . R—Q 8 ch., 7. K—K 7.

Diagram 53.

In this instructive position White, with the move, wins.

	WHITE.	BLACK.
1.	R—B 4	R—R 8
2.	R—K 4 ch.	K—Q 2
3.	K—B 7	R—B 8 ch.
4.	K—Kt 6	R—Kt 8 ch.
5.	K—R 6	R—R 8 ch.
6.	K—Kt 5	R—Kt 8 ch.
7.	R—K Kt 4	

And White wins.

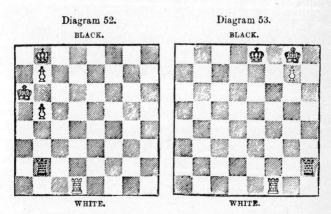

Diagram 52.

BLACK.

WHITE.

Diagram 53.

BLACK.

WHITE.

ROOK AGAINST ONE OR MORE PAWNS.

WE have already seen (p. 451) that a Pawn at its 7th square, defended by its King, and with the adverse King at a distance, may in some cases draw the game against the Queen. It will be obvious that, in a similar position, it must be much more easy to do so against a Rook. The latter, indeed, must speedily be sacrificed for the Pawn to prevent the loss of the game. When, however, the Pawn is not quite so far advanced, and especially if supported by a second one, many cases of the greatest difficulty occur, and which demand the utmost nicety and precision of calculation.

The following examples will serve in some degree to illustrate this, and they might easily be varied and increased to an indefinite extent.

Diagram 54.

White loses, even with the move.

Suppose :—

WHITE.	BLACK.
1. R—K 8	K.—Q 2
2. K—K 3	P—Q 8 (Q)

&c., &c.

Diagram 54.	Diagram 55.
BLACK.	BLACK.

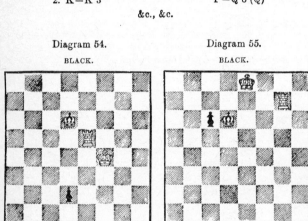

WHITE.　　　　　　　WHITE.

Diagram 55.

Here White can win the Pawn, and therefore the game.

WHITE.	BLACK.
1. R—Kt 6 ch.	K—Q 4
2. K—Q 7	P—B 4
3. R—Q 6 ch.	K—B 5
4. K—B 6	K—Kt 5
5. K—Q 5	P—B 5
6. R—Kt 6 ch.	K—B 6
7. R—Q B 6	

And White wins.

Two united Pawns at their 6th square, supposing the Kings to be at a distance, will win against a Rook if they have the move, or even without the move, providing they are not at the moment attacked. (See Diagram 56.)

Black having to play, moves :—

WHITE.	BLACK.
1.	P—Kt 7
2. R—B 1	P—B 7
3. R—Kt 1 ch.	K—R 6
4. K—B 3	Either Pawn " Queens."

&c., &c.

Diagram 56.   Diagram 57.

BLACK.   BLACK.

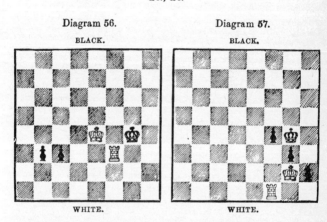

WHITE.   WHITE.

Three united Pawns, defended by their King, win against a Rook, unless the adverse King can be soon played in front of the Pawns. In the present instance (see Diagram 57) the Pawns win, even under that disadvantage.

WHITE.	BLACK.
1.	P—B 6 ch.
2. R×P	P—R 8 (Q) ch.
3. K×Q	K×R
4. K—Kt 1	P—Kt 7
5. K—R 2	K—B 7 and wins.

Or,

1.	P—B 6 ch.
2. K—R 1	P—Kt 7 ch.
3. K×R P	P×R (Kt) ch. and wins.

It is evident that were Black to make a Queen, his opponent would be stalemated.

Even when, as in the next position (see Diagram 58), the Pawns are one square less advanced, Black, by careful play, will be able to draw the game.

WHITE.	BLACK.
	K — B 3
1. R — B 2	K — Kt 3
2. K — B 4	K — B 2
3. R — K 2	K — Kt 3
4. R — K 5	K — Kt 2
5. R — K 6 ch.	
6. R — Q 6	

(White dare not play K — Kt 5, as Black would then advance R P,
afterwards supporting it with Kt P.)

6.	K — B 2

His best move ; were he to play K — R 2 he would lose ; thus,—

6.	K — R 2
7. *K — Kt 5*	*K — Kt 2*
8. *R — Kt 6 ch.*	*K — R 2*
9. *R — R 6 ch.*	*K — Kt 2*
10. *R — R 5*	

And wins.

7. R — K R 6	K — Kt 2
8. R — R 5	K — Kt 3
9. R — Kt 5 ch.	K — R 3
10. R — Kt 8	

If White takes the Pawn, Black wins, through the advance of
the R P.)

10.	K — R 2
11. R — Q 8	K — Kt 3
12. R — Q 6 ch.	

And can only draw.

Diagram 58.

BLACK.

WHITE.

Diagram 59.

BLACK.

WHITE.

Had Black, however, played up his King to support the Pawns, he would have lost (*e.g.*).

WHITE.	BLACK.
1. R—B 2	K—Kt 3
2. K—B 4	K—R 4
3. R—Q 2	K—R 5
4. R—Q 6	K—R 4
5. R—K 6	P—R 7
6. R—K 8	P—R 8 (Q)
7. R—R 8 ch.	

And wins.

Diagram 59.

With the move Black wins.

WHITE.	BLACK.
1.	R—B 1
2. K—R 6	K—B 3
3. R×R	P—R 7
4. K—R 7	P—R 8 (Q)
5. K—Kt 8	Q—R 3
6. R moves	Q mates

ROOK AGAINST TWO ROOKS.

THE two Rooks, in all ordinary cases, win with ease against one Rook, for you are speedily able to force an exchange. As in almost every rule which can be laid down in chess, however, occasional exceptions occur.

Diagram 60.

BLACK.

WHITE.

This ingenious position is first given by Stamma, and has been copied by many subsequent writers. With the move, Black gives mate at once; and even without this advantage, it would at first sight appear that he may draw the game, because White cannot at the same time defend against the threatened mate and protect his attacked Rook. By the following mode of play, however, it will be seen that, with the move, White may win the game.

WHITE.	BLACK.
1. R—K R 5	R × R
2. R—R 6 ch.	K moves
3. R—R 5 ch.	K moves
4. R × R	

And wins.

The most important class of cases in which the single Rook is enabled to draw the game, is that where his King is placed in a position of stalemate by the two Rooks; the weaker force has then only to persist in giving a perpetual check, and offering to sacrifice his Rook as often as the opportunity arises. Diagram 61 is an example. Suppose:—

WHITE.	BLACK.
1.	R—Kt 2 ch.
2. K—K 8	R—Kt 1 ch.
3. K—Q 7	R—Q 1 ch.
4. K—B 7	R—B 1 ch., &c.

And it is obvious that White cannot avoid the check without stalemating his adversary.

Diagram 61.

BLACK.

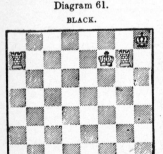

WHITE.

Diagram 62.

BLACK.

WHITE.

Diagram 62.

Here, with the move, White wins the game.

WHITE.	BLACK.
1. P—B 7	R—K B 1

(If 1.   P—B 7
   2. P--B 8 (Q) and wins.)
   2. R—B 2   R × P
(If 2.   P—B 7
   3 R × P, followed by 4 R—K 2.)
   3. R × R   K—Kt 1
   4. R—B 7

And wins.

ROOK AGAINST ROOK AND BISHOP.

The long-pending controversy, whether the King, Rook, and Bishop can win by force from any indifferent position against the King and Rook alone, appears at length to be definitely settled in the negative. The merit of this interesting discovery, which may be said to set at rest a question upon which the leading players of Europe have been at issue for above two hundred years, is mainly due to the unwearying industry and penetration of the late Mr. Kling, a German amateur who was long domiciled in England.

PHILIDOR'S POSITION.

Diagram 63.

BLACK.

WHITE.

In 1749 Philidor demonstrated that in the above position (Diagram 63), White won as follows :—

WHITE.	BLACK.
1. R—B 8 ch.	R—Q 1
2. R—B 7	R—Q 7

(This is Black's only play to prevent White winning immediately, for as will be seen presently, when once you can compel him to move the Rook to your Q 1, or Q 3, the only two other squares open to him, the game can be won in a few moves.)

    3. R—Q Kt 7   R—Q 8

(Here observe that he was obliged to occupy one of the objectionable squares, since if he played his Rook off the file, you mated at once.)

    4. R—Kt 7   R—K B 8 (or Var. I.)
    5. B—Kt 3   K—B 1 (or Var. II.)

(You play the Bishop thus to prevent his checking when he moves the Rook, and at the same time to force him to take up a less advantageous position.)

    6. R—Kt 4   K—K 1

(He returns his King thus, because you now threaten to win directly by B—Q 6 ch., and afterwards R—K Kt 8, &c.)

    7. R—Q B 4   R—Q 8 (or Var. III.)
    8. B—R 4   K—B 1
    9. B—B 6   R—K 8 ch.
  10. B—K 5   K—Kt 1
  11. R—K R 4

And he cannot save the game.

VARIATION I.
Beginning at Black's 4th move.

WHITE.	BLACK.
4. R—Kt 7	K—B 1
5. R—K R 7	R—K Kt 8

(Black is compelled to play his R—Kt 8, in order to interpose when you check with Rook, and the result is that you win his Rook.)

    6. R—Q B 7   K—Kt 1

(This is Black's best move; if he plays R—Kt 3 ch., you interpose the Bishop, and he cannot escape.)

    7. R—B 8 ch.   K—R 2
    8. R—R 8 ch.   K—Kt 3
    9. R—Kt 8 ch.

Winning the Rook.

VARIATION II.
Beginning at Black's 5th move.

WHITE.	BLACK.
5. B—Kt 3	R—B 6
6. B—Q 6	R—K 6 ch.
7. B—K 5	R—K B 6

(If 7.	K—B 1
8. R—K R 7 !)	
8. R—K 7 ch.	K—B 1
(If 8.	K—Q 1
9. R—Q Kt 7)	
9. R—Q B 7	K—Kt 1
10. R—Kt 7 ch.	K—B 1
11. R—Kt 4	K.—K 1
(If 11.	R--K 6
12. R—R 4)	
12. B—B 4	

And wins.

VARIATION III.
Beginning at Black's 7th move.

WHITE.	BLACK.
7. R—Q B 4	K—B 1
8. B—K 5	K—Kt 1
9. R—K R 4	

Winning.

In playing over the variations just submitted, it is impossible to avoid being struck by the elegance and accuracy of this analysis, but, as Lolli and other writers observe, "the general proposition laid down by Philidor, of the Rook and Bishop winning against a Rook, can only be sustained on the supposition that the adversary can always be forced into this or a similar position," and this, though attempted by Philidor in his edition of 1777, has never been demonstrated, and in the opinion of every player who is conversant with the subject, is an impossibility.

Lolli has subsequently given three positions, in two of which White can win by force, but the third is one where, with the best possible play, he can only draw. As these positions are well known, and are besides comprehended in one or other of the categories in Mr. King's demonstration, it is not necessary to give them here. In addition to these, Mr. Cochrane has given three situations, which were sent by two players of Lille to the Café de la Régence, in Paris, as examples where White can only draw the game.

In later times Mr. Szen, the celebrated player of Hungary, put forth a position wherein Black can maintain his defence and draw the game. (See Diagram 64.)

Again, we have had the admirable analysis of Mr. Zytogorski, in which an attempt, all but successful, was made to prove that the superior force should always win. From this able analysis we take one of the most important positions, where Mr. Zytogorski thought he demonstrated a win for White, but which Mr. Kling has shown to be an error. (See Diagram 65.)

MR. SZEN'S POSITION.　　MR. ZYTOGORSKI'S POSITION.

Diagram 64.　　Diagram 65.

BLACK.　　BLACK.

WHITE.　　WHITE.

As these positions are included in one or other of the classes into which Mr. Kling divides the subject, it is needless to append their manifold variations, but it may be well to give the particular one of Mr. Zytogorski's, in which the error before alluded to, occurs. Place the Pieces as in Diagram 65.

WHITE.	BLACK.
1. R—K 8 ch.	R—B 1
2. R—K 7	R—B 8
3. R—Q 7	R—B 7
4. R—Q B 7	R—B 8
5. B—B 6	R—Kt 8 ch.
6. K—B 5	R—Kt 7
7. B—K 5	R—Q R 7
8. R—Kt 7 ch.	K—B 1
9. R—Q 7	K—Kt 1
10. K—B 6	R—R 3 ch.
11. B—Q 6	R—R 8
12. R—Kt 7 ch.	K—R 1
13. R—Kt 2	R—B 8 ch.
14. K—Kt 6	K—Kt 1
15. B—B 5	R—B 5
16. R—Kt 5	R—Q R 5
17. K—B 6 (d. ch.)	K—R 2
18. B—K 3	R—Q B 5
19. R—Kt 7	K—R 1
20. R—Q Kt 7	K—Kt 1

It is at this 20th move of Black, according to Mr. Kling, that Mr. Zytogorski's mistake occurs.

Nothing can be more beautiful and correct than the foregoing play, but at this point, instead of directing Black to move his King as above, Mr. Zytogorski makes him play 20. R—B 3 ch., and by that means lose the game.

21. R—Kt 8 ch.	K—R 2
22. R—Kt 6	R—B 2
23. B—Q 4	R—B 2 ch.

This is his only move to draw the game; and now, whether White take the Rook or not, Black will succeed in saving the game.

MR. KLING'S ANALYSIS.

First Chapter.

The positions found in the following Chapter will show how the player with the Rook and Bishop can drive his adversary to the end of the board, and at the same time will point out the surest method that Black can adopt to arrive at a position for drawing the game.

First Position.   Diagram 66.

BLACK.

WHITE.

We start from a position which the Black can always be compelled to occupy.

WHITE.	BLACK.
1. B—K 5	R—Kt 2
2. R—R 6	R—Q 2
3. B—Q 6	R—Q 1 (see Var. 1 and 3)
4. R—K B 6 ch.	K—Kt 2
5. B—B 4	R—Q 2
6. K—K 6	R—Q 8

(This move is bad, and loses the game.   See Variation II.)

7. B—K 5	K—R 2
8. R—B 7 ch.	K—Kt 3
9. R—Kt 7 ch.	K—R 3
10. R—Kt 4	K—R 2
11. K—B 7	R—Q 2 ch
12. K—B 6	R—Q Kt 2
13. K—B 5	R—Q 2
14. R—Kt 1	R—B 2 ch.
15. B—B 6	R—Q 2
16. R—R 1 ch.	K—Kt 1
17. K—K 6	R—K R 2
18. R—Kt 1 ch.	K—B 1
19. R—Q 1 and wins.	

This variation shows that Black's 6th move loses the game; the other variations lead to drawn games.

VARIATION I.

WHITE.	BLACK.
3.	K—Kt 2
4. R—Kt 6 ch.	K—B 2
5. R—B 6 ch.	K—Kt 1
6. K—K 6	R—R 2
7. R—B 8 ch.	K—R 2
8. R—B 1	K—Kt 1
9. B—K 5	R—R 3 ch.
10. K—B 5	R—R 3
11. R—Kt 1 ch.	K—B 2
12. R—Kt 7 ch.	K—B 1
13. B—B 6	R—R 7
14. R—Q R 7	R—Q B 7
15. B—K 7 ch.	K—K 1
16. B—Q 6	K—Q 1
17. K—K 6	K—B 1

It now becomes a position of the second class, the defence of which will be found in the Third Chapter.

VARIATION II.

WHITE.	BLACK.
6.	R—Q R 2
7. B—R 6 ch.	K—Kt 1
8. B—B 8	R—R 3 ch.
9. B—Q 6	R—R 2
10. R—B 8 ch.	K—R 2
11. R—B 1	R—R 3
12. R—K Kt 1	K—R 3

This is now a position of the first class, the defence of which will be found in the following Chapter.

VARIATION III.

WHITE.	BLACK.
3.	K—K 1
4. R—K 6 ch.	K—Q 1
5. R—K B 6	K—B 1 (a)
6. R—B 8 ch.	K—Kt 2
7. K—K 6	R—K R 2
8. K—Q 5	R—R 4 ch.
9. B—K 5	K—Kt 3
10. R—Kt 8 ch.	K—R 4

Again a position of the first class.

SECOND CHAPTER.

First Class.

The division of the different positions into classes is made to estimate their value with regard to the possibility of defence.

The first and second class give us the easiest method of defence, and we shall see that we can arrive at the one or the other by playing the correct moves ; we shall also show that one can be changed to the other. If, however, the second player does not play very well,

Diagram 67.

BLACK.

1   2 WHITE. 3

Diagram 68.

BLACK.

WHITE.

First, Second, and Third Position.—The White Rook occupying the same square in the three positions.

Fourth Position.—This last position is the only exception in the first class, in which White can win by playing K—Kt 6.

(a) If Black plays R—K R 2, it will still resolve into a position of the first class.

he can be forced into a position belonging to the other classes, which gives to the first player a better chance of forcing the game.

We have only made use of the Queen's Bishop in the several positions—it being evident that the King's Bishop would lead to similar positions on squares of the other colour.

The other positions are played as follows.

FIRST POSITION.

This is one of the most difficult of this class for the defence, the Black King being so near the Rook's square. It is evident that White would win, were the Black King placed on Q R 1, and his Rook on Q R 8, and White's King on Q R 5—B on Q R 4—R on K R 7, the position being the same on the left side of the board as that of the fourth position on the right.

WHITE.	BLACK.
1. K—B 5	K—R 1 (or Var. 1
2. B—Q 2	R—Kt 2
3. R—R 1	R—K 2
4. B—Kt 5	R—Q Kt 2
5. B—B 6	R—Q R 2
6. B—Q 4	R—B 2 ch.
7. K—Q 5	K—Kt 2
8. B—K 5	R—B 2
9. K—K 6	R—B 7
10. R—Kt 1 ch.	K—B 3
11. R—B 1 ch.	K—Kt 4
12. K—Q 5	R—B 4
13. R—Kt 1 ch.	K—R 4

This is a position of the same class, and one more favourable for the defence than the first position.

VARIATION I.

WHITE.	BLACK.
1.	R—B 8 ch.
2. K—Kt 6	K—B 1
3. B—B 5	K—Q 1
4. K—B 6	R—K 8
5. R—K B 7	R—K 3 ch.
6. B—Q 6	R—K 8
7. R—B 6	

This is not so well defended as the other, but it is still a drawn game, as we shall see in the third position of the third class. The best method of defence is only given, the variations being too numerous and too similar to excite any interest.

THIRD CHAPTER.

Second Class.

In this class there is only one position won for the White. Besides the five regular positions, we have added one where the White King attacks the adverse Rook at the first move, which gains White a move and the game.

This position is solely to show with what precision the Black Rook ought to be played.

FIRST POSITION.   Diagram 69.   SECOND POSITION.   Diagram 70.

BLACK.   BLACK.

WHITE.   WHITE.

THIRD POSITION.   Diagram 71.   FOURTH POSITION.   Diagram 72.

BLACK.   BLACK.

WHITE.   WHITE.

FIFTH POSITION. Diagram 73.   SIXTH POSITION.   Diagram 74.

BLACK.   BLACK.

WHITE.   WHITE.

This fifth position is the only one of this class which is lost for
Black. The Black Rook is placed on K Kt 5—the game being lost
on any other square on the same line; were he on the K Kt 3, White
could give mate in three moves, which would be still worse.

White to play.

WHITE.	BLACK.
1. R—R 8 ch.	K—R 2
2. K—B 5	R—Kt 1
3. R—R 7 ch.	K—R 3
4. R—R 1	

Winning.

The third of these positions (Diagram 71) may be played in the
following manner:—

WHITE.	BLACK.
1. R—K Kt 7	K—Q 1

By this move Black loses the position of the second class and is
obliged to take one of the third, which however is still defensible.

SIXTH POSITION.

WHITE.	BLACK.
1. K—Q 5	B—B 8
2. B—B 5	K—Kt 1 (a)
3. R—R 7	R—K 8
4. K—B 6	R—K 3 ch.
5. B—Q 6 ch.	K—R 1
6. R—R 1	

Winning.

(a) If Black plays K—Q 1, White plays K—B 6, and can occupy
a winning position in four moves.

FOURTH CHAPTER.

Third Class.

Although there is only one winning position in the five given in this class, the defence is more difficult than those of the preceding classes.

FIRST POSITION.   Diagram 75.

BLACK

WHITE.

White plays in this position.

WHITE.	BLACK.
1. R—Q 7	R—B 7
2. R—K R 7	K—B 1

This is now a position of the second class, and can be resolved into a position similar to the one we start from.

SECOND POSITION.   Diagram 76.   THIRD POSITION.   Diagram 77.

BLACK.   BLACK.

WHITE.   WHITE.

FOURTH POSITION.   Diagram 78.

BLACK.

WHITE.

This fifth position is lost for the Black (*e.g.*).

WHITE.	BLACK.
1. R—R 8 ch.	R—Kt 1
2. R—R 4	R—Kt 6
3. R—R 4	K—Kt 1
4. R—R 8 ch.	K—R 2
5. R—R 8	

Winning.

It is won, because the Black Rook has not so many squares to play to as in the preceding variations.

FIFTH POSITION.   Diagram 79.

BLACK.

WHITE.

FIFTH CHAPTER.

Fourth Class.

In this Chapter two positions out of five are favourable for White, the third and fifth.

FIRST POSITION.   Diagram 80.

BLACK.

WHITE.

	WHITE.		BLACK.
1.	R—B 7		R—K 3
2.	R—Q 7		R—Q B 3
3.	R—Q 2		R—B 8
4.	R—Q 6		

It is now a position of the third class; but if Black for his first move plays R—Q 8, White can win.

SECOND POSITION.   Diagram 81.   THIRD POSITION.   Diagram 82.

BLACK.   BLACK.

WHITE.   WHITE.

In this third position, White can win in the following manner :—

	WHITE.	BLACK.
1.	R—B 2	R—R 3
2.	R—K R 2	K—B 1
3.	R—Q Kt 2	R—R 1
4.	R—Kt 6	K—Q 1
5.	R—B 6	K—K 1 (a)
6.	R—B 1	K—Q 1
7.	B—K 7 ch.	K—K 1
8.	R—B 1	R—R 3 ch.
9.	B—Q 6	R × B
10.	K × R	K—Q 1
11.	R mates.	

SIXTH CHAPTER.

Fifth Class.

FIRST POSITION.   Diagram 83.   SECOND POSITION.   Diagram 84.

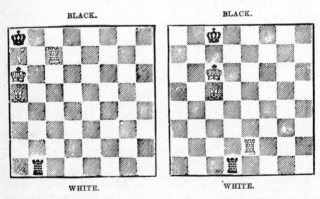

BLACK.   BLACK.

WHITE.   WHITE.

(a) The game is equally lost if Rook moves to R 2.

THIRD POSITION.   Diagram 85.   FOURTH POSITION.   Diagram 86.

All the positions of this class are won for White, with the exception of the last, which, however, is the most difficult to defend. Some of these positions have been analysed by Philidor and Lolli. The last was thought to be a won game by Mr. Kling, and many of the best players; a profound analysis has demonstrated the impossibility of winning. Mr. Kling subsequently endorsed the opinion of Lolli, La Bourdonnais, and others, who have declared the following position a drawn game.

Diagram 87.

We shall see that this position is nearly the same as No. 4 of this class.

Lolli, as also La Bourdonnais, give no instruction with regard to the manner of playing it. The last says, in his work, pp. 186, 187 : "It is to be regretted that Lolli has not given the principal moves. This position of Lolli is fertile of 'pats,' and I think that Black, by playing correctly, can always hinder their adversary from occupying, with their King and their Bishop, the position where the winning of the game is shown (viz. K on K 6, B on K 5) ; but I conceive also that White can easily force the Black King on the other line, in a position where he will no longer have a defence."

La Bourdonnais, however, has not given any proof of his opinion, and we show the manner which demonstrates the impossibility. He continues :—" It is a pity that Lolli has not proved his assertion by a demonstration. That would have facilitated the study of this difficult position."

We are now going to give the defence of this position.

FIRST POSITION.   Diagram 88.

BLACK.

WHITE.

Here White forces Black to take the first position of the fifth class in two moves, and wins the game.

WHITE.	BLACK.
1. R—Kt 6 ch.	K—R 1
2. R—R 6	R—Q Kt 8
3. R—R 8 ch.	R—Kt 1
4. R—R 4	R—Kt 8 (a)

(a) Had Black played R—K 1 the game would equally have been lost, and had he moved R—Kt 2, the game would continue thus,—

WHITE.	BLACK.
5. R—K Kt 4	R—R 2 ch.
6. K—Kt 6	R—Kt 2 ch.

5.	B—Kt 4	K—Kt 1
6.	K—Kt 6	K—B 1
7.	K—B 6 and wins.	

It is evident that had Black played K—B 1 on the first move White
would win by R—Q 6.

In the SECOND POSITION of this Class (see Diagram 84, page 482),
White plays,—

WHITE.		BLACK.
1.	R—K 8 ch.	R—Q 1
2.	R—K 7	R—Q 7
3.	R—K B 7	R—Q 8
4.	R—Q R 7	R—Q Kt 8
5.	R—K 7	R—Q 8
6.	B—K 3	R—Q 6

(If Black plays 6 R—Q 1, White replies with R—K 5, and wins more
speedily.)

7.	B—Kt 6	R—B 6 ch.
8.	B—B 5	R—Q 6
9.	R—B 7 ch.	K—Q 1
10.	R—Q R 7	K—K 1
11.	R—K 7 ch.	K—Q 1
12.	R—K 4	K—B 1
13.	B—Q 4	

And wins.

THIRD POSITION.   (See Diagram 85, page 483.)

WHITE.		BLACK.
1.	R—Kt 8 ch.	R—B 1
2.	R—Kt 7	R—B 7
3.	R—K R 7	R—B 8
4.	R—Q B 7	R—Q 8
5.	B—B 3	R—Q 6

(If Black plays 5. R—Q 1, the answer is 6. R—B 4, winning more
easily.)

7.	K—B 6	R—Kt 1 (a)
8.	B—B 7	R—Kt 2
9.	R—K R 4, and wins.	

(a) If Black moves—

		K—R 2
	B—B 7	R—R 1
	R—K R 4, and wins.	

6. B—B 6	R—K 6 ch.
7. B—K 5	R—Q 6
8. R—K 7 ch.	K—Q 1
9. R—K R 7	K—B 1
10. R—B 7 ch.	K—Q 1
11. R—B 4	

And wins.

FOURTH POSITION.   (See Diagram 86.)

[This position, with the leading variation, which deserves the most attentive consideration, has already been given in the introductory observations to Mr. Kling's Analysis.   (See page 472, and Diagram 65.)]

The variations springing from this last position are so numerous that it would be impossible to give them all; we only add two, where Black having played incorrectly, has taken a lost position.

Diagram 89.   Diagram 90.

BLACK.   BLACK.

WHITE.   WHITE.

Diagram 89.

WHITE.	BLACK.
1. R—Q R 3	R—Kt 7 ch.
2. B—Kt 3.	K—B 1
3. K—B 6	K—Kt 1
4. R—R 8 ch.	K—R 2
5. R—R 7 ch.	K—R 3 (or Var. 1)
6. R—K Kt 7	K—R 4
7. R—Kt 5 ch.	K—R 3
8. R—Kt 4	K—R 2
9. K—B 7, and wins.	

VARIATION I.

From Black's 5th move.

5.	K—Kt 1
6. R—Kt 7 ch.	K—R 1
7. R—Kt 1	R—Q R 7
8. B—K 5	K—R 2 (*a*)
9. R—Kt 7 ch.	K—R 1
10. R—Kt 1	K—R 2
11. R—R 1 ch.	K—Kt 1
12. B—Q 4	R—R 3 ch.
13. K—K 7	R—R 3
14. R—Kt 1 ch.	K—R 2
15. White mates in six.	

Diagram 90.

WHITE.	BLACK.
1. R—Kt 7 ch.	K—B 1
2. R—Q B 7	R—Q Kt 8
3. B—Q 4	R—Q 8
4. B—K 5	R—Q Kt 8
5. R—Q 7	K—Kt 1
6. K—B 6	R—Kt 3 ch.
7. B—Q 6	R—Kt 8
8. B—B 5	R—Kt 6
9. R—Kt 7 ch.	K—R 1
10. R—Kt 1	R—B 6 ch.
11. K—Kt 6	K—Kt 1
12. R—Kt 4	R—B 6
13. B—Q 6	R—B 3
14. K—B 6 d. ch.	K—R 2
15. R—Kt 7 ch.	K—R 1
16. R—Q 7	R—B 8
17. B—K 5	R—B 3 ch.
18. K—B 7 d. ch.	K—R 2
19. R—Q 8	K—R 3
20. B—B 6	R—B 2 ch.
21. B—K 7	K—R 2
22. R—Q 4	R—B 3
23. B—Q 6	

And wins.

There are many other methods of varying the moves, but those given are the most interesting, and sufficiently develop the principle of the defence.

From these it is evident that White can force his adversary's King to the extreme line of the board, but it is equally apparent

---

(*a*) If he plays R—B 7 ch., he is equally lost.

that he cannot win, if the defence be correctly played,—it is also shown that Black can always make a drawn game, even after losing the advantage of the positions of the first and second class, and being driven into one of the other less favourable situations; those are only exceptions where White has won.

Kr. Kling concludes his very able and interesting examen (which leaves little to be desired beyond a more distinct and methodical arrangement of the matter), by declaring his conviction, after the most laborious investigation of the subject, that " *the Rook and Bishop against the Rook constitute a drawn game.*"

ROOK AGAINST ROOK AND KNIGHT.

THIS species of termination has not received one tithe of the attention and study which has been bestowed on the very similar one we have just been discussing. It seems to have been taken for granted that the single Rook, in such positions, can draw the game. The late Mr. Forth, however, gave much consideration to the subject, and is of opinion, and, we think, has satisfactorily proved, that " the Rook and Knight exercise a more effective power against the Rook than that Piece does in opposition to the Knight, or than King and two Knights can do against King and Pawn."

We proceed to give a few examples, for which we are mainly indebted to the demonstrations of Mr. Forth, and we commend this particular study, as one still fertile in discoveries, to the consideration of amateurs.

Diagram 91.

White, with the move, will win the Rook in four moves.

WHITE.	BLACK.
1. Kt—K 6 ch.	K—Q 4

(If instead Black plays K—K 5, White will play R—Kt 4 ch.)

2. R—Q 8 ch.	K—K 5
3. R—Q 4 ch.	K moves
4. K × R	

Many instances of this kind might obviously be given if necessary, but it is more important to understand the mode of action when the Pieces are at the side of the board, or may be driven there.

Diagram 92.

In this instance, White, with the move, will win in ten moves.

WHITE.	BLACK.
1. R—B 7 ch.	K—K 1 !
2. K—K 6	K—Q 1

(If to B 1, White plays R—B 7 ch., and on the K moving to Kt 1, mates in two more moves.)

3. R—Q 7 ch.	K—B 1
4. Kt—K 7 ch.	K—Kt 1
5. K—Q 6	R—Kt 3 ch.

(His best move to delay the mate.)

| 6. Kt—B 6 ch | R × Kt ch. |

(If K—B 1, White may move R—Q R 7.)

7. K × R

And mates in three more moves.

Diagram 91.   Diagram 92.

BLACK.   BLACK.

WHITE.   WHITE.

Diagram 93.

This example is much more difficult than the preceding one. "It will be seen," says Mr. Forth, "that when the Black King is on the Rook's, Knight's, or Bishop's square, it is comparatively easy to force the game, but the difficulty is materially enhanced when he is on the King's or Queen's square, where it is, at present, an undecided question whether mate can be forced in general situations. The positions where the Rook and Knight exercise the greatest power, are those in which the adverse Rook is on the same half of the board as that on which the Kings stand, and the White Knight can be moved to the next square to his King for the purpose of interposing when check is given. Such situations are, for the most part, decisive; care, however, must be taken to keep the Kings near each other, that time may not be lost in gaining the opposition at the proper moment."

In the present position White can win in twenty moves (*e.g.*)—

WHITE.	BLACK.
1. Kt—Q 6 ch.	K—B 1 !
2. R—Q 7	R—Kt 1 (or A.)
3. R—Q R 7	R—Q 1

It is necessary to force the Black Rook on to this square, in order
to prevent his checking the King when White moves his Knight.)

4. Kt— B 5	R—Q Kt 1 !
5. Kt—Kt 7	R—Kt 3 ch.
6. Kt—K 6 ch.	K—Kt 1
7. R—K 7	R—Kt 6
8. K—Kt 6	R—Kt 1
9. R—Q 7	R—Q R 1
10. R—Q 6	R—K 1
11. R—Q B 6	R—Q R 1
12. Kt—Kt 5	K—B 1
13. R—K 6	K—Kt 1
14. Kt—R 7	R—Q Kt 1
15. R—K 7	R—Kt 3 ch.
16. Kt—B 6 ch.	R × Kt ch.

And White wins in four more moves.

(A.)

2.	K—Kt 1
3. K—Kt 6	K—B 1
4. R—B 7 ch.	K—Kt 1
5. Kt—K 4	Any move.
6. Kt—B 6	

&c., &c.

Diagram 93.	Diagram 94.
BLACK.	BLACK.

WHITE.	WHITE.

Diagram 94.

This position is from Lolli, and is an example of a drawn game White having the move plays,—

WHITE.	BLACK.
1. P—Q 7	R × P
2. R × B	R—Q 7
3. R—B 4 ch.	K × R

And White is stalemated.

Chapter IV.

ENDINGS WITH KINGS AND PAWNS ONLY.

When, towards the end of a game, a few Pawns only, with their respective Kings, are left upon the board, it might at first sight be supposed from the limited nature, and the simplicity and uniformity of their moves, that little difficulty could arise, and no great study or examination be necessary. If, indeed, the value of the Pawns, like that of the superior Pieces, were to be estimated only by the power they originally possessed, such a supposition would doubtless be correct; but the peculiar privilege by which, under certain conditions, they may be elevated to the rank of the most valuable Pieces, brings a new and very interesting element into the calculation, and renders this particular species of termination at once one of the most difficult and most important branches of chess strategy. It is at the same time one which is generally very imperfectly understood by amateurs; and perhaps it is amongst finished players only that its essential importance is fully recognised, because from that class chiefly those well-contested and equal games proceed which are most frequently brought to pawn endings. Amongst the best players it frequently happens that the slightest miscalculation leads to the loss of an otherwise secure battle. Nothing can well be conceived more trying to the nerves and temper, than after hours of intense mental effort, and when a difficult game has been successfully conducted through danger, and against a superior force, until it is safely reorganised with victory in view, to see the well-earned conquest suddenly fall from your hands by some momentary lapse of the overstrained attention, or some paltry artifice which a tyro would have penetrated.

A remarkable example of this kind occurred in the eleventh game of the match between Staunton and St. Amant played in Paris in the year 1843. After a long and severe struggle, conducted by the English player with some inferiority of force (his opponent having gained an advantage at the commencement), the following position (see Diagram 95) occurred; Black (Staunton) having to play.

Diagram 95.

BLACK.

WHITE.

We think there can be little doubt that, under ordinary circumstances, Black would have played the correct move of K×P, and
have won the game with ease. Instead of this, however, from
momentary inadvertence, the consequence of nine or ten hours'
incessant mental exertion, he moved K—K 5, and the game was
pursued as follows:—

WHITE.	BLACK.
1.	K—K 5
2. K—Q 1	K—Q 6
3. P—Q 5	P—K 7 ch.
4. K—K 1	K—B 7
5. P—Q 6	K×P
6. P—Q 7	P—B 6
7. P—Q 8 (Q)	P—B 7
8. Q—Q 2	

And wins.

But had Black, on the contrary, played as already suggested, he
would have won the game; thus,—

WHITE.	BLACK.
1.	K×P
2. K—Q 1	

(If, in place of this move, he advance K—Kt P, Black will equally
  win by playing K—K 5, then taking the Kt P in another move
  or two, and afterwards returning with his King in sufficient time
  to defend his own K P.)

2.	K—Q 6
3. P—K Kt 4	P—K 7 ch.
4. K—K 1	K—B 7

5. P—K Kt 5	K×Kt P
6. P—K Kt 6	P—B 6
7. P—K Kt 7	P—B 7
8. P—Kt 8 (Q)	P—B 8 (Q) ch.
9. K×P	Q—B 5 ch.
10. Q×Q	P×Q

And must evidently win.

The student will naturally enquire how a proficiency in the art of playing Pawns may be best attained ? And whether he can hope to gain much benefit in it from books ? We can only say, that it is a matter exceedingly difficult to generalise upon, or to reduce to rules, and that, therefore, great and incessant practice is the grand requisite ; but it should never be forgotten that the required practice may be obtained equally, and perhaps even in a superior degree, by the study of those critical and ingenious positions which are given by our best authors, as by actual play, and we strongly recommend attention, therefore, to the selection of situations which form the subject of the present Chapter.

KING AND PAWN AGAINST KING AND PAWN.

WE have already seen (p. 430) the method of playing a single King against a King and Pawn. When a Pawn is left on each side, and both are able to Queen at the same time, the result is usually a drawn game ; there are, however, exceptions of some importance which, before exchanging the last Pieces, it is necessary to bear in mind. These may arise either through one of the Pawns giving check on Queening, or from the King of the party Queening last being on the same file as his Queen, so that his opponent checks, and wins the Queen. The following, from Lolli, will be a sufficient illustration.

Diagram 96.

BLACK.

WHITE.

Here, Black having the move, may draw the game by P—Q 7;
if, on the contrary, he plays R × P ch., expecting to Queen his Pawn,
he will lose it (*e.g.*)—

WHITE.	BLACK.
1.	R × P ch.
2. R × R	P—Q 7
3. R—Q 5	

(A remarkably neat *coup*.)

3.	K × R
4. P—Q 7	P—Q 8 (Q)
5. P—Q 8 (Q) ch.	

And wins.

KING AND TWO PAWNS AGAINST KING AND PAWN.

USUALLY the two Pawns win, but many cases occur where the game
is drawn.

The first position (see Diagram 97) is by Philidor. If Black has
the move, White will win, but if otherwise the game is drawn. This
instance forcibly exemplifies the importance in similar cases of
gaining the opposition with your King, or of so placing him opposite
the adverse one, with one square between them, that Black, having
to play first, is compelled to retreat and leave you to take up the
position you may require.

First, suppose White moves :—

WHITE.	BLACK.
1. K—Q 4	K—Q 3

(If 1. . . . K—B 4, White wins by K—K 3.)

2. K—Q 3	K—Q 2
3. K—K 3	K—K 2
4. K—Q 4	K—Q 3
5. K—K 4	K—K 3

And the game is drawn.

But suppose Black has to play :—

WHITE.	BLACK.
1.	K—Q 3
2. P—B 5	K—K 2

(If 2.   P × P

3. K × P and wins easily by playing ultimately K—R 7.)

3. P—B 6 ch.

(If you had taken his Pawn, he would have drawn the game.)

3.	K—K 3
4. K—Q 4	K—Q 3

5. P—B 7	K—K 2
6. K—K 5	K×P
7. K—Q 6	K—B 1
8. K—K 6	K—Kt 2
9. K—K 7	K—Kt 1
10. K—B 6	K—R 2
11. K—B 7	K—R 1
12. K×P	K—Kt 1
13. K×B 6	K—R 2
14. K—B 7	K—R 1
15. K—Kt 6	K—Kt 1
16. K—R 6	K—R 1
17. P—Kt 6	

And wins.

Diagram 97.   Diagram 98.

BLACK.   BLACK.

WHITE.   WHITE.

Diagram 98.

Here White wins by sacrificing his Q P at the proper moment; thus,—

WHITE.	BLACK.
1. K—B 6	K—Q 1
2. P—Q 7	K×P
3. K—B 7	K—Q 1
4. K—K 6	K—B 2
5. K—K 7	K—B 1
6. K—Q 6	K—Kt 2
7. K—Q 7	K—Kt 1
8. K×P	

And wins.

The chance of a drawn game is greater for the single Pawn when it is a Rook's Pawn opposed to the adverse Rook's and Knight's Pawns. In the present instance (see Diagram 99), White, however, wins, but had the Pawns and Kings been one step further advanced, the game would only have been drawn.

	WHITE.	BLACK.
1.		K—B 4
2.	K—Q 3	K—Q 4
3.	K—K 3	K—K 4
4.	K—B 3	K—Q 4

(Black still keeps up the opposition, but dare not move any further from the Pawns.)

	WHITE.	BLACK.
5.	K—B 4	K—Q 3
6.	K—K 4	K—K 3
7.	K—Q 4	K—Q 3
8.	K—B 4	K—B 2
9.	K—Q 5	K—Kt 3
10.	K—Q 6	K—Kt 2
11.	K—B 5	K—B 2
12.	P—Kt 6 ch.	

And wins.

Diagram 99.   Diagram 100.

BLACK.   BLACK.

WHITE.   WHITE.

Diagram 100.

The game is drawn. If Black has to move he takes up the opposition, and suppose, on the contrary, White plays,—

	WHITE.	BLACK.
1.	K—Q 4	K—K 3

(Any other move would lose the game.)

	WHITE.	BLACK.
2.	K—K 4	K—Q 3

And White cannot do more than draw the game.

Diagram 101.

The move is quite immaterial, the game in either case being easily drawn. If White has to play, and move P—R 6, he can never force his adversary to abandon the possession of the Rook's and Knight's squares, and if he plays :—

WHITE.	BLACK.
1. P—Kt 6	P—R 3

(By taking the Pawn he would lose the game.)

2. P—Kt 7 ch.	K—Kt 1

And the game is drawn.

Diagram 101.　　　　　　　　Diagram 102.

BLACK.　　　　　　　　BLACK.

WHITE.　　　　　　　　WHITE.

From this it will appear that in nearly all cases, when the Rook's and Knight's Pawns are advanced to their fifth squares, the opposite Rook's Pawn, with its King near, will draw the game. The only exception appears to be when the White King is on K R 6, and the Black King occupies the corner, as in the present diagram, White has to play. Thus, suppose White's King here to be on R 6, he will play :—

WHITE.	BLACK.
1. P—Kt 6	K—Kt 1

(If he take the Pawn, the result is obviously the same.)

2. P—Kt 7	K—B 2
3. K × P, &c.	

And wins.

But if Black had the move, in this same position, the game would be drawn, because, after the exchange of Pawns, White's remaining

Pawn, on being advanced to its 7th sq., would give check, after which White cannot win, as already shown (p. 431).

Diagram 102.

Here also the game is drawn, whoever moves first. Suppose Black has to play:—

WHITE.	BLACK.
1.	K—R 1

(Had he played the Pawn, or K—Kt 1, he would have lost.)

2. K—R 6	K—Kt 1
3. P—R 5	K—R 1
4. P—Kt 5	

(Had this Pawn been unmoved, or moved only one square, White would now have won. This applies to many similar cases, and proves that if White can place his King at R 6, with either of his Pawns unmoved, he must win, because he has then the option of moving them one or two squares at pleasure, and thus gaining a move.)

4.	K—Kt 1
5. P—Kt 6	

And the game is drawn, as in the last example.

Diagram 103.

This position was given by some of the earliest writers, who, however, erroneously supposed that in all cases the game should be drawn. The error was clearly demonstrated by Lolli, who shows that, with the move, White can win. We give some of the principal variations, the minor details will be easily supplied.

WHITE.	BLACK.
1. K—K 5	P—R 4 (or A.)
2. P—Kt 5	K—B 2
3. K—Q 6	K—B 1

(It is quite immaterial, as you will readily discover, where the King is played to.)

4. K—K 6	K—Kt 2
5. K—B 5	K—B 2
6. P—Kt 6 ch., &c.	

And wins.

(A.)

1. K—K 5	K—Kt 2 :
2. P—R 5	

(Had Black, instead of his last move, played K—B 2, White plays 2 K—B 5.)

2.	K—B 2
3. K—B 5	K—Kt 2

4. K—K 6	K—R 1
5. K—B 6	K—R 2
6. K—B 7	K—R 1
7. K—Kt 6	

And wins.

Diagram 104.

This situation has been the occasion of much discussion. The older writers, by whom it was introduced, considered that White ought to win, but this opinion has been controverted, at least so far as relates to cases where White has the move. We are indebted to the indefatigable authors of the "Handbuch" for a copious analysis, which appears to us to set the question at rest, and to prove, that with proper play, the game must always be drawn, it being only requisite for the weaker party to advance his Rook's Pawn at the critical moment.

Diagram 103.   Diagram 104.

BLACK.   BLACK.

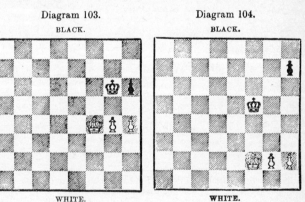

WHITE.   WHITE.

First, suppose White moves:—

WHITE.	BLACK.
1. K—Kt 3	

(This is the move usually given to White, and it does not appear that he has anything better.)

1.	K—Kt 4
2. P—R 3 (or A.)	P—R 3
3. K—B 3	K—B 4
4. P—Kt 4 ch.	K—B 3

(If instead you play this Pawn one square only, Black advances his Pawn another square, and maintains the opposition.)

5. K—B 4	K—Kt 3
6. K—Kt 3	K—Kt 4
7. P—R 4 ch.	K—Kt 3
8. K—B 3	K—B 2
9. K—K 4	K—K 3

Drawn game.

(A.)

WHITE.	BLACK.
1. K—Kt 3	K—Kt 4
2. P—R 4 ch.	K—B 4
3. K—B 3	

(Should White instead play K—R 3, Black will still play P—R 4.)

3.	P—R 4
4. P—Kt 3	K—K 4
5. K—K 3	K—B 4

And Black must draw.

Now, suppose Black plays first,—

WHITE.	BLACK.
1.	K—B 5
2. K—K 2 (or A)	K—K 5
3. P—R 3	P—R 3
4. K—B 2	K—B 5
5. P—Kt 3 ch.	K—B 4
6. K—B 3	P—R 4

Drawn game.

(A.)

| WHITE. | BLACK. |
| 2. P—R 3 | |

Lolli now makes Black move K—B 4, and then shows that he must
    lose.   It is evident that he ought to play :—

| 2. | P—R 3 |

And will always be able to draw the game.

We cannot here afford space to follow the " Handbuch " through
all the details, but what we have now given will be a sufficient clue
to the student, and enable him to discover, without much difficulty,
the proper defence for Black in any given variation.

Diagram 105.

White having the move, the game is drawn.

WHITE.	BLACK.
1. K—B 5	K—B 2
2. P—Kt 6 ch.	K—Kt 1

3.	K—Q 6	K—B 1
4.	K—K 7	K—Kt 1
5.	K—Q 7	K—R 1
6.	P—R 6	K—Kt 1

And draws.

Diagram 105.   Diagram 106.

BLACK.   BLACK.

WHITE.   WHITE.

Diagram 106.

If Black moves, he can draw the game by K—Kt 1, but if White plays first, he wins as follows :—

WHITE.		BLACK.
1.	K—B 5	K—Kt 1
2.	K—Kt 6	K—R 1
3.	K—B 7	K—R 2
4.	P—R 6	

And wins.

Had Black played 1. K—R 1, White still plays 2. K—Kt 6, Black must then move 2. K—Kt 1, and you advance R P, and if he refuse to take it, play K—B 7.

Diagram 107.

White wins with or without the move.

First, suppose he has the move :—

WHITE.		BLACK.
1.	K—B 5	P—Kt 3 ch.
2.	K—Q 5	K—Q 2
3.	P—Kt 5	K—B 2
4.	K—K 6	

And wins.

If Black moves first :—

1.		K—B 1
2.	K—Kt 6	K—Kt 1
3.	P—Kt 5	K—R 1
4.	K—B 7	K—R 2
5.	P—R 5	K—R 1
6.	K—Q 8	

(Then you gain a move, and place your King in the proper position before advancing the Pawn.)

6.		K—Kt 1
7.	K—Q 7	K—R 2
8.	K—B 8	K—R 1
9.	P—R 6	P—Kt 3
10.	K—B 7	K—R 2
11.	K—B 6	

And wins.

Diagram 107.   Diagram 108.

BLACK.   BLACK.

WHITE.   WHITE.

Diagram 108.

White wins with or without the move.

WHITE.		BLACK.
1.		K—Kt 5
2.	K—K 4	K—B 5
3.	K—K 3	P—Kt 5
4.	K—K 4	P—Kt 6
5.	P—R 3	

White wins.

Diagram 109.

In this position also White wins.

WHITE.	BLACK.
1. P—B 5	K—B 1

(Had he advanced the Pawn, White would not have taken it, but
moved P—B 6.)

| 2. K—Kt 6 | K—Kt 1 |
| 3. P—B 6 | K—R 1 |

(He would equally lose by taking the Pawn.)

1. K—B 7

And wins.

Diagram 109.

BLACK.

WHITE.

Diagram 110.

BLACK.

WHITE.

Diagram 110.

With the move Black may draw the game, without it he must
lose.

White having the move plays : —

WHITE.	BLACK.
1. K—B 3	P—Q 4 (or A.)
2. P—K 3	K—B 3
3. K—Q 4	K—Q 3
4. P—B 3	K—B 3
5. P—B 4	P × P
6. K × P	

And wins.

(A.)

| 1. | K—Q 4 |
| 2. K—Q 3 | P—Q 3 |

3. P—B 3	K—B 4
4. P—K 4	P—Q 4
5. P—K 5	

And wins.

But if Black moves first, he plays :—

1.	K—B 5
2. P—B 3	P—Q 4
3. P—K 3	K—B 4
4. K—Q 3	K—B 3
5. P—B 4	K—Q 3

And the game is drawn.

KING AND TWO PAWNS AGAINST KING AND TWO PAWNS.

SOME interesting cases occur under this head, where the game may be won or drawn by correct play.

Diagram 111.

This is a well-known position of Philidor's, who supposed, that if Black had the move, he would lose the game. This opinion, however, has been proved to be erroneous, the game being drawn whoever plays first. If White moves, he plays :—

WHITE.	BLACK.
1. K—K 3	K—K 4
2. K—B 3	K—B 4
3. K—Kt 3	K—K 4
4. K—Kt 4	K—B 3
5. K—Kt 3	K—K 4

And the game is drawn.

If Black moves, he plays :—

| 1. | K—K 4 |
| 2. K—K 3 | K—Q 4 |

(Were he to move K—B 4, you would win by 3. K—Q 4.)

3. K—B 3	K—K 4
4. K—Kt 3	K—K 3
5. K—Kt 4	K—B 3

And by continuing to play thus Black may always draw the game.

Diagram 112.

With the move Black wins.

WHITE.	BLACK.
1.	K—B 6
2. K—K 2	K—Kt 7
3. K—Q 2	K×P
4. K—B 2	P—B 5

And wins.

Diagram 111.	Diagram 112.
BLACK.	BLACK.

WHITE.   WHITE.

Diagram 113.

White, with the move, wins.

WHITE.	BLACK.
1. Kt—Q 7 ch.	K—K 2
2. Kt×B	B P×Kt
3. P—Kt 5	K—B 2

(**If 3.** K—B 3, White moves K—K 4, and the position becomes the same as under in another move.)

4. K—K 5	K—K 2
5. P—B 6 ch.	K—B 2
6. K—Q 6 or B 5	

And wins.

Diagram 114.

With the move White wins.

WHITE.	BLACK.
1. P—Kt 7	P—R 7
2. P—Kt 8 (Q)	P—R 8 (8) ch.

3. Q—K 5 ch.	Q×Q ch.
4. P×Q	P—Kt 5
5. P—K 6	P—Kt 6
6. P—K 7	P—Kt 7
7. P—K 8 (Q) ch.	

And wins.

Diagram 113.   Diagram 114.

BLACK.   BLACK.

WHITE.   WHITE.

KING AND TWO PAWNS AGAINST KING AND THREE PAWNS.

Diagram 115.

With or without the move Black wins.

First, with the move:—

WHITE.	BLACK.
1.	P—Kt 6
2. P—R 3 (or A.)	K—Q 5
3. K—B 3	

(If you play instead K—Q 2, he plays P—B 6.)

| 3. | K—K 4 |
| 4. K—K 2 | |

(Had you here moved K—Kt 4, he would win by K—K 5 and K 6, and afterwards playing P—B 6.)

| 4. | K—K 5 |
| 5. K—B 1 | K—Q 6 |

6. K—K 1	K—K 6
7. K—B 1	K—Q 7
8. K—Kt 1	K—K 7
9. K—R 1	P—B 6
10. P×P	K—B 7

And wins.

(A.)

2. P×P	R P×P
3. K—B 1	K—K 6
4. K—K 1	K—Q 6
5. K—B 1	K—Q 7
6. K—Kt 1	K—K 7
7. K—R 1	P—B 6

And wins.

Diagram 115.   Diagram 116.

BLACK.   BLACK.

WHITE.   WHITE.

Next, if White move first he must equally lose.

WHITE.   BLACK.

1. K—B 2

(You have nothing better; if you play P—Kt 3, Black plays R P×P, and wins as before.)

1.	P—Kt 6 ch.
2. K—Kt 1	K—K 6
3. K—R 1	P—B 6
4. P×B P	K—B 7, &c.

And wins.

Diagram 116.

The game is drawn.

WHITE.	BLACK.
1. K—Kt 4	K—Kt 3
2. K—B 4	K—B 2
3. K—B 5	K—K 2
4. K—Kt 4	K—K 3
5. K—B 4	K—K 2

Drawn game.

KING AGAINST THREE PASSED PAWNS.

We now come to a species of termination which has occupied very much of the attention of the chess world, viz., the power of the King as opposed to three united Pawns, the opposite King not being able to come to their aid. Without going through the multitude of positions and variations which have appeared on the subject, we shall endeavour to make it as clear as our space will permit. The first question to be considered, and it is one which well understood will very much simplify all the rest, is the proper method of playing the King in situations such as the following (see Diagram 117), or where the White King is on any square in front of the Pawns. Formerly it was supposed that the three Pawns could advance to Queen by their own force, when thus opposed to a King only, but this opinion is now known to have been incorrect. The fact is, that the King, when he occupied any square in front of the Pawns, or when he is within three moves of his Kt 3, which from its importance has been called the master square of the position, can invariably stop the Pawns. (It is important to recollect that Black is always understood to be unable to move his King so as to gain a move when necessary.)

Diagram 117.

BLACK.

WHITE.

We now proceed to analyse some of the situations arising from this description of end game, beginning with the one above given. The White King, being here less than three moves from his Kt 3 wins in all cases.

WHITE.	BLACK.
1.	P—B 4 (see Var.)
2. K—Kt 2	P—R 4 (B.)
3. K—Kt 3	P—Kt 4 (A.)
4. K—Kt 2	

(In all cases like this, where the King is in front of the three equally advanced Pawns, with one square between, he immediately arrests them by retreating one square, providing they are not further advanced then to their fifth squares.)

4.	P—B 5

(If P—R 5, the King is played to R 3; and if P—Kt 5, to Kt 3.)

5. K—B 3	P—R 5
6. K—Kt 4	

And wins; because whatever Pawn is moved, the King takes it.

(A.)

3.	P—Kt 3

(This is the strongest position (the adversary having to move) the Pawns can assume, and were they one step further advanced, White could not stop them.)

4. K—Kt 2	P—Kt 4

Had Black moved P—B 5 or R 5, you win thus :—

4.	P—B 5
5. K—B 3	P—Kt 4
6. K—B 2	P—R 5
7. K—Kt 2	P—Kt 5
8. K—Kt 1, &c.	

5. K—Kt 3	P—Kt 5

(If Black play P—R 5 or B 5, you play King in front of it.)

6. K—Kt 2	P—B 5
7. K—B 2	

If he move P—Kt 6, you play K—B 3, and if

7.	P—R 5
8. K—Kt 1, &c.	

(B.)

2.   P—Kt 4
3. K—Kt 3

(If 3. P—R 4, see first variation, if P—R **3**, White moves 4. K—B 3.)

3.   P—Kt 5
4. K—B 4   P—R 3

(If to R 4, White wins at once by 5. K—Kt 3.)

5. K—Kt 3   P—R 4
6. K—Kt 2

And wins, as before.

VARIATION.

On Black's 1st move.

It is obvious that the moves already given will equally apply if
Black plays P—R 4 or B 4 ; therefore, suppose,—

WHITE.	BLACK.
1.	P—Kt 4
2. K—Kt 2	P—Kt 5
3. K—Kt 3	P—B 4
4. K—B 4 or R 4	

And the position is the same as in Variation (B.)

A careful examination of this analysis will speedily enable the
student to understand the proper method of playing the King so
as to prevent the Pawns advancing to Queen.

We give a few more positions by way of illustration.

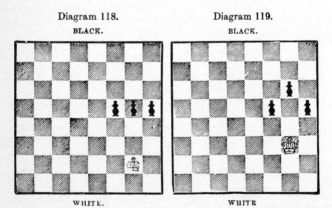

Diagram 118.   Diagram 119.

BLACK.   BLACK.

WHITE.   WHITE

In these four instances, the King wins either with or without the move, but in all of them he does so most readily if the Pawns play first; and in all of them, if the Pawns were one square further advanced, with the King in the same relative position, the party having to move would lose. Suppose, then, the King moves:—

Diagram 118.

WHITE.	BLACK.
1. K—Kt 3	P—Kt 5
2. K—Kt 2	P—B 5
3. K—B 2	P—R 5

(If instead he had played P—Kt 6, you move K—B 3, or if P—B 6, K—Kt 3.)

| 4. K—Kt 1 | P—B 6 |
| 5. K—B 2, &c. | |

Diagram 119.

WHITE.	BLACK.
1. K—Kt 2	P—B 5

(If 1. P—Kt 4, the position is the same as the last.)

| 2. K—B 3 | P—Kt 4 |
| 3. K—B 2 | |

(If to Kt 2, the Pawns win.)

| 3. | P—R 5 |

(If to Kt 5, see Diagram 121.)

| 4. K—Kt 2 | P—Kt 5 |
| 5. K—Kt 1 | |

And wins.

Diagram 120.

BLACK.

WHITE.

Diagram 121.

BLACK.

WHITE.

Diagram 120.

WHITE.	BLACK.
1. K—Kt 2	

And the situation is the same as at the 2nd move of Diagram 118.

Diagram 121.

WHITE.	BLACK.
1. K—B 2	P—Kt 5
2. K—Kt 2	P—Kt 6

(If P—R 5, see Diagram 119.)

3. K—B 3	P—R 5
4. K—Kt 2	

Black must lose.

We have already observed that in similar positions, but one step further advanced, the King, if he has to move, would lose. The student having examined the above will find the solution easy. We only, therefore, give four more examples, where in all cases the Pawns win.

Diagram 122.   Diagram 123.

BLACK   BLACK.

WHITE.   WHITE.

Diagram 122. If Black has the move he plays P—B 6, or, if K moves, and is played to Kt 2, then 1. P—R 5, if K—R 2, then P—B 6.

Diagram 123. Black having the move plays P—B 4; on the contrary, had White to move, this Pawn would play to B 3 only, thereby gaining a move.

Diagram 124. Here also the unmoved Pawn advances one or two squares, according, as the King has or has not the first move. If Black moves first :—

WHITE.	BLACK.
1.	P—B 3
2. K—B 3	P—B 4
3. K—Kt 2	P—B 5, &c.

Winning.

Diagram 125. The position is similar to the two preceding ones. The Pawns winning by their power of playing the unmoved Pawn one or two squares at pleasure. For example:—

WHITE.	BLACK.
1.	P—Kt 3
2. K—Kt 2	P—Kt 4

&c., &c.

Had the King here originally stood at B 3 or R 3, the party moving first would have won.

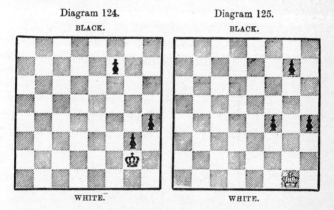

Diagram 124.	Diagram 125.
BLACK.	BLACK.
WHITE.	WHITE.

It would obviously be easy to multiply these examples to an indefinite extent ; the foregoing, however, will be sufficient to exemplify the principle with which we set out, viz., that the King can always stop the Pawns when he is originally upon any square in front of them, or when he can reach his Kt 3 within three moves. It will also be clear (from the three last positions) that whenever two of the Pawns can succeed in advancing unattacked to their fifth squares, with the third unmoved, they invariably win, wherever the adverse King may be.

Suppose, then, that the White King originally stood on Q 1 (the Pawns being unmoved), it follows that whoever has the move must win; because, if the King moves he has time to place himself on the Kt 3 within three moves, but if the Pawns move they will be able to prevent his doing so; thus:—

WHITE.	BLACK.
1.	P—R 4
2. K—K 2	P—B 4
3. K—B 3	P—R 5
4. K—B 4	

(If the King retreat, Black will play P—B 5, &c.)

4.	P—Kt 4 ch.
5. K—B 3	

&c., &c.

The Pawns win as in a former example.

The foregoing examples naturally lead us to the consideration of the still more complex positions arising from King with Rook's, Knight's, and Bishop's Pawns unmoved, against a similar opposing force.

KING AND THREE PASSED PAWNS AGAINST KING AND THREE PASSED PAWNS.

Diagram 126.

BLACK.

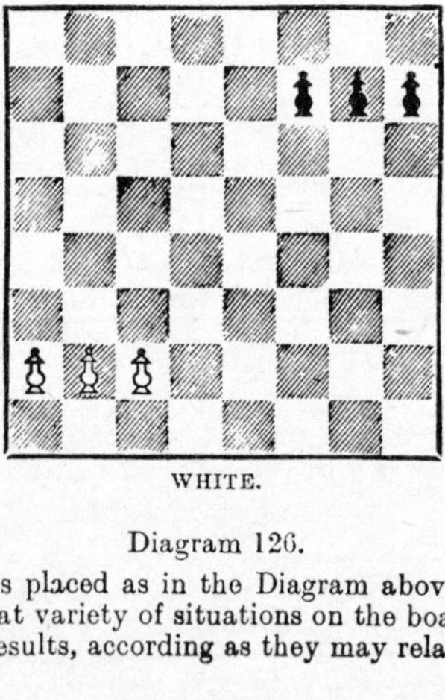

WHITE.

Diagram 126.

With the Pawns placed as in the Diagram above, the two Kings may occupy a great variety of situations on the board, producing, of course, different results, according as they may relatively be more or less advantageously situated. However varied the position of the two Kings, either player may, nevertheless, readily discover whether his position be a winning or a losing one, by observing the following rules.

To simplify the matter, all the possible positions that may be assumed for the two Kings are divided and classed under the two following cases :—

Case 1. When both the Kings are more than three moves distant from their respective master squares.

Case 2. When one or both Kings are within three moves of their master squares.

With respect to the first case, it has already been shown that, under the conditions named, the King cannot prevent the adverse Pawns from going to Queen. Each party will, therefore, make a Queen, and the game ought to be drawn, unless one of the Kings happen to occupy a square in the royal rank, in which case he would lose, as the adversary would Queen a Pawn, checking, &c. None of the positions falling under the first case produce any interesting situations, nor afford much scope for play.

The game, however, becomes totally altered in its character in all the numerous situations included in *Case* 2, wherein the party should win whose King is most advanced in the game, and to ascertain which of the two Kings is so in advance, observe the following General Rule (*a*). "Victory will be in the hands of the party who can first play his King into its master square." The power of arriving first to this square will result either from the advantage of the first move, or from being originally placed nearer to it.

The proper mode of play is the following :—The player having the winning position (which suppose to be the White), should have in view to advance his Pawns until they are stopped by the Black King. White will then stop the Black Pawns, which will compel the Black King to move out of position and the White Pawns will afterwards go forcedly to Queen. (This will be shown in the 1st Example.)

In cases where the Black (when losing player) would force his Pawns to be stopped first, the White would still win, for the Black would not afterwards be able to stop the White Pawns. This is shown in the 1st Variation to the 1st Example.

In conducting his game the player having the winning position must be cautious of two things, and which, it is probable, were the chief difficulties that had so long retarded the solution of the "Three Pawn Problem."

1st. Before advancing his Pawns he must take care that his King be near enough to the adverse Pawns to prevent two of them reaching their 5th squares with the third Pawn unmoved. Were this permitted, the game would be drawn, as shown in the 1st Variation to the 2nd Example. When, therefore, his King is three moves distant

---

(*a*) An exception to this Rule is, when one of the Kings stands so near the adversary's Pawns as to prevent them being moved two squares without being captured.

from the master square, he must begin by moving his King, and not his Pawns, as the 2nd Example and its 1st Variation will prove.

2nd. The winning player must be careful when advancing his King to oppose the adverse Pawns, to stop them in the fewest possible number of moves, for the loss of a move would be the loss of the game. As an error of this kind may be easily committed, two examples are given as Illustrations. (See 2nd and 3rd Variations to 1st Example.)

First Example.

Greco's Position.   Diagram 127.

BLACK.

WHITE.

Diagram 127.

This situation has been handed down to us by Greco, in his "Treatise on Chess." It was considered by him, and for long afterwards, by all chess-players to be a drawn game, whoever had the move.

This fallacy was first discovered by M. Szen, the celebrated Hungarian player, and afterwards by others. On viewing the position, it will be perceived that the White King can first reach the master square, even if the Black begins. White should, therefore, according to the rule, win the game, whether he moves first or not.

Suppose, then, Black to have the first move, and to play :—

WHITE.	BLACK.
1.	K—Q 2
(As he might have played a Pawn.	See Variations.)
2. P—R 4	K—B 3
3. P—R 5	K—Kt 4
4. P—Kt 4	P—R 4

5. P—B 4 ch.	K—R 3
6. P—B 5	K—Kt 4
7. K—B 2	P—R 5
8. K—Kt 2	P—Kt 4
9. K—R 3	P—B 4

(Better than P—B 3 ; but it may be observed here, that no advantage can be derived from playing an unmoved Pawn one or two squares, unless the other two Pawns have reached their 5th square.

| 10. K—R 2 | |

(K—Kt 2 would lose.)

10.	P—B 5
11. K—Kt 2	P—Kt 5
12. K—Kt 1	P—B 6
13. K—B 2	P—R 6
14. K—Kt 3	Is obliged to move his King, and one of the White Pawns will Queen.

VARIATION I.

WHITE.	BLACK.
1.	P—R 4
2. K—B 2	P—R 5
3. K—Kt 2	

(If 3. K—B 3, you would lose the game ; see 2nd Variation.)

3.	P—Kt 4
4. K—R 3	P—B 4
5. P—R 4	P—B 5
6. K—Kt 4	K—Q 2
7. P—R 5	K—B 3 (best, as most
8. P—B 4	likely to mislead).

P—Kt 4 would have lost the game. See (A.)

| 8. | K—Kt 2 |

(If K—B 4, you check with Kt P, and then advance R P).

| 9. P—B 5 | |

Two of the Pawns being now at their 5th squares, with the third unmoved, one of them must Queen. If Black now play K—Kt 1, you move P—Kt 3, not Kt 4, and if K to any other square, you advance B or R P according to circumstances.

(A.)

8. P—Kt 4	K—Kt 4
9. P—B 3 (best)	K—R 3
10. P—B 4	K—R 2
11. P—Kt 5 (has nothing better)	K—Kt 2

12 P—R 6 ch.	K—Kt 3
13. P—B 5 ch.	K—R 2
14. P—B 6	K—Kt 3

White is now forced to move his King, and cannot afterwards stop
the Pawns.

VARIATION II.

WHITE.	BLACK.
1.	P—Kt 4
2. K—B 2	P—R 5
3. K—B 3	

(This move loses the game.)

3.	K—Q 2

(No other move would win.)

4. K—Kt 4	P—Kt 4
5. P—R 4	P—B 4 ch.
6. K—R 3	K—B 3
7. P—R 5	K—Kt 4
8. P—Kt 4	P—B 5
9. K—Kt 4	K—R 3
10. P—B 4	K—R 2
11. P—B 5	K—Kt 2

Stops the Pawns, and wins.

VARIATION III.

WHITE.	BLACK.
1.	P—R 4
2. K—B 2	P—Kt 4
3. K—Kt 3	P—R 5 ch.
4. K—Kt 4	

(This move loses, because Black gains a move by checking with B P.
White ought to have played K—R 3.)

4.	P—B 4 ch.
5. K—R 3	K—Q 2

(He might also play P—B 5.)

6. P—R 4	K—B 3
7. P—Kt 4	P—B 5
8. K—Kt 4	

(Unless you made this move, you could not stop the Black Pawns.)

8.	K—Kt 3
9. P—Kt 5	K—B 4
10. P—B 3 (best)	K—Kt 3
11. P—B 4	K—Kt 2
12. P—B 5	K—R 2 or B 2

Stops the Pawns, and wins.

Second Example.

Diagram 128.

Szen's Position.

This position was first introduced to the notice of chess players by M. Szen. It only differs from that of Greco in the situation of the White King. Here the two Kings are equidistant from their master square, *i.e.* the K Kt 3 for White, and Q Kt 3 for Black. According to the rule, therefore, the first player must win. Suppose White begins :—

WHITE.	BLACK.
1. K—K 2	

(This is the only winning move ; had a Pawn been played, the game would have been drawn. See 2nd Variation.)

1.	P—R 4

(He might have played the King. See 1st Variation.)

2. K—B 3	P—Kt 4
3. P—R 4	P—R 5
4. K—Kt 4	P—B 4 ch.
5. K—R 3	P—B 5
6. K—Kt 4	K—Q 2
7. P—R 5	K—B 3
8. P—B 4	

And the Pawns will Queen, as in the 1st Variation of the last Example

Diagram 128.

BLACK.

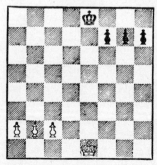

WHITE

VARIATION I.

WHITE.	BLACK.
1. K—K 2	K—Q 2
2. P—R 4	K—B 3
3. P—R 5	K—Kt 4 or (A.)
4. P—Kt 4	P—R 4
5. P—B 4 ch.	K—R 3
6. P—B 5	K—Kt 4
7. K—B 3	P—R 5
8. K—Kt 4	

And will stop the Black Pawns, throwing the move upon Black, who must then lose.

(A.)

3. P—R 5	P—R 4
4. K—B 3	P—R 5
5. K—Kt 4	P—Kt 4
6. P—B 4	P—B 4 ch.
7. K—R 3	P—B 5
8. K—Kt 4	K—Kt 2
9. P—B 5	He cannot stop the White Pawns.

VARIATION II.

WHITE.	BLACK.
1. P—R 4	P—R 4

(Had he played the King, he would not have taken proper advantage of the error of White's first move.)

2. P—R 5	K—Q 2
3. P—Kt 4	K—B 3
4. P—R 6	K—Kt 3
5. P—Kt 5	P—R 5
6. K—K 2	P—Kt 4
7. K—B 2	P—R 6
8. K—Kt 3	P—Kt 5
9. K—R 2	K—R 2

The party who first plays his unmoved Pawn will lose, because his adversary will gain the move by advancing his unmoved Pawn either one or two squares. As, therefore, each party will play the King only, the game will be drawn (a).

(a) For this clear and simple resolution of the celebrated problem "King and Three Pawns *versus* King and Three Pawns," we are indebted to the skilful industry of Capt. W. D. Evans, the inventor of the beautiful opening called the Evans' Gambit.

APPENDIX

BY

R. F. GREEN.

INDEX TO THE OPENINGS.

Allgaier Gambit. 1. $\dfrac{\text{P}-\text{K }4}{\text{P}-\text{K }4}$; 2. $\dfrac{\text{P}-\text{K B }4}{\text{P}\times\text{P}}$; 3. $\dfrac{\text{Kt}-\text{K B }3}{\text{P}-\text{K Kt }4}$; 4. $\dfrac{\text{P}-\text{K R }4}{\text{P}-\text{Kt }5}$; 5. $\dfrac{\text{Kt}-\text{Kt }5}{}$.

Allgaier-Kieseritzky Gambit. See *Kieseritzky Gambit.*

Allgaier-Thorold Gambit. 1. $\dfrac{\text{P}-\text{K }4}{\text{P}-\text{K }4}$; 2. $\dfrac{\text{P}-\text{K B }4}{\text{P}\times\text{P}}$; 3. $\dfrac{\text{Kt}-\text{K B }3}{\text{P}-\text{K Kt }4}$; 4. $\dfrac{\text{P}-\text{K R }4}{\text{P}-\text{Kt }5}$; 5. $\dfrac{\text{Kt}-\text{Kt }5}{\text{P}-\text{K R }3}$; 6. $\dfrac{\text{Kt}\times\text{P}}{\text{K}+\text{Kt}}$; 7. $\dfrac{\text{P}-\text{Q }4}{}$.

Anderssen's Counter Attack in the Salvio Gambit. 1. $\dfrac{\text{P}-\text{K }4}{\text{P}-\text{K }4}$; 2. $\dfrac{\text{P}-\text{K B }4}{\text{P}\times\text{P}}$; 3. $\dfrac{\text{Kt}-\text{K B }3}{\text{P}-\text{K Kt }4}$; 4. $\dfrac{\text{B}-\text{B }4}{\text{P}-\text{Kt }5}$; 5. $\dfrac{\text{Kt}-\text{K }5}{\text{Q}-\text{R }5\text{ ch.}}$; 6. $\dfrac{\text{K}-\text{B }1}{\text{Kt}-\text{K R }3}$; 7. $\dfrac{\text{P}-\text{Q }4}{\text{P}-\text{Q }3}$.

Anderssen's Counter Attack in the Scotch Gambit. 1. $\dfrac{\text{P}-\text{K }4}{\text{P}-\text{K }4}$; 2. $\dfrac{\text{Kt}-\text{K B }3}{\text{Kt}-\text{Q B }3}$; 3. $\dfrac{\text{P}-\text{Q }4}{\text{P}\times\text{P}}$; 4. $\dfrac{\text{B}-\text{Q B }4}{\text{B}-\text{B }4}$; 5. $\dfrac{\text{Castles}}{\text{P}-\text{Q }3}$; 6. $\dfrac{\text{P}-\text{Q B }3}{\text{B}-\text{K Kt }5}$.

Anderssen's Counter Attack in the Sicilian Defence.

1. $\dfrac{P-K\,4}{P-Q\,B\,4}$; 2. $\dfrac{Kt-K\,B\,3}{P-K\,3}$; 3. $\dfrac{P-Q\,4}{P\times P}$; 4. $\dfrac{Kt\times P}{Kt-K\,B\,3}$.

Anderssen's Opening. 1. $\dfrac{}{P-Q\,R\,3}$.

Avalos-Salvio Gambit. See *Salvio Gambit*.

Barnes's Defence in the Ruy Lopez. 1. $\dfrac{P-K\,4}{P-K\,4}$; 2. $\dfrac{Kt-K\,B\,3}{Kt-Q\,B\,3}$;

3. $\dfrac{B-Kt\,5}{P-K\,Kt\,3}$.

Ben Oni's Counter Gambit. 1. $\dfrac{P-Q\,4}{P-Q\,B\,4}$.

Benima's Defence in the Scotch Game. 1. $\dfrac{P-K\,4}{P-K\,4}$:

2. $\dfrac{Kt-K\,B\,3}{Kt-Q\,B\,3}$; 3. $\dfrac{P-Q\,4}{P\times P}$; 4. $\dfrac{Kt\times P}{B-K\,2}$.

Berlin Counter Attack in the Ruy Lopez. 1. $\dfrac{P-K\,4}{P-K\,4}$;

2. $\dfrac{Kt-K\,B\,3}{Kt-Q\,B\,3}$; 3. $\dfrac{B-Kt\,5}{Kt-B\,3}$.

Berlin Defence in the King's Bishop's Opening. 1. $\dfrac{P-K\,4}{P-K\,4}$;

2. $\dfrac{B-B\,4}{Kt-K\,B\,3}$.

Berlin Defence in the Ruy Lopez. 1. $\dfrac{P-K\,4}{P-K\,4}$; 2. $\dfrac{Kt-K\,B\,3}{Kt-Q\,B\,3}$;

3. $\dfrac{B-Kt\,5}{Kt-K\,B\,3}$.

Bertin's Gambit. See *Cunningham Gambit*.

Bird's Defence in the Ruy Lopez. 1. $\dfrac{P-K\,4}{P-K\,4}$; 2. $\dfrac{Kt-K\,B\,3}{Kt-Q\,B\,3}$;

3. $\dfrac{B-Kt\,5}{Kt-Q\,5}$.

Bird's Opening. See *Dutch Opening*.

Bishop's Gambit. See *King's Bishop's Gambit*.

Bishop's Gambit, Limited. See *Little Bishop's Gambit*.

Blackburne's Attack in the Four Knights' Game. 1. $\frac{\text{P}-\text{K }4}{\text{P}-\text{K }4}$;

2. $\frac{\text{Kt}-\text{K B }3}{\text{Kt}-\text{Q B }3}$; 3. $\frac{\text{Kt}-\text{B }3}{\text{Kt}-\text{B }3}$; 4. $\frac{\text{B}-\text{Kt }5}{\text{B}-\text{Kt }5}$; 5. $\frac{\text{Castles}}{\text{Castles}}$;

6. $\frac{\text{Kt}-\text{Q }5}{\text{B}-\text{B }4}$; 7. $\frac{\text{P}-\text{Q }4}{}$.

Blackburne's Attack in the Scotch Gambit. 1. $\frac{\text{P}-\text{K }4}{\text{P}-\text{K }4}$;

2. $\frac{\text{Kt}-\text{K B }3}{\text{Kt}-\text{Q B }3}$; 3. $\frac{\text{P}-\text{Q }4}{\text{P}\times\text{P}}$; 4. $\frac{\text{Kt}\times\text{P}}{\text{B}-\text{B }4}$; 5. $\frac{\text{B}-\text{K }3}{\text{Q}-\text{B }3}$;

6. $\frac{\text{P}-\text{Q B }3}{\text{K Kt}-\text{K }2}$; 7. $\frac{\text{Q}-\text{Q }2}{}$.

Blackmar Gambit, No. 1. 1. $\frac{\text{P}-\text{Q }4}{\text{P}-\text{Q }4}$; 2. $\frac{\text{P}-\text{K }4}{\text{P}\times\text{P}}$; 3. $\frac{\text{P}-\text{K B }3}{\text{P}\times\text{P}}$;

4. $\frac{\text{Kt}\times\text{P}}{}$.

Blackmar Gambit, No. 2. 1. $\frac{\text{P}-\text{Q }4}{\text{P}-\text{K B }4}$; 2. $\frac{\text{P}-\text{K }4}{\text{P}\times\text{P}}$;

3. $\frac{\text{P}-\text{K B }3}{\text{P}\times\text{P}}$; 4. $\frac{\text{Kt}\times\text{P}}{\text{Kt}-\text{K B }3}$; 5. $\frac{\text{B}-\text{Q }3}{}$.

Boden-Kieseritsky Gambit. 1. $\frac{\text{P}-\text{K }4}{\text{P}-\text{K }4}$; 2. $\frac{\text{B}-\text{B }4}{\text{Kt}-\text{K B }3}$;

3. $\frac{\text{Kt}-\text{K B }3}{\text{Kt}\times\text{P}}$; 4. $\frac{\text{Kt}-\text{B }3}{}$.

Boden's Defence in the Philidor. 1. $\frac{\text{P}-\text{K }4}{\text{P}-\text{K }4}$; 2. $\frac{\text{Kt}-\text{K B }3}{\text{P}-\text{Q }3}$;

3. $\frac{\text{P}-\text{Q }4}{\text{P}\times\text{P}}$; 4. $\frac{\text{Q}+\text{P}}{\text{B}-\text{Q }2}$.

Boden's Defence in the Ruy Lopez. 1. $\frac{\text{P}-\text{K }4}{\text{P}-\text{K }4}$; 2. $\frac{\text{Kt}-\text{K B }3}{\text{Kt}-\text{Q B }3}$;

3. $\frac{\text{B}-\text{Kt }5}{\text{B}-\text{B }4}$; 4. $\frac{\text{P}-\text{B }3}{\text{Q}-\text{K }2}$.

Bradford Attack in the French Defence. 1. $\frac{\text{P}-\text{K }4}{\text{P}-\text{K }3}$; 2. $\frac{\text{P}-\text{Q }4}{\text{P}-\text{Q }4}$;

3. $\frac{\text{Kt}-\text{Q B }3}{}$.

Brien's Counter Gambit. 1. $\dfrac{P-K4}{P-K4}$; 2. $\dfrac{P-KB4}{P+P}$;

3. $\dfrac{B-B4}{P-QKt4}$.

Calabrais Counter Gambit. 1. $\dfrac{P-K4}{P-K4}$; 2. $\dfrac{B-B4}{P-KB4}$.

Calabrais Gambit. 1. $\dfrac{P-K4}{P-K4}$; 2. $\dfrac{P-KB4}{P\times P}$; 3. $\dfrac{Kt-KB3}{P-KKt4}$;

4. $\dfrac{B-B4}{B-Kt2}$; 5. $\dfrac{P-KR4}{P-KR3}$; 6. $\dfrac{P-Q4}{P-Q3}$; 7. $\dfrac{Kt-B3}{P-QB3}$;

8. $\dfrac{P\times P}{P\times P}$; 9. $\dfrac{R\times R}{B\times R}$; 10. $\dfrac{Kt-K5}{\quad}$.

Centre Counter Gambit. 1. $\dfrac{P-K4}{P-Q4}$.

Centre Gambit. 1. $\dfrac{P-K4}{P-K4}$; 2. $\dfrac{P-Q4}{\quad}$.

Classical Defence in the K B Gambit. 1. $\dfrac{P-K4}{P-K4}$; 2. $\dfrac{P-KB4}{P\times P}$;

3. $\dfrac{B-B4}{Q-R5\,ch.}$.

Classical Defence in the K B Opening. 1. $\dfrac{P-K4}{P-K4}$; 2. $\dfrac{B-B4}{B-B4}$;

Cochrane's Attack in Petroff's Defence. 1. $\dfrac{P-K4}{P-K4}$;

2. $\dfrac{Kt-KB3}{Kt-KB3}$; 3. $\dfrac{Kt\times P}{P-Q3}$; 4. $\dfrac{Kt\times P}{\quad}$.

Cochrane's Attack in the Scotch Game. 1. $\dfrac{P-K4}{P-K4}$;

2. $\dfrac{Kt-KB3}{Kt-QB3}$; 3. $\dfrac{P-Q4}{P\times P}$; 4. $\dfrac{B-QB4;}{B-Kt5\,ch.}$ 5. $\dfrac{P-QB3}{P\times P}$:

6. $\dfrac{P\times P}{\quad}$.

Cochrane Gambit. 1. $\dfrac{P-K4}{P-K4}$; 2. $\dfrac{P-KB4}{P\times P}$; 3. $\dfrac{Kt-KB3}{P-KKt4}$;

4. $\dfrac{B-B4}{P-Kt5}$; 5. $\dfrac{Kt-K5}{Q-R5\,ch.}$; 6. $\dfrac{K-B1}{P-B6}$.

Cochrane-Schumoff Defence in the Scotch Gambit. 1. $\frac{P-K\,4}{P-K\,4}$;

2. $\frac{Kt-K\,B\,3}{Kt-Q\,B\,3}$; 3. $\frac{P-Q\,4}{P\times P}$; 4. $\frac{B-Q\,B\,4}{B-B\,4}$; 5. $\frac{Kt-Kt\,5}{Kt-R\,3}$;

6. $\frac{Kt\times K\,B\,P}{Kt\times Kt}$; 7. $\frac{B\times Kt\,ch.}{K\times B}$; 8. $\frac{Q-R\,5\,ch.}{P-K\,Kt\,3}$; 9. $\frac{Q\times B}{P-Q\,4}$.

Compromised Defence in the Evans' Gambit. 1. $\frac{P-K\,4}{P-K\,4}$:

2. $\frac{Kt-K\,B\,3}{Kt-Q\,B\,3}$; 3. $\frac{B-B\,4}{B-B\,4}$; 4. $\frac{P-Q\,Kt\,4}{B\times Kt\,P}$; 5. $\frac{P-B\,3}{B-R\,4}$;

6. $\frac{P-Q\,4}{P\times P}$; 7. $\frac{Castles}{P\times P}$.

Count Vitzthum's Attack in the Scotch Gambit. 1. $\frac{P-K\,4}{P-K\,4}$;

2. $\frac{Kt-K\,B\,3}{Kt-Q\,B\,3}$; 3. $\frac{P-Q\,4}{P\times P}$; 4. $\frac{B-Q\,B\,4}{B-B\,4}$; 5. $\frac{Kt-Kt\,5}{Kt-R\,3}$;

6. $\frac{Q-R\,5}{\quad}$.

Cozio's Attack in the K B Gambit. 1. $\frac{P-K\,4}{P-K\,4}$; 2. $\frac{P-K\,B\,4}{P\times P}$;

3. $\frac{B-B\,4}{Q-R\,5\,ch.}$; 4. $\frac{K-B\,1}{P-K\,Kt\,4}$; 5. $\frac{Q-B\,3}{\quad}$.

Cunningham Gambit. 1. $\frac{P-K\,4}{P-K\,4}$; 2. $\frac{P-K\,B\,4}{P\times P}$; 3. $\frac{Kt-K\,B\,3}{B-K\,2}$.

Damiano Gambit. 1. $\frac{P-K\,4}{P-K\,4}$; 2. $\frac{Kt-K\,B\,3}{P-K\,B\,3}$; 3. $\frac{Kt\times P}{\quad}$.

Danish Gambit. 1. $\frac{P-K\,4}{P-K\,4}$; 2. $\frac{P-Q\,4}{P\times P}$; 3. $\frac{P-Q\,B\,3}{\quad}$.

Double Fianchetto. 1. $\frac{P-K\,4}{P-K\,Kt\,3}$; 2. $\frac{P-Q\,4}{B-Kt\,2}$; 3. $\frac{P-K\,B\,4}{P-Kt\,3}$;

4. $\frac{P-Q\,B\,4}{B-Kt\,2}$.

Double Ruy Lopez. 1. $\frac{P-K\,4}{P-K\,4}$; 2. $\frac{Kt-K\,B\,3}{Kt-Q\,B\,3}$; 3. $\frac{B-Kt\,5}{Kt-K\,B\,3}$;

4. $\frac{Kt-B\,3}{B-Kt\,5}$.

Dutch Opening. **1.** $\dfrac{\text{P—K B 4}}{}$.

E. Morphy's Defence in the Kieseritsky Gambit. **1.** $\dfrac{\text{P—K 4}}{\text{P—K 4}}$;

2. $\dfrac{\text{P—K B 4}}{\text{P} \times \text{P}}$; **3.** $\dfrac{\text{Kt—K B 3}}{\text{P—K Kt 4}}$; **4.** $\dfrac{\text{P—K R 4}}{\text{P—Kt 5}}$; **5.** $\dfrac{\text{Kt—K 5}}{\text{P—Q 4}}$.

English Game. See *Staunton's Opening*.

English Knight's Game. See *Staunton's Opening*.

English Opening. **1.** $\dfrac{\text{P—Q B 4}}{}$.

Evans' Gambit. **1.** $\dfrac{\text{P—K 4}}{\text{P—K 4}}$; **2.** $\dfrac{\text{Kt—K B 3}}{\text{Kt—Q B 3}}$; **3.** $\dfrac{\text{B—B 4}}{\text{B—B 4}}$;

4. $\dfrac{\text{P—Q Kt 4}}{}$.

Evans' Gambit Declined. **1.** $\dfrac{\text{P—K 4}}{\text{P—K 4}}$; **2.** $\dfrac{\text{Kt—K B 3}}{\text{Kt—Q B 3}}$; **3.** $\dfrac{\text{B—B 4}}{\text{B—B 4}}$;

4. $\dfrac{\text{P—Q Kt 4}}{\text{B—Kt 3}}$.

Falkbeer's Counter Gambit. **1.** $\dfrac{\text{P—K 4}}{\text{P—K 4}}$; **2.** $\dfrac{\text{P—K B 4}}{\text{P—Q 4}}$.

Fegatello. **1.** $\dfrac{\text{P—K 4}}{\text{P—K 4}}$; **2.** $\dfrac{\text{Kt—K B 3}}{\text{Kt—Q B 3}}$; **3.** $\dfrac{\text{B—B 4}}{\text{Kt—B 3}}$; **4.** $\dfrac{\text{Kt—Kt 5}}{\text{P—Q 4}}$;

5. $\dfrac{\text{P} \times \text{P}}{\text{Kt} \times \text{P}}$.

Fianchetto di Donna. **1.** $\dfrac{\text{P—Q Kt 3}}{}$.

Fianchetto di Re. **1.** $\dfrac{\text{P—K Kt 3}}{}$.

Fianchetto Defence (King's). **1.** $\dfrac{\text{P—K 4}}{\text{P—K Kt 3}}$.

Fianchetto Defence (Queen's). **1.** $\dfrac{\text{P—K 4}}{\text{P—Q Kt 3}}$.

Fleissig's Attack in the Four Knights' Game. **1.** $\dfrac{\text{P—K 4}}{\text{P—K 4}}$;

2. $\dfrac{\text{Kt—K B 3}}{\text{Kt—Q B 3}}$; **3.** $\dfrac{\text{Kt—B 3}}{\text{Kt—B 3}}$; **4.** $\dfrac{\text{B—Kt 5}}{\text{B—Kt 5}}$. **5.** $\dfrac{\text{Kt—Q 5}}{\text{B—B 4}}$;

6. $\dfrac{\text{P—B 3}}{}$.

Fleissig's Attack in the Scotch Gambit. 1. $\frac{P-K4}{P-K4}$; 2. $\frac{Kt-KB3}{Kt-QB3}$; 3. $\frac{P-Q4}{P\times P}$; 4. $\frac{Kt\times P}{B-B4}$; 5. $\frac{B-K3}{Q-B3}$; 6. $\frac{P-QB3}{KKt-K2}$; 7. $\frac{Kt-B2}{\quad}$.

Four Knights' Game. 1. $\frac{P-K4}{P-K4}$; 2. $\frac{Kt-KB3}{Kt-QB3}$; 3. $\frac{Kt-B3}{Kt-B3}$.

Fraser's Attack in the Evans' Gambit. 1. $\frac{P-K4}{P-K4}$; 2. $\frac{Kt-KB3}{Kt-QB3}$; 3. $\frac{B-B4}{B-B4}$; 4. $\frac{P-QKt4}{B\times Kt P}$; 5. $\frac{P-B3}{B-B4}$; 6. $\frac{Castles}{P-Q3}$; 7. $\frac{P-Q4}{P\times P}$; 8. $\frac{P\times P}{B-Kt3}$; 9. $\frac{Kt-B3}{B-Kt5}$; 10. $\frac{Q-R4}{\quad}$.

Fraser's Attack in the Scotch Gambit. 1. $\frac{P-K4}{P-K4}$; 2. $\frac{Kt-KB3}{Kt-QB3}$; 3. $\frac{P-Q4}{P\times P}$; 4. $\frac{Kt\times P}{Q-R5}$; 5. $\frac{Kt-KB3}{\quad}$.

Fraser's Counter Attack in the Muzio Gambit. 1. $\frac{P-K4}{P-K4}$; 2. $\frac{P-KB4}{P\times P}$; 3. $\frac{Kt-KB3}{P-KKt4}$; 4. $\frac{B-B4}{P-Kt5}$; 5. $\frac{Castles}{P\times Kt}$; 6. $\frac{Q\times P}{Q-B3}$; 7. $\frac{P-K5}{Q-B4}$.

Fraser and Möller's Defence in the Greco Counter Gambit. 1. $\frac{P-K4}{P-K4}$; 2. $\frac{Kt-KB3}{P-KB4}$; 3. $\frac{Kt\times P}{Kt-QB3}$.

Fraser-Macdonnell Attack in the Bishop's Gambit. 1. $\frac{P-K4}{P-K4}$; 2. $\frac{P-KB4}{P\times P}$; 3. $\frac{B-B4}{Q-R5}$ ch.; 4. $\frac{K-B1}{P-KKt4}$; 5. $\frac{Kt-QB3}{B-Kt2}$; 6. $\frac{P-KKt3}{P\times P}$; 7. $\frac{Q-B3}{\quad}$.

Fraser-Mortimer Attack in the Evans' Gambit 1. $\frac{P-K4}{P-K4}$; 2. $\frac{Kt-KB3}{Kt-QB3}$; 3. $\frac{B-B4}{B-B4}$; 4. $\frac{P-QKt4}{B\times Kt P}$; 5. $\frac{P-B3}{B-B4}$;

6. $\dfrac{\text{Castles}}{\text{P}-\text{Q 3}}$; 7. $\dfrac{\text{P}-\text{Q 4}}{\text{P}\times\text{P}}$; 8. $\dfrac{\text{P}\times\text{P}}{\text{B}-\text{Kt 3}}$; 9. $\dfrac{\text{Kt}-\text{B 3}}{\text{B}-\text{Kt 5}}$;

10. $\dfrac{\text{Q}-\text{R 4}}{\text{B}-\text{Q 2}}$; 11. $\dfrac{\text{Q}-\text{Kt 3}}{\text{Kt}-\text{R 4}}$; 12. $\dfrac{\text{B}\times\text{P ch.}}{\text{K}-\text{B 1}}$; 13. $\dfrac{\text{Q}-\text{B 2}}{\qquad}$.

French Defence. 1. $\dfrac{\text{P}-\text{K 4}}{\text{P}-\text{K 3}}$.

French Knight's Game. See *Philidor's Defence.*

From's Gambit. 1. $\dfrac{\text{P}-\text{K B 4}}{\text{P}-\text{K 4}}$.

Fyfe Gambit. 1. $\dfrac{\text{P}-\text{K 4}}{\text{P}-\text{K 4}}$; 2. $\dfrac{\text{Kt}-\text{Q B 3}}{\text{Kt}-\text{Q B 3}}$; 3. $\dfrac{\text{P}-\text{Q 4}}{\qquad}$.

Ghulam Kassim's Attack in the Muzio Gambit. 1. $\dfrac{\text{P}-\text{K 4}}{\text{P}-\text{K 4}}$;

2. $\dfrac{\text{P}-\text{K B 4}}{\text{P}\times\text{P}}$; 3. $\dfrac{\text{Kt}-\text{K B 3}}{\text{P}-\text{K Kt 4}}$; 4. $\dfrac{\text{B}-\text{B 4}}{\text{P}-\text{Kt 5}}$; 5. $\dfrac{\text{P}-\text{Q 4}}{\qquad}$.

Giuoco Piano. 1. $\dfrac{\text{P}-\text{K 4}}{\text{P}-\text{K 4}}$; 2. $\dfrac{\text{Kt}-\text{K B 3}}{\text{Kt}-\text{Q B 3}}$; 3. $\dfrac{\text{B}-\text{B 4}}{\text{B}-\text{B 4}}$.

Göring's Attack in the Evans' Gambit. 1. $\dfrac{\text{P}-\text{K 4}}{\text{P}-\text{K 4}}$;

2. $\dfrac{\text{Kt}-\text{K B 3}}{\text{Kt}-\text{Q B 3}}$; 3. $\dfrac{\text{B}-\text{B 4}}{\text{B}-\text{B 4}}$; 4. $\dfrac{\text{P}-\text{Q Kt 4}}{\text{B}\times\text{Kt P}}$; 5. $\dfrac{\text{P}-\text{B 3}}{\text{B}-\text{B 4}}$;

6. $\dfrac{\text{Castles}}{\text{P}-\text{Q 3}}$; 7. $\dfrac{\text{P}-\text{Q 4}}{\text{P}\times\text{P}}$; 8. $\dfrac{\text{P}\times\text{P}}{\text{B}-\text{Kt 3}}$; 9. $\dfrac{\text{Kt}-\text{B 3}}{\text{Kt}-\text{K 4}}$;

10. $\dfrac{\text{B}-\text{K Kt 5}}{\qquad}$.

Göring Gambit. 1. $\dfrac{\text{P}-\text{K 4}}{\text{P}-\text{K 4}}$; 2. $\dfrac{\text{Kt}-\text{K B 3}}{\text{Kt}-\text{Q B 3}}$; 3. $\dfrac{\text{P}-\text{Q 4}}{\text{P}\times\text{P}}$;

4. $\dfrac{\text{P}-\text{B 3}}{\qquad}$.

Greco Counter Gambit. 1. $\dfrac{\text{P}-\text{K 4}}{\text{P}-\text{K 4}}$; 2. $\dfrac{\text{Kt}-\text{K B 3}}{\text{P}-\text{K B 4}}$.

Greco-Philidor Gambit. 1. $\dfrac{\text{P}-\text{K 4}}{\text{P}-\text{K 4}}$; 2. $\dfrac{\text{P}-\text{K B 4}}{\text{P}\times\text{P}}$;

3. $\dfrac{\text{Kt}-\text{K B 3}}{\text{P}-\text{K Kt 4}}$; 4. $\dfrac{\text{B}-\text{B 4}}{\text{B}-\text{Kt 2}}$.

Grimm's Attack in the Bishop's Gambit. 1. $\dfrac{\text{P—K 4}}{\text{P—K 4}}$;

2. $\dfrac{\text{P—K B 4}}{\text{P}\times\text{P}}$; 3. $\dfrac{\text{B—B 4}}{\text{Q—R 5 ch.}}$; 4. $\dfrac{\text{K—K B 1}}{\text{P—K Kt 4}}$; 5. $\dfrac{\text{Kt—Q B 3}}{\text{B—Kt 2}}$;

6. $\dfrac{\text{P—Q 4}}{\text{P—Q 3}}$; 7. $\dfrac{\text{P—K 5}}{\text{P}\times\text{P}}$; 8. $\dfrac{\text{Kt—Q 5}}{\text{K—Q 1}}$; 9. $\dfrac{\text{Kt—K B 3}}{\text{Q—R 4}}$—;

10. $\dfrac{\text{P—K R 4}}{\text{P—K R 3}}$; 11. $\dfrac{\text{K—Kt 1}}{}$.

Gunsberg's Defence in the Scotch Gambit. 1. $\dfrac{\text{P—K 4}}{\text{P—K 4}}$;

2. $\dfrac{\text{Kt—K B 3}}{\text{Kt—Q B 3}}$; 3. $\dfrac{\text{P—Q 4}}{\text{P}\times\text{P}}$; 4. $\dfrac{\text{Kt}\times\text{P}}{\text{B—B 4}}$; 5. $\dfrac{\text{B—K 3}}{\text{Q—B 3}}$;

6. $\dfrac{\text{P—Q B 3}}{\text{K Kt—K 2}}$; 7. $\dfrac{\text{B—Q Kt 5}}{\text{Kt—Q 1}}$.

Hampe-Allgaier Gambit. 1. $\dfrac{\text{P—K 4}}{\text{P—K 4}}$; 2. $\dfrac{\text{Kt—Q B 3}}{\text{Kt—Q B 3}}$; 3. $\dfrac{\text{P—B 4}}{\text{P}\times\text{P}}$;

4. $\dfrac{\text{Kt—B 3}}{\text{P—K Kt 4}}$; 5. $\dfrac{\text{P—K R 4}}{\text{P—Kt 5}}$; 6. $\dfrac{\text{Kt—K Kt 5}}{}$.

Hampe-Allgaier-Thorold Gambit. 1. $\dfrac{\text{P—K 4}}{\text{P—K 4}}$; 2. $\dfrac{\text{Kt—Q B 3}}{\text{Kt—Q B 3}}$;

3. $\dfrac{\text{P—B 4}}{\text{P}\times\text{P}}$; 4. $\dfrac{\text{Kt—B 3}}{\text{P—K Kt 4}}$; 5. $\dfrac{\text{P—K R 4}}{\text{P—Kt 5}}$; 6. $\dfrac{\text{Kt—K Kt 5}}{\text{P—K R 3}}$;

7. $\dfrac{\text{Kt}\times\text{B P}}{\text{K}\times\text{Kt}}$; 8. $\dfrac{\text{P—Q 4}}{}$.

Hampe Opening. See *Vienna Game*.

Harvey's Attack in the Evans' Gambit. 1. $\dfrac{\text{P—K 4}}{\text{P—K 4}}$;

2. $\dfrac{\text{Kt—K B 3}}{\text{Kt—Q B 3}}$; 3. $\dfrac{\text{B—B 4}}{\text{B—B 4}}$; 4. $\dfrac{\text{P—Q Kt 4}}{\text{B}\times\text{Kt P}}$; 5. $\dfrac{\text{P—B 3}}{\text{B—B 4}}$;

6. $\dfrac{\text{Castles}}{\text{P—Q 3}}$; 7. $\dfrac{\text{P—Q 4}}{\text{P}\times\text{P}}$; 8. $\dfrac{\text{P}\times\text{P}}{\text{B—Kt 3}}$; 9. $\dfrac{\text{R—K 1}}{\text{Kt—R 4}}$;

10. $\dfrac{\text{B}\times\text{P ch.}}{}$.

Hollandish Defence. 1. $\dfrac{\text{P—Q 4}}{\text{P—K B 4}}$.

Holloway's Defence in the Muzio Gambit.   1. $\dfrac{P-K4}{P-K4}$;

2. $\dfrac{P-KB4}{P\times P}$;   3. $\dfrac{Kt-KB3}{P-KKt4}$;   4. $\dfrac{B-B4}{P-Kt5}$;   5. $\dfrac{Castles}{P\times Kt}$;

6. $\dfrac{Q\times P}{Kt-QB3}$.

Horny's Defence in the Allgaier Gambit.   1. $\dfrac{P-K4}{P-K4}$;

2. $\dfrac{P-KB4}{P\times P}$;   3. $\dfrac{Kt-KB3}{P-KKt4}$;   4. $\dfrac{P-KR4}{P-Kt5}$;   5. $\dfrac{Kt-Kt5}{P-KR3}$;

6. $\dfrac{Kt\times P}{K\times Kt}$;   7. $\dfrac{Q\times P}{Kt-KB3}$;   8. $\dfrac{Q\times BP}{B-Q3}$.

Hungarian Defence.   1. $\dfrac{P-K4}{P-K4}$;   2. $\dfrac{Kt-KB3}{Kt-QB3}$;   3. $\dfrac{B-B4}{B-K2}$.

Hunt Opening.   1. $\dfrac{P-QKt4}{\rule{1.5cm}{0.4pt}}$.

Indian Opening.   1. $\dfrac{P-KKt3}{P-K3}$;   2. $\dfrac{P-Q3}{\rule{1.5cm}{0.4pt}}$.

Inverted Hungarian Game.   1. $\dfrac{P-K4}{P-K4}$;   2. $\dfrac{Kt-KB3}{Kt-QB3}$;

3. $\dfrac{B-K2}{\rule{1.5cm}{0.4pt}}$.

Italian Defence in the Bishop's Opening.   1. $\dfrac{P-K4}{P-K4}$;

2. $\dfrac{B-B4}{B-B4}$;   3. $\dfrac{P-QB3}{Q-Kt4}$.

Italian Game.   1. $\dfrac{P-K4}{P-K4}$;   2. $\dfrac{Kt-KB3}{Kt-QB3}$.

Jaenisch's Counter Attack in Philidor's Defence.   1. $\dfrac{P-K4}{P-K4}$;

2. $\dfrac{Kt-KB3}{P-Q3}$;   3. $\dfrac{P-Q4}{Kt-KB3}$.

Jaenisch's Counter Gambit.   1. $\dfrac{P-K4}{P-K4}$;   2. $\dfrac{Kt-KB3}{Kt-QB3}$;

3. $\dfrac{B-Kt5}{P-B4}$.

Jaenisch's Counter Game.   1. $\dfrac{\text{P—K 4}}{\text{P—K 4}}$;   2. $\dfrac{\text{Kt—K B 3}}{\text{Kt—Q B 3}}$;

3. $\dfrac{\text{P—Q B 3}}{\text{Kt—B 3}}$.

Jerome Gambit.   1. $\dfrac{\text{P—K 4}}{\text{P—K 4}}$;   2. $\dfrac{\text{Kt—K B 3}}{\text{Kt—Q B 3}}$;   3. $\dfrac{\text{B—B 4}}{\text{B—B 4}}$;

4. $\dfrac{\text{B×P ch.}}{\quad\quad}$.

Kann's Defence.   1. $\dfrac{\text{P—K 4}}{\text{P—Q B 3}}$.

Kieseritsky's Attack in the Two Knights' Defence.   1. $\dfrac{\text{P—K 4}}{\text{P—K 4}}$;

2. $\dfrac{\text{Kt—K B 3}}{\text{Kt—Q B 3}}$;   3. $\dfrac{\text{B—B 4}}{\text{Kt—B 3}}$;   4. $\dfrac{\text{Kt—Kt 5}}{\text{P—Q 4}}$;   5. $\dfrac{\text{P×P}}{\text{Kt—Q R 4}}$;

6. $\dfrac{\text{P—Q 3}}{\quad\quad}$.

Kieseritsky's Counter Gambit.   1. $\dfrac{\text{P—K 4}}{\text{P—K 4}}$;   2. $\dfrac{\text{P—K B 4}}{\text{P×P}}$;

3. $\dfrac{\text{B—B 4}}{\text{P—Q Kt 4}}$.

Kieseritsky Gambit.   1. $\dfrac{\text{P—K 4}}{\text{P—K 4}}$;   2. $\dfrac{\text{P—K B 4}}{\text{P×P}}$;   3. $\dfrac{\text{Kt—K B 3}}{\text{P—K Kt 4}}$;

4. $\dfrac{\text{P—K R 4}}{\text{P—Kt 5}}$;   5. $\dfrac{\text{Kt—K 5}}{\quad\quad}$.

K B P Opening.   See *Bird's Opening*.

King's Bishop Gambit.   1. $\dfrac{\text{P—K 4}}{\text{P—K 4}}$;   2. $\dfrac{\text{P—K B 4}}{\text{P×P}}$;   3. $\dfrac{\text{B—B 4}}{\quad\quad}$.

King's Bishop's Opening.   1. $\dfrac{\text{P—K 4}}{\text{P—K 4}}$;   2. $\dfrac{\text{B—B 4}}{\quad\quad}$.

King's Fianchetto.   See *Fianchetto di Re*.

King's Gambit.   1. $\dfrac{\text{P—K 4}}{\text{P—K 4}}$;   2. $\dfrac{\text{P—K B 4}}{\quad\quad}$.

King's Knight's Defence in the K B Opening.   See *Berlin Defence*.

King's Knight's Gambit.   1. $\dfrac{\text{P—K 4}}{\text{P—K 4}}$;   2. $\dfrac{\text{P—K B 4}}{\text{P×P}}$;

3. $\dfrac{\text{Kt—K B 3}}{\quad\quad}$.

King's Rook's Pawn's Gambit. 1. $\frac{P-K4}{P-K4}$; 2. $\frac{P-KB4}{P\times P}$;

3. $\frac{P-KR4}{}$.

Kling and Horwitz's Counter Attack. 1. $\frac{P-K4}{P-K4}$; 2. $\frac{P-KB4}{P\times P}$;

3. $\frac{Kt-KB3}{P-KKt4}$; 4. $\frac{B-B4}{P-Kt5}$; 5. $\frac{Kt-B3}{Q-K2}$.

Koch and Ghulam Kassim's Attack. See *Ghulam Kassim's Attack.*

Kolisch's Defence in the Kieseritsky Gambit. 1 $\frac{P-K4}{P-K4}$;

2. $\frac{P-KB4}{P\times P}$; 3. $\frac{Kt-KB3}{P-KKt4}$; 4. $\frac{P-KR4}{P-Kt5}$; 5. $\frac{Kt-K5}{P-Q3}$.

Lewis Counter Gambit. 1. $\frac{P-K4}{P-K4}$; 2. $\frac{B-B4}{B-B4}$; 3. $\frac{P-QB3}{P-Q4}$.

Lichtenheim's Counter Attack. 1. $\frac{P-K4}{P-K4}$; 2. $\frac{P-KB4}{P\times P}$;

3. $\frac{B-B4}{Kt-KB3}$.

Little Bishop's Gambit. 1. $\frac{P-K4}{P-K4}$; 2. $\frac{P-KB4}{P\times P}$; 3. $\frac{B-K2}{}$.

Lopez Counter Gambit. 1. $\frac{P-K4}{P-K4}$; 2. $\frac{Kt-KB3}{P-Q3}$; 3. $\frac{B-B4}{P-KB4}$.

Lopez Gambit. 1. $\frac{P-K4}{P-K4}$; 2. $\frac{B-B4}{B-B4}$; 3. $\frac{Q-K2}{Kt-QB3}$;

4. $\frac{P-QB3}{Kt-B3}$; 5. $\frac{P-B4}{}$.

Lopez-Philidor Defence. 1. $\frac{P-K4}{P-K4}$; 2. $\frac{Kt-KB3}{Kt-QB3}$; 3. $\frac{B\quad Kt5}{P-Q3}$.

Lord's Defence in the Philidor. 1. $\frac{P-K4}{P-K4}$; 2. $\frac{Kt-KB3}{P-Q3}$;

3. $\frac{P-Q4}{Kt-Q2}$.

Macdonnells' Attack in the K B Gambit. 1. $\frac{P-K4}{P-K4}$; 2. $\frac{P-KB4}{P\times P}$; 3. $\frac{B-B4}{Q-R5 ch.}$; 4. $\frac{K-B1}{P-KKt4}$; 5. $\frac{Kt-QB3}{B-Kt2}$; 6. $\frac{P-KKt3}{\quad}$.

Macdonnell's Attack in the Muzio Gambit. 1. $\frac{P-K4}{P-K4}$; 2. $\frac{P-KB4}{P\times P}$; 3. $\frac{Kt-KB3}{P-KKt4}$; 4. $\frac{B-B4}{P-Kt5}$; 5. $\frac{Kt-B3}{\quad}$.

Macdonnell's Double Gambit. 1. $\frac{P-K4}{P-K4}$; 2. $\frac{B-B4}{B-B4}$; 3. $\frac{P-QKt4}{B\times Kt P}$; 4. $\frac{P-B4}{\quad}$.

Maurian's Defence in the K B Gambit. 1. $\frac{P-K4}{P-K4}$; 2. $\frac{P-KB4}{P\times P}$; 3. $\frac{B-B4}{Kt-QB3}$; 4. $\frac{P-Q4}{Q-R5 ch.}$.

Max Lange's Attack. 1. $\frac{P-K4}{P-K4}$; 2. $\frac{Kt-KB3}{Kt-QB3}$; 3. $\frac{B-B4}{B-B4}$; 4. $\frac{Castles}{Kt-B3}$; 5. $\frac{P-Q4}{\quad}$.

Meadow Hay Opening. 1. $\frac{P-QR4}{\quad}$.

Minckwitz's Defence in the Steinitz Gambit. 1. $\frac{P-K4}{P-K4}$; 2. $\frac{Kt-QB3}{Kt-QB3}$; 3. $\frac{P-B4}{P\times P}$; 4. $\frac{P-Q4}{Q-R5 ch.}$; 5. $\frac{K-K2}{P-QKt3}$.

Modern Classical Defence in the K B Gambit. See *Classical Defence.*

Mortimer's Attack in the Evans' Gambit. See *Fraser-Mortimer Attack.*

Mortimer's Defence in the Ruy Lopez. 1. $\frac{P-K4}{P-K4}$; 2. $\frac{Kt-KB3}{Kt-QB3}$; 3. $\frac{B-Kt5}{Kt-B3}$; 4. $\frac{P-Q3}{QKt-K2}$.

Muzio Gambit. 1. $\frac{P-K4}{P-K4}$; 2. $\frac{P-KB4}{P\times P}$; 3. $\frac{Kt-K3}{P-KKt4}$; 4. $\frac{B-B4}{P-Kt5}$; 5. $\frac{Castles}{\quad}$.

Neumann's Defence in the Kieseritsky Gambit. 1. $\frac{\text{P—K 4}}{\text{P—K 4}}$;

2. $\frac{\text{P—K B 4}}{\text{P} \times \text{P}}$; 3. $\frac{\text{Kt—K B 3}}{\text{P—K Kt 4}}$; 4. $\frac{\text{P—K R 4}}{\text{P—Kt 5}}$; 5. $\frac{\text{Kt—K 5}}{\text{Kt—Q B 3}}$.

Normal Position in the Evans' Gambit.

BLACK.

WHITE.

1. $\frac{\text{P—K 4}}{\text{P—K 4}}$;   5. $\frac{\text{P—B 3}}{\text{B—B 4}}$;

2. $\frac{\text{Kt—K B 3}}{\text{Kt—Q B 3}}$;   6. $\frac{\text{Castles}}{\text{P—Q 3}}$;

3. $\frac{\text{B—B 4}}{\text{B—B 4}}$;   7. $\frac{\text{P—Q 4}}{\text{P} \times \text{P}}$;

4. $\frac{\text{P—Q Kt 4}}{\text{B} \times \text{Kt P}}$;   8. $\frac{\text{P} \times \text{P}}{\text{B—Kt 3}}$.

Old Classical Defence in the K B Gambit. 1. $\frac{\text{P—K 4}}{\text{P—K 4}}$;

2. $\frac{\text{P—K B 4}}{\text{P} \times \text{P}}$; 3. $\frac{\text{B—B 4}}{\text{P—K B 4}}$.

Ouroussoff's Attack. See *Prince Ouroussoff's Attack.*

Paulsen's Attack in the French Defence. 1. $\frac{\text{P—K 4}}{\text{P—K 3}}$;

2. $\frac{\text{P—Q 4}}{\text{P—Q 4}}$; 3. $\frac{\text{Kt—Q B 3}}{\qquad}$.

Paulsen's Attack in the Scotch Gambit. 1. $\frac{\text{P—K 4}}{\text{P—K 4}}$;

2. $\frac{\text{Kt—K B 3}}{\text{Kt—Q B 3}}$; 3. $\frac{\text{P—Q 4}}{\text{P} \times \text{P}}$; 4. $\frac{\text{Kt} \times \text{P}}{\text{B—B 4}}$; 5. $\frac{\text{B—K 3}}{\text{Q—B 3}}$;

6. $\frac{\text{P—Q B 3}}{\text{K Kt—K 2}}$; 7. $\frac{\text{Q—Q 2}}{\qquad}$.

Paulsen's Attack in Philidor. 1. $\frac{\text{P—K 4}}{\text{P—K 4}}$; 2. $\frac{\text{Kt—K B 3}}{\text{P—Q 3}}$;

3. $\frac{\text{P—Q 4}}{\text{P} \times \text{P}}$; 4. $\frac{\text{Kt} \times \text{P}}{\text{P—Q 4}}$; 5. $\frac{\text{P} \times \text{P}}{\qquad}$.

Paulsen's Attack in the Vienna. 1. $\dfrac{P-K\,4}{P-K\,4}$; 2. $\dfrac{Kt-Q\,B\,3}{Kt-Q\,B\,3}$; 3. $\dfrac{P-K\,Kt\,3}{}$

Paulsen's Counter Attack in the Ruy Lopez. 1. $\dfrac{P-K\,4}{P-K\,4}$; 2. $\dfrac{Kt-K\,B\,3}{Kt-Q\,B\,3}$; 3. $\dfrac{B-Kt\,5}{K\,Kt-K\,2}$; 4. $\dfrac{Kt-B\,3}{P-K\,Kt\,3}$; 5. $\dfrac{P-Q\,4}{P\times P}$; 6. $\dfrac{Kt\times Q\,P}{B-Kt\,2}$.

Paulsen's Counter Attack in the Sicilian Defence. 1. $\dfrac{P-K\,4}{P-Q\,B\,4}$; 2. $\dfrac{Kt-K\,B\,3}{P-K\,Kt\,3}$; 3. $\dfrac{Kt-B\,3}{B-Kt\,2}$.

Paulsen's Defence in the Kieseritsky Gambit. 1. $\dfrac{P-K\,4}{P-K\,4}$; 2. $\dfrac{P-K\,B\,4}{P\times P}$; 3. $\dfrac{Kt-K\,B\,3}{P-K\,Kt\,4}$; 4. $\dfrac{P-K\,R\,4}{P-Kt\,5}$; 5. $\dfrac{Kt-K\,5}{B-Kt\,2}$.

Paulsen's Defence in the Muzio Gambit. 1. $\dfrac{P-K\,4}{P-K\,4}$; 2. $\dfrac{P-K\,B\,4}{P\times P}$; 3. $\dfrac{Kt-K\,B\,3}{P-K\,Kt\,4}$; 4. $\dfrac{B-B\,4}{P-Kt\,5}$; 5. $\dfrac{Castles}{P\times Kt}$; 6. $\dfrac{Q\times P}{Q-B\,3}$; 7. $\dfrac{P-K\,5}{Q\times P}$; 8. $\dfrac{P-Q\,3}{B-R\,3}$; 9. $\dfrac{Kt-B\,3}{Kt-K\,2}$, 10. $\dfrac{B-Q\,2}{Q\,Kt-B\,3}$; 11. $\dfrac{Q\,R-K\,1}{Q-K\,B\,4}$.

Petroff's Counter Attack. See *Petroff's Defence.*

Petroff's Defence. 1. $\dfrac{P-K\,4}{P-K\,4}$; 2. $\dfrac{Kt-K\,B\,3}{Kt-K\,B\,3}$.

Philidor's Attack in the Bishop's Opening. 1. $\dfrac{P-K\,4}{P-K\,4}$; 2. $\dfrac{B-B\,4}{B-B\,4}$; 3. $\dfrac{P-Q\,B\,3}{}$.

Philidor's Counter Gambit. 1. $\dfrac{P-K\,4}{P-K\,4}$; 2. $\dfrac{Kt-K\,B\,3}{P-Q\,3}$; 3. $\dfrac{P-Q\,4}{P-K\,B\,4}$; 4. $\dfrac{P-K\,R\,4}{P-B\,5}$; 5. $\dfrac{Kt-K\,5}{Kt-K\,B\,3}$.

Philidor's Defence.   1. $\dfrac{\text{P—K 4}}{\text{P—K 4}}$;   2. $\dfrac{\text{Kt—K B 3}}{\text{P—Q 3}}$.

Philidor's Defence in the Kieseritsky Gambit.   1. $\dfrac{\text{P—K 4}}{\text{P—K 4}}$;

2. $\dfrac{\text{P—K B 4}}{\text{P×P}}$;   3. $\dfrac{\text{Kt—K B 3}}{\text{P—K Kt 4}}$;   4. $\dfrac{\text{P—K R 4}}{\text{P—Kt 5}}$;   5. $\dfrac{\text{Kt—K 5}}{\text{Kt—K B 3}}$;

Pierce Gambit.   1. $\dfrac{\text{P—K 4}}{\text{P—K 4}}$;   2. $\dfrac{\text{Kt—Q B 3}}{\text{Kt—Q B 3}}$;   3. $\dfrac{\text{P—B 4}}{\text{P×P}}$;

4. $\dfrac{\text{Kt—B 3}}{\text{P—K Kt 4}}$;   5. $\dfrac{\text{P—Q 4}}{}$.

Polerio Gambit.   1. $\dfrac{\text{P—K 4}}{\text{P—K 4}}$;   2. $\dfrac{\text{P—K B 4}}{\text{P×P}}$;   3. $\dfrac{\text{P—Q 4}}{}$.

Polerio's Defence in the Kieseritsky Gambit.   1. $\dfrac{\text{P—K 4}}{\text{P—K 4}}$;

2. $\dfrac{\text{P—K B 4}}{\text{P×P}}$;   3. $\dfrac{\text{Kt—K B 3}}{\text{P—K Kt 4}}$;   4. $\dfrac{\text{P—K R 4}}{\text{P—Kt 5}}$;   5. $\dfrac{\text{Kt—K 5}}{\text{B—K 2}}$.

Ponziani's Counter Gambit.   1. $\dfrac{\text{P—K 4}}{\text{P—K 4}}$;   2. $\dfrac{\text{Kt—K B 3}}{\text{Kt—Q B 3}}$;

3. $\dfrac{\text{P—Q 3}}{\text{P—B 4}}$.

Ponziani's Game.   See *Staunton's Opening.*

Potter's Defence in the Allgaier Gambit.   1. $\dfrac{\text{P—K 4}}{\text{P—K 4}}$;

2. $\dfrac{\text{P—K B 4}}{\text{P×P}}$;   3. $\dfrac{\text{Kt—K B 3}}{\text{P—K Kt 4}}$;   4. $\dfrac{\text{P—K R 4}}{\text{P—Kt 5}}$;   5. $\dfrac{\text{Kt—Kt 5}}{\text{P—K R 3}}$;

6. $\dfrac{\text{Kt×P}}{\text{K×Kt}}$;   7. $\dfrac{\text{P—Q 4}}{\text{P—Q 4}}$;   8. $\dfrac{\text{B×P}}{\text{P×P}}$;   9. $\dfrac{\text{B—B 4 ch.}}{\text{K—Kt 2}}$;

10. $\dfrac{\text{Castles}}{\text{Kt—K B 3}}$;   11. $\dfrac{\text{Q—Q 2}}{\text{Kt—B 3}}$;   12. $\dfrac{\text{Kt—B 3}}{\text{B—Q 3}}$.

Prince Ouroussoff's Attack in the Allgaier Gambit.   1. $\dfrac{\text{P—K 4}}{\text{P—K 4}}$;

2. $\dfrac{\text{P—K B 4}}{\text{P×P}}$;   3. $\dfrac{\text{Kt—K B 3}}{\text{P—K Kt 4}}$;   4. $\dfrac{\text{P—K R 4}}{\text{P—Kt 5}}$;   5. $\dfrac{\text{Kt—Kt 5}}{\text{P—K R 3}}$;

6. $\dfrac{\text{Kt×P}}{\text{K×Kt}}$;   7. $\dfrac{\text{B—B 4 ch.}}{}$.

Pulling's Counter Attack in the Scotch Gambit. 1. $\dfrac{P-K4}{P-K4}$; 2. $\dfrac{Kt-KB3}{Kt-QB3}$; 3. $\dfrac{P-Q4}{P\times P}$; 4. $\dfrac{Kt\times P}{Q-R5}$.

Quaade Gambit. 1. $\dfrac{P-K4}{P-K4}$; 2. $\dfrac{P-KB4}{P\times P}$; 3. $\dfrac{Kt-KB3}{P-KKt4}$; 4. $\dfrac{Kt-QB3}{P-Kt5}$; 5. $\dfrac{Kt-K5}{Q-R5\ ch.}$; 6. $\dfrac{P-KKt3}{P\times P}$; 7. $\dfrac{Q\times P}{}$.

Queen's Bishop's Pawn's Defence in the K B Opening.

1. $\dfrac{P-K4}{P-K4}$; 2. $\dfrac{B-B4}{P-QB3}$.

Queen's Bishop's Pawn's Game. See *Staunton's Opening*.

Queen's Fianchetto. See *Fianchetto di Donna*.

Queen's Gambit. 1. $\dfrac{P-Q4}{P-Q4}$; 2. $\dfrac{P-QB4}{}$.

Queen's Knight's Opening. See *Vienna Game*.

Queen's Pawn's Counter Gambit. 1. $\dfrac{P-K4}{P-K4}$; 2. $\dfrac{Kt-KB3}{P-Q4}$.

Queen's Pawn's Defence in the Q B P Game. 1. $\dfrac{P-K4}{P-K4}$; 2. $\dfrac{Kt-KB3}{Kt-QB3}$; 3. $\dfrac{P-QB3}{P-Q4}$.

Queen's Pawn's Game. See *Scotch Gambit*.

Rice Gambit. 1. $\dfrac{P-K4}{P-K4}$; 2. $\dfrac{P-KB4}{P\times P}$; 3. $\dfrac{Kt-KB3}{P-KKt4}$; 4. $\dfrac{P-KR4}{P-Kt5}$; 5. $\dfrac{Kt-K5}{Kt-KB3}$; 6. $\dfrac{B-B4}{P-Q4}$; 7. $\dfrac{P\times P}{B-Q3}$; 8. $\dfrac{Castles}{}$.

Richardson's Attack in the Evans' Gambit. 1. $\dfrac{P-K4}{P-K4}$; 2. $\dfrac{Kt-KB3}{Kt-QB3}$; 3. $\dfrac{B-B4}{B-B4}$; 4. $\dfrac{P-QKt4}{B\times KtP}$; 5. $\dfrac{P-B3}{B-R4}$; 6. $\dfrac{Castles}{Kt-B3}$; 7. $\dfrac{P-Q4}{Castles}$; 8. $\dfrac{Kt\times P}{}$.

Rivière's Counter Attack in the Kieseritsky Gambit. 1. $\dfrac{P-K\,4}{P-K\,4}$;

2. $\dfrac{P-K\,B\,4}{P\times P}$; 3. $\dfrac{Kt-K\,B\,3}{P-K\,Kt\,4}$; 4. $\dfrac{P-K\,R\,4}{P-Kt\,5}$;

5. $\dfrac{Kt-K\,5}{Kt-K\,B\,3}$; 6. $\dfrac{Kt\times Kt\,P}{P-Q\,4}$.

Rivière's Opening. 1. $\dfrac{P-Q\,4}{P-K\,B\,4}$.

Rosentreter Gambit. 1. $\dfrac{P-K\,4}{P-K\,4}$; 2. $\dfrac{P-K\,B\,4}{P\times P}$; 3. $\dfrac{Kt-K\,B\,3}{P-K\,Kt\,4}$;

4. $\dfrac{P-Q\,4}{P-Kt\,5}$; 5. $\dfrac{Kt-K\,5}{Q-R\,5\,ch.}$; 6. $\dfrac{P-K\,Kt\,3}{P\times P}$; 7. $\dfrac{Q\times P}{\quad}$.

Rosenthal's Defence in the Kieseritsky Gambit. 1. $\dfrac{P-K\,4}{P-K\,4}$;

2. $\dfrac{P-K\,B\,4}{P\times P}$; 3. $\dfrac{Kt-K\,B\,3}{P-K\,Kt\,4}$; 4. $\dfrac{P-K\,R\,4}{P-Kt\,5}$; 5. $\dfrac{Kt-K\,5}{Q-K\,2}$.

Russian Defence. See *Petroff's Defence.*

Ruy Lopez' Knight's Game. 1. $\dfrac{P-K\,4}{P-K\,4}$; 2. $\dfrac{Kt-K\,B\,3}{Kt-Q\,B\,3}$;

3. $\dfrac{B-Kt\,2}{\quad}$.

Salvio's Defence in the Kieseritsky Gambit. See *Polerio's Defence.*

Salvio Gambit. 1. $\dfrac{P-K\,4}{P-K\,4}$; 2. $\dfrac{P-K\,B\,4}{P\times P}$; 3. $\dfrac{Kt-K\,B\,3}{P-K\,Kt\,4}$;

4. $\dfrac{B-B\,4}{P-Kt\,5}$; 5. $\dfrac{Kt-K\,5}{\quad}$.

Sander's Defence in the Evans' Gambit. 1. $\dfrac{P-K\,4}{P-K\,4}$;

2. $\dfrac{Kt-K\,B\,3}{Kt-Q\,B\,3}$; 3. $\dfrac{B-B\,4}{B-B\,4}$; 4. $\dfrac{P-Q\,Kt\,4}{B\times Kt\,P}$; 5. $\dfrac{P-B\,3}{B-R\,4}$;

6. $\dfrac{Castles}{P-Q\,3}$; 7. $\dfrac{P-Q\,4}{B-Q\,2}$.

Schliemann's Counter Gambit. See *Jaenisch's Counter Gambit.*

Schmidt's Attack in Staunton's Opening. 1. $\dfrac{P-K\,4}{P-K\,4}$;

2. $\dfrac{Kt-K\,B\,3}{Kt-Q\,B\,3}$; 3. $\dfrac{P-B\,3}{P-B\,4}$; 4. $\dfrac{P-Q\,4}{P-Q\,3}$; 5. $\dfrac{P-Q\,5}{\quad}$.

Schulze-Müller Gambit. 1. $\dfrac{P-K4}{P-K4}$; 2. $\dfrac{Kt-KB3}{Kt-QB3}$; 3. $\dfrac{Kt \times P}{Kt \times Kt}$; 4. $\dfrac{P-Q4}{}$.

Scotch-Evans' Attack in the Scotch Gambit. 1. $\dfrac{P-K4}{P-K4}$; 2. $\dfrac{Kt-KB3}{Kt-QB3}$; 3. $\dfrac{P-Q4}{P \times P}$; 4. $\dfrac{B-QB4}{B-B4}$; 5. $\dfrac{Castles}{P-Q3}$; 6. $\dfrac{P-QKt4}{}$.

Scotch Gambit. 1. $\dfrac{P-K4}{P-K4}$; 2. $\dfrac{Kt-KB3}{Kt-QB3}$; 3. $\dfrac{P-Q4}{}$.

Scotch Game. See *Scotch Gambit.*

Sicilian Defence. 1. $\dfrac{P-K4}{P-QB4}$.

Soerensen's Gambit. 1. $\dfrac{P-K4}{P-K4}$; 2. $\dfrac{P-KB4}{P \times P}$; 3. $\dfrac{Kt-KB3}{P-KKt4}$; 4. $\dfrac{P-Q4}{P-Kt5}$; 5. $\dfrac{Kt-B3}{}$.

Spanish Game. See *Ruy Lopez.*

Stanley's Attack in the Evans' Gambit. 1. $\dfrac{P-K4}{P-K4}$; 2. $\dfrac{Kt-KB3}{Kt-QB3}$; 3. $\dfrac{B-B4}{B-B4}$; 4. $\dfrac{P-QKt4}{B \times KtP}$; 5. $\dfrac{P-B3}{B-R4}$; 6. $\dfrac{P-Q4}{}$.

Staunton's Opening. 1. $\dfrac{P-K4}{P-K4}$; 2. $\dfrac{Kt-KB3}{Kt-QB3}$; 3. $\dfrac{P-B3}{}$.

Steinitz's Attack in the French Defence. 1. $\dfrac{P-K4}{P-K3}$; 2. $\dfrac{P-K5}{}$.

Steinitz's Attack in the Sicilian Defence. 1. $\dfrac{P-K4}{P-QB4}$; 2. $\dfrac{P-KKt3}{Kt-QB3}$; 3. $\dfrac{B-KKt2}{}$.

Steinitz's Defence in the Giuoco Piano. 1. $\dfrac{P-K\,4}{P-K\,4}$;

2. $\dfrac{Kt-K\,B\,3}{Kt-Q\,B\,3}$; 3. $\dfrac{B-B\,4}{B-B\,4}$; 4. $\dfrac{Castles}{Kt-B\,3}$; 5. $\dfrac{P-Q\,3}{P-Q\,3}$;

6. $\dfrac{B-K\,Kt\,5}{P-K\,R\,3}$; 7. $\dfrac{B-R\,4}{P-K\,Kt\,4}$.

Steinitz Gambit. 1. $\dfrac{P-K\,4}{P-K\,4}$; 2. $\dfrac{Kt-Q\,B\,3}{Kt-Q\ \ 3}$; 3. $\dfrac{P-B\,4}{P\times P}$;

4. $\dfrac{P-Q\,4}{}$.

Stonewall Opening. 1. $\dfrac{P-Q\,4}{P-Q\,4}$; 2. $\dfrac{P-K\,B\,4}{}$.

Stone-Ware Defence in the Evans' Gambit. 1. $\dfrac{P-K\ \,4}{P-K\ \,4}$;

2. $\dfrac{Kt-K\,B\,3}{Kt-Q\,B\,3}$; 3. $\dfrac{B-\,B\,4}{B-B\,4}$; 4. $\dfrac{P-Q\,Kt\,4}{B\times Kt\,P}$; 5. $\dfrac{P-B\,3}{B-Q\,3}$.

Swedish Gambit. See *Danish Gambit.*

Thorold's Attack in the Allgaier Gambit. See *Allgaier-Thorold Gambit.*

Two Bishops' Opening. 1. $\dfrac{P-K\,4}{P-K\,4}$; 2. $\dfrac{B-B\,4}{B-B\,4}$.

Two Knights' Defence. 1. $\dfrac{P-K\,4}{P-K\,4}$; 2. $\dfrac{Kt-K\,B\,3}{Kt-Q\,B\,3}$; 3. $\dfrac{B-B\,4}{Kt-B\,3}$.

Three Knights' Game. 1. $\dfrac{P-K\,4}{P-K\,4}$; 2. $\dfrac{Kt-K\,B\,3}{Kt-Q\,B\,3}$; 3. $\dfrac{Kt-B\,3}{}$.

Three Pawns' Gambit. 1. $\dfrac{P-K\,4}{P-K\,4}$; 2. $\dfrac{P-K\,B\,4}{P\times P}$; 3. $\dfrac{Kt-K\,B\,3}{B-K\,2}$;

4. $\dfrac{B-B\,4}{B-R\,5\ ch.}$; 5. $\dfrac{P-K\,Kt\,3}{P\times P}$; 6. $\dfrac{Castles}{}$.

Van't Kruy's Opening. 1. $\dfrac{P-K\,3}{}$.

Vienna Defence. 1. $\dfrac{P-K\,4}{P-Q\,B\,3}$.

Vienna Defence in the Salvio Gambit. 1. $\dfrac{P-K\,4}{P-K\,4}$;

2. $\dfrac{P-K\,B\,4}{P\times P}$; 3. $\dfrac{Kt-K\,B\,3}{P-K\,Kt\,4}$; 4. $\dfrac{B-B\,4}{P-Kt\,5}$; 5. $\dfrac{Kt-K\,5}{Q-R\,5\ ch.}$;

6. $\dfrac{K-B\,1}{Kt-Q\,B\,3}$.

Vienna Game. 1. $\dfrac{P-K\,4}{P-K\,4}$; 2. $\dfrac{Kt-Q\,B\,3}{\quad\quad}$.

Vitzthum's Attack. See *Count Vitzthum's Attack.*

Waller's Attack in the Evans' Gambit. 1. $\dfrac{P-K\,4}{P-K\,4}$;

2. $\dfrac{Kt-K\,B\,3}{Kt-Q\,B\,3}$; 3. $\dfrac{B-B\,4}{B-B\,4}$; 4. $\dfrac{P-Q\,Kt\,4}{B\times Kt\,P}$; 5. $\dfrac{P-B\,3}{B-R\,4}$;

6. $\dfrac{Castles}{P-Q\,3}$; 7. $\dfrac{P-Q\,4}{P\times P}$; 8. $\dfrac{Q-Kt\,3}{\quad\quad}$.

Wing Gambit. 1. $\dfrac{P-K\,4}{P-K\,4}$; 2. $\dfrac{B-B\,4}{B-B\,4}$; 3. $\dfrac{P-Q\,Kt\,4}{\quad\quad}$.

Zukertort's Attack in the Philidor. 1. $\dfrac{P-K\,4}{P-K\,4}$; 2. $\dfrac{Kt-K\,B\,3}{P-Q\,3}$;

3. $\dfrac{P-Q\,4}{P-K\,B\,4}$; 4. $\dfrac{Kt-B\,3}{\quad\quad}$.

Zukertort's Opening. 1. $\dfrac{Kt-K\,B\,3}{\quad\quad}$.

INDEX TO PLAYERS.

ALAPIN, 373
Alechin, 192, 196, 402, 417
Alvensleben, 407
Anderssen, 138, 152, 154 (2), 156 (2), 185, 270, 316, 318 (2), 320, 343, 345 (2), 351, 411
Attwood, 70

BARDELEBEN, 145, 200
Barnes, 77
Berger, 386, 411
Bernstein, 420
Bihn, 306 (3)
Bilguer, 250, 276
Bird, 185, 272, 396, 398
Blackburne, 188, 196, 370, 398 (2), 411, 417, 420
Bledow, 245 (2), 250, 268
Boden, 77, 223
Boncourt, 70, 393
Bonetti, 245
Bourdonnais, de la, 70, 241, 285, 300, 341 (3), 363, 383
Brahmin Moheschunder Bonnerjee, 103
Brien, 83, 228 (2), 396
Buckle, 71, 135, 138
Burn, 140, 143
B., Dr., 243

CALVI, 314
Capablanca, 190, 192 (3), 196 (2), 203, 420
Charousek, 164, 171, 351 (2)
Cochrane, 103, 113, 152, 213 (2), 216, 241, 262, 285, 316, 383 (2)
Cook, 359

DANIELS, 243
Delmar, 158
"Delta," 347
De Riviere, 80, 154, 218, 270
Deschappelles, 213
Devinck, 343, 357
Discart, 245
Dubois, 270
Dufresne, 154
Duras, 111

EHRICH, 138
Englisch, 370
Evans, 225, 262, 316

FALKBEER, 228, 396, 408, 411
Fritz, 158
Froelick, 411

"GAMMA," 347 (2)
Ghulam Kassim, 300
Goltz, der, 272, 349
Greville, 216, 218
Guretzki-Comitz, 407
Gunsberg, 185, 200

HAMPE, 77, 80, 407, 408 (2)
Harmonist, 143
Harrwitz, 74 (2), 86, 225 (2), 393
Heineman, 140 (2)
Hert, 302
Heydebrand und der Laza, 98, 168 (2), 243, 245 (2), 268 (2), 272, 276, 285, 298, 300, 302, 314, 316, 349, 402
Hoffmann, 86
Horwitz, 71, 101 (3), 128 (3), 152, 225 (2), 250 (2), 383, 386, 393
H., 268, 285, 314, 402

JAENISCH, 74, 98, 113, 135, 138, 158, 185, 218, 345
Janowski, 190, 386
Janssens, 228
Jorowski, 359
Journoud, 247
Judd, 188

KENNEDY, Captain, 71, 185, 216
Kieseritsky, 152, 218, 247, 250, 287, 314 (2), 316, 318, 343, 351, 357, 393
Kipping, 152, 220
Kolisch, 143

LAROCHE, 80, 218
Lasker, 145, 160, 190 (2), 192, 203, 351, 373 (2), 375 (2), 402, 417, 420
Lee, 398
Lehner, 164
Leonhardt, 252
Lindehn, 260
Lipschutz, 370
Lock, 71
Locock, 359
Lowenthal, 80, 86, 132, 154, 270, 347, 386, 402, 407, 408

MACKENZIE, 158, 200, 396
Maczowski, 260
Marco, 252, 359, 375

Martinez, 111
Maroczy, 252
Marshall, 143, 252, 260, 386
Mason, 164, 396
Max Lange, 86, 138, 140 (2), 343, 345 (2), 357 (2), 407 (2)
Mayer, 156, 302
McDonnell, 241, 300, 341 (3), 363, 383
Michelet, 287
Mieses, 103, 257, 260, 411
Milliard, 220
Morphy, 74 (2), 77 (2), 103, 154, 156, 200, 220, 223, 270, 318 (2), 320, 349, 386
Mucklow, 347
M. G., 276
M——t, 276
M., 168

Newmann, 111
Niemzowitch, 417

Ourousoff, 135 (2), 158, 220, 306 (3)

Paulsen, L., 200
Paulsen, W., 143
Petroff, 98, 113
Philidor, 70
Pillsbury 105 (2), 164, 375
Pollock, 111, 164, 188, 200, 398
Popert, 216 (2), 241
Potier, 103
Potter, 257

Ralli, 132
Ranken, 347
Rinne, 357
Rousseau, 247

Saalbach, 156
St. Amant, 132, 262 (2), 370, 393, 396
Schallopp, 103, 171, 185
Schiffers, 143, 164, 370
Schlechter, 105, 252, 257, 359, 375
Schulder, 135
Schulten, 250, 349
Schumoff, 74, 135, 138, 218, 220, 345
Schwarz, 398
Showalter, 188
Smith, 272
Stanley, 247, 270
Staunton, 71, 101 (3), 113, 128 (3), 132, 152, 168, 216, 225, 241 (2), 262, 298, 302, 316, 343, 370, 383 (3), 386, 402
Steinitz, 145 (2), 188, 190 (2), 373 (2), 375
Sternfeld, Baron, 302
Szen, 77, 80, 298, 300, 318, 393

Tarrasch, 192, 420
Taubenhaus, 140, 171
Tchigorin, 105, 160, 171, 287, 351, 359
Teichmann, 252
Tinsley, 373

Walker, 213, 243, 262, 314
Wayte, 168
Weiss, 188
Wilkinson, 220
Williams, E., 71
Williams, 168
Wilson, 70
Winawer, 287

Zukertort, 158, 420
Z., 83

CONSULTATION GAMES.

Lowenthal and Falkbeer, 241
————————
Staunton and Rankin
Staunton and Barnes, 268
————————
Lowenthal and Owen
Blackburne, Winawer, and Bird
L. Paulsen, W. Paulsen, & Zukertort, 287
Morphy, Walker, and Greenaway,
Lowenthal, Mongredien, and Medley, 349
Harrwitz, Sazias, and Another
————————
Kieseritzky, Henderson, and Kling, 363
Lowenthal and "Alter", 408
Staunton and Barnes
———————— 83
B., M. and W.
H., M. and Z.
Morphy and Barnes
———————— 83
Staunton and Owen
De Riviere and Journoud, 156
————————
Morphy

CORRESPONDENCE GAMES.

Buda Pesth, 98
————
Paris
Amsterdam, 132
————
London
Edinburgh, 213
————
London
Posen, 243
————
Berlin

NOTES

NOTES

NOTES

NOTES

NOTES

NOTES

NOTES